A Guid
HALF
AND LARGE CENTS
History • Varieties • Populations • Values

Q. David Bowers

Foreword by
Harry E. Salyards

Whitman
Publishing, LLC
PUBLISHING SINCE 1934
www.whitman.com

A Guide Book of
HALF CENTS AND LARGE CENTS

www.whitman.com

© 2015 Whitman Publishing, LLC
3101 Clairmont Road, Suite C, Atlanta, GA 30329

THE OFFICIAL RED BOOK is a trademark of Whitman Publishing, LLC.

Correspondence concerning this book may be directed to the publisher, attn: Half Cents and Large Cents, at the address above.

ISBN: 0794843166
Printed in China

Disclaimer: Expert opinion should be sought in any significant numismatic purchase. This book is presented as a guide only. No warranty or representation of any kind is made concerning the completeness of the information presented. The author, a professional numismatist, regularly buys, sells, and sometimes holds certain of the items discussed in this book.

Caveat: The value estimates given are subject to variation and differences of opinion. Before making decisions to buy or sell, consult the latest information. Past performance of the rare coin market or any coin or series within that market is not necessarily an indication of future performance, as the future is unknown. Such factors as changing demand, popularity, grading interpretations, strength of the overall coin market, and economic conditions will continue to be influences.

About "Bowers-Whitman numbers": For cross-referencing to other listings and ease of use, Bowers-Whitman or "BW" numbers have been assigned to each entry (except for cents 1816-1857). In addition, the standard popular references in use are listed adjacent, such as the S (Sheldon), N (Newcomb), C (Cohen), or B (Breen) number. It is expected that the deserved popularity of these traditional numbers will continue. However, anyone desiring to do so is welcome to use BW numbers in conjunction with them.

Collect all of the books in the Bowers Series: more than a dozen volumes individually covering Morgan dollars, Buffalo nickels, Indian Head cents, and many other popular U.S. coins. Visit your local bookstore or shop online at www.Whitman.com.

For a complete catalog of numismatic reference books, supplies, and storage products, visit Whitman Publishing online at www.whitman.com.

CONTENTS

Foreword

This was the beginning. All the hundreds of designs, in more than a dozen denominations, struck at the federal mints of the United States over the past 207 years had their genesis in these pieces, the humble copper cents and half cents.

From their inception, they were at once familiar and unfamiliar. Familiar in the sense that the American population—of some three million in 1793—was accustomed to a variety of British and state coppers in circulation, many of them far underweight for the value they were supposed to represent. The large cents and half cents of that inaugural year had specific counterparts in large and small English coppers, the halfpence and farthings, and would have represented about the same purchasing power.

But they were unfamiliar, too—first and foremost in their embodiment of Liberty as a female figure on the obverse. Even the state coppers of the 1780s, after all, had generally placed a lumpy imitation of King George on their obverses! Plus, with an idealism befitting a fresh start, these new cents were to contain full metal weight of value in copper—11 pennyweights, or 264 grains, according to the Mint Act of 1792. Even after Congress reduced this weight to 208 grains, about two months before the first Chain cents were struck, these were still thick, substantial coins. Another unfamiliar feature was their insistent decimalization: 1/100 on the reverses of all cents through 1807, and 1/200 on the reverses of all half cents through 1808. No longer were Americans to think in terms of 12 pence per shilling and 20 shillings per pound. This very public reminder of a new way of reckoning was repeated on the edges of many varieties of 1793 to 1795 (ONE HUNDRED [or TWO HUNDRED] FOR A DOLLAR), until an additional weight reduction to a 168-grain cent standard took place, resulting in thinner coins with largely plain edges thereafter.

Yet one could argue that these coins failed to make much of an impression on the American monetary consciousness. Many, including one of the founding architects of the American decimal system of coinage, Thomas Jefferson, continued reckoning various accounts in pounds, shillings, and pence long after 1808, as shown in his *Memorandum Books*. And the Spanish milled silver coinage, with its reckoning in eighths of a dollar, lasted in American circulation as long as the large copper cents and half cents. In addition, these cents and half cents spent most of their circulating life north of the Mason-Dixon line and east of the Mississippi. They were never a legal tender in their own time. By the time settlement spilled as far west as "Bleeding Kansas," they were on their last legs: too cumbersome, too expensive to produce—refrains we've heard in our own time for the (once) "frankly token" small cent coinage that succeeded them.

So why the ongoing fascination with these coins? The answer, I believe, lies today, as it lay in 1857 when they were being withdrawn from circulation, in their very commonplace nature. To any American, whether born in 1800 or 2000, the word *cent*—or its ubiquitous misnomer, *penny*—means familiar money. Whereas, unless we grew up in the Intermountain West, even 50 years ago silver dollars were curiosities—Christmas gifts, perhaps, but not familiar, everyday money. And unless you're over 85, you probably don't remember gold as money in circulation, either. Even then, it was probably only the occasional half eagle that came your way—at least, that's what my grandmother told me back in the early 1960s: middle-class folks just didn't see any higher denominations in their day-to-day experience.

But cents? They're a different matter. That same grandmother set aside Indian Head cents for my mother, which were passed on to me as the foundation of my first collection. Did *her* grandmother, in turn, cast a nostalgic eye on those large coppers of the

1850s? She may have. They also counted for something, in real purchasing power, back then. And they certainly represented something even more valuable to those coin press operators at the first United States Mint in Philadelphia, who earned $1.29 per day for an 11-hour workday, six days a week. That's $30.96 per month to support a family, for relatively skilled labor. To reckon their *hourly* wage in the coppers they produced, they would have earned barely more than 10 of those newly minted Chain cents, which dropped from the coining press in March 1793. So of course they were spent, and spent, and spent again—and worn down to the point where, by the time the public at large was paying any attention, as they were disappearing from daily view, overall survival percentages (for the dates before 1815, at least) were on the order of 3 percent. Thus, the nostalgia of 1857—a nostalgia for "the first familiar memories of childhood," as Sheldon put it—was the first stimulus to their collection and study.

The second wave of fascination with these coins—what I'll call the nostalgia of 1967, when Early American Coppers (EAC) was founded—grew out of the childhood memories of those of us who came of age in the middle decades of the 20th century. Over the 11 intervening decades back to 1857, whole shelves of books and monographs had been written about these early coppers, but most of the interest was focused among a small, shifting cast of collectors in the Boston–New York–Philadelphia corridor. But by 1967, a whole generation of us had grown up, coast-to-coast, plugging Lincoln and Indian cents into Whitman folders. What could be more natural than to look to the earlier series of cents? What could be more stimulating to that project than meeting and sharing questions and answers with other, like-minded collectors? Thus the study of early American coppers has become a truly national endeavor, with EAC members currently in every state.

Yes, the operative word is *study*. For all that has been written about these coins over the decades—and they are certainly the most deeply researched field of American numismatics—new discoveries continue to be made. That was never more apparent to me than in working with Dave Bowers on this book as it evolved over several months. It truly seemed that the more answers we got from collaborators with expertise in particular areas, the more questions were raised for further research. And as Dave has pointed out, the coins are plentiful enough to allow for a continuing broad base of collecting and research.

And yet, they are not common—not common in the sense that Statehood quarters or Morgan dollars are common. That, too, is part of the fascination. Many examples exist of an obverse die that is extremely common with one reverse die, but very rare with another. Of such awareness comes the collector's dream of cherry-picking a rarity for a common-date price. There is also a significant gradient in rarity between the latest dates and the earliest.

To look at the cents specifically, a bit more than 156 million were struck altogether between 1793 and 1857. But more than 56 percent of those, or about 88 million, were struck from 1836 to the end of the series. Almost 47 million, or another 29 percent of the total, were struck between 1816 and 1835. Only 22.5 million altogether were struck between 1793 and 1814. If only 3 percent of those cents survived, that would be about 675,000 coins to share among today's collectors. Or consider the half cents: two-thirds of their total production, all of 5.25 million, are represented by the years 1793 through 1811; 3 percent of those surviving would represent only 157,000 coins. So, with all the collector interest in them, could it be possible that United States large cents and half cents are still underappreciated?

Let's look at another couple of comparisons. The 1795 plain-edge cents have a generally accepted mintage of 501,500—about the same as the 1909-S V.D.B. Lincoln cent (484,000). According to one current price guide, a 1795 grading Very Good will cost you $480, while the key-date Lincoln in the same grade will set you back $800. Not only are you paying more for a well-worn example of a modern coin, but that Lincoln cent was *hoarded* in Mint State from the date it was struck! So what about a modern scarcity that was not hoarded, the 1916-D dime? Its mintage of 264,000 compares closely to that of the 1809 cent (222,867). Well, you could theoretically purchase *three* 1809 cents in Fine-12 (at $775 apiece) for the cost of a single 1916-D dime in the same grade ($2,600). But for a variety of reasons, which Dave relates in this book, it is a serious collecting challenge to find a *single* pleasing, light-brown Fine 1809 cent; there just aren't that many out there! Therein, too, lies part of the fascination with large cents and half cents: no matter how deep your pockets, you can't just take a wad of money to a major coin show and come home with a respectably complete collection, as you could with many a modern American series.

So, why yet another book on these coins? Because up until now, modern references have been fragmented by denomination (large cents *or* half cents), and among the cents in particular, by runs of dates. Recall that I mentioned "shelves of books and monographs"; you can't take a shelf full of references with you to a coin show! *Walter Breen's Encyclopedia of Early United States Large Cents 1793–1814* offers a treasure trove of detail but as a book weighs six pounds by itself! Some volumes on that shelf full of references are guilty of repeating the same hearsay-become-fact of still earlier publications. Some of the other references, while technically quite accurate, make for dry-as-dust reading. That will never be said of the volume you hold in your hands. Dave, with suggestions from a number of us who have worked with him on this project, has tried very hard to separate myth from documented fact while at the same time capturing the spirit that has animated this field of collecting for a century and a half.

I believe that he has succeeded. In fact, I believe that this book will become the first work in the field of American numismatics since Sheldon's *Penny Whimsy* to be dipped into, time and time again, not just for the technical details on some particular coin, but for sheer reading pleasure.

Harry E. Salyards
Hastings, Nebraska

INTRODUCTION

To be *dynamic* a numismatic specialty has to have multiple factors. These include the following, *all* of which are present with copper half cents and large cents.

A dynamic specialty has to offer inexpensive coins in addition to rarities. Affordable coins (or tokens, medals, or pieces of paper money) need to be in the majority so that a person of modest means can have the satisfaction of building a fine collection.

A collection of half cents and large cents is indeed affordable—not a complete collection with every rarity or variety, but a very nice collection within the series. A set of Braided Hair half cents of the circulation issues of 1849 to 1857, in a grade such as Extremely Fine, can be built for relatively low expense and is very interesting to own. A group of copper half cents of the year 1804, with interesting die varieties as described in Ron Manley's *Half Cent Die State Book 1793–1857*, can be inexpensive to form, at least in large part, and yet provide an evening's worth of discussion with a fellow collector.

In contrast, the specialist in early American gold coins of the era from 1795 to 1834 needs to have hundreds of thousands of dollars just to form a set of the basic types—forget about dates and varieties! Necessarily, such specialists are few. Only one person can own an 1822 half eagle, as there are only three of this date in existence, and two are in the Smithsonian Institution. If the owner of the single coin in private hands should elect to sell it, what would it cost? Five million dollars? Ten million? In contrast, the Holy Grail date among copper cent dates is the 1799, of which nearly a thousand exist. A collectible example can be bought for a few thousand dollars, but most other dates cost in the hundreds, or even less. For a major type within a date the palm goes to the 1793, Liberty Cap, cent of which just over 11,000 were struck, but only about 350 examples remain. Of these only 40 to 45 are Very Fine or better. The cost of any of these is probably $40,000 and up, but well-worn examples can be had for less than $10,000.

A dynamic specialty has to be interesting to contemplate, going far beyond the simple aspects of price and rarity. The items must give feedback, so that when studied they provide enjoyment—perhaps even suggesting mysteries. And, mysteries are aplenty in numismatics. Hardly a year passes in the hobby without someone presenting a new slant on some minting procedure, or a curious aspect of a certain variety.

A dynamic specialty has to have challenges. How about this one? No one has ever completed a collection of die varieties of large copper cents, although some have come close, most notably Daniel W. Holmes Jr., who gathered all but two—one being a unique 1793 in the collection of the American Numismatic Society (ANS), and the other being a later date discovered in modern times. Some of Holmes's rarer pieces are in grades such as About Good, Good, and Very Good—not unusual, for there are any number of varieties for which the finest-known example falls short of Fine.

This adds to the challenge part. If you were able to write a check and buy a complete collection of half cents or large cents in gem Mint State, as you can indeed do for many modern series, the interest in collecting them would fade, and quickly. Instead, because perfection is impossible in the field of early coppers, you come to a new appreciation of these coins that have seen honest wear, where the thrill of the chase can literally involve finding a choice Fine coin to upgrade your banged-up Good: truly a lifetime endeavor.

There needs to be an active marketplace for a specialty to be dynamic. With half cents and large cents this is a wonderful panorama ranging from single offerings on eBay or in club auctions to landmark sales of great collections crossing the auction block. In the meantime, the essence of copper commerce is thousands of transactions large and small at conventions and coin shops and through mail-bid sales and advertisements. Someone wanting to spend money can start right away. Someone wanting to sell will find many eager buyers.

A system of grading and a system of pricing are each essential. With coppers, these also provide an element of challenge. Show a 1797 half cent to 10 different specialists and ask them to grade and appraise it, and you will probably receive 10 different answers. This is great for collectors, as it enables cherrypicking—the reviewing of many different offerings to select pieces that seem to have unrecognized or unappreciated potential. And yet there are approximate guidelines. The same 10 specialists might not agree if the 1797 coin is VF-20, F-15, or whatever, but none will say it has been worn down to VG-8 or is so well preserved as to be AU-50. More about grading later, of course.

Camaraderie and fellowship are essential. Early American Coppers (usually called EAC), formed in 1967, has been a focal point for annual meetings, auctions, and other opportunities to gather ever since. No one cares whether you work in an executive suite or on a farm in Kansas, or whether you have a PhD or simply a high school education. Everyone with an interest in collecting is welcome, and everyone has a good time.

Another essential part of a dynamic specialty is information. Half cents and large cents have no end to this, what with news coming bimonthly in the pages of *Penny-Wise*, published by EAC. The latest convention gossip, or die-variety discovery, or auction sale review, or . . . ? Every issue is different. Added to these are articles in other magazines and newspapers, and enough books, current as well as out of print, to fill a shelf. Add catalogs of famous collections of the past and you can fill several more shelves.

All of the preceding contribute to the staying power of the fascination of half cents and large cents. It is not uncommon for a specialist to be active in the series for 10, 20, or even more years. Some started young, as did John Kraljevich, who as a teenager mounted an exhibit of Matron Head cents (and was also a finalist in the World Series of Numismatics held at an American Numismatic Association convention). Others started late—for example, Clarence Bement discovered copper coins when he was on the far side of 70 but went on to build a great collection.

*　　　*

Half cents and large cents are meant to be *enjoyed*. Any combination of the ways just given will be fine. The more the better. Along the way, history and tradition are among the greatest keys. This is the story written by a numismatist whose love of copper coins began in 1846:

> I don't just remember when I began to collect coins, but I think it was about 1846. Strange to say it was during a spell of sickness, and my bank of coppers was the means of lighting the dormant spark into flame. I was a child of six or seven years, and while in my sick bed my mother gave me the contents of my "bank" to amuse me. I remember it was an old-fashioned sugar bowl, for this was before the day of elaborate and intricate designs.
>
> The pennies then were all in copper, mostly our own country, a few Canadian, New Brunswick, or Nova Scotia half-pennies or pennies, with an occasional King George half-penny that some of his soldiers had probably left behind while on a hasty visit some 30 or 60 years previously.
>
> I suppose all beginners in coins in the United States first try to obtain the series of cents. My first effort was to obtain one bearing the date of my birth, an easy task; then those bearing the dates of birth of my father and mother; here I found to get an 1821 was not so easy. My next ambition was to get all the dates of the cents, and by trading my duplicates for others, I ere long had a very respectable list. The half-cents, though regularly issued at this time, I found hard to obtain.
>
> I here feel constrained to say, and do so without fear of contradiction, that there is nothing more beautiful in the numismatic line than that drawer in your cabinet of Fine to Proof U.S. cents from 1793 to 1857. How they glow in their different shades—red, brown, olive, gray, and black. There is no coin more beautiful than an Uncirculated copper with its color softened or toned down by time, and per contra there is nothing uglier than a poor one. Your silver and gold series in monotonous color may represent more intrinsic value, but in beauty the coppers surpass, as they often do in fictitious value.
>
> Have we in any series of coin, foreign or domestic, a more beautiful head of Liberty than on our cents from 1793 to 1807 and from 1808 to 1814? Have you anything in your cabinet better in design or die execution than is shown in our cents of the 1840s or 1850s?

My voice is still for the collecting of the U.S. cent—the old-fashioned cent—in series; and from what I can learn, and the price they are bringing these days when in good condition, I am assured they still hold a warm place in the hearts of most collectors. And so my first confession will be a weakness for the copper of my boyhood days, the best we ever had.

The first full series of our cents I ever saw was one I used to see when a boy in the main hall of a then prominent business college in the East. The coins were arranged *ad seriatem* in a large frame with many others and held in place with round-headed tacks, the tacks being driven close to the edge of the coin, holding it in place by the overlapping head. I remember this frame well for it was the first effort of the kind I had ever seen or heard of, and it stimulated me in my efforts to complete my set. Pieces were in an ordinary condition, the most of them, though the dates were distinct. There had been a space left for the 1815, and the probabilities are that the getter-up of the collection was not aware that no cents were struck in that year.[1]

As to my personal involvement, I have had the pleasure of either personally cataloging or having my company present some of the finest collections ever to cross the auction block.[2] After I discovered numismatics in 1952, while still a teenager, I read as much as I could, including about cents. These were a specialty for some dealers back then, perhaps the most notable being the Copley Coin Company, which was the successor to the Sheraton Coin Company—or at least handled its remaining inventory. The latter was the brainchild of Robert Henderson, founder of the Sheraton Hotels chain, who collected copper cents. I was a friend of Maurice M. Gould and Frank Washburn, who operated Copley upstairs on Boylston Street in Copley Square in Boston. In that decade, Charles Ruby, Emery May Holden Norweb, Louis E. Eliasberg, James O. Sloss—all of whom frequented the American Numismatic Society, which I joined in 1958—and most of the other luminaries in the field of coppers were acquaintances, and many were friends.

I remember well when Mrs. Norweb mentioned to me that she had read Walter Breen's feature on Proof coins in Raymond's *Coin Collector's Journal*, and she wanted me to help find for her pieces now called "First Restrike" and "Second Restrike." It was many years before anyone else became even the slightest bit interested in these—restrikes were simply "Small Berries." Period. I later handled Mrs. Norweb's estate.

Byron White and Bob Schuman, not often recalled today in this context, were large-cent aficionados back then. Doug Smith always had a trade deal for me, sort of like trading his two alley cats for my American Kennel Club–registered spaniel, it often seemed, but usually we worked things out. Oscar G. Schilke had a very impressive collection of half cents and cents, which Empire Coin Company (in which Jim Ruddy and I were partners) bought piecemeal and sold privately over a span of years. Dorothy Paschal, ever on the prowl for nice-looking early cents (eye appeal was everything), was always in a hurry—sometimes reminding me of a bird flitting from bush to bush. She was rather frail, or seemed to be, but always a lady of the highest degree.

Kenneth Fuller, an old-timer at the Empire State Numismatic Society, specialized in large cents and one day asked Jim Ruddy and me to visit and pick up his collection. The time had come. The same thing happened with Edward Gilroy, whose cabinet included the finest 1793, AMERI., cent to appear on the market for a long time, Sylvester S. Crosby's 1799, and Hillyer C. Ryder's 1804, among other outstanding coins. Charles

W. Foster of Rushville, New York, who styled himself the "Suitcase Dealer," since he carried much of his inventory with him, was the epitome of a nice old-timer and always had a bunch of Randall Hoard cents to sell me.

The Rittenhouse Society, which Ken Rendell, Walter Breen, Ken Bressett, Grover Criswell, George Fuld, Dick Johnson, Eric P. Newman, and I organized in the late 1950s, had its first official meeting at the American Numismatic Association Convention in Boston in 1960, and it is still going strong today. The group emphasizes research and writing. Remarkably for any organization in existence for a half century, there has never been even the slightest argument or controversy in any of its meetings—again the camaraderie and fellowship mentioned earlier.

I could not afford to collect "regular" large cents in the mid-1950s, as even back then a nice 1793 would cost into the hundreds of dollars. However, well within my budget were counterstamped cents bearing advertisements, political slogans, and other notices. These often cost just a dollar or two, rarely more than five dollars. When the Marquis de Lafayette paid a return trip to the United States in 1824, thousands of copper cents were stamped with his portrait on one side and Washington's on the other. I have perhaps a half-dozen different cent dates with such. Whitten's Golden Salve, a long-forgotten product, is memorialized today on a counterstamped cent I've owned for many years, keeping good company with a hundred or more silversmiths' hallmarks impressed on coppers.

VOTE THE LAND FREE, a plentiful counterstamp, evokes a presidential election campaign of the 1840s—double entendre, as adherents thought the government should provide free land to homesteaders and, separately, that the land of America should be free from slavery. Dr. G.G. Wilkins, a dentist in Pittsfield, New Hampshire, was America's most prolific user of counterstamped cents to promote his business—far more active than Dr. Shattuck's Water Cure in Maine, which also advertised the same way. Fascinated by what the story might have been on both, I wrote a monograph about Wilkins and a large book about Shattuck. John J. Ford Jr., of whom more will be said later, thought this was one of the best esoteric numismatic studies he ever read.

Perhaps significant: I find counterstamped cents every bit as interesting and fascinating today as I did in the 1950s, when, a few years after meeting the proprietors of the Copley Coin Company, I bought Maurice Gould's personal collection of these—which had been featured in the pages of the *Numismatist* and elsewhere. I still cherish the coins.

Since then a lot has happened. In my wildest dreams in the 1950s I would never imagine that I could be responsible for bringing the Garrett, Norweb, and Eliasberg collections to market, each one with absolutely unforgettable half cents and large cents. Many other collections bring fond memories as well.

First minted in 1793 and last issued in 1857, these coppers were coins of the people. Just about everyone had a few. A pocketful of pennies, as everyone called them, could buy a lunch, a coach ride, a small article of clothing, or admission to a circus.

When in 1857 the half cents were discontinued forever and the large copper cents were replaced by the small Flying Eagle version, a wave of nostalgia swept across America. Finding one of each different date was the goal for burgeoning collectors. Many if not most newly created numismatists were successful, back to the date 1816 for the cents, although the scarce 1823 might have been the last one found. No one could find an 1815, but surely a few must be somewhere, it was probably thought. Early cents were found now and again, including well-worn examples of the first year, 1793.

This nostalgia, the yearning for "pennies" from the carefree days of childhood, generated much interest in this specialty. By 1860, such cents and, to a lesser extent, half cents (for as a class they were always much harder to find), were front row center in numismatics. When the first photographic plate of coins was published in the *American Journal of Numismatics* in 1869, it depicted large cents of 1793.

Since that time, the passion for these issues has endured. I hope the following pages can communicate my enthusiasm to you along the way, as these coins of long ago entice you to learn their histories and those of the people who knew them.

HOW TO USE THIS BOOK
PRICES AND GRADES

The valuations in this book—taken from the contributions of multiple half and large cents experts, listed in the credits and acknowledgements section of this book (all of whom are active in the real marketplace)—are intended to be middle of the road. These are not conservative; nor are they optimistic. It is hoped that as of press time, a valuation of a coin graded, say, AU-50, is about what such a coin might cost if sold by a leading auction house or dealer. The quality is "average." Similar to Jack H. Robinson's outlines in his popular *Copper Quotes by Robinson*, a high-quality coin will bring more, and an unattractive coin or coins with problems will bring less.

In the marketplace you will find many coins listed or certified as AU-50, but hardly ever, perhaps never, will you see "unattractive," "low quality," or other such negatives. It is up to you to determine that. You may see a coin listed enthusiastically, such as "AU-50, marvelous quality, one of the finest in existence." In that instance you need to determine whether the adjectives have merit.

Moreover, the assignment of a grade reflects the *actual wear* a coin has received. It does not reflect whether it is glossy and beautiful or dull and porous. It does not reflect whether the hair of Miss Liberty or the obverse stars are flat in areas, or whether they are needle sharp. It does not reflect whether the coin has been struck from relatively new dies, or whether the dies were "tired" (well worn, so as to impart a grainy or streaky character to the fields).

In addition to those factors, prices can change. Two identical coins sold at auction at about the same time can bring different prices. The market can move up or down, as can the prices of individual coins. Before making purchases, check elsewhere in the marketplace to verify current values. Those in this book are intended as a general guide as of the time the book was prepared.

The grading definitions are adapted from Whitman Publishing's *Grading Coins by Photographs: An Action Guide for the Collector and Investor*, which is compiled from input from many collectors and dealers.

The information on the highest grades known for each variety is from various sources. For expanded information see texts by John R. (Bob) Grellman Jr., William C. Noyes, Jack Robinson, and others listed in the selected bibliography. Grading data in various texts and catalogs can be very inconsistent, depending on whether the observer uses liberal or conservative interpretations. Many coins described as About Uncirculated in certain of these studies, and also the present text, have been certified as Mint State by the commercial third-party grading services. For additional information in this regard consult the reports published by the Numismatic Guaranty Corporation of America (NGC) and the Professional Coin Grading Service (PCGS).

All photograph pairs show the obverse and reverse of the same coin; there are no composites.

Bowers-Whitman Numbers

For cross-referencing to other listings and ease of use, Bowers-Whitman or "BW" numbers have been assigned to each entry (except for cents 1816–1857). In addition, the standard popular references in use are listed adjacent, such as the S (Sheldon), N (Newcomb), C (Cohen), or B (Breen) number. It is expected that the deserved popularity of these traditional numbers will continue. However, anyone desiring to do so is welcome to use BW numbers in conjunction with them.

Catalog Listings

The coins in this study are organized by year of issue. However, within each year-by-year section, the die varieties are not listed chronologically. The use of BW numbers is a convenience to readers in cross-referencing half cents within each year-by-year section of the text, as these numbers begin anew in each section.

Charts giving typical values for the cents of one year may appear at the beginning of the catalog for that year. Some coins are priced individually in charts following their catalog entries. Charts begin with the certified population from NGC, average grade, and percent of Mint State coins for each variety.

Mintage Figures

The mintage figures in this book are a combination of the *calendar-year* data presented in the *Annual Report of the Director of the Mint*, and, in some instances, estimates by the author and consultants (and so identified). It seems to be the case that until Robert Maskell Patterson became director of the Mint in July 1835, dies of certain years were kept in use in later years until they became unfit. In many instances, calendar-year figures are one thing, while the number of coins struck with a given date is unknown. Examples include the Mint listing for 12,170 half cents delivered on April 6, 1799, although no half cents of that date are known. Presumably, dies with earlier dates were used. There is no recorded mintage at all for cents in calendar year 1823, yet coins of that year exist (though they are scarce).

Estimated Populations

These are estimates based on the opinion of the author and the consultants to the book, although not everyone agreed on certain figures. From time to time in *Penny-Wise* and elsewhere, studies have been performed to evaluate the ratio of certain dates offered in the marketplace. These can be useful to contemplate. It is likely that many, if not most, high-grade and valuable half cents and cents have been recorded by students of the series, while hundreds of thousands of lesser-grade coins have not. That said, if a population estimate for one variety is given as 35 to 50 coins and for another as 250 to 350, it is virtually certain that the first coin is much scarcer than the second.

New discoveries are constantly being made. There are any number of cent varieties that William H. Sheldon viewed as unique or that had just two or three known examples when *Early American Cents* was published in 1949, but for which many more are known today. An outstanding example is the 1796 cent known as Sheldon NC-4, in this listing 1796, T Over Junction of Hair and Forehead, Reverse of 1795 (BW-20). Today it is estimated that 30 to 45 are known. On the other hand, there are many varieties that were considered very rare in 1949 and are still rare today.

THE FIRST
PHILADELPHIA MINT
AND THE AMERICAN SCENE

EARLY AMERICAN COINAGE
COINS OF THE COLONIES AND STATES

The first coins struck in what is now the United States were silver threepence, sixpence, and shillings first produced in Boston in 1652 under the authority of the Massachusetts Bay Colony.[1] Based on the British monetary system, these bore the imprint NE on one side, for New England, and the denomination as III, VI, or XII (pence) on the other. In time, the designs evolved to include what numismatists designate as Willow Tree, Oak Tree, and Pine Tree coins. The early NE coins were not dated. Nearly all of the other issues were dated 1652, in observation of the year of their authorization. The mint master was John Hull, who received a commission based on the face value of the pieces struck. In time he became a wealthy man. The Pine Tree shilling is the most famous of these early issues and is perhaps the iconic colonial coin; Nathaniel Hawthorne even wrote a story about these coins. Pine Tree coins were last made in 1682.

In time, several other colonies had coins made under contract for circulation in their district, and some companies and private individuals made them as well. In 1658 and 1659 silver coins depicting Lord Cecil Calvert were struck in England for the Maryland colony in denominations of 4, 6, and 12 pence. From 1722 to 1724, the English entrepreneur William Wood obtained a license (or patent) from the British Crown allowing him to strike coins for circulation in the New World. These pieces, of halfpenny, penny, and twopence values, bore the portrait of King George I and, on the reverse, the inscription ROSA AMERICANA, or the American rose. Wood also struck copper halfpence and pennies for circulation in Ireland, but shipped many to America as well.

In the 18th century, many British halfpence, genuine—or "regal"—as well as counterfeit, were imported into America, where they were generally known as *pennies*, inserting this term into the language.

After the Revolutionary War, several states had their own copper coins produced under contract, the first being Connecticut in 1785, followed by New Jersey in 1786. Vermont, not yet a state (this would not happen until 1791), authorized a copper coinage in 1785. Machin's Mills, a private enterprise near Newburgh, New York, turned out many coins, including imitations of other state issues and British halfpence. Connecticut was the most prolific issuer; today, well over 300 die varieties are known. These various coppers bore no denomination, were the size of British halfpence, and again were known as pennies.

Coins dated 1787 and 1788 were struck by a state-operated mint in Massachusetts—a different facility from the one used in the previous century. Joshua Witherle was mint master. Important to the present text, the coins were imprinted HALF CENT and CENT, the first use of these terms on coins struck in the United States. The mint closed in 1789 when it was realized that each coin cost twice its face value to produce. The dies were cut by Joseph Callender of Half Square, State Street, in Boston for a payment of £4 4s. each. This was considered to be too expensive, and Jacob Perkins of Newburyport did the same work on a commission basis for a royalty of one percent of the face value of the coinage struck from the dies he cut.

Perkins is one of the most famous figures in the annals of numismatics. In 1800 he engraved the dies and struck the "He Is In Glory, the World In Tears" Washington funeral medals. He was best known as a bank-note engraver and inventor of the siderographic process for reproducing engraved plates. In the early 19th century his plant in Newburyport was one of the largest producers of paper money for banks.

EARLY FEDERAL COINS

In 1776 a pewter dollar was struck, depicting on one side a sundial and the word FUGIO (for "I fly," referring to the rapid passage of time), with CONTINENTAL CURRENCY around the border. On the reverse, a series of rings bore state names and abbreviations. The design was taken from a sixth-dollar paper bill issued by the Continental Congress.

Curiously, today no documentation has been found concerning this coinage, how the contract (if there was one) was awarded by the Continental Congress, and how many were made. It is presumed to be official, as the production of $1 paper notes was suspended when the coins were made. Continental paper depreciated rapidly in value and was nearly worthless by 1781. This cast a pall on any prospect for federal currency in the near future. Citizens demanded "hard" money in the form of coins.

Robert Morris as depicted in *The National Portrait Gallery of Distinguished Americans,* engraved by T.B. Walsh after a painting by James B. Longacre, who copied a portrait by R.E. Pine. (Longacre was publisher of the *Gallery* series.)

Robert Morris, superintendent of finance, proposed a national coinage and the establishment of a mint. He corresponded on the subject with Benjamin Dudley, an Englishman living in Boston, who came to Philadelphia on October 23, 1781. Five weeks later, a shipment of copper arrived in Philadelphia from Boston on the brigantine *Active*, sailing under Captain Hodge. On January 15, 1782, Morris sent a memorandum to Congress:

> Shortly after my appointment, finding there was a considerable quantity of public copper at Boston, I ordered it around to this place. It is safely arrived, and will when coined amount to a considerable sum. If Congress are of the opinion with me that it would be proper to coin money I will immediately obey their ideas and establish a mint.[2]

Morris recommended that a decimal system be adopted. The two prevailing currencies in use in America at the time were the Spanish *escudos* and *reales* and the British pounds, shillings, and pence. Dudley "produced dies and sample pattern pieces of the intended coins" and drew plans for a mint building. Morris thought that the unoccupied former Dutch Reformed Church, which had been purchased by the Methodists and was currently known as St. George's, might be a suitable site, and the Masonic Lodge was considered as well. In February Congress approved Morris's plan. No mint materialized at the time, however, and today nothing is known about the nature or location of Dudley's patterns.

Morris continued his efforts and on May 5, 1783, paid A. Dubois $72 for making a pair of dies for the "Public Mint." John Jacob Eckfeldt, a German immigrant, was also paid for work the same year. It is believed that the patterns produced at the time are what we know as the 1783 Nova Constellatio coinage based on a 1,000-unit mark and decimal subdivisions.

Despite intense efforts, an actual mint did not materialize, and the pieces produced remained patterns with no regular-issue counterparts. On July 6, 1785, Congress approved the dollar as the basic currency unit with decimal subdivisions, but no action to establish a mint was taken.

In 1787 James Jarvis, an entrepreneur, was awarded a contract to strike copper coins, today called Fugio coppers, bearing a sundial motif and somewhat similar in design to the 1776 Continental dollar. Many were made, and they circulated widely.

After the Morris effort to establish a federal mint there were several further proposals for contract coinages in the manner of that given to Jarvis. The federal government had little in the way of manufacturing expertise and owned no buildings, it was argued by those seeking such business. It was logical that the making of coins be delegated to the private sector, similar to the construction of guns, furniture, paper, and other items needed by the government.

Several individuals and firms in the United States and England produced tokens or coins on speculation in hopes of receiving contracts. These coins include several dated 1791 and 1792 depicting President George Washington.

On April 15, 1790, Congress instructed secretary of the Treasury Alexander Hamilton to draft plans to establish a national mint. On January 20 of the following year, a report was submitted to Congress, and on March 3, President Washington approved the joint resolution of Congress to establish a coining facility.

This legislation was the direct result of entrepreneur John Hinckley Mitchell's proposal to Congress to strike American coins from his unnamed mint in Europe. Mitchell had a private agreement with coiner Matthew Boulton to get a fee if the application was successful. The proposal had been sent to Secretary of State Jefferson, who advised strongly against it.[3]

Attempts by individuals to privatize American coinage continued for some years afterward. On March 10, 1793, Thomas Digges of Birmingham, England, sent a "book of medals and coins" to secretary of state Thomas Jefferson via Thomas Pinckney, United States minister to Great Britain. The samples were numbered and marked, but the composition of the group is not known today. Digges's commentary on the collection ran, in part, "As I know you have made the American Mint and coinage much your study, they may serve as assistant samples towards perfection, those of Mr. Boulton's being of a very superior kind." Digges also described Boulton's highly efficient, steam-powered coining press. Neither Jefferson nor Congress were inclined to put the nation's coinage into private hands, much less overseas, and nothing came of the inquiry.[4]

In the meantime, commerce was mainly conducted with foreign coins bearing imprints of Mexico (in particular), Peru, Chile, England, Holland, Italy, Portugal, and other lands. Certain of these were given legal tender status by Congress. There were hundreds of different combinations of silver and gold coin denominations, types, and issuers, and the purity (fineness) of coins varied considerably.

To keep track of these differences, merchants relied on charts listing coin values and used balance scales to be sure that coins were of approximately the correct weight. Just about every leading newspaper had a column titled "Prices Current," which listed the values of commodities and, often, silver and gold coins. In practice, anything copper and about the size of a "penny" traded for a penny—whether it was new, well worn, light-weight, or heavy. Similarly, most crown-size coins (as numismatists call them), such as the eight-real coins of Spanish America, were valued at a dollar.

THE FIRST PHILADELPHIA MINT
ESTABLISHING THE MINT

In his third annual message to Congress, on October 25, 1791, President George Washington said:

> The disorders in the existing currency, and especially small change, a scarcity so peculiarly distressing to the poorer classes, strongly recommend the carrying into immediate effect the resolution already entered into concerning the establishment of a Mint. Measures have been taken pursuant to the resolution for procuring some of the necessary artists, together with the requisite apparatus.[5]

The Mint Act of April 2, 1792, provided for the establishment of a federal coining facility. The legislation also established a monetary system based on dollars and the decimal system, and gave weights and finenesses for various issues from the copper half cent to the gold $10 or eagle. Most pertinent to the present text were the rules regarding copper coinage:

> Cents—each to be of the value of one-hundredths part of a dollar, and to contain 11 penny-weights of copper.

Nothing was stated concerning their being legal tender, a point that surfaced years later in various inquiries and court cases.

The Mint Act, originally written in the Senate, specified the following:

> Upon one side of each of the said coins, there shall be an impression or representation of the head of the president of the United States for the time being, with an inscription which shall express the initial or first letter of his Christian or first name,

and his surname at length, the succession of the presidency numerically, and the year of the coinage.

It also provided that the reverses of the gold and silver coins were to bear the figure or representation of the eagle with the inscription THE UNITED STATES OF AMERICA, and the reverses of the copper coins were to be with an inscription expressing the denomination.

On March 24 the House of Representatives formed the "Committee of the Whole House on the bill sent from the Senate." The House moved to amend the Senate's suggestion, specifying that "upon one side of each of the said coins there shall be an impression emblematic of liberty, with an inscription of the word, LIBERTY."

This passed and was sent to the Senate, which disagreed with the change and returned it to the House. After discussion, the House resolved to keep the new wording, after which the Senate took no further action.[6]

President Washington chose Secretary of State Jefferson to be in charge of organizing the Mint, as he had been involved with various coinage proposals earlier. Otherwise, Treasury Secretary Hamilton would have been the logical choice, although Hamilton was very busy with other matters. In a way the Mint was also a consolation prize for Jefferson, as Hamilton had recently been put in charge of the post office. Jefferson set about finding a competent engraver for a staff position.

On April 14, President Washington commissioned David Rittenhouse to be the director of the Mint. Rittenhouse was a talented scientist, astronomer, engraver (he signed the border of the £6 note plate for the New Jersey issue of March 25, 1776, and did ornamentation on clock faces, among other work), and maker of scientific instruments, and a man with high stature in the scientific and social circles of Philadelphia.

The follow-up Act of May 8, 1792, provided for a copper coinage. Section 1 directed:

> that the Director of the Mint, with the approbation of the President of the United States be authorized to contract for and purchase a quantity of copper, not exceeding one hundred and fifty tons, and that said Director, as soon as the needful preparation shall be made, cause the copper by him purchased to be coined at the Mint into cents and half cents . . . thence to issue into circulation.

Section 2 of the act stated that "no copper coins, or pieces whatsoever, except the said cents and half cents, shall pass current as money," making the copper coinage produced at the Mint the only copper authorized for trade. Whether "current as money" made them legal

Director of the Mint David Rittenhouse as depicted in *The National Portrait Gallery of Distinguished Americans,* **engraved by James B. Longacre after a portrait by Charles Willson Peale.**

tender was later debated, as noted earlier. In 1836 the director of the Mint, Robert Maskell Patterson (son of former director Robert Patterson), asked Congress to make copper coins legal tender to the amount of 10 cents, but objections by Representative John Quincy Adams and others killed the idea.[7]

Despite this intention, a flood of nonfederal copper coins continued in circulation for many years thereafter, such pieces consisting of British halfpennies; "bungtown" coppers; imitation Irish and British halfpennies; a large number of coins issued earlier by Massachusetts, New Jersey, Vermont, and Connecticut; and coins and tokens of many other styles, types, and varieties. Indeed, some of these state coins remained in the channels of commerce for the next half century.

PATTERNS AND COINS

In September 1861, *Historical Magazine* provided the following account:

> John Harper, an extensive manufacturer of saws, at the corner of Sixth and Cherry streets, caused dies to be made under the direction of Robert Birch. The coins of 1791 were made in the cellar of Mr. Harper's shop on a press which it is supposed was imported from England. The coins of 1792 were struck on a press which was set up in an old coach-house in Sixth Street above Chestnut, directly opposite Jayne Street. This last described press was made by Adam Eckfeldt.[8]

There are no federal coins known with the date of 1791, and it is supposed that this account mistakenly referred to what numismatists call the Washington Large Eagle and Small Eagle cents, which were made on speculation in Birmingham, England. Other errors, including the Birch and Eckfeldt mentions, are explained in the note. In 1861 there was a great appetite for numismatic information, and much appeared in print that was later found to be incorrect.

In 1792 Joseph Wright made a pair of dies for a pattern quarter dollar. Likely these patterns were later struck at the Mint—not in an old coach house, as has been suggested. In the same year, an artist with the surname of Birch produced several dies for

A typical 18th-century screw press. Two men pulled the straps at the ends of the weight arm, driving the screw downward to strike a coin.

pattern coins, including large-diameter copper and white-metal patterns signed BIRCH. The portrait style on the 1792 half disme is similar to these, suggesting a possible attribution to him.

Pattern quarter dollar by Wright, in 1792. Around the reverse is a circle of five-pointed stars.

Large-diameter pattern cent by Birch, in 1792.

Peter Getz, an engraver and mechanic from nearby Lancaster, expressed interest in working for the Mint. He furnished a pair of scales to Rittenhouse and also made scales for the Bank of the United States. Montroville W. Dickeson provided a sketch of the engraver's life in the *American Numismatical Manual*, 1859, reprinting text furnished by J. Franklin Reigart of Lancaster (adapted):

> Mr. Peter Getz was born in Lancaster, Pa.; his occupation was that of a silversmith; but he was, otherwise, a very skillful mechanic and remarkable for his ingenuity. He excelled as a seal-engraver, and an engraver on steel, and was the inventor of a very ingenious hand-vise. He built the three first fire-engines for his native town, the *Active, Sun*, and another, which is still in existence in the county, and invented an improved printing press—noticed in the *Lancaster Journal*, January 8, 1810—worked by rollers instead of the screw, which, by printers was considered a great improvement.
>
> Mr. Getz died December 29th, 1809, at 47 years of age, leaving a large family. . . . Mr. Getz was personally complimented by Washington for his artistic skill in producing the die for what is called the "Washington Cent," and it was also officially recognized by the government.

Getz is not known to have been interviewed by Washington on the subject of speculative coinage for 1792, nor has any contemporary documentation survived. However, certain copper and silver coins, unsigned but widely attributed to Getz by numismatists, have G. WASHINGTON PRESIDENT. 1. / 1792 around the obverse border, and on the reverse is an adaptation of the Great Seal of the United States, with 15 stars above the eagle, an olive branch to the observer's left, arrows to the right, and UNITED STATES OF AMERICA around the border.

As Kentucky became the 15th state on June 1, 1792, the number of stars would seem to place this coinage after that time. This particular issue, known in copper as well as silver, may have been intended for federal coinage, as it follows an early proposal that the president be depicted. However, by June 1792, the Mint Act of the preceding April had changed that. There seems to be no reason to connect Getz with any official 1792 Mint patterns.

Jacob Perkins may have been a candidate for the position of engraver as well, per a newspaper notice from July 10, 1792: "We hear that the ingenious Mr. Perkins, of Newburyport, has been sent for to Philadelphia, to execute the coinage of the United States."[9] Perkins did go to Philadelphia and hoped for Mint work, but the records (such as they are: surviving early documentation is very sparse) are silent as to any actual involvement he may have had. He had talents as an engraver, mechanic, and coiner. Perkins remained in Philadelphia for several months and came to like the city, making it his home for a time years later.

For a long time in numismatic literature, Jean Pierre Droz—a Swiss engraver, clock maker, and constructor of automaton figures—was considered by some to be the Mint's engraver. In *Early American Cents*, William H. Sheldon devoted considerable space to Droz's talents and Thomas Jefferson's efforts to induce him to come from Europe to take the engraver's post at the Mint. Droz, who also worked in England, never crossed the Atlantic.[10]

President Washington wrote to Director Rittenhouse on July 9, 1792.

> Having had under consideration the letter of the Director of the Mint for this day's date, I hereby declare my approbation of the purchase he has made of the house and lot for the Mint, of the employment of Mr. Voigt as coiner; of the procuring fifteen tons of copper and proceeding to coin the cents and half cents of copper.

THE MINT BUILDING

On July 31, 1792, the first foundation stone was laid for the Mint in Philadelphia, then the seat of the federal government. The two main buildings, eventually three stories high, fronted on North Seventh Street and extended 33 feet to the rear. A popular myth is that the stone-laying ceremony was led by President Washington, whose temporary residence was less than three blocks away. However, he was at Mount Vernon in Virginia at the time.[11] Likely, Director Rittenhouse and his associates at the Mint were on hand.

In the meantime, between July 11 and 13,[12] silver five-cent pieces, called half dismes (the *disme* designation was later changed to *dime*, the term used today), were struck for the government. It is believed that about 1,500 were made. The dies were probably by Birch, as the female portrait resembles that on a copper pattern cent signed BIRCH. The coins were struck at the nearby residence of John Harper, a local saw maker and machinist with a factory in Trenton, New Jersey. At the time, incoming equipment and other items were stored with Harper.

Frank H. Stewart described the principal buildings of the new Mint facility in his *History of the First United States Mint:*

> Facing on Seventh Street was the so-called Office Building. Behind it was a yard 18 feet wide, with an alley to one side. The Coinage Building measured 30 by 35 feet and was in the rear. The first floor of the Coinage Building measured 28 feet, 11 inches in width, 32 feet, 3 inches in depth, and 11 feet, 1 inch in height. All inside measurements. The second floor was 29 feet, 2 inches in width, 31 feet, 10 inches in depth, 12 feet, 1 inch high on the front and 9 feet, 10 inches high on the back. One vault in the Coinage Building was 6 feet, 5 inches in length, 5 feet, 7 inches in width, and 6 feet high.[13]

The Mint was ready for occupancy on September 7. As Rittenhouse was in ill health, it was left to Henry Voigt to begin the Mint's operation. As early as September 3, he ran

Artist Edwin Lamasure's conception of what the Mint looked like in the 1790s, an image commissioned by Mint historian Frank H. Stewart and painted in 1914. The offices of the Mint are at the right. Behind is the coinage building. The top of this building had been destroyed in a fire on November 15, 1868 (when it was being used for other purposes), and thus it was not known what it looked like. The cupola was an added touch, as many other Philadelphia buildings had similar features. In the far back is the plant for making metal into the strips from which planchets were cut.

a notice for copper in *Dunlap's Daily Advertiser*: "The highest price will be given for old copper at the Mint, No 29 North Seventh Street." Space for similar advertisements was also purchased in *Bache's General Advertiser*.

On October 6, 1792, Voigt brought 15 gallons of rum to the Mint, and another 15-1/2 gallons on October 17. This was the standard drinking supply for those working in the Mint, a popular fringe benefit. Jacob Bay, who cut letter and digit punches for the Mint, was twice fined for drunkenness on the job. Years later, the Mint began supplying employees domestic beer instead.

On September 10, 1792, some old copper of six pounds' weight was purchased by Voigt, this being the first metal acquired for coinage. Later in the same month, a "heavy press" was set up, and by September 25, 1792, Thomas Flude was busy trimming it.[14] Little is known about presses at the Mint at the time, although at least one of them had been purchased from John Harper the preceding August. These presses were not of large capacity, but they worked for coining cents.

Photograph of the first Mint building taken in 1854 by "B" and published in the *American Journal of Numismatics* in November 1868.

On October 16, Voigt was able to purchase 1,451 pounds of copper from James and Shoemaker, and, on November 26, he purchased 4,140 pounds from Gustavus and Hugh Calhoun. During this period, several varieties of copper pattern cents were struck. Those of the largest diameter were made from dies by Birch. The plan at the time was to have each cent contain its full intrinsic value of metal.

Some weeks later a smaller and more convenient version of the cent, with a silver plug, was coined from dies cut by Voigt. In his account book, on December 17, Voigt wrote, "Struck off a few pieces of copper coins." On the next day Jefferson wrote to Washington:

> Th. Jefferson has the honor to send the president 2 cents made on Voigt's plan by putting a silver plug worth three-fourths of a cent into a copper worth one-fourth of a cent.
>
> Mr. Rittenhouse is about to make a few by mixing the same plug by fusion with the same quantity of copper. He will then make of copper alone of the same size and lastly he will make the real cent as ordered by Congress four times as big. Specimens of these several ways of making the cent may now be delivered to the committee of Congress now having the subject before them.

Silver-center pattern cent, dated 1792, with a plug of silver at the center.

These are what numismatists know today as 1792 silver-center cents and fusible-alloy (silver and copper mixed together) cents.[15]

The price of copper began to rise. It became necessary for Rittenhouse to petition Congress to reduce the amount of copper metal required for each cent and half cent. As a result, the Act of January 14, 1793, was passed, changing the weight of the proposed copper coinage. It stated that "every cent shall contain two hundred and eight grains of copper, and every half cent shall contain one hundred and four grains of copper" and that the earlier act with regard to the weight of copper coinage should be repealed. The January act therefore reduced the copper in the cent to 8-1/2 pennyweights from the original specified weight of 11.

CENTS MADE FOR CIRCULATION

Although pattern coins in copper had been struck in 1792, including several of the cent denomination, it was not until February 1793 that quantity production commenced. These were the Chain AMERI. cents, the first examples of which were delivered by the coiner on March 1.

The difference between the cost of copper metal plus the cost of production and the face value represented a profit to the Mint, a point repeatedly emphasized in later years in the *Annual Report of the Director of the Mint.* Accordingly, there was a great effort to locate supplies of the metal in the early days. It fell to Voigt to find this metal. Once, after being unable to contact the director in a timely manner, he took a horse and cart and went on a search for copper, inadvertently violating Mint rules that workers were not to leave the premises without permission. This caused a stir at the time.

Sources included copper coins struck elsewhere, rough sheet, and various scrap. The quality necessarily varied depending upon impurities. It was the coiner's duty to make occasional assays of the copper and to monitor the weight of the coins. From the appearance of existing half cents and cents, this task seems to have been done on an erratic and inconsistent basis in the early years.

Half cents were first issued in July 1793. In the summer, Joseph Wright, a highly accomplished portrait artist, seems to have been hired as the first staff engraver, freeing coiner Voigt to tend to the regular duties of his office. It is known that Wright did engraving work for the Mint (a 1792 pattern quarter and a medal for Henry Lee), but no documentation exists as to his specifically making coinage dies. It is virtually certain that he created the Liberty Cap cent.

In November, $10,000 worth of copper ordered by Thomas Jefferson through minister to England Thomas Pinckney arrived in port aboard the *Pigon* and *Mohawk* from a European source, possibly Sweden.[16] This delivery was of good quality, if cents of late 1793 and early 1794 are indicative.

On June 3, 1794, a press used by Matthias Ogden to strike New Jersey copper coins in the late 1790s was sold to the Mint by his widow Hannah, for $47.44. As the Mint had larger, newer presses and others on order, likely the Ogden press was used for cutting planchets or for spare parts. Like Ogden, Mint assayer Albion Cox had also been involved in the New Jersey coinage.[17]

YELLOW FEVER

On September 18, 1793, the Mint was closed as yellow fever raged through Philadelphia, its cause unknown. This was the first such epidemic since 1762.[18] On the same day there was a delivery of cents by the coiner to the treasurer. Many citizens went to the country to stay with friends or relatives or to live in tents along the Schuylkill River to avoid the fever. Unfortunately, Joseph Wright died about this time from the dreaded disease, and his wife succumbed shortly thereafter. Joseph Whitehead and Jacob Bay, who did work for the Mint, died as well, as did Jonathan Dickinson Sargeant, son-in-law of Director Rittenhouse.[19]

At the time, no one knew much about the plague or that it was transmitted by the common mosquito, *Aedes aegypti*. A century would pass before Walter Reed made the connection. Interestingly, on August 29, 1793, the *American Daily Advertiser* suggested that bites from mosquitoes further distressed those infected, and that "common oil" added to rainwater casks and cisterns would destroy their breeding places. Sometimes tar was burned in the streets to counter noxious vapors that might be transmitting the disease. It was later recalled that on July 24, 1793, the sloop *Amelia* arrived with a group of refugees from Santo Domingo, a Caribbean island where disease was common. On August 16, the Danish ship *Henry* arrived, with the captain and two sailors suffering with what was later identified as yellow fever.

In 1796 there was another severe epidemic, but the Mint's response is not known today.[20] On August 28, 1797, the facility was closed and remained so into the autumn. Starting on August 20, 1798, the Mint was idled for three months for the same reason, and in 1799 it was locked from August 24 to October 23. In 1802 the Mint director wrote that "fever was within 500 yards of the Mint," but no record has been found that it closed. On September 16, 1803, the Mint was shut down for six weeks.[21]

Among many suggestions for preventing the fever was the quarantining of ships when the first case of the disease was learned, as the outbreaks often originated near the docks on the Delaware River and then spread block by block throughout the city. This was done, and after 1804 the problem subsided. Scourges were not limited to Philadelphia. Yellow fever epidemics occurred elsewhere, as did plagues of dreaded cholera.[22]

On November 23, 1793, with the Mint now back in operation, Robert Scot succeeded the unfortunate Wright as engraver, a post he would retain until October 30, 1823.[23]

ALBION COX

In May 1793, Albion Cox, who had been involved with the making of New Jersey coppers in 1786, was hired as assayer. It was to be Cox's task to melt and test incoming silver and gold and evaluate them for fineness and worth. Silver and gold coins were not to be struck for the Mint's own account, but for depositors of the metal, who could specify the denominations desired. Surety bonds of $10,000 each for Voigt and Cox were required before they could work with these particular metals. This was an exceedingly high sum for the era, and Cox was stymied for a time. Copper was under the charge of Voigt, and its coinage was not delayed.

Cox remembered the recent yellow fever epidemic in a letter of December 16, 1793, to Caleb Camp, Esq., of Newark, and also noted that Congress was aware of the surety restriction preventing him from work on deposited precious metals:

> Very shortly after I saw you here—from the increase of the malignant fever we closed this Mint and departed the city from that time until the latter part of the last month when we returned. All communication was cut off. I therefore had no opportunity of writing to you. Unfortunately, I was taken ill the second day after my return and confined to my room three weeks. I had the fever a few days after I quitted the city, but with good nursing and a clear air I recovered with the assistance of medicine.
>
> My last complaint was inward bloody boils, which the doctors inform me were the remains of the fever, and was a happy circumstance, as it so tormented me that a return of the fever would have without doubt carried me off. It remains to be determined whether our lost time is to be paid. In justice we ought to be paid as our

expenses were very high, as every imposition in house rent and for provisions was practiced by the country people.

I trust from all these circumstances you will be patient until our matters are finally determined. I expect every moment to be called on before Congress as some alteration in the law respecting the Mint will take place in my favor. We have also a large quantity of metal arrived from Europe and the West Indies which has caused a large increase of business and must be attended to very strictly. The moment I have settled my matters in Congress and received my salary you shall be acquainted.

I am not by any means as well as before the fever attacked me, but I trust with care I shall soon recover. Numbers who have recovered from the fever are still in a malingering state. All the officers in the Mint have now two quarters' salary unsettled.[24]

Upon the workers' return they were given partial pay for the furlough period during the epidemic. However, Cox's surety requirement was not met until the amount was lowered to $1,000 in 1794. Cox was then able to perform his duties as assayer, including for the first silver half dollars and dollars of autumn 1794 and the first gold half eagles in the summer of 1795.[25] He would serve until his unexpected death by apoplexy at a dinner party at his home on November 27, 1795. "His residence was a handsome mansion on Green Hill, which, during his only too brief occupancy of it, was the seat of a generous and refined hospitality."[26]

WITHIN THE MINT

Regulations specified that dies for use in coining presses were to be received from the director and kept safely under custody of the coiner until defaced (canceled and rendered unfit for further use) or broken, at which time they were to be returned. During closings for yellow fever, the dies, important documents, and other items were placed in a strongbox and deposited with the Bank of the United States. A resident watchman remained as a guard at the Mint.

When the items were returned it seems that certain unused dies became mixed with ones that had already been employed, resulting in intermittent combinations of dies rather than continuous use until a die became unfit. Another possibility is that the intermittent use of dies during this time could have been caused by taking the dies out of a press so that another denomination could be coined, then replacing them in another combination later.

Most duties at the Mint required strong body and temperament. Work began at six in the morning in the warmer months and at seven in the winter and continued for an 11-hour stint—this for six days a week. Rum was provided, although drunkenness was not allowed. A coining press operator earned about $1.29 per day. These presses were operated by human muscle. Horses provided the power to operate the roller mill, which converted copper ingots into flat strips. A dog named Nero, purchased for $3, helped guard the Mint while a watchman remained through the night.[27] Lighting was first provided by candles and whale-oil lamps, later augmented by lanterns.

On December 27, 1794, James Davy, an Englishman who sought commercial involvement in coinage, sent these observations to the secretary of state:

I shall offer my opinions on the Mint of the United States of America. . . . I find the supply of copper has not been regular, that the power now applied is not adequate, nor are many parts of the machinery adapted for performing the work to the best advantage.

Other observations might have been made, & Improvements suggested, if I had seen the whole of the machinery at work, or had the opportunity of a more minute inspection of the Mint; There is no doubt but that the coinage may be much improved, by rendering the cents brighter, and clearer from rough black streaks which much disfigure many of them, the expenses considerably diminished & a greater quantity of coins produced; besides laying a foundation for other important advantages to this country, by adopting the plan herein offer'd.

If it should appear that my services will be of use, I shall be happy to engage my attention to the execution of the improvements suggested, & in procuring materials, & the necessary workmen in addition to those already engaged, some of whom appear to possess considerable merit.

THE 1795 INVESTIGATION

Others were critical of the Mint as well. In 1794 and 1795, Congress conducted an extensive investigation of it, concluding in response that the operation had cost a lot of money to operate but had struck relatively few coins. Indeed, in 1793 and most of 1794, only half cents and cents had been made. Outsiders, including John Harper, petitioned to take over the work on private contract.

On February 9, 1795, Congressman Elias Boudinot issued a report from the committee appointed to investigate the state of the Mint. Included was an inventory of equipment, which read in part:

> 2nd. The present state and progress of the works. The houses are built on three lots of ground, in Seventh street, between Market and Arch streets, the fee simple of which is vested in the United States, and one in the Northern Liberties, taken by the Director, on a lease for five years, at the trifling rent of five shillings per annum.
>
> The works consist of two rolling machines, one for hot and the other for cold metal, worked by four horses, and require five hands constantly to attend them, while in operation. There is a third, nearly completed, to be appropriated to the smaller coinage. A drawing machine for the purpose of equalizing the strips for cutting the planchets, and are worked by the same hands as are last mentioned. Three cutting presses for the planchets of larger and smaller coins, which are worked by one man each. A milling machine, which is intended to be worked by the horse mill, but, at present, requires one hand.
>
> Three coining presses, with the improvement for supplying and discharging themselves by machinery. Six hands will attend three, if in one room. A fourth, for dollars and medals, in particular, will be finished in about three months. Two turning lathes for dies, and a boring machine for making holes in the large frames, screws for presses, stakes, rollers, and an infinite variety of instruments and tools, necessary to carry on the coinage. There are, besides three annealing and one boiling furnace, with two forges, the assay, melting and refining furnaces.
>
> The net produce of these works, from the establishment of the mint to this time, consists of one million and eighty-seven thousand five hundred cents, paid into the treasury of the United States, equal to ten thousand eight hundred and seventy-five dollars; in silver coins delivered, thirty-five thousand one hundred and sixty-five dollars. The future produce, it is said, will be about two hundred thousand cents per month.[28]

CHANGES AT THE MINT

In failing health, David Rittenhouse resigned as director of the Mint in June 1795. Henry William DeSaussure was appointed in his place and began his duties on July 8, 1795, and served only slightly more than three months. He resigned in September and stayed until October 27, 1795, by which time a replacement had been found.[29] During that interim the first gold coins were struck, beginning with half eagles in July. Elias Boudinot, the prominent member of Congress who earlier reported on the Mint investigation, was given the directorship on October 28, 1795, and served for nearly 10 years.

On October 10, 1795, Adam Eckfeldt, who had done work as a mechanic from time to time since 1792, was given full-time employment as a "die sinker and turner" for $500 per year. Soon afterward, he was named assistant coiner at $700 per year. His duties, as defined, were to "personally forge, turn, and harden all dies and hubs and to do, or direct to be done everything necessary thereto, except the engraving and polishing."[30]

Mint director Elias Boudinot as depicted in *The National Portrait Gallery of Distinguished Americans,* **engraved by J.W. Paradise after a portrait by Samuel L. Waldo and William Jewett.**

The Mint was closed after August 28, 1797, during another plague of yellow fever. Eckfeldt stayed at the facility to guard it and to work on a coining press.[31] His improvements are not specifically known today, but may have included a mechanism to automatically feed planchets and eject finished coins. In January 1800, Boudinot stated that the typical daily output of a press was 14,000 pieces.

In the late 1790s the typical die seems to have had a production life of 100,000 impressions, more or less, with great variation among individual dies. This seems to have changed dramatically within the year 1800 with the use of much-improved die steel, as evidenced by a production of half cents in that year that surpassed 200,000. Similar high figures can be estimated by comparing mintage figures with the number of different dies used in subsequent years.

In this era the monetary system in the United States was in complete synchrony. Copper, silver, and gold coins could be exchanged at par for other denominations, and notes of the Bank of the United States were likewise at par.

Benjamin Rush, signer of the Declaration of Independence and famous physician of Philadelphia, became treasurer of the Mint in 1800 after yellow fever caused the death of his predecessor, Nicholas Way. Rush and Director Boudinot had a mutual relative who died and whose original will left a considerable sum of money to Boudinot's side of the family. The relative had an all-night deathbed session with Rush, however, in which the will was changed to Rush's favor. By 1800 the two men were barely speaking. Rush even went to the trouble of making formal charges against Boudinot, including theft of Mint property. The "property" in question was horse dung, which Boudinot had arranged to have hauled from the Mint for nothing. The result of the charges was an unpleasant inquiry, but no action came of the hearings.[32]

THE CAPITAL MOVES TO WASHINGTON

The year 1800 was a time of transition. Early in the year many parades and public gatherings were conducted to mourn the passing of George Washington, who had died at his Mount Vernon estate on December 14, 1799. During the summer of 1800, the capital of the United States was moved from New York City to Washington, D.C., with

123 federal clerks participating in the move. Congress met in Washington for the first time on November 17, 1800, the same day President John Adams moved into the executive mansion. Congressional discontent with the Mint, which had faded since an investigation in 1794 and 1795, was renewed. Some thought it illegal for the facility to remain in Philadelphia and felt that it should be relocated to the new capital.

The move-the-Mint-to-Washington movement was ended on March 3, 1801, when Congress authorized the Mint to remain in Philadelphia for a further two years. However, it was clear that the matter had not gone away, and subsequent discussions were held.

In 1800 the second federal census revealed a population of 5,308,483, mostly along the Atlantic coast. Of this number, 896,849 were slaves. In the presidential election, Democratic-Republican Thomas Jefferson won 73 Electoral College votes, as did Aaron Burr, followed by 65 for President John Adams and 64 for Charles Pinckney. After a ballot by the electors, the outgoing Federalist-controlled Congress swung the majority to Jefferson's side in February 1801.

CONTINUING PROBLEMS WITH COPPER

In the early days, copper for coining was very scarce in America, and chief coiner Henry Voigt's problems in obtaining enough were unabated. There were no significant known domestic sources for quantities of the metal, although by that time mines had been operated in Simsbury, Connecticut, and elsewhere. Across the Atlantic, Sweden had generous supplies of the metal, as did England (from mines in Wales). As noted, Voigt had to make do with what he could find in the way of assorted scrap and other sources, none of them steady or reliable.

In 1795 a large quantity of Talbot, Allum, & Lee copper tokens had been purchased, and half cent planchets cut from them, yielding a supply that lasted into 1797. Scrap was melted and converted into strip, then planchets for cents. Misstruck cents often had half cent planchets punched from them, eliminating the need to reprocess the metal, except for the scrap. Although weights were specified by statute for half cents and cents, it seems that the rules were observed casually at times, for some coins of this era varied in this regard.

A Talbot, Allum, & Lee token, denominated as ONE CENT, similar to those purchased in quantity by the Mint in 1795. Planchets for coining half cents were cut from them and used to strike half cents dated 1795 and 1797.

The copper problem eased when arrangements were made to buy casks filled with planchets made by Boulton & Watt at the Soho Manufactory in Birmingham, England. These first arrived in 1797. Another English source was tried and found to be more expensive, and their planchets were found to be of poor quality. Some sheet copper was obtained domestically from 1798 to 1800, but the amounts were negligible.[33] In autumn 1801, Director Boudinot wrote to Matthew Boulton to request that he send out "by the first spring ships, from 20 to 25 tons of planchettes, and to repeat it every spring and fall."

A memorandum from Boudinot, February 27, 1802, noted the following:

As to importing the cents complete from Europe, it can certainly be done for a trifling sum above the price of the planchettes, say about £20 sterling per ton, did the policy of government admit of it. Of this I would not venture to determine, the

Legislature alone being competent to that purpose. I once stated it to a Committee of both Houses, but they determined that it would be a dangerous measure, and would not hearken to it.

Half cents were made at the Mint through 1797, after which the next delivery was 12,170 on April 6, 1799, but from earlier-dated dies.[34] Coins from dies dated 1800 were followed by continuous coinage from 1802 until 1811, after which none were struck until years later in 1825. Copper cents were made continuously with dates through 1814 (some were minted in late 1815, but likely dated 1816), although the quantities from dies dated 1799 and 1804 were small, creating rarities that would later be highly prized by numismatists.

As the Mint made half cents and cents for its own account and banked any profits, it seems likely that the officers opted to make cents in preference, as the production cost was less than making two half cents for the same face value. The public accepted half cents readily enough, as evidenced by the extensive wear seen today on most of the earlier ones. However, years later, the subject as to whether half cents were popular or unpopular with the citizenry engendered debate among numismatists.

INTO THE NEXT CENTURY

In the spring of 1801, Robert Leslie, a watchmaker, clock maker, and inventor from London, visited Philadelphia in an attempt to solve a major challenge: to produce more coins. While the coin shortage had been a frequent complaint, the quantity of silver and gold coins, constituting the greatest value of production, was dependent on depositors, not on the capabilities of the Mint. Thomas Jefferson was told of a device proposed by Leslie, and Director Boudinot was informed about it. The Mint was asked to give it a trial.

The supposed innovation proved to be simply a variation of the old European roller die system (in which coins are struck by being squeezed between cylindrical dies rotated on their axes). Leslie was informed that his invention was useless and was told to bring in bullion, not dies, the next time he wanted to improve the institution![35] A conventional press for one-cent pieces could turn out about 14,000 per day—a capacity that was never fully utilized on a yearly basis.

On June 30 of the same year, the officers at the Mint were ordered to discharge all employees who had been idled because of the lack of incoming bullion for coinage.[36] The continuing coinage of copper cents paid expenses. No half cents were struck that year. In the meantime, on February 17, Thomas Jefferson was elected president of the United States by the House of Representatives, succeeding John Adams, who had held the post since Washington's retirement. Jefferson was inaugurated on March 4, 1801.

ABOLISHING THE MINT

In 1802 there was such a vigorous call for closing the Mint that it impaired the efficiency and work of the employees and officers. Pressure became intense, and on March 22 Director Boudinot drew up an inventory of assets for Congress to study. This included equipment such as "five striking presses with machinery, three cutting presses, one milling machine, five pairs of rollers great and small, one drawing machine," and "a large number of hubs and dies on hand, of different denominations."

The tide soon turned for the better. Boudinot's *Annual Report* dated January 1, 1803, included this:

To the President of the United States.

The Director of the Mint of the United States, begs leave respectfully to make his annual report on the issues of the state of the Mint.

He is happy to inform the President, that the bullion deposited in the Mint during the past year, has far exceeded what was expected at the beginning of it, notwithstanding the considerable check given to deposits for some time, by frequent reports from the seat of government, during the last session of Congress, that the Mint would be abolished.

Since the first day of January, 1802, there has been issued from the Mint a sum, amounting in the whole, to five hundred and sixteen thousand one hundred and fifteen dollars, eighty-three cents . . . which has been added to the current coin of the Union. Of this sum, one hundred and twenty-nine thousand seven hundred and thirty dollars, and ninety-one cents, in value, in gold, have been coined from bullion and gold dust imported into the United States, and collected to the Mint, as a center, from the different parts of the Union. The balance of the gold coinage has been coined from clipped, plugged, and otherwise spoiled foreign coins, which have been sent to the Mint as bullion. Had not this whole sum been coined in the United States, it must have been remitted to the European markets; in which case the freights, insurance, and commissions, with the profits on the cents, would have amounted to a sum nearly equal to the current expenditures of the Mint. . . .

The current expenses of the Mint for the past year, have amounted to seventeen thousand four hundred and sixty-two dollars and sixty-five cents, as will appear from Schedule, No. III, from which the profits on the copper coinage, amounting to five thousand six hundred and forty-four dollars and thirty-three cents, should be deducted.

Besides the cents on hand, we have near twenty-four tons of copper planchets ready for striking; the coinage of which are in daily operation, at the rate of fifteen thousand cents a day.

It is a duty incumbent on the Director of the Mint, respectfully to call the President's attention to the expiration of the law of the United States for continuing the Mint at Philadelphia, on the fourth of March next, by its own limitation. It therefore becomes absolutely necessary that the subject should be brought before Congress so early, that provisions may be made for the contingency. If Congress should rise without doing anything therein, the Mint could not be continued in Philadelphia with propriety; neither could it be removed to the seat of government, for want of a law to authorize it.

It is but doing justice to merit to say, that the officers of the Mint, concerned in the coinage, and the workmen, have greatly increased in their professional knowledge, and have acquitted themselves with strict integrity, and particular attention to their several departments, for many years past;—so that not a dollar has been lost, except in one solitary instance, when the culprit was detected by their assiduity and care, prosecuted, and punished; and it was by their exertions that the Mint was kept open during the late distress of the city, by the fever of last summer.

If the Mint should remain in its present situation, there will be a necessity of at least two additional horses, and some repairs to the machinery, part of it having been repaired the past year, from necessity. At least five hundred dollars will be necessary in that case, to be added to the usual estimate, to be appropriated for the purchase of horses, and further repairs to the present machinery.

All which is respectfully submitted to the President, by his very obedient and humble servant,

Elias Boudinot, Director

On March 3, 1803, the authorization was extended for five years, and it was extended again on April 1, 1808, for five more years, then again on December 2, 1812, until March 4, 1818. Other acts covered January 4, 1818, to March 4, 1823, and March 3, 1823, to March 4, 1828. Finally, legislation provided for the Mint to remain in the city of its origin from March 10, 1828, until otherwise provided by law.

A NEW DIRECTOR

In 1805 Boudinot resigned as director, and Mint treasurer Benjamin Rush applied for the post but was told by President Thomas Jefferson that another man, Robert Patterson, had already been chosen. The irony of this was that Rush had been offered the director's post in 1795 (after the resignation of David Rittenhouse) and had declined it at the time because of his lucrative medical practice. To add insult to injury, before their falling out, Rush had loaned Boudinot some chemistry textbooks to study when the latter became director in October of the same year!

In 1807 medal engraver John Reich, a German immigrant who had been doing contract work since 1801, was hired as an assistant engraver at the Mint. In 1808 he created the Classic Head cent design, which was also used on the half cent beginning in the following year.

During this time, ships of England and France were intercepting American vessels and impressing (kidnapping) sailors, as well as committing other offenses.[37] The Embargo Act signed by President Jefferson on December 22, 1807, mandated that no American ships visit foreign ports, an action intended to make England and France relax their oppression of American commerce and cease aggression toward American ships.

However, the embargo and the subsequent Non-Intercourse Act had the salient effect of angering just about everyone engaged in the shipping trade in America, as well as manufacturers and commodities brokers who were now denied overseas markets. Many East Coast shippers took evasive actions, including the preparing of false registers and bills of lading, the loading of ships in small ports or off the coast, and more. A large smuggling trade took place with Canada to the north, a district that was under the control of Great Britain. This was widely reported in the press. Many citizens felt that those in maritime commerce had no alternative.

A pall fell upon the American economy. Hardest hit were port cities, where ships were idled and thousands thrown out of work. Retailers and other merchants suffered, as did manufacturers. West India goods, as they were called, imported from the Caribbean, disappeared from shops. Later historians would view the legislation as a mistake.

The situation changed for the better by 1810, at least for certain manufacturers. The continuing restrictions in maritime commerce caused many factories to enter the production of goods formerly imported from Europe, yielding profits to that sector of the economy (but doing little for shipping merchants). Secretary of the Treasury Albert Gallatin estimated the value of American manufactured goods at $120,000,000 and noted that for many products imports were no longer necessary.

Still, the economy was slow overall, and many merchants continued to suffer. In the same year the third federal census revealed a population of 7,239,881 inhabitants, including 1,211,364 slaves, 186,746 free blacks, and about 60,000 immigrants. Planchets for copper cents continued to be imported from Boulton & Watt, which delivered the best quality for the lowest price.

THE WAR OF 1812

On January 24, 1811, the House of Representatives voted 65 to 64 to postpone the renewal of the charter of the Bank of the United States, which had been established in

1791 and was the largest depot for depositing coins struck at the Mint. In the Senate the vote was 18 to 17. Thus, the bank perished. Earlier, John Jacob Astor, an enemy of the bank, stated that he and his acquaintances would put $2 million at the disposal of the government for financial use if the bank would be discontinued. It is probably the case that the First Bank of the United States, in operation from 1791 to the expiration of its charter in 1811, was beneficial to the citizens of the United States and the stability (such as it was) of the monetary system, but was counter to many personal investments, private bank connections, and the interests of many politicians.

This did not adversely affect the Mint, as it developed. Director Robert Patterson reported:

> With the exception of a few weeks, after the expiration of the charter of the Bank of the United States, the supply of bullion, now furnished chiefly by the other banks in this city, has never been more abundant. . . . From the treasurer's statement of last year's coinage, which is herewith transmitted, it will appear that during that period there have been struck and issued—in gold coins, 99,581 pieces, amounting to $497,905.

On the high seas, sailors from British vessels continued to board American ships. On December 9, Representative Felix Grundy of Tennessee called for war against England, setting the scene for events of the following year. The United States declared war on June 18, 1812, initiating a conflict that became known as the War of 1812. During the next three years, many engagements were fought on the Atlantic Ocean, while other battles took place on Lake Erie and Lake Champlain and on American soil.

Shipments of copper planchets from Boulton & Watt in Birmingham ended, and the Mint worked with its remaining inventory until it ran out. Copper rose in value. On November 13, 1813, Treasurer Thomas T. Tucker contacted the Mint through his Philadelphia agent, Tench Coxe, who related the message that "he judges it advisable at present to abstain from any further distribution of copper coin."

Niles' Weekly Register, March 19, 1814, reported this regarding Representative Adam Seybert from Pennsylvania:

> Mr. Seybert stated that many persons in the United States were in the habit of melting our copper coins, in consequence of the price that the material was now selling at. He stated that for the years 1810, 11, 12, and 13, the value of the cents and half cents coined at the Mint was equal to $33,090.[38]

Seybert offered a resolution "that a committee be appointed to enquire into the expedience of altering the copper coins of the United States." The resolution was subsequently adopted.

This engendered some discussion, which ended when Director Robert Patterson said that changing the standard was infeasible. No half cents had been coined since 1811. In addition, the supply of planchets for cents was running low, and market conditions made it unprofitable to seek more.

The Seybert comment was echoed in a January 19, 1816, congressional motion made by Representative Erastus Root of New York, in which he stated that there was a scarcity of copper coin because these had often used by manufacturers "for the purpose of being melted up for sheets, bolts, or stills, etc." As copper was an important commodity for warfare, the melting was caused by a spike in the copper price during the War of 1812 to 80 cents per pound, or nearly twice face value![39]

No one knows how many cents and half cents disappeared, but the general low grade of extant Classic Head cents suggests that a significant proportion disappeared into the melting pot.

On October 27, 1814, chief coiner Adam Eckfeldt delivered 357,830 cents, the total amount on hand. These had been coined in recent times, perhaps to keep Mint employees busy.[40]

From the viewpoint of many Americans, the conflict with Britain was a war that few people wanted—a maritime dispute that had been blown far out of proportion. Once commenced, both sides fought bitterly, losses were sustained, and many soldiers and sailors were killed. The Capitol and White House in Washington were burned by British troops in late summer 1814, and Baltimore would have been ravaged as well, had it not been for its valiant defense by Fort McHenry (of "The Star-Spangled Banner" fame).

From the onset of the war, a huge quantity of gold coins was exported—this despite the blockade of American ports at certain times by British ships. This situation lasted for the next several years.[41] Various Eastern banks were accused of aiding the British by making specie (the universal Treasury and banking term for silver and gold coins, but not applicable to copper) available to them. This was done under subterfuge as well as through open violations of the law, including shipments to Canada—which was prohibited trade with "the contiguous British provinces."

The conflict caused hoarding of silver and gold coins and the issuance of a flood of mostly worthless paper money. The American monetary system began a long period of stress, strain, and duress. After 1813, gold coins disappeared from circulation, and except for some intermittent episodes before 1821, they were not seen again in the channels of commerce until autumn 1834. A flood of paper bills during the war prompted the hoarding of copper and silver coins as well.

On December 24, 1814, the Treaty of Ghent was signed in Europe, ending the conflict, but news traveled slowly, and fighting continued into the next year, culminating in January 1815 at the Battle of New Orleans with Andrew Jackson's victory for the United States. It was certain that the economy would recover, silver and gold would again be seen in circulation, and good times—the first since the Embargo Act—would return. In February 1815, such coins were seen in some cities, but only briefly.

The flood of paper money continued, and gold and silver stayed in hiding. By July it took an average of $115 in paper to buy $100 in silver half dollars (dollars had not been struck since 1804). During the year, deposits of precious metal were low at the Mint. The only silver coins delivered were quarter dollars. No cents were struck with this date, and gold coins were limited to just 635 half eagles. Half dollars dated 1815 exist (and are scarce), but were not struck until 1816.[42]

CENT COINAGE RESUMES

The Mint did not acquire a supply of copper until late in 1815, by which time there was a slowing of business everywhere. The expected postwar boom had not occurred. On January 1, 1816, Director Patterson reported that the outlook was better for the coming year, though production fell markedly short of his projections here:

> The high price of gold and silver bullion, for some time past, in the current paper money of the country, has prevented, and as long as this shall continue to be the case, must necessarily prevent deposits of these metals being made for coinage, to any considerable amount.
>
> But a fresh supply of copper having lately been received at the Mint, we have again resumed the coinage of cents; and it is believed that we shall, in the course of the year, should no failure in the expected supply of copper take place, be fully able to coin fifty tons weight, amounting to nearly 47,000 dollars; and that with a regular supply of

copper, which can readily be procured on terms highly advantageous to the government, we can continue to coin fifty tons per annum, as long as it may be judged expedient.

The circulation of these copper coins, and of those heretofore issued from the Mint, (amounting to 251,646 dollars,) and which must be still nearly all in the country, would, it is presumed, soon supply, in a great measure, the place of the small silver coins, which have now almost totally disappeared.[43]

In 1816 the Matron Head design was instituted for the cent, and it would be continued through the mid-1830s. Robert Scot is generally attributed as the engraver, but this is not certain, as his eyesight was failing at the time. If it was not Scot, then John Reich probably did the work.

THE MINT FIRE AND REBUILDING

Early in the morning of January 11, 1816, hot ashes placed by a neighbor in a wooden barrel burst into flame next to a Mint building. Within the hour the "mill house" was severely damaged, and some other facilities were scorched or burned. The *United States Gazette* carried this account later in the same day:

> About two o'clock this morning fire broke out in a part of the back buildings belonging to the Mint of the United States, the cause totally unknown. The machinery employed in preparing the gold and silver bullion for coinage has suffered considerable injury, but little or no loss, even the bullion or coins or the precious metals, will be sustained. The front part of the buildings, containing the coining presses, the books and clerk's office, with the engraver's and assayer's apartments, is uninjured.
>
> The director and other officers of the establishment can tender their warmest thanks to the fire companies and other vigilant citizens for their prompt and successful exertions in extinguishing this alarming fire.[44]

Inspection revealed that the equipment for rolling metal strip was a loss, as were many of the tools and machines used for assaying and refining. As happenstance would have it, this was a slow period at the Mint: deposits of metal continued to be very small, and in early 1816 the number of workmen on hand was lower than normal.

As part of the rebuilding of the facilities, improved machinery was ordered from England.[45] Director Robert Patterson reported that the net loss from the fire was slight, as the mill building was in poor repair and the destroyed machinery was so worn that it would have needed replacement soon. It is assumed that no coins other than 1815-dated half dollars and 1816-dated cents were made in 1816, although earlier-dated dies could have been used as well (matching dated dies to use in a calendar year does not seem to have been Mint policy until Robert's son Robert Maskell Patterson became director in late summer 1835, and even after then there were some discrepancies).

In 1816 the Second Bank of the United States commenced business under a 20-year charter granted by Congress. As with the first such bank, which operated from 1791 to 1811, political and commercial dislike of the institution was prevalent, as it was felt that banks should be operated privately and owned by stockholders. While the majority of the stock in both of the Bank of the United States entities was actually owned privately, because the federal government owned a large stake in the stock and had a say in policies, they were widely viewed as national banks.

Branches were opened in more than two dozen cities. Bankers in the private sector viewed the competition as unfair, as the national bank was perceived as being sound and well run, with no chance of failure. In contrast, state-chartered banks often failed due to poor management, an unfavorable economic climate, or for other reasons. Also distressing was the fact that the bills of most private banks were worth par only in the regions in which the banks were located. Elsewhere they traded at a discount. In contrast, notes of the Bank of the United States were worth par everywhere. When the time came, the charter of the Second Bank of the United States was not renewed, mainly due to opposition in the early 1830s by President Andrew Jackson, and the charter would expire in 1836.

The *Mint Report* for the calendar year 1817 noted the following:

> It is expected that the coinage for the next year will be much greater, a considerable quantity of bullion being deposited for the purpose—and arrangements have been made for better supplies of copper. A steam engine is substituted for the horse power heretofore employed.

The steam engine and related iron castings were provided by Oliver Evans, famous in the annals of steam machinery, who on June 24, 1817, was paid $6,508.52 for them.[46] Steam was not used for coining presses until March 1836, and minting continued using manual force on hand-operated screw presses. The rolling mills were ordered from Belles & Harrold in England. As there is no record of purchase, the planchet presses and draw bench were likely made locally under Mint supervision.[47]

In addition to Boulton & Watt, which continued to supply planchets until 1837, Belles & Harrold furnished planchets from 1816 until 1834.[48] In time, firms in Connecticut and Massachusetts supplied planchets in lieu of the British companies.

In 1818 the economy recovered, and silver and gold coins were once again available at par, but not in quantity. Millions of dollars in specie arrived from foreign ports, including many silver five-franc pieces from France.[49] Many shipments were for the Bank of the United States. Regardless, silver coins were rarely seen in circulation, and gold coins remained scarce. This sense of well-being did not last for long, and a business depression took place in 1819 and lasted for the next several years.[50]

The *Annual Report of the Director of the Mint* for 1819 included an enthusiastic mention of the prospect of coining many cents, a profit center:

> Within the year the coinage has been, in gold, 51,723 pieces, amounting to 258,515 dollars.[51] . . . The amount of coinage would have been considerably greater had a sufficient supply of bullion been regularly furnished; but, for four or five months, no deposits of any consequence were received. During this interval, however, the men were advantageously employed in completing and improving the buildings and machinery belonging to the establishment, and the Mint is now, it is believed, fully competent to coin all the gold and silver which it is probable will hereafter be received, as well as to carry on the copper coinage to any desirable amount, for, even with a single press, at the rate it is now working, eighty tons (seven and a half millions of cents) may be coined in the course of a year.

Separately, in answers to queries posed by John H. Eppes, chairman of the Committee of Finance, Director Robert Patterson commented concerning cents: "The copper coinage is continuing in constant operation, striking at least 100,000 cents per week."[52]

THE EARLY 1820S

Large quantities of cents continued to be struck from imported planchets. In fact, there were so many that they could not effectively be placed into circulation. The Annual Report for 1820 noted, "The press employed in the copper coinage did not continue in operation more than six months; as the quantity of copper coins had accumulated far beyond the public demand."

The Mint paid out cents to all comers, in exchange for silver coins, including foreign issues that were legal tender, and at par for notes from any bank whose currency was accepted at face value by the Bank of the United States.[53]

At the time, copper cents seem to have circulated mainly in the Northeast, as related in various Mint and other reports. They were seldom found in the West (at that time defined as Ohio and beyond) or in the deep South. In those places the smallest denomination of coin was the silver half dime, keeping company with the Spanish-American *medio* (half real) valued at 6.25¢. The Mint was only partially successful in promoting expanded use of cents, including free shipping to remote places. Production slumped, and in calendar year 1823 none were coined (although cents from dies of this date were coined later, probably in 1824).

The price of gold increased on international markets. After 1820 it cost more than face value in bullion to make a $5 gold coin, the highest denomination at the time. These, however, continued to be struck in quantity for the export trade. The face value made no difference, as these coins traded at metal value alone, and banks and others active in foreign exchange deposited much bullion to have them produced. These coins were melted overseas, which accounts for their rarity today. This situation did not change until the Act of June 28, 1834, reduced the gold content of coins, after which time they became plentiful in domestic commerce.

In the 1820s, Proof or "master coins" were struck from dies polished to yield a mirrorlike surface. The earliest-dated full set known of these is of 1821 and is in the National Numismatic Collection at the Smithsonian Institution. It became Mint policy to make Proof coins for presentation on special occasions and to provide numismatists with specimens for their cabinets. For half cents and large cents, neither denomination was struck in Proof finish every year, and in 1853 none at all are known to have been made.

A NEW DIRECTOR AND ENGRAVER

In 1824 Samuel Moore succeeded his father-in-law, Robert Patterson, as director of the Mint. Moore remained in office until July 1835, when he was succeeded by Robert Maskell Patterson, of the same family. During this era, the position of director was usually given to someone with a knowledge of the Mint and its operations, sometimes a relative, as here.

In the same year, chief engraver Robert Scot, who had drawn his last pay on October 30, 1823, was succeeded by William Kneass. Another change was to come to the Mint on January 1, 1825, when it was announced that no workman "can be permitted to bring spirituous liquors into the Mint. Any workman who shall be found intoxicated within the Mint must be reported to the Director, in order that he may be discharged."[54]

Also in 1824, Marquis de Lafayette, French hero of the American Revolution, visited the United States and was declared by Congress to be "the Nation's Guest." Before he returned to France in 1825, he visited each state in the Union. Many copper cents and silver half dollars were counterstamped from nine-millimeter dies with his portrait on one side and that of Washington on the other. The dies were cut by Joseph Lewis, a New York City engraver.[55] A few other coins were stamped as well, including an 1807 half cent now in a Missouri collection. For unrelated reasons, cents became scarce in circulation. It was not until the autumn of 1825 that these coins, which were "much wanted," became "abundant," according to *Niles' Weekly Register*.

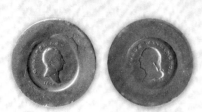

An 1807 half cent counterstamped with dies depicting Lafayette on the obverse and Washington on the reverse. This is the only example of this counterstamp shown on this denomination known to the author. As both the coin and the counterstamped images are well worn, this coin must have remained in circulation for decades after 1824.

An 1822 copper cent counterstamped with Washington on the obverse and Lafayette on the reverse. In 1824 and 1825, thousands of cents and a lesser number of half dollars, as well as a few other coins, were counterstamped to mark the return visit of Lafayette, the French hero of the American Revolution, to America. This example shows little wear and was probably kept as a souvenir.

As the Mint earned a profit on half cents (the coinage of which was resumed in 1825) and cents, it continued to offer free shipping to buyers, as described in this statement in the *Annual Report of the Director of the Mint* for 1827:

> The amount of copper coins distributed within the last year, is $21,910. They are forwarded, as heretofore, at the expense and risk of the government, to all parts of the United States, accessible by regular means of transportation, on receiving the value thereof here, or a certificate of deposit, to the credit of the treasurer of the United States, for the requisite amount, in any of the banks authorized to receive deposits of public money.

And this from the 1828 report:

> Copper coins have been distributed within the last year to the amount of $27,566.34, with a profit thereon of nearly $8,000. The profit thus accruing on the issue of copper coins is regularly paid into the Treasury of the United States; and is an effective reimbursement of so much of the amount annually expended for the support of this establishment.

For this reason, the production of cents continued to be steady and extensive, limited only by the ability of commerce to receive them. In contrast, silver and gold mintages varied widely, depending on deposits.

In 1828 a New Hampshire citizen went on a trip to Philadelphia and entered this in his diary:

> I and Mr. Fisk went to see the United States Mint. There they were, striking off half dollars in one room, and cents in another. The other part of the works were not in operation. I enquired how many half dollars they struck off in a minute, and they said 43.[56] The pieces of silver were plated out and cut to the right size previously, so that they were only given the impression. It took three men to do this; all of them had hold of the machine at a time, and it appeared to be pretty hard labor.[57]

Overview of the Mint in 1829

Director Samuel Moore prepared a report on the Mint to accompany a bill in the House of Representatives, dated January 25, 1829. While some elements were incorrect and are deleted here, it gives a view of the various buildings at the time (adapted):

At first a house and lot on 7th Street and one other lot fronting on a fourteen foot alley, were purchased. Under a subsequent Act of January 2, 1795, a third lot, marked C, was purchased, fronting on the alley and extending northward to a private court and separated from the lots before mentioned by a four foot alley, and all the property bounding it. Other areas were rented but no others were purchased.

Buildings 1 and 2 on the chart are built of brick three stories high, combined as a single unit. Under it are vaults. On the first floor is a receiving and weighing room and one press room. A second floor is all of the officers except the assayers, three of whom have one apartment. The third floor furnishes the office of the assayer, a location exceedingly inappropriate for the character of the chemical agents employed but no other arrangement has been practical.

This building is after the most ordinary manner as customary 50 years ago without any pretensions as design or arrangement. The stairway by which all must reach the office is a dark winding passage in which a lamp is kept burning through the day.

Number 3 is a two story brick building erected in 1816 when steam power was first substituted for that of horses for the purpose of rolling the ingots etc. It contains the steam engine and the machinery pertaining to it thereto skillfully arranged. This department of the works has hitherto been found competent to its design and is even capable of more than had been required. The engine is of the power of about ten horses.

Number 4 is a small frame building rudely constructed, formerly a stable and of little value. It is, however, a place for deposit for nearly all of our coined and uncoined copper.

Number 5 is a two story brick building which contains melting and refining furnaces. So efficient in its dimensions although the refining furnace occupies a cellar that all dependent operations are often retarded by the inefficiency of its accommodation. How silly it was that this building had to be erected on a lot leased which expired some time since. The building and lot are now rented year to year.

Number 6 is a small two story frame building that's lightly constructed. It contains on the first floor the press by which most of our silver is coined and is in daily use for this purpose.

Number 7 is a small two story brick house, old and dilapidated in which the cent coinage is executed. Above these two is a shop for making and repairing machinery.

Number 8 is a smith shop and number 9 is a coal house, both roughly boarded and covered in the same manner.

The whole range presents an aspect singularly unsuited to the important uses which some parts of it have been for so many year appropriated. Lot E has no building on it but is employed as a wood yard.

You recommended that enlarged operations be done with "machinery devised and executed by Mr. Boulton and adopted in some of the mints in Europe." This topic has been the subject of some preliminary inquiries addressed to Mr. Boulton in 1827. From his reply it appears that so much of his system of machinery as might be desirable to introduce would cost about seven thousand pounds at Liverpool. It is understood that machinery of this description, constructed by Mr. Boulton for a Mint in South America, is in New York for sale. If this should be found adapted to our purposes it would be judicious to embrace the opportunity of securing it, the expense it is presumed would be low as the price charged by Mr. Boulton at Liverpool.[58]

THE SECOND PHILADELPHIA MINT AND THE AMERICAN SCENE

LAYING THE CORNERSTONE

On March 2, 1829, Congress appropriated funds for a new mint. Land on Chestnut Street above 13th Street, near the corner of Juniper Street, was purchased. The frontage was 150 feet and the depth 204 feet. The cornerstone was laid on July 4 of the same year.

Designed by well-known architect William Strickland, a personal friend of chief engraver William Kneass (who named one of his children after Strickland), the building was in the Greek Revival style so popular at the time.[1] Six large columns graced the front and upheld the pediment. Many other government and bank buildings of the time were made to look like incarnations of Greek temples, the Bank of the United States (Philadelphia) and the Sub-Treasury (New York City) being but two of numerous examples.

Niles' Weekly Register, July 18, 1829, carried this account:

> The Mint of the United States. From the *Philadelphia Gazette*.
>
> The foundation stone of the edifice about to be erected, under the provisions of the law for extending the Mint establishment, according to a plan thereof approved by the president, was laid, on the morning of the 4th of July, at 6 o'clock, in the presence of the officers of the Mint, and a number of distinguished citizens.
>
> Within the stone was deposited a package, securely enveloped, containing the newspapers of the day, a copy of the Declaration of Independence, of the Constitution of the United States, and of the farewell address of general Washington; also, specimens of the national coins, including one of the very few executed in the year 1792, and a half dime coined on the morning of the 4th, being the first of a new emission of that coin, of which denomination none have been issued since the year 1805.[2]

No half dimes at all had been made since 1805, and now, in the wee hours of the morning of July 4, 1829, the Mint was aglow with activity as sparkling new coins were stamped out in time for the special cornerstone laying. Why the half dime? It was a logical choice, as the smallest authorized silver coin of the United States. These would make ideal souvenirs for those attending, it was thought. And they did! In attendance were various Mint officers and employees, as well as local dignitaries.

THE NEW MINT

The building was ready for occupancy in January 1833. While balance scales, serviceable screw presses, and certain scientific apparatus were brought from the old Mint to the new, most equipment was newly manufactured.[3] In this way the equipment at the old Mint, much of which was in poor condition or obsolete, could be continued in use at the old site while the new Mint was being built and set up for operation. Afterward the old machinery was sold at auction.[4] A steam plant provided power for rolling ingots into strips from which planchets were cut, but coining continued to be done by hand-operated presses.

Production of half cents continued at the new Mint in 1833. In 1834 and 1835 thousands were made, after which minting of this denomination was discontinued until 1849, except for Proofs. There was little demand for them from banks and others, and a generous supply remained on hand from earlier times. Production of copper for Mint profit was more efficient with the cent denomination. On August 1, 1834, the Mint commenced striking gold coins of the new lightweight standard, permitting them to circulate once again. By autumn they were seen in commerce, but it took several years of production before the $2.50 and $5 coins were plentiful. The design was by chief engraver William Kneass and was a loose copy of the head that John Reich had created in 1808 for the cent.

The second Philadelphia Mint, which was occupied for
coinage from January 1833 to autumn 1901, shown in 1897.

Late in the year 1833 there was a pause in the economy. On February 8, 1834, *Niles' Weekly Register* reported that the "value of lands and their productions, of buildings, and of stocks of all sorts, and commodities, in general, has fallen an average of not less than 15 percent since the first October last—perhaps 20 percent." This was soon forgotten, and good times resumed. America enjoyed an era of unbridled prosperity spurred by the building of railroads and the sale of federal lands in the West—in the districts beyond Pennsylvania. In 1835 the Treasury declared a surplus, and money was returned to the states (to this day a unique occurrence).

In August 1835, chief engraver William Kneass suffered a stroke, after which he became partially incapacitated. Christian Gobrecht, who was an accomplished artist and engraver in the private sector, was hired to do the work. For a decade he had done contract projects for the Mint, and the quality of his output was well known and appreciated. Although Kneass had been laid low by his stroke, chief technology officer (so to speak) Franklin Peale wrote to Director Robert Maskell Patterson on December 16, 1836, noting that "new dies were executed with all necessary enthusiasm by Messrs Kneass and Gobrecht and hardened then by Mr. Eckfeldt all complete for striking this morning."[5] Thus, it appears that Kneass had recovered somewhat and was capable of at least assisting. These were probably dies for the first Liberty Seated silver dollars (Gobrecht dollars, as we call them today).

Although copper, silver, and gold coins all circulated side by side in the mid-1830s, most trade was conducted with paper money issued by nearly a thousand state-chartered banks. These had no specific backing in gold or silver but were issued on the promise to redeem them in coins upon presentation. Banks kept only small amounts of coins on hand for this purpose, as funds were employed in investments and loans in order to generate profits for stockholders. So long as a bank had a good reputation, most notes remained in circulation in their region. When there was concern about a bank's strength, sometimes a run would occur, more paper would be presented than could be redeemed, and the institution would fail.

The prosperity of America attracted many foreign investors, and international commerce flourished. Shipping notices continually reported large quantities of silver and gold coins arriving at New York, Philadelphia, Boston, and other ports. The coins of choice for trade were Spanish-American issues, particularly the eight-real silver "dollar" and the eight-escudo gold doubloon, which were legal tender by various acts of Congress. Despite the domestic mintage of coins since 1793, in 1836 it was estimated that only one-sixth of the circulating silver coinage in New York was American made.[6] Gold coins were even scarcer. Copper coins were dominated by American cents, to which were added other issues, including state coppers that were made in the 1780s, and which were by now well worn.

Improved Technology

Steam power came into increased use, and by 1835 much equipment in American factories was driven by this force—exceptions including mills located on usable waterways. It seemed appropriate to harness such energy to run more equipment at the Mint, in addition to steam-powered roller mills.

In 1833 Director Samuel Moore arranged for Franklin Peale, a son of local artist and museum proprietor Charles Willson Peale, to go to Europe and visit the various mints there. He left in May and was abroad for nearly two years. While there, he examined coining equipment and assaying processes in England, France, and elsewhere. Upon his return, the Mint ordered certain equipment, the most important being a Contamin portrait lathe, or *tour à portrait de Contamin*. This device aided in the making of metal hubs by transfer or pantograph from larger images in brass or iron. The Contamin unit remained in use past the era of copper half cents and cents.

In 1836 steam power was used to drive an improved model of a milling machine, which took flat planchets and, by compressing them between a roller and curved metal plate, put a raised or "upset" rim on them. This facilitated coining, as less metal flow was needed in the press to fully strike up the rim. How important this was to copper coinage is not known, as planchets ordered from private suppliers such as Crocker Brothers were supplied with raised rims already in place.

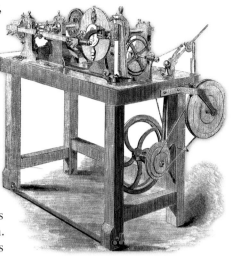

A Contamin-style portrait lathe in use at the Philadelphia Mint.

STEAM FOR COINAGE

By this time, mints in Europe had come to use a knuckle-action coining press invented in Prussia by D. Uhlhorn, the design of which had been improved by Thonnelier. Peale reported:

> Presses on similar principles are in use in more than one city in Germany, and their successful operation was witnessed in Carlesruhe [Karlsruhe] in the Grand Duchy of Baden. Particular advantage has been derived from a careful examination of the coining presses of Monsieur Thonnelier, of Paris. It is just to observe that none of these presses were perfectly satisfactory. I have, therefore, made my own distribution and proportion of parts, thrown off whatever was complex, and added such as were necessary to its perfection.

By September 1835, a model had been constructed in Philadelphia under Peale's supervision. In the same city the firm of Merrick & Agnew, makers of heavy equipment including fire engines, was commissioned to construct such a machine for the Mint, with Rufus Tyler (who became chief coiner at the New Orleans Mint when it opened in 1838) as the lead mechanic. It was Mint practice over the years to keep old presses on hand as new presses were added, so that at any given time the age of the equipment was mixed. Power was generated by a vertical "steeple" type steam engine located at a distance in the building and transmitted to the press via shafts and pulleys.[7]

Peale continued, listing the advantages of the new press recently constructed:

> A few familiar facts are added as evidences of the peculiar adaptation of the toggle-joint to coining, as proved by the operation of the press which is the subject of this notice.

> 1. The pressure acts with increasing force until the close of the operation, at which time its intensity is greatest, and it is always carried to the same extent.

2. No injury occurs from the absence of a blank from between the dies when the blow is given, an accident that results in the destruction, or great injury, to one, if not both of the dies, in presses of the ordinary construction.

3. An immense saving of labour. From trial, we have ascertained that a man, with one hand applied by means of a common winch handle, can coin eighty pieces per minute (the experiment was tried upon cents, which have a diameter of 1 and 1/10 inches). A boy, fourteen years of age, was able to coin sixty per minute, without any unusual exertion; and, lastly, it was impossible for the operator to tell, by the resistance offered to his exertions, whether the pieces were being coined or not.

It was hoped to have the new steam-powered coining press ready to demonstrate on February 22, 1836, George Washington's 104th birthday. Christian Gobrecht prepared a small medal with this date to be struck and distributed at the ceremony. In this era, the two grand national holidays were Washington's Birthday and Independence Day (July 4). Each furnished the opportunity for orations, parades, and festivities.[8] The press was not ready, however, and the opportunity was missed. The reverse die was altered to the date of March 23, when the ceremonial striking finally took place.

In time, other presses were made, in three capacities, the medium-size being suitable for striking eagles, quarter dollars, and cents, as demonstrated on March 23. The units had automatic feed by a vertical tube that stored planchets.[9]

The steam-powered presses were very successful. Director Patterson wrote to secretary of the Treasury Levi Woodbury on June 30, 1837, commenting, "One of the steam-presses has coined 400,000 cents within the last few weeks, without interruption or accident, and our largest press has been coining half dollars with perfect success."[10]

An impression from the dies of the February 22, 1836, medalet by Christian Gobrecht. When the ceremony was postponed, the reverse die was altered to read March 23, 1836. (Massachusetts Historical Society)

The first steam-powered coining press installed at the Mint in 1836, first used that March for coining copper cents.

CROCKER BROTHERS

William A., Samuel L., and George A. Crocker associated as Crocker Brothers and began processing copper near Norton Center, Massachusetts, on a mill on the Wading River. In 1831 the brothers joined with Daniel Brewer, Nathaniel Crandell, and others to form the Taunton Copper Manufacturing Company, under the name of Crocker Brothers & Co., capitalized at $200,000. Seeking to expand the business, the company sent a letter of inquiry to the Mint on March 19, 1832. A contract to manufacture planchets was arranged. The first shipment of samples to the Mint was made in October of the same year. These were found to be fully equal to the Boulton & Watt quality, and could be purchased at a lower price. The English firm continued to be a supplier, however. Within the Crocker factory, William Allen West was in charge of this activity and operated the devices, including one or more milling machines, to create raised rims.

Not only did Crocker Brothers make planchets, they also worked with the Mint in distributing finished cents in New York and the New England states. These were sent from Philadelphia to Norton Center in the same casks that Crocker had used for the planchets. In 1838, Mint Director Patterson ended the Mint's arrangement with Boulton & Watt. The Crocker Brothers continued their arrangement with the Mint through the end of the era of half cents and copper cents in early 1857, although they were not the only supplier.[11]

THE PANIC OF 1837

In 1836 by many outward appearances the American economy continued to be prosperous. However, business reports increasingly told of problems with banks, manufacturers, and credit. Many large loans were past due. The land boom in the West had slowed to nearly a standstill that summer after President Andrew Jackson issued the Specie Circular, which mandated that land purchases be paid for only in gold or silver coins and that paper money was no longer acceptable.

The Second Bank of the United States wound down its operations, sold its buildings, and closed. The slack was taken up by state-chartered banks without any problems. Nicholas Biddle, president of the bank, formed the deceptively named Bank of the United States of Pennsylvania, but dropped "of Pennsylvania" from most publicity. The venture ultimately failed, bringing disgrace to Biddle, who had been a pillar of Philadelphia society.

As the year 1837 commenced, the prices of everyday goods kept rising. On February 15, a crowd of several thousand people gathered in New York City in a park near City Hall to protest the high costs of bread, meat, and fuel. Unemployment was increasing, and many families were having difficulty making ends meet. Flour in particular had risen sharply in value, from $7 and $8 per barrel to $12. Many believed, with partial justification, that this was due to hoarding and speculation, but a poor wheat crop the year before was the main cause.

The Flour Riot ensued. Warehouses were broken into, including one owned by Eli Hart that held 53,000 barrels, and flour and wheat were destroyed. About 40 rioters were eventually captured, tried, and sent to prison for short terms. The damage had unintended consequences. Flour increased in scarcity and promptly rose in price another 50 cents per barrel.[12]

In March stock prices on Wall Street fell across the board. Anxiety gripped the financial community. New Orleans, the trading center of the Mississippi Valley, was hard hit, and in that southern port Herman Briggs & Company, a leading cotton brokerage house, failed. In a domino effect, other brokers and factors went bankrupt, and banks experienced a cash shortage. The era of prosperity was over.

At a March 1837 meeting in New York City, Daniel Webster told a crowd that the growing financial problems were due to government interference with private bank notes in general and, in particular, the Specie Circular. Few questioned his statement. Appeals were made by various business interests to newly inaugurated President Martin Van Buren, complaining that real estate values in the country had dropped by $40 million within the past six months.

At the time there were 788 banks in the United States, with a total capital of $291 million. These institutions had $149 million worth of paper money in circulation, backed by only $37.9 million worth of gold and silver coins. Deposits totaled $127 million. Outstanding loans amounted to $525 million.[13]

It was evident from such figures that of every $100 in paper bills in circulation, only about $23 in coins was available for redemption. Bankers hoped against hope that the notes would stay "out there" in commerce.

The credit and cash crunch went from bad to worse: increasing demands were made to redeem paper money, and on May 10, 1837, New York banks suspended specie payments under a state law that permitted them to do this for a one-year period. By this time there were about 100 bank failures in the city—an amazing number—causing a loss of about $15 million. Philadelphia banks suspended the payment of gold and silver coins on May 11. After this action virtually every bank elsewhere in the United States suspended paying out coins.

By the end of the year it was estimated that at least 618 banks had failed nationwide. Many of these had assets of dubious value, and some had no assets at all—except a printing press or, more likely, some bank-note ordering-forms from one or another of the engraving and printing firms, who in turn were all too eager to deliver as many notes as were requested without doing much in the way of checking credentials. The country was awash in "broken bank" notes not worth the paper they were printed on. In Michigan, considerably more than 80 percent of the dozens of banks were in this category. An estimated 39,000 citizens went bankrupt, $741 million were registered in business losses, and all but one textile mill in New England closed down.[14] Adding to the general misery was the continuing high price of flour, caused by a combination of speculation and expensive importation from the Mediterranean area.

Coins of all kinds disappeared from circulation, including copper cents, and in order to maintain commerce, paper shinplasters were issued by merchants, banks, towns, and others. Most of these became as worthless as the broken bank notes they supplemented.

New Kinds of "Cents"

Cent-size copper tokens were made by the millions and helped fill the need for small change. These were the Hard Times tokens that numismatists so dearly love today. Scovill's mint and button factory in Waterbury, Connecticut, made many of these tokens, selling keg lots at well under face value to merchants who wanted to spend them or give them out in change. Many tokens bore advertisements of merchants; others bore anti-Jackson or anti–Van Buren inscriptions, including references to the failure to recharter the now-defunct Second Bank of the United States. Others had a Liberty Head on the obverse and a wreath on the reverse, similar in general appearance to contemporary cents but with slightly different inscriptions. Newspapers denounced the tokens as counterfeits. They were not legal tender, but neither were large cents in the view of many, as contemporary federal law had made no such provision. Recipients could refuse either variety of copper, but if they did there was the risk of receiving worthless paper scrip instead.

Tokens may or may not have been in contravention to this law approved on March 3, 1825:

> SEC. 21. And be it further enacted, That, if any person, or persons, shall falsely make, forge, or counterfeit, or cause or procure to be falsely made, forged or counterfeited, or willingly aid or assist in falsely making, forging, or counterfeiting any coin, in the resemblance or similitude of any copper coin which has been, or hereafter may be,

coined at the Mint of the United States; or shall pass, utter, publish, or sell, or attempt to pass, utter, publish, or sell, or bring into the United States, from any foreign place, with intent to pass, utter, publish, or sell, as true, any such false, forged, or counterfeited coin, with intent to defraud any body politic, corporate, or any other person, or persons, whatsoever; every person, so offending, shall be deemed guilty of felony, and shall, on conviction thereof, be punished by fine, not exceeding one thousand dollars, and by imprisonment, and confinement to hard labour, not exceeding three years.[15]

While most Hard Times tokens were copper and of cent size, there were a few exceptions to this format, including in particular those of Feuchtwanger's composition. These are especially important in the annals of copper coinage, as their manufacturer petitioned Congress to do away with current copper cents and use his alloy instead.

Lewis Feuchtwanger, a scientist, metallurgist, and druggist, had compounded the alloy, which was variously known as American silver and Feuchtwanger's composition. It was a variety of the class of metal generally known as German silver. It had a silver-gray color, giving it the impression of having value, but its composition was of nickel, copper, and tin—none of them precious.[16]

In New York City, Feuchtwanger became an exhibitor at the yearly fairs of the American Institute, a trade association that awarded medals and certificates for noteworthy products. In 1834 he took home a silver medal for his display of implements made of his composition, which was said to be useful as a substitute for silver in any application, including tableware.

In 1837 Feuchtwanger issued a token that was probably distributed by the hundreds of thousands, if not to the extent of more than a million. This volume is evidenced by the availability today of Feuchtwanger tokens in many different die varieties. The obverse depicted an eagle pouncing on a rattlesnake, with the date below. The reverse was lettered FEUCHTWANGER'S COMPOSITION around the border, and bore ONE / CENT within a wreath at the center. The edge was reeded. He advertised to redeem these cents on demand at his business at 2 Courtlandt Street in lower Manhattan.

In late summer and autumn 1837, Feuchtwanger spent much time and effort trying to interest Congress in adapting his alloy to make coins. His ideas were outlined in a petition dated September 13, 1837, which noted the following:

An 1837 Hard Times token, SUBSTITUTE FOR SHIN PLASTERS, a copper, cent-size issue of a type that became common in circulation after payment of specie (silver and gold coins) was suspended beginning on May 10. Bank notes were often called shinplasters, a derisive term suggesting that they were not much good for anything except applying plaster to a hurt leg. The phoenix, a mythical bird that arose from its own ashes, perhaps expressed hope that the monetary system would revive.

A Hard Times token made in imitation of the contemporary cent design. The inscription NOT ONE CENT was included on the reverse to evade charges of counterfeiting. The phrase was used generations earlier as a patriotic refusal when the pirates of Tripoli in the Mediterranean Sea demanded tribute to allow American ships to pass safely.

That your memorialist after repeated labors, has succeeded in making and perfecting a metallic composition, known as German silver, of clean, white, and durable material, of specific value, from which coins and all articles can be advantageously manufactured, as are now wrought out of pure silver.

Your memorialist proposes to your honorable body to substitute this composition for the copper currency of the country, by striking off pieces of the size of a dime, and of the value of one cent, specimens of which he has prepared for inspection.

Your memorialist proposes to furnish this substitute for copper as cheaply as copper is now furnished to the Mint, and is confident that the "silver cent" thus proposed as a substitute for the cent pieces will be more acceptable, more portable, and would be more generally used in making up the fractional parts of a dollar.

Your memorialist prays your honorable body to take the subject under your consideration, and, as in duty bound, will ever pray.[17]

In Congress on the same day, September 13, Senator Thomas Hart Benton of Missouri presented Feuchtwanger's proposal "accompanied by specimens" for distribution to fellow legislators.[18] To advance his proposal, the inventor prepared a "Circular," as it was titled, enclosing an example of a "silver penny" made of his alloy, and with this text:

I submit for your consideration a specimen of a one-cent piece made of American Composition, known by the name of German Silver, equivalent in value to One Cent in Copper, which I propose with the authority of Congress, to substitute for the existing unclean and unhealthy Copper Currency by which a handsome current coin may be obtained answerable for the fractional parts of a Dollar, and acceptable in the operations of trade and local purchases.

If this "Silver Penny" as I wish to have it designated shall be approved by Congress as a substitute for the one Cent pieces, I shall in that case, propose to remunerate the Mint for any loss sustained by the United States by the withdrawal of the Copper Coin. I am ready to contract for the delivery at the Mint of any amount of the Composition which Congress may authorize to be coined.

Dr. Lewis Feuchtwanger,
New-York City[19]

The response was lukewarm at best. The idea continued to command the attention of Senator Benton, however, who on October 14 wrote to Mint Director Patterson to endorse the idea. On January 4, 1838, Patterson replied that the alloy was of uncertain standard, that the government would not want to buy metal from a monopolist, and so on. Perhaps most important, he reminded Benton:

An 1837 cent of Feuchtwanger's composition issued by Lewis Feuchtwanger. These were made in large quantities and circulated widely. A strong effort was made to have Congress adopt the metal for federal coinage purposes, but this was blocked for several reasons, including the Mint's reliance on copper coinage to earn a profit. (Shown at 125%.)

On the whole, it is my decided opinion that it would not be proper to abandon our copper coinage in favor of the proposed substitute, and you

will observe that, in presenting this opinion, I have not thought it necessary to bring to your view the many advantages belonging to the copper coinage; its profit to the Government, (the only pecuniary offset to the expense of the Mint).

GOBRECHT AND THE COPPER CENTS

The year 1838 opened with generally unfavorable business conditions left over from the year before. The malaise would last for several years. In time, surviving banks resumed paying out coins, and in 1843 the economy turned upward to a new era of prosperity.

In June 1838, the Mint Cabinet, a collection of coins, medals, and minerals, was formed at Philadelphia with a stipend of $1,000 in the Treasury Department's budget for that year. Mint assayers Jacob Reese Eckfeldt and William E. Dubois took charge of gathering specimens, including some said to have been furnished by old-time employee Adam Eckfeldt (Jacob's father). However, most were culled from incoming deposits of silver and gold coins. In addition to numismatic specimens the Cabinet included ores and some items wrought from precious metals.

In the same year the first branch mints were opened in Charlotte, North Carolina; Dahlonega, Georgia; and New Orleans, Louisiana. The first two produced only gold coins, and the last struck both silver and gold.

In the mid-1830s some adjustments, attributed to Christian Gobrecht, were made to the Matron Head design on the cent. In 1837 the plain hair cord of Miss Liberty was replaced by strings of beads. In 1839 the Booby Head and Silly Head portraits, as collectors call them, were introduced and made for a short time. The culmination the same year was an entirely new portrait by Gobrecht, the Braided Hair type, which was continued until 1857. The same motif was used on half cents from 1840 to 1857.

Copper cents were used at this time mainly in the Northeast, and also west to Michigan, but they were not popular beyond that point. To the south, such coins circulated in Virginia but were not often seen in the lower states. Several accounts have been found of unopened kegs of cents that had been sent to the South being returned.

Adam Eckfeldt—who had been appointed as chief coiner by President James Madison on February 15, 1814, and who had been on the staff since 1795—resigned early in 1839, and Franklin Peale was named his replacement on March 29.

On March 15, 1839, subscriptions amounting to $180 were raised by various Mint officials in Eckfeldt's honor. The money was used to strike a gold medal, which honored his service. Two were made in silver for the president of the United States and the secretary of the Treasury, and bronze examples were made available to others.[20] According to Mint refiner and melter Richard S. McCulloh, Eckfeldt visited the Mint frequently in his retirement. He died on February 5, 1852.

The May 1846 issue of *Hunt's Merchants' Magazine and Commercial Review* included this general commentary on the Mint, part of a description of business activities in Philadelphia:

> Another edifice of considerable magnitude, and although under the administration of the general government, yet devoted to objects connected with commerce, is the United States Mint. This edifice is constructed of white marble, and was finished in 1830. It exhibits a front of about one hundred and twenty-two feet upon Chestnut-street, and the same upon Centre Square, decorated with six lofty Ionic columns.
>
> All the steps connected with the coining of money from the bar of gold, silver and copper, to the stamped eagle, dollar or penny, are here prosecuted, and all the processes of assaying, refining and coining, are performed, both in the preparing and stamping the metal. The apartments of the building are elegantly arranged, and the finished and effective machinery by which all those operations are conducted, is propelled entirely by steam-power.[21]

Cents as Legal Tender

In November 1846, *Banker's Magazine* reported this, under the title of "Legal Tender":

> In a case pending before Baltimore County Court, sitting as a court of appeals, Judge Purviance presiding, a question arose as to whether cents are a legal tender. From the evidence, it appeared that the appellant had tendered, in payment of a debt amounting to upwards of $20 a bag of cents, which were refused.
>
> On the part of the appellee it was contended, upon the authority of a decision of the Supreme Court of South Carolina, that cents are not legal tender in payment of any debt amounting to more than four cents, as the smallest silver coin is the half dime or five-cent-piece, and as the Constitution of the United States uses only the words gold and silver.
>
> For the appellant it was maintained, that the act of the Assembly of Maryland, 1812, makes the coins of the United States current money, which may be tendered in payment of debts in Maryland, and that cents are as much the coins of the United States as any coins issued from the Mint.
>
> In the course of the evidence it appeared that the tender was not made to a person authorized to receive it, and therefore the case passed off upon this point. The learned judge, however, in the course of his opinion, intimated that no difficulty could exist as to the fact of cents being a legal tender, and in support of his opinion referred to a note to 2 Greenleaf on Evidence, page 496,—an able work, sanctioned by the approbation of the late Judge Story—in which it is declared "copper cents and half cents are established as part of the currency, and by implication made a legal tender, by stat. 1792, ch. 39, sec. 2."
>
> The case was ably and elaborately argued by W. P. Preston, Esq., for the appellant, and W. H. Collins and J. C. Blackburn, Esq., for the appellee.

In January 1848, gold was discovered in quantity at Sutter's Mill on the American River in California. Beginning in 1849, large deposits of the metal were received at the Philadelphia Mint. This ushered in a new era of activity, and coinage presses were kept busy for the next decade. In 1849 half cents were made for circulation again, for the first time since 1835.

The price of copper was rising in the marketplace, and although the Mint had no difficulty obtaining planchets, the profit from coinage diminished. Abundant quantities of the metal were available from mines in the Lake Superior district and elsewhere. Much of this copper was processed in Connecticut and Massachusetts. Although several different companies furnished cent planchets after the mid-1840s, most were supplied by Crocker Brothers, who provided all of the half cent planchets after 1848.

Beginning in 1850, many experiments were made with lighter-weight, pattern versions of the cent. The Act of February 21, 1853, reduced the silver content of coins from the half dime to the half dollar (but not the dollar). Subsequently, coinage in these metals yielded a profit to the Treasury Department. No longer were cents the only significant source of such revenue.

Politics and Scandals

Also in 1853, in response to political pressure and a changing administration in Washington, Robert Maskell Patterson (the first Robert Patterson's son) resigned as director of the Mint. This resignation triggered a long string of political rather than merit-based

appointments to the post, a sad state of affairs indeed. Unlike Patterson, most later directors entered the office with very little knowledge of coinage, manufacturing, or monetary history. An October 1853 article in *Banker's Magazine* included this:

> In these days, when the simple dogma, that to the victors belong the spoils, governs appointments to office, and partisanship outweighs all higher claim, it is a public misfortune that the leaven of tried worth cannot remain in some departments of the public service.
>
> In view of the vast business of the Mint, the scientific and technical nature of its operations, the government should have made it consistent with Mr. Patterson's interest to remain. He takes out of it, however, a reputation for high talents and perfect probity; and, personally, he must be the gainer by the voluntary withdrawal from a place, which is no longer secure against the periodical squabbles of needy politicians.

Robert Maskell Patterson, the last of the learned Mint directors—men who had knowledge of science and mechanics prior to their appointment. Later, the directorship became a political plum.

The coining room at the Philadelphia Mint as it appeared in the 1850s and early 1860s. (*Harper's Monthly*, December 1861)

For a long time chief coiner Franklin Peale had been using Mint employees and equipment during regular working hours to conduct his private business of making dies for and striking medals. Sometimes employees were sent to Peale's house to do carpentry, plastering, and other jobs. One of the Mint workmen was ordered to drive Peale's daughter Anna around in a carriage. In other instances Mint workmen were assigned to fix tents and make bows and arrows for an archery club to which Peale belonged. In 1853, charges were preferred against Peale. He survived this, but in late 1854 there was an incident involving medal dies, and he was fired. Peale then petitioned Congress for $30,000 for all the work and improvements he had done at the Mint. Many, if not most, of the Mint employees felt his dismissal was incorrect. Peale was widely liked, was prominent in Philadelphia society and scientific circles, and for years afterwards he was mentioned by his former fellow workers as being responsible for many of the innovations at the Mint.[22] His daughter continued the fight for compensation after Peale's death in early 1870 and obtained $10,000 from Congress in March 1873.[23]

In spring 1854, the Philadelphia *North American* reported that the Mint was becoming secretive:

> We are unable to present to-day our customary exhibit of the operations of the Mint for the month of April, in consequence of an order, from the Treasury Department, forbidding the officers of the institution furnishing the information for publication. In future, we understand, the information is only to be communicated to the Secretary of the Treasury, who will exercise his own discretion to the time and form of publication.
>
> This, we cannot but think, is a reform backward, and apparently without any object, unless it be the object of the honorable secretary to withhold facts from the business and financial portions of the country at large, and in which they have a deep interest.[24]

Part of this criticism may have had to do with a major investigation within the Philadelphia Mint, in which many irregularities and illegal acts were discovered. It was learned that the weigh clerk had complete control of incoming shipments, without audit, and others were similarly unsupervised. A devastating report many pages in length included this:

> In the melting-room there are always several operatives at work, and they, to a certain extent, would seem as a check against depredations, but not a certain preventive, as each deposit is under the charge of a single workman, who, if so disposed, might readily slip out of the pan a California slug or other valuable piece of gold. Thus, from the time the deposit is first made until placed in the crucible to be melted, it is exposed to the depredations of the several parties who have access to the weigh-room, to the vault, and to the melting room.
>
> An abstraction of one-fourth of one per cent. only from an annual deposit of fifty millions of bullion, would produce $125,000; and yet, from the variable character of the deposits, differing, as they do, in their results, from the one-half of one per cent. up to six and seven per cent., it will readily be perceived that an abstraction of one, two, and even three per cent., might be made from the deposits without detection, and almost without suspicion; for as the loss will fall on the depositor, they might readily be made to believe, or to suppose, that the bullion contained a larger portion of the baser material than was supposed.
>
> From this it will be seen what an enormous sum might be abstracted from the deposits; and as the character of the Mint is at stake, every possible effort should be made to preserve its good name. As the vault is open to several persons connected

with the weigh-room, it would be an easy matter for any of these persons to take from the boxes containing the deposits, pieces of California slugs, or lumps of gold; and to equalize the loss among the several depositors, they might filch a small portion of the dust in the different boxes and deposit the same in the boxes from which the slugs or lumps of gold were taken.[25]

From secret observations and more than 100 pages of testimony, it was learned that for *several years,* dating back to at least December 1851, a Mr. Negus of the department had been stealing; he was pinpointed as the greatest offender. During the investigation it was found that from a single shipment in April 1854, Negus had "filched a portion from each of the sixteen boxes," and 72.80 ounces of gold was found in "the bag in his private vault." His total defalcations made him a wealthy man, garnering more than a quarter-of-a-million dollars over the course of his employment—at minimum! Negus's thievery was reported to the Treasury, but by the time the secretary of the Treasury sent orders to have Negus arrested, it was found that he had fled the country.[26]

The Closing Chord

Elsewhere within the Mint, experiments with patterns of lighter-weight cents culminated in the Act of February 21, 1857, which included this:

> SEC. 4. And be it further enacted, That from and after the passage of this act, the standard weight of the cent coined at the mint shall be seventy-two grains, or three-twentieths of one ounce troy, with no greater deviation than four grains in each piece; and said cent shall be composed of eighty-eight per centum of copper and twelve per centum of nickel, of such shape and device as may be fixed by the director of the mint, with the approbation of the Secretary of the Treasury; and the coinage of the half cent shall cease.

In anticipation of this, copper half cents and cents were last coined in January 1857, at which time they slipped into history.

An 1850 pattern cent from dies reflecting a silver content of 10 percent in a mixture of silver and copper called *billon.* The hole in the center permitted the coin to be of larger diameter than would otherwise be the case. The dies were made up quickly to test the concept (Judd-119).

In 1853, pattern cents were made of a nickel alloy by combining a regular quarter eagle obverse die with a hastily made reverse (Judd-150).

In 1854 the Contamin portrait lathe was used to trace over an already-struck Liberty seated dollar to create a smaller hub to be used to strike pattern cents. The pantograph tracing was done quickly, some of the star details were lost, and the 4 in the date resembled a 1. A reverse die was prepared, and patterns were struck of a smaller diameter and weight than the circulating coppers (Judd-157).

Seemingly, for the Mint it was good riddance, per this comment in the *Annual Report of the Director of the Mint*, 1860:

> The new cents have heretofore been issued in exchange for the fractions of the Spanish and Mexican dollar, and for the old copper cents. As the Spanish and Mexican pieces were received at their nominal value, large amounts of these coins have been brought to the melting-pot, and thus the community has been relieved from an irregular and depreciated currency. . . . In order to accelerate the process of relieving the community from the cumbrous and inconvenient copper cents, the Mint now pays the expenses of transportation on them, and will make returns in the new issues. This arrangement will tend to relieve the country from a burdensome currency, without increasing the amount of circulation of that denomination of coins.

In 1854 pattern cents were made of the Braided Hair / Matron Head type, but with a reduced diameter and without obverse stars (Judd-161).

A reduced-diameter pattern cent of 1855, using as the obverse a motif Christian Gobrecht had created for an 1838 pattern half dollar. Similar Flying Eagle patterns were also made in 1854 (Judd-172).

The pattern production terminated with the 1856, Flying Eagle, cent of 72 grains weight. More than 800 of these were made for distribution to congressmen, newspaper editors, and others of influence. Later, 2,000 or more restrikes were privately made for sale through favored dealers. These coins resulted in passage of the Act of February 21, 1857, discontinuing the copper half cent and cent.

PEOPLE AND PROCESSES WITHIN THE MINT

ENGRAVERS AT THE MINT

ARTISTS AND DESIGNS

The appearance of copper half cents and cents reflected the taste and artistry of the engraver. There were few hard and fast rules, other than Congress's stipulation that "upon one side of each of the said coins there shall be an impression emblematic of liberty, with an inscription of the word, LIBERTY." Generations later, sculptor August Saint-Gaudens, contemplating this, noted that here was no definition of what "an impression" should be, and suggested that a "young boy leaping" might be representative.

By 1792 a female head was chosen, which in later Mint notes was referred to as an "ideal head," or a depiction of no person in particular. Women had been depicted on coins since ancient times, including Athena on the famous silver "owl" of Athens, as well as Cleopatra, Queen Anne of England, and others. However, these represented specific goddesses or monarchs.

In colonial America, continuing into the Confederation period, the obverses of coins depicted many subjects, including pine trees on Massachusetts silver coins and New Hampshire coppers, rocky landscapes on Vermont coins, a horse head and plow on coppers of New Jersey, a volcanic peak on the Brasher doubloon, and a sundial on Fugio coppers. The goddess Columbia was depicted on certain coppers of 1785 to 1787, King George II and King George III on Connecticut coppers, and Lord Baltimore on Maryland silver. Indians were illustrated on the obverse of certain Massachusetts and New York copper coins. George Washington was the motif of some tokens dated in the 1780s and early 1790s.

The patterns of 1792 each showed a female head on the obverse, with several interpretations, each quite different. These became known as Liberty heads. The inspiration may have been issues of France, where Miss Liberty had been used on the Libertas Americana medal, commissioned for the United States by Benjamin Franklin.

Whatever the reason, Miss Liberty in various representations was used on the obverse of all half cents and cents from 1793 to 1857, and on the reverse of each was a wreath, UNITED STATES OF AMERICA, and the denomination. Interpretations were by various artists and were usually of their own design, although the Draped Bust motif first used on the cents of 1796 and later the half cents of 1800 was from a sketch by artist Gilbert Stuart, who was not associated with the Mint.

Some of the most important engravers are discussed in the following sections.

HENRY VOIGT

The engraver of the dies for the 1793 Chain cents, Wreath cents, and perhaps the Liberty Cap half cents was Henry Voigt, the coiner at the Mint.[1] He performed this function until Joseph Wright was hired in the summer of 1793—probably in mid- to late August.[2] Voigt also forged, turned, and hardened the die steel, per Mint records.

In the past, some have forwarded Adam Eckfeldt as the artist responsible for the Liberty Cap design—these numismatists include Frank H. Stewart (author of *First United States Mint, Its People and Its Operation*, 1924) and, after him, Walter Breen (although he later revised his opinion on the matter). Eckfeldt was a mechanic, and no record has been found of his having any engraving talent or expertise. Eckfeldt was paid for some smith work on December 14, 1792, after which he does not appear in Mint records until April 3, 1795. Further mention of Eckfeldt is made later in the section on Robert Scot.

Voigt (also spelled in the Anglicized version of Voight in many citations) was born in Pennsylvania in 1738 and died there on February 7, 1814.[3] Circa 1755 to 1765 he was in Saxony, in northern Germany, where his family had its roots. During this time he studied, and also held a position as a workman, at the Saxe-Gotha Mint—a facility remembered today for the excellence of its products, including some coins with proof-like surfaces. While there he familiarized himself with all branches of the mint machinery and operation and was able to make several improvements that resulted in increased efficiency and the reduction of expense.

Back in America, he learned the watchmaker's trade and also became proficient in engraving. David Rittenhouse was a friend, and Voigt worked with him in the construction of philosophical (*scientific* in modern terminology) apparatus, including an orrery, which is a mechanical device showing the sun, moon, and known planets in motion. In 1780 he went to Reading, Pennsylvania, where he built and conducted a factory for the making of woolen and cotton cards. He then returned to Philadelphia, where he operated a clock-making business at 149 North Second Street with his brother Sebastian. Among other activities, Voigt was associated with John Fitch, pioneer builder of steam-powered boats, in the construction of machinery. Steam was important in the expanding technology of the era, but the state of the art was more advanced in England than in the United States.

On April 13, 1792, Voigt applied for a position with the Philadelphia Mint, then in its planning stages, following authorization by the Mint Act of April 2. Rittenhouse, appointed as director of the Mint by President Washington, enlisted Voigt to be superintendent and chief coiner. Voigt's appointment was an easy choice as his talents were a known entity. His duties were to include receiving all metal for coinage and causing that metal to be prepared into strips, planchets to be cut from it, and coins to be subsequently struck. He was to have several assistants, including one to forge, turn, and harden dies (after they had been engraved). He was also to maintain records of coinage, expenses, and other data.

JOSEPH WRIGHT JR.

It is probably true that more attention has been spent by numismatic writers on Joseph Wright than on any other person associated for such a brief time with the Mint. He is known to have cut the dies for a 1792-dated pattern quarter dollar and a medal of Henry Lee. Given the aforementioned Mint record, dating his official hire to mid-1793 and the fact that the Liberty Cap cent dies are sunk from device hubs (rather than engraved by hand, as were the earlier issues), Wright seems to be another logical candidate for the engraver who created the Liberty Cap portrait used on the third design for 1793 large cents. No documentation has been found to confirm this theory. Whoever its creator, the beautiful Liberty Cap cent motif became the standard for the next several years, creating a numismatic favorite for all time.

Joseph Wright Jr. was born in Bordentown, New Jersey, on July 16, 1756, the son of Joseph Wright Sr. and Patience Lowell Wright. His father died in May 1769. In the early 1770s, Patience took the family to London, where she became well known as a modeler of wax heads for museum display. These were very popular in an era in which there were very few printed representations of famous people. Her income was sufficient that she provided an education for Joseph, who in April 1775 commenced study at the Royal Academy of Arts, including with portraitist John Hoppner under the supervision of Benjamin West. His talents were recognized, and commissions were received from many patrons. The Prince of Wales (later to become King George IV) sat for him.

In 1781 Wright went to Paris, where he met Benjamin Franklin, who introduced him to others in his circle. Late in 1782 he sailed from Nantes, France, and—after a shipwreck and other delays—he reached Boston early in 1783, after which he made his home in Philadelphia. In October of that year he went to Rocky Hill, New Jersey, and painted General and Mrs. Washington under a commission from Congress. He also made a life mask of Washington in plaster. Tradition has it that he completed a later depiction of Washington by observing the general at worship in St. Paul's Church. In April 1786, he moved to New York City, where he maintained a studio on Pearl Street. On December 5, 1790, he married Sarah Vandervoort, the daughter of his landlady. In 1791 he went back to Philadelphia, where he continued as a portraitist.

Wright engraved the dies for the Comitia Americana medal presented to Major Henry Lee for the capture of Paulus Hook in 1775. The full extent of his medallic work is not known. This comment was published in 1872, adapted from an account of 1814:

> Joseph Wright, by profession a painter, belonging to Philadelphia, many years since exercised his ingenuity in making a die, from which he struck one copy of Washington's head, which is now in the possession of the Hon. Ebenezer Hazard, Esq. It is unique, and is particularly valuable, being considered the best medallic profile likeness of the illustrious Washington, which has ever been taken. The artist, in attempting to make a second impression, unfortunately broke his die. . . .[4]

For the fledgling Philadelphia Mint he created the eagle-on-globe 1792-dated pattern for a quarter dollar. This work has a certain delicacy to it, similar in a way to the 1793 Liberty Cap cent. In 1793 he received a commission as draughtsman and engraver at the Mint. It is not known whether he was ever officially installed, although letters from Jefferson and Washington do refer to him as the Mint's engraver.[5] It seems likely that he was employed there in the summer of that year.

On September 18, 1793, the Mint was shuttered as yellow fever plagued the city. One of the victims was Wright. A letter from Moid Wetherill, September 11, 1793, told of his condition:

> Joseph Wright being very ill and not expected to recover requested the subscriber to make a memorandum as follows: that the said Joseph Wright had presented an account against the United States for cutting a medal, amount 50 guineas. Two essays of a quarter dollar, cut by direction of David Rittenhouse Esq. and presented to him (broke in hardening) value about 40 guineas.[6]

The eagle-on-globe reverse die of 1792 is cracked on an existing specimen, which seems to verify Wetherill's letter. There was no mention of money due for any recent coin engraving work, and Mint records are silent on that aspect. However, Director Rittenhouse could have paid Wright from his own pocket to do Liberty Cap cent dies.

Wright died on September 13 (or 14, or in late September; accounts vary). His wife died at the same time.

Robert Scot

Appointed as engraver at the Mint on November 23, 1793, as the successor to the late Joseph Wright, Robert Scot remained in the post until October 30, 1823. During his term he continued the Liberty Cap motif in the copper series, introduced the Draped Bust, and created the Matron Head. How much of this work was done by Scot and how much by his assistants is an open question.

Born in the British Isles about the year 1750, Scot became a watchmaker there.[7] In the early 1780s he came to Philadelphia, where he did engraving work. An early commission was the engraving of the frontispiece to a Masonic sermon given by William Smith, D.D., and printed by Hall & Sellers (numismatically remembered as the printer of early paper money, including Continental currency). For the same firm he created illustrations of buildings in Philadelphia and nearby districts. He billed himself as the "late engraver to the state of Virginia," and in 1785 was paid £16 for engraving work by the state of Pennsylvania. It is believed that Scot cut the dies for the Great Seal of the United States in the early 1780s at the direction of Charles Thomson.[8]

Alexander Lawson, a contemporary, commented, "He first drew in all his work with a point, and then cut it with the graver. He had no knowledge of animals or figures. He engraved a whole length of Washington, after C.W. Peale, certainly not very flattering to so handsome a man. He was chosen die-sinker to the Mint, which office he filled for many years."[9]

In 1791 Scot was listed as an engraver at 36 Chestnut Street. Later, he moved to 2 Carter's Alley. After his appointment at the Mint, Scot was still listed as an "engraver and copper plate printer" in Philadelphia directories. Some early maps bear his imprint. While employed at the Mint he was also a partner with Samuel Allerdice in the firm of Scot & Allerdice, preparers of architectural plates and other illustrations for Dobson's edition of *Rees' Encyclopedia* during the period from 1794 to 1803.

On April 3, 1795, mechanic Adam Eckfeldt, who had last done work for the Mint in 1792, was paid for smith work on the presses, punches, and die cups. He gained a full-time staff position in 1795. The Mint record describing his appointment specifically states that he shall not perform engraving and polishing. In later years, Eckfeldt communicated extensively with historians and numismatists—more than any other early Mint employee. He never claimed to have engraved dies, but did say that he *made* them, referring to forging and turning, *not* engraving. From this a scenario was contrived by some later writers that credited Eckfeldt for designing and making dies for the coinage of 1792, and much else. In recent times, this has been discredited. This is not to the detriment of Eckfeldt, who made no such claims to begin with. He is viewed as a friend to the hobby, and decades later he continued to help collectors with their needs. He was also important in the June 1838 formation of the Mint Cabinet.

Poulson's Advertiser, April 28, 1806, contained an obituary notice for the wife of Scot, "engraver to the Mint." Scot's private business was later transferred to Murray, Draper, Fairman & Company, bank-note engravers in the same city. Some claim that Scot engraved plates for printing bank notes for the Bank of North America in the 1790s, but this has not been confirmed.[10]

Scot's eyesight is said to have been failing after 1820, making it difficult to do engraving for the Mint.[11] In any event, there were no new coin designs at that time, and medals were created by others. Facts are scarce and theories (sometimes not presented as such) are abundant. Scot died in 1823.

JOHN SMITH GARDNER

John Smith Gardner worked at the Mint as an acting assistant engraver as early as November 1795, at slightly more than $2.25 per day. On August 11 he requested that Director Henry William DeSaussure increase the amount to $4. Historian Stewart wrote that Gardner "had the [duty of] making all the punches together with the types necessary for the dies, also all the hubs from the original dies and the striking of all the hubs and dies. He also engraved all the reverses of each kind of die . . . and put the border and legend on all the head [obverse] dies, assisted in hardening each and partly the glossing of them."[12]

This would suggest that he created reverses for half cents and cents along with his other work. By the end of 1794 the denominations for which dies had been made included the half cent, cent, half dime, half dollar, and silver dollar. Gardner worked for several months in that year and in 1796, by which time his daily rate was $3.[13] Records show that he was paid in total for 234 days of work.[14]

JOHN REICH

Among the assistant engravers who worked at the Mint for a long period of time, John Reich (Johann Matthaus Reich) is one of the best remembered today. The John Reich Collectors Society, devoted to the numismatic aspects of Capped Bust (primarily) coinage, bears his name. The Classic Head design used on half cents from 1809 to 1836 and cents from 1808 to 1814 was his work.

John Reich was born in 1768 in Fürth, Bavaria, where his father was a prolific medalist of indifferent talent. After working in his father's shop he emigrated from Hamburg to America aboard the *Anna*, arriving in Philadelphia in August 1800.

After a year's indenture to a Philadelphia coppersmith, Reich was "freed" by Henry Voigt, chief coiner at the Mint. For the Mint, he engraved an illustrious series of medals, including Indian peace medals with the portraits of Thomas Jefferson and James Madison (the reverse was used years afterward on other peace medals), congressional award medals to Commodore Edward Preble for valiant action in the bombardment of pirates at Tripoli and to Captain Isaac Hull for the capture of the British frigate *Guerriere*, and others—including a Declaration of Independence medal with Jefferson and a medal of Franklin. For Joseph Sansom, a Philadelphia entrepreneur, he cut dies for several Washington medals, including the famous American Beaver. Among the Sansom commissions, in January 1806 this was advertised:

> A medal in honor of the memory of Washington has been struck at Philadelphia, under the direction of J. Reich, a German artist. The face, a head of General Washington, in his uniform. Inscription, GENERAL WASHINGTON, C.C.A.U.S. (Commander in Chief of the Armies of the United States). Reverse, under the date of the acquisition of Independence, the American eagle, with the thunder-bolt in its claws and the olive branch in its beak, descending upon the section of the globe, on which the United States are delineated by their boundaries.[15]

A Washington medal using the Gilbert Stuart portrait, known today as the Presidency Relinquished medal, was sold as the work of "the celebrated artist John Reich," issued in Philadelphia on October 9, 1806, "in commemoration of the retirement of Washington." These were offered in *Poulson's Advertiser* as being available in silver.

Mint Director Robert Patterson wrote to President Jefferson on March 25, 1807:

> Our present Engraver, Scot, though indeed a meritorious and faithful officer, is yet so far advanced in life, that he cannot very long be expected to continue his labors. In the event of his sickness or death, the business of the Institution would probably be stopped for some time, since few, if any one could be found qualified to supply his place except Mr. Reich, an artist with whose talents, I presume, you are not unacquainted; and this gentleman not finding business here sufficient for his support, is, I understand, about to remove to Europe.
>
> A small salary would, however, retain him in the country, and secure his services to the Mint. And, in truth, the beauty of our coins would be greatly improved by the assistance of his masterly hand.
>
> An assistant engraver was formerly employed by Mr. Rittenhouse, and by Mr. DeSaussure—and with your approbation, Sir, I would immediately employ Mr. Reich in that capacity. He is willing for the present to accept of the moderate compensation of six hundred dollars per annum; and should this gentleman be employed, perhaps more than his salary would be saved to the public, in which is usually expended on the engraving of dies for medals, but which might then be executed by an artist in their own service, with little or no additional experience.[16]

On April 2, 1807, Patterson again wrote to President Jefferson:

> With your approbation I have employed Mr. John Reich as an assistant engraver in the Mint at the annual salary of six hundred dollars. He has covenanted to execute any work in the line of his profession, that may be required of him either by the Director or Chief Engraver, whether for the immediate use of the Mint, or for that of the United States, when ordered by any special resolution or Act of Congress for that purpose, or by the President, provided that in the execution of any such work, no extraordinary hours of labor or attendance be required without an adequate compensation therefor, so that if any seals should be wanted for the public Offices, or dies for the purpose of striking Indian or other medals, they can now be executed in the best stile at the Mint, without any extra expense to the government.
>
> Mr. Reich is now preparing a set of new dies in which some improvements in the devices will be introduced, (adhering, however, strictly to the letter of the law) which it is hoped will meet with public approbation.[17]

Reich went to work on his "new dies" and other tasks. In 1808 his medal for the New York chapter of the Washington Benevolent Society was struck at the Mint and widely distributed. In the same year his completely revised design for the cent, the Classic Head obverse with a continuous wreath on the reverse, was made. In the next few years Reich prepared many dies from existing hubs and punches, quite skillfully, as evidenced by few errors during this period. Business at the Mint slowed in 1815, with only quarter dollars and a few half eagles minted that year, followed by only half dollars (dated 1815) and cents in 1816. In the latter year Reich was troubled by failing eyesight.[18] On March 31, 1817, he resigned.

Reich was one of the founders of the Society of Artists (1811) and one of the first group of Pennsylvania Academicians (1812). After leaving the Mint, he traveled to the West (such as it was at the time) in search of a more favorable climate to restore his health, and he settled in Pittsburgh, Pennsylvania. The artist died circa 1832.[19]

Among the products of all Mint engravers who prepared designs for half cents and cents for the first Philadelphia Mint, Reich's medallic work has no comparison.

WILLIAM KNEASS

Scot was succeeded as chief engraver by William Kneass, who was appointed on January 29, 1824, chiefly on the recommendation of Adam Eckfeldt. Kneass was born in Lancaster, Pennsylvania, in September 1781. During the War of 1812 he served as a volunteer with a company of field engineers who constructed fortifications on the west side of Philadelphia. Shortly after the war, in 1815, Kneass engraved a plate representing a plan of the works erected in the defense of the city.

In the early 1820s, Kneass was an engraver of illustrated plates for books, with an office on Fourth Street near Chestnut. In the 1810s and early 1820s he was involved in at least two partnerships in the general engraving business, Kneass & Dellaker (or Delleker) and Young & Kneass & Co. Among his products were printing plates for bank notes. As early as 1820 he did commission work for the Mint, at one time employing punches provided by John Reich (who had left the Mint in 1817).

As chief engraver, he did not produce any new designs that are memorable to numismatists today. He is best remembered for the Classic Head $2.50 and $5 gold coins of 1834, which were copied from Reich's Classic Head cent design of 1808. For cents he may have made some portrait modifications in what we know as the Matron Head design.

Kneass was at his station at the Philadelphia Mint until August 27, 1835, when he suffered a major stroke and was incapacitated to a degree. It seems that his die work after this time was reduced, although he did prepare coinage dies. True to Mint tradition, he retained the title of chief engraver and collected his salary until his death on August 27, 1840.[20]

Patterson DuBois wrote of him in the *American Journal of Numismatics*, July 1883 (excerpt):

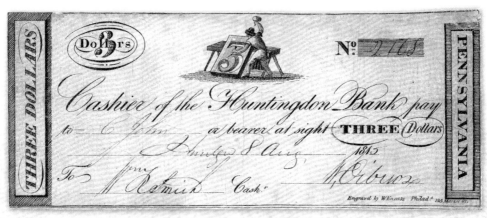

$3 note for the Huntingdon Bank of Pennsylvania, 1815,
from a plate engraved and signed by William Kneass.

Mr. Kneass is well remembered as an affable, genial "gentleman of the old-school," who had the rare quality of engaging and winning the esteem and affection of children and youth, in whose companionship he found rich delight. Prior to his appointment he had an engraving office on Fourth above Chestnut Street, Philadelphia, which was a well-known rendezvous for the leading wits and men of culture, for which Philadelphia was then eminent.

CHRISTIAN GOBRECHT

Christian Gobrecht was born in Hanover, Pennsylvania, on December 23, 1785, the son of the Reverend John C. Gobrecht, who had come to America in 1755 from Hesse in Germany. Gobrecht's mother, Elizabeth Sands, could trace her lineage to Plymouth colony as far back as 1642.

After serving an apprenticeship in Manheim, Pennsylvania, he became an engraver of ornamental clock faces and works in Baltimore, later moving to Philadelphia in 1811 and joining the bank-note engraving firm of Murray, Draper, Fairman, and Company, circa 1816. In 1817, Gobrecht made improvements to his 1810 invention of a medal-ruling machine by which a three-dimensional medal or bas-relief object could be converted to a two-dimensional illustration for use in a publication, using a linear process. At another time he constructed and demonstrated a talking doll, and another effort was made on improvements for the parlor reed organ. Gobrecht married Mary Hamilton Hewes on May 31, 1818.

In 1824 he prepared dies for the Franklin Institute medal of the same date, signed C. GOBRECHT F. below the bust of Franklin.[21]

A Mint ledger reveals that on January 27, 1825, Gobrecht was paid $25 for "letters and figures for the engraver," the latter referring to Kneass, then at his post for nearly a year.[22] Gobrecht furnished "designs and models of die" to the Mint as early as 1826.[23]

On the day after Kneass's stroke, Mint Director Robert Maskell Patterson, who had been in the post since July, wrote to Treasury Secretary Levi Woodbury to request emergency permission to hire Gobrecht as an engraver. Gobrecht was employed beginning in early September. However, problems arose as he did not want to be referred to as an "assistant," because his talents far exceeded those of Kneass.

Numismatic researcher Craig Sholley found a copy of a strongly worded September 29, 1835, letter from Patterson to Gobrecht in which Patterson reminds Gobrecht that he has accepted the assistant engraver position as offered and is obligated to continue in that position. Patterson went on to state that he cannot convince Congress of the need for a "new engraver" at $1,500 per year and then falsely threatens that if Gobrecht breaks the contract, the Mint will contract dies out to Europe as it is cheaper to have them made there anyway! Sholley notes that it seems to be this letter and the subsequent negotiations that led to a solution of the title matter. Gobrecht was named second engraver (not assistant) and received part of Kneass's stipend.[24]

In the next several years Gobrecht did most if not all of the artistic engraving work for coinage. Part of Kneass's salary, $250 per year, was paid over to him, in addition to his regular stipend.

From late summer 1835 onward, much work was done by Gobrecht, including the creation of the Liberty Seated silver coinage. After Kneass's death, Gobrecht served as chief engraver, appointed on December 21, 1840. In the mid- and late 1830s Gobrecht experimented with the portrait of Miss Liberty on the cent, creating several variations. Changes in head styles including the Silly Head and Booby Head variations, culminating in the Braided Hair motif in 1839—which was subsequently used on the half cent beginning in 1840—can be attributed to his hand.

Gobrecht died on July 23, 1844. He was succeeded by James B. Longacre, who assumed the post on September 6, 1844. The Braided Hair design remained unchanged through the end of the series in 1857 and was not influenced by Longacre.

JAMES B. LONGACRE

James Barton Longacre was born in Delaware County, Pennsylvania, on August 11, 1794, by which time the Mint had been striking half cents and cents for a year. As an apprentice to James F. Watson, he learned the basics of engraving. He then apprenticed to George Murray, a principal of the highly successful Murray, Draper & Fairman Company of bank-note engravers. He learned further skills in that art, then gained his freedom in 1819. An early work—a portrait of Andrew Jackson, the hero of New Orleans, engraved after a painting by Thomas Sully—was published in Philadelphia in 1820, to wide acclaim. By that time Longacre had created multiple illustrations for S.F. Bradford's *Encyclopedia*. During the next decade he did much work, including engraving plates for bank notes. In the early 1830s, in partnership with James Herring, he began work on the *National Portrait Gallery of Distinguished Americans*. Longacre and other engravers created large portraits of eminent military heroes, politicians, and other public figures. Accompanying each was a biography. The *Gallery* was issued in multiple volumes over a period of several years. This master work had no equal in its era. In the same decade he was a partner in Draper, Toppan, Longacre & Co., highly successful bank-note engravers with offices in Philadelphia and New York City.

James B. Longacre, from a 19th-century engraving.

On September 16, 1844, Longacre was appointed engraver at the Mint. So far as is known, he had no prior experience in making hubs for coins or medals, or engraving dies for these. He learned while doing. Longacre received heavy criticism from others at the Mint, especially for his difficulty in engraving proper dies for the 1849 double eagle, his first major coin design, and the smaller gold dollar with the same obverse motif. This $20 coin was to be America's largest gold coin, and problems arose in making the relief of the obverse portrait suitable.

Undaunted, Longacre persevered. During the era of cents and half cents he went on to produce designs for the 1853 silver three-cent piece, or trime; the 1854 $3 gold coin; a redesign of the gold dollar, in the same year; and in 1856 a pattern Flying Eagle cent (with the obverse design adapted from Gobrecht), this in addition to various pattern motifs that were never adopted.

For the copper coins from 1844 onward he had no involvement with the designs, and no modifications were made. The coiner's department, under Franklin Peale, controlled many of the hubs and also prepared working dies. Accordingly, Longacre had no connection with blundered dates on dies of this era.[25] After 1857, he went on to create more new coinage motifs than any engraver before or since, including the Indian Head cent, the two-cent piece, the nickel three-cent piece, the Shield nickel, modifications to existing designs, and many patterns. In addition, he did work for others on a contract basis, including the government of Chile.

In the meantime, except for the reverse of a medal for Captain Duncan Ingraham, he had others do the work for medals. Anthony C. Paquet, William H. Key, P.F. Cross, and William Barber worked as his assistants over a period of years, though none dealt with half cents or large cents. Longacre died on January 1, 1869, and was widely mourned. At noon on January 4 the entire staff gathered at the Mint to pay tribute. William Barber delivered a eulogy, and William E. Dubois presented resolutions.[26]

Die Work by Assistants

While hubs for half-cent and cent portraits and reverse wreaths were made by talented artists, including John Reich and Christian Gobrecht, who were not chief engravers at the time, much routine die work was probably done by mechanics. This involved impressing the design hubs into the dies and punching individual letters and numerals (and, for 1840 and later, four-digit date logotypes).

There is no reason to believe that the chief engraver or other engraving artist did all of this work. Indeed, enough clumsily made die work took place (much to the delight of numismatists today) that it is almost certain that other workers were involved. A poster example is the 1794 "Fallen 4" variety, well known as Sheldon-63 (in the present text also 1794 Bowers-Whitman–84). Large-cent specialist George Clapp called this the "Drunken Diecutter's Obverse," while he gave the designation "Office Boy Reverse" to another die with amateurish features. On June 17, 1794, Frederick Riche was paid $18 for 18 days of work "sinking dies." Likely, he dealt with lower denominations, as he is not known to have had any particular skills.[27]

We can only wonder who made the 1817 cent with 15 obverse stars instead of 13— perhaps a newcomer to the Mint? In the half-cent series we have the 1797 1 Over 1 variety, a die-cutting goof par excellence, and the odd "Low Head" die, among others. The 1828 half cent with 12 stars instead of 13 is another memorable blunder.

Unfortunately, while Mint records are often extensive with regard to the chief coiner and the assayer, they are sparse for the engraver, who was directly supervised by the director. Accordingly, the names and roles of various helpers the engraver may have had were apt to remain off the books. The same is true for many activities of the directors.

After 1840, when four-digit logotypes came into use, on at least two occasions the diesinker punched it in upside down on cent dies, then corrected it: the 1844 Over 81 and the 1851 Over 81. In 1847 there were "Large 7 Over Small 7" cents, with traces of smaller figures (made by misplaced partial impressions of the logotype not far into the dies). Walter Breen attributed these and other errors to the alleged inexperience of Longacre, but such mistakes occurred before that engraver took his post, such as on 1843 quarter eagles with the 18 small and 43 much larger.

Making Dies
The Steel Die

Copper half cents and cents were struck from steel dies. These were used in pairs, one with the obverse design and the other with the reverse. A bar of high-quality steel was forged by hand, then turned on a lathe to create a cylindrical form with a large shank tapering to a smaller diameter just below the die face. After the blank die was created, it was heated to a cherry-red temperature, then allowed to cool slowly. This had the effect of softening the steel so that designs could be engraved on it.

The die was then given to an engraver, who added designs (of which more will be said). Then it was returned to a mechanic, who heated it again to cherry-red and quenched it quickly in water or oil. This hardened the steel but rendered it too brittle for use, so the die was then heated to a straw color and allowed to cool slowly, thus tempering the steel. If all went well and the steel was of good quality, the metal would be more or less uniform to a depth of an eighth of an inch or so. However, if the die forger had not inspected and selected the steel carefully or was careless in his forging technique, the die could crack while hardening or crack, sink, and bulge when used to strike coins.

After tempering, the die was dressed by lightly polishing the face to remove scale and any irregularities and to set the basin, or curvature of the die. It was then ready for coinage use.[28]

Engraving a Chain Cent Die in Early 1793

Under good light and with a magnifying glass nearby, an engraver set to work to create the design. The obverse required a portrait of Miss Liberty, lettering, and the date. Around the edge, beads were added for artistic effect, framing the interior motifs. Such beads were only used in 1793, for half cents and for the Wreath and Liberty Cap cents. The very first coppers—the 1793, Chain, cents delivered in March 1793—had plain borders.

The engraver of the Chain cent dies cut the portrait of Miss Liberty into the die face by hand, like carving a cameo in reverse. All features were intaglio, or recessed. Probably, wax impressions were taken at regular intervals to monitor the progress. The head itself was likely the first process. After a satisfactory portrait was made, hair strands and other details were finessed—a painstaking task, as all of the hair in a given strand had to be parallel to adjacent strands.

When the portrait was finished, separate letter and number punches were employed to add LIBERTY and the date 1793. No inscribed circle guidelines seem to have been used, although they could have been. Nonetheless, spacing of the letters and numerals, their alignment, and their distance from the border varied from one die to another.

The reverse die for a Chain cent was an easier task: only punches were used, with no hand engraving necessary. A tiny dot called the "center dot" was made in the center for one arm of a compass. This dot is often quite visible on these, and other, reverse dies. The other arm was a stylus used to inscribe a light circle around the border—or perhaps more than one—for use in aligning the letters.

Near the center, a small elongated punch in the form of a single chain link was impressed into the die 15 times, overlapping to create the chain motif intended to represent the 15 different states in the Union. Within the circle of links, ONE / CENT was impressed with individual letter punches, and the fraction 1/100 was created below. Around the border, UNITED STATES OF AMERI. was punched on the very first die, soon changed to the full AMERICA. Again, the border was plain.

Using Design Hubs for Liberty Cap and Draped Bust Coins

The engraving of portraits directly into the dies soon gave way to the use of punches or hubs depicting Miss Liberty and giving basic elements of the reverse wreath. The hub for the Liberty Cap dies, and eventually several of these were made, had the head and cap. The pole was added by hand, and hair strands were often strengthened or finessed, particularly at the back of the head. The letters of LIBERTY and the date numerals were added by hand.

The Liberty Cap motif varied widely in size and style in the half cent series, with the first issues (those of 1793) facing left. Half cents from 1794 to 1797 and all cents from 1793 to 1796 had Miss Liberty facing to the right. Liberty Cap hubs in the cent series were all about the same size, but their relief varied, as did their eye appeal. To numismatic eyes, the earlier ones seem to be more delicate and attractive.

The Draped Bust motif was first used in 1796, having been employed on silver dollars in 1795. Several hubs were made, mostly with differences in the hair. It seems to have been the practice to make up the dies in advance, adding the first three digits, but omitting the last until the die was ready for use. This is evidenced by certain 1800 cent dies that were made by overdating dies that had been predated with 179. Similarly, certain half cents of 1805 have the last digit in a tiny font, compared to the first three, suggesting that it was added at a later time.

Although no records exist, it is assumed that if an obverse die with a given date had been hardened for use, it was kept in service until it cracked or was rendered unfit for further service—sometimes into the next calendar year or so. Forensic examination of existing coins shows much evidence of this. One of the most famous examples of this practice is a 1795-dated obverse in the $5 gold series that was mated with a reverse design created in 1797 or 1798. In the cent series, there are various examples, many of which are delineated in *Walter Breen's Encyclopedia of United States Half Cents*. Such instances include certain 1798-dated coins known to have been made after 1799-dated coins, as the 1799 coins show the reverse die in an earlier state or condition.

The wreath hubs became more sophisticated as time went on. The earliest ones required that stems below the bow, berries and their stems, and leaves be added. As time progressed, the leaves were rendered complete on the hub and, eventually, the berries were as well. The inscription within the wreath, HALF / CENT for the smaller denomination and ONE / CENT for the larger, was added by single letter punches, as was UNITED STATES OF AMERICA around the border. Spacing between the letters often varied, as did the position of the letters with respect to the wreath elements. Less often, certain letters were higher or lower than others. The fractions, 1/200 and 1/100, were punched in by hand with individual numerals, and an engraving tool was used to make the bar. This bar might consequently be light or heavy, long or short, and level or tilted. In the cent series after 1797, the fractions were apt to have the most easily observable differences to aid in numismatic attribution.

Dentils were added by hand along the border of both dies. This was perhaps done two or three dentils at a time or with the help of a jig, as most (but hardly all) are of uniform width, length, and spacing on any given die. However, from die to die they vary from long and thin to short and rounded. Some are spike-like.

Beginning in the period from 1800 to 1802, the Mint used a more durable die steel. As Adam Eckfeldt became accustomed to the forging requirements, the new steel dramatically increased the life of a die to about 200,000 or so impressions. This caused some problems related to overestimating the number of dies to be prepared.[29] After this time, fewer dies were needed, resulting in fewer coin varieties for a given production quantity from this point onward.

LATER HALF CENT AND CENT DIES

As the years passed, the making of dies became more sophisticated. The Classic Head motif designed by John Reich was first used on cents in 1808 and half cents in 1809, in combination with a new wreath (continuous, rather than open at the top, and without a fraction below it). More features were incorporated into the hubs, leaving fewer to be added by hand.

This state of affairs continued well into the 19th century. Eventually, with the Braided Hair design introduced on cents in late 1839 and half cents in 1840, the only operation done by hand was the adding of the date. During 1840, the use of four separate digit punches was discontinued, and logotype or gang punches with all four digits became standard. After that time, the main variable was the position of the date with regard to the bust and the dentils.

THE COINAGE LIFE OF DIES

The life of coinage dies rose steadily over the years. At the beginning of the 1793, Chain, cent coinage, the life was about 3,000 impressions, rising to about 10,000 as coinage continued. In 1794, under chief coiner Henry Voigt, the average for cents was about 20,000. The figure rose to 40,000 on average from 1795 to 1798, following the hiring of Adam Eckfeldt, who improved the method of forging the steel.

Eckfeldt experimented with steel from 1799 to 1801 or so. By 1802 and 1803 the average die life was about 200,000 impressions, as noted earlier, followed by about 350,000 from 1805 to 1808. Figures for 1809 to 1814 are anomalous, planchets were scarce, and the die life was about 250,000 strikes. From 1816 to 1830 the life was about 320,000 impressions, after which, continuing to 1857, it was about 400,000. Within any of these averages, some dies broke quickly, and others lasted for a long time.[30]

MAKING PLANCHETS
RECEIVING AND PROCESSING METAL

Metal was received at the Mint in various forms, including copper sheeting (used elsewhere for roofs and for ship bottoms), dented and damaged silverware, old coins, ingots, and scrap. The incoming metal was melted and assayed, the latter through a chemical process that determined its purity so that the depositor of the metal could be paid the proper amount. To be rendered useful for coinage, silver and gold had to be refined and made into an alloy of fixed standard, usually 90 percent precious metal and 10 percent copper—the latter to add strength.[31] Copper was melted, and the impurities were skimmed off the top of the cauldron, after which the copper was deemed satisfactory for Mint use.

Melted copper and refined silver and gold were cast into pigs or ingots. These were then reduced into thin, long strips by running them between two steel rollers in a series of operations during which the space between the rollers was gradually decreased. Finally, the strip was pulled through the drawbar to create the desired thickness.

THE PUNCH PRESS AND EDGE LETTERING

This thin strip was then passed through a punch press, and planchets were cut out one at a time, much in the manner of a cookie cutter. Planchets were processed through a milling machine, which slightly reduced the diameter of the planchet while giving it a raised rim on both sides. Coins struck from these planchets had plain (not lettered) edges unless vertical ribs (reeds) were impressed by the use of a Castaing-type machine (similar to that used for lettering edges).

Planchets for early half cents and cents (1793 through part of 1795—though the practice continued for half dollars and silver dollars from 1794 onward) were then run through an edge-lettering machine of the French Castaing type, consisting of two parallel bars, each inscribed in raised letters with half of the message to be imprinted on the edge of the planchet, such inscription being TWO HUNDRED FOR A DOLLAR for half cents and ONE HUNDRED FOR A DOLLAR for cents.

Striking Coins
Hand-Operated Presses

Two dies—one for the obverse and one for the reverse—were fitted into a coining press. A screw-type press was used in the early years. Depending on the size of the press, one to four men would tug on straps fitted to heavy iron balls at the ends of a cross arm, causing the cross arm to move in a circular path, driving the top or *hammer die* downward to impact the blank disc or planchet, which was resting on top of the fixed bottom or *anvil die*. In some instances, the workmen pushed on the outer part of the arm itself. By the late 1790s, and possibly earlier, planchets were fed into the press by a hopper and "feed fingers," the latter developed by John Harper.[32]

In the early years, the Mint had several presses in operation. These were of domestic manufacture and had sufficient capacity to strike cents as well as slightly larger-diameter coins, such as the Birch pattern cents of 1792. On March 25, 1794, the Mint paid John Rutter & Co. for a coining press weighing 13 hundredweight (1,456 pounds). This was probably used to coin silver half dollars and dollars in the following autumn. First struck were silver dollars, delivered on October 15. All had weak striking, and of perhaps 2,000 struck, only 1,758 were released. On December 1, the first delivery of half dollars was made, amounting to 5,300.

On February 2, 1795, Samuel Howell was paid for two small presses and one large press, the latter weighing 1 ton, 11 hundredweight (3,232 pounds). This was suitable for properly coining large-diameter dollars.

Watching Coins Being Struck

The coining process and attendant activities furnished the subject of a reminiscence of a visit to the Mint in 1812 by a *very* young (born in 1808) George Escol Sellers, who was later to become a well-known mechanical engineer:

> The old U.S. Mint in Philadelphia was on the east side of Seventh Street, in one of those areas called in Philadelphia a city block, these blocks being bounded on their four sides by the principal streets, and perhaps subdivided into smaller blocks by alleys or courts. . . . The building used for the Mint had very much the appearance of an ordinary three-story brick dwelling house of that period, the back building and yard extending on the alley. In a rear room, facing on the alley, with a large, low-down window opening into it, a fly press stood; that is a screw-coining press mostly used for striking the old copper cents.
>
> Through this window the passersby in going up and down the alley could readily see the bare-armed vigorous men swinging the heavy end-weighted balanced lever that drove the screw with sufficient force so that by the momentum of the weighted ends this quick-threaded screw had the power to impress the blank and thus coin each piece. They could see the rebound or recoil of these end weights as they struck a heavy wooden spring beam, driving the lever back to the man that worked it; they could hear the clanking of the chain that checked it at the right point to prevent its striking the man, all framing a picture very likely to leave a lasting impression, and

there are no doubt still living many in Philadelphia who can recollect from this brief notice the first mint. . . .

One day in charge of my elder brother I stood on tip-toe with my nose resting on the iron bar placed across the open window of the coining room to keep out intruders, watching the men swing the levers of the fly press; it must have been about noon, for Mr. Eckfeldt came into the room, watch in hand, and gave a signal to the men who stopped work. Seeing me peering over the bar, he took me by the arms and lifted me over it. Setting me down by the coining press, he asked me if I did not want to make a cent, at the same time stopping the men who had put on their jackets to leave the room.

A cent of 1812.

He put a blank planchet into my hand, showed me how to drop it in, and where to place my hand to catch it as it came out; the lever and weights were swung, and I caught the penny as we boys called cents, but I at once dropped it. Mr. Eckfeldt laughed and asked me why I dropped it. Because it was hot and I feared it would burn me; he picked it up and handed it to me, then certainly not hot enough to burn; he asked if it was not cold when he gave it to me to drop into the press; he told me to look and see there was no fire, and feel the press that it was cold; he then told me I must keep the cent until I learned what made it hot; then I might if I liked spend it for candy. . . .

The little yard in the rear of the old mint was a very attractive place to us youngsters; its great piles of cordwood, which by the barrow load was wheeled into the furnace room and thrust full size in the boiler furnace, which to my young eyes appeared to be the hottest place on earth. There almost daily was to be seen great lattice-sided wagons of charcoal being unloaded, and the fuel stacked under a shed to be used in the melting and the annealing furnaces.

As I grew older and better able to understand, my interest in all the various processes increased; from the fuel yard to the melting room to see the pots or crucibles charged with the metals and their fluxes placed in the furnaces and the fires started, and when melted to see the man with his cage-jawed grasping tongues lift the crucible out of the fiery furnace and pour the melted metal into the ingot molds. Then rolling these ingots into strips of sheet metal, splitting and turning them into narrow strips by revolving cutting shears. Thinning or pointing the end of the strips by rollers with flatted spaces on them, so that the strips can be inserted between the regulated and fixed dies of the draw-bench to equalize their thickness as they are seized by a pair of nippers or gripping tongues, the hooked handle of which the operator at once engages in a link of the constantly traveling chain by which the strip is drawn through between the dies, the operator then by hand pushed the grippers back into place to take a grip on another strip.

These strips were fed by hand into the planchet cutting-out presses, and it required practice to attain the adroitness to so handle the strips to cut them out to the best advantage so as to leave the least metal to be returned to the melting pots. Silver planchets by the rolling and drawing process become too hard for coining without first annealing. Then the hand-milling press was a very interesting one to watch, it was raising and notching or lettering the rim of the planchet as a preventive against clipping or robbing. This was done by rolling between grooved and notched parallel rulers or bars, one being fixed, the other movable endways by a pinion working into a rack. The operator after placing two planchets one in advance of the other between the parallel bars, then by a partial turn of a hand-crank the movable bar is thrust ahead sufficiently to entirely rotate the planchets, when they are taken out and two others put in.

Every gold and silver planchet as cut out was passed through the hands of an adjuster; if overweight reduced by a file, a leather pouch in front of his bench catching the filings; if too light they were returned to the melter.

I have no recollection of ever having seen the copper planchets for cents being made in the Mint, but I have a vivid recollection of small iron hooped casks filled with copper planchets for cents and half cents. I have the impression that they were imported as copper in that condition and only stamped or coined in the mint. These casks were similar to the casks in which card wire was imported from England at that period.[33]

In the present context it is important to note that Sellers watched *cents* being struck. Some other presses were operated differently.

In 1829 B.L.C. Wailes of Natchez, Mississippi, visited the Mint and toured the facility, entering this in his diary regarding a coining press in the process of striking half eagles:

This is a very powerful, ingenious, simple (though very perfect) piece of machinery. It consists (like the cutting machine) of a very powerful upright screw, to the top of which is affixed a heavy and strong lever worked with great apparent ease by one man at each end, and by which the screw is made to make about one-fourth of a revolution and returning instantly to its former position.

At the lower end of the screw is affixed the die which gives the impression on the upper side, and immediately under it, the die considering the impression of the reverse of the coin, around which a pair of nippers (which gives the milling or impression on the edges), and by which placing as a rivet in the manner of shears emits the introduction of the coin before and its injection after it receives the impression.

Near the lower end of the screw stands a tube sufficiently large to admit a considerable number of the coins, one on top of the other, which may be termed the hopper, at the bottom of which is an apparatus sufficiently large to admit the passage of the coin, one at a time. The lower end in the file or hopper is struck out with great accuracy by a thin piece of iron made to strike edgewise at each movement of the lever and is conveyed by a channel formed for

A steam-driven (by means of shafts and pulleys) coining press as in use at the Mint in the 1850s.

this purpose and is conveyed directly on and under the die. The screw is brought down and the nippers close with such a force that makes the impression. The lever is instantly brought back, the nippers open, the stamped coin is struck out of its place and conveyed to a box by a spout (or conductor) as the screw rises, and another unstamped coin takes its place, and the screw comes down again.[34]

Although Wailes mentions that "nippers" (i.e., feed fingers) were applying the reeding, this observation was incorrect, as gold coins were struck in a reeded collar at the time.[35]

Steam-powered coinage came to the Mint on March 23, 1836, as described in chapter 2. Cents were struck on presses of this type from this time until the coppers were discontinued in 1857.

SPECIMEN, MASTER, AND PROOF COINS

Proof coins, as they were widely designed in America by the late 1850s, had European antecedents generations older. To create coins or sets suitable for presentation or for sale to museums and collectors, coinage dies were given special treatment. Typically, they were finished to a high polish in the fields of the obverse and reverse, to provide a mirror background to the portrait and other features of the coins. In many instances the planchets were polished or carefully prepared. Many examples could be cited. In 1746, full sets of British silver coins were given mirror finish, and in the same century many patterns and special coins were made. Often, the occasion for making Proofs, such as a coronation or a military victory, was documented. In the 1790s the Soho Manufactory operated by Boulton & Watt in Birmingham turned out thousands of mirror Proofs of exquisite quality for collectors and for presentation. Examples include the 1796 P.P.P. Myddelton token in copper and silver for the proposed American settlement in Kentucky, various Copper Company of Upper Canada issues, and the beautiful Washington "Seasons" Indian peace medals, all of which have American connections. Minting of Proof half cents and copper cents was done on screw presses, slowly so as to squeeze gently rather than with a quick, violent impact. In some instances, more than one impression was made in order to sharpen the features. Screw presses continued to be used for this purpose even after steam coinage was implemented (1836). Hydraulic presses were first employed to strike Proofs in the 1890s, years after the half cent and copper cent era.

John Dannreuther (discussed later in the section "Sholley and Dannreuther Commentary") suggests that the term *Proof* may have been first employed at the Mint in 1860 in connection with United States federal coins by James Ross Snowden, who served as director from 1853 to 1861. The Mint was a latecomer, for by that time the designation was in common use with collectors and dealers. Prior to the early 1850s, such terms as *Master Coin* and *Specimen* were sometimes used, along with *Cabinet Coin* (not usually capitalized at that time, but capitalized here as per modern numismatic practice). Such pieces were in contrast to *circulation strikes*, produced for commerce, with no attention paid to any special finish or quality. There was no agreed-upon definition for any of these terms, and use was erratic.

Today some certification services as well as collectors and dealers use "Specimen" to denote what they consider is a special coin apart from circulation strike. Such coins may have a partial Proof surface or some other special characteristic. "Presentation coin" is sometimes used, especially for high-quality coins from the early years of the Mint.

As for the focus of this book, no records have been found of any half cents or copper cents being specially struck for such a purpose. Today, for these two denominations,

1849, Small Date, half cent with mirror-Proof finish. This variety was struck only in Proof format.

1857, Small Date, copper cent. Proof with mirror surfaces.

numismatists are mainly interested in so-called mirror Proofs, years ago called the *brilliant Proofs.* As brilliant Proofs can become toned and no longer have a bright surface, the nomenclature is somewhat confusing.[36] In any event, such pieces when toned still have their mirror surface.

The author's definition of a Proof is one struck by a squeeze strike (as was used in hubbing dies), not a quick stroke, and with the planchet in a closed collar, imparting a mirror edge. The confining of metal in the collar and between the dies pushed it up to fill all details, including star centers, high areas of the hair and leaves, and the dentils. Any similar strikes that do not meet these requirements are elusive of definition and could be special strikes, or they could just as well not be. This includes certain cents of the Matron Head type that have mirrored surfaces and sharp rims, but occur with flatness on certain stars. Some, but not all, coins that are cataloged as Proofs may have been made in Proof format. Opinions differ.

It is a matter of debate when the first Proof coins (the nomenclature we will continue to use in this text when referring to coins fitting the modern definition of mirror Proofs) were struck at the Philadelphia Mint. There has been a lot of fiction printed in this regard, which is not worthy of repeating here.

As can be seen by inspecting the coins themselves, certain coins of 1796 have highly mirrorlike surfaces. Most quarter dollars of this year have fields that are nearly equal to the deliberately made Proofs of generations later. However, they were not struck for any purpose other than for passing into commerce. The dies were simply given a high polish by the engraver. This raises the question, still debatable today: can a coin be a Proof if it looks like one, even if it was clearly made for circulation? In some instances, such as with Gobrecht silver dollars dated 1836, the answer is clearly yes, in the author's opinion.[37] For the 1796 quarter, most catalogers today use *prooflike* (not capitalized) or *Specimen. Presentation coin* enters into the area of contrived ceremonies, not at all documented, such as the one Walter Breen presented in his Proof coin *Encyclopedia:* supposedly, when the very first 1795 $5 half eagles were struck, Director Henry William DeSaussure was so delighted that he had such coins struck specially. The same text creates scenarios for many other presentations that likely are fictional.

In many instances, including in the 1820s and later, clash marks, or die injuries, occurred when two dies came together in a coining press without a planchet in between. The dies were then relapped, or lightly ground down to remove these marks, and then polished to refresh the surfaces. What might be called inadvertent or unintentional Proofs were created. The widely studied denomination of half dollars provides many examples among Capped Bust issues of the 1820s and with Liberty Seated coins from relapped dies (a process that removed certain other lower-relief features, such as drapery; the mirrored-surface 1877-S half dollar is a poster example).

Among half cents and large cents, relapping to create prooflike surfaces is seen in various years. The most egregious are half cents of 1833, which are often found with highly prooflike surfaces. Many have been sold as Proof over the years. A reflection of modern scholarship on the subject is provided by Ronald P. Manley in the *Half Cent Die State Book 1793–1857*:

> The existence of Proof half cents dated 1825, 1826, 1828, and 1829 is alluded to by Walter Breen (half cent *Encyclopedia*, pages 322, 323, 325, 330, 331, 335). However, these are, in my opinion, more likely Uncirculated business strikes from freshly polished (or repolished) dies. As of January 1998 neither of the two leading professional grading services, NGC or PCGS, had certified a single half cent Proof of any of these dates.

Similarly, Manley writes this in reference to so-called Proofs of 1832:

> Possibly, five Proofs exist according to Walter Breen's Proof Census (half cent *Encyclopedia*, pp. 350–351). However, I am skeptical of Breen's claims for Proofs with this die combination. The first specimen Breen listed, from the Mint Cabinet collection at the Smithsonian Institution, is described as "somewhat impaired." It has been cleaned and thus may be a business strike.

Manley goes on to discuss what he calls a Proof from the collection of the Honorable and Mrs. R. Henry Norweb. When it was auctioned in 1987, it was described as a circulation strike. A third "Proof" in the Breen listing was likely prooflike, and the two remaining were not available for study. Certification services would seem to be of little help, with such instances such as 1811 "restrike" half cents from rough dies and no prooflike surface being certified as Proof.

THE BEGINNING OF PROOF COINAGE

Exactly when the first Proofs of any denomination were indeed deliberately made for numismatic or presentation purposes at the Philadelphia Mint is not known. The Mint used closed collars for cents beginning in 1816, giving such pieces vertical edges (when viewed edgewise) rather than slightly rounded ones. However, on circulation strikes these edges were not mirrorlike. This comment applies to all circulation strikes. *Walter Breen's Encyclopedia of United States and Colonial Proof Coins 1722–1989* states:

> This year [1817] . . . was notable for the installation of various items of new equipment. . . . The manufacture of unquestionable Proofs appears to have begun on a consistent basis in this year. On these Proof coins 2 to 4 blows from the dies in a screw press can usually be demonstrated, dies and blanks having been polished to unusual brilliance.

This claim is not verifiable elsewhere. Breen cites no original sources, and no records of new equipment have been found.[38]

Similarly, a statement of Breen's for 1825 Proof coins, "There are more of the smaller denominations than of the half dollars. Occasion: the visit to the USA of Marquis de Lafayette, July 1824 to September 1825," seems to be pure fiction. There are many detailed accounts of Lafayette's visit, but none mention the Philadelphia Mint making Proof coins in this connection.

It is the opinion of most scholars that the several Breen works with information on Proof half cents and large cents contain much valuable information, but that many statements of "fact" that cannot be confirmed should be taken with a large grain of salt. Many of his listings of existing Proofs are taken from very old auction listings of coins not evaluated later. Breen himself had very little expertise in either grading or determining Proof status.[39]

The earliest full set of unquestioned Proof coins is dated 1821 and is in the Smithsonian Institution, the repository of the former Mint Cabinet. This contains the cent, dime, quarter dollar, $2.50 coin, and $5 coin, these being the full range of denominations that were regularly made that year. No special equipment is known to have been installed for making such coins. It is presumed that they were made by quick squeezing on regular hand-operated presses, but with care and by the use of planchets that had been carefully selected and perhaps lightly polished. They are Proofs of the mirror style.

During the period under study for half cents and cents, ending in 1857, the Mint kept no known records of the number of Proofs made. The coiner struck such pieces, or had an assistant do so, replacing the copper, silver, or gold with other planchets, so that no deficiency was recorded. This was not a subterfuge or evasion, but was simply the policy at the time. Often, the same practice was followed for medals struck at the Mint. Accordingly, the production of such Proof coins is nowhere given in any *Annual Report of the Director of the Mint* during that era.

There were *very* occasional exceptions in internal Mint records (now available at the National Archives). From 1834 an account is preserved of special sets (which we now know were of Proof format) made and fitted into cases, given to Edmund Roberts, who set sail for the far side of the world, to present them as diplomatic gifts to the Sultan of Muscat and the King of Siam, among others. Each set had a half cent and cent in addition to other coins. Gobrecht silver dollars were made with mirror surfaces from dies dated 1836 and 1839 and were duly entered in the account books (although without mention of their Proof surfaces, though all were made that way). Most of these dollars were placed into circulation at face value, although some were kept for presentation, including two of the first 1836 dollars given to President Andrew Jackson.

COINS FOR NUMISMATISTS

In 1841 Baltimore numismatist Robert Gilmor Jr. exchanged letters with former Secretary of War Joel Roberts Poinsett, who was involved in establishing the National Institute for the Promotion of Science to house American collections and other treasures. The National Cabinet of Curiosities owned by the government was given to the Institute's care, as were some other properties. Gilmor suggested that collections be formed to illustrate coinage of the Mint as well as the various states. In a letter dated April 14, 1841, Gilmor shared some thoughts with Poinsett and told of his experiences with the Mint:

> The Mint has aided me considerably, and has even provided desiderata from the old dies, when I require it—Mr. Eckfeldt of the Mint has been of great service to me, and was stimulated by my attempt to commence one for the Mint itself, which really ought not to be without a specimen of every one of its coins—by timely attention to the subject by whoever has charge of the Department may soon make a considerable advance towards obtaining those in circulation, but no time should be lost, as the old gold coin is gradually disappearing by being coined into the new. The Mint would no doubt aid you in this, and coin your deficiencies.

The National Institute, however, did not flourish and in time was replaced by the Smithsonian Institution, which later acquired the Institute's collections.[40]

Coining "deficiencies" meant restriking, per Gilmor's correspondence. Many such restrikes are known to have been made in Proof format, including many half cents, dated as early as 1831. Where there are die differences, in which restrikes vary from originals, these are detectable by numismatists today. Examples are the half cents struck only in Proof finish in 1831; 1836; 1840 to 1848; 1849, Small Date; and 1852. Original Proofs from 1840 onward have large berries in the reverse wreath, while restrikes are distinguished by small berries. Such differences were not noticed by collectors at the time but attracted attention when the study of die varieties developed after 1860. Certain Proof cents of the 1840s seem to have been restruck as well, using a common reverse die.

The preceding circumstance reflects the extent to which Mint officers were friendly with collectors—although this has no particular connection to Proofs or special finishes, except, by implication, that restrikes had prooflike surfaces. Otherwise, Proof coins and sets are believed to only have been supplied to numismatists and other applicants if dies had already been made for this purpose. One reason for striking Proofs may have been to furnish display pieces for the Mint Cabinet. If so, this practice was not followed consistently, as it is likely that no sets were made in 1851, 1852, or 1853—although some denominations were made with prooflike finish.

Beginning in 1854 Proofs attracted wider attention from collectors. In 1858, director of the Mint James Ross Snowden instituted a policy that Proof coins be made available early in the year, so as to reduce the need for correspondence with collectors who requested such coins.[41] This was at the beginning of the great growth era of the hobby that was catalyzed by the discontinuation of the large copper cent in early 1857.

While a very few sets were made, with denominations from the half cent upward to gold, many half cents and cents were minted individually, likely in yearly quantities of 100 or more, beginning in 1854. Silver Proofs were made in smaller numbers, and production of gold Proofs, especially for larger denominations, was minuscule and sometimes did not occur at all. In 1857 probably 200 to 300 Proof half cents and large cents were struck, but no Proof $20 coins are known to have been made.

The Mint remained a haven for collectors through early 1859. At that point, Director Snowden—in office since 1853, and in 1859 busy acquiring Washington tokens and medals for the Mint Cabinet—determined to restrike coins in quantity and to create rarities, such as unnecessary patterns. Distribution of these went underground, and profits benefitted Mint officers. It was later estimated that in only two years, 1859 and 1860, about $50,000 worth of pattern coins were "struck and disposed of at the Mint, without any benefit to the government, at whose expense they were coined. Copies were not even put into the government collection of its own coins."[42] This was many multiples of the total value of coins, tokens, and medals auctioned during this 24-month period! This scenario has been widely described elsewhere.

SHOLLEY AND DANNREUTHER COMMENTARY

Craig Sholley and John Dannreuther have each studied early Proofs with care, Dannreuther mostly from examination of the coins themselves, and Sholley primarily through the use of National Archives records and other data. Certain of their comments are given here (edited to avoid repetition).

According to Sholley:

> The Mint began using a collar for copper in 1816 and it was very tight by 1827. It is unclear if this is related to the new Rush-Muhlenberg press in 1827. I do agree that the pre-1821 "Proofs" do not look like Proofs. They do not have the polish that post-1821 coins do, they don't have the rims and edges, and they don't appear to be struck twice. I question if polished planchets were used. . . .
>
> "Specimen" coins are fairly well documented in the records. I would still use the Mint terms "Specimen" or "Master Coin," not Proof, in describing such pieces. The Specimen, Master Coin, and Proof periods overlap.

> From what I've seen Specimen coinage was simply a nice coin struck with fairly fresh dies on a better planchet that was either hand selected or specially burnished (but not polished), and given a single strike.
>
> The Master Coin period begins use of polished dies but not polished planchets. It appears that sometimes the Mint did not use polished reverse dies, so we get Master Coins with only obverse polished dies. However, these could be simply circulation strikes using dies previously used for Master Coins. By the time we reach the "Proof" period we have the fully polished dies and planchets along with double strikes. During this period the Mint stops using special dies for circulation strikes.[43]

Dannreuther notes:

> Until the tight close collars were introduced (different times for different series), it was very difficult to strike these special coins. The tight close collar makes true Proofs, in my opinion. The exact time of tight close collars is tough to call, as the "Proof" 1820 large cents don't really look like Proofs, while those of 1821 do. It is telling that the first complete Proof set in the Smithsonian is 1821, *and* there are no large cents there before 1821 that are even remotely close to being Proofs.[44] This indicates that the Mint did something different in 1821. The collars for large cents seemed to have been "tightened" over the years. The collar used on 1827 and 1828 Proof large cents is a single, very tight close collar.
>
> The December 1827 introduction of the Rush-Muhlenberg press may have been instrumental in the "tightening" of the close collars. I am still researching the changing of the collars. It also appears that all the reeded-edge coins from 1794 onward [silver beginning in 1794, gold in 1795] used close collars (again, they were tightened over time, until 1827 to 1828, when they became very tight, and rims were introduced). Thus, some have argued that 1827 and 1828 represent the time frame when true Proofs were made. Certainly, coins struck in tight close collars with rims are Proofs.
>
> The Mint did not charge for Proofs until 1860 (per James Snowden's circular of December of that year limiting Proof set purchases to one per customer at a premium; obviously the limit was not enforced). The term *Proof* was adopted by the Mint around this time, although the term Master Coin was used in the 1859 circular, as was Proof, so the terms were interchangeable to Mint officials.

Inconsistent Early Usage

In the 19th century—the cradle days of the hobby's popularity, when there was little information available relating to Proofs—it was not unusual for a cataloger to use Proof to describe certain coins with "nice" surfaces, such as what today we would call "gem Mint State" or "Mint State, prooflike". In such catalogs, one can find just about any series, from 1793 copper cents onward, called Proof. Such descriptions as "Extremely Fine, almost Proof," and even "Uncirculated, was Proof," can be found.

About the year 1857, Augustus B. Sage, who at that time was prominent in numismatics and in 1859 would be, briefly, America's most important coin auction cataloger, encountered John Cooper Vail, a fellow collector who was known as a poet and entrepreneur. Long thereafter, Sage reminisced:

> Vail, I believe, was the first man in this country to advertise for rare coins, and he obtained by that means numbers of the rarer specimens of our earlier coinage. Often have I conversed with him, and with wonder-wrought countenance envied him the pleasure of ever having *seen* so many gems. How he would dwell upon the pine tree six-pences, *perfect*, *almost Proof*, and the *Washington dollar* that "came from an old woman at the circus."[45]

In 1859 Sage issued this, as per the cover inscription: *Catalogue of the Valuable and Extensive Collection [of] Coins, Medals & Numismatic Works, the Property of Henry Bogert, Esq. Which will be sold at public auction, by Messrs. Bangs, Merwin & Co. at their rooms, No. 13 Park Row, on February 28th, 1859, and the five following days.* The catalog was a 93-page affair, plus covers. This listing typified the casual use of Proof at the time:

> Lot 1231. Dime, 1805. Extremely fine, nearly a Proof. [sold for $1.75]

Similarly, on July 20, 1866, Charles Clay, a prominent numismatist in Manchester, England, sent to the American Numismatic and Archaeological Society in New York a catalog he had prepared of his collection, which he was seeking to sell.[46] A few years later, E.B. Mason Jr., one of several dealers active in Philadelphia, went to England to search for coins and paid Clay a call, afterwards publishing this comment: "[I was] much pleased with the different series and surprised to find a number of pieces unknown in America. The United States cents, 1793 to 1814, are remarkably fine, but not Proofs, as Dr. Clay has claimed in his pamphlet describing the collection, and published for circulation."[47]

Almost countless examples of the misuse of the term *Proof* in auction catalogs could be cited. The 1795 $5 gold half eagle alone is a playground for such misusages, including these (from a much longer list):

> June 1883, John W. Haseltine, 69th Sale, William J. Jenks Collection: Lot 324: "1795 Very close date. Reverse, large wreath in eagle's beak. A rare variety in beautiful, nearly Proof condition."

> January 1884, W. Elliott Woodward, the Hon. Heman Ely Collection: Lot 809: "1795 Small eagle reverse; Unc. Almost Proof, the first issue of this coin, very scarce."

> May 1885, W. Elliott Woodward, 78th Sale, J. Colvin Randall Collection: Lot 997: "1795 Date touches the bust; Extremely Fine, nearly Proof."

A Proof coin cannot become Uncirculated (Mint State), nor can the opposite occur. Also, a coin cannot be "almost Proof." It either is or is not a Proof. Circulation strikes and Proofs each represent a different method of manufacture, as stated.

AVAILABILITY OF PROOFS

As to the market desirability of true Proofs among later generations of numismatists, until the 1950s, the vast majority of collectors considered Proof to be a *better* quality than Uncirculated. Sometimes—as was often done with, for example, Indian Head cents—an Uncirculated coin would be acquired as a stopgap until a Proof could be found as an "improvement." There were a few exceptions among collectors, such as F.C.C. Boyd, who built parallel collections of some series–one containing circulation strikes and the other Proofs. It was through the repeated commentaries of John J. Ford Jr. and Walter Breen in New Netherlands Coin Company catalogs that the tide turned. Today, Proofs are appreciated as a different type of production.

In American numismatics there are many coins that are readily available with Proof finish, but very rare in Mint State. The opposite is also true. As examples, a gem Proof of the 1901 Morgan silver dollar is easily enough obtained, but a gem Mint State coin may become available only once in every several years.

A set of nickel three-cent pieces from 1865 to 1889 could be assembled in Proof format in less than a month, but a gem-quality set of circulation strikes would likely take several years to complete. Similarly, a set of Proof silver three-cent pieces, or trimes, of the Type III design minted from 1858 to 1873 could be completed quickly, but a decade might be required for a gem Mint State collection, and even then the challenge might remain unfulfilled.

Of course, for most series, Proofs are rarer, often much rarer, than circulation strikes. Countless thousands of Uncirculated 1936 Washington quarters exist from a mintage of 41,300,000, but only 3,837 Proofs were struck. More than five million Uncirculated 1921 Morgan silver dollars exist, but there are fewer than 30 mirror Proofs.

In the series of half cents, today Proofs are available for the Proof-only years of 1831; 1836;

1821, Proof (N-1), cent with mirror surfaces and sharply struck stars and other features. This cent has a long pedigree ranging from Thomas L. Elder's sale of the Peter Mougey Collection in 1910 to the Larry and Ira Goldberg sale of the R.E. (Ted) Naftzger Jr. Collection in 2009.

1840 to 1848; 1849, Small Date; and 1852, and are eagerly sought. Proofs from 1854 to 1857, years in which circulation strikes were also produced, were made in fair quantity and appear on the market regularly. Prooflike circulation strikes of dates in the 1820s and 1830s have been widely offered as Proofs, per the Ronald P. Manley comment quoted earlier.

For Proof large cents the situation is vastly different. As a class they are far rarer than half cents, this being true for the years prior to 1854. There are no "Proof only" years. Proofs of cents were made of many, if not most, dates from the 1820s to the 1840s, but in small numbers, for use at the time. Most Proofs of the 1840s share a common reverse die and may include restrikes. Proofs from 1854 to 1857 were made in significantly larger numbers and are the dates most often encountered today.

There are many false Proofs in the marketplace. These typically are very dark in appearance, but when held at an angle to the light show reflective surfaces. While some of these are prooflike circulation strikes, most are coins with the fields carefully polished or burnished, then artificially toned. Some years ago, a major New York collection of cents had many such so-called Proofs from 1817 to 1839.[48] Supposed Proofs have been offered of certain Braided Hair cents of the 1840s and 1850s, but many listed by Walter Breen have been debunked by John R. (Bob) Grellman Jr., in *The Die Varieties of United States Large Cents*, and by others elsewhere.

How, then, should a *real* Proof copper half cent or cent be defined?

For the author, to qualify as a Proof a cent must conform to Proof *half* cents of 1831, 1836, and the other Proof-only years, each of which is unquestioned. There are no "weak" Proofs among these, nor are there any with traces of mint luster. A Proof should have sharply struck stars (often a huge problem with coppers called Proof now, but with weak stars), sharp dentils (not as much of a problem), sharply struck hair and leaves, and a mirror edge (when viewed edge-on). No doubt other special coins were struck whose distribution intent is not known today. These might well be called Specimens at the pleasure of their owners, certification services, and others, as opinions vary, and facts will probably forever remain unknown.

A very few carelessly struck Proof restrike half cents are known with some weakness, including an 1831 with the incorrect reverse of 1840.

Similarly, it is important to emphasize that not everyone has the standards described here. Denis Loring, who has written extensively on the subject of Proof large cents, cites 1833 Newcomb-4, seen with evidence of at least four blows from the press—a coin with mirrored surface, but with weak stars.[49]

True Proof half cents and large cents are rare, beautiful, and a delight to own. However, great care should be exercised in their acquisition.

Numismatics in
the 19th Century

Collecting American
Coins in Europe

In the 1790s, when the Philadelphia Mint began operation, there was no organized interest in numismatics in America. Several museums had displays of medals and relics, and a few individuals enjoyed the pursuit. There is no record of anyone showing a particular interest in copper, silver, and gold coins contemporaneously struck at the Mint.

In contrast, there was a great interest in numismatics in Europe. Collectors and museums in England, France, Germany, and elsewhere sought coins for their cabinets, with ancient Greek and Roman issues being a particular focal point and the subject of several books. In England, from about 1786 through the late 1890s, there was a great passion for collecting halfpenny-size copper tokens. The size of an American cent, these tokens were made by different workshops in London, Birmingham, and elsewhere. Near Birmingham, the Soho Manufactory, which was operated by Matthew Boulton and James Watt, was particularly active. As noted earlier, the same enterprise furnished planchets to the Philadelphia Mint.

While many of these halfpence were used as small change in circulation, many others were numismatic delicacies, specifically made to sell to collectors. Today, these are generally classified as Conder tokens, so named because James Conder, a British collector, prepared a listing of them in 1798. His was not the first listing, but happens to be the one that posterity smiled upon. Conder lived in Ipswich, Suffolk. His book was titled *An Arrangement of Political Coins, Tokens, and Medalets, issued in Great Britain, Ireland, and the Colonies, Within the Last Twenty Years: From the Farthing, to the Penny Size.*

Some relatives of these tokens, not necessarily described by Conder, have American themes and have been adopted by numismatists this side of the Atlantic. Examples include the 1792, Roman Head Washington, cent, the 1796 P.P.P. Myddelton token, the undated (circa 1798) Theatre in New York tokens, and a fair number of others, mostly in the Washington series. Some of these can be very expensive.

British-made tokens of the 1790s furnished a platform for humor and satire. James Spence, a London entrepreneur and publisher, issued dozens of varieties lampooning politics and other subjects.

Another maker created what is called the Token Collector's Halfpenny. It depicts on one side a numismatist seated at a table strewn with halfpennies (presumably). Smoking a cigar, and with a glass of wine in front of him and Father Time standing behind, the man seems to be having a good time. On the other side we see two numismatists, Don Quixote–like, brandishing swords and riding jackasses at high speed. Above is ASSES RUNNING FOR HALFPENCE. The satire is, of course, on numismatists paying high prices for Conder tokens.

Token Collector's Halfpenny, a satirical Conder token issued in England in 1796. At the time halfpenny tokens (the size of an American copper cent) were all the rage with collectors.

America furnished a destination for English writers and other travelers, several of whom visited New York City, Philadelphia, and other places, then published travelogues upon their return. Sometimes they brought coins back with them. British numismatists desired to add United States issues to their collections, representing examples from former colonies.

It seems that, sometime late in 1795, an Englishman visited America, perhaps calling on the Mint. In any event, he returned home with two Mint State 1794 silver dollars and three of like quality dated 1795, as well as several dozen other coins. These were eventually added to Greek, Roman, and other coins in a cabinet. In 1964 the coins were auctioned in London, bringing to the market many specimens of remarkable quality, including memorable half cents and large cents.[1]

THE EARLY YEARS IN AMERICA

The Library Company of Philadelphia had a collection of ancient coins and medals by 1764, some of which were the gift of Thomas Penn of England.[2] Quite possibly, this was the first American numismatic cabinet of importance.

In April 1782, the Swiss émigré Pierre Eugène Du Simitière opened the American Museum in Philadelphia. A voracious collector of books, broadsides, and the history of the American Revolution, Du Simitière was one of the earliest numismatists in the United States, and he dedicated an entire section of his museum to coins and paper money. After his death in October 1794, his museum collection was sold at public auction on March 19, 1785, including his coins, medals, and paper money. This was the earliest known public auction of numismatic items in the United States.[3]

John Allan, an accountant by profession, enjoyed buying, selling, and collecting coins and other historical items and was probably the first rare coin dealer in the United States.[4] In New York City he supplied coins to many clients, including Philip Hone, a wealthy man who in 1826 served a term as mayor. Other clients at the time included Pierre (or Peter) Flandin and Michael Moore. In 1831 Charles Cushing Wright, a well-known engraver and die sinker, gave lectures on classical coins and medals at the National Academy of Design at Clinton Hall in New York City. Samuel J. Beebee, an exchange broker at 22 Wall Street, dealt in specie in the 1830s, and at a later date he is known to have surveyed incoming items to select pieces of numismatic value. Several dozen other brokers plied their trade and were suppliers to collectors.

James Mease, of Philadelphia, was interested in numismatics at an early time. In his 1811 book, *The Picture of Philadelphia, Giving an Account of Its Origin, Increase and Improvements in Arts, Sciences, Manufactures, Commerce, and Revenue*, he devoted space to the Mint and its operations and listed the officers. In 1821 his article "Description of Some of the Medals Struck in Relation to Important Events in North America" was published in *Collections of the New York Historical Society*, possibly the first article on American numismatics to reach print in the United States.[5]

Robert E. Bache, of Brooklyn, was active in numismatics by 1829, apparently continuing in the hobby until his death in England in 1834.[6] Years later his collection, long in storage in an iron box in the Atlantic Bank in Brooklyn, was purchased intact and auctioned by W. Elliot Woodward, whose auction sale of December 19, 1865, included this:

A typical 19th-century wooden cabinet for housing a collection of coins, tokens, and medals.

Lot 2678: A coin cabinet, 2 feet 4-1/2 inches high, 20 inches wide, and 20 inches deep, outside measurement; contains 29 drawers, running in grooves for economy of space. The material is rosewood, with ebony trimmings, elegantly inlaid with mother-of-pearl; the drawers are lined with flannel and numbered on tablets of mother-of-pearl. This cabinet belonged to the late Robert E. Bach [*sic*], of Brooklyn, is of English manufacture, was purchased by him in London, in 1830, and cost 30 guineas.[7] It is in excellent order, and most desirable, being thoroughly built, and very elegant in appearance.

The Philadelphia Museum, founded in the city in 1784 by Charles Willson Peale, displayed a selection of coins and medals and issued an admission token which is quite collectible today. The Peale family operated museums in New York and Baltimore, each with numismatic displays.

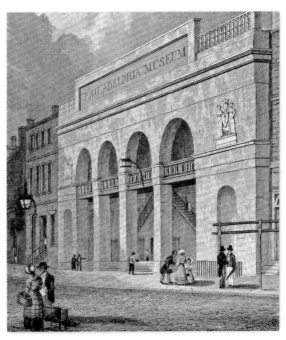

The Philadelphia Museum had a selection of coins and medals on view. (Fenner, Sears & Co., London, 1831)

Admission token to Peale's Philadelphia Museum. Dies by Christian Gobrecht. Struck at the Philadelphia Mint.

In Washington, D.C., from 1816 to 1839, the Columbian Institute for the Promotion of Arts and Sciences, chartered by Congress, had a small cabinet of numismatic specimens among its possessions.[8] In the same city, John Varden set up an exhibit of coins by 1829, lamenting that prior to that year there had been three collectors of note in the district, but that they had moved away, taking their collections with them.

INTO THE 1830S

In the 1830s, John Rodman Coxe, a professor at the University of Pennsylvania, had a collection of copper coins including many pieces he purchased at Moses Thompson's Auction Store at the northeast corner of Third and Chestnut Streets, Philadelphia.[9] In Baltimore, Robert Gilmor Jr., scion of a wealthy shipping and mercantile family, was an avid numismatist. Among other treasures he owned a 1787 Brasher doubloon.

Joseph B. Felt, a doctor of divinity who lived in Salem, Massachusetts (later moving to Boston), wrote an important book of 259 pages, published in 1839 by Perkins & Marvin: *An Historical Account of Massachusetts Currency.* This is notable as the earliest-dated numismatic work of any large size to be published in the United States.[10] Also in Salem, the East India Marine Society, founded in 1799 and incorporated in 1801, had a display of coins, a description of which was mentioned in an 1821 catalog. In 1823, Admiral Sir Isaac Coffin presented a case of 111 medals to the Society, and in 1846 John Pickering donated a collection of ancient coins.[11]

By 1830 William Gordon Stearns, of Boston, was a coin collector. A letter from him dated March 18, 1840, was published in the *Numismatic Chronicle* in London and gave a superficial overview of North American coinage. Harrington's Museum, in Boston, must have had some interesting coins, medals, and paper money in the 1830s, for some specimens were offered a few years later at auction in a catalog dated July 11, 1842, under the imprint of N.A. Thompson & Co.[12]

Another early collector, Joseph B. Cooper, was mentioned in a diary entry by Isaac Mickle, of Philadelphia, on October 18, 1838:

> This morning I got up (as all good citizens should) and, after breakfast, went to Philadelphia on business which it not expedient for the reader to know. Upon my return Mr. Joseph B. Cooper, a lover of antiquities, called to show me his Cabinet of Curious Coins, which, by the by, is large and interesting. He undertook to translate some of the inscriptions, but between his stammering and his ignorance, I was reminded of the fable of the blind leading the halt.[13]

THE MINT CABINET

By any measure the preeminent American museum holding of rare coins during the 19th century was the Mint Cabinet, later called the Mint Collection, and known today as the National Coin Collection. Beginning about 1824, Adam Eckfeldt—and possibly others at the Philadelphia Mint—started saving specimens of current coinage, according to a later reminiscence by Edward D. Cogan, who must have heard this from some officer of the institution.[14] A supply of copper cents, medals, and other items was kept on hand for sale or exchange to interested visitors and collectors. In addition, the Mint willingly produced restrikes of earlier issues upon request—such as from Baltimore numismatist Robert Gilmor—if appropriate old dies were on hand. Gilmor claimed to have furnished the original encouragement to Eckfeldt to mount a display of the institution's own coinage.

In June 1838, the Mint Cabinet was formally organized, and on March 3, 1839, Congress recognized the growing collection and voted an annual appropriation for its maintenance. Among the earliest visitors to the display was Alexandre Vattemare, of France. Stopping by in 1838, he observed that silver dollars on hand did *not* include a specimen dated 1804, which was later to be recognized as a rarity.[15] By the early 1840s, Jacob Reese Eckfeldt and William E. Dubois superintended the pieces on display. In 1846 a 138-page catalog of the holdings was written by Dubois and published as *Pledges of History: A Brief Account of the Collection of Coins Belonging to the Mint of the United States.* In the second edition of this work, 1851, the Mint display was described as follows:

> The suite of apartments in the Mint appropriated to the exhibition of coins, ores, and national medals occupies the front of the building in the second story, and measures 16 feet wide by 54 feet long. Originally there were three rooms, connecting with each other by folding-doors; the removal of these has made one large saloon, with recesses, very commodious and suitable for the use to which it is applied.
>
> The eastern and western rooms are of uniform size and construction; the central one has a dome and skylight, supported by four columns; with a corresponding window in its floor (protected by a railing) to light the hall of the entrance below. The ancient coins are displayed in eight cases, mitred in pairs, and placed erect against the walls in the wide doorways and the middle room. The modern coins are variously arranged; part (including all those of the United States) being in a nearly level case which surrounds the railing above mentioned; and part being in upright cases, disposed along the walls of the middle and west rooms. The ores, minerals, and metallic alloys are placed in the west room; in the eastern are shown the national and other medals, and the fine beams used for the adjustment of weights. The middle room also contains portraits of the directors of the Mint, beginning with Rittenhouse, the first director. All the cases are fronted with glass, and, besides allowing an inspection of every specimen, present an agreeable coup d'oeil on entering the room, especially by the middle door.
>
> Visitors are admitted at prescribed hours, if attended by an officer or conductor of the institution. The collection was commenced in June 1838. Long before that date, however, Adam Eckfeldt, formerly chief coiner, led as well by his own taste as by the expectation that a conservatory would some day be established, took pains to preserve master-coins of the different annual issues of the Mint, and to retain some of the finest foreign specimens, as they appeared in deposit for recoinage.[16] As soon as a special annual appropriation was instituted for this object by Congress (which was as soon as it was asked), the collection took a permanent form, and from the nucleus above mentioned, has gone on in a continual course of augmentation ever since. It is now nearly as large as we expect or wish to have it, excepting, however, that specimens of new coinage, domestic or foreign, must be added as they appear. For effecting this purpose we have had singular facilities. A great majority of the coins—almost all of those not over 300 years old—have been culled from deposits, and consequently have cost us no more than their bullion value. They are, moreover, the choicest of their kind; and perhaps there are few cabinets where so large a proportion of the pieces are in so fine preservation, as well the ancient as the modern. We have also the advantage of the correspondence and aid of gentlemen abroad, some of them officially related to our government, and all of them experienced in this business, and disposed to respond to our wishes. . . .
>
> At the present time the aggregate of specimens is about 650 in gold, 2,100 in silver, 1,200 in billon [an alloy of silver and copper, the latter predominant], brass, copper, &c.; in all 3,950. Of these, the ancient Greek and Roman number 82 in gold, 503

in silver, and 480 in other metals; in all, 1,065. Compared with the numismatic cabinets of Europe, our collection is indeed but a dwarf in size, and may stand second, in that respect, to some in this country. But it was not our purpose to amass an immense store of coins, the very multitude of which might deter from its examination. We are rather willing to be the first to set an example of moderation in a pursuit which has its temptations to extravagance and excess.

In 1842 a handsome quarto volume was issued under the imprint of the Assay Office of the U.S. Mint: *A Manual of Gold and Silver Coins of All Nations, Struck Within the Past Century*. This became known among collectors as the Assay Manual. Engravings to illustrate the work were done by Joseph Saxton's medal-ruling machine, a pantograph device that employed a stylus to trace over the surface of a coin or medal and translate the three-dimensional object to a two-dimensional representation.[17] While the *Assay Manual* was not intended as a numismatic volume, it did have certain information of interest to collectors, but nothing in the way of rarity or value data—or anything relating to half cents and cents.

For a long time Dubois in particular was the spokesperson for the Mint on matters numismatic. His expertise was reinforced in 1846 by the publication of a pamphlet, rare today, titled *Pledges of History: A Brief Account of the Collection of Coins Belonging to the Mint of the United States; More Particularly of the Antique Specimens*, which described the Mint Cabinet. Again, there was little of interest to present-day collectors of early coppers.

THE 1840s

In Washington in early 1840, Joel Roberts Poinsett, the secretary of war, sought to establish the National Institute for the Promotion of Science in Washington, D.C. By May a constitution for the National Institute had been written, and within a year the United States government's National Cabinet of Curiosities and the specimens from the United States Exploring Expedition to the Southern Pacific were under the National Institute's care. Poinsett hoped to secure the endowment received in 1838 under the will of James Smithson, but Congress elected to establish (in 1846) the Smithsonian Institution instead. In 1858, the National Institute's coins began to be transferred to the Smithsonian (which today houses the National Numismatic Collection).

In the 1840s the coins and related items in Peale's Philadelphia Museum were sold to showman P.T. Barnum, and afterward were displayed along with items acquired from Scudder's Museum in Barnum's American Museum, one of the great tourist attractions in lower New York City.

Matthew Adams Stickney was one of the most important figures on the 19th century numismatic stage. Born in Rowley, Massachusetts, on September 23, 1805, he later moved to South Danvers (today's Peabody), where he was employed in the counting rooms of Sawyer & Pierce, dealers in West Indian (Caribbean) goods. Two years later Stickney went into the same business, which he pursued there and, later, in the nearby seaport of Salem, where he resided. An intellectual, as we might call him today, he studied avidly after leaving the public schools, and gained proficiency in Latin and became familiar with the classics.

> As a boy he was greatly interested in ornithology, and it is said that before he was ten years old he had gathered a collection of nearly two thousand eggs—thus early giving evidence of "the collector's instinct." As he grew older, his love of antiquarian pursuits developed, and inheriting from his grandfather a large amount of Continental currency, which had been paid him for services in the Revolution, he was led to make a collection of Colonial and Continental coins and money.[18]

From an early age, possibly in 1817, he vigorously pursued numismatics, traveling and corresponding widely to seek specimens of interest, combining the pleasure of their acquisition with his appreciation of history.[19] He is said to have found *two* specimens struck from the 1785 Immune Columbia dies, but in gold instead of copper, in New York City at the cost of bullion. Both were numismatic concoctions: one was a restrike over a British guinea, likely as a numismatic fantasy, and the other was fabricated with a different reverse.[20]

On May 9, 1843, he visited the Philadelphia Mint to inquire about a most curious coin: an *1804* silver dollar he had seen illustrated in the 1842 Assay Manual. A bargain was struck, and Stickney exchanged several coins—including the gold Immune Columbia overstrike—for the 1804 dollar.[21] In a later reminiscence, he included information about his collecting activities:

> It [the 1804 dollar] was not then considered any more valuable than any other of the series, and I only desired it to help make up the chronological series which I perhaps was the first to attempt to make of U.S. coins.
>
> Jacob G. Morris Esq. of Phila. (lost on board of the "Arctic" on his return from Europe in 1854) whom I visited at the same time, in a letter received from him soon after, writes, "I have never cared for making a collection of American coins of each year's coinage, it is only where the style has been altered, or where there is any peculiarity in the coin, differing from those in general circulation that I have cared for them, nor do I see the utility of it to a collector." Dr. Roper & others were of the same opinion. . . .
>
> I have been for nearly fifty years a systematic collector of coins, and for a very long period almost without a competitor, and very many of the rare coins which now enrich other cabinets were by great solicitation obtained from me.[22]

The following recollection of Stickney is from John Robinson, who "knew him well":

> Stickney made his money in a grocery shop not far from his home, the house in which his two daughters still reside. By offering to accept the copper "Brummies"[23] of the date at the cent value, he acquired many rare coins, and he also had an arrangement with a New York firm of brokers to reserve for him any unusual pieces of gold and silver, and thus at comparatively little cost he gathered his great collection in the 1840s and 1850s.
>
> We boy collectors in Salem used to call on him to see his rarities, but did not always get in. Later we learned a trick which opened both his door and his heart. We took him bright Civil War tokens and little medals which, shut up as he was, he had no means of obtaining, and so beneath his beaming smiles we got our reward by glimpses of olive-colored, Uncirculated 1793s and by actually holding in our hands the Massachusetts Janus head 1776, and that rarity of rarities, the Brasher doubloon, which brought the unheard of sum of $6,000 at the sale of Stickney's collection.
>
> When S.S. Crosby applied to me as a Salemite to know how he could induce Stickney to permit him to make rubbings of the colonial rarities for his forthcoming work on the "Early Coins of America," I gave him the strategy of our boyhood. Crosby tried it and wrote me the next week a letter of thanks—it worked to a charm; Crosby got all he wanted.[24]

Samuel Abbott Green began collecting coins circa 1846 when he found a rare 1799 cent in circulation.[25] His interest grew, and in time he became prominent in the Boston Numismatic Society, served on the 1870 and 1872 Assay Commissions, and served as a coeditor of the *American Journal of Numismatics*.

No doubt a truly comprehensive list of collectors active in the 1840s would include more than 200 names.

THE 1850s

The first American auction sale of numismatic importance featured the cabinet of Lewis Roper of Philadelphia. Roper was active in numismatics in the 1840s and was one of the collectors known to Mint officials Eckfeldt and Dubois. An adventurer at heart, it seems, he headed off to join the Gold Rush. Seeking to return via Panama in 1850 aboard the SS *Panama*, out of San Francisco, he caught fever, died, and was buried at sea. His properties were auctioned via a 24-page catalog on February 20, 1851, under the title of *Executors' Sale: Valuable Collection of Gold and Silver Coins and Medals, Etc., Catalogue of the Entire Collection of Rare and Valuable Coins, Medals, Autographs, Mahogany Coin Case, Etc., Late of Doctor Lewis Roper, Deceased.*

Offered were 698 lots, the last 45 of which were autographs. The realization was $1,172.47, the first American coin sale definitely known to have crossed the $1,000 level.[26] The sale took place in the auction room of Moses Thomas & Son, Philadelphia. At the auction an Uncirculated 1793 Chain cent was awarded to Boston numismatist Ammi Brown for all of ten cents![27]

In the same era, Charles I. Bushnell, an attorney in New York City, was particularly active in numismatic research and corresponded with collectors and historians about colonial coinage. The New-York Historical Society on Chambers Street, at Broadway, had a library of 10,000 volumes and a valuable collection of coins and minerals. Peale's Museum and Gallery of the Fine Arts and Barnum's American Museum also had displays of coins among their other curiosities.

Token in white metal issued by P.T. Barnum's American Museum, New York City. The reverse advertises coins and medals among the museum's many attractions.

England was beginning to become a fertile hunting ground for American collectors and dealers. Perhaps the earliest foray for which we have a record today was the trip taken by Jacob G. Morris of Philadelphia, who had been well known in numismatics since at least the early 1840s. He was a passenger aboard the SS *Arctic* when it went down in the North Atlantic Ocean on its way back from Europe on September 27, 1854. Presumably, he had made the rounds of the dealers in London and perhaps elsewhere. On the same ill-fated vessel was a coin destined for Bushnell, the 1733 Rosa Americana pattern twopence. A later chronicler, in connection with this prime rarity, noted that he knew of the existence of only four—now three—specimens:

> The fourth was purchased in England for the sum of £7, or $35, for Charles Bushnell, Esq., of New York City, unfortunately placed on board the steamer *Arctic*, to be transmitted to him, on her last and fatal voyage, and its pigmy proportions are now added to the vast accumulations that lie imbedded in the sands of the Atlantic Ocean.[28]

In the 1820s, Pierre (Peter) was an active numismatist in New York City.[29] Apparently, his interest continued for many years thereafter. Finally, he tired of the pursuit, and on June 6, 1855, his collection was auctioned by Bangs, Brother & Co., of the same city, the first truly notable numismatic sale held by what would become, in various incarnations, a very long-lived auction house. The offering comprised 230 lots containing a total of

1,195 pieces and sold for the aggregate sum of $736.02.[30] The owner's name was not mentioned on the title page of the listing titled *Catalogue of a Valuable Collection of American and Foreign Coins and Medals in Gold, Silver, Copper and Bronze*. Items relating to early federal coppers were so general that they have little meaning today:

> Lot 184: Two 1793 cents, one with 15 links of a chain; and a cent of 1795, equal to a proof, *very rare.*
>
> Lot 189: 20 various American cents, *fine.*
>
> Lot 190: 8 various half cents, *fine.*

Except by dedicated bibliophiles, the Flandin catalog is all but forgotten today.

Not so with the collection of A.C. Kline, which crossed the block on June 12, 1855, just six days after the Flandin Collection was sold in the same room.[31] The 92-page catalog did not mention the owner's name. The sale included many notable half cents and large cents. Lot 11 was an "1815" cent "of the highest rarity," that sold for an astounding $5.50, or more than twice the realization for a 1799 cent described as "Fine and rare."[32] The pages offered 1,712 numbered lots, to which were appended two addenda of 137 and five lots each. The realization totaled $1,753 for the main catalog plus $299.14 and $10.37 for the addenda. This became the first American coin auction sale, including addenda, to cross the $2,000 level.

Numismatic historian Joel J. Orosz described its importance:

> It was the first American sale to attract buyers from across the nation. Joseph Mickley and Dr. Edward Maris led the hometown Philadelphians, but Charles Bushnell represented New York, and Boston had a relatively large contingent of buyers that included Jeremiah Colburn, Ammi Brown, and Henry Cook. Truly, everyone who was anyone in antebellum American numismatics was vying for Kline's coins.
>
> The Kline sale quite simply rewrote the record books, nearly doubling the realization of the Roper sale ($2,062 to the previous high of $1,172). The numbers sound

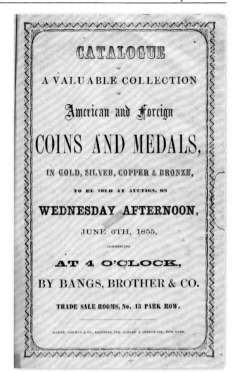

Cover panel of the Flandin Collection catalog, June 6, 1855.

The Trade Sale Rooms at 13 Park Row, New York City, where Bangs, Brother & Co. conducted the Flandin and other sales. The firm suspended business in October 1857 amid the Panic of 1857. It later reopened as Bangs, Merwin & Co. in the same premises. The firm sold antiques, estate effects, art, and quantities of recently published books (this being the way the book trade acquired inventory at the time). Coin offerings were infrequent. This illustration is from an 1859 catalog. In 1860 the company relocated to the Irving Buildings at 594–596 Broadway.

insignificant today, but one must take into account the way in which inflation has ravaged the value of the nation's currency.[33]

The Kline sale in particular was of further importance in American numismatic history in that the prices were widely publicized in newspapers. Beyond the numismatic community, bankers, brokers, and exchange houses were alerted, precipitating an intense search for rare varieties that might be found in general circulation.

COLLECTING COPPERS IN THE 1850s

In the mid-1850s several hundred collectors, or even more, were active. Usually, copper cents were a focal point of interest, less so for half cents. Specialties were wide ranging, from coins of ancient Greece and Rome, to "crown" or dollar-size coins of Europe, to current issues of various countries. Proof coins could be obtained as a courtesy from the Philadelphia Mint, apparently for face value upon application. Half cents and large cents were quite popular, and it is thought that up to two or three hundred were made each year beginning in 1854, the larger figures being for the later years.

John E. Burton recalled the era:

> I began collecting coins (cents and half cents) in 1854. I lived in my native village of New Hartford, New York. There were four boy collectors in the village—Charlie Millard, Stevie Childs, Byron Case and myself. I was fortunate in Jimmie Dobie, who was a saloonkeeper where my grandfather, Asa Allen, a soldier of the War of 1812, took his "nip" daily, and Dobie told me I could come in each day after school and look over all the cents and half cents in the till and take out any I wanted and put another in its place. I secured in a few years a considerable collection of these. By 1857 I had the best in town.[34]

In Philadelphia, Joseph N.T. Levick was an enthusiastic numismatist. Many fine coins came from the Mint, until the Flandin and Kline auctions made the officials aware of market values. According to Levick:

> Cents in those days [prior to the 1855 Kline sale] were easily found in circulation in such condition as to satisfy a collector; always excepting, of course, those rare dates of 1799 and 1804, which were considered scarcer than the 1793s, and even those dates were to be had of collectors by exchanging.
>
> I quite well remember what an advantage the Mint was to us who lived in Philadelphia, for we had the privilege of going to the institution and selecting from trays or drawers subdivided for each date. From these I procured some excellent specimens of cents for their face value; and many of us collectors, knowing this channel, thus secured cheap cents. We also took the precaution to lay aside quantities of fine pieces to trade with, and for some years afterwards, the market was well stocked with cents.
>
> The employees of the Mint, however, soon learned to know the increasing value of these coins, and also commenced laying aside the finer pieces and more unusual dates. Our game was blocked by this discovery, for we saw thenceforward that the desirable cents were missing.[35]

Frederick M. Bird started collecting coins as a lad in the 1850s, when he lived in Philadelphia:

> I took the numismatic fever when a small boy, away back in the fifties. That was the golden age of the young collector. The big red cent was the circulating medium, and

anything of its size passed for it; smaller pieces went for a half cent. One could gather a very decent set of "colonials" at par, for all sorts of copper were in circulation then, and there was not much competition in taking them out of it. I used to make interest with groceries and candy shops, whose soft-hearted proprietors would put by their "queer" or "bad pennies" for me.

During the week I would save my limited share of the coinage of the realm, and on Saturdays would make my rounds and exchange it for these antique or foreign specimens. Once I got a fair bronze of Lincinius for half a cent, and once a nearly Uncirculated Washington cent (large eagle), with another piece, for three cents; the man behind the counter thought he was making large profits that time. An uncle of mine, cashier of a bank in Delaware, took at face value a fine Pine Tree shilling, and an uncommon silver Hessian coin; the former had come from the stocking of some farmer's wife, the latter had been dug up near the field of Brandywine.[36]

Bird lived close to Joseph J. Mickley, one of the leading numismatists in the city. Born on March 24, 1799, as a young man he learned the art of piano tuning and repair, soon expanding to other musical instruments. Once, he repaired, but at the same time carefully preserved, two violins that had been the property of George Washington. About the year 1816 he desired to find a cent of the year of his birth—easy enough to do, he thought. Reality proved otherwise, and it took a long time.

By the 1850s, Mickley's home at 927 Market Street, where he had lived since 1842, was a social center for collectors, including Bird, who seems to have seen his cents of 1799 and 1804, costing Mickley "a half dime each." He continued:

I became his frequent visitor. This was easy, for he was very good natured and accessible, and his place was the resort of harmless loafers, whom he used to address as "friends and fellow-pitchers." . . . He lived in a large house on the north side of Market Street, below Tenth. The ground floor was a grocery, I think; the second story was occupied by pianos, though I never heard of any one going there to see them. His time was spent in a shop or office in the back building, corresponding to the dining room in most Philadelphia houses, with the kitchen beneath it. Back of this was a smaller room, where he kept old almanacs, directories, local histories, and the like; these were a minor hobby with him. I saw nothing of his family, whom he doubtless met at meal-times. Morning, noon, and evening he had (or was likely to have) a stream of visitors of all ages and conditions, with whom he loved to gossip.

Most of Mr. Mickley's coins were not arranged, in my time, but stored away in a desk, where they were of no use to him or anyone. I doubt if he knew what he had. The exceptions were in a large cabinet in his second floor back. Here he kept some few Romans (if I remember all right) and his splendid series of the issues of our Mint in gold and silver, for every year or near it. The large sum—in intrinsic value alone— here locked up impressed my youthful mind; on my remarking that these dollars and eagles must have cost him fabulous prices, he answered with much feeling, "No, no, they were real prices."

Among numismatists of this era, Mickley has been chronicled more than any other. At one time he bought a large lot of old Mint dies as "scrap iron." One way or another, fantasy restrikes were made from them, including an 1811 half cent obverse combined with an irrelevant reverse die, and mismatched cents dated 1804 and 1823. These are often called Mickley restrikes, but no evidence has been found of his actually having made such coins. Perhaps he loaned out the dies for a time.

In 1858 he published a four-page leaflet, *Dates of United States Coins, and Their Degrees of Rarity*, which was a useful guide for bankers and others as to what to keep and what to spend. No prices were given.

After sustaining a robbery of many of his foreign coins valued as much as $10,000, Mickley sold his American issues and others to W. Elliott Woodward, of Roxbury, Massachusetts, who auctioned them in 1867. In 1869, Mickley went on a grand tour of Europe, staying for three years and visiting at least 24 mints.[37] He died on February 15, 1878, by which time he was the most honored numismatist of his era.[38]

Lorin G. Parmelee, another collector who would become very well known, began his interest in the 1850s, not with a rare 1799, but with quantities of various dates. In Boston he was the leading supplier of baked beans to restaurants, hotels, and other public places. Each day he would deliver a new pot or two and pick up the empties. It seems that his passion for coin collecting began in 1855, at which time the value of key cents was already realized:

> In 1855, hearing that there was a premium on old copper cents, he began the process of looking over his pile (which was always a big one) every Monday, laying aside the best ones. He generally came to market Mondays with his old red pail full of copper cents, stopping on his way at State Street to dispose of the fine ones at the brokers, receiving 10 to 25 cents each for them. At that time 1793 cents sold at the toll gates for 25 cents each, and at the brokers for double that amount, although occasionally an extra fine one would bring as high as a dollar. Five dollars was considered an extraordinarily fancy price for the finest cents procurable.
>
> 1799 cents were always scarce, and five dollars was not considered exorbitant for a good one. 1804 cents brought from two to three dollars. For a long time Mr. Parmelee contented himself to saving the best of the cents that he picked up, selling or exchanging his duplicates, until he discovered that he had, with three or four exceptions, a complete date of cents in Very Fine to Uncirculated condition.[39]

In contrast to the well-chronicled Mickley, Parmelee, Levick, and certain other early collectors, today little is known about A.F. Walcott and his activities other than this:

> About 1856–7, Mr. A.F. Walcott of Salem, Mass., a young collector of coins, was presented with a bag of "bright cents" by a relative, Mr. William Pickman of that city. They had been laid away for many years—quite forgotten—and when found were as bright as the day they were coined. Of the Mint series there were those of 1795, 1796, 1797, and 1798, a number of half-cents of 1797, 1798 [*sic*], and 1800, also a few Massachusetts Indian cents.
>
> Mr. Walcott exchanged them with various collectors and at the Mint, where they were looked upon with suspicion and inquiries made as to where they came from, etc., etc. We remember that several collectors looked upon them doubtingly, thinking that some expert had been making them. The prices paid for some of these pieces at the present time would astonish our friend if he were in this part of the world.[40]

THE ACT OF FEBRUARY 21, 1857

In 1850 the Mint began extensive experiments to reduce the weight of the copper cent. The price of the metal was rising, and these coins, a profit center for the institution, seem to have had a dim future in this regard. The situation was ameliorated by the Act of February 21, 1853, which reduced the weight of certain silver coins and provided that the Mint could make these for its own account, rather than only for depositors. These new coins were profitable to produce. Trials with the cent continued, however. After several pattern issues were produced in other formats, in 1854 a reduced-size copper cent was made to the extent of hundreds of patterns, for distribution to interested congressmen and collectors, and in two major designs: a Liberty Head motif similar to that currently being used and a Flying Eagle design (adapted from the silver dollar of 1836, by Christian Gobrecht). Further experimentation occurred in 1855.

Finally, in 1856 nearly a thousand patterns were made of a motif and format that would be adopted on February 21, 1857: a small-diameter cent with a Flying Eagle motif, made of copper-nickel, an alloy of 88 percent copper and 12 percent nickel. Pattern 1856, Flying Eagle, cents were widely distributed to newspaper editors, congressmen, and others of influence. Notices appeared here and there in the popular press, such as in *Harper's Illustrated Weekly* magazine.

As news spread concerning the coming of the copper-nickel cent, nostalgia swept across the land. The copper cents of childhood were about to disappear! Excitement prevailed, and thousands of people looked through their pocket change, cabinets, banks, and elsewhere, and endeavored to string together sets of as many different dates as they could find.

Playing upon the public's interest, the varied displays of the Boston Museum featured "COINS" and "MEDALS" among its exhibits (see ribbon at lower right of this June 23, 1857, broadside).

For many who had persistence, a collection of one cent each from 1816 through 1856 was gathered, with the 1857 cents being generally unavailable, as they were not in general circulation, because few had been released from the mint. Among those that could be found in change, the most elusive by far was the 1823, followed by the 1821. Cents dated in the 1850s were generally available in grades that collectors would come to call Extremely Fine, About Uncirculated, and Uncirculated (the last term later popularized to Mint State). Coins of the 1840s were apt to be more worn, say Fine to Very Fine, and those dating back to 1816 might be Good (mostly worn smooth with the date, lettering, and major features visible in outline format), Very Good, or occasionally Fine.

THE DYNAMIC YEAR OF 1858

The momentum gained force, and in 1858, Joel Munsell, an Albany printer, published *An Historical Account of American Coinage*, by John Howard Hickcox. This slim book contained 151 numbered pages, plus introductory material and five pages of plates (by J.E. Gavit of Albany, including some illustrations used in the 1850 *Documentary History of the State of New York*, by O'Callaghan).

Hickcox's book was produced only to the extent of 200 copies in the regular edition, plus five copies on large paper. Apparently, most were distributed to historians and libraries rather than numismatists. The text was used subsequently as the basis of several commentaries by contributors to *Historical Magazine*. It had little in the way of impact in the growing community of collectors, nearly all of whom were unaware that the work existed.

The Philadelphia Numismatic Society, organized on December 28, 1857, held its first official meeting on January 1, 1858. In the meantime, in New York City a group of collectors led by Augustus B. Sage discussed forming a club. On March 8, 1858, Sage and four friends—Henry O. Hart, James D. Foskett, Edward Groh, and James Oliver—affixed their names to a circular letter that invited interested collectors to meet at Sage's family residence, rooms upstairs at 121 Essex Street, New York City, at 7:30 p.m., March 15, to establish what became the American Numismatic Society (ANS). At about two months shy of his 17th birthday, Sage became a founding member.

The meeting took place as planned, the society's membership expanded, and during the next two years it held meetings in various rooms around the city. Then, in December 1859, it expired, or seemed to. Meetings ceased, and no more was heard.

Sage went into the rare coin business in 1858. In the autumn of that year he launched a string of medalets, Sage's Odds and Ends, from dies by George H. Lovett. The first featured the Crystal Palace in flames, commemorating, or at least observing, its destruction in October of that year. Another followed, showing the Old Sugar House, a building that British troops occupying New York used as a prison during the Revolution. The third depicted Paul Morphy, the chess-playing sensation of America and Europe. These were discontinued, and Sage's Historical Series was initiated, going on to depict more than a dozen subjects, most of which were connected with Revolutionary War history. Sage's Numismatic Gallery honored well-known collectors of the time, starting with Charles I. Bushnell.

In 1859, with three sales, Sage became the first professional numismatist to issue a coin auction catalog, the few earlier ones being produced by art auction houses. After 1860, Sage faded from the scene, leaving a rich legacy.

The December 1858 issue of *The Banker's Magazine* tells of the ever-growing passion for collecting old copper cents:

Since the circulation of the new "nickels," coin collectors have been eagerly searching for rare coppers of the old kind, for they will soon be very scarce. We know of one collector who boasts of every copper known to be struck in America, except three or four. Numismatics has become as much a "rage" as opera-going, chess-playing, sailing on the Delaware, rowing on the Schuylkill, exercising in the gymnasium; and the votaries of the fancy pursue it with a zeal and ardor worthy of the immortal old buck.

One collector was indefatigable enough to pick out of nearly 100,000 coins a cabinet of 400 or 500, which he considered at least worth $500; but just after he had made his selection his premises were broken open, and the rare and precious coins were carried off by some rascally burglar, who valued them at about the price of old copper.

IDLER AND COGAN

Meanwhile, in Philadelphia, William K. Idler catered to many clients. Idler began his rare coin dealership in 1858 at 111 North Ninth Street, having started his shop earlier in the year with a stock of minerals and relics, drawing upon his extensive studies in mineralogy (including a 15-year stint in South America, during which time he secured many specimens). He added jewelry to his stock, then old coins. Circa 1859 he seems to have made arrangements with certain Mint officers to act as a secret outlook for restrikes, rare patterns, and other freshly minted coins, an activity beyond the purview of the present text except to mention that Proof restrike half cents were among such delicacies.

Also in Philadelphia, English immigrant Edward D. Cogan conducted an art shop that sold prints, frames, and the like. A boastful but highly accomplished sort, he later claimed to be the first rare coin dealer in the United States. This assertion was later repeated many times, making him "the father of the rare coin trade in America" to historians who did not bother checking earlier references. Here is the story in his own words:

> I have been engaged in the coin trade since the latter part of 1856. Quite late in the year 1856 a friend of mine brought into my store in Philadelphia an electrotype Washington cent of 1792, and persuaded me to buy it for 25¢; upon showing it, as a curiosity, to a gentleman, he offered me 50¢ for it—and the curiosity was gone. . . .
>
> I immediately set about collecting an entire set of United states cents, but had not the most distant idea, at that time, of ever making it a business.[41] I continued collecting from that time till the latter end of 1858. When finding the demand increasing, and the supply quite equal to it, I commenced selling my duplicates, and from that period have followed the coin trade, almost exclusively,[42] as a matter of business.

By the "latter end of 1858," Charles B. Norton (who issued his first price list in 1856), Augustus B. Sage (active in the trade by early 1858), and John K. Curtis (a bidder in the Flandin sale in 1855 and certainly in business as a dealer in 1857) were well established—and this is just a short list dating back to professional numismatist John Allan in the 1820s.

Considered on the merits of its contents, a mail-bid sale of "duplicates" conducted by Cogan on November 1, 1858, would be worthy of but brief mention, if any notice at all. However, this particular listing of old copper cents from his personal collection, comprising just 77 lots that realized $128.63, became the subject of so much later puffery that an explanation is necessary. Cogan was fond of citing this mail-bid listing as the watershed event that launched the popularity of coin collecting in America, this being based on mention of it in some metropolitan newspapers at the time. To forward this claim he reprinted the newspaper article, with commentary, in 1863, and distributed it widely in the numismatic community. Hokum published by Cogan and other dealers would continue for generations afterward, furnishing many investigative opportunities for numismatic researchers of a later time.

Notwithstanding his seemingly natural inclination to bloviate, Cogan was a very important figure in the coin business during the growth years of auction sales, the 1860s and 1870s. From his November 1, 1858, cent offering onward, he conducted at least 70 sales under his own name and may have done some cataloging for others. He described coins simply and with little in the way of flourish, letting the bidders add their own spice. Fiercely proud, he was genial and kind to most everyone, but could mount a bitter attack if challenged, such as during a notable encounter with Ebenezer Locke Mason Jr. in which both men exchanged fisticuffs and were rolling around together on the auction room floor!

Retiring in November 1879, four years after his highly acclaimed auction of the Col. Mendes I. Cohen Collection, Edward D. Cogan sought to have his business continued by his son George, but events proved that the younger Cogan lacked the requisite numismatic knowledge, business savvy, or both, and the business soon ended.

A Pioneer Listing of 1793 Cent Die Varieties

The *Historical Magazine*, which made its debut in January 1857, was the closest that any wide-circulation publication of the era came to a numismatic periodical. Quite frequently, subscribers using initials or noms de plume posed questions relating to early American coins and currency, and, often, these elicited replies that were published in later issues. The New-York Historical Society and other New York connections appear with some frequency in this magazine, as do the names and initials of collectors of the era.

To the *Boston Evening Transcript*, March 1, 1859, "A.S. Brookline" (for Augustine Shurtleff, Brookline being fictitious) contributed a detailed listing of 1793 cents, plus comments on other cents through 1857. The information concerning the first issues included this:

> The act for the establishment of the United States Mint, was passed April 2, 1792, and it went into operation the same year; being more or less experimental until 1795.
>
> Although a small trial piece for a cent, with a silver centre, was struck in 1792, and the disme and half disme in the same year—there seems to be no doubt that the first regular issue of the currency was the cent of 1793. Of this there are eleven varieties struck in the following order:
>
>> 1st—Obverse, a head with fine flowing hair, copied from the French ideal of Liberty; beneath, the date, with figures wide apart; above, the word 'Liberty.' Reverse, an endless chain of fifteen links, inclosing the words 'one cent,' and the fraction 1-100. Around it 'United Slates of Ameri.' Edge divided into alternate sections of leaf work and milling.
>>
>> 2d—Same as first on obverse. Reverse, reads 'United States of America,' in full.
>>
>> 3d—Hair longer, and bust running out to a fine point; date close in the figures, and piece slightly larger.
>>
>> 4th—Obverse, head bolder in the features, hair flowing straight back, in long, thick locks. Under the neck a twig, with three broad leaves, nearly at right angles with each other. Large date below, 'Liberty' above. Reverse, a wreath of

two branches, united by a ribbon, inclosing words 'one cent.' Around it 'United States of America;' below, the fraction 1-100. Obverse and reverse both surrounded by a finely beaded line near the edge.

5th—Hair a little fuller; leaves on the twig inclined forward. Figures in the date, and letters in the word 'Liberty; much smaller and closer. Reverse, same as No. 4.

6th—Hair rather shorter in middle part of the head. Leaves on the twig much more slender, and in position like No. 4. Reverse, leaves in wreath longer, and bow in knot larger.

7th—Obverse, like the last in head, but the leaves on the twig quite small, and pointing symmetrically upwards. Reverse, varies slightly in wreath.

8th—Obverse same as No. 7. Reverse differs in the wreath, and has 'one cent' exactly in the centre, instead of slightly above it, as before. Fraction closer, in figures.

9th—Obverse like No. 8, except that the leaves on the twig are more pointed, and all incline forward. Reverse, wreath varies again in form and arrangement of the leaves.

10th—Precisely like No. 9, except that now, for the first time, the edge is changed; and, instead of the device mentioned in No. 1, bears the words 'One hundred for a dollar.'

11th—A much larger piece, with more of the bust; the hair is rolled off from the forehead, and combed smooth, falling down over the back; on the left shoulder is the staff and liberty-cap; the twig of leaves under the neck is omitted. Reverse, the wreath is much longer in the leaves, and the bow-knot is very different; the beaded line on both sides is preserved, and the edge is lettered as in No. 10.

The varieties of this year, as above described, are distinguishable at a glance, in good specimens, which are, however, somewhat difficult to obtain. Nos. 3, 5 and 8, are the most common.

While it is always dangerous to state something is *first*, certainly this March 1, 1859, listing is among the earliest technical descriptions of large cent dies, and with a listing in presumed order of issue no less! Shurtleff had been a founder of the Boston Numismatic Society in December 1857.[43] Certainly, by 1859 he had engaged in deep scholarship on the subject.

Norton's Literary Letter, issued from October 1857 to 1860 by New York City bookseller Charles B. Norton, also contained many items of numismatic interest.

THE 1815 CENT AND THE
AMERICAN NUMISMATICAL MANUAL

The aforementioned Augustus B. Sage contributed a coin-collecting column to the *New-York Dispatch* in 1857. He fielded many questions from readers and gave much useful information in an era in which there was not a single book giving the availability or value of United States coins. Indeed, it was not even known whether certain pieces had actually been made. Since the Mint often reused still serviceable dies from previous years, the coinage figures in the *Report of the Director of the Mint* dealt with calendar years, not with the actual dates on the coins. As an example, an earlier *Report* stated that 12,170 half cents were made in 1799, which may have been true, but they were dated 1797 or earlier.

In the *New-York Dispatch* of September 13, 1857, a reader styling himself as "Outsider" took exception with the statement that no cents dated 1815 existed: "William Long of Philadelphia has in his cabinet an American cent dated 1815 in very fine condition. It is not an altered date but a genuine article. We do not recollect of ever having seen any other of that date, so we will put 1815 down as something rare."

On March 2, 1859, at a meeting of the ANS, then barely a year old, "Mr. [William] Bramhall moved the following resolution—whereas—The question as to the coinage of the American cent in the year 1815, remains a matter of doubt and dispute, therefore—Resolved that the Committee on American Coins be and is hereby instructed to investigate and report regarding the same—which was carried."[44]

Soon afterward, the *American Numismatical Manual*, by Montroville W. Dickeson, was published. This lavish large-size book was illustrated with color plates, with reddish-brown added to sketches of cents, silver to silver coins, and gold ink to coins in that metal. For a certain coin he noted:

> Cent. 1815. In this year, we are satisfied that there was no coinage of either cents or half cents, or even a pattern piece gotten up for either. Most numismatologists and others concur in this opinion, though a few contend that pattern pieces were struck off at the Mint, and urge as a reason for their not being coined in volume and circulated, the destruction of the Mint by fire in this year.
>
> It will be found, by referring to the newspapers of that time, that the fire did not occur till January 1816, and that it then only destroyed a portion of the shed adjoining the mint-house, in which the rolling was done. The true reason for the non-coinage was, we believe, the want of copper, occasioned by the European agents not sending it forward in time for use. A few amateur collectors, however, boast of genuine specimens, and cite tests and proofs; but if the coins could tell their own story, they would not impute their origin to the United States Mint. Those *we* have examined, bearing the date of this year, are clearly alterations of the cent of 1813, rendered scarce, as we have heretofore remarked, by this very operation.

On the same subject, in his discussion of *1813* cents he commented, "So many of the best of this emission have been altered to 1815, that it is difficult to obtain good specimens."

Years later on April 4, 1882, a sheet issued by auctioneer M. Thomas & Sons, Philadelphia, told of items to be offered that day, *Sale of Coins, Medals, &c. Catalogue of Rare American and Foreign Silver & Copper Coins, Medals, Pattern Pieces &c., Chiefly Composed of Long's Philadelphia Museum Collection*.

On January 27, 1886, Thomas conducted the *Second Sale of The Collection Formerly Known as "Long's Museum," Catalogue of Revolutionary and Rebellion Relics*. The sale included two complete runs of large cents, but each without the 1809 (a date that is scarce, but hardly a major rarity). Among the curious cents were an "1815" altered from an 1813, three altered "1799" cents, and two altered cents of "1804." The "1815" was the same "not an altered date but a genuine article" coin that "Outsider" wrote about in the September 13, 1857, issue of the *New-York Dispatch*.

As to the museum, in the 1850s William W. Long operated the Museum Hotel at 376–380 South Third Street in Philadelphia. In *An Arrangement of Tradesmen's Cards, Political Tokens, also Election Medals, Medalets, &c. Current in the United States of America for the Last Sixty Years, Described from the Originals, Chiefly in the Collection of the Author,* the first book ever written on this numismatic subject, written in 1858 by Charles I. Bushnell and published that date, a token issued by Long was described: "Pistol & Rifle Galleries. Billiards & Bowling. Bagatelle & Shuffle Boards. Liquors, Oysters, Segars, &c. Refectory & Museum Hotel."

PLATE XVII.

Plate illustrating large cents and other coins printed in colored ink in the *American Numismatical Manual*, Montroville W. Dickeson, 1859.

As to the forgotten genre of museum hotels, in America before the Civil War—an era of curiosity and wonderment in which P.T. Barnum and others flourished and the first widely circulated illustrated newspapers were published—several overnight stopping places found that an exhibit of interesting things drew patrons. In New York City, Thomas Riley conducted the Fifth Ward Museum Hotel on the west corner of West Broadway and Franklin Street from 1826 until his death in 1858. Located at a busy intersection near the Hudson River piers, the place was one of the city's most popular attractions. Riley was a numismatist, a bidder in the sale of the Pierre Flandin Collection in 1855, but nothing has been found concerning coins and medals that were likely on display in his business.[45]

After about 1860, as more information became available through auction catalogs and dealer knowledge, the idea of a genuine 1815 cent existing was dismissed. Modern texts note that none were minted with that date; the *Guide Book of United States Coins* (the Red Book), for example, states that "a lack of copper prevented production."

The *American Numismatical Manual* was the first book treating half cents and large cents in detail. As noted, the first edition was in 1859. This was a good seller for publisher Lippincott, and subsequent editions were issued in 1860 and 1865, with the central word in the title changed slightly to *Numismatic*. This work treated coppers date by date and gave comments concerning types and varieties.

Dickeson was starting nearly from scratch in knowledge, as no useful texts had been published up to that time. It does not seem that he was aware of the information published in either the *Boston Evening Transcript* or the *Historical Magazine*. He seems to have relied on his own observations and, likely, on inquiries placed with others. Alternatively, much of his research may have been done earlier, as he had been active for a long time. The volume, which was impressively printed and contained embossed colored illustrations, was a tour de force in publishing. Although many articles, monographs, and books revised and corrected errors in Dickeson, nothing of such an impressive format appeared in print for the next century, a remarkable tribute. Dickeson had many interests, including archaeology, and was prominent in the exploration of Indian mounds in the Mississippi River watershed. He was also an artist of some accomplishment. As a side note, he was the landlord for the shop that Ebenezer Locke Mason Jr. opened in Philadelphia in 1860.

A white-metal medal issued by Dickeson advertising his coin and medal safe, a cabinet suitable for storing and displaying a collection.

By that time, Mason had been scouring the countryside for rare coins for several years, as he related in a reminiscence, "The Coin Trade":

> During the years 1857, '58 and '59, the writer was connected with a very popular exhibition, traveling from North to South and visiting all the important cities and towns en route. While thus engaged we made it a daily practice to visit all the old junk shops, confectioners, bakers, grocers, etc. and collect all the old and curious coins we could find—at the same time leaving a card with address to establish future trade; and this practice led to a very general hunt in the places aforesaid, for coins, and in many instances we were surrounded at the opening of the exhibition with men and boys eager to dispose of large quantities of old cents, etc.

In one instance while passing through North Carolina, we purchased 10,000 copper pieces; 64 brass Washington tokens of 1783, and 46 Connecticut coins, besides a large quantity and variety of both foreign and American. . . .

The gathering of coins afforded us an agreeable pastime, as well as a profitable occupation; and the constant accumulation of coins led us to enter the field as a dealer in this city in 1860. While thus occupied we advertised very extensively in the large cities, offering what appeared to be fabulous prices for rare U.S. cents. Many of our friends will remember the advertisements, headed with glaring capitals: $25 PAID FOR U.S. CENTS OF 1799.[46]

ATTENDING AN AUCTION IN 1859

Joseph N.T. Levick, who lived in Philadelphia at the time, but would soon move to New York, remembered a sale of 1859 and compared prices to what some of the same varieties sold for a few years later:

On one of the first visits to New York, in '59, to attend a coin sale, I rather astonished many of the New Yorkers, by the spirited manner in which I bid for pieces. I gained a bargain, however, as I purchased for one dollar, a '95 thick die cent, which set the Philadelphians wild when I exhibited it to them. That piece afterwards realized the sum of $11, at my sale, and was bought by Mr. Wm. J. Jenks. It is, I presume, now owned by Mr. Seavey, of Massachusetts; I should like to buy it of him for double that price. I question if there is another of that type its equal in the country; at least, I never saw or heard of one.

The '96 half-cent in my sale sold for $12. Oh! How cheap, alongside of the one I bought at the McCoy Sale for $120. In this manner I could go on to enumerate piece after piece, that sold low, in comparison with what they now bring, but it would necessitate the taking up of almost the entire catalogue.

Among the principal and most enthusiastic buyers at my sale, for cents, was Mr. M.G. Gronberg, who purchased with a determination to secure most of my best cents. In a very short period he afterwards acquired a collection unsurpassed by any in Philadelphia. He sold this collection to George F. Zehnder, of Philadelphia, for not less than $300, which was at that time said to be a high figure; and it was the subject of laughter that any one could be found so insane as to pay such a price. But what would be said of a collection in this city, owned by Mr. M.L. Mackenzie, which has cost him not less than twelve hundred dollars?[47]

MARKET PRICES IN 1860

Copyrighted in 1860 and published in 1861, *Coins, Medals, and Seals, Ancient and Modern,* by W.C. Prime, was widely distributed by Harper & Brothers. The author, like most other numismatists of his era, was a person of many interests. The title page of his work noted that he was also author of *Boat Life in Egypt and Nubia, Tent Life in the Holy Land,* "etc., etc., etc.," all of the etceteras indicating that the volumes mentioned were but a fraction of his output.[48] *Coins, Medals, and Seals, Ancient and Modern* appeared close on the heels of Dickeson's *American Numismatical Manual,* at a time when there were very few books available to guide the coin collector. The study, which does not seem to have been widely used by numismatists of the era, included prices "at recent sales by auction," sometimes adding "Proof" or "Uncirculated." Up to this time no book had included such extensive information on prices of half cents and cents:

Half cents:

1793: $4.13

1794: $1

1795: $0.75

1796: $12

1797: $1

1800: $0.70

1802: $2.13

1803: $0.30

1804: $1.38

1805: $0.45

1806: $0.30

1807: $0.25

1808: $0.40

1809: $0.30

1810: $0.70

1811: $1.88

1825: $0.22

1826: $0.22

1828: $0.22

1829: $0.22

1831, Proof: $10.50

1832: $0.25

1833, Proof: $0.25

1834: $0.25

1835: $0.25

1836, Proof: $5.25

1841, Proof: $4.50

1842, Proof: $9.50

1843: $4

1844: $5

1845: $4.75

1846, Proof: $8.75

1847, Proof: $8.25

1848, Proof: $5.75

1849: $0.25

1850, Proof: $1.10

1851: $0.05

1852, Proof: $5.50

1853: $0.45

1854: $0.05

1855: $0.05

1856, Proof: $1.10

1857, Proof: $0.65

Cents:

1793: $10

1794: $1

1795: $11.00

1796: $4.50

1797: $4

1798: $2.50

1799: $11

1800: $2

1801: $2

1802: $2.63

1803: $0.75

1804: $8

1805: $0.80

1806: $3.75

1807: $2.13

1808: $1

1809, Proof: $4.50

1810: $0.70

1811: $2

1812: $1

1813: $2

1814: $0.80

1816: $0.80

1817: $0.80

1818: $0.30

1819: $1.60

1820: $2.55

1821, Proof: $8

1822: $1

1823: $0.80

1824, Uncirculated: $2.13

1825, Uncirculated: $3.25

1826, Uncirculated: $3

1827, Uncirculated: $4

1828: $1.13

1829, Proof: $5.13

1830: $2

1831, Proof: $3.25

1832, Uncirculated: $4

1833, Uncirculated: $1.75

1834: $1.25

1835, Uncirculated: $1.85

1836: $0.65

1837, Proof: $3

1838: $0.55

1839: $1.62

1840, Proof: $5

1841, Proof: $3.38

1842, Uncirculated: $2.50

1843, Proof: $4

1844, Uncirculated: $2.13

1845, Uncirculated: $1.25

1846, Uncirculated: $1.88

1847, Proof: $4.88

1848, Proof: $4.50

1849, Uncirculated: $1.13

1850, Uncirculated: $0.40

1851: $0.35

1852, Uncirculated: $0.35

1853, Uncirculated: $0.15

1854, Proof: $4

1855, Proof: $3.50

1856, Proof: $2.37

1857, Proof $2.25

W. Elliott Woodward

In 1860 the first extensive guide to the prices of American coins was published by George Jones. The 41-page effort was *The Coin Collectors' Manual, Containing a Description of the Gold, Silver, Copper and Other Coins of United States With an Account of Actual Sales in Philadelphia and New York.* As to whether this manual was widely distributed is not known, for few citations have been found concerning it.

After 1860, when Sage faded from the numismatic scene, the auction mantle—as light as it was, in view of Sage's having presented only three sales in 1859—passed to W. Elliot Woodward and Edward D. Cogan. Woodward was born in Oxford, Maine, on November 29, 1825. He spent the early years of his life there. In 1848 he moved to Roxbury, a town adjacent to Boston. By 1852 he established the Eustis Street Pharmacy (name soon changed to the Mount Pleasant Apothecary Store), and for the rest of his life he was a druggist by profession.

Well-read and with a penchant for scholarship, he became very knowledgeable in numismatics. In 1860 he issued his first auction catalog. Others followed. In an era when little printed information was available to collectors, and much of that was misleading, Woodward included much truly valuable commentary in his auction catalogs. In 1862 Woodward issued the four-page *Remarks. A Table Giving the Year of Coinage of All American Coins, and The Prices at Which I Will Purchase Them. Table Giving Brief Descriptions of Rare American Coins.*

An 1864 sale of more than 3,100 lots described in a 160-page catalog had this notice on the cover:

> The Entire Collection of American Coins, Medals, &c. made by John F. McCoy, Esq., of New York City, and now owned by W. Elliot Woodward, of Roxbury, Mass., together with a few Fine Foreign Coins and Medals, and the whole of Mr. Woodward's Private Collection of Coin Catalogues, American and English, and other Papers and Pamphlets, relating to American coins and coinage. Sold at Auction by J.E. Cooley, George A. Leavitt, Auctioneer, at the Trade Sales Rooms, 498 Broadway, New York, on Tuesday and the Four Following Evenings, May 17th, 18th, 19th, 20th, and 21st, 1864, Commencing each day precisely at five o'clock.

Among the offerings were many copper half cents and cents, including these (with modern comments added in brackets). The prices realized are noted:

> Lot 657. 1793 [cent]. Flowing hair, links, Ameri, the hair touched by circulation in the slightest degree, the reverse absolutely perfect, with a beautiful almost proof surface; a splendid cent, one of the best ever offered, extremely rare. $18.50.

> Lot 663. 1795 [cent]. Thick die, lettered edge, perfectly uncirculated, with fine polished surface, the finest known, extremely rare. $13.00.
>
> [Obviously, this was a very nice coin. "Thick die" meant thick planchet. Numismatic nomenclature, then in its formative era, was often quite casual. "Fine polished surface" probably meant a "nice prooflike surface" in today's parlance, not a coin that had been polished.]

> Lot 670. 1799 [cent]. One of the finest existing, the best ever offered at auction, excessively rare. $27.00. [No grade was given. This was not particularly unusual for Woodward or for other catalogers of the time. Nearly all bidding was done by people who attended in person and viewed the coins.]

> Lot 757. 1796 [half cent]. Uncirculated, the finest specimen existing. One hundred dollars has been offered and refused for this half cent. $120.00.
>
> [Is this the variety with pole to cap, or is it without? It paid Woodward to wait: he gained an extra $20.]

> Lot 760. 1802 [half cent]. Good for date, but not worthy of a place in this collection. $1.25.
>
> [Now, how often does an auctioneer state that a coin is "not worthy"? Such a comment is as rare as the elusive half cent itself. $1.25 was about equal to a working man's daily pay in 1864.]

Lot 2064. [counterstamp]. Small head, "General Lafayette, 1824," by Wright; struck on United States cent of 1818, fine, and very rare. $1.00.

Lot 2460. [1792 Washington Roman Head cent]. Obv. Naked bust facing right, having very little resemblance to any acknowledged likeness of Washington, the hair being in curls, tied with a band, the ends of which fall loosely behind the neck, "Washington, President, 1792." . . . In perfect, almost proof condition, and of the utmost rarity. This piece, the celebrated Roman or Naked bust Washington Cent, of 1792, the owner considers far more desirable and valuable than any other American coin or medal. Three specimens only are known in the country. $480.[49]

THE *AMERICAN JOURNAL OF NUMISMATICS*

When the *American Journal of Numismatics* was published beginning in May 1866, thus becoming the country's first numismatic periodical, Woodward was frequently consulted on matters of numismatic history and facts. He became sufficiently familiar to the readers of that journal that he simply signed some submissions as "W." In time, Woodward went from one numismatic success to another, including the purchase and cataloging of the Joseph J. Mickley Collection in 1867. In October 1867, the *Journal* referred to him in a headline as "The Lion of the Day," noting that "his movements, like those of the forest-king, attract the eyes and excite the interest of his kind."

In November 1866, the *Journal* printed this submission from "C.," presumably Jeremiah Colburn, who suggested to readers:

> who may have occasion to issue catalogues of their coins, that they adopt a uniform style of printing; and I would recommend that Mr. W.E. Woodward's catalogues be the criterion by which they will be guided. In point of typographical appearance, Mr. Woodward's catalogues are far ahead of anything of the kind yet issued, and in numismatic literary merit and information they excel all other works yet published in the United States, not even excepting Prime and Dickeson. It costs no more to print a good-looking catalogue than a poor one. For instance, if the Chilton catalogue [sold by Bangs, Merwin & Co., New York City, March 1865] had been printed in the Woodward style, a difference in favor of the customer would have been made in the items of paper, press work, and binding. If my suggestion is carried out, I think it will please all those collectors who preserve catalogues for reference.

W. Elliot Woodward went on to catalog many other sales, comprising 111 in all. On January 5, 1892, W. Elliot Woodward passed to his final reward, following a long illness.

THE BOSTON SCENE

Henry Cook, a seventh-generation *Mayflower* descendant, was born in 1821, entered the maritime trade, and was employed on the west coast of South America and later as mate on a trading vessel in the Pacific Ocean. By the 1840s he was an avid coin collector.[50] In the 1850s he relinquished seafaring for the security of an on-land occupation in Boston and entered the boot and shoe trade at 74 Friend Street. He was fond of looking through copper half cents and cents in circulation and picking out coins with scarce dates, which he displayed in a counter in his shoe shop. It seems that he was active in the rare coin business by the mid-1850s. He remained a factor for many years, acquiring many fine properties along with much miscellany. When desirable coins were acquired, he often consigned them to the sale room through a printed catalog. A sale held in Boston on November 24, 1863, at Leonard & Co., included an offering of large cents prefaced by this note:

> The following perfect collection of American copper coins is believed to be equal, if not superior, to any cabinet collection in the country, having been selected by the owner for these many years past, from the thousands that have passed under his observation.

Highlights of the coppers:

> Lot 461, "1793 13 [an error; should be 15] link chain, 'United States of America.' Very fine specimen and a rare variety." $4.50.

> Lot 466: "1797 Uncirculated; equal to proof; rare." $3.25.

> Lot 468: "1799 Uncommonly good specimen for this extremely rare date." $6.25.

> Lot 473: "1804 But very slightly rubbed by circulation; the most perfect specimen we have ever seen of this very rare cent." $4.25.

Boston was a hub of numismatic activity from the 1850s onward, with the Boston Numismatic Society and the Massachusetts Historical Society being focal points for activity. William Sumner Appleton, born to a wealthy family on January 11, 1840, was one of the more prominent figures. He never sought employment, but instead he spent his time in intellectual pursuits and hobbies. By the age of 19 he was sufficiently informed in numismatics to join such veteran collectors as Winslow Lewis, Joseph M. Finotti, John Kimball Wiggin, Jeremiah Colburn, Henry Davenport, William Eliot Lamb, Augustine Shurtleff, Henry Dearborn Fowle, and George Williams Pratt in the formation of the Boston Numismatic Society.

Meetings were held the first Saturday of each month at 13 Bromfield Street, only a few steps from the site where Massachusetts silver coins had been minted in the 17th century. Appleton would serve as secretary for 38 years. At the October 4, 1866, meeting of the society he reported on his recent trip to Europe, noting that in London he bought a 1793 Wreath cent in "perfectly brilliant condition," among other treasures.

THE LEVICK PLATE AND CROSBY LISTING OF 1793 CENTS

Joseph N.T. Levick, who lived in Philadelphia in the 1850s and in New York City from the 1860s onward, was a man of varied talents. In the early 1860s he was a banker, dealer in government securities, and broker at 44 Wall Street. Among his activities he traded in gold and silver specie, which at the time sold at a sharp premium in terms of federal greenback notes. During the Civil War, as Lieutenant Levick of Sickle's Brigade, New York, he served as an observer in a reconnaissance balloon. On December 14, 1865, he joined the American Numismatic and Archaeological Society and rapidly became active in its projects. On March 8, 1866, he made a proposal which eventually led to the publication of the *American Journal of Numismatics*.

He was one of the most knowledgeable collectors in the fields of early copper cents, Civil War store cards, and medals. Levick issued a number of interesting medals for his own account, the most distinctive being "The Smoker." The obverse depicts a happy old duffer holding a cigar and exhaling a cloud of smoke. This inscription is around the border: NO PLEASURE CAN EXCEED / THE SMOKING OF THE WEED.

In 1868 Levick and Sylvester S. Crosby of Boston collaborated on the production of an illustrated catalog of cents of the year 1793, a worthy successor to the listing printed in the *Boston Evening Transcript* back in 1859. As a start, in the *American Journal of Numismatics,* October 1868, Levick presented "A Table Exhibiting the Prices Paid for the Five Types of the 1793 Cent of the United States, Selected from Twenty of the Most Prominent Coin Sales in the Country from 1855 to 1868." Long titles were in vogue at the time, and the words on the cover or first page of an auction catalog could fill a good-sized paragraph.

Levick commenced with the cents offered in the John W. Kline Collection in 1855, noting that he was "believed by most to be A.C. Kline" (possibly the initials of John's wife), and concluded with the Mickley Collection auctioned by Woodward on October 28, 1867 (despite the 1868 title of the article). The collections selected were those with outstanding examples, Levick noted, but there were many other offerings "too ordinary to note." The high point of the market was from 1863 to 1866, this being true for 1793 cents and all other coins. Those were heady times when many people hesitated to hold greenbacks and placed their money into hard assets.

Levick noted:

> Previous to the Kline Sale I find but one lot in which a '93 was sold. This appears in the Dr. Roper Sale, February 20, 1851, and that piece, it seems, sold as low as ten cents. Its condition may have been poor. Mr. Kline's sale, therefore, is made my starting point, being the first in which the '93s receive some attention. I find, in this sale, that four types are put up in one lot, and sold for $3.20, or 80 cents each, to Mr. Burtiss of New York.

In actuality, Roper's solitary 1793 was not "poor," but was the Uncirculated coin sold to Ammi Brown, as noted earlier.

Crosby prepared narrative descriptions to be published. Two photographic montages of cents, obverses and reverses, were to be featured, pasted on a regular page. Extra photographs were to be made, to be offered for sale for $1 per pair from Edward D. Cogan. Levick was generous with credits to those who provided information, a listing of which provides a window on leading numismatists of the day:

> Those gentlemen who so kindly rendered me much assistance I am too happy to thank, but cannot use language strong enough to express my esteem for them, and take pleasure to mention here their names: Messrs. Mortimer L. Mackenzie, L. Bayard Smith, Charles I. Bushnell, John Hanna, Edward and Henry Groh, Robert Hewitt, Jr., and John K. Curtis, New York City; Benjamin Betts, John A. Nexsen, and J. Carson Brevoort, Brooklyn, N.Y.; S.S. Crosby, Boston, George F. Seavey, Cambridgeport, Matthew A. Stickney, Salem, Mass.; Thomas Cleneay, Timothy C. Day, and Joseph Reakirt, Cincinnati, Heman Ely, Elyria, Ohio; E.J. Farmer, Cleveland, Ohio; Col. M.I. Cohen, Baltimore, Md.; Charles Gschwend, Pittsburg, Robert C. Davis and Emil Cauffman, Philadelphia, Pa.; Michael Moore, Trenton Falls, N.Y.; Richard B. Winsor, Providence, R.I.
>
> I should mention, also, Messrs. Edward Cogan and W. Elliot Woodward as being too ready to aid me, but not being collectors, or rather not then owning fine specimens of '93s they could do me no good further than their good wishes or sympathy.

"The Cents of 1793" was published in the *American Journal of Numismatics* in April 1869. The single photograph (apparently instead of the two announced) was superb, and extra details could be discerned with the aid of a low-power glass. Crosby prepared a careful listing, assigning numbers to obverses and letter to reverses, such as 1-A, 4-C, and the like.

Not long afterward, in June, Edward D. Cogan issued the *Catalogue of Coins and Medals, the Property of Mortimer Livingston Mackenzie, Esq.*, with five photographic plates, the first for any American auction sale. Included were six high-grade 1793 cents including Mickley's Chain AMERI.

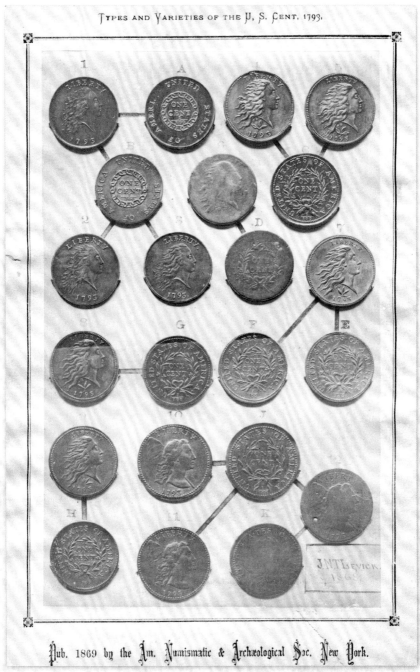

The photographic plate from "The Cents of 1793," published in the *American Journal of Numismatics*, April 1869. The coins were assembled in 1868 by J.N.T. Levick, who used specimens provided by leading collectors of the time.

In the same year, Edward Maris, of Philadelphia, issued a 17-page monograph, *The Cents of 1794*, describing 39 varieties and giving names to them, such as *Egeria* and *Patagonian*, variously inspired by his studies of the classics and his medical knowledge of the human physique. In 1870 a supplement described four more. From this time onward the cents of 1794 became a focal point of interest for many. Those of 1793 were more diverse, but some were rare or expensive or both. In contrast, nearly all of the 1794s were affordable in grades such as Fine and Very Fine.

Melting Cents

In the meantime, old cents were being returned to the Mint in record numbers. Fortunately, numismatists were allowed to look through them. E.B. Mason Jr., in *Mason's Coin & Stamp Collectors' Magazine*, included occasional items about this activity, such as in 1871:

> A large quantity of the old U.S. cents has been received at the Mint, in this city, from various parts of the country. Among 20,000 cents but one Uncirculated coin was found, and that was an 1837. Nothing rare or fine in such a quantity is a very convincing argument that numismatology is spreading, and the people of this country are well informed in regard to the value of rare coins.

And more about that year appeared in the July 1872 issue:

> The U.S. Mint in 1871 redeemed and destroyed 1,005,215 copper one-cent pieces, bearing dates prior to 1858. Thus far in 1872, about 1.5 million coppers additional have been redeemed.

There was no particular interest in bulk cents, and as related in the discussion of the Randall Hoard in chapter 11, in New York City in the late 1860s a quantity of thousands of pieces was sold at 90¢ per hundred when the owner could find no one to take them for face value. Over the years various court actions confirmed that large quantities of "pennies" could be refused by merchants. Legal tender value of one-cent pieces ranged from nothing to a total of four cents, then ten cents.

Clinton Hall at Astor Place, New York City, was host to many auction sales held by George A. Leavitt & Company and associated firms and presented collections cataloged by W. Elliot Woodward, Edward D. Cogan, and others. Coins were spread out on long tables on the third floor, where they could be examined before and during the sales. Earlier, in 1859, the ANS held a meeting in one of its rooms. The building also housed the Mercantile Library.

J. Ledyard Hodge had been active in the hobby in Philadelphia in the 1850s and had corresponded with collectors about prices and availability of coins, what was happening at the Mint, and so on. Later he moved to Washington, D.C., to work at the Pension Office. He was caught, tried, and convicted of embezzlement, and his assets were seized. On October 23, 1871, the Washington auction firm of W.L. Wall & Co., with offices "at the New Marble Building, corner Pennsylvania Avenue and 9th Street," sold off Hodge's prizes. The offering consisted of 356 pieces, "many of them Proofs, all being U.S. coins of silver, copper, and nickel."[51] A review of the sale appeared in the *American Journal of Numismatics*, January 1872. Items of interest to the present text included Proof sets of 1846 ($25), 1854 ($19.50), 1855 ($18), 1856 ($18), and 1857 ($14); Proof cents of 1821 ($9.50), 1854, 1856, and 1857 (prices not recorded); and a group of Proof half cents 1840 to 1848 plus 1852 for $90. Nearly everything rare was carried home by E.L. Mason Jr. The only other numismatist in attendance was John Jay Knox, who spent $9.25.[52]

FROSSARD ON CENTER STAGE

The decades of the 1870s and 1880s saw a great increase in the number of professional numismatists. Earlier, Woodward was the leading cataloger of auctions, with Cogan second. Others filled in the ranks, some conducting sales, others not. Now, new faces became prominent, and the art and science of numismatics moved forward to new levels.

Édouard Frossard, whose name usually appeared in print as Ed. Frossard, was at one time or another highly visible as a dealer, very outspoken, extremely knowledgeable, honest in most (though dishonest in some) dealings, and jealous of his competitors. With this diverse and sometimes opposing mixture of talents and attributes, he was well liked or despised by other numismatists on a purely individual basis. His personality must have been very complex. However, without a doubt, he was one of the most important dealers on the numismatic scene from the 1870s until his death in 1899.

He served in the Civil War, was wounded, taught languages in New York City, and later established a school at Irvington-on-Hudson. In 1872 he discovered numismatics. He read avidly and learned quickly. Within a few years he could hold his own with experts. He entered the trade with George W. Merritt as his best customer. Merritt lived not far away in a mansion earlier occupied by Jay Gould (the financier who failed in 1873). In 1875, Frossard became the first editor of J.W. Scott's *Coin Collector's Journal*, commuting by train to Scott's store in New York City. In 1877, alienated from Scott, he started his own business. In the same year he began issuing *Numisma*, an outspoken journal on subjects numismatic. Considering himself to be more knowledgeable that his perceived enemies and low-level competitors, at one time or another he insulted or published negative things about many if not most of them. A summation of *Numisma* was given by numismatic book dealer Charles Davis:

> An often acid, often scholarly, always entertaining journal with important, although sometimes axe-grinding observations on the business practices of his competitors, and invaluable for reports on contemporary auctions with notices of overgrading and counterfeits liberally sprinkled in. Arrows were shot at, among others, *Doctor* Woodward (the apothecary unable to sell the false talisman to the children of Knicker), Charley Steigerwalt (the plagiarist with his big journal), *Brother* Mason (the only original Moses in the coin trade), J.W. Scott (the Fulton Street octopod), the Chapmans (who produce quarto catalogues with margins sufficiently large for corrections), and David U. Proskey (with a level head and an India rubber conscience).[53]

In 1879 Frossard's work was published in New York City, titled *Monograph of United States Cents and Half Cents Issued Between the Years 1793 and 1857: To which is added a table of the principal coins, tokens, jetons, medalets, patterns of coinage and Washington pieces, generally classed under the head of colonial coins. A contribution to the numismatic history of the United States.* Soon after, however, Woodward roundly criticized the Frossard work in his April 1881 catalog, describing it as being of no value and containing many errors! The coins in the monograph were mainly from the collections of George W. Merritt and Lorin G. Parmelee. This was the first comprehensive guide to large cents until Doughty's *Cents of the United States* was published in 1890. Curiously, unsold copies of the Frossard work were later purchased by Woodward.

In early 1881 Woodward was busy in his den in Roxbury, Massachusetts, writing descriptions for a sale to be conducted on June 22 and 23, including the Clogston collection of mostly ordinary half cents, but with Proofs of 1842, 1843, and 1847. These Proofs gave Woodward the opportunity for a long dissertation, in the form of a satire on "The Legend of Sleepy Hollow," about Frossard, calling him the Sage of Sleepy Hollow, stating that certain of his credentials were false, that he was never a colonel in the Civil War, that his former residence in Paris could not be verified, and so on.

Frossard picked up the challenge, writing on October 17, 1881 (published in *Numisma* the following January):

> In a former catalogue Mr. Woodward mentions that he knows no difference between the original and restrike half cents. You, wishing to impart wisdom to all ye mortals who seek it, kindly call his attention to the fact that there is really such a thing, and he like a wise man accepts the information and imparts it again in his Burton catalogue as though he knew it since childhood. Therefore let all give thanks to you and [the goddess of our hobby] Numisma! Thanks for good opinion. We lay no claim to the discovery of differences in half cents. These have always been known and recognized among well posted coin dealers and collectors. The greater part of the half-cents were restruck at the Mint at a time when the governing officers desired to increase the collection of Washington medals at the Mint by exchange, and were coined with that object in view, not as is generally supposed for speculative purposes.

Harlan P. Smith got into the fray, and in his June 4–5, 1885, catalog of the Douglas Steward Collection commented on the quality of cents there offered, apparently very nice examples, by including this seemingly provocative and certainly not necessary comment: "None of these cents have been oiled to produce 'Baltimore Proofs;' none have been scoured with Irvingtononhudson brick, to make them 'bright red.'" The "Baltimore Proofs" referred to George Massamore of that city, while "Irvingtononhudson" referred, of course, to Frossard.

On September 10–13, 1888, a catalog titled *W. Elliot Woodward's One Hundred and First Sale. Greek and Roman Coins, with a Superb and Excessively Rare Collection of Pattern Coins of the United States, Assay Medals, etc. Also a Fine Numismatic Library*, 1,557 numbered lots, contained the notation "catalogued by W. Elliot Woodward, assisted by Ed. Frossard, Esq., of New York City." Apparently, the old rift between the two dealers had been patched.

In 1893 a monograph by Frossard and W.W. Hays, *Varieties of United States Cents of the Year 1794, Described and Illustrated*, was published (a revised edition was published years later in 1910 by Elder and Gilbert).

Frossard made his share of mistakes, including "authenticating" fake coins, which delighted his competitors, who must have rubbed their hands with glee. By the time of his passing on April 14, 1899, in addition to 59 issues of *Numisma*, which ran to 1891, he had turned out 160 auction catalogs. Despite the preceding controversy, these are viewed today as one of the most valuable archives of their time.

ANDREWS AND LATER-DATE CENTS

While die varieties of cents of 1793, 1794, and other early dates had attracted a lot of numismatic attention, later-date cents from 1816 onward were collected only by dates and a few obvious varieties. That changed in 1881 when *A Description of 268 Varieties of U.S. Cents, 1816–1857, in the Collection of Frank D. Andrews*, was published in Vineland, New Jersey. Only 40 were distributed, mainly to his friends, although extras were for sale at twenty-five cents each. This scenario was published more than a century later by Charles E. Davis in connection with the offering of a copy in the 1994 and 1995 Bowers & Merena sale of the Armand Champa Library:

> Elliot Woodward, the Boston dealer currently in the middle stages of his well-chronicled feud with Ed. Frossard, used Andrews' work to launch a full-scale attack on his enemy, who two years earlier had published *A Monograph of United States Cents and Half Cents*, a lavish production which touched on similar ground. Having bought from Andrews all unsold copies, Woodward praised it *ad nauseam*.
>
> In his 37th Sale catalogue (April 8–9, 1881), he wrote: "This unpretending little book of fifty-four pages is the work of an original investigator, and is a real and not a pretended contribution to numismatic science."
>
> He then submitted a full-page book review to the editors of *The American Journal of Numismatics*, stating "The author's method of identification is so simple, and his descriptions are so clear that they cannot be mistaken." He compared it to Frossard's work which "was written for show, but without a *show* of preparation or knowledge."
>
> This exuberance generated a full-page defense of Frossard in the next issue of the *AJN* with a rebuttal signed simply "De Saugy." Such notoriety was certainly unanticipated by Andrews, but it may have given him the incentive to revise and expand the work two years later with a second edition that was to remain the standard classification guide for 60 years.

Perhaps enjoying the attention and in any event broadening his horizons, Andrews joined the American Numismatic and Archaeological Society on June 6, 1883.

ELSEWHERE ON THE SCENE

David U. Proskey, of the "India rubber conscience," was one of the most active dealers in the late 19th century. Important to the present text, he was editor for a long time of Scott's *Coin Collector's Journal*, for which he wrote a serial article on early copper cents that formed the basis of a book later written by Francis Worcester Doughty and published in 1890. George Clapp, whose fine cabinet of cents originated with the Ellsworth collection, once said that Proskey knew more about large cents than any other man he had ever met.[54] Without a doubt, Proskey was a person of great numismatic knowledge, but—as was later the case with certain other geniuses in the field (Virgil M. Brand and F.C.C. Boyd come to mind)—most of what he knew never reached print.

D.C. Wismer, an old-time numismatist best remembered today for his long-running series on obsolete paper money in *The Numismatist* in the 1920s and 1930s, reminisced about the early days of his collecting, including these experiences with early coppers in the late 1880s:

I commenced to hunt around the city of Philadelphia for coppers, etc., becoming acquainted with Mr. Mason, who had a small store on the corner of Filbert Street and Penn Square; the Chapman brothers and their father; Dr. Maris, who made the most complete list of the New Jersey cents at the time; Mr. Idler, who had a jewelry store on South 11th Street, and a Frenchman whose name, as near as I can recollect, was Beller-leau, who had a store on North 3rd Street near Race Street. From these dealers and the sales of the Chapmans I acquired most of my coins, also traveling around the country, in Allentown, Bethlehem, Easton and other places, buying such items as were for sale.

    In Bethlehem I purchased about 1,200 large coppers from a shoemaker. In Quaker-town, I bought 1,400 large copper cents from the executor of a man who had been toll-gate keeper on the Bethlehem Pike at Chestnut Hill, where he accumulated his large coppers. In Norristown was Gus Egolf, who gathered coins and had quite a col-lection. I purchased a collection of large copper cents from him that were fastened in recesses of a board surrounded with putty, which held them fast after it had become hardened, showing only the obverse.[55]

In the meantime, in 1878, brothers Samuel Hudson Chapman and Henry Chapman Jr. entered the coin business in Philadelphia. Born in 1857 and 1859, as teenagers they worked in the shop of John W. Haseltine, son-in-law of William K. Idler who contin-ued and expanded Idler's inside connections with Mint officials. From an early time they issued special editions of their catalogs, with photographic plates, an unusual but not exclusive practice at the time. One such issuance was *The Collection of Mr. Samuel A. Bispham, of Philadelphia, Containing Many Rare Pieces.* Included was an outstanding col-lection of large cents. The venue for this and other early Chapman sales was Bangs, Merwin & Co., in New York City, though later Philadelphia was their venue of choice.

Beginning with their controversial sale of the Charles I. Bushnell Collection in 1882 (their competitors sneered at the $5 price for the special edition, and nitpicked every misstatement they could find), the Chapmans rose to numismatic glory, later selling many fine properties. Any comprehensive library of auction catalogs featuring half cents and large cents must of necessity contain many with the Chapman imprint.

In 1890 Proskey collaborated with Francis W. Doughty in the production of the 115-page work, *The Cents of the United States: A Numismatic Study. Extensively Illustrated from Selected Specimens,* published by Scott Stamp & Coin Company. Although bearing Doughty's name, most historians believe the work was largely by Proskey. There were many errors in the book, but its use endured until it was superseded by William H. Shel-don's *Early American Cents* in 1949.[56]

From June 25 to 27, 1890, the New York Coin & Stamp Company (David U. Proskey and Harlan P. Smith) offered one of America's greatest collections through the 96-page *Catalogue of the Finest Existing Collection of American Coins, the Property of Mr. Lorin G. Par-melee, of Boston, Mass.* The catalog was well illustrated with 10 photographic and four col-lotype plates, and the sale presented many important half cents and large cents, including the finest-known 1793, Strawberry Leaf, cent. Except for the estate collection of T. Har-rison Garrett, this was the finest private cabinet of coins in America at the time.

This was a hard time in the American economy—the prelude to the Panic of 1893—and the coin market was in a slump. Parmelee bought back many of the rarities in the sale, after which he parceled them out to buyers for the next several years.

In 1894 Édouard Frossard and W.W. Hays issued an 18-page monograph with two plates, *Varieties of United States Cents of the Year 1794 Described and Illustrated,* which added to the available information about this popular date. The "Hays numbers" became popular with specialists.

In 1896 and 1897, the *American Journal of Numismatics* published Sylvester S. Crosby's "The United States Coinage of 1793 Cents and Half Cents," which was later issued as a stand-alone reference. This updated his work that had been published in the same magazine in 1869. Twenty-one varieties were described in detail, accompanied by the last-minute footnoted discovery (in Frossard's April 1897 sale) of a hitherto unknown Wreath cent die combination.

Plate of copper large cents (plus a 1787 Fugio at the upper left) from the 1890 Parmelee catalog. The finest known (then and now) 1793, Strawberry Leaf, cent, lot 671, is in the second row, second from the left.

THE 20TH CENTURY AND BEYOND

EARLY COPPER COLLECTING FLOURISHES

Continuing the trend that had stretched without a misstep from the 1850s to the late 1890s, interest in collecting and studying early half cents and cents remained intense into the 20th century. During the next 100 years, more fine collections would be formed, more articles and books would be written, and more numismatists would be active in these specialties than ever before.

Sometimes, collectors specialized in coppers, but more often they collected these in connection with other series. Such numismatists as H.O. Granberg, Virgil M. Brand, Waldo C. Newcomer, James Ellsworth, John Work Garrett, Hillyer C. Ryder, Wayte Raymond, Colonel Edward H.R. Green, F.C.C. Boyd, William H. Dunham, William Cutler Atwater, Will W. Neil, Christian A. Allenburger, Louis E. Eliasberg, Floyd Starr, James Stack, and others, to take the list up to about 1950, had very diverse cabinets, but their holdings of copper half cents and cents were rich indeed.

Often, the coins of these collectors were memorialized in auction catalogs that remain of absorbing numismatic interest today. Other times, as in the case of the Brand, Newcomer, Raymond, Green, and Boyd holdings, they were sold privately, leaving to the imagination what they contained, although in some instances inventories or purchase records survive. For some others, selected coins crossed the auction block, while others were placed privately.

HALF CENTS IN PARTICULAR

The collection of Hillyer C. Ryder is an example of the last possibility. A collector as well as a student, Ryder had a fondness for coppers. Beginning in the early 1890s, he often took the train from his home in Carmel, New York, to visit New York City. There he made the rounds of the dealers and attended auctions, staying at the Broadway Central Hotel, a superannuated place by that time, but inexpensive, this seemingly good for his coin budget (which was substantial anyway). When not chasing colonial coppers, half cents, and large cents, he attended vaudeville shows, another passion. From January 17 to February 18, 1914, the American Numismatic Society (ANS) held a memorable event, the "Exhibition of United States and Colonial Coins," which was described in a handsome catalog and to which he loaned specimens.

In 1908 the society moved into an elegant new building on Audubon Terrace, 155th Street and Broadway, which was part of a complex paid for by Archer Huntington, scion of a famous railroad family. On the architrave or frieze around the top of the building were lettered the names of famous numismatists, all but one being scholars in the fields of foreign and ancient coins—these were the passions of Huntington, who took advantage of the opportunity to dictate policy. The exception among the lettering was "CROSBY." Huntington also financed the Hispanic Society of America's building on the same terrace. At the time, its location in Morningside Heights, near Columbia University, was a society center of the city. Years later in the 1950s, the society would become the repository for the George Clapp collection of copper cents, of which more will be said later.

In 1919 Ryder and Henry C. Miller collaborated on a study of die varieties published in book form by the society under the title of the *State Coinage of New England*. Ryder tackled the Vermont and Massachusetts coppers, and Miller did the Connecticuts.

On February 11, 1928, Ryder died at his home, at age 77. Subsequently, the administrator of his estate contacted Wayte Raymond, who by that time was one of the top several New York City dealers, to appraise the coins. Afterward, the collection was forgotten, until one day in 1944 Raymond received a telephone call from the current holder of the coins, which had remained untouched for nearly a generation. "Would you be interested in buying the coins at the appraisal price?" Yes, indeed! The market had advanced considerably. Raymond later sold the collection, after extracting desired pieces in the colonial series, to the New Netherlands Coin Company. Much was sold privately, including to John J. Ford Jr., who was partner in the company, and to Emery May Holden Norweb. The rest was auctioned on September 26, 1953, and June 23, 1954. The collection of half cents was particularly impressive and included Mint State examples of certain varieties of the years 1793 to 1797.[1]

During Ryder's lifetime, half cents formed a specialty with some others, although these coins have always been harder to find in numismatic circles, and thus the number of devotees has been fewer.

On April 13 and 14, 1917, Thomas L. Elder, who conducted auctions and also operated the most active coin shop in New York City, published a catalog titled *Splendid Collection of United States and Foreign Coins Formed by Henry C. Miller, Esq. of New York City. Remarkably Large and Complete Set of U.S. Cents and Half Cents in the Finest Condition Obtainable.* Many treasures Miller had found in Europe were included—notably, a gem 1796 half cent without pole to cap.

Today the name of Ebenezer Gilbert is still associated with half cents because of his 1916 study, by far the finest up to that time, *The United States Half Cents. From the First Year of Issue, 1793, to the Year When Discontinued, 1857. All Dates and Varieties Described and Illustrated.* Elder was the publisher. For the next several decades this was the standard reference, although its use was restricted by the rarity of available copies. Gilbert's personal collection, which included 55 varieties of 1794 cents, had been cataloged and auctioned by Elder in October 1910, at the time that both men were preparing a revision of the 1893 text by Édouard Frossard and W.W. Hays on the 1794 cents. In 1909 Gilbert and Elder had issued a 12-page listing, *The Varieties of the United States Cents of 1796.*

During the second and third decades of the century, Elder handed many outstanding half cents and cents at auction. Although Elder was one of the most technically and historically knowledgeable dealers of the era, his catalogs were often arranged erratically, seemingly in order of consignments as they came in, with little in the way of serious scholarship. Elder once boasted that he could catalog 1,000 lots in a single day. How other consignors reacted to this claim is not known. At the same time, Elder wrote many fine articles for his own magazines (published under several titles) and for *The Numismatist*. He advocated the study of history in connection with numismatics. Both Elder and Gilbert were interested in varieties of cents as well, and studied them.

THE CHAPMAN BROTHERS AND COPPER COINS

Brothers Samuel Hudson and Henry Chapman, who started their rare coin partnership in 1878, were at the top of the profession by the early 20th century. Their catalogs, the special editions of which had photographic plates, set the standard for quality. The duo continued to handle many important collections, including those with memorable half cents and large cents. In the summer of 1906 their business was dissolved, after which each went his own way, and with success. Samuel Hudson remained active until the late 1920s, and Henry until his death in 1935.

From June 25 to 29, 1907, Henry Chapman sold the estate collection of pioneer numismatist Matthew A. Stickney, who had died at his home in Salem, Massachusetts, 13 years earlier, on August 11, 1894. The catalog was an impressive production of 222 pages describing 3,026 lots, the best old-time cabinet to cross the auction block up to then and a competitor to the 1890 sale of the Lorin G. Parmelee Collection. The event created a sensation. In July *The Numismatist* reported in "Numismatics at High Tide" that more than 1,000 collectors were represented at the event, which saw record prices. Among copper coins these were mentioned:

> 1793 Chain AMERI. cent, Fine, $41; 1796 cent, Uncirculated, $40; 1804 cent, broken dies, Extremely Fine, $100; 1821 cent, Proof, $77.50; 1842 half cent, original, Proof, $125; Proof sets of U.S. coins from the half cent to the dollar: 1843 $170, 1844 $190, 1845 $250, 1846 $340, 1847 $210, 1848 $200, 1849 $220, and 1850 $30.

S. Hudson Chapman's auction of the William F. Gable Collection, sold in Philadelphia in May, furnished the topic for a detailed listing of prices realized in *The Numismatist*. Among early cents, a 1793 Chain AMERI., Crosby 1-A, in Fine grade sold for $23, and an 1804 cent described as Uncirculated was bid up to $130.

On May 29, 1916, Henry offered the collection of Clarence Bement, a presentation of some of the finest large cents ever to be auctioned. Bement had not discovered numismatics until he was a septuagenarian. He made good use of his time after then. Interestingly, his collection of minerals is remembered today as one of the finest in that specialty. In June 1918, Chapman offered the estate collection of Allison W. Jackman, which was laden with superb half cents and large cents in addition to rarities in many other series.

It was S. Hudson's turn in April 1923 to catalog and offer at auction the Henry W. Beckwith Collection, which had the highest average quality of any cabinet of cents to be presented up to that time. Uncirculated coins, including gems, were the rule. In the same year, Hudson published a study, *The United States Cents of the Year 1794*, in an edition estimated as 100 copies.[2] There were many errors, and Chapman made an effort to recall as many copies as possible. In 1926 a revised edition was published.

**The William F. Gable Collection was auctioned in Philadelphia in 1914.
The gathering included a veritable who's who in American numismatics,
including copper specialists J.H. Cornell, Clarence S. Bement, Hillyer C. Ryder,
and H.W. Beckwith. Young dealers William Pukall and B. Max Mehl, both
at the left, would each remain active in the trade into the 1950s.**

A truly marvelous collection of half cents crossed the block on June 9, 1924, via
S. Hudson's catalog titled *The Superlative Collection of United States Half Cents Complete
in all Dates and Varieties of the Late F.R. Alvord, Esq. of York, Penna.*

George P. French
and His Collection

In 1911 the annual convention of the American Numismatic Association (ANA) was held
in Chicago. At a business meeting it was reported that there were 552 active members
in the group, a decline from 608 the year before. Edgar H. Adams, one of America's
foremost numismatic scholars of the time, later wrote about the exhibits on display,
including that of George P. French of Rochester, New York, the most detailed description of any cent display to reach print up to this time:

> The exhibit of this gentleman consisted almost exclusively of his cent collection, which
> was pronounced by those who are expert in this line as being without a doubt the fin-
> est and best series of this denomination on record. The exhibit embraced about 440
> specimens, all different, numerous ones being the very best preserved pieces known.
>
> He showed 15 varieties of the 1793 cent, 14 of which were Extremely Fine to
> Uncirculated. Among these was a Chain cent, with periods, with some original red,
> and a Wreath cent. Crosby 9-G, also with original red. Crosby 9-H was a semi-Proof,
> and Crosby Liberty Cap, 12-K, which is the only Uncirculated specimen known.
>
> There were 45 1794 cents, 32 being in Extremely Fine to Uncirculated condition.
> There were six specimens of the 1795, two varieties of the thick planchet being Uncir-
> culated, and one of them showing much original red. There was also a 1795 thin plan-
> chet, with a berry on each side of wreath, an extremely rare variety, in any condition, but
> this specimen is in Proof condition, and the only one known in this state of preservation.
>
> Of 1796 there were 11 varieties. One of them, Gilbert 8, is probably one of the best
> specimens known. Two other 1796 Liberty Caps were Extremely Fine to Uncirculated,

Gilbert 15, with fillet head, is the finest known, being a semi-Proof. Also an Extremely Fine specimen of Gilbert No. 16, of which there are only three specimens known. There were also two unique specimens of this date, being Gilbert 26 and 27 being the identical pieces from which Mr. Gilbert wrote his descriptions.

French's 1822 cent, Newcomb-1, a coin exhibited at the ANA convention in 1911 and at the ANS in 1914, sold as lot 431 in B. Max Mehl's offering of the French Collection in 1929; the coin was later owned by Howard R. Newcomb, Floyd Starr, Bertram Cohen, J.R. Frankenfield, Chris Victor-McCawley, and Jeff Gresser. In modern times it was graded as MS-64 by NGC. It is called a Proof in *Walter Breen's Encyclopedia of United States and Colonial Proof Coins.*

Of 1797 there were 13 varieties, 12 of them being Uncirculated and one Extremely Fine. Among the Uncirculated ones were the stemless wreath and the knob-less 9, being the only specimens known in this condition. There were 22 of the 1798 cents, including the three varieties over '97, two of which are Uncirculated, and the only specimens known in this condition. These also include the milled edge variety, the boldest known, and in Uncirculated condition.

The rare 1799 was represented by three beautiful specimens. The variety over '98 is in Extremely Fine condition and has some mint bloom on the reverse. Another over '98 has the broken obverse die, of which but two are known, and this is the best of the two. The 1799 perfect die is an unusually bold and evenly struck coin, and one of the best known.

Of the cents dated 1800 there were nine specimens, among them 1800 over 1798, in Extremely Fine condition, probably the best known; 1800 over 1799, Uncirculated, and the finest known; two specimens of the unfinished die, 1800 over 1790, Extremely Fine to Uncirculated. The other varieties of 1800 were Uncirculated, some of them showing original red. There were two specimens of the 1804, the perfect die being Uncirculated, light olive in color, with much of the original red. The broken die was a beautiful, gold light olive specimen, and About Uncirculated. Briefly, the 1801, 1802, and 1803 contained all the rare varieties, the 1806, 1807, 1808, 1809, 1810, 1811, 1823 were mint red specimens.

All the other dates were shown in Uncirculated mint red and Proof condition. To describe this wonderful collection of cents in such detail as would adequately lay stress upon the merit of the individual specimens, would occupy too much space, but it is sufficient to say that it was probably the finest collection of the kind ever assembled and exhibited. The series of half cents, almost complete, was shown in from Uncirculated to Proof condition.[3]

In May 1929 *The Numismatist* included this:

The collection of large cents formed by Dr. George P. French, of Rochester, N.Y., has been sold to B. Max Mehl, of Fort Worth, Texas. The sale took place on March 21 during a business trip through the East, by Mr. Mehl. The price paid is said to be $50,000. The Dr. French collection of cents is one of the largest and finest ever formed. Parts of it have been exhibited at ANA conventions and admired by collectors on account of the condition of the coins and the number of varieties it contains.

Although the large cents comprise only 64 dates, the collection contains 832 cents, each a distinct die variety. Three of the cents are said to be valued at $5,000 each. Dr. French has been about 40 years in drawing the coins together. The price paid for the collection is said to be the largest ever recorded for a single series of United States coins.

Several months later, in August, the same magazine had some "how to pick them out" comments about those planning to attend the forthcoming ANA convention: "If you see a heavy-set man with a serious expression on his face gently lead different members to one side and tell them numismatic stories, you will know that is Dr. George P. French, of Rochester." In 1930 Mehl cataloged the cents, apparently without calling upon experts (as Mehl, an expert marketer, was not a technically oriented numismatist), producing a 139-page fixed-price catalog.

A modern commentary on this sale by Charles Davis appeared in *The Asylum*, Spring 1994, and quoted notes from a copy of the French catalog annotated by George H. Clapp, the Pittsburgh specialist discussed in the next section. In the following samples, references are to Mehl's coin numbers in the French catalog:

> No. 17: Mehl: Only three or four specimens known. Clapp: Of which I have four or five.
>
> No. 72: Mehl: Both obverse and reverse are perfect dies. Only the faintest die break is visible on the reverse. Clapp: How can reverse be perfect if it shows a die break?
>
> No. 86: Mehl: Unique—the only known specimen. Clapp: Bunk! I have three of them.
>
> No. 117: Mehl: Very rare variety. Clapp: About the commonest.
>
> No. 123: Mehl: Seldom found good. Clapp: Correct! Generally *better* than good.
>
> No. 227: Mehl: Originally classed as Uncirculated. Clapp: I suppose this was when it left the mint.
>
> No. 301: Mehl: Hardly perceptible nicks due to cabinet friction. Clapp: Must have his cabinet lined with broken stone.

Such things contribute to the enjoyment of copper coin tradition down to the present day.

THE ELLSWORTH AND CLAPP COLLECTIONS

In the late 19th century, Col. James W. Ellsworth quietly assembled one of the finest cabinets of American coins. He made a fortune with Ames & Company, a coal mining concern; was on the board of directors of the World's Columbian Exposition in the early 1890s; and later in the same decade served as president of the National Bank of Chicago. On November 19, 1892, as a member of the board of directors of the World's Columbian Exposition, he was on hand in Philadelphia to witness the striking of the first 1892 Columbian half dollar and received the first coin made. In 1894 Ellsworth served on the Assay Commission, which met in Philadelphia to review the quality and integrity of the coinage produced the preceding year. Under the pseudonym "Hercules" he was a major buyer in auctions. He was hardly known to other collectors in Chicago and New York, cities where he maintained residences, among others, such as one house in Switzerland and a villa in Palmieri, Italy, near Florence.

On March 7, 1923, his collection was sold to Wayte Raymond and John Work Garrett through Knoedler & Co. for $100,000. The transaction included about 2,000 specimens, among which were two 1804 dollars, the finest known 1787 Brasher doubloon, the largest collection of 1792 pattern coins, and more. Garrett, who financed the deal, had first pick of anything he wanted, but his early coppers were already of high quality, so those went to

Raymond. He placed most with stockbroker Charles Clapp, who experienced a financial reversal in the same year and subsequently sold his cent collection to his brother George.[4]

Whatever interest Charles Clapp may have had in early cents was eclipsed by the later efforts of George. The founder and president of the Aluminum Company of America (now known as Alcoa), he had ample funds with which to indulge his numismatic desires. Cents were his passion, and leisure hours were spent contemplating his treasures. In 1931 his 64-page study, *The United States Cents of the Years 1798–1799*, was distributed by Philadelphia dealer James G. Macallister. At the August 1935 ANS convention, held in Pittsburgh, Clapp was general chairman. He and his wife hosted convention visitors at their mansion in nearby Sewickley, where his collection was on display for all to enjoy, along with tables of food and beverages.

In 1937 he declared his intention to donate his cents to the ANS, but at a later date, as he wanted to add to it and enjoy the coins in the meantime. The gift was finalized in December 1946, when his cabinet of 1,452 cents from 1793 to 1857 was delivered to the society. In the next year he was coauthor with Howard R. Newcomb of *The United States Cents of the Years 1795, 1796, 1797, and 1800*, published by the ANS. Clapp died on March 31, 1949, at the age of 90.

The Clapp cents were available for study at the society to scholars and other interested people, including William H. Sheldon, who was heavily influenced by Clapp, and who, in 1949, paid respect to him with references in *Early American Cents*. At a slightly later time young Walter Breen, on the ascendancy in numismatic research and writing, examined the Clapp collection at the society and, surprisingly, found "G.H.C.'s collection being so defective in a number of instances."[5] Actually, the Clapp collection had not been defective in any way, but one of its frequent visitors at the society was indeed defective in a mental way, as related in the following section.

SHELDON, *THE* BOOK, AND KOSOFF

William Herbert Sheldon Jr., who appeared as William H. Sheldon in print, and who caught the excitement of cent collecting from his numismatically inclined father, was in residence at Columbia University in New York City for many years. He had both PhD and MD degrees, but his career in medicine had been limited by the poor judgment he had shown in the mid-1930s when his fiancée, a girl named Starlight, ran off to marry another man. Sheldon wrote a very threatening letter to her husband, who sent copies to several leading universities.[6] Whether Sheldon had mental problems seems to have been a subject brought up only many years later (as discussed in a moment); it does not appear in the many printed mentions of him in the 1940s and 1950s. When not involved in numismatics, Sheldon invented body-classification system known as somatotyping and was busy measuring bodies of men and women and classifying them as *endomorphs, mesomorphs,* and *ectomorphs.*

Important to numismatics, he loved large cents, especially those dated from 1793 to 1814. He was admirably placed to indulge in their study: it was just a short walk from Columbia to the ANS building on Audubon Terrace. In the city in the 1930s and 1940s Sheldon was also a constant visitor to Stack's, the New Netherlands Coin Company, the Numismatic Gallery, and other dealers who might have either a few new coppers to offer or coins to be viewed in an upcoming sale. Sometimes, notably at Stack's, he would contribute some comments to the proprietors or aid in classifying varieties by Hays, Newcomb, or some other numbers.[7]

Among the leading players in Sheldon's numismatic life was Abe Kosoff, who usually styled himself as A. Kosoff in print. Kosoff studied to be an accountant but became a part-time dealer in rare coins in New York City beginning in 1929, while still a teen-ager. In 1937 he entered the profession full time, eventually calling his business the Numismatic Gallery. Julius Guttag was an early friend and patron, and he consigned items for Kosoff's first auction in 1940.

The Numismatic Gallery had the lion's share of the flash in New York during the 1940s. Abner Kreisberg was taken in as an equal partner in 1944, and in that year he and Kosoff joined Robert Friedberg in the formation of Coin Associates, a group organized primarily to sell coins to King Farouk of Egypt.

Of an amiable nature, Kosoff was more of a "people person" than a numismatic scholar, although he did appreciate history and tradition. Technicalities he left to others. In addition to socializing, Kosoff had a penchant for advertising, publicity, and merchandising. More than any other of his peers in the city, he had lunches and dinners with important collectors and dealers, including F.C.C. Boyd, whose collection he sold privately and at auction from 1943 to 1946, including two sales under the title of "The World's Greatest Collection." That it wasn't: many rarities and mintmarked coins were absent, and there were no half cents or large cents at all (these were sold before the auctions)—but the title sounded good. Kosoff also had a weekly lunch date with Wayte Raymond.

Oscar J. Pearl, who in his thirties was attracted to large cents, began his career as a banker and later went to work for Burroughs, a manufacturer of business equipment, after which he started a dealership in that line.[8] In 1944, the Numismatic Gallery offered the Oscar J. Pearl Collection of copper cents in a fixed-price catalog, which indirectly credited William L. Clark (of the ANS), George H. Clapp, and strong competitors Joseph and Morton Stack as "the publishers of *The Numismatic Review* for making available the new work by Howard R. Newcomb." The introduction to the cent offering noted the following:

> Mr. Pearl recognized the beauty and scarcity of the coins in this series and endeavored to obtain as many varieties and in as fine a condition as possible. His series of 1793 cents is undoubtedly one of the finest in existence; the 1794 series is almost complete. He is especially proud of the 1845 Newcomb-14. This Proof gem is the specimen used by Mr. Newcomb in describing the N-14 variety and was discovered in Mr. Pearl's collection. It is probably unique.

Following are some selections from the Pearl catalog (cross-referenced to the later Sheldon and the current Whitman numbers):

> 1793 Crosby 1-A. The finest known specimen of this extremely rare variety. From the Mickley, McKenzie, Hall, and Brand collections. This coin has been described as a Proof. It is a magnificent specimen with a beautiful glossy surface. The Dr. French Collection did not have a Crosby 1-A. $1,850 [1793, Chain AMERI.; BW-1, S-1]
>
> 1793 Crosby 4-C. A sharp Uncirculated specimen from the Hall Collection, with dark, even coloring. Undoubtedly one of the finest in existence. $850 [1793, Chain AMERICA, Period After LIBERTY and Date; BW-5, S-4]
>
> 1793 Crosby 6-F. A superb Uncirculated Wreath cent with light chocolate coloring. Excessively rare. This is the original Crosby specimen. $1,400. [1793, Wreath Type, Vine and Bars Edge; BW-11, S-5]
>
> 1793 Crosby 9-G. An Uncirculated gem with original red. Perfectly centered, this is the original Crosby specimen. We doubt that this one can be equaled. $1,200. [1793, Wreath Type, Vine and Bars Edge, Triangular Ribbon Bow, ONE / CENT High; BW-18, S-8]

1793 Crosby 9-H. An Uncirculated gem with original red. Perfectly centered, this is the original Crosby specimen. A gem of the first water. Extremely rare. $1,150. [1793, Wreath Type, Vine and Bars Edge, Widest Ribbon Bow; BW-17, S-9]

1794 Hays-8, Chapman-30. Variety with the numerous stars on the reverse. Unusually good for this rarity. Very Fine and exceedingly rare. Not more than 2 finer specimens known. $135. [1794, Left Edge of Neck Ends in Sharp Tip, Starred Reverse; BW-59, S-48]

1794 Hays-46a, Chapman-48. Uncirculated and undoubtedly one of the finest known specimens. Very rare. $200. [1794, Shielded Hair, Missing Fraction Bar; BW-87, S-64]

1795 Jefferson Head of 1795. Obverse differs entirely from all Liberty Cap cents. Fine. Probably not more than 2 better specimens known to exist. An extreme rarity, seldom offered. $300. [1795, Jefferson Head, Plain Edge; BW-16b, S-80]

1799 Doughty-138, Clapp 2. The Perfect Date variety with an even dark steel surface. Probably one of the best three or four 1799 cents known. This is the original Crosby specimen. An Eastern collector paid $2,500 for a slightly better specimen. Extremely Fine and rare. $900. [1799; BW-1, S-189]

1804. Doughty-198. There is only one variety of the 1804 cents. This is the famous Beckwith specimen. An Uncirculated gem struck from the perfect dies. Probably the finest specimen of this rarity in existence. $1,100. [1804, Original; BW-1a, S-266a]

1821 Newcomb-1, Andrews-1. Perfect Brilliant proof. Probably the finest known. The Beckwith specimen. Has a beautiful iridescent surface. Cost Mr. Pearl $165 some time ago. Extremely rare. $200.

1845 Newcomb-14, not in Andrews. Proof. . . . This specimen was used by Mr. Newcomb in describing the N14 variety. It is believed to be unique. A dark brown surface with bluish tint. $125.

1841, Proof, Newcomb-1, mirror surfaces. Lot 366 in the Pearl Collection catalog, this was sold to Will W. Neil, a Kansas pharmacist. At B. Max Mehl's sale of the Neil Collection, June 1947, it went to Warren Snow. It sold again at Stack's sale of the Snow Collection in 2008.

Sheldon was on hand, too, but either did not help with the cataloging or elected not to be credited (for Kosoff was always generous in the latter department). The availability of the Pearl coins is said to have catalyzed his organizing of notes, which by 1947 had developed into the first "condition census" listings. These consisted of a specific enumeration of the six finest of each variety known to be in numismatic hands. Meanwhile, Sheldon had been diagnosed with Hodgkin's disease, not fatal, but limiting to certain activities.

In any event, Kosoff and Sheldon had been friends for years, and Kosoff more than anyone else urged the doctor to collate his research and publish it. In time, a manuscript was created. Sheldon gave the dealer an advance set of proofs received from Harper & Brothers, which proved to be of good advantage. A commentary by Kosoff in *The Numismatist*, August 1949, included this:

> Now comes one book that is complete within itself and is not only a list—it is a new treatment of the series. Order and system were applied to the identification, grading, and valuing of every known variety of early cent. Reference to the plates and tables makes it simple for even a novice to accurately identify and appraise the value of any of the early copper cents.

Early American Cents, priced at $10, was released soon thereafter. At the time, interest in large copper cents was widespread, as it had been since day one in the hobby, but the numismatic market was in a slump. The heady times of World War II, when cash was common and products were rare, had been replaced by saturation of the market for appliances, new houses, and the like. Unemployment was high and spirits were low, a malaise that began in 1947 and relentlessly continued far longer than anyone expected.

Coin auctions were having lackluster results. Early in 1948, Kosoff and Kreisberg moved the Numismatic Gallery to 8943 Wilshire Boulevard, Beverly Hills, California, keeping the New York premises at 42 East 50th Street for a time, then closing them a few months later in view of the economic conditions. What was supposed to be a showcase auction, the Memorable Sale—laden with gems in the gold series, from early issues to rarities to Proofs, which had all been consigned by Jacob Shapiro (also known as Jake Bell), one of the most impressive such offerings ever!—attracted very few bidders and was a dud. It was Kreisberg's duty to shepherd the disconsolate Shapiro around the tourist, shopping, and dining spots of Southern California to keep him away from lot viewing at the office, where only a few people, instead of the expected crowds, were on hand.

Early American Cents was favorably received upon its publication, but the interest was much less than it would have been in earlier times. Still, those who bought and read it were impressed. No book of this scope had ever been published before, and Sheldon's comments on the aspects of collecting and appreciating coppers had no precedent.

In time, the market improved. Things started looking up in 1950, and a long-term rise in values took place until a market collapse in 1964 and 1965. During this time, particularly beginning in the year 1960, *investment* buyers became more important than numismatic buyers. However, the prices of copper half cents and cents remained steady, as investors, schooled that "gem" silver and copper were the key to profits, were not apt to have much interest in a well-worn 1793 cent.

By the early 1950s, *Early American Cents* was well known, especially after the New Netherlands Coin Company (discussed later) ignited wide interest in numismatic scholarship. Those who read the book quickly found it to be—not even *arguably*—the most enticing, captivating text ever written on an American numismatic specialty. To read the book was to want to own some of the cents described, preferably a 1793, 1799, or 1804, but a 1798 or 1803 would be okay as well. Today, it is still viewed as one of the best books for anyone interested in becoming a serious numismatist.

In 1954 Sheldon's *Atlas of Men: A Guide and Handbook on Somatotyping* was published, comprising 357 pages and 19 charts explaining his body-classification system. This system was soon relegated to the realm of quackery, and after only a few years, the market-value formula that he developed for coins, combining grading numbers and basal values, was viewed as worthless. Separate from that system, however, his grading numbers had a life of their own, and still do.

In 1958 Harper & Brothers, working with John J. Ford Jr., issued a new version of *Early American Cents*, retitled *Penny Whimsy*. Walter Breen and Dorothy I. Paschal contributed additional material to the original Sheldon work. Sheldon and Paschal took somewhat casual advisory positions. Virtually everything new was added by Breen. This update had been in the works for quite a few years, but delays, typical with the publication of Breen's research, had ensued.

John W. Adams remembered Sheldon's secretary Paschal thus:

> "Dr. Dorothy," as she was known to those familiar with her, was an ardent collector
> of early date large cents. Aesthetically, her collection was one of the finest assembled

as she valued appearance and beauty over all other characteristics, including condition. She became interested in large cents after meeting Dr. William H. Sheldon.[9]

Paschal came from an old-line family of means. She was an eager scout for cents, emphasizing, as Adams related, the eye appeal of the coins. Once I acquired a bright red 1811 cent, a year for which full mint color on cents is scarcely ever seen, and sold it to her. She was very excited and could hardly wait to show it to Sheldon, to whom she might or might not sell it, she said.

In 1956 she was among those attending Abe Kosoff's sale of the T. James Clarke Collection of large cents. By that time she lived in Ohio. In 1957, the New Netherlands Coin Company sold the Judge Thomas L. Gaskill Collection of large cents to her in a private transaction. At the ANA convention in New Orleans in the summer of 1972, Ray Chatham sold her collection. Gordon Wrubel purchased many pieces for R.E. (Ted) Naftzger Jr.[10] On April 19, 1972, without publicity, Naftzger also purchased Sheldon's cent collection for $300,000.

THE FALL OF SHELDON

The late Ted Naftzger was one of the greatest figures in American numismatics, but at the same time one of the least chronicled. As is sometimes the case, his numismatic career included controversy. He was a man of great wealth. Combining his fortune with a warm personality, he contributed much to his friends and acquaintances, but not to the printed record. Without a second thought, he would mail a prized 1793 cent or some other treasure to a specialist who asked about its features. Abe Kosoff was his main outlet in numismatics, and he commissioned Kosoff to sell rarities, specialized collections, and other properties, including the Thomas G. Melish Collection of gold coins auctioned in 1956. Other gold coins went to Jeff Browning in Texas, known as the Dallas Bank Collection. Intrigued with the excitement surrounding the 1933 double eagle in the 1940s, Naftzger bought four of them.[11]

In 1973 Sheldon moved out of New York. In the same year, Naftzger collated his holding of cents and shipped duplicates off to the New Netherlands Coin Company to be auctioned. By that time, he realized that Sheldon had failed to deliver some of the coins from his collection and had given false pedigrees to others. In 1976, ever the gentleman, Naftzger enlisted cent specialist Denis Loring to casually approach Sheldon and buy any coins that Naftzger still needed. In 1977 Sheldon died in Cambridge, Massachusetts. He was widely mourned at the time, and by all indications his place in the pantheon of large cents seemed secure.

In time it became widely known that somewhere along the line, Sheldon's passion for large copper cents had gotten the best of him. Naftzger independently determined that the doctor had stolen or switched many high-grade early cents from a variety of parties. Del Bland's research in the late 1980s at the ANS revealed that a number of choice pieces from the George Clapp Collection donated to the society had been switched out and replaced by inferior specimens. It was stated that at one time, Sheldon, a close friend of and frequent visitor to the society, had been allowed to store his personal collection in its vaults. No wonder Breen had found the collection to be "defective." Unfortunately, Naftzger allowed some of the coins from Sheldon's collection to pass to new owners with their false pedigrees attached.

Court actions and hard feelings were the result. Who had the proper title to what? Could a curator of the society have traded cents with Sheldon? This was viewed as unlikely. Viewed from any angle, Sheldon was an out-and-out thief. Eventually, many of the ANS's cents were repatriated, partially through extensive efforts by Eric P. Newman, who was then a trustee of the society.[12] Discouraged by all of this, Naftzger, who had known of Sheldon's switching at an early date but had endeavored to conceal his knowledge of the matter when it went to court, sold his collection of early cents to Stack's. In time, they became widely distributed, with dealer Eric Streiner in the forefront of activity.

As Shakespeare wrote in *Julius Caesar*, "The evil that men do lives after them; the good is oft interred with their bones." Nevertheless, *Early American Cents* lives on, and we all use Sheldon numbers, his Rarity Scale, and the now-pervasive Sheldon Numerical Grading System. As for somatotyping, a quick search on the Internet will reveal that today it is considered a pseudoscience.

WALTER BREEN

Today the name of Walter Breen is inextricably woven into the literature of numismatics from the 1950s to the present. He was the main reviser of *Early American Cents* in 1958, published under the new title of *Penny Whimsy*, and years later presented *Walter Breen's Encyclopedia of United States Half Cents* and *Walter Breen's Encyclopedia of Early United States Cents 1793–1814*. By any evaluation, he was one of the most prolific contributors to research and publication in the field of early coppers.

In 1947 he had discovered numismatics and was immediately captivated by the blend of history, technology, research, and the milieu of collectors, dealers, and writers. He read avidly, committing to memory just about everything he encountered. The earliest numismatic mention of Breen I have found is this account from the ANA convention held in Boston, August 21 to 25, 1948: "Talented Walter Breen, one of the younger members of the ANA, was in demand at all times, especially by the women who never could hear enough of his remarkable piano playing."[13]

Born in San Antonio, Texas, on September 5, 1930, Breen grew up in an orphanage in Wheeling, West Virginia, and in two Catholic monasteries and endured childhood abuses which no doubt affected his brilliant mind. Although he was a polymath who could compose as well as play music, who could recite from memory the basic biography of just about anyone in world politics and literature, and whose talents were immense in several other fields, he was very troubled. He was institutionalized for a time as a teenager.[14]

In 1948 and 1949 Breen spent much time in New York City and in Washington, D.C. He visited numismatic scholars and discussed what he considered to be the woeful lack of historical and technical numismatic information in print. The works of Newcomb, Clapp, Doughty, Beistle, Adams and Woodin, Haseltine, and others were viewed as simply a recitation of details observed on coins, with little as to how coins were made and distributed, and hardly anything on minting procedures. During this early time of learning about coins, Breen lived from hand to mouth, so to speak, and did not own a presentable suit of clothes. Friends usually furnished meals and accommodations.

In November 1950, following recommendations made by Stuart Mosher, numismatic curator at the Smithsonian Institution; Raymond H. Williamson, a highly regarded researcher; and, especially, John Jay Ford Jr., Breen was hired by Wayte Raymond to do numismatic research and writing. In the January–February 1951 issue of *The Coin Collector's Journal*, Raymond wrote:

> Your editor recently engaged Walter Breen, a young numismatist with considerable ability in the research field, to make a thorough examination of the early records of the U.S. Mint now on deposit in the Hall of Archives, Washington, D.C. Mr. Breen has largely completed his research covering an enormous number of documents and

record books. The results have been outstanding, and much information is now available for the first time.

This led to Raymond's publication of much important information concerning die varieties, mintage figures, and other data, some findings revising conventional wisdom in the hobby. In the early 1950s, certain of this appeared in *The Coin Collector's Journal.* "Research in the Archives: Report on Proofs, Essais, Restrikes & Related Material" in the March–April 1951 issue appeared first, followed in May–June 1951 by "Revised Copper Coinage Figures 1793–1857," and, later, others. Certain issues of the journal were stand-alone monographs by Breen on such subjects as early Proof coins, the patterns of 1792, minor coinages from 1792 to 1916, and Gobrecht coinages.

Breen's article "More About Longacre's Indian Cent Model" appeared in April 1951 in the *Numismatic Scrapbook Magazine,* an early entry in what would become many contributions to that popular monthly. During the decade he also created monographs published by Hewitt Brothers (imprint of the *Scrapbook*), such as *New Varieties of $1, $2.50 and $5.00 United States Gold.*

In 1952 at Johns Hopkins University, Baltimore, by his own account, Breen completed a four-year course of study in 10 months, by taking and passing required exams, and he graduated that year. He was awarded a Phi Beta Kappa key (humanities), which he wore with pride for much of the rest of his life. For a time in the 1950s, under the recommendation of Sheldon, he studied premed at Columbia University, New York City.

In September 1952, he joined the staff of the New Netherlands Coin Company as a full-time employee, following his work for hire on the ANA convention auction catalog of that summer (of which more will be said). In an article in *The Numismatist* the following December, Oliver Eaton Futter noted that when investigating a research matter for which he could not find the answers he was seeking at the ANS, he naturally sought the counsel of that "very unusual student of coins, Walter Breen."

The "very unusual student" continued his research, with his three main areas of interest—possibly with the idea of writing books on each of them someday—being half cents, large cents, and copper coins of New Jersey. In this decade he contributed the "Cent Collector's Forum" column to *The Numismatist.* He was very critical of most dealers (who were interested in making money, not in numismatic tradition), other researchers (who often ranged from naïve to just plain stupid), etc. Needless to say, he soon became controversial.

Wayte Raymond

Wayte Raymond, who changed the life of Breen by hiring him in 1950, was by then a grand figure in numismatics. He still maintained an office in New York City, but was in the twilight years of his activity. Often, he and his wife Olga would go out to Montauk at the eastern tip of Long Island and relax in their "other" home there.

Raymond, born in 1886 in Connecticut and interested in coins since he was a teenager, could look back on many accomplishments. By 1904 he was selling by mail order, supplementing his income as a bank clerk. In January 1909 he attended the first regular meeting of the New York Numismatic Club, and in 1912 he entered an agreement with B. Max Mehl, the Texas dealer, to form a combined dealership in New York City. This company lasted for only a month or two, after which Raymond expanded his own business, including forming the United States Coin Company, with Elmer Sears providing financial backing.

In 1917 Raymond handled the auction sale for the annual ANA convention. In May 1918 he moved into the new building of the Anderson Studios at Park Avenue and 59th

Street, which later evolved into Anderson Galleries, the American Art Association, then years later into Parke-Bernet Galleries, and finally into the American branch of Sotheby's. Raymond was closely affiliated with Anderson through the 1920s. In 1922 he partnered with John Work Garrett to buy the earlier-mentioned Ellsworth Collection. During the decade he bought vast quantities of bank-wrapped rolls of cents (mainly), nickels, and other coins from old-time sources, including David U. Proskey and others.

In the early 1930s Raymond kept his office on Park Avenue but also conducted the coin part of the Scott Stamp & Coin Company at 1 West 47th Street. He also did cataloging for J.C. Morgenthau & Co., a Scott enterprise, this in combination with Philadelphia dealer James G. Macallister. The output comprised at least 53 catalogs, nearly all of which were simply listings of dates, mintmarks, grades, and, sometimes, a word or two about desirability. There was no significant scholarship. Similar to the situation with Elder, this belied Raymond's own research goals and his interest in numismatic education.

In the early 1930s, despite the ongoing Depression, New York City was alive with numismatic activity. This dynamism was provided by a half dozen or so coin stores, including one operated by brothers Joseph and Morton Stack since 1933; the camaraderie fostered by the New York Numismatic Club, organized at Keen's English Chop House, 72 West 36th Street, on December 11, 1908;[15] and the availability of the ANS's library and research facilities.

Raymond published various price lists, informational booklets, and studies, culminating in 1934 with the first edition of the *Standard Catalogue of United States Coins and Currency*, a hardbound volume that retailed at $2.50 and for the first time gave mintage figures, market prices, and illustrations in a single volume. In the same era Raymond's line of "National" cardboard album pages, made by M.L. Beistle in Shippensburg, Pennsylvania, made its debut and revolutionized the coin hobby. Now collecting coins could be like filling in a crossword puzzle: empty spaces beckoned and made it instantly obvious which coins were still needed. This brought significant profits to Raymond, who found a ready market for his huge holding of coins in bank-wrapped rolls.[16] Earlier, collectors usually stored coins in two-by-two-inch paper envelopes or in cabinet drawers. In May 1934, Raymond revived the title of *The Coin Collector's Journal*, founded by J.W. Scott in 1875 and discontinued in 1888. He extended the publication's run by 160 issues, ending in 1958.

In the 1950s Raymond sold much inventory through the New Netherlands Coin Company. He died on September 23, 1956, after a long illness. His estate collection was purchased by John J. Ford Jr. and the New Netherlands Coin Company.[17]

Another highly important person in the numismatic excitement of the Depression years was Lee F. Hewitt, who launched the *Numismatic Scrapbook Magazine* in Chicago in January 1935. This quickly became the most popular periodical the hobby had ever seen, and it kept that position until the advent of *Coin World* in 1960. The *Scrapbook* kept going until it was discontinued in February 1976. Today, a file of copies is particularly valuable for the well-researched articles of R.W. Julian, many of which relate to half cents and large cents.

THE RISE OF THE NEW NETHERLANDS COIN COMPANY

On September 15, 1936, there was a new entry on the New York City scene: the New Netherlands Coin Company, founded by Moritz Wormser, opened for business on 17th Street. The firm was to have been named New *Netherland*, an early designation given to Manhattan, but an "s" was added by mistake.[18]

Wormser, whose nickname was "Mike," was born in 1878. In August 1913 he became a member of the New York Numismatic Club. On October 17, 1913, Wormser joined the ANS. In August 1921 he was elected president of the American Numismatic *Association*, whose journal gave this information:

> Mr. Wormser has been a resident of New York and vicinity for about 25 years. He is a graduate of Columbia University in the class of 1899. He took a course in Colorado College and received his M.A. from Columbia in 1903. He specialized in civil engineering, but after a short experience in that field he turned his attention to banking, in which he is now engaged in New York City. His home is at Woodmere, Long Island. He has been a collector since he was 13 years of age. He is also a member of the American Numismatic Society, the New York Numismatic Club, the Rochester Numismatic Association and several foreign numismatic societies. He was elected a member of the Board of Governors of the ANA at the Rochester convention in 1917, and at the Philadelphia convention last year.[19]

Wormser went on to serve five one-year terms as president of the ANA, an accomplishment still without equal (today, there is a lifetime two-term limit).

Joining him at New Netherlands in an office at the prestigious address of 95 Fifth Avenue were his two sons, Charles M. and Sam, and David Marks Bullowa.[20] A month after the doors opened, disaster struck. A massive burglary took place, and most of the inventory was carried off—a mystery never solved. The elder Wormser died in 1940. Son Charles signed on with the United States Navy (eventually rising to the rank of commander). Bullowa conducted the business until he joined the army in 1942. In the meantime, the firm's first auction was held on November 24, 1940, comprising 815 lots in a catalog that is of no numismatic importance today. With various staffers under the direction of Stuart Mosher, the operation was continued until Charles resumed charge after returning from the war. In 1945 the numismatic department of Scott Stamp & Coin, conducted by Wayte Raymond on the fourth floor at 1 West 47th Street (one level above the stamp operation), was turned over to New Netherlands. All inventory of Raymond's books, albums, publications, and supplies was included. The Scott name continued to be used in tandem with New Netherlands.

In *The Numismatist* in June 1950 an advertisement boasted, "Our auction sales are growing!!" The sales were said to have "more consignments, more bidders' mail and sales, conservative classifications, insignificant returns, and prompt settlement."

JOHN JAY FORD JR.

In November 1950, Charles M. Wormser hired John J. Ford Jr., who had been an enthusiastic numismatist since childhood.

Ford's father had ambition and drive that he passed on to his son. Orphaned at an early age, the elder Ford was placed in the care of his grandparents, who with all good intentions sent him off to a monastery to learn about the Catholic religion and, hopefully, become a priest. Family tradition has it that he escaped this confinement and headed west, where he arrived in San Francisco just in time to experience the April 1906 earthquake and fire. Fortune attended his efforts, and in time he acquired a vineyard in California, then went into the oil business in Texas—not to overlook his work with the business offices of film studios! At one time he was owner of a circus. He then moved to New York City, where he bought and sold investment securities. He also maintained a home in the West. The elder Ford appreciated art, crystal, antiques, and other fine things. Among his favorite possessions was a Herschede grandfather's clock that won a grand prize at the Panama-Pacific International Exposition in 1915.[21]

John Jay Ford Jr. was born in 1924 and during an interview with the author described his early years in his own words:

> I was born in Hollywood, California. My father had moved out there in the early 1920s and was quite flush with money as he was involved with the United Artists film people—Charlie Chaplin, Mary Pickford, Douglas Fairbanks, Sr.—as a money raiser or money man or something. . . . We moved again, to New York, about 1926 because in 1925 and 1926 he had some business misfortune in California. I was only two years old at the time. By 1932, when the Depression got really bad, we were living in Jackson Heights in Queens, which is about four or five miles from New York City. My father's partner had committed suicide in 1929, and my father was wiped out; he was really scrounging. Money was very, very tight in 1932, when I was eight years old.

By 1935 Ford was a coin collector, and in the next few years he traveled regularly by train to New York City, where he scouted the various shops looking for bargains. In the meantime he bought, sold, and traded coins as what was called a "vest-pocket dealer." In 1939, at the age of 15, he was hired by Stack's to work on off-hours when he was not attending high school. In 1942 he joined the army and worked in the intelligence service. Returning to the United States, he continued dealing in coins part-time while working for Lever Brothers and in other activities, including as an aerial photographer (he came close to losing his life in a crash). He married Joan McDonald, bought a home in Levittown, and set about raising a family, including, in time, daughters Leslie, Susan, and Kimberly.

In one memorable incident, Ford purchased a 1793, Chain, cent that had been cleaned to a bright orange. He stripped it down to remove any grease, and then set about rehabilitating it by placing it on an outside window sill, where, surely, the atmosphere would soon tone it to an attractive brown. Unfortunately, on one fine day a painting crew came through the neighborhood to finish up some detail work for the buildings, and the cent disappeared. The family later moved to 176 Hendrickson Avenue, Rockville Centre, Long Island.

Now and again, Ford found time to contribute articles to various magazines and journals, including *The Numismatist*, one of which was the obituary of cent specialist Homer K. Downing published in August 1951. Born in 1898, Downing died on May 29, 1951, by which time he and Ford had been close friends for many years. Excerpts from the obituary follow:

> It was about 11 years ago when Homer Downing became actively interested in numismatics. Originally, as is the habit of many beginners, his interests covered a major portion of the various issues of United States coins. During the summer and fall of 1941, his enthusiasm became intense and gradually resolved into an ardent interest concerning our early copper cents.
>
> About that time he carefully canvassed the New York dealers and eventually made the many contacts and friendships that he later valued so highly. In 1942, following a keen desire to learn fully about his hobby, he joined several of the metropolitan coin clubs and in the latter part of that year made the acquaintance of the late Henry C. Hines.
>
> In the fascinating world of large cents, Henry Hines was long recognized, together with Howard Newcomb and George Clapp, as one of the "Big Three." From the first day of their meeting, he and Homer Downing were fast friends. During the years that followed, many a trip was made from 939 Woodycrest Avenue to the Newark Athletic Club. On those pleasant Friday evenings, copies of Crosby and Hays, Gilbert and

Clapp, Newcomb and Andrews, were all carefully perused and Mr. Hines displayed his treasures to an apt and completely absorbed pupil. It was during this period that H.K.D. became acquainted with something more than die deviations or rare varieties. The careful examination of the older sale catalogues and the recollections of an aged collector brought forth a desire to trace the history of famous collections and magnificent coins.

Shortly before the death of Henry Hines, late in 1946, Homer Downing met Dr. William Sheldon. The fruits of this meeting will always be of inestimable value to the American numismatist. For many years, Dr. Sheldon had, with painstaking study and deliberation, prepared an exhaustive work on the early coppers, 1793–1814. Homer Downing's valued collaboration in the completion of this famous work need not be mentioned here. . . . Many Saturdays, during the latter years of his life, were spent at the American Numismatic Society museum in New York. Old friends were greeted, catalogues and files were carefully scrutinized and many happy hours were dedicated to the Clapp collection housed there. . . .

It is almost impossible to record all the activities of a man who loved his hobby as did Homer Downing. At the time of his death he was completing work on a detailed photographic record of the finest-known specimens of the early cents. This, coupled with an intense desire to trace the individual owners of such choice pieces, took up a great deal of his time. Pedigree, or the history of ownership, was a very important part of numismatics to H.K.D. His records were so complete and so accurate that he could often trace one coin through half-a-dozen or more collections. It is ironic that only a month previous to his untimely death, he carefully inked in the "H" and "D" on the edge of each of his prized 1794 cents. This was, in his words, "To insure proper identification" of pieces from his collection. Homer Downing utilized his extremely orderly mind with the exacting intensity so characteristic of members of his profession. He investigated methods of cleaning, improving and preserving cents; of displaying, labeling and housing them and, most of all, of organizing factual data in such a manner as to permit its future publication. Many cannot take our hobby as seriously as did he.

In January 1951, John Ford went to work as a partner with Charles M. Wormser in the New Netherlands Coin Company. By the early 1950s, when I first visited it, the New Netherlands office was somewhat basic and minimal—probably not having seen the hand of a decorator for a generation. After alighting from the elevator and walking across a hard asphalt-linoleum-type floor for a few feet, a visitor was confronted with a door with a frosted-glass pane. Upon opening it a counter could be seen, done at a right angle, the form of a carpenter's square, with several chairs arranged in front. The counter was low, and under a glass top were various tokens, sheets of obsolete paper money, and other items of interest. A protective wall was behind the counter at both angles, with a two-way glass permitting a view of the goings-on by anyone who wished to view from the back.

The staff basically consisted of three people: Wormser, who was president of the company and the greeter of most customers (unless they had a technical numismatic interest), his secretary, and Ford.

Ford's office was in the back. Walter Breen had a desk but was rarely there. Instead, he worked by making notes and doing his writing in his local apartment. However, on occasion he was on premises, to examine and classify coins, or to meet selected clients. Auction catalogs were rough-cataloged by Breen, then edited by Ford. Breen could not sell his way out of a paper bag, so to speak, but Ford was a consummate salesman and promoter. Born with a natural gift for enthusiasm and salesmanship, Ford could make just about anything seem interesting to anybody, and he did. Accordingly, encouragements and admonitions to bid as high as possible were added by Ford, who at the same time had to delete many libelous statements about the ethics of other dealers, the stupidity of certain collectors, and other negatives that Breen had inserted. Finally the work, usually far behind schedule at this point, was sent off to the printer to be set into type. In time, long strips of white paper called galley proofs would be received and marked up.

Each day Ford commuted to the city from Rockville Centre on the Long Island Railroad. This was a welcome method for him, as he could catch up on his reading, one of his favorite pursuits. Numismatic things were tucked here and there in Ford's home, usually in piles, but not sorted or arranged. Ford always talked of the future—of books he was going to write, projects he was going to do. In the meantime, a perfectionist by heart, Ford was occupied with the latest New Netherlands catalog or other matters of the moment. He never did find time to expand and dig into the many publishing projects he envisioned, although he did facilitate others, leading to the inclusion of this commentary in the present book. In 1958 his Ford Numismatic Publications was responsible for publishing *Penny Whimsy.*

In 1952 Homer K. Downing's widow Anna consigned his large cents to New Netherlands. With the help of Walter Breen, Ford was determined to outdo any former presentation of early coppers. The venue was to be the ANA's annual convention, held that year at the Statler Hotel in New York City. The auction privilege was awarded to a consortium of dealers consisting of Numismatic Fine Arts (Edward Gans), Hans M.F. Schulman, Henry Grunthal, and New Netherlands, an arrangement with nothing comparable before or since.

New Netherlands succeeded in spades. The Downing large cents brought many thousands of dollars more than expected, and the numismatic community was electrified. Breen was soon hired full-time, and for the next decade the firm's catalogs were a gold mine of numismatic details, research findings, and simply good and often entertaining reading.

To the August 1954 issue of *The Numismatist,* Ford contributed this:

> Collectors of cents, half cents and colonials were present by the dozen as New Netherlands' 44th Sale (their first evening sale since the 1952 Convention) began on the evening of June 23. Those who came expecting to see fireworks were not disappointed. The catalogue represented a gamble on the proposition "half cents and colonials are now about ready to come into their own." The prices realized by a few of the outstanding items speak for themselves.
>
> [The account gave these prices, among others:] 1793 cent, Crosby 9-H, About EF $145; Uncirculated 1817 cent, Newcomb-2 and N-9-1/2 each $19; 1822 cent, N-12, Uncirculated $34; 1793 half cent, Gilbert-3, MS-60 $315; 1794 half cent G-9, AU-55, $220; 1796 With Pole half cent, Uncirculated, $1,600; 1796 half cent, No Pole, Fine $700; 1843 half cent, Gilbert 1-B, $125.
>
> Of this auction, John Ford of the New Netherlands Co., said, "If this sale proves anything, it proves that collectors are starting to turn away from the highly touted but really commonplace coins, and to turn their attention more and more to series that until lately were dormant. We predict that despite the manifest hysteria, this is only a beginning."

At the time most other coin catalogs were very basic in their descriptions—simply giving dates, mintmarks, and a word or two about the grade. Not so with New Netherlands, which would nearly always have a paragraph describing even the most ordinary coin, and sometimes much more than that.

To *The Numismatist,* June 1960, Breen submitted a lengthy commentary about a sale his employer had conducted recently. O. Rundle Gilbert was at the podium. A current "slump" in the market for cents was noted. Recently, this had been painfully evident at Abe Kosoff's sale of the James O. Sloss cents. Excerpts from Breen's commentary follow:

Amid considerable excitement the two day New Netherlands 54th Sale began, somewhat late, on Friday evening, April 22nd, with auctioneer Gilbert offering the Canadian 15 sols of 1670. This went at $1,325 to a floor buyer, who was later heard to say that he was executing a buy-bid and would have been prepared to go many thousands of dollars higher. The performance of this lot and of the other colonials which started this auction apparently refutes the old theory that one must begin an auction with inexpensive material to allow the audience to get warmed up and to give big buyers time to arrive. . . . Copper of all kinds seemed to be enjoying a revival from an earlier slump, particularly large cents. . . .

Large cents showed surprising strength. Two 1793 Chains, S-2 and S-3, close to EF and VF or better but both rough, brought $420 and $350; three Wreaths, VF or better (S-5, 6, 9), $440, $320 and $235. Almost any early date better than VF went for full book or higher. A Condition Census 1794 S-51, VF-30, brought $195 (book value $180 plus), for example. The stemless 1797, S-131, almost EF, went to a dealer at $290; 1798 S-156 (Rarity-7), just Good, $41; 1798 S-177, F-15, $82.50; 1800 S-199, almost VF, $135; 1801 common three errors but rare perfect die, VF-30, $185; an Uncirculated 1803 S-251, $215; an AU 1803 S-256, $125; a VF perfect die 1804, $280 to a dealer; an almost EF but buffed broken die 1804, $380 to the same dealer; an AU 1806, $140. Really choice late dates were also in strong demand. An 1816 N-5 brought $47, the unpublished 1816 N–6-1/2 (double profile) $60, and a nice but hardly Uncirculated 1816 N-8, $66. The 1822 Proof was bid up to $650, the EF 1823 to $325, the Mint State 1824 wide date to $190, a "gem" first strike of 1829 to an astounding $210, and the unique Proof 1835 N-7 sold for $700.

Half cents generated a good deal of excitement. An EF 1794 of common die went to a dealer at $160, and this man also bid in the 1795 overstruck on a large cent at $170. Two Uncirculated 1800s, the former a red one from the Boston find, soared to $130 and $90. An original 1840 Proof, weakly struck, went to a dealer at $320; a VF 1845, $130; and an 1847 restrike, $160.

Not long afterward, Breen left New Netherlands. Don Taxay, a protégé of both Ford and Breen, was hired freelance to help with cataloging, which he did until spring 1964, when he took a post as curator of the Chase Manhattan Bank Money Museum. Jon Hanson, an eager and talented numismatist from California, did much valuable work for the firm. The firm's catalogs record many outstanding half cents and cents and are essential to any comprehensive library on these specialties.[22]

In 1971 Ford left the company and retired, or at least so he said, to his home in Rockville Centre, Long Island. Later in his life he became in a bitter and extended controversy regarding the authenticity of certain gold ingots, mostly purchased from his scout and agent, Paul Franklin, who claimed to have bought them from sources in the West, from the Blake estate in Massachusetts, and other places.[23]

Ford and his wife Joan moved to Phoenix, Arizona, where he died on July 7, 2005. During his lifetime, and continuing with his estate, his collection was auctioned by Stack's in a series of sales that brought close to $70 million, far and away the most valuable collection ever to cross the block by 2013. As to his legacy, it is probably true that Ford, in combination with Breen, forever raised the standards of American numismatic cataloging by encouraging of research and study as a key to enjoyment and success in numismatics.

Walter Breen's Career

After the freelance work Breen had done on the Downing catalog descriptions garnered wide acclaim, John J. Ford Jr. hired him fulltime as a member of the New Netherlands staff. As noted, this changed the course of numismatic auction cataloging in America.

Later New Netherlands catalogs, issued regularly, continued the scholarship. By 1955 they became the focal point of the hobby, still without any competition to speak of. On the personal side, Breen was a friend to nearly everyone, gladly asked questions and shared information, and was appreciated by most who knew him. On the business side, he remained contemptuous of most dealers and scholars. His lifestyle was that of a hippie, or bohemian, to use a term of his era. In addition he preferred the company of men to that of women, which brought him some criticism.

The desire for information grew throughout the hobby as Breen's writing became widespread and enjoyed. He was by no means the only scholar in the field—such figures as Eric P. Newman, Raymond H. Williamson, and others were widely respected before Breen's name was known, but their output was modest in terms of printed works. Through his position with New Netherlands in New York City, his frequent appearances at conventions, his voluminous correspondence, and a continuing stream of articles in print, Breen captured the lion's share of attention. Soon, dealers and collectors turned to him to evaluate coins and write letters concerning their history and authenticity, for a modest fee. This coin was "the finest seen," that coin was "an unquestioned Proof," and so on.

In September 1960, Breen left New Netherlands, ending what had been, behind the scenes, a tempestuous relationship with Ford. Breen was casual when Ford wanted precision. Breen was sloppy in personal habits and appearance, while Ford was immaculate. Breen liked to gossip and talk about varieties and history to customers, and Ford wanted him to *sell* coins. And so it went. It was what might be called a love-hate relationship. Ford needed Breen's scholarship, and Breen needed Ford's paychecks.

In the spring of 1961, Breen told his friends that he had joined the Metropolitan Coin Company, recently formed by Lynn Glaser and Paul Weinstein, and would be the editor of the projected bimonthly magazine, *The Metropolitan Numismatic Journal*—to contain an unprecedentedly high level of scholarship and authoritative articles. The arrangement proved to be short-lived. In 1962 he asked the present author and James F. Ruddy, then partners in the Empire Coin Company, to publish an update on the 1916 work by Ebenezer Gilbert on half cents, but he wanted to remain anonymous, as he was afraid that he would be sued by Ford for using information gained while employed by New Netherlands. Now, on his own, Breen despaired of its ever being published. It was issued as a small and quite forgettable monograph under the title of *United States Half Cents 1793–1857*. This would at least be getting something into print, until his master work on half cents could be completed, scheduled for a few years hence.

On June 2, 1964, Breen married the recently divorced Marion Zimmer Bradley (who lived from June 3, 1930, to September 25, 1999). Bradley was a science-fiction writer of high acclaim, and today her work remains classic. Breen did much of the research for Bradley's *Mists of Avalon*, which was published soon after their marriage.

In the 1960s Breen worked off and on as a cataloger for Lester Merkin. The 1964 catalog of the Louis Helfenstein collection of large copper cents, with its full-color cover (unusual at the time) depicting an assortment of such coins, created a sensation. The photography inside and out was by Marty Bauman, himself a collector. A publicity blurb noted the following:

> Lester Merkin takes great pride in presenting to the numismatic fraternity the famous Louis Helfenstein Collection of large cents, 1793–1857. Of a total of 332 lots, 319 are Uncirculated, 10 are AU and three are below AU. Practically every piece is a Condition Census specimen. Many are the finest or equal to the finest known of the particular variety involved. This is without doubt the most outstanding collection of large

cents to be auctioned since the Parmelee Sale in 1890. Such a collection may never appear again at public auction in our lifetime. A magnificent catalogue with full color cover, and approximately 200 photographs of the actual coins are in black and white.

Breen lived in California for the most part, where, in 1966, he was awarded a Master of Arts degree in sociology by the University of California at Berkeley. In 1967 he moved back to New York with his family, set up a home on Staten Island, and commuted daily to Merkin's office.

In 1968 a new entity emerged on the scene with much pomp and fanfare. That was Harmer, Rooke Numismatists, Ltd., New York City, a branch of a stamp company founded in 1903. A lavish gallery was fitted out, including "a $75,000 electronic laboratory (the only one of its kind in the world). At present material is not being accepted for authentication from the general public. Prior announcement will be made when these unique facilities are available for public use."[24]

The large staff included numismatists D. Paul (Don) Taxay and William T. Anton Jr. Lending guidance were Donald D'Amato, the well-known New York auctioneer (a regular for Stack's sales), and Walter Breen. At Harmer, Rooke someone stole Breen's extensive manuscripts (or else he misplaced them) on half cents, colonial coins, New Jersey coppers, and Proof coins, which he carried in a timeworn leather briefcase. In any event, these hundreds of sheets typed on onion-skin paper with many penciled annotations disappeared, and no copies had been kept. Later, Breen endeavored to reconstruct as much as he could from memory.

Breen left Harmer, Rooke and finally landed a contract with Stanley Apfelbaum, president of First CoinVestors in Albertson, New York. In the 1970s, while on the staff of First CoinVestors, he lived with his family in Berkeley, California. During this time he readily consented to signing authentications, documents for investment clients, and so on, some of which seem to have been prepared without his carefully inspecting the items in question. Breen was also involved in Pine Tree Auction Co., developed by First CoinVestors.

In 1983 Jack Collins, trading as the American Institute of Numismatic Research, published *Walter Breen's Encyclopedia of United States Half Cents 1793–1857*, an impressive work of more than 500 pages, with enlarged illustrations of all die varieties and a page or often several devoted to each of them. In 1988 Doubleday & Company published *Walter Breen's Complete Encyclopedia of United States and Colonial Coins*, under the sponsorship of First CoinVestors. Most of the work had been done years earlier, but it took a long time to get into print. In a way this was a successor to Montroville W. Dickeson's 1859 *American Numismatical Manual*: large, impressive, and filled with information. It was well received in the hobby.

At the 1989 ANA convention, Breen was front-row center in a Numismatic Theatre presentation, "Walter Breen Answers Your Questions About Numismatics," with Harry W. Bass Jr. as the moderator. The event drew a large audience and probably could have lasted far longer than the hour allotted if there had been time and space in the facility. Although no one realized it at the time, this marked the height of Breen's career. The days of his numismatic activities were numbered. In 1989 he was arrested and convicted for child molestation and given three months of probation. No information about this was published in any numismatic journal. In 1990 he was arrested again, with a different victim, and was convicted and sent to jail. While there he corresponded extensively with numismatists, usually on long sheets of yellow tablet paper. On April 28, 1993, he died of cancer in prison in Chino, California. By that time he was divorced from his wife and estranged from his children.

In 1994 his friend Jack Collins contributed "In Remembrance of Walter Breen" to *Rare Coin Review* No. 100. These excerpts reflect some aspects of his life not mentioned earlier in the present text:

> Breen was considered an anomaly, with a phenomenal memory that could digest an entire page of a Manhattan telephone directory in just a few minutes, and then moments later recite upon command any address and telephone number when prompted with the resident's name. Then, the capacity of his mind was virtually limitless. He was capable of speaking and writing in at least five languages.
>
> For the most part of his adult life, especially his later years, he was a lonely and depressed man, with long bouts of suicidal contemplation. He only found solace in classical music, to which he was chronically addicted all during his waking hours. To combat loneliness, he became a workaholic, endlessly researching, writing and rewriting. During his dark emotional period, he produced much of his classic work. . . .
>
> Walter was possessed of a very complex personality, as appears to be the case with most geniuses. Bizarre and eccentric personality traits appear to be inherent with being a genius. When it came to numismatics, he was a genius without peer—quite possibly the first and only one to ever appear in the field of numismatics.

In July 1999, his contributions to numismatics remained sufficiently important that after conducting a poll, *COINage* named him as one of 18 "Numismatists of the Century." In 2000, *Walter Breen's Encyclopedia of Early United States Cents 1793–1814*, edited by Mark Borckardt, was published, as Breen would have wished.

In recent times there has been a reevaluation of his work. Many comments have appeared in *Penny-Wise* and elsewhere regarding data that seems to have been imaginary, of opinions given as facts, and more. One observer said, "Probably only about 10 percent of his writings are wrong, but I don't know which 10 percent that is!"

The preceding said, the numismatic world was changed forever by the catalog style initiated by Breen in the 1950s. Today, the data he incorporated in his books on half cents and cents are not even remotely challenged by any other texts. A reading of both will impart a wealth of useful information. However, errors are common. To twist the old saying, the details can be devilish—and cause problems.

His contributions should be viewed as immense and exceedingly valuable, but not to be relied upon as the last word.

ABE KOSOFF IN LATER YEARS

In 1948 Abe Kosoff moved to California, where Numismatic Gallery opened an office in Beverly Hills, while Kreisberg tended the New York City business. Within the year, all operations were centered in California. The firm lasted until 1954, after which the partners went their separate ways, each with success. Kosoff moved to Encino, then to Palm Springs.

Kosoff continued his flair for publicity, and his news releases were among the most interesting to reach print in his time. The following excerpt is from *The Numismatist*, July 1956. As was true of many auction reports, one needed a program to tell the players, in this instance copies of Crosby and Hays (or the Sheldon cross-reference) for the 1793 and 1794 cents, Sheldon for the others, and Gilbert for the half cents.[25]

> Total prices realized at the auctions of the T. James Clarke large cents and the Thomas G. Melish collections set what is undoubtedly a record for any American sales.[26] Over $212,000 worth of rare coins went under the hammer of A. Kosoff of Encino, California in four auction sessions.

April 21st, Kosoff sold the Clarke cents at the Statler Hotel in New York City. Collectors and dealers had congregated from all parts of the country and had been examining the lots for several days prior to the sale. Interest was keen and bidding brisk as the 1793 Crosby 1-A was sold to Al McDowell of Ohio for $350. Morton Stack of New York paid $700 for the Crosby 3-C, and then Jim Sloss of Pennsylvania went to $1,650 for the gem 6-F. The 7-F maintained the pace at $1,200, as did the 9-G at $850. The 10-I sold high at $500, as did the 1794 Hays 17 at $275. A record price of $500 was paid for the Hays 46a [Missing Fraction Bar], which was out of the Pearl Collection, and the 1796 Liberty Cap, Gilbert A, fetched $310, another top figure.

The Judge Moll 1799 cent went reasonably at $1,100, although the rare variety with the heavily cracked obverse, ex-French, realized a high $600, Mrs. Paschal being the buyer. Mrs. Norweb reached a bit for the 1800, S-197, at $180 and the 1802, S-235, at $400. The 1804 cents went reasonably at $525 and $475, but considerable interest sent the 1806 to $250. Undoubtedly a very new high was established when Manny Taylor of New York bid $550 for the 1807 Comet cent; previous high was about half that figure.

The first 140 lots through 1814 fetched over $26,000, and the 493 lots in the session went for over $43,000 with splendid results evidenced when the extraordinary offering of the late Proofs were put on the block. The 1825 N-9 sold for $155, 1828 N-5 at $255 and a second one at $250, 1831 N-3 at $125, 1837 N-3 at $175, 1837 N-10 at $125; 1838 N-11 went for $230 and 1840 N-2 at $165.

Closing the New York session were 47 lots of half cents. A superb 1795 fetched a record $325, but the splendid 1796 With Pole sold for a very reasonable $850. Proofs did very well with the 1831 G-1 at $275, the G-2 at $200 and the 1832 G-1 at $200. The Proofs in the 1840s ranged between $120 and $175.

In *The Numismatist*, January 1960, an account was carried of another Kosoff sale featuring outstanding copper coins. The author was on hand at this event. Interest was good, but not quite as exciting as this narrative suggests:

The long-awaited auction of the Dr. James O. Sloss Collection of U.S. large cents was held before a full house at the Park Sheraton Hotel, New York City. The 350 cents realized a total of $69,318.35.

When the opening bid of $1,400 on the 1793 Crosby 1-A shot to $1,900, it set the pace and when the Crosby 1-C (Lot No. 2) started at $3,850, a new record for any large cent had already been set. This specimen carried a splendid pedigree—Beckwith, Earle, Jackman, Newcomb, and now Sloss. The cataloguer, Abe Kosoff of Encino, California, had predicted a runaway price for this coin and the hammer fell at $5,500. This new record for any large cent was to be short-lived though.

The 1793 3-C, estimated at $1,250, fetched $1,600 and the 4-C brought $1,400 against an $1,150 estimate. The 6-F out of the Miller, Newcomb, T.J. Clarke collections was estimated at $2,400, brought $2,500. The first five lots had already realized $12,900.

In the 1794 group, some prices realized were: S-25: $90, S-31: $190, S-44: $230, S-63: $85. A splendid AU-55 of the S-70 variety went for $350 and a superb MS-60 of the same variety went to a Brooklyn collector at $675 after spirited bidding.

A magnificent 1795, S-75 went to a New England dealer at $675. The 1796s provoked much competition as the S-84 realized $310, the S-91: $150, S-92: $400, S-119: $625, an MS-70.

Another predicted runaway on the 1797 S-121 materialized. Opening at $700 against a number of floor bidders this finest known MS-65 went to a New York dealer, representing a splendid collection, a record $2,100.

The crowd grew expectant as the unprecedented offering of 1799 cents was at hand. The famous Proskey-Hines overdate opened at a low $2,100 but soon reached higher levels selling well above the $2,500 estimate. A charming lady was disappointed when her final bid of $3,400 was topped by a $3,500 book bid. The Hall-Brand-Pierce-Barnhart overdate went reasonably at $2,300 and the Dr. French overdate, a VF-25 was a comparatively cheap purchase at $850.

Then came Lot 50, the highlight of the sale, the "King of Cents," the Hines 1799, perfect date. This, the most famous and most desirable of the large coppers, is head and shoulders superior to any other specimen. This remarkable combination of rarity, pedigree and condition smashed the record set by the 1793 Crosby 1-C earlier in the evening. Smashed is the word for the $5,500 on the 1793 was exceeded by bids represented on the floor of $8,100 out of New Jersey, $9,000 out of California, and $10,000 out of New York. The book had a top bid of $11,500 and the lucky purchaser was awarded this plum at $10,500: a new high record for any large cent.[27] It seems likely that if this record is ever topped, it will take this same Hines 1799 to do it!

Other noteworthy items were 1800 S-197: $380, 1801 S-214: $295, S-220: $250, 1802 S-62: $700, and S-228: $360. The 1803s, S-243: $150, S-250: $380, another S-250: $600, S-260: $475. The 1804s went at $1,100 and $850. A superb 1805 S-267 fetched $300.

The 1806: $180 and the 1807 S-271, the popular Comet, smashed the former $550 record, going to $900. The 1808s went at $265 and $400 and the superb 1809 MS-65 went for a record $700. An 1810 S-285 brought $675 and a superb 1811 S-287 set an all time high at $850.

Records for 1812, too, at $475, $360 and $300 and $150 for 1813, $260 for 1814. When Lot 123 was sold ending the offering of early cents the total realized to that point was $58,600.

The 1817: 15 star: $115, 1821 Newcomb-1: $320, 1822 N-4: $220, 1823 over 22, the Winsor, Earle, Bement, Ryder, Sloss coin fetched a record $1,100, 1824 N-2-1/2: $205, 1825 N-3: $170, N-4: $160, 1826 N-5: $170, 1827 N-6: $105.

The late dates included many MS-70 and MS-65 grade coins. They induced spirited competition reflecting the condition-conscious collecting trends. The total sale realized just short of $70,000, the predicted figure of the cataloguer. Collectors await the special library edition being prepared by the cataloguer.

In 1955 Kosoff was the prime mover in the founding of the Professional Numismatists Guild. In 1959 he was the chief force in publishing a new book on pattern coins by J. Hewitt Judd. Later, he was a columnist for *Coin World* and co-compiler of the *Official ANA Grading Standards for United States Coins*. The collection of large cents formed by Admiral Worthington S. Bitler during the late 1940s and the 1950s was bought by him in 1960 and resold. The Edward H. Schwartz collection of cents comprising 1,170 lots was auctioned in 1961.

Later in his life, he lived in semiretirement, but quite a few coin deals came his way, especially from old-time customers. His traditional method as agent was to invite three dealers to come to Palm Springs to examine the coins at his bank and then submit a firm bid in writing. The highest bid won. Many important properties were handled that way.

Kosoff died in 1983 and was widely mourned by the collecting community. The present author wrote his book-length biography, *Abe Kosoff: Dean of Numismatics*, which was published in 1984, and worked with his family in auctioning his numismatic estate.

STACK'S

In 1933 the Stack brothers, Joseph and Morton, entered the rare-coin business in New York City. These were difficult times in the depth of the great Depression, probably not an ideal year for a start-up. Through local advertising and a reputation gained for fair trading and quick decisions in buying scrap gold, jewelry, and rare coins, the company flourished. In 1935 they held their first auction sale.

Within the decade, Stack's became a gathering place for advanced collectors and researchers to exchange information and share ideas. The surroundings were warm and cozy, causing many participants to later recall these meetings as a pleasure and also an inspiration. In the 1940s, Stack's published the *Numismatic Review*, conducted by professor Thomas Ollive Mabbott. Research articles on all phases of numismatics were presented. Today, a set of these volumes is still a standard reference.

In time, the majority of "name" collections would come Stack's way. Often these were cataloged in house by John J. Ford Jr., on staff in the late 1930s and early 1940s; Vladimir Clain-Stefanelli, who later left with his numismatically talented wife Elvira to take charge of and reorganize the National Numismatic Collection at the Smithsonian; James C. Risk; and many others, including to this day some of the most highly accomplished and qualified experts in numismatics. Harvey Stack, son of Morton, joined the company full-time in 1947. Recently, he likened the firm to a "university of numismatics."

Many auctions, indeed hundreds of them, contained important half cents and large cents, as did and do the auctions of any long-running firm. The few catalogs focusing on especially important offerings that are discussed here are but a *very short* listing that could include many, many more. One such is the Anderson-Dupont Collection, cataloged by consultant William H. Sheldon and presented in 1954. The title was the combination of the surnames of the consignors, an estate collection from an earlier owner not revealed. This was the first market test of the Sheldon system of grading in combination with "basal values" proposed by him in *Early American Cents* in 1949. A cent in a grade such as EF-40 with a basal value of $2 was estimated to bring 40 times $2, or $80. The audience was enthusiastic, prices soared, and the Sheldon system was left in the dust. *Penny Whimsy* offered a revised version in 1958, but it did not gain market acceptance. Of course, although the system ended, the grading lingered on.

In 1963 Stack's published a fixed-price catalog, *United States Half Cents (The Collection of Joseph Brobston)*, with 12 large photographic plates illustrating both sides of 192 half cents. The introduction included this:

> There has never been a collection to equal it offered for sale, either by private contract or public auction. We make this statement with full knowledge of the fine pieces contained in the famous Alvord Sale in 1924 and the later Dupont and Ryder Sales.

And the statement was true.

In 1969 an encore deluxe was provided by another catalog in the same genre, *The Philip M. Showers Collection of United States Half Cents: A Written and Photographic Inventory*, which had 141 half cents depicted on two photographic plates.

A June 1975 Stack's catalog was titled *United States Large Cents Featuring the Robert J. Kissner Collection of U.S. Large Cents With Other Important Consignments*, a significant offering in its time.

All bets were off in June 1984, when holders of the catalog titled *The Floyd T. Starr Collection of United States Large Cents, United States Half Cents*, comprising 893 lots, fought to outdo each other. The Early American Coppers (EAC) group describes it on their Web site:

Dubbed "Starr Wars," the collection commanded considerable interest among large cent collectors. Highlights included the unique Strawberry leaf cent of 1793 (NC-2) and one of three known examples of NC-3. C. Douglas Smith was the primary cataloguer. He was assisted by Denis Loring and Jules Reiver. The collection had been built from the Hines and Newcomb late date collections.

This was at a very slow time in the investment end of the coin market, but enthusiasm for coppers was unabated. In March 1988, the Herman Halpern Collection of cents, 774 lots, cataloged by staffer Carl C.W. Carlson, created its share of excitement. Not that it made any difference with copper specialists, but the general market had improved by then. Record prices were set.

SUPERIOR GALLERIES

On the West Coast, Superior Stamp & Coin Company, established in 1930 in Los Angeles by the Goldberg family, was fairly quiet on the auction scene for many years. Then in the 1970s, under the direction of Larry, Ira, and Mark Goldberg, with offices in Beverly Hills, the company hit its stride with what developed into a long list of "name" collection offerings.

Early out of the gate was the offering of Part I of the Charles Ruby Collection, formed by a professor at California State University at Fullerton. Ruby was a people person, and his pet 1793 favorites were widely shared at club and convention gatherings. The cataloging was done by Walter Breen and Denis Loring. Unusual in the copper specialty before and since, the listed grades were viewed as conservative by many bidders and in commentary in *Penny-Wise*. Soon, many had been graded higher by their new owners and others.

Among the Superior sales, the autumn 1986 Robinson S. Brown Jr. Collection, featuring outstanding cents from 1793 to 1857, was one of the most important. The consignor, known as Robbie Brown to everyone, had been and continued to be a frequent attendee at EAC gatherings. As the chairman of Brown-Forman Distillery in Kentucky, he had ample funds for this specialty. As have been nearly all well-financed members of EAC, he was a down-home regular guy. All of the regular Sheldon-numbered varieties were present, plus 29 of the noncollectibles, some of which had become *now*-collectibles, giving in total the largest number of different 1793 to 1814 cents ever to appear in a single offering. Cataloged by Jack Collins, this set the place for a string of later notable copper sales.

The pace was maintained in January 1989, when the Jack H. Robinson Collection of half cents and large cents crossed the block, with all Sheldon-numbered varieties, many in multiples to illustrate die states. The consignor was also the cataloger for the most part, with some expertise added by Del Bland. Robinson was and is well known for his *CQR* publication, a nickname for *Copper Quotes by Robinson*, a guide to availability in different grades and with price estimates at three different levels of quality within a given grading number. The Thomas Chalkley Collection was sold in January 1990 and had outstanding cents of later dates. The Dennis Mendelson Collection sale of February 1991 was cataloged by Del Bland and created a lot of attention, as did the G. Lee Kuntz Collection in October 1991.

In January 1992, the estate collection of Roger S. Cohen Jr., consigned by his daughter Debbie, included every variety among the circulation strikes. Most were in medium grade levels, affording opportunities to a wide audience. In the same month the John J. Nicholas Jr. Collection was offered. Del Bland graded the coins by so-called EAC standards, not specifically defined, but still used today as a name for a very conservative evaluation. The coins were submitted to Professional Coin Grading Service for another view. Collectors had the opportunity to compare both grades assigned. At the time the very idea of encapsulating early copper coins was viewed negatively by many specialists, although newcomers to the hobby embraced the concept warmly.

The J.R. Frankenfield Collection was sold by Superior in February 2001. It was billed as the most complete combined collection of half cents and early cents ever offered. The Robinson S. Brown Jr. Collection of 1839 to 1857 late-date cents was sold in June 2002.

IN MODERN TIMES

Several years earlier, in June 1998, two former principals left Superior, by which time it had undergone ownership changes (and later would continue to do so), and formed Larry & Ira Goldberg, Coins & Collectibles. The Goldbergs soon picked up the mantle of copper coin specialty and handled several important collections. Notable are the R.E. (Ted) Naftzger Jr. Collection of middle-date cents 1816 to 1839 and the 2009 offering of the Daniel W. Holmes Jr. Collection.

Chris Victor-McCawley and John R. (Bob) Grellman Jr. have been partners with the Goldbergs in these presentations, bringing with them many years of expertise in early copper coins, including catalogs for EAC and for the Colonial Coin Collectors Club. When this manuscript was begun, they were cataloging the collection of Daniel W. Holmes Jr., absolutely complete in early varieties with all of the Sheldon-numbered varieties and all of the noncollectibles except for one unique 1793 held by the ANS. This represented an unprecedented accomplishment.

Heritage Auctions in Dallas, captained by James Halperin and Steve Ivy, emerged in the late 20th century as the largest-volume numismatic auction house. The Wes Rasmussen Collection (2005) and the Jules Reiver Collection (2006), cataloged by Mark Borckardt and Denis Loring, are among Heritage's memorable offerings. In February 2008 the firm presented the Walter Husak Collection of early cents, 1793 to 1814, remarkable for its quality, including the finest collection of 1794s ever assembled.

The story is ongoing. Every two months *Penny-Wise* brings the latest news on early coppers. A file of the issues of the past 40 years gives extensive information about many other fine collections that have been auctioned or otherwise sold, in addition to those mentioned here. If even a paragraph were to be devoted in this book to all of the copper auctions, happenings, discoveries, etc., several chapters would need to be added. The reader is referred to past issues *Penny-Wise* for more coverage of events of the last 40 years.

REMINISCENCES

As to my own activities, these are chronicled well enough in publications of the past. With Empire Coin Company, Bowers and Ruddy Galleries, and Bowers and Merena Galleries, of which I was an owner at one time, I had the privilege of personally cataloging, and in many other instances working with staffers in the presentation of, many memorable properties. The Garrett Collection sold for The Johns Hopkins University had coppers of incredible quality, as did the collection of the Honorable and Mrs. R. Henry Norweb. The Louis E. Eliasberg Collection will forever remain one of a kind.

I have written books on all three of these collections, to which I will refer the reader in lieu of reiterating the highlights here. In recent times I have been a partner in Stack's, as discussed earlier, which is now Stack's Bowers Galleries.

While I have many recollections of past coins and collections, it is memories of coin people that I most treasure.

GRADING HALF CENTS AND LARGE CENTS

THE SHELDON SYSTEM
SHELDON GRADING NUMBERS

Determining the grade of a half cent or large cent is important, as it is a key element in evaluating a coin's market price. As the next chapter explains in detail, numbers are only a part of the equation, and other factors can be equally or more important. But first, the numbering system, how it originated, and guidelines for grading coins today.

In his 1949 book *Early American Cents*, William H. Sheldon devised a market formula in which a particular die variety of copper cent dated from 1793 through 1814 (he considered no other coins) could be reduced to numbers, enabling a numismatist to quickly calculate the market value.

As die varieties vary considerably in their value, and such issues as the 1793, Chain AMERI.; 1793, Liberty Cap; and 1799 are more valuable than, say, a common variety of 1803, different basal values were set up. For purposes of illustration here, a variety that was not particularly rare may have been given a basal value of $1 in 1949, while a scarce or rare piece might have been assigned $5. (Basal values are no longer used, but if they were, the prices would be *much* higher.)

Sheldon's idea was to determine a pricing scale by numbers, so that if the grading number were multiplied by the basal value of the variety, a precise market value could be obtained. It is seen that Sheldon was not really creating a *grading* scale at all, but a pricing scale! This aspect is not well known today. Back then the emphasis on Uncirculated coins was not as strong as it is today. While, of course, collectors back in 1949 would rather have a coin in Uncirculated grade than one in, say, Extremely Fine, most specialists in the field of copper cents were content to have a "nice" example in a grade they could afford. It was often the case that an Uncirculated piece would sell for just slightly more than one in Extremely Fine or About Uncirculated.

All of this changed, and dramatically so, in later years when Uncirculated coins, which Sheldon called Mint State (a term dating back to the 19th century), were avidly collected for this category alone, and prices broke away sharply from circulated grades. In 1949 there was not a tremendous premium for a typical early cent. In *Penny Whimsy*, 1958, Sheldon made some revisions to the market system, but these proved to have little lasting value.

Sheldon's scale from 1 to 70, later adapted and revised as the American Numismatic Association's (ANA) Official Grading Standards, was simple enough at first glance. Per his logic, a rare cent with a basal value of $5, if in VF-30 grade, would be worth $5 times 30, or $150. A coin in MS-60 would be worth twice as much, or $300. On the other hand, a coin with a basal value of $2, if in EF-40 grade, would be worth $80. And so it went.

The grading numbers from 1 to 70 were created in 1949 *to fit the prices then in effect*. It may have worked for a very short while. At the time the coin market was in a slump, licking its wounds from a postwar boom, and just beginning to revive. In the early 1950s, a new surge of interest emerged, prices rose sharply across the board, and more emphasis was placed on Mint State coins.

By the 1940s, when *Early American Cents* was published, Sheldon was well known professionally for his involvement with grouping human beings into physical categories, known as somatotyping. This he carried on for a long time. A mention of it is appropriate here, as it gives an insight to his interest in formulas. Liam O'Connor's article "How Shape Shapes Your Life: 100,000 Bodies Can't Be Wrong" told this:

> Dr. William H. Sheldon, director of the Constitution Laboratory at Columbia University . . . has been investigating body build and temperament for about 25 years. Thus far he and his associates have produced three monumental volumes: *The Varieties of Human Physique*, *The Varieties of Temperament*, and *Varieties of Delinquent Youth* (published by Harper & Brothers).
>
> Four more books are now in preparation. About 30 medical schools, hospitals, and other institutions are cooperating with Dr. Sheldon. The Rockefeller Foundation recently made a grant of $100,000 for further research. He and his co-workers already have photographed and studied more than 100,000 individuals. Dr. Sheldon classifies people into three constitutional types.

These were designated as *endomorphs* ("fatties"), *mesomorphs* ("muscle men"), and *ectomorphs* ("nervous types"). Endomorphs were great at parties, it was said, but had little sexual drive. In contrast, mesomorphs were eager to bed down members of the opposite sex but were not particularly social.

To classify a person, Dr. Sheldon rates the nude body for fat, muscles, and nerves— always in that order—on a seven-point scale. On this scale 1 represents the minimum, 7 the maximum, and 4 the average. The extreme *endomorph* or fatty therefore has 7-1-1 as his *somatotype* (body build) number. If he were less fat, more muscular, and more nervous, his somatotype might be 6-2-2 or 5-3-3.[1]

Later, Sheldon's classification system for bodies was dismissed as a pseudoscience (much about this can be found on the Internet).

From the preceding it is easy enough to understand how it was a short jump for Sheldon to group copper cents by grade numbers, rarity, and specific values. For good measure, the "condition census" indicated the grades of the top six specimens known.[2]

One might ask why the numbers were not abandoned as well when the market-price system failed. By any evaluation, they were and still are almost as much of a pseudoscience as somatotyping. The answer is that they were convenient shorthand and also appeared to have a mathematical basis, implying precision.

A coin described by adjectives alone, such as Very Good, might indicate a satisfactory coin but not much else. Similarly, a newcomer to the hobby might not necessarily know that an About Uncirculated coin is nicer than one described as Very Fine or Extremely

Fine. By using Sheldon numbers such as VG-8, VF-20, EF-40, and AU-50, just about anyone could quickly figure that an EF-40 coin was not as good as an AU-50 piece, but seemingly far finer than one in VG-8. Moreover, such numbers evoke images of a numismatic scholar situated in a laboratory, assigning a precise number based on extensive knowledge and study—perhaps as an astronomer, using scientific principles, might assign a number to a star to indicate its apparent magnitude.

It was and is very comforting to a newcomer in the hobby to think that a VF-20 grade has been assigned after much care by the numismatic equivalent of a rocket scientist. Anyone can call a coin Very Fine, it might be thought, but to be able to identify its grade precisely as VF-20 might require years of scholarship plus experience in the field. As noted throughout this book, grading is highly subjective, and experts who make their living by grading a coin can call the same specimen AU-58 or MS-64. Not much science here!

Today, the Sheldon numbers, which originally had just three steps to cover Mint State coins (MS-60, MS-65, and MS-70), have been expanded to include intermediate designations as well. Consider them to be shorthand, not scientific, and subject to interpretation, and you will know as much as the experts.

The following guidelines are from Whitman's *Grading Coins by Photographs*. For additional information see *The Official American Numismatic Association Grading Standards for United States Coins*. I was the author of the former and coauthor with Kenneth E. Bressett of the recent editions of the latter. In addition to the grades listed, it is common practice for collectors and dealers in the field of early coppers to assign further intermediate grades such as G-5, 6, and 7. Note also that for some Mint State coins the grade is followed by BN (brown), RB (red and brown), or RD (red), indicating the presence of original mint color.

GRADING GUIDELINES
HALF CENTS, 1793–1857
LIBERTY CAP, HEAD FACING LEFT, HALF CENTS (1793)

Striking and Sharpness. Half cents of this type are often light brown and on fairly smooth planchets, indicating that a good quality of copper was used. Borders on both sides are raised beads, an unusual feature not used later in the series. Sometimes certain beads can be weak, but this is the exception, not the rule. The Cohen-1 (Bowers-Whitman–1) variety is often lightly defined at HALF CENT on the reverse, due to a combination of striking and shallow depth of letters in the die. On some coins, up to and including VG-8, these words may be completely missing. Accordingly, this feature cannot be used in assigning a grade.

Availability. Half cents of this date are usually seen in lower grades, AG-3 to Fine-12 or so. Extremely Fine and About Uncirculated examples are rare, and Mint State coins are very rare. When encountered, which is not often, Mint State coins are apt to be in ranges from MS-60 to MS-63. Within a given grade the quality is usually quite satisfactory. In the marketplace, grading is often liberal.

MS-60 to 65 (Mint State). *Obverse:* In the lower ranges, MS-60 and 61, some slight abrasions can be seen on the higher areas of the portrait. Luster in the field is incomplete, particularly in the center of the open areas. At the MS-63 level, luster should be complete, with no abrasions evident. In higher levels, the luster is deeper, and some original mint color may be seen. *Reverse:* In the lower ranges

1793 (Bowers-Whitman–4, Cohen-4, Breen-4). Graded MS-63.

some abrasions are seen on the higher areas of the leaves. Generally, luster is complete in all ranges, as the open areas are protected by the lettering and wreath. Otherwise, the same comments apply as for the obverse.

Illustrated coin: An exceptional coin, well centered and with most details very sharp. One of the finest seen.

AU-50, 53, 55, 58 (About Uncirculated). *Obverse:* Friction is seen on the higher parts, particularly on the rounded cheek and on the higher strands of the hair. Friction and scattered marks are in the field, ranging from extensive at AU-50 to minimal at AU-58. Luster may be seen in protected areas, minimal at AU-50, but sometimes extensive on an AU-58 coin. Border beads, if well

1793 (BW-3, C-3, B-3). Graded AU-50.

struck, are separate and boldly defined. *Reverse:* Friction is seen on the higher wreath leaves and (not as easily discernible) on the letters. The fields, protected by the designs, show friction, but not as noticeably as on the obverse. At AU-55 and 58 little if any friction is seen. The reverse may have original luster, toned brown, minimal on lower About Uncirculated grades but sometimes extensive at AU-58. Border beads, if well struck, are separate and boldly defined. Grading at the About Uncirculated level is mainly done by viewing the obverse.

Illustrated coin: This grade would probably be viewed as conservative by many. A well-struck coin with excellent detail in most areas, but with the beads light on the right obverse rim. Light wear is seen on the higher areas.

EF-40, 45 (Extremely Fine). *Obverse:* Wear is seen on the portrait overall, with reduction or elimination of some separation of hair strands on the highest part. The cheek is ever so slightly flat on the highest part. Some leaves will retain some detail, especially where they join the stems. Luster is minimal or nonexistent at EF-40 but may sur-

1793 (BW-2, C-2, B-2). Graded EF-40.

vive in traces in protected areas at EF-45. *Reverse:* Wear is seen on the highest wreath and ribbon areas and on the letters. Luster is minimal but likely more noticeable than on the obverse, as the fields are protected by the designs and lettering.

Illustrated coin: This coin is perhaps conservatively graded. The coin has a decent strike on both sides except for some blending of border beads, which is not unusual at this grade level.

VF-20, 30 (Very Fine). *Obverse:* Wear on the portrait has reduced the hair detail to indistinct or flat at the center on a VF-20 coin, with slightly more detail at VF-30. The thin, horizontal (more or less) ribbon near the top of the hair is distinct. The border beads are blended together, with many blurred or missing. No luster is seen. *Reverse:* The leaf details are

1793 (BW-1, C-1, B-1). Graded VF-20.

nearly completely worn away at VF-20, with slight detail at VF-30. The border beads are blended together, with many indistinct. Some berries in the sprays may be worn away, depending on the strike (on strong strikes they can be seen down into Very Good and Good grades). No luster is seen. HALF CENT may be weak but is fully readable on certain coins (such as the illustrated 1793, BW-1), in which this feature was shallowly cut into the dies.

Illustrated coin: A sharp coin, with lightly granular surfaces. HALF CENT is weak on the reverse due to the shallowness of the letters in the die on this particular variety, not due to wear.

F-12, 15 (Fine). *Obverse:* The hair details are mostly worn away, with about one-third visible, mainly at the edges. Border beads are weak or worn away in areas. F-15 shows slightly more detail. *Reverse:* The wreath leaves are worn flat, but their edges are distinct. HALF CENT may be missing on variety 1793, BW-1 (this is also true of lower grades). Border

1793 (BW-2, C-2, B-2). Graded F-15.

beads are weak or worn away in areas. F-15 shows slightly more detail.

Illustrated coin: Scattered planchet flaws from the strip-rolling process are not unusual but must be mentioned.

VG-8, 10 (Very Good). *Obverse:* The portrait is well worn, although the eye can be seen, and the hair tips at the right show separation. Border beads are worn away, and the border blends into the field in most if not all of the periphery. LIBERTY and 1793 are bold. VG-10, not an official ANA grading designation, is sometimes applied to especially nice Very

1793 (BW-2, C-2, B-2). Graded VG-8.

Good coins. *Reverse:* The wreath, bow, and lettering are seen in outline form, and some leaves and letters may be indistinct in parts. Border beads are worn away, and the border blends into the field in most if not all of the periphery.

Illustrated coin: The raised rim beads are gone, and the rim blends into the field in areas. The outside areas of the letters are worn.

G-4, 6 (Good). *Obverse:* The portrait is worn smooth and is seen only in outline form, although the eye position can be discerned. LIBERTY and 1793 are complete, although the date may be weak. Reverse: Extensive wear is seen overall. From half to two-thirds of the letters in UNITED STATES OF AMERICA and the fraction numerals are worn away.

1793 (BW-4, C-4, B-4). Graded G-6.

The reverse shows more evidence of wear than does the obverse and is key in assigning this grade. G-6 is often used to describe finer examples in this category.

Illustrated coin: A well-worn example, but one showing the portrait, LIBERTY, and date very clearly. The reverse shows fewer details.

AG-3 (About Good). *Obverse:* Wear is more extensive than on the preceding. The portrait is visible only in outline. LIBERTY is weak but usually fully discernible. 1793 is weak, and the bottoms of the digits may be worn away. *Reverse:* Parts of the wreath are visible in outline form, and all but a few letters are gone. Grading of AG-3 is usually done by the reverse.

1793 (BW-2, C-2, B-2). Graded AG-3.

Illustrated coin: This is a well-worn and somewhat porous example. For the one-year 1793 type this is still a very numismatically desirable coin.

Fair-2 (Fair). *Obverse:* Worn nearly smooth. Date is partly visible, not necessarily clearly. Head of Miss Liberty is in outline form. Some letters of LIBERTY are discernible. *Reverse:* Worn nearly smooth. Peripheral letters are nearly all gone, with only vestiges remaining. Wreath is in outline form. HALF CENT ranges from readable to missing (the latter on certain die varieties as struck).

1793 (BW-4, C-4, B-4). Graded Fair-2.

Illustrated coin: This coin is well worn and granular but identifiable as to date and distinctive type. Highly marketable in this low grade as a filler for type-set purposes.

LIBERTY CAP, HEAD FACING RIGHT, HALF CENTS (1794–1797)

Striking and Sharpness. Half cents of 1794 are usually on dark planchets with rough surfaces, and usually of low aesthetic quality overall. Most 1795 half cents are on high-quality planchets, smooth and attractive, this being truer of the later plain-edge type than of the early thick-planchet issue. The individual listings by die varieties in the half cent section give more information. Striking can be weak in areas, and often the dentils are incomplete on one or both sides. Many Small Head coins of 1795 to 1797 have very little detail on the hair, even in higher grades. Half cents of 1796 are great rarities; quality varies, but higher-grade pieces are usually attractive. Half cents of 1797 are usually seen in low grades and on poor planchets; striking varies widely but is usually weak in areas. Dentils can be either weak or prominent in various circulated grades, down to the lowest; on certain varieties of 1795 they are prominent even on well-worn coins.

Care must be taken in the assigning of any grade, combining knowledge of a given die variety and the relief or sharpness of the die with observations of actual wear. Because of variance of opinion among experts, grades of certified coins can vary widely in their interpretations. The astute buyer must take die-variety idiosyncrasies into consideration. Generally, grading guidelines follow those of the half cent of 1793, but more expertise is required.

Availability. As a general type, this issue is scarce but available. Most are in lower grades, but Very Fine and Extremely Fine coins come on the market with regularity. About Uncirculated and the occasionally seen Mint State coins are usually very attractive.

MS-60 to 70 (Mint State). *Obverse:* On MS-60 and 61 coins there are some traces of abrasions on the higher areas of the portrait. Luster in the field is incomplete, particularly in the center of the open areas. At MS-63, luster is complete, and no abrasions are evident. At higher levels, the luster is deeper, and some original mint color may be seen. At MS-65 there are some scattered con-

1794, High Relief Head (BW-9, C-9, B-9). Graded MS-65.

tact marks and possibly some traces of fingerprints or discoloration, but these should be minimal and not at all distracting. Above MS-65, a coin should approach perfection. *Reverse:* In the lower ranges some abrasions are seen on the higher areas of the leaves. Generally, luster is complete in all ranges, as the open areas are protected by the lettering and wreath. Otherwise, the same comments apply as for the obverse.

Illustrated coin: A spectacular coin of a year seldom seen in Mint State. Die with High Relief Head, used on 1794, BW-7 to BW-9. Both sides have rich brown surfaces. On the obverse the luster is light, while on the reverse it is not as noticeable. On these varieties the high-relief obverse will sustain wear better than the low-relief reverse. Each die variety must be studied during the grading process.

AU-50, 53, 55, 58 (About Uncirculated). *Obverse:* Friction is seen on the higher parts, particularly the center of the portrait. Friction and scattered marks are in the field, ranging from extensive at AU-50 to minimal at AU-58. To reiterate: knowledge of the die variety is important. For certain shallow-relief dies (such as 1797) an About Uncirculated coin may appear to be in a

1797, 1 Above 1 in Date
(BW-1, C-1, B-1). Graded AU-58.

lower grade. Luster may be seen in protected areas, minimal at AU-50, but sometimes extensive on an AU-58 coin. *Reverse:* Friction is seen on the higher wreath leaves and (not as easy to discern) on the letters. The fields, protected by the designs, show friction, but not as noticeably as on the obverse. At AU-55 and 58 little if any friction is seen. The reverse may have original luster, toned brown, minimal on lower About Uncirculated grades but sometimes extensive on higher. Grading at the About Uncirculated level is mainly done by viewing the obverse.

Illustrated coin: This variety was caused by a die-cutting error. This coin has lustrous light-brown surfaces. It was struck from a buckled and cracked obverse die. It has a decent strike overall and excellent eye appeal—rare for a half cent of this date, although this particular variety is often more attractive than most others of the year.

EF-40, 45 (Extremely Fine). *Obverse:* Wear is seen on the portrait overall, with reduction or elimination of some separation of hair strands on the highest part. This varies by die variety, as some are better delineated than others. The cheek shows light wear. Luster is minimal or nonexistent at EF-40 but may survive in traces in protected

1794 (BW-1a, C-1a, B-1a). Graded EF-45.

areas (such as between the letters) at EF-45. *Reverse:* Wear is seen on the highest wreath and ribbon areas and on the letters. Luster is minimal but likely more noticeable than on the obverse, as the fields are protected by the designs and lettering. Sharpness will vary depending on the die variety. Expect certain issues of 1794 and 1797 to be lighter.

Illustrated coin: This coin's dies were cut in shallow relief and with low rims. This makes the coin much less sharp overall than the one illustrated for Mint State. As is true of other early half cents, the characteristics of a given variety need to be studied as part of the grading process.

VF-20, 30 (Very Fine). *Obverse:* Wear on the portrait has reduced the hair detail to indistinct or flat at the center. The border dentils are blended together, with many indistinct. No luster is seen. Again, knowing details of the die variety is important. A VF-20 or VF-30 1797 is very different in appearance from a 1794, Large Head, in the same grade. *Reverse:* The leaf details are nearly completely

1795, "Punctuated Date" (1,795), Plain Edge
(BW-5, C-4, B-4). Graded VF-20.

worn away at VF-20, with slight detail at VF-30. The border dentils are blended together, with many indistinct. No luster is seen. The sharpness of details depends on the die variety. Half cents of 1797 require special care in their study.

Illustrated coin: The date is "punctuated" due to a die flaw. The dentils are prominent on the left side of the obverse and from light to missing on the right side. The center of HALF CENT is slightly light due to the die, not to wear. The die is sunken at ER of AMERICA, as made.

F-12, 15 (Fine). *Obverse:* The hair details are mostly worn away, with about one-third visible, mainly at the edges. Border dentils are weak or worn away in areas. F-15 shows slightly more detail. *Reverse:* The wreath leaves are worn flat, but their edges are distinct. Border dentils are weak or worn away in areas. F-15 shows slightly more detail.

1795, "Punctuated Date" (1,795), Lettered Edge
(BW-2, C-2a, B-2a). Graded F-12.

VG-8, 10 (Very Good). *Obverse:* The portrait is well worn, although the eye can be seen, and the hair tips at the left show separation. Border dentils are worn away on some issues (not as much for 1795 coins), and the border blends into the field in most, if not all of, the periphery. LIBERTY and the date are bold. VG-10, not an official ANA grading designation, is

1794 (BW-2b, C-2b, B-2b). Graded VG-10.

sometimes applied to especially nice Very Good coins. *Reverse:* The wreath, bow, and lettering are seen in outline form, and some leaves and letters may be indistinct in parts. Border dentils are worn away, and the border blends into the field in most, if not all of, the periphery. In certain die varieties and die states, especially those of 1797, some letters may be very weak or missing.

Illustrated coin: This coin has fairly strong features overall for the grade and shows some granularity.

G-4, 6 (Good). *Obverse:* The portrait is worn smooth and is seen only in outline form, although the eye position can be discerned. LIBERTY and the date are complete, although the date may be weak. Dentils are gone on some, but not all, die varieties. *Reverse:* Extensive wear is seen overall. From half to two-thirds of the letters in UNITED STATES OF AMERICA, and the

1795, Pole to Cap, Lettered Edge
(BW-1, C-1, B-1). Graded G-4.

fraction numerals, are worn away. Certain shallow-relief dies may have letters missing. G-6 is often assigned to finer examples in this category.

Illustrated coin: This coin shows smooth, even wear. It was struck on a dark planchet. HALF CENT is light due to being shallowly cut in the die.

AG-3 (About Good). *Obverse:* Wear is more extensive than on the preceding. The portrait is visible only in outline. LIBERTY is weak but usually fully discernible. The date is weak, and the bottoms of the digits may be worn away. *Reverse:* Parts of the wreath are visible in outline form, and all but a few letters are gone. Grading of AG-3 is usually done by the reverse, as the obverse typically

1795, "Punctuated Date" (1,795), Plain Edge
(BW-5, C-4, B-4). Graded AG-3.

appears to be in a slightly higher grade. If split grading were used, more than just a few half cents of this type could be designated as G-4 / AG-3 or even G-6 / AG-3.

Illustrated coin: The obverse, if graded separately, would be a clear G-4 or even G-6, although it has some light scratches. The reverse is worn down to AG-3.

Draped Bust Half Cents (1800–1808)

Striking and Sharpness. Striking varies. Weakness is often seen at the center of the obverse and on the wreath leaves on the reverse. Planchet quality is often porous and dark for 1802, 1803, 1807, and 1808 due to the copper stock used, but this is not described on the labels of certified coins. Here is another cherrypicker's delight, made possible by the fact that certified holders only list the alphanumerical grade.

Availability. As a type, Draped Bust half cents are available in any grade desired, up to and including Mint State, the latter usually dated 1806 (occasionally 1800 and, less often, 1804), by virtue of old-time hoards. The year 1804 includes many different die varieties and die states. Apart from aspects of strike, cherrypicking for surface quality is especially essential for 1802, 1807, 1808/7, and 1808.

MS-60 to 70 (Mint State). *Obverse:* In the lower grades, MS-60 and 61, some slight abrasions can be seen on the higher areas of the portrait. Luster in the field is incomplete, particularly in the center of the open areas, which on this type are very extensive. At the MS-63 level, luster should be nearly complete, and no abrasions evident. In higher levels, the luster is complete and deeper, and some orig-

1804, Crosslet 4, Stems to Wreath
(BW-9, C-10, B-9). Graded MS-60.

inal mint color may be seen. MS-64 coins may have some slight discoloration or scattered contact marks. A well-graded MS-65 or higher coin has full, rich luster; no marks visible except under magnification; and a blend of brown toning or nicely mixed (not stained or blotchy) mint color and natural brown toning. *Reverse:* In the lower Mint State ranges some abrasions are seen on the higher areas of the leaves. Generally, luster is complete in all ranges, as the open areas are protected by the lettering and wreath. Sharpness of the leaves can vary by die variety, so this aspect should be checked. Otherwise, the same comments apply as for the obverse.

Illustrated coin: This is well struck at the centers but shows some lightness at the inner rims—an attractive coin with lustrous, rich, light-brown surfaces.

AU-50, 53, 55, 58 (About Uncirculated). *Obverse:* Friction is seen on the higher parts, particularly the hair of Miss Liberty. Friction and scattered marks are in the field, ranging from extensive at AU-50 to minimal at AU-58. Luster may be seen in protected areas, minimal at AU-50 with more at AU-58. At AU-58 the field may also retain some luster. In all instances, the luster is lesser in area

1806, Large 6, Stems to Wreath
(BW-4, C-4, B-4). Graded AU-58.

and depth than on the reverse of this type. *Reverse:* Friction is evident on the higher wreath leaves and (not as easy to discern) on the letters. Again, the die variety should be checked. The fields, protected by the designs, show friction, but not as noticeably as on the obverse. At AU-55 and 58, little if any friction is seen. The reverse may have original luster, toned brown, minimal on lower About Uncirculated grades but often extensive at AU-58.

EF-40, 45 (Extremely Fine). *Obverse:* Wear is seen on the portrait overall, with reduction or elimination of some of the separation between hair strands on the highest part. The cheek shows light wear. Luster is minimal or nonexistent at EF-40 but may survive among the letters of LIBERTY at EF-45. *Reverse:* Wear is seen on the highest wreath and ribbon areas and on the letters. Luster is

1804, Plain 4, Stems to Wreath
(BW-12, C-11, B-12). Graded EF-40.

minimal but likely more noticeable than on the obverse, as the fields are protected by the designs and lettering.

Illustrated coin: Probably lightly cleaned years ago, this coin's obverse has a slightly orange hue.

VF-20, 30 (Very Fine). *Obverse:* Wear on the portrait has reduced the hair detail to indistinct or flat at the center. The border dentils are blended together, with many indistinct. No luster is seen. *Reverse:* The leaf details are nearly completely worn away at VF-20, with slight detail at VF-30. The border dentils are blended together, with many indistinct. No luster is seen.

1804, Crosslet 4 "Spiked Chin," Stems to Wreath (BW-5, C-8, B-7). Graded VF-20.

Illustrated coin: One of several "Spiked Chin" die combinations.

F-12, 15 (Fine). *Obverse:* The hair details are mostly worn away, with about one-third visible, mainly at the edges. Border dentils are weak or worn away in areas. F-15 shows slightly more detail. *Reverse:* The wreath leaves are worn flat, but their edges are distinct. HALF CENT may be missing on variety 1804, Crosslet 4, Stems to Wreath (BW-1)—also true of lower grades. Border dentils are weak or worn away in areas. F-15 shows slightly more detail.

1804, Crosslet 4 "Spiked Chin," Stems to Wreath (BW-4, C-6, B-6). Graded F-12.

Illustrated coin: The reverse of this coin was struck from an overused die, which caused the cud breaks around the rim.

VG-8, 10 (Very Good). *Obverse:* The portrait is well worn, although the eye can be seen, as can hints of hair detail (some at the left shows separation). Curls now appear as mostly solid blobs. Border dentils are worn away on most varieties, and the rim, although usually present, begins to blend into the field. LIBERTY and the date are bold. VG-10, not an official ANA grading designation, is

1805, Small 5, Stems to Wreath (BW-3, C-3, B-3). Graded VG-8.

sometimes applied to especially nice Very Good coins. *Reverse:* The wreath, bow, and lettering are seen in outline form, and some leaves and letters may be indistinct in parts. The border may blend into the field on some of the periphery.

Illustrated coin: This coin has smooth, even wear. The obverse die has a bulge in the right field that is usually seen on this variety.

G-4, 6 (Good). *Obverse:* The portrait is worn smooth and is seen only in outline form, although the eye position can be discerned. LIBERTY and the date are complete, although the date may be weak. The border blends into the field more extensively than on the preceding, but significant areas of border can still be seen. *Reverse:* Extensive wear is seen overall. From half to two-thirds of the

1805, Small 5, Stems to Wreath
(BW-2, C-2, B-2). Graded G-4.

letters in UNITED STATES OF AMERICA and the fraction numerals are worn away. G-6 is often assigned to finer examples in this category.

   Illustrated coin: The coin shows much wear, but the key features for G-4 are present. The surfaces are dark and lightly porous and should be described as such in a listing.

AG-3 (About Good). *Obverse:* Wear is more extensive than on the preceding. The portrait is visible only in outline. LIBERTY is weak but usually discernible. The date is weak, and the bottoms of the digits may be worn away, but must be identifiable. *Reverse:* Parts of the wreath are visible in outline form, and all but a few letters are gone.

1802, 2 Over 0, Reverse of 1802, 1 Leaf Left, 2 Leaves
Right at Wreath Apex (BW-2, C-2, B-2). Graded AG-3.

   Illustrated coin: The obverse is clearly G-4 or so, but the overall grade is defined by the reverse, which is AG-3.

CLASSIC HEAD HALF CENTS (1809–1836)

Striking and Sharpness. Coins of 1809 to 1811 usually have areas of light or incomplete striking. Grading coins of the early years requires special care and expertise. Sometimes coins as high as Mint State appear blurry in areas due to the dies and striking. Those of later years are often found well struck and are easier to grade. Areas to check include the dentils and rims on both sides, the star centers and hair detail on the obverse, and the leaf detail on the reverse.

Availability. As a type this issue is easily enough found, although 1811 is scarce and 1831 and 1836 are notable rarities. Mint State coins from old hoards exist for certain of the later dates, particularly 1828, 1833, and 1835, but often have spotting, and many seen in the marketplace are cleaned or recolored. Care is advised. Although 1809 to 1811 half cents are often seen with extensive wear, those of the 1820s and 1830s are not often seen below Very Fine, as they did not circulate extensively.

MS-60 to 70 (Mint State). *Obverse:* In the lower grades, MS-60 and 61, some slight abrasions can be seen on the portrait, most evident on the cheek, as the hair details are complex on this type. Luster in the field is complete or nearly complete. At MS-63, luster should be complete, and no abrasions are evident. In higher levels, the luster is complete

1833 (BW-1, C-1, B-1). Graded MS-65RD.

and deeper, and some original mint color may be seen. MS-64 coins may have some slight discoloration or scattered contact marks. A well-graded MS-65 or higher coin has full, rich luster—with no marks visible except under magnification—and has a nice blend of brown toning or nicely mixed (not stained or blotchy) mint color and natural brown toning. Coins dated 1809 to 1811 may exhibit significant weakness of details due to striking (or, in the case of most 1811s, porous planchet stock) on both the obverse and the reverse. *Reverse:* In the lower Mint State grades, some abrasions are seen on the higher areas of the leaves. Mint luster is complete in all Mint State grades, as the open areas are protected by the lettering and wreath. Sharpness of the leaves can vary by die variety, so this aspect should be checked. Otherwise, the same comments apply as for the obverse.

Illustrated coin: This coin, a survivor from a hoard of this particular date, has nearly full original mint red-orange on both sides. Many examples are spotted, unlike the present coin.

AU-50, 53, 55, 58 (About Uncirculated). *Obverse:* Friction is seen on the higher parts, particularly the cheek and hair (under magnification) of Miss Liberty. Friction and scattered marks are in the field, ranging from extensive at AU-50 to minimal at AU-58. Luster may be seen in protected areas, minimal at the AU-50 level, with more showing at AU-58.

1809, Normal Date (BW-4, C-6, B-6). Graded AU-58.

At AU-58 the field may retain some luster as well. *Reverse:* Friction is seen on the higher wreath leaves and (not as easy to discern) on the letters. Again, half cents of 1809 to 1811 require special attention. The fields, protected by the designs, show friction, but not as noticeably as on the obverse. At AU-55 and 58, little if any friction is seen. The reverse may have original luster, toned brown, minimal on lower About Uncirculated grades but often extensive at AU-58.

Illustrated coin: Brown luster with unusual blue color as well. The bottom five stars on the left are weak, as struck, and the dentils are light in that area. As this die combination does occur sharply struck, a cherrypicker will want to seek such a coin. Certified holders do not mention the quality of strike.

EF-40, 45 (Extremely Fine). *Obverse:* Wear is seen on the portrait overall, with reduction or elimination of some separation of hair strands. The cheek shows light wear. Luster is minimal or nonexistent at EF-40 but may survive among the letters of LIBERTY at EF-45. *Reverse:* Wear is seen on the highest wreath and ribbon areas and on the letters. Luster is

1811 (BW-2, C-2, B-2). Graded EF-40.

minimal but likely more noticeable than on the obverse, as the fields are protected by the designs and lettering.

   Illustrated coin: This coin is a typical strike, showing some lightness at the star centers, although wear caused some of the lightness. The surfaces are lightly granular.

VF-20, 30 (Very Fine). *Obverse:* Wear on the portrait has reduced the hair detail, but much can still be seen (in this respect the present type differs dramatically from earlier types). *Reverse:* The wreath details, except for the edges of the leaves, are worn away at VF-20 and have slightly more detail at VF-30.

   Illustrated coin: This coin has

1811 (BW-2, C-2, B-2). Graded VF-20.

gray-brown surfaces. At this grade and lower, the sharpness of the original strike diminishes in importance, as star centers, hair, leaves, and so on show significant wear.

F-12, 15 (Fine). *Obverse:* The hair details are fewer than on the preceding, but many are still present. Stars have flat centers. F-15 shows slightly more detail. *Reverse:* The wreath leaves are worn flat, but their edges are distinct. F-15 shows slightly more detail.

   Illustrated coin: Smooth, even wear characterizes this example of

1811 (BW-2, C-2, B-2). Graded F-15.

the scarce 1811 half cent. Some light porosity or granularity is normal at this grade level.

VG-8, 10 (Very Good). *Obverse:* The portrait is well worn, although the eye and ear can be seen, as can some hair detail. The border is well defined in most areas. *Reverse:* The wreath, bow, and lettering are seen in outline form, and some leaves and letters may be indistinct in parts. The border is well defined in most areas.

1811 (BW-1, C-1, B-1). Graded VG-8.

Illustrated coin: Here is a poster example of this grade—smooth, with even wear, a nice planchet, and overall attractive appearance.

G-4, 6 (Good). *Obverse:* The portrait is worn smooth and is seen only in outline form. Much of LIBERTY on the headband is readable, but the letters are weak. The stars are bold in outline. Much of the rim can be discerned. *Reverse:* Extensive wear is seen overall. Lettering in UNITED STATES OF AMERICA ranges from weak but complete (although

1811 (BW-2, C-2, B-2). Graded G-4.

the ANA grading guidelines allow up to half of the letters to be unreadable; also note that the ANA text illustrates the words in full) to having perhaps a third of the letters missing. HALF CENT is usually bold.

AG-3 (About Good). *Obverse:* Wear is more extensive than on the preceding. The portrait is visible only in outline. A few letters of LIBERTY are discernible in the headband. The stars are weak or worn away on their outer edges. The date is light. *Reverse:* The wreath is visible in outline form. Most or even all of UNITED STATES OF AMERICA is worn away. HALF CENT is usually readable.

1828, 12 Stars (BW-3, C-2, B-3). Graded AG-3. The famous 12-star variety.

Illustrated coin: A well-worn example. Although many details are gone, it is still clearly identifiable.

Braided Hair Half Cents (1840–1857)

Striking and Sharpness. Many if not most are well struck, and nearly all are on good planchet stock. Points to check for sharpness are the denticles on both sides, the star centers and hair detail on the obverse, and the leaf detail on the reverse.

Availability. As coins of this design did not circulate after the 1850s, and as circulation strikes were not made until 1849, such pieces never acquired extensive wear. Typical grades are from EF-40 upward. Coins in lesser grades are seen now and again but are not in particular demand, as Extremely Fine and About Uncirculated coins are relatively inexpensive.

MS-60 to 70 (Mint State). *Obverse:* In the lower Mint State grades, MS-60 and 61, some slight abrasions can be seen on the portrait, most evidently on the cheek. The tip of the coronet should be checked as well. Luster in the field is complete, or nearly so. At MS-63, luster should be complete, and no abrasions evident. At higher levels, the luster is com-

1854 (BW-1a, C-1, B-1). Graded MS-63RB.

plete and deeper, and some original mint color may be seen. Mint frost on this type is usually deep, sometimes satiny, but hardly ever prooflike. MS-64 coins may have some slight discoloration or scattered contact marks. A well-graded MS-65 or higher coin has full, rich luster; no contact marks visible except under magnification; and a nice blend of brown toning or nicely mixed (not stained or blotchy) mint color and natural brown toning. The late Walter Breen stated that he had never seen an 1853 (common date) half cent with extensive *original* mint color, but these are plentiful with brown-toned surfaces. *Reverse:* In the lower Mint State grades some abrasions are seen on the higher areas of the leaves. Mint luster is complete in all Mint State grades, as the open areas are protected by the lettering and wreath.

Illustrated coin: A hoard coin from this year, with original mint color mixed with natural light-brown toning. Full details on both sides. Such grading is highly subjective, and the same coin might be designated as MS-64RB or even MS-65RB. This provides an opportunity for the astute buyer to cherrypick, for if it were offered as MS-65RB the price would be much higher.

AU-50, 53, 55, 58 (About Uncirculated). *Obverse:* Wear is evident on the cheek, the hair above the forehead, and the tip of the coronet. Friction is evident in the field. At AU-58, luster may be present except in the center of the fields. As the grades go down to AU-50, wear is more evident on the portrait. Wear is seen on the stars but is not as easy

1851 (BW-1, C-1, B-1). Graded AU-58.

to discern as it is elsewhere. At AU-50 there is either no luster or only traces of luster close to the letters and devices. *Reverse:* Wear is most evident on the highest areas of the leaves and the ribbon bow. Luster is present in the fields. As the grades go downward from AU-58 to 50, wear increases and luster decreases. At the AU-50 level there is either no luster or traces of luster close to the letters and devices.

Illustrated coin: This coin is sharply struck on both sides and has eye-pleasing light-brown surfaces.

EF-40, 45 (Extremely Fine). *Obverse:* Wear is more extensive on the portrait, including the cheek, hair, and coronet. The star centers are worn down slightly. Traces of luster are minimal, if at all existent. *Reverse:* The centers of the leaves are well worn, with detail visible only near the edges of the leaves and nearby, and the higher parts worn flat. Letters show significant wear. Luster, if present, is minimal.

1854 (BW-1a, C-1, B-1). Graded EF-40.

VF-20, 30 (Very Fine). *Obverse:* Wear is more extensive than on the foregoing. Some of the strands of hair are fused together. The center radials of the stars are worn nearly completely away. *Reverse:* The leaves show more extensive wear, with details visible at the edges, and only minimally and not on all leaves. The lettering shows smooth, even wear.

1855 (BW-1, C-1, B-1). Graded VF-20.

LARGE COPPER CENTS, 1793–1857

Note that early copper coins of all kinds may exhibit tooling (engraving done outside the Mint in order to simulate worn-away or weakly struck details). These old coppers have also sometimes been burnished to smooth out areas of porosity. Learn to recognize the signs of these alterations. They are considered to be damage, and they significantly decrease the coin's value.

CHAIN REVERSE CENTS (1793)

Striking and Sharpness. The details of Miss Liberty's hair are often indistinct or missing, even on many higher-grade specimens. For all grades and varieties, the reverse is significantly sharper than the obverse. Hence, if split grading were popular today (as it once was), a Chain AMERI. cent might be correctly graded as VG-8 / F-12, or similar. An enlightened cataloger will carefully describe both sides of an offered coin. In the marketplace, grading interpretations are often quite liberal. The portrait of Miss Liberty is shallow and is often weak, especially on the 1793, Chain AMERI., BW-1 variety (which is often missing the date). Each coin is apt to have its own personality within an assigned grade, certified or otherwise. Some expanded comments about this are given below.

Availability. All varieties are rare in the context of the demand for them: probably fewer than 1,000 or so survive today. Most are in lower grades, from Fair-2 to VG-8. Even Fair and About Good coins are highly collectible, for although the date may be worn away, the chain device identifies the type. Very Fine and Extremely Fine coins are few and far between, and About Uncirculated and Mint State coins are very rare.

MS-60 to 70 (Mint State). *Obverse:* In the lower Mint State grades, MS-60 and MS-61, some slight abrasions can be seen on the higher areas of the portrait. The large open field shows light contact marks and perhaps a few nicks. At MS-63 the luster should be complete, although some very light abrasions or contact marks may be on the portrait. At MS-64 or higher—a nearly impossible level for

1793, Chain AMERICA, Period After LIBERTY and Date (BW-5, Sheldon-4, B-5). Graded MS-65BN.

a Chain cent—there is no sign of abrasions anywhere. Mint color is not extensive on any known Mint State coin, but traces of red-orange are sometimes seen around the rim and devices on both sides. *Reverse:* In the lower Mint State grades some abrasions are seen on the chain links. There are some abrasions in the field. At MS-63, luster should be unbroken. Some abrasions and minor contact marks may be evident. In still higher grades, luster is deep, and there is no sign of abrasion.

Illustrated coin: This variety has a distinctive obverse with a period after the date and LIBERTY.

AU-50, 53, 55, 58 (About Uncirculated). *Obverse:* Light wear is seen on the highest areas of the portrait. Some luster is seen in the large open fields at the AU-58 level, less at AU-55, and little if any for AU-53 and 50. Scattered marks are normal and are most evident in the field. At higher levels, some vestiges of luster may be seen among the letters and numerals and between the hair tips.

1793, Chain AMERI. (BW-1, S-1, B-1). Graded AU-50. The famous AMERI. reverse.

Reverse: Light wear is most evident on the chain, as this is the most prominent feature. The letters show wear, but not as extensive. Luster may be seen at the AU-58 and 55 levels, usually slightly more on the reverse than on the obverse. Generally, the reverse grades higher than the obverse, usually by a step, such as an AU-50 obverse and an AU-53 reverse (such a coin would be listed as the lower of the two, or AU-50).

Illustrated coin: Described by an auction cataloger: "Very well defined, some softness on the usually weak highest point of the hair, other fine details well delineated. Some very faint planchet granularity is seen, and a few short parallel fissures are noted around the central reverse. Some scattered nicks, old thin curved scratch from nose through chin and below, another pin scratch on the high forehead."

EF-40, 45 (Extremely Fine). *Obverse:* The center of the portrait is well worn, with the hair visible only in thick strands, although extensive detail remains in the hair tips at the left. No luster is seen. Contact marks are normal in the large expanse of open field but should be mentioned if they are distracting. *Reverse:* The chain is bold and shows light wear. Other features show wear, as well—

1793, Chain AMERICA
(BW-2, S-2, B-2). Graded EF-40.

more extensive in appearance because the relief is lower. The fields show some friction, but not as much as on the obverse.

    Illustrated coin: A cut or void is seen in Miss Liberty's hair, as are some pinpricks and marks. Light scratches are seen at the top of the head. The reverse is especially bold. Surfaces are microscopically granular on both sides.

VF-20, 30 (Very Fine). *Obverse:* More wear is seen on the portrait, with perhaps half or slightly more of the hair detail showing, mostly near the left edge of the hair. The ear usually is visible (but might not be, depending on the sharpness of strike). The letters in LIBERTY show wear. The rim remains bold (more so than on the reverse). *Reverse:* The chain shows more wear than on the preced-

1793, Chain AMERICA
(BW-4, S-3, B-4). Graded VF-20.

ing but is still bold. Other features show more wear and may be weak in areas. The rim may be weak in areas.

    Illustrated coin: Nice detail is seen in the hair strands at the left. There are some marks near the neck and in the right field, not unusual for this grade. The reverse has a dig below the T in CENT.

F-12, 15 (Fine). *Obverse:* The hair details are mostly worn away, with about one-third visible, that being on the left. The rim is distinct on most specimens. The bottoms of the date digits are weak or possibly worn away. *Reverse:* The chain is bold, as is the lettering within the chain. Lettering around the border shows extensive wear but is complete. The rim may be flat in areas.

1793, Chain AMERI. (BW-1, S-1, B-1). Graded F-15.

    Illustrated coin: This coin has a planchet flaw and many tiny pin scratches, with a few heavier scratches above the portrait. Overall, this coin is better than F-15, but the grade compensates for the scratches. This points to the necessity for astute buyers to go beyond an alphanumeric grading number and study the coin itself. The same can be said for *most* early copper cents.

VG-8, 10 (Very Good). *Obverse:* The portrait is well worn, although Miss Liberty's eye remains bold. Hair detail is gone at the center but is evident at the left edge of the portrait. LIBERTY is always readable but may be faded or partly missing on shallow strikes. The date is well worn, with the bottom of the numerals missing (published standards vary on this point, and it used to be the

1793, Chain AMERICA, Period After LIBERTY and Date (BW-5, S-4, B-5). Graded VG-8.

case that a full date was mandatory). *Reverse:* The chain remains bold, and the center letters are all readable. Border letters may be weak or incomplete. The rim is smooth in most areas.

Illustrated coin: Certified as F-12 but more closely fitting VG-10, perhaps, if one deducts for overall porosity. Sometimes, early copper cents cannot be neatly pigeonholed into grade categories.

G-4, 6 (Good). *Obverse:* The portrait is worn smooth and is seen only in outline form, although the eye position can be discerned. LIBERTY may be weak. The date is weak, but the tops of the numerals can be discerned. *Reverse:* The chain is fully visible in outline form. Central lettering is mostly or completely readable, but light. Peripheral lettering is mostly worn away.

1793, Chain AMERICA (BW-4, S-3, B-4). Graded G-4.

Illustrated coin: The presence of the date at the bottom can barely be discerned, but LIBERTY is sharp. The reverse is a poster example of the grade. Remarkably, for a coin so extensively worn, bumps and marks are absent. Few G-4 coins are this nice overall.

AG-3 (About Good). *Obverse:* The portrait is visible as an outline. LIBERTY and the date are mostly or even completely worn away. Contact marks may be extensive. *Reverse:* The chain is fully visible in outline form. Traces of the central letters— or, on better strikes, nearly all of the letters—can be seen. Around the border all letters are worn away.

1793, Chain AMERICA (BW-4, S-3, B-4). Graded AG-3.

Illustrated coin: The date is completely worn away, but most of LIBERTY is readable. Two edge bumps on the left are not unusual for this low grade. The reverse is quite bold, and some peripheral lettering can be seen.

Wreath Reverse Cents (1793)

Striking and Sharpness. These cents are usually fairly well struck, although high-grade pieces often exhibit some weakness on the highest hair tresses and on the leaf details. On lower-grade pieces these areas are worn, so the point is moot. Planchet quality varies widely, from smooth, glossy brown to dark and porous. The lettered-edge cents are often seen on defective planchets. Consult the Sheldon text and photographs to learn the idiosyncrasies of certain varieties. Some detailed auction listings reflect the truism that among early cents a grading number is only part of the story, as advanced collectors know well. The borders have raised beads, an artistic touch; on high-grade pieces these are usually very distinct, but they blend together on lower-grade coins and can sometimes be indistinct. The beads are not as prominent as those later used on the 1793, Liberty Cap, cents.

Availability. At least several thousand examples exist of the different varieties of the type. Most are in lower grades, from AG-3 to VG-8, although Fine and Very Fine pieces are encountered with regularity. Choice Extremely Fine, About Uncirculated, and higher coins are highly sought numismatic prizes. Some Mint State coins have been billed as specimen or presentation coins, but this is supposition, as no records exist.

MS-60 to 70 (Mint State). *Obverse:* On MS-60 and 61 coins there are some traces of abrasions on the higher areas of the portrait, most particularly the hair. As this area can be lightly struck, careful inspection is needed for evaluation, not as much in Mint State (as other features come into play), but in higher circulated grades. Luster in the field is incomplete at lower Mint State levels but should be

1793, Wreath Type, Vine and Bars Edge, Widest Ribbon Bow (BW-17, S-9, B-12). Graded MS-65BN.

in generous quantity. At MS-63, luster should be complete and no abrasions evident. At higher levels, the luster is deeper, and some original mint color may be seen. At MS-65 there might be some scattered contact marks and possibly bare traces of fingerprints or discoloration. Above MS-65, a coin should approach perfection. A Mint State 1793, Wreath, cent is an object of rare beauty. *Reverse:* In the lower Mint State grades some abrasions are seen on the higher areas of the leaves. Generally, luster is complete in all grades, as the open areas are protected by the lettering and wreath. In many ways, the grading guidelines for this type follow those of the 1793 half cent—also with sprays of berries (not seen elsewhere in the series).

   Illustrated coin: This is a coin to die for, so to speak, and is described thus in a catalog: "What can be said about this coin? Adjectives including *marvelous, exceptional, wonderful,* and just about anything else, seem to fall short of the incredible and absolute beauty of this piece. Here, indeed, is a coin for posterity, a 1793 cent the likes of which would be difficult to duplicate elsewhere for any price."

AU-50, 53, 55, 58 (About Uncirculated). *Obverse:* Friction is seen on the highest areas of the hair (which may also be lightly struck) and the cheek. Some scattered marks are normal in the field, ranging from more extensive at AU-50 to minimal at AU-58. *Reverse:* Friction is seen on the higher wreath leaves and (not as easy to discern) on the letters. The fields, protected by the designs (including sprays of berries at the

1793, Wreath Type, Vine and Bars Edge, Triangular Ribbon Bow, ONE / CENT High (BW-18, S-8, B-13). Graded AU-50.

center), show friction, but not as noticeably as on the obverse. At AU-55 and 58, little if any friction is seen. Border beads, if well struck, are separate and boldly defined.

Illustrated coin: Offered at auction with this description: "Glossy dark steel brown with appealing surface quality. Under a strong glass, the surfaces show extremely fine granularity . . . only really notable near the borders. A natural planchet flaw at the rim above the O in OF is a reminder of the tribulations the Mint endured in its first year of full operations. The marks that are present are utterly inoffensive, with just a dull scrape under 17 of the date and a minor old scratch under the last S of STATES. . . . The overall eye appeal, both in hand and under careful scrutiny, is very nice."

EF-40, 45 (Extremely Fine). *Obverse:* More extensive wear is seen on the high parts of the hair, creating mostly a solid mass (without detail of strands) of varying width in the area immediately to the left of the face. The cheek shows light wear. Luster is minimal or nonexistent at EF-40 but may survive in traces in protected areas (such as between the letters) at EF-45. *Reverse:* Wear is seen on the

1793, Wreath Type, Vine and Bars Edge, Widest Ribbon Bow (BW-17, S-9, B-12). Graded EF-40.

highest wreath and ribbon areas and on the letters. Luster is minimal but likely more noticeable than on the obverse, as the fields are protected by the designs and lettering. Some of the beads blend together.

Illustrated coin: This coin shows some granularity and contact marks and is of a lighter brown color than is usual.

VF-20, 30 (Very Fine). *Obverse:* Wear on the hair is more extensive and varies depending on the die variety and sharpness of strike. The ANA grading standards suggest that two-thirds of the hair is visible, which in practice can be said to be "more or less." More beads are blended together, the extent of which depends on the striking and variety. Certain parts of the rim are smooth, with

1793, Wreath Type, Vine and Bars Edge, Widest Ribbon Bow (BW-17, S-9, B-12). Graded VF-25.

beads scarcely visible at all. No luster is seen. The date, LIBERTY, and hair ends are bold. *Reverse:* The leaf details are nearly completely worn away at VF-20, with slight detail at VF-30. The border beads are blended together, with many indistinct. Some berries in the sprays are light, but nearly all remain distinct. No luster is seen.

Illustrated coin: Note some tiny pin scratches and overall planchet granularity. The sharpness is better than that usually seen at this grade.

F-12, 15 (Fine). *Obverse:* The hair details are mostly worn away, with about one-third visible, mainly at the edges. The ANA grading standards suggest that 50 percent are visible, seemingly applying to the total area of the hair. However, the visible part, at the left, also includes intermittent areas of the field. Beads are weak or worn away in areas. F-15 shows slightly more detail. By this

1793, Wreath Type, Vine and Bars Edge, Widest Ribbon Bow (BW-17, S-9, B-12). Graded F-12.

grade, scattered light scratches, noticeable contact marks, and the like are the rule, not the exception. These are not mentioned at all on holders and are often overlooked elsewhere, except in some auction catalogs and price lists. Such marks are implicit for coins in lower grades, and light porosity or granularity is common as well. *Reverse:* The wreath leaves are worn flat, but their edges are distinct. Border beads are weak or worn away in areas. F-15 shows slightly more detail.

Illustrated coin: This is a sharp coin, but it shows some minor (nondistracting) pits near the base of the obverse. It has even color, superb visual appeal, and a mostly smooth surface.

VG-8, 10 (Very Good). *Obverse:* The hair is well worn toward the face. Details at the left are mostly blended together in thick strands. The eye, nose, and lips often remain well defined. Border beads are completely gone, or just seen in traces, and part of the rim blends into the field. LIBERTY may be slightly weak. The 1793 date is fully visible, although there may be some light-

1793, Wreath Type, Vine and Bars Edge, Widest Ribbon Bow (BW-17, S-9, B-12). Graded VG-8.

ness. Scattered marks are more common than on higher grades. *Reverse:* The wreath, bow, and lettering are seen in outline form, and some leaves and letters may be indistinct in parts. Most of the berries remain visible, but weak. Border beads are worn away, and the border blends into the field in most if not all of the periphery.

Illustrated coin: This is an attractive example for the grade, with just one tiny pit near the top of the 3 and some minor granularity.

G-4, 6 (Good). *Obverse:* The hair is worn smooth except for the thick tresses at the left. The eye, nose, and lips show some detail. LIBERTY is weak, with some letters missing. The date is discernible, although partially worn away. The sprig above the date is usually prominent. The border completely blends into the field. *Reverse:* Extensive wear is seen overall. The wreath is seen in outline form, with

1793, Wreath Type, Vine and Bars Edge, Widest Ribbon Bow (BW-17, S-9, B-12). Graded G-4.

some areas weak. Usually ONE CENT remains readable at the center. The border letters and fraction show extensive wear, with some letters very weak or even missing, although the majority should be discernible. Dark or porous coins may have more details on both sides in an effort to compensate for the roughness. Marks, edge bumps, and so on are normal.

Illustrated coin: This coin's certified holder noted that the surfaces are "corroded," a rather harsh term (*oxidized* or *deeply oxidized* might be gentler). At G-4, problems are expected. The date is weak, but most other features are discernible.

AG-3 (About Good). *Obverse:* Wear is more extensive than on the preceding. The eye, nose, and lips may still be discernible, and the sprig above the date can usually be seen. LIBERTY may be very weak or even missing. The date is gone, or just a trace remains. *Reverse:* Parts of the wreath are visible in outline form. ONE CENT might be readable, but this is not a requirement. Most bor-

1793, Sprung Die, Wreath Type, Vine and Bars Edge (BW-12, S-6, B-7). Graded AG-3.

der letters are gone. If a coin is dark or porous it may be graded AG-3 and may be sharper than just described, with the porosity accounting for the lower grade.

Illustrated coin: This piece is toned gray overall and has porous surfaces. The date is gone, but other features on both sides are discernible, making for easy attribution as to die variety.

Liberty Cap Cents (1793–1796)

Striking and Sharpness. The depth of relief and striking characteristics vary widely, depending on the variety. Points to check are the details of the hair on Miss Liberty, the leaf details on the wreath, and the dentils on both sides. Generally, the earlier, thick-planchet issues are better strikes than are the thin-planchet coins. Plain-edge 1795 cents often have low or shallow rims. To determine the difference between lightness caused by shallow dies and lightness caused by wear, it is necessary to study the characteristics of the die variety involved.

Availability. Cents of this type are readily available, although those of 1793 are rare and in great demand, and certain die varieties of the other dates are rare and can command high prices. Typical grades range from About Good upward to Fine, Very Fine, and, less often, Extremely Fine. Attractive About Uncirculated and Mint State coins are elusive, and when found are usually dated 1795, the thin planchet variety.

MS-60 to 70 (Mint State). *Obverse:* On MS-60 and 61 coins there are some traces of abrasions on the higher areas of the portrait. Luster is incomplete, particularly in the field. At MS-63, luster should be complete, and no abrasions evident. At higher levels, the luster is deeper, and some original mint color may be seen on some examples. At the MS-65 level there may be some scattered contact marks and possibly

1795, LIBERTY Not Hyphenated, 5 Touches Neck, 2 Leaves at Apex, ONE / CENT High, Plain Edge (BW-8, S-76b, B-4b). Graded MS-63BN.

some traces of fingerprints or discoloration, but these should be very minimal and not at all distracting. Generally, Liberty Cap cents of 1793 (in particular) and 1794 are harder to find with strong eye appeal than are those of 1795 and 1796. Mint State coins of 1795 often have satiny luster. Above MS-65, a coin should approach perfection, especially if dated 1795 or 1796. Certified Mint State cents can vary in their strictness of interpretation. *Reverse:* In the lower Mint State grades some abrasions are seen on the higher areas of the leaves. Generally, luster is complete in all grades, as the open areas are protected by the lettering and wreath. Often on this type the reverse is shallower than the obverse and has a lower rim.

Illustrated coin: This problem-free coin with great eye appeal was struck on a high-quality planchet with glossy, semi-prooflike surfaces. The reverse is lower, from a shallower die. Some lightness of strike can be seen in the dentils.

AU-50, 53, 55, 58 (About Uncirculated). *Obverse:* Very light wear is evident on the highest parts of the hair above and to the left of the ear. Friction is seen on the cheek and the liberty cap. Coins at this level are usually on smooth planchets and have nice eye appeal. Color is very important. Dark and porous coins are relegated to lower grades, even if AU-level sharpness is present. *Reverse:* Very

1794, Lower Lock a Circle (BW-97, S-70, B-62). Graded AU-50.

light wear is evident on the higher parts of the leaves and the ribbon, and, to a lesser extent, on the lettering. The reverse may have original luster, toned brown, varying from minimal (at lower About Uncirculated grades) to extensive. Grading at the About Uncirculated level is mainly done by viewing the obverse, as many reverses are inherently shallow from lower-relief dies.

Illustrated coin: On this particular die variety the obverse rim dentils are particularly bold, which helped to shield the field from wear. The motifs and inscriptions on both sides are cut deeply into the dies. Some porosity can be seen in the dentils above I of LIBERTY. This coin has excellent eye appeal overall.

EF-40, 45 (Extremely Fine). *Obverse:* The center of the coin shows wear or a small, flat area for most dies. Other hair details are strong. Luster is minimal or nonexistent at EF-40 but may survive in traces in protected areas (such as between the letters) at EF-45. *Reverse:* Wear is seen on the highest wreath and ribbon areas and the let-

1794 (BW-98, S-71, B-63). Graded EF-40.

ters. Luster is minimal but likely more noticeable than on the obverse, as the fields are protected by the designs and lettering. Sharpness varies depending on the die variety but is generally shallower than on the obverse, this being particularly true for many 1795 cents.

Illustrated coin: This coin has attractive light-brown surfaces. The flatness at the center of the obverse is partly from striking, not entirely from wear. Marks are evident, and on the reverse there is a rim bruise near the U in UNITED.

VF-20, 30 (Very Fine). *Obverse:* Wear on the portrait has reduced the hair detail to indistinct or flat at the center, and on most varieties the individual strands at the left edge are blended together. One rule does not fit all. The ANA grading standards suggest that 75 percent of the hair shows, while Professional Coin Grading Service (PCGS) suggests 30 per-

1793, Liberty Cap (BW-27, S-13, B-20). Graded VF-20.

cent to 70 percent on varieties struck from higher-relief dies, and less than 50 percent for others. Examples such as this reflect the artistic, rather than scientific, nature of grading. *Reverse:* The leaf details are nearly completely worn away at VF-20, with slight detail at VF-30. Some border letters may be weak, and ditto for the central letters on later varieties of this type. The border dentils are blended together with many indistinct. No luster is seen. The sharpness of details depends on the die variety.

Illustrated coin: This is the rarest of the three major types of 1793, and it is eagerly sought in all grades. Unlike later Liberty Cap cents, those of 1793 have raised beads instead of dentils at the borders. This one has a dark planchet with some scattered marks, both of which not unusual for this date and type.

F-12, 15 (Fine). *Obverse:* The hair details are mostly worn away, with about one-third visible, mainly at the lower edges. Border dentils are weak or worn away in areas, depending on the height of the rim when the coin was struck. F-15 shows slightly more detail. Reverse: The wreath leaves are worn flat, but their edges are distinct. Border dentils are weak or worn away in areas. F-15 shows slightly more detail. At this level and lower, plan-chet darkness and light porosity are common, as are scattered marks.

1794, Exact Head of 1795, Tip of Lowest Lock Points Downward (BW-101, S-72, B-65). Graded F-12. This style was made later in the 1794-dated coinage.

Illustrated coin: Some lines and contact marks are expected for this grade.

VG-8, 10 (Very Good). *Obverse:* The hair is more worn than on the preceding, with detail present only in the lower areas. Detail can differ, and widely, depending on the dies. Border dentils are worn away on some issues (not as much for 1793 and 1794 coins), and the border will blend into the field in areas in which the rim was low to begin with or in areas struck slightly off center. LIB-

1794, Left Edge of Neck Ends in Sharp Tip, Closed Wreath (BW-61, S-49, B-41). Graded VG-8.

ERTY and the date are bold. VG-10 is sometimes applied to especially nice Very Good coins. *Reverse:* The wreath, bow, and lettering are seen in outline form, and some leaves and letters may be indistinct in parts. Border dentils are worn away, and the border blends into the field in most if not all of the periphery. In certain die varieties and die states, especially of 1797, some letters may be very weak or missing.

Illustrated coin: This coin is sharp in some areas but is lightly struck at the upper-right border and on the corresponding part of the reverse, probably because the die faces were not parallel in the coining press. Note scattered light pitting and marks.

G-4, 6 (Good). *Obverse:* The por-trait is worn smooth and is seen only in outline form, although the eye and nose can be discerned. LIBERTY and the date are complete, although the date may be weak. Dentils are gone on varieties struck with low or shal-low rims. *Reverse:* Extensive wear is seen overall. From half to two-thirds of the letters in UNITED STATES OF AMERICA and the fraction

1796, Triple Leaf Opposite AM (BW-4, S-83, B-4). Graded G-4.

numerals are worn away. Certain shallow-relief dies may have letters missing. G-6 is often assigned to finer examples in this category. Darkness, porosity, and marks characterize many coins.

Illustrated coin: Note the dark and lightly porous planchet. ONE CENT is not visible on the reverse due to the shallow die and striking (such situations can vary from one die to another). Otherwise, this coin is close to VG-8.

AG-3 (About Good). *Obverse:* Wear is more extensive than on the preceding. The portrait is visible only in outline. LIBERTY will typically have some letters worn away. The date is weak but discernible. *Reverse:* Parts of the wreath are visible in outline form, and all but a few letters are gone. Grading of AG-3 is usually done by the reverse, as the obverse typically appears to be in a slightly higher grade.

1794, Bisecting Obverse Die Crack
(BW-95, S-68, B-60). Graded AG-3.

Illustrated coin: This coin is fully G-4 on the obverse but is weak on the reverse, prompting a more conservative grade. It has no serious marks or edge bumps (somewhat unusual for an AG-3 coin).

DRAPED BUST CENTS (1796–1807)

Striking and Sharpness. Most were struck on high-quality planchets, many of which were imported from Boulton & Watt of Birmingham, England. (This high-quality planchet is less predictable for varieties of 1796, and almost never present for those of 1799 and 1800.) Sharpness of details varies among the die varieties. When weakness is found, it is most likely on the hair behind the forehead, on the leaves in the upper part of the wreath, and among the dentils. However, lightness can occur in other areas as well. Many if not most coins of this type are not perfectly centered, with the result that dentils can be bold on one side of a die and light or even missing on the opposite side; this can occur on the obverse as well as on the reverse. Not much attention has been paid to this, and values are unaffected. Certain Draped Bust cents of 1796 and 1797 have semi-prooflike surfaces and can be traced to the Nichols find. Those of 1799 often have rough or porous surfaces and are found in lower grades (the finest is the Henry Hines Collection About Uncirculated coin).

Availability. As a type, cents of this style are readily available, although the 1799, 9 Over 8, and 1799 are the keys to the series, and the 1804 is elusive. A different scenario evolves when considering engraving errors, repunched dates, and recut letters and numerals; many of these varieties are very difficult to locate. The eye appeal of these rarities is apt to be below par. Other years are generally available in Very Fine and higher grades, are well struck (except for some reverse leaves, in instances) on high-quality planchets, and have excellent eye appeal. The quality of lower grades varies, depending on the rigors of circulation. Dark and porous coins are plentiful among coins graded below Very Fine. True Mint State coins tend to be in lower levels, MS-60 to MS-63, when found.

MS-60 to 70 (Mint State). *Obverse:* In the lower Mint State grades, MS-60 and 61, some slight abrasions can be seen on the higher areas of the portrait, especially the cheek, and on the hair behind the forehead. Luster in the field is incomplete, particularly in the center of the open areas, which on this type are very open, especially at the right. At MS-63, luster should be nearly complete, and no abrasions evident. In higher levels, the luster is complete

1807, "Comet" Variety, Small Fraction, Bar Not Connected to Ribbon (BW-1, S-271, B-1). Graded MS-65RB. The famous "Comet" variety, so called from a die break behind the head.

and deeper, and some original mint color should be seen. MS-64 coins may have some slight discoloration or scattered contact marks. A well-graded MS-65 or higher coin will have full, rich luster; no marks visible except under magnification; and a nice blend of brown toning or nicely mixed (not stained or blotchy) mint color and natural brown toning. *Reverse:* In the lower Mint State ranges some abrasions are seen on the higher areas of the leaves. Generally, luster is complete in all Mint State ranges, as the open areas are protected by the lettering and wreath. Sharpness of the leaves can vary by die variety, so this aspect should be checked. Otherwise, the same comments apply as for the obverse.

Illustrated coin: Much *original* mint color is seen on both sides.

AU-50, 53, 55, 58 (About Uncirculated). *Obverse:* Friction is seen on the higher parts, particularly the hair of Miss Liberty and the cheek. Friction and scattered marks are in the field, ranging from more extensive at AU-50 to minimal at AU-58. Luster may be seen in protected areas, minimal at AU-50 and more visible at AU-58. At AU-58 the field may retain some luster, as well. In many instances, the luster is smaller in area and lesser in depth than on the reverse of this type. Cents of this type can be very

1803, Lump Under Chin, Point on Left Wreath Stem, Short Fraction Bar (BW-29, S-247, B-5). Graded AU-50. Small Date, Small Fraction.

beautiful in About Uncirculated. *Reverse:* Friction is seen on the higher wreath leaves and (not as easy to discern) on the letters. Again, the die variety should be checked. The fields, protected by the designs, show friction, but not as noticeably as on the obverse. At AU-55 and 58, little if any friction is seen. The reverse may have original luster, toned brown, minimal on lower About Uncirculated grades but often extensive at the AU-58 level. General rules for cents follow the half cents of the same type.

Illustrated coin: This is the popular "Mumps" variety, so named because of the bulge below the chin. The coin has many tiny scattered marks but is pleasing overall.

EF-40, 45 (Extremely Fine). *Obverse:* Wear is seen on the portrait overall, with reduction or elimination of some separation of hair strands on the highest part. By the standards of Early American Coppers (EAC), if the spit curl in front of Liberty's ear is missing, the coin is not Extremely Fine. The cheek shows more wear than on higher grades, and the drapery covering the bosom is lightly

1803, 3 Touches Drapery
(BW-24, S-256, B-15). Graded EF-40.

worn on the higher areas. Often weakness in the separation of the drapery lines can be attributed to weakness in striking. Luster is minimal or nonexistent at EF-40 but may survive among the letters of LIBERTY at EF-45. *Reverse:* Wear is seen on the highest wreath and ribbon areas and on the letters. Luster is minimal but likely more noticeable than on the obverse, as the fields are protected by the designs and lettering. The ANA grading standards state that at EF-45 nearly all of the ribbing (veins) in the leaves is visible, and that at EF-40 about 75 percent is sharp. In practice, striking plays a part as well, and some leaves may be weak even in higher grades.

Illustrated coin: This is a high-level coin in terms of sharpness, with details perhaps befitting AU-50, but the grade is reduced slightly due to some planchet porosity. The coin has nice eye appeal overall.

VF-20, 30 (Very Fine). *Obverse:* Wear on the portrait has reduced the hair detail further, especially to the left of the forehead. The rolling curls are solid or flat on their highest areas, as well as by the ribbon behind the hair. The border dentils are blended together, with many indistinct. No luster is seen. *Reverse:* The leaf details are nearly completely worn away at VF-20, with slight detail at

1803, Small Date, Large Fraction, Fraction Bar Closer to Left Ribbon (BW-14, S-260, B-19). Graded VF-20.

VF-30. The ANA grading standards are a bit stricter: 30 percent remaining at VF-20 and 50 percent at VF-30. In the marketplace, fewer details can be seen on most certified coins at these levels. The border dentils are blended together with many indistinct. No luster is seen.

Illustrated coin: The wreath is bold, but the high parts on most leaves are worn flat.

F-12, 15 (Fine). *Obverse:* Many hair details are worn away, with perhaps half to one-third visible, mainly at the edges and behind the shoulder. Border dentils are weak or worn away in areas. F-15 shows slightly more detail. Porosity and scattered marks become increasingly common at this level and lower. *Reverse:* The wreath leaves are worn flat, but their

1799, 9 Over 8 (BW-2, S-188, B-2). Graded F-12.

edges are distinct. Little if anything remains of leaf vein details. Border dentils are weak or worn away in areas. F-15 shows slightly more detail.

Illustrated coin: Note the gray, toned surfaces, with very light porosity and some scattered marks. The date is full and clear (sometimes a challenge to find in this variety). Cents of 1799, 9 Over 8, and 1799 are the keys to the series and in the marketplace are often graded liberally.

VG-8, 10 (Very Good). *Obverse:* The portrait is well worn, although the eye can be seen, as can hints of hair detail. Some hair at the left shows separation. Curls now appear as mostly solid blobs. Border dentils are worn away on most varieties, and the rim, although usually present, begins to blend into the field. LIB-ERTY and the date are bold in most areas, with some lightness toward the rim. VG-10 is sometimes applied

1803, "Unicorn Variety," 3 Embedded in Drapery (BW-6, S-245, B-2). Graded VG-8. Small Date, Small Fraction.

to especially nice Very Good coins. *Reverse:* The wreath, bow, and lettering are seen in outline form, and some leaves and letters may be indistinct in parts. The border may blend into the field on some of the periphery. The strength of the letters is dependent to an extent on the specific die variety.

Illustrated coin: This coin was struck from an overused die: note the cud break near the rim on the lower-right of the reverse.

G-4, 6 (Good). *Obverse:* The portrait is worn smooth and is seen only in outline form, although the eye position can be discerned and some curls can be made out. LIBERTY is readable, but the tops of the letters may fade away. The date is clearly readable, but the lower part of the numerals may be very weak or worn away. The border will blend into the

1799 (BW-1, S-189, B-3). Graded G-4.

field more extensively than on the preceding, but significant areas will still be seen. *Reverse:* Extensive wear is seen overall. From half to two-thirds of the letters in UNITED STATES OF AMERICA and the fraction numerals are worn away. On most varieties, ONE CENT is fairly strong. G-6 is often assigned to finer examples in this category.

Illustrated coin: Note the dark planchet, as is typical for this variety, and some light porosity.

AG-3 (About Good). *Obverse:* Wear is more extensive than on the preceding. The portrait is visible only in outline. LIBERTY is weak, partially worn away, but usually discernible. The date is weak, and the bottoms of the digits may be worn away, but the date must be identifiable. *Reverse:* Parts of the wreath are visible in outline form, and all but a

1799, 9 Over 8 (BW-2, S-188, B-2). Graded AG-3.

few letters are gone. ONE CENT is usually mostly or completely discernible, depending on the variety.

Illustrated coin: The obverse, if graded separately, would qualify as G-4, but the reverse does not come up to that level.

CLASSIC HEAD CENTS (1808–1814)

Striking and Sharpness. Striking sharpness varies but is often poor. The cents of 1809 are notorious for having obverses much weaker than their reverses. Points to look for include sharpness of the dentils (which are often mushy, and in most instances inconsistent), star centers (a key area), hair details, and leaf details. These cents are often dark and porous due to the copper stock used.

Availability. Examples are readily available in grades from well worn to Very Fine and Extremely Fine, although overall quality often leaves much to be desired. About Uncirculated and Mint State coins are elusive, and a true Mint State coin with Full Details on a high-quality planchet is a first-class rarity. Grading numbers do not mean much, and connoisseurs might well prefer a high-quality EF-45 to a poorly struck MS-63. Overall eye appeal of the obverse and reverse is often subpar, a characteristic of this type. Cherrypicking is the order of the day, with a wide field open, for most buyers in competition are not aware of differences in quality.

MS-60 to 70 (Mint State). *Obverse:* In the lower Mint State grades, MS-60 and 61, some slight abrasions can be seen on the portrait, most evidently on the cheek, as the hair details are complex on this type. Luster in the field is complete or nearly complete; the field is not as open on this type as on the Draped Bust issues. At MS-63, luster should be complete,

1810 (BW-4, S-285, B-2). Graded MS-65BN.

and no abrasions evident. In higher levels, the luster is complete and deeper, and some original mint color may be seen. MS-64 coins may have some slight discoloration or scattered contact marks. A well-graded MS-65 or higher coin will have full, rich luster; no marks visible except under magnification; and a nice blend of brown toning or nicely mixed (not stained or blotchy) mint color and natural brown toning. Incomplete striking of some details, especially the obverse stars, is the rule. *Reverse:* In the lower Mint State grades, some abrasions are seen on the higher areas of the leaves. Mint luster is complete in all Mint State grades, as the open areas are protected by the lettering and wreath. Sharpness of the leaves can vary by die variety, so this aspect should be checked. Otherwise, the same comments apply as for the obverse.

Illustrated coin: The stars are flatly struck at the left, typical for this variety and generally representative of the Classic Head type. The dentils are off center, again typical for this coin. The eye appeal is superb.

AU-50, 53, 55, 58 (About Uncirculated). *Obverse:* Friction is seen on the higher parts, particularly the cheek. The hair will have friction and light wear, but these will not be as obvious as in lower grades. Friction and scattered marks are in the field, ranging from more extensive at AU-50 to minimal at AU-58. Luster may be seen in protected areas, min-

1813 (BW-1, S-292, B-2). Graded AU-50.

imal at AU-50 but more visible at AU-58. At AU-58 the open field may retain some luster, as well. *Reverse:* Friction is seen on the higher wreath leaves and on the letters. Fields, protected by the designs, show less friction. At the AU-55 and AU-58 levels little if any friction is seen. The reverse may have original luster, toned brown, minimal on lower About Uncirculated grades but often extensive at AU-58.

Illustrated coin: Note the dark planchet, which is typical of the variety because of the copper stock used that year. The light striking at the star centers is normal, and some lightness of strike is seen on the hair, especially above LIBERTY. The dentils on Classic Head cents are nearly always off center on one side or the other—here on the reverse.

EF-40, 45 (Extremely Fine). *Obverse:* Wear is seen on the portrait overall, but most hair detail will still be present. The cheek shows light wear. Luster is minimal or nonexistent at EF-40 but may survive in among the letters of LIBERTY at EF-45. *Reverse:* Wear is seen on the highest wreath and ribbon areas and on the letters. Leaf veins are visible

1814, Plain 4 (BW-2, S-295, B-2). Graded EF-40.

except in the highest areas. Luster is minimal but likely more noticeable than on the obverse, as the fields are protected by the designs and lettering.

Illustrated coin: A very attractive coin, far above average in sharpness, but with some "old oxidation" seen around certain of the elements.

VF-20, 30 (Very Fine). *Obverse:* Wear on the portrait has reduced the hair detail, especially on the area to the right of the cheek and neck, but much can still be seen. *Reverse:* The wreath details, except for the edges of the leaves and certain of the tips (on leaves in lower relief), are worn away at VF-20, with slightly more detail at VF-30.

1810, 10 Over 09 (BW-1, S-281, B-1). Graded VF-35.

Illustrated coin: This is an attractive example that is conservatively graded. The VF-35 grade is not official in either the Sheldon or the ANA system but is widely used.

F-12, 15 (Fine). *Obverse:* The hair details are fewer than on the preceding, but many are still present. The central hair curl is visible. Stars have flat centers. F-15 shows slightly more detail. The portrait on this type held up well to wear. *Reverse:* The higher areas of wreath leaves are worn flat, but their edges are distinct. F-15 shows slightly more detail.

1812, Large Date (BW-2, S-289, B-4). Graded F-12.

Illustrated coin: Note that the planchet is lightly porous, as is often seen on cents of this type.

VG-8, 10 (Very Good). *Obverse:* The portrait is well worn, although the eye and ear can be seen clearly. The hair is mostly blended, but some slight separation can be seen in areas. The border is raised in most or all areas. *Reverse:* The wreath is more worn than on the preceding grade, but there will still be some detail on the leaves. On most coins, ONE CENT

1809 (BW-1, S-280, B-1). Graded VG-8.

is bold. Border letters are light or weak but are fully readable. The border is well defined in most areas.

Illustrated coin: This is a dark and somewhat porous example of what is considered to be the scarcest issue of the Classic Head type, although on an absolute basis the date is not rare.

G-4, 6 (Good). *Obverse:* The portrait is worn smooth and is seen only in outline form. Much or even all of LIBERTY on the headband is readable, but the letters are weak. The stars are weak, only in outline form, and several may scarcely be discerned. *Reverse:* Extensive wear is seen overall. Lettering in UNITED STATES OF AMERICA is weak but

1814, Plain 4 (BW-2, S-295, B-2). Graded G-4.

completely discernible. The wreath is in outline, but still fairly bold, and ONE CENT is usually strong.

AG-3 (About Good). *Obverse:* Wear is more extensive than on the preceding. The portrait is visible only in outline. Most letters of LIBERTY are discernible, as this feature is in low relief. The stars are weak or worn away on their outer edges, and the date is light. *Reverse:* The wreath is visible in outline form but remains fairly strong. Most or even all of

1808 (BW-3, S-279, B-3). Graded AG-3.

UNITED STATES OF AMERICA is worn away. ONE CENT is usually easily readable.

MATRON HEAD CENTS (1816–1839)

Striking and Sharpness. Planchet quality is generally very good for this type. Color tends to be lighter on coins of the 1830s than on earlier dates. Striking can vary. Points to check include the obverse stars (in particular), the highest hair details, and the leaves on the reverse. Dentils can range from sharp to weak, and centering is often irregular. The reverse design is essentially the same as that used on the earlier type of 1808 to 1814, and can be graded the same way. This motif stood up to circulation particularly well. For idiosyncrasies of striking, refer to auction catalogs and pictorial reference guides; the Newcomb book does not treat this aspect.

Availability. As a type, cents of these years are easily available. The scarcest date by far is 1823 (and the related 1823, 3 Over 2, overdate). Cents of 1816 to 1820 (particularly 1818 and 1820) are readily available in Mint State, mostly from the famous Randall Hoard. Otherwise, Mint State coins are generally scarce, although those of the 1830s are more readily available than those of the 1810s and 1820s. Circulated examples exist in approximate relationship to their mintages. Planchet quality and striking sharpness vary in all grades, and careful selection is recommended. Enough coins with excellent eye appeal exist that forming a specialized collection can be a pleasure.

MS-60 to 70 (Mint State). *Obverse:* In the lower Mint State grades, MS-60 and 61, some slight abrasions can be seen on the portrait, most evidently on the cheek, which on this type is very prominent. Higher areas of the hair can be checked, particularly the top and back of Liberty's head, but this should not be confused with lightness of strike. Luster in the

1820, Large Date (Newcomb-13). Graded MS-63BN.

field is complete or nearly complete. At MS-63, luster should be complete, and no abrasions are evident. In higher levels, the luster is complete and deeper, and some original mint color may be seen. MS-64 coins may have some minimal discoloration or scattered contact marks. A well-graded MS-65 or higher coin will have full, rich luster; no marks visible except under magnification; and a nice blend of brown toning or nicely mixed mint color and natural brown toning. Randall Hoard coins of the 1816 to 1820 years usually have much mint red and some black spotting. *Reverse:* In the lower Mint State grades some abrasions are seen on the higher areas of the leaves. Mint luster is complete in all Mint State grades, as the open areas are protected by the lettering and wreath. Sharpness of the leaves can vary by die variety, so this aspect should be checked. Otherwise, the same comments apply as for the obverse.

Illustrated coin: A die crack links the stars, as is always seen on this plentiful variety. This coin is probably from the famed Randall Hoard, as are nearly all Mint State cents of this date.

AU-50, 53, 55, 58 (About Uncirculated).

1819, 9 Over 8 (N-1). Graded AU-50.

Obverse: Friction is seen on the higher parts, particularly the cheek. The hair has friction and light wear, usually most notable in the general area above BER of LIBERTY. Friction and scattered marks are in the field, ranging from extensive at AU-50 to minimal at AU-58. Luster may be seen in protected areas, minimal at the AU-50 level but more visible at AU-58. At AU-58 the field may retain some luster as well. *Reverse:* Friction is seen on the higher wreath leaves and on the letters. Fields, protected by the designs, show friction. At the AU-55 and 58 levels little if any friction is seen. The reverse may have original luster, toned brown, minimal on lower About Uncirculated grades but often extensive at AU-58.

Illustrated coin: Note the medium-brown obverse color and the lighter-brown reverse.

EF-40, 45 (Extremely Fine).

1829, Large Letter (N-6). Graded EF-40.

Obverse: Wear is seen on the portrait overall, but most hair detail is still present, except in higher areas. The cheek shows light wear. Luster is minimal or nonexistent at EF-40 but may survive among the letters of LIBERTY at EF-45. *Reverse:* Wear is seen on the highest wreath and ribbon areas and on the letters. Leaf veins are visible except in the highest areas. Luster is minimal but likely more noticeable than on the obverse, as the fields are protected by the designs and lettering.

Illustrated coin: Here is a well-centered coin. On this variety the obverse dentils are larger (reducing the area of the field somewhat) than are those on the reverse.

VF-20, 30 (Very Fine). *Obverse:* Wear on the portrait has reduced the hair detail, especially on the area to the right of the cheek and neck, but much can still be seen. *Reverse:* The wreath details, except for the edges of the leaves and certain of the tips (on leaves in lower relief), are worn away at VF-20, with slightly more detail at VF-30.

1839, 9 Over 6 (N-1). Graded VF-20.

Illustrated coin: Some light granularity is most noticeable on the reverse. This coin was made by overdating an 1836 die with Plain Hair Cords, otherwise not used on cents of the year 1839. It is scarce in any grade, and even rarer above Fine.

F-12, 15 (Fine). *Obverse:* The hair details are fewer than on the preceding, but still many are present. Wear is extensive above and below the LIBERTY coronet, with the area from the forehead to the coronet worn flat. Stars have flat centers. F-15 shows slightly more detail. *Reverse:* The higher areas of wreath leaves are worn flat, but their edges are distinct. F-15 shows slightly more detail.

1823 (N-2). Graded F-15.

Illustrated coin: This is the scarcest date of this design type.

VG-8, 10 (Very Good). *Obverse:* The portrait is well worn, although the eye and ear can be seen clearly. The hair is mostly blended, but some slight separation can be seen in lower areas. The border is raised in most or all areas. *Reverse:* The wreath is more worn than on the preceding, but still there is some detail on the leaves. On most coins, ONE CENT is bold. Bor-

1823, 3 Over 2 (N-1). Graded VG-8.

der letters are light or weak but are fully readable. The border is well defined in most areas.

Illustrated coin: Note the tiny scratches on the cheek and the many tiny marks in the field. This coin has a pleasing light-brown color and overall good eye appeal.

G-4, 6 (Good). *Obverse:* The portrait is worn smooth and is seen only in outline form. Much or even all of LIBERTY on the headband is readable, but the letters are weak, and L may be missing. The stars are weak. The rim is usually discernible all around. *Reverse:* Extensive wear is seen overall. Lettering in UNITED STATES OF AMERICA is weak but

1831 (N-12). Graded G-6.

completely discernible. The wreath is in outline, but still fairly bold, and ONE CENT is usually strong. The rim is usually faded into the field in many areas (depending on the die variety).

Illustrated coin: Here, an advanced die state caused a cud break at the lower right of the obverse, and cracks connect most of the stars. Note the double profile of the portrait, caused by die chatter during the coining process.

AG-3 (About Good). *Obverse:* Wear is more extensive than on the preceding. The portrait is visible only in outline. Most letters of LIBERTY remain discernible in the headband, as this feature is in low relief. The stars are weak or worn away on their outer edges, and the date is light. *Reverse:* The wreath is visible in outline form but remains

1818 (N-6). Graded AG-3.

fairly strong. Most of UNITED STATES OF AMERICA is worn away. ONE CENT is usually readable, but light.

Illustrated coin: The obverse on its own qualifies as G-4, but the wear on the reverse places the coin in the AG-3 category overall.

BRAIDED HAIR CENTS (1839–1857)

Striking and Sharpness. Sharpness can vary. On the obverse, the star centers can be a problem, especially for dates in the 1850s; less often, there can be lightness on the front of the coronet and the hair. On the reverse the leaves can be light, but most are well struck. The dentils can be mushy and indistinct on either side, this being particularly true of dates in the early and mid-1850s. Flaky or laminated planchets can be a problem, again among coins of the 1850s, in which tiny pieces of metal fall away from the surface, leaving areas in the field that interrupt the luster on Mint State coins. As grading numbers do not reflect sharpness of strike, once again there is ample opportunity for cherrypicking.

Availability. All dates are readily available, with the 1857 somewhat less so (it was minted in January 1857 in low quantity; seemingly not all were released). The delicate-featured issues of 1839 to 1843 are becoming more difficult to find in Extremely Fine or finer conditions without surface problems. Cents dated in the 1850s are usually seen in Very Fine or higher grades. Certain die varieties attributed by Newcomb numbers can be scarce or rare. For issues in the 1850s the differences can be microscopic, thus limiting their numismatic appeal and making them unattributable unless in high grades. Hoards were found of some dates, particularly 1850 to 1856, making Mint State coins of these years more readily available than would otherwise be the case. Grades below VF-20 are not widely collected and, for many issues, are too worn to attribute by die variety. Lower grades are not analyzed here.

MS-60 to 70 (Mint State). *Obverse:* In the lower Mint State grades, MS-60 and 61, some slight abrasions can be seen on the portrait, most evidently on the cheek. The tip of the coronet and the hair above the ear should be checked, as well. Luster in the field is complete or nearly so. At MS-63, luster should be complete, and no abrasions evident. If there is

1855, Upright 55 (N-4). Graded MS-65RD.

weakness on the hair, it is due to light striking, not to wear; this also applies for the stars. In higher levels, the luster is complete and deeper, and some original mint color may be seen. Mint frost on this type is usually deep, sometimes satiny, but hardly ever prooflike. MS-64 coins may have some slight discoloration or scattered contact marks. A well-graded MS-65 or higher coin will have full, rich luster; no marks visible except under magnification; and a nice blend of brown toning or nicely mixed (not stained or blotchy) mint color and natural brown toning. MS-64RD or higher coins with original color range from scarce to very rare for dates prior to 1850, but those of the 1850s are seen regularly (except for 1857). *Reverse:* In the lower Mint State grades some abrasions are seen on the higher areas of the leaves. Mint luster is complete in all Mint State ranges, as the open areas are protected by the lettering and wreath. The quality of the luster is the best way to grade both sides of this type.

    Illustrated coin: Showing relatively few tiny flecks, this is an above-average example at this grade. The stars are weak in areas, as is nearly always seen in Mint State hoard coins of this year.

AU-50, 53, 55, 58 (About Uncirculated). *Obverse:* Wear is evident on the cheek, the hair above the ear, and the tip of the coronet. Friction is evident in the field. At AU-58, luster may be present except in the center of the fields. As the grade goes down to AU-50, wear becomes more evident on the cheek. Wear is seen on the stars, but it is not as easy to dis-

1849. Graded AU-58.

cern as it is elsewhere, and, in any event, many stars are weakly struck. At AU-50 there will be either no luster—or only traces of luster—close to the letters and devices. *Reverse:* Wear is most evident on the highest areas of the leaves and the ribbon bow. Luster is present in the fields. As the grade goes down from AU-58 to 50, wear increases and luster decreases. At AU-50 there will be either no luster or just traces close to the letters and devices.

    Illustrated coin: Some friction is present, but the coin has nearly full luster and outstanding eye appeal. Note some lightness of strike on the stars, as is usual for this variety (and not reflective of the grade).

EF-40, 45 (Extremely Fine). *Obverse:* Wear is more extensive on the portrait, including the cheek, the hair above the ear, and the coronet. The star centers are worn down slightly (if they were sharply struck to begin with). Traces of luster are minimal, if at all existent. *Reverse:* The centers of the leaves are well worn, with detail visible only near

1856, Slanting 5. Graded EF-40.

the edges of the leaves and nearby, and the higher parts are worn flat. Letters show significant wear. Luster, if present, is minimal.

Illustrated coin: Note the light wear on the higher areas, as well as the lightly struck stars, which is typical for the variety. This coin has attractive light-brown surfaces.

VF-20, 30 (Very Fine). *Obverse:* Wear is more extensive than on the preceding. Some of the strands of hair are fused together at the top of the head, above the ear, and on the shoulder. The center radials of the stars are almost completely worn away. *Reverse:* The leaves show more extensive wear. Details are visible at the leaves' edges only minimally and not on all the leaves. The lettering shows smooth, even wear.

1855, Upright 55. Graded VF-20.

Illustrated coin: These coins were gone from circulation by 1861, suggesting that this piece, with its smooth, even wear, must have circulated actively up to that time.

F-12, 15 (Fine). *Obverse:* About two-thirds of the hair detail is visible. Extensive wear is seen below the coronet. On the coronet the beginning of the word LIBERTY shows wear, with L sometimes only partially visible. The hair behind the neck is flat. The stars are flat. *Reverse:* The leaves show more wear and are flat except for the lower areas. The ribbon has very little detail.

1857, Large Date. Graded F-12.

Illustrated coin: This is one of only a handful of this scarce year known at the Fine level. (Perhaps they circulated in Canada?) Most are Extremely Fine to Mint State.

PROOF HALF CENTS AND LARGE CENTS

Mirror-surface Proofs were made for collectors and presentation purposes. These are discussed in detail in chapter 3.

In the half cent series, Proofs are known of certain dates from the 1830s to 1857. Proof cents are known of certain dates from the 1820s to 1857. Most often seen are those dated from 1854 to 1857. Attribution of earlier Proofs, especially for issues of the 1820s and 1830s, is sometimes controversial, this including certain coins certified as Proof. A degree of awareness is needed when contemplating the purchase of any Proof half cent or cent. A good step is to consult with several experts.

Proof-60 to 70. *Obverse and reverse:* Superb gems at PF-65 and 66 show hairlines only under high magnification, and at Proof-67 none are seen. The fields are deeply mirrorlike. There is no evidence of friction. At lower levels, hairlines increase, with a profusion at PF-60 to 62 (and also a general dullness of the fields). Typical color for an undipped coin ranges from light or iridescent brown to brown with some traces of mint color. Except for issues in the 1850s, Proofs are nearly always BN or, less often, RB.

Illustrated coins: The half cent is a very-high-quality coin with a generous amount of original mint color, this piece could be designated PF-64RD just as easily, for some RD coins do not have this much color. Some light hairlines keep this from a higher grade. Excellent eye appeal.

1852, First Restrike, Small Berries, Proof, half cent. Graded PF-64RB.

1855, Slanting 55, Proof, cent (N-10). Graded PF-65BN.

The same die pair used to strike this cent was used to make circulation strikes. John R. (Bob) Grellman Jr., an authority on Braided Hair cents, stated that Proofs were made of this variety, but that it is "extremely difficult" to differentiate certain circulation strikes from Proofs.

How to Be a Smart Buyer

Beyond the Numbers
Reliance on Numbers Can Be Dangerous

The numerical grade for a half cent or large cent is of course important. Generally, an AU-50 coin is in a higher grade than an EF-40, and both are better than VF-20, and much better than Good-4. Such numbers are all that are needed by many buyers, especially newcomers. They desire simplicity, and the Sheldon system, easy enough to understand, seems to give the assurance that a grade, which could be fuzzy if just called Good or Very Fine, is scientifically precise. Certainly, the gurus in numismatics who offer a 1793 half cent as MS-61 grade have determined that it is better than an MS-60, but is not quite as desirable as an MS-62.

In the field of Buffalo nickels, for example, for a scarce issue such as a 1926-D in Mint State, the buying and selling rules involve numbers and numbers only for 95 percent of the buyers in the marketplace. One 1926-D nickel might be certified as MS-63 and another as MS-65. The MS-63 might be lustrous, needle-sharp in its details, and have superb eye appeal. The MS-65 might be flatly struck on both sides (most of this particular date and mintmark are) and be from worn-out dies. The MS-65, priced at multiples of the MS-63, will sell more quickly and attract more attention! Moreover, the "registry sets," so popular on the Internet, glorify a high-number coin, even if it is poorly struck or downright ugly, and ignore a truly rare, sharply struck coin with great eye appeal only a couple of grades lower.

Moreover, there is no scientific or consistent way to assign such numbers. To be scientific a system needs to be clearly defined, so that anyone reading a set of rules will automatically call a nickel MS-63, AU-50, or whatever the case may be. This has never happened. This inconsistency has given rise to the seemingly illogical situation that a grading service may call a coin MS-63 one time, then on resubmission, designate it as MS-64, 65, or 63 again. This happens all the time. As has been said, if you call a cow a horse, it does not become a horse. It is still a cow. If a coin is in a holder marked MS-65, then it *is* MS-65 in the view of many. In numismatics, a cow *can* become a horse!

For you, the preceding state of events is *wonderful!*

Although the going is a bit more challenging in the field of early coppers than it is for Buffalo nickels, Morgan dollars, or Standing Liberty quarters, you will find that in the majority of instances numbers are used when offering half cents and large cents, and hardly anything is said about weak striking, grainy dies with flow lines, or the like.

The secret is that as a smart buyer you can spend $1,000 for a great coin in, say, EF-40 grade and obtain a more desirable (in my opinion) coin than someone who spends $5,000 for an overgraded MS-60 with low eye appeal.

DIFFERENT NUMBERS, DIFFERENT QUALITY

Early coppers exist in a wide variety of appearances. Some are dark and porous; others are light brown and glossy. It is worthwhile to know that this can make a difference in value. Time was when hardly any half cents or large cents were in certified holders. Today, many are, and the trend is increasing. This is neither good nor bad. It is simply the situation. Often, when an experienced collector, such as a longtime member of Early American Coppers (EAC), desires to consign coins to an auction, he or she requests that they be certified. This is not illogical or contradictory. It simply broadens the market and the number of bidders, for it is a fact that quite a few buyers will buy *only* certified coins.

The purpose of this chapter is to deal with reality and at the same time share my opinions as to the *advantage* this can be for you, as an alert buyer.

AT LEAST THREE SCHOOLS OF THOUGHT

In the field of half cents and large cents, there seem to be at least three different schools of thought as to grading early coppers, perhaps ideally exemplified by the Larry and Ira Goldberg sale of the R.E. (Ted) Naftzger Jr. Collection of middle-date large cents, in 2009—a spectacular presentation cataloged by Chris Victor-McCawley and John R. (Bob) Grellman Jr.

Each coin was given *three* grades. First, there was what is called EAC grading by conservative standards (although these standards have never been defined); second there was the grade that catalogers Victor-McCawley and Grellman, plus the Goldbergs, thought to be correct; and third there was certification by PCGS. Although the catalog speaks for itself, the following illustrations may reflect the challenge facing the present author, a committee, or anyone endeavoring to compile a guide of values.

An 1821 cent, Newcomb-2, was graded by PCGS as MS-60, but in a census prepared by Del Bland, one of the best-known longtime copper experts, it was called a Proof. Bill Noyes, another expert, called it "net AU-50" in a published survey. The catalogers, not assigning their own grade, stated, "We are reluctant to say this is a Proof . . . but the look of this piece certainly leads you in that direction."

In the same memorable sale an 1839, 1839 Over 1836 (N-1), cent was graded by PCGS as MS-65BN, by Victor-McCawley and Grellman as MS-63, and by Bill Noyes as "MS-63 in one of his lists, MS-60 in another," according to the catalog.

An 1839, N-5, cent was MS-66 by PCGS, MS-64 by Victor-McCawley and Grellman, MS-61 in another listing, and MS-63 in the Noyes census.

An example of the famous 1794, Starred Reverse, cent provides another instance of grading variations. This particular example surfaced in the late 1980s when it was sent unattributed to the American Numismatic Association (ANA) Certification Service in Colorado Springs by James Evans. It was quickly identified as a rarity. The coin was consigned to David W. Akers, who offered it in Auction '90 as lot 1508, graded at VF-20. It has since been graded by PCGS as VF-25. In the meantime, Walter Breen in his *Encyclopedia* (2000) designated it as "sharpness of VF, but a dent opposite the neck and some handling marks." In 2003 at the ANA convention sale it was graded F-12. *The Official Condition Census for U.S. Large Cents 1793–1839*, by Bill Noyes, Del Bland, and

Dan Demeo (2005), lists it as the eighth finest known, at VG-10 net, otherwise VF-20. Whatever the grade, the all-important stars are especially well delineated on the reverse.

Obverse and reverse, plus detail of the reverse, of one of the finer examples of the famous 1794, Starred Reverse—in this book, the 1794, Left Edge of Neck Ends in Sharp Tip, Starred Reverse (BW-59, S-48, B-38). Graded VF-25 (PCGS), this coin has been ranked as either the sixth or eighth finest known. It is one of relatively few that have all of the stars well defined.

Many similar examples could be cited. All one needs to do is have an auction catalog in one hand and a copy of *Penny-Wise* in another. To these comments I add William H. Sheldon's comment that ownership is worth five points!

Some years ago Barry J. Cutler, director of the Bureau of Consumer Protection of the Federal Trade Commission, addressed a forum at an ANA convention. Sellers of investment coins in particular had been claiming that grades assigned by professional services were absolute. Cutler noted, "I have been a coin collector for more than 35 years and a litigator and counselor on numismatic matters for more than five years." After telling more of his background, he went on to say, "One very thick cloud is the underlying premise that grading now is sufficiently objective to support a traditional sight-unseen market for rare coins."

Seeking to test this, he asked a group of experts who made their living by grading coins to assign their opinions to the same common-date Saint-Gaudens double eagle. The expert opinions ranged from AU-58 to MS-64.

DISCUSSION OF DIFFERENT METHODS

As I see it, and although there are exceptions to every category, old-line EAC grading is very conservative. What I, Victor-McCawley, Bob Grellman, or another active cataloger in the current market, might call MS-63 (not that all of us agree on the same number) might be conservatively graded by someone else under the so-called EAC standards as AU-55, AU-58, or MS-60.

At the same time, a coin that I might call MS-63BN might be certified by Numismatic Guaranty Corporation of America (NGC) or PCGS as MS-65. Some buyers will write out a check instantly at the MS-65 price if so certified, but they might not want to even consider acquiring the same coin if not certified and graded at least as high as my grade, MS-63. However, it could be certified as MS-62, or lower than my grade. Certified grades seem to be quite liberal, on average, but there are exceptions.

Conservative graders have their point of view, and that is fine. Market catalogers have theirs. The grading experts at the certification services may agree or disagree, and that is fine as well. We are all part of the same field.

If you expect *precision* and are not finding it, consider that in such dynamic collecting fields as the world of antique furniture, ancient artifacts, antique jewelry, minerals, the specialty of antique prints, old and rare books, fossils, collectible clocks and watches, documents and manuscripts, and modern art as well as old masters—the list could go on and on—there are *no* grading standards in some cases, and in others there is wide disagreement.

If you were seeking a first printing of Edgar Allan Poe's *Tamerlane*, a book dealer, say a distinguished member of the Antiquarian Booksellers Association of America, might say, "This is a very fine copy, intact, bright, and completely original." If you asked, "Could you tell me if it is EF-45, AU-50, or AU-53?" the concept would seem strange and foreign.

And yet, the combined collecting activity in the fields just mentioned, and the total amount of business transacted, completely overwhelms the volume of numismatic direct sales and auctions combined. Somehow, dealers in and collectors of prints, art, books, fossils, clocks, manuscripts, antiquities, and dozens of other fine arts and collectible fields are getting along just fine without either numbers or generally agreed-upon grading systems.

Although this comment will seem strange to anyone who has entered numismatics with the mind-set that certified coins are definitive, I believe that different grading opinions are *very desirable* for the hobby. I dare say that longtime members of EAC or of the Colonial Coin Collectors Club are as a group more intelligent and more sophisticated than are collectors of certified 20th-century coins. Of course, there are exceptions in both categories. Sophisticated buyers are *forced* to learn about grading, and that is good! You are part of the class that includes legendary collectors of the past, who had to do the same thing.

Certified Coins and Their Practicality

With the foregoing as an introduction, now to the challenges and, yes, the *pleasures* of evaluating early coppers. As to what *you* should do—and this constitutes the majority of EAC members and also longtime clients of most of the auction companies—your task is to evaluate the coin on its own. Study the photographs of both sides, examine it in person or have an agent do so, and if it is certified as MS-66 but you consider it to be MS-63, bid an MS-63 price. This always works. However, if you are super-conservative and consider that a coin certified as MS-66 is really just MS-60, and bid an MS-60 price, the chances are virtually certain that you will not be a buyer. Accordingly, you need to be practical.

The late Richard Picker was a dealer in early American coins from the 1950s until his passing in 1983. He handled many outstanding half cents and large cents, had a fine professional reputation, and enjoyed a wide clientele. He made it a policy *never* to assign a grade to a coin. Instead, he priced each one: "That is a thousand-dollar 1794 cent."

The most practical policy for you is to learn about grading coppers by studying a lot of pictures and viewing coins in person—doing fieldwork. This is a pleasant exercise. Given a few weeks of practice, you should become quite proficient. At the ANA's annual Summer Seminar in Colorado Springs, there is a week-long course on basic grading. Many attendees come with little knowledge of the subject. By week's end they have learned a lot.

Copper Quotes by Robinson

For conservative grading, a very handy guide is a publication called *Copper Quotes by Robinson (CQR)*, by Jack H. Robinson, who is a contributor to the present book (not to pricing but to general editorial matters). Using conservative EAC grading, he has compiled a listing (now in its 19th edition) in which he gives guidelines for grading, not quite following ANA or Sheldon standards, but for Good, having G-5 instead of G-4. For each category he classifies three levels: Choice, Average, and Scudzy. Here are some excerpts of what he says for Fine-12:

> Choice—The color should be an original pleasing brown, the surfaces should be smooth, with no corrosion or porosity, the rims should be free of defects such as dings and/or nicks. There should be noticeable "eye appeal." The piece should not have been *cleaned*. There should be no significant marks or damage to the piece, and the mint should have used prime materials in striking the piece. Laminations, fissures, etc. do detract. Remember, this is condition, not a grade.
>
> There could be marks but they must be very few or insignificant as the Net Grade must equal the Sharpness Grade. This condition of Choice is not intended to specify

absolute perfection, but rather to represent those as close to perfection and still remain within tolerance levels. This condition is not impossible, but [is rather rare].

This excerpt is less than half of the narrative for Fine-12 Choice in *CQR*. Then follows Fine-12 Average with a discussion also of Average Plus and Average Minus. Robinson concludes with an even more detailed discussion of the Scudzy category, of which this is but the introduction, a small portion of the whole:

> SCUDZY—A term, being applied to early U.S. copper, by *CQR*. It could apply to a VF-30 piece that is so porous as to be expected to be called a Net F-12 or VG-10 or G-6, whatever. This becomes an area of negotiation between parties, and anyone who wants to pin this down any tighter is welcome to try to do so.
>
> This area of condition is up for grabs in negotiation, but is generally not as hotly contested as Choice and Average. Everything has a value!

Having "been there, done that," Robinson goes on to say, "there will be many outraged owners of scudzy coins who will feel *CQR* has done them wrong."

Even these brief excerpts from many pages of narrative material in *CQR* demonstrate that, indeed, there is more to determining the value of a coin than just looking at its number. Hopefully, by now you are convinced!

Again, the nice part is that all of this is a *great advantage* for you. Really.

KNOWING THE TERRITORY

In the evaluating of our prices, Jack Robinson's, or anyone else's, it is important to have knowledge of the individual coin itself. A half cent of 1797 of the Low Head variety with Lettered Edge (the variety known as Cohen-3b, cross referenced here as BW-3) usually comes dark and porous, perhaps not quite Scudzy, but usually not up to Average. To find a Choice example with full, sharp legends and devices, and with pleasing color and smooth surfaces, is almost an impossibility. If you were to find one, it might be worth two or three times the price listed!

In contrast, an 1849, Large Date, half cent is *usually* Choice. A Scudzy or dark and porous coin would be a rarity (not that anyone cares). The point is that a Choice 1849 half cent is worth about the price listed. No further excitement.

You also want to know what to expect. There is no use in seeking an Extremely Fine specimen of a half cent variety of which the best grade recorded is Fine. On the other hand, if hundreds of Mint State 1850 cents exist, and if you want to buy one, you will have ample opportunity.

You can see that you've "got to know the territory," as the Music Man said in the Broadway show of the same name.

Knowledge is not optional. It is absolutely necessary! Otherwise it is nearly impossible, except by luck, to acquire choice examples of many early issues. This book is a *guide*, not the be all and end all. The same is true of any other accepted text in the field. Read, absorb, and then do some work in the field. Examine half cents and large cents at shows, look at pictures in catalogs, and check images on the Internet.

Do this, and you will become a knowledgeable buyer. You will become *sophisticated*.

This book will be your introductory map to the territory.

THE GREAT ADVANTAGE FOR YOU!

All of the preceding can be viewed two ways: either as a great complication that is difficult to solve and understand, or as an *opportunity*.

The *opportunity* word beckons, and cherrypicking for quality—examining coins in person and seeking out pieces with Choice surfaces, from fresh dies, and well struck—can be very challenging to do, but enjoyable as well, and it will yield superb coins for your collection.

To me this is a far better situation than having everything automatically well struck from nice planchets and certified in high grades. Put another way, there is a great challenge in cherrypicking for, say, nice half cents of 1808 or cents of 1797, whereas there is no challenge at all in finding superb ultragem MS-70 commemoratives minted last year.

SEEKING HIGH QUALITY
SHARPNESS

It goes without saying, or it should, that a sharply struck coin is more desirable than one that has weak details. Among half cents and cents, many dies were not made with needle-sharp features. In such instances, a struck coin cannot be sharper than the dies from which it was struck. However, most dies were indeed sharp.

Within a given variety, the striking sharpness sometimes varied. This related to how far the top or anvil die came down on the planchet, and how deeply the planchet was struck or squeezed. Did the metal flow into every recess of both the obverse and reverse dies? On some varieties it did not. On others it did. General theoretical guidelines follow:

Obverse. The portrait of Miss Liberty should be sharply detailed. This includes separation of all of the hair strands, this usually being the key aspect. If it is a later type with stars at the border, the center of each star should be sharp and show radial lines. The word LIBERTY should be sharp, as should the digits in the date. The dentils or serrations around the border should be present and distinctly separated from each other.

Reverse. On the reverse the first place to look is the higher relief areas of the leaves. They should be sharp and show veins or details. Next, look at the dentils. Then inspect the lettering and other features.

A weakly struck obverse on a 1797, Berries: 5-4 (only die) (BW-15, S-136, B-7), cent. Notice the letters in LIBERTY. This particular variety can be found weakly struck, as here, or sharply struck. Many varieties do not offer this option, and weak striking is a characteristic of all known specimens.

A sharply struck obverse on a 1797, Berries: 5-4 (only die) (BW-15, S-136, B-7), cent. In the marketplace the certification services and many, if not most, sellers pay no heed to sharpness, which provides ample opportunity for cherrypicking.

A weakly struck obverse on an 1812, Small Date (BW-3, S-290, B-2), cent. Weak striking is characteristic of this variety, although the sharpness and weakness can vary. This cent is from a tired, overused die and shows flow lines and distended stars.

This 1812, Small Date (BW-3, S-290, B-2), cent has some weak stars, as is usual, but it is from an early stage of the dies, and, shows crisp details in most areas.

PRACTICAL ASPECTS OF SHARPNESS

The preceding guidelines define an *ideal* half cent or large cent. In practice, very few coins are ideal! In addition to the preceding, many coppers were struck from tired dies that should have been taken off the press. These show grainy fields or flow lines (streaks) instead of rich, frosty luster. In reviewing several thousand high-resolution images in connection with selecting pictures for this book, I was quite surprised to learn that fewer than 10 percent of the Matron Head and Braided Hair cents were sharply struck throughout, from dies that were not worn out! In contrast, *most* Braided Hair half cents displayed complete details.

At this point it is again necessary to know the territory. For a given die combination the easiest way to do this is to study pictures in standard references and on the Internet. For most of the varieties you will have multiple opportunities. If you review 10 pictures of a given large cent in auction catalogs and on the Internet and all have weak stars, study the situation more closely. If some have two weak stars and others have six or seven, your objective will be to find one with just two or three weak ones. For that particular variety there may be no such thing as one with needle-sharp details. On the other hand, if photographs reveal that for a certain variety well-struck coins exist, then try to find an example.

As to tired dies with grainy fields, this aspect cannot be determined as easily from photographs. However, all dies were fresh at one time. For some dies that were mated with multiple obverses or reverses, all of the examples from a late variety may be from tired dies, and that is acceptable for that variety—there being no other choice. In most instances, you can determine among early coins when a given obverse or reverse was first used. For later coins, most obverses and reverses had only one mate. Accordingly, finding a coin from dies with good surfaces is a realistic objective for the later issues.

PLANCHET QUALITY

Planchet quality is discussed throughout the specialized listings. Generally, coins of 1816 onward are on high-quality planchets, smooth and attractive. Roughness and porosity are not usually factors. For coins from 1793 to the second decade of the 19th century, those struck on planchets imported from Boulton & Watt in England are

The 1829, Large Letters (N-7), cent is typically flatly struck in areas. However, there are choices among offered coins, and cherrypicking may yield a sharper piece. This and the accompanying 1829, Large Letters (N-7), coin were both certified as MS-64. Which would you pick?

Another 1829, Large Letters (N-7), cent with weakness in areas, but decidedly finer than the other in this set. Curiously, overall quality often is overlooked in the marketplace, and a variety within a given grade is apt to be priced about the same, regardless of this aspect.

This 1852 cent is weakly struck from a tired, overused die. The dentils are so mushy that they can hardly be seen, and most stars are flat. However, it has superb original mint color.

This 1852 cent is well struck from a fresh die, has excellent dentils and decent stars, and is quite sharp overall. However, it has no original mint color. In the marketplace this coin would likely be priced for a fraction of the figure assigned to the other 1852 cent shown here.

almost always nice. Coins struck on planchets made from miscellaneous scrap copper or scattered sources can be dark, rough, and porous. In some instances, misstruck large cents had half cent planchets cut from them. Most of these are porous.

There are some general guidelines. Many half cents of 1797 have problems, as do half cents of 1802. In contrast, half cents of 1800, 1803, and 1804 are usually an attractive medium brown, with smooth surfaces. Large cents of 1812 to 1814 are often dark and somewhat porous, while those of 1816 are not. Study of what is available in the marketplace will be a useful guide to identifying which die combinations are often found with problems.

ASPECTS OF COLOR

An ideal half cent or large cent would seem to be one with a brown color, from light to dark, evenly blended. Gray and even black are acceptable for some varieties, especially if otherwise the planchet is smooth and problem free.

Mint State coins often have traces of original color. This is a shade of orange that is usually called *red* and abbreviated on certified holders as RD. The key to eye appeal here

A Group of Very Fine
1793 Half Cents

Depicted is a group of half cents certified in the Very Fine range. In the marketplace, price guides are apt to give a single number, such as VF-20 or whatever. In practice, eye appeal can vary widely. As you review these half cents and the grades assigned, if you were picking one to include in a type set, would you be guided more by the certified number, or would eye appeal take precedence? There are many real decisions such as this to be made when buying coins.

1793 (Bowers-Whitman–1,
Cohen-1, Breen-1), half cent.
Certified as VF-20.

1793 (BW-3, C-3, B-3), half cent.
Certified as VF-20.

1793 (BW-3, C-3, B-3), half cent.
Certified as VF-25.

1793 (BW-4, C-4, B-4), half cent.
Certified as VF-25.

is a blending of the colors, such as red and brown (RB). If one or the other color is blotchy, the result will not be pleasing. For many high-grade Mint State coins with much original color, tiny black or gray flecks and specks are to be expected, especially on coins from hoards. These can vary in their intensity, giving the opportunity to cherrypick examples with these at a minimum.

Many coins have been recolored. In *Early American Cents*, Sheldon gives detailed instructions. The procedure can be desirable, such as when a cent has been dipped by a novice to produce a brilliant but unnatural-appearing color. Recolored or toned to a rich brown, the result can be a very attractive cent. It seems to be the rule that skillful recoloring, call it *conservation*, is not mentioned or even noticed when assigning grades, including by certification services. Conservation can enhance the appearance of an early copper, but the very mention of it is apt to be made in secret, if at all. In contrast, conservation of posters, documents, old masters' paintings, and many other items of collecting desirability is routinely mentioned and is highly appreciated in those specialties.

A Group of Extremely Fine Draped Bust Large Cents

Shown is a group of Draped Bust large cents certified in the Extremely Fine range. As can be seen, eye appeal varies greatly.

1797, Stemless Wreath (BW-7, S-131, B-27), cent. Certified as EF-40.

1798, Style 2 Hair, Small 8, High Top Serif on 7 (BW-51, S-184, B-45), cent. Certified as EF-45.

1802, Lower-Right Serif of T Is Slightly Over Forehead, Berry Directly Right of Top Serif of O of ONE (BW-12, S-237, B-10), cent. Certified as EF-40.

1803, Small Date, Large Fraction, Leaf Tip Under Left Serif of E of UNITED (BW-12, S-258, B-17), cent. Certified as EF-45.

For encapsulated Mint State coins the grade is followed by BN (brown), RB (red and brown), or RD (red). Often a coin that is RB will sell for a significantly higher price, and one that is RD will sell for even more. The secret is that often a lustrous BN coin can be more attractive than either an RB or an RD, another opportunity for cherrypicking.

Unlike nickel, silver, or gold, a worn copper coin can be just as beautiful as a Mint State one! This is part of the appeal of coppers mentioned so many times by writers in the field.

ASPECTS OF EYE APPEAL

Does a half cent or large cent look *nice?* Is it pleasing? Does it have good eye appeal? This is a separate aspect from sharpness of strike or grade. A cent can be needle-sharp but as ugly as a toad. Or it can be lightly struck on some of the stars or leaves but have a glossy, lustrous brown surface so attractive that the coin almost says, "Buy me!"

The best way to learn about eye appeal is to view many coins or photographs of them. This is easy enough to do. A handy rule is that the words *but* or *except* should not be needed as part of a detailed description. Consider: "This is a beautiful 1803, Cohen-1, cent, except for the green spot near the date," or "This Chain AMERI. cent is one of the nicest VG-8 coins I have seen, except for the scratch in the right obverse field."

You can be very sure that when the time comes for you to sell your coins, buyers will notice these "but" and "except" things. Except for rare varieties for which there is no choice, avoid such pieces unless they are available at a *deep* discount. Even then, you might want to let them pass by.

BUYING EARLY COPPERS: FOUR STEPS TO SUCCESS
A SYSTEM THAT WORKS

Variations of the Four Steps to Success have been used in some of my other Whitman books, and reports from readers and users have been enthusiastic across the board. These are the steps that I have used for years. They are easy to follow, and they work every time!

By this point in the book you know what to look for in a half cent or large cent—what to expect, what to avoid, and when compromises may be needed. You are all set to go out into the marketplace, checkbook or credit card in hand, and *buy* some coins!

I suggest that you go slowly in the beginning. It is always easier to buy coins than to sell them. What you do *not* want to do is have a box full of coins that six months from now, when smarter than you are now, you wish you didn't own. At the same time it is human nature to jump in and test the water, to buy something, or a few things. Although auctions are a wonderful way to buy coins, and I have been in the coin-auction business for many years, I suggest that for starters you purchase coins by direct sale, with a return privilege if you change your mind within a reasonable time, say a few days. Most mail-order dealers will allow this. At a coin shop this might be possible as well. In contrast, at shows and conventions, sales are usually considered to be final.

My advice here is to pick common varieties that are available well struck and with good eye appeal. If you like half cents, buy some in the 1850s and not in the 1790s, even if you can afford the earlier and rarer varieties. There will always be the opportunity to buy. There is no rush.

Here we go:

Step 1: Numerical Grade Assigned to the Coin

When you visit a coin shop or a convention, or contemplate a catalog or Internet offering, have an approximate grade in mind for each coin you are seeking. If you would like a half cent of 1807, study the price in various grades, in this book and elsewhere. Determine how much money you want to spend and what grade level is appropriate, whether Good-4, VF-20, EF-40, or some other level. If you are like most copper specialists, or hope to be like them, you might rather have 10 different half cents in VF-20 grade than a single MS-60 for the same price. Most Fine and Very Fine coins have all the features that define a variety clear.

Although at the outset you cannot determine everything you may eventually want to buy, it is good to have a fairly wide selection in mind. Before you start on your hunting expedition, zero in on a dozen or two dozen different early half cents or cents you might like to own.

Once you determine an objective, say VF-20, then ask to view coins graded from Fine-12 to VF-30. This will give you an idea of the differences in these ranges. You may well find that one VF-20 coin is nicer than another VF-30. If seeking later dates, then Extremely Fine and About Uncirculated might be the grades you want, or even MS-60.

I suggest that you only buy coins from a dealer who is expert in early coppers and is recognized as such by his or her peers. Ask around to find some candidates. Usually there are at least several at a convention, and even more through mail order.

Review a given coin and determine if you think it to be a good representative of the grade you are seeking. This will involve using grading guidelines plus some experience you have already had by looking at coins or images of them.

Now, with a half cent or large cent offered in the grade you are seeking, you have a candidate *for your further consideration.*

Step 2: Eye Appeal at First Glance

Now comes eye appeal. Is it pretty? Is it a coin you find attractive overall, without an *except* or *but?* I discussed eye appeal earlier, so I will not dwell on it here.

If the coin is attractive to your eye, then in some distant future year when the time comes to sell it, the piece will be attractive to the eyes of other buyers, which is an important consideration. Now, with a properly graded, attractive coin in hand, you have a candidate *for your further consideration.*

Step 3: Evaluating Sharpness and Related Features

Now comes the technical part. Check the overall sharpness. While one with needle-sharp details would be ideal, perhaps for this particular variety all have some weak stars. If so, this coin is still a "buy" candidate. On the other hand, if this coin has some weak stars and others you have seen are needle sharp, stop your search here and start with another coin. Again, you need to know the territory. This is easy enough to do, but it cannot be accomplished instantly.

If examples from fresh dies are available, do not buy one that has grainy fields or flow lines, streaky star points, or the like. Again, you need to know what is or is not available.

If you are buying by mail order, you can evaluate the coin at your leisure. A good method is to tell the dealer at the outset, "Please send me only coins that are problem free and attractive." The dealer will know what you mean.

If the half cent or large cent under consideration has passed the preceding tests, it is ready *for your further consideration*. Chances are good that you are holding a very nice coin in your hand, one that the most particular member of EAC would be proud to own!

Step 4: Establishing a Fair Market Price

Now, to the price you should pay. For starters, use this book or one or several other handy market guides for a ballpark estimate (unless you are buying a used copy long after the publication date). Most varieties of half cents and large cents are actively traded, and there is no lack of information. This book will be a good start, but as prices often change, it is best to get current values and updates. Be sure to consult the most recently published edition of any book you use.

Also, a coin with a large population will have a price that is more standard than that for a rare issue. Prices for rarities as well as coins that are in exceptional grades can vary widely. However, at the outset, you are not seeking these.

If the coin is common enough in a given grade, with sharp details, fine planchet quality, and good eye appeal, then the market price is very relevant, as you can shop around. For example, circulation strike Braided Hair half cents from 1849 to 1857 are widely available. Further, most are sharply struck and attractive. If the average market price is $400 for the grade you are seeking, then probably a $250 coin will have problems or will be overgraded (go back to step 1 and review it more carefully), and if it is offered at $700, it is overpriced.

Don't be a bargain hunter, for inevitably you will end up with lower-grade coins. Don't be foolish and overpay either. If the coin is worth $400, then probably any price from, say, $375 to $450 would be okay. As to paying $450, or a bit more than the standard price, by this time you have a half cent (or large cent) in your possession that has passed all of the tests with flying colors. Buy it, and now on to the next.

Congratulations. You now own a *wonderful* coin!

Other Elements of Collecting Early Coppers
Die Varieties

Raymond H. Williamson, in "Collecting U.S. Large Cents," *The Numismatist*, June 1949, made this point:

> A person needs very little numismatic knowledge to form a type collection of cents, or even a date collection. But when he seriously undertakes variety collecting, he must begin to study his coins and the literature with careful discrimination. If our collector is imbued with a normal amount of curiosity, he will soon want to know why the varieties differ and this quest for information is very likely to lead to a study of the history of early U.S. coinage methods and procedures—metallurgy, mechanics, sources of metal supply, coinage authorizations, etc.
>
> Such analysis inevitably involves a knowledge of the people of the times and their economic and political thinking. This study and research is fascinating and it is endless in scope. In short, our collector has become a numismatist, rather than merely an accumulator of coins.

Indeed, die varieties, not widely popular when Williamson wrote this, became very popular when *Early American Cents* was published in the same year. Since then, interest has increased steadily. Today, die varieties are the core of collecting half cents and cents.

OTHER WAYS TO COLLECT

Forming a type set of early coppers is a challenging pursuit and can be the doorway to more specialized interests. Major varieties, such as those listed in the *Guide Book of United States Coins* (the Red Book), are a very popular way to collect—they are easy to understand and require only a fraction of the number of coins that a complete or nearly complete variety set would require. Comments about these ways are given in chapters 8 and 10.

Various states of dies, or progressions as the dies are used, can be interesting to collect. In the half cent series this specialty is quite well known among 1804 issues in particular, of which there are many, several of which can be collected in multiple states. For large copper cents, states are also interesting to study and can be found for most of the early combinations. While relatively few specialists endeavor to collect 1793 cents by die state, for certain of the later issues, such as at the turn of the 19th century, this can be a fascinating pursuit that does not require a large outlay of funds. Among early dates many of the advanced die states, with multiple breaks, cuds, and the like, are typically found in lower grades, hardly ever in such preservation as Extremely Fine or finer.

OBSERVING A COIN'S CHARACTERISTICS

"You can see a lot by just looking," observed baseball catcher and philosopher Yogi Berra. And, indeed, when looking at half cents and cents carefully, there are many interesting details to contemplate. The earlier dates especially offer a wonderland of opportunities. Shown here are some variations found on cents, including border treatments, fractions, and other interesting characteristics.

BORDER TREATMENTS ON COPPER CENTS

Plain border (area inside of the rim) on a 1793, Chain AMERICA (BW-2, S-2, B-2), cent.

Beaded border on a 1793, Wreath Type, Vine and Bars Edge (BW-11, S-5, B-6), cent.

Beaded border on a 1793, Bisecting Obverse Crack, Liberty Cap (BW-24, S-14, B-17), cent.

Denticles on a 1794, Head of 1793, Double Chin (BW-2a, S-18a, B-2a), cent. These heavy, closely spaced denticles are among the first to be added to an early cent die. This general style was used in 1794 and 1795.

Long, thin denticles characterize Liberty Cap dies of 1796, as with this 1796, Triple Leaf Opposite AM (BW-4, S-83, B-4), cent. Draped Bust dies also have long, thin denticles, but only the ends of the denticles are usually seen, making them appear to be short.

Denticles at the top of a 1797, Reverse of 1795, Plain Edge (BW-3b, S-121b, B-3b), cent are probably from the same denticle punch as those at the bottom (see related illustration here).

Denticles at the bottom of the same 1797, Reverse of 1795, Plain Edge (BW-3b, S-121b, B-3b), cent probably appear heavier and thicker due to the depth of punching into the die and possible relapping of the die.

Curiously shaped denticles on the obverse of a worn 1797, Berries: 5-4 (only die) (BW-15, S-136, B-7), cent. Compare to the next cent.

Denticles on the obverse of a high-grade 1797, Berries: 6-5 (BW-16, S-137, B-8), cent from the same die as 1797, Berries: 5-4 (only die) (BW-15, S-136, B-7), but now with a different appearance. They are irregular, but this aspect is not as noticeable here as on the other cent.

An off-center striking of 1797, Fused Denticles at 4 O'Clock, Berries: 5-5, E of ONE Directly Over T (BW-25, S-126, B-16), showcases the full length of the denticles. In practice, on a given coin of this era, only the inner ends show, sometimes just a small part, giving them the appearance of being short. As a general rule, cents with Style 1 Hair, used from 1796 through part of 1798, have long, thin denticles.

Long, tapered (or wedge-shaped) denticles on the reverse of a 1798, 8 Over 7, Closely Spaced Overdate, 8 Touches Drapery (BW-1, S-150, B-6), cent.

Denticles of medium length on the reverse of a 1798, Style 1 Hair, Large 8, 1 Lower Than First 0 in Fraction, Second 0 Almost Touches Ribbon (BW-9, S-147, B-4), cent.

This 1801 (BW-2, S-214, B-2), cent shows a new style with short denticles. This became the standard and is seen on most dies with Style 2 hair from 1798 onward.

The border ornaments on the 1812, Small Date (BW-4, S-291, B-1), cent are in the form of pellets or beads.

The denticles on the reverse of the 1816 (N-5) cent are in the form of tabs. With slight variations this style continued until the end of the large cent series in 1857.

Fractions on Copper Cents

Fraction on a 1793, Chain AMERICA (BW-2, S-2, B-2), cent. It seems that the engraver paid little attention to symmetry, as the bar is too long and extends too far to the left, and the digits are different distances from the bar.

Fraction on a 1794, Marred Field, Long Fraction Bar (BW-24, S-31, B-13), cent with an exceptionally long horizontal bar and with misaligned digits.

This crudely executed fraction is on the reverse of a 1795, LIBER-TY Hyphenated, 5 Does Not Touch Neck, ONE / CENT High, Lettered Edge (BW-1, S-73, B-1), cent.

OTHER DIE CHARACTERISTICS

Detail of the reverse of a 1793, Wreath Type, Vine and Bars Edge (BW-11, S-5, B-6), cent. The artistry is of a high degree of excellence and shows carefully formed laurel leaves interspersed with tiny maple leaves (trefoils in the literature) and sprays of berries. The ribbon is very bold, and the beaded border adds a nice touch. This and other 1793, Wreath, cent dies are attributed to Henry Voigt.

Crudely aligned date on a 1794, Head of 1793, Close Straight Date, Reverse Letters Close to Denticles (BW-4b, S-20b, B-4b), cent. A lot of die work for early cents seems to have been done by mechanics and other workmen, not by engravers.

Die rust caused this rough surface on a 1794, Scarred Head, Full Cheeks (BW-16, S-24, B-8), cent.

Amateur die cutting on a 1794, Long Tail on Right Ribbon (BW-20, S-29, B-11), cent. The stems are of unequal length, and the ribbon ends are differently styled and of different lengths.

Prominent clash marks above the hair on a 1794, Marred Field, Long Tail on Right Ribbon (BW-22, S-30, B-12), cent. The obverse and reverse dies came together without an intervening planchet, and leaves from the reverse die were impressed into the obverse die.

Prominent clash marks and a large die crack at the upper left of the reverse of a 1794, Up-turned Locks (BW-30, S-32, B-18), cent.

On the reverse of the 1794, 7 Tilts to Right, Closed Wreath (BW-70, S-54, B-46), cent the ribbon bow is incomplete due to relapping, there is no bow knot, and the two tails of the ribbon seem to be formed differently.

A section of the die became weakened on this 1794, Fallen 4 in Date (also With Button on Cap) (BW-84, S-63, B-37), cent and dropped to the lower left, creating this unusual cud break. The die piece was still present, as traces of the denticles can be seen.

Detail of the reverse of a 1796, Date Hyphenated 17-96, Reverse of 1795 (BW-26, S-93, B-34), cent showing severe damage, including clash marks from the obverse and the breaking away of parts of the die to form cuds.

A rim cud on the obverse of a
1796, Three Leaves Opposite OF,
Reverse of 1794 (BW-47, S-110,
B-16), cent. Being so close to the
rim, the letters in LIBERTY caused
weakness on many dies, and this
resulted in cuds over various letters.

This example of
an 1812, Small Date
(BW-3, S-290, B-2),
cent was struck from
worn-out dies and
exhibits strong flow
lines and streaks.

Early American Coppers

In the introduction to this book I suggested that to be *dynamic* a collecting specialty has to have multiple facets and appeal to many different people. One of the most important is interaction with other enthusiasts. Early American Coppers fills such a need, and in a wonderful manner.[1] This can be a great way to "collect"—to collect friends who share your interest. A good friend is a treasure forever.

The group was the brainchild of Herbert A. Silberman, who as an afterthought in an advertisement of duplicate cents for sale in *Coin World*, November 9, 1966, added this tag: "If you collect large cents, please write. We are trying to start a mail club to trade and discuss this series."

This was late in the roster of specialized groups, as the *Colonial Newsletter* (bringing together devotees of early American coins), the Society of Paper Money Collectors, the Token and Medal Society, and other clubs were well underway, most formed in the early 1960s during the great boom in coin collecting.

William H. Sheldon was given charter membership number 1, although he never took a very active role in the group—an exception being his article, "The 'Big Four' of the Old Copper Cents."

By fortunate circumstance, Warren A. Lapp, of Brooklyn, New York, volunteered to edit a journal. What should it be called? In view of Sheldon's *Penny Whimsy* being the bible of the hobby, the *Penny* word came to the forefront as in suggested titles such as *Pennyworth*, *Penny Royal*, and *Penny Ante*, among others. Lapp later recalled that the would-be publisher William J. (Bill) Parks, of distant Orlando, Florida, came up with *Penny-Wise*, which made its debut with the dateline of February 15, 1967. Seventy-five copies were printed, to be distributed by all of 39 people who had signed up. The rest were parceled out as new members joined, the group reaching 93 members by year's end.

Lapp was the ideal editor. He respected scientific inquiry and abstruse theories, and he published them, while at the same time devoting space to stories by Denis Loring or other contributors about trips to a convention or auction, the hotel and travel accommodations enjoyed (or endured), and the news of the day. *People* were always at the forefront. The publication was egalitarian—no lofty pretensions, no stated requirements of what might or might not be of interest to readers. More and more people enrolled.

In 1972 the group formally incorporated as Early American Coppers, Inc.; EAC it was then and is now. In 1977 it received tax-exempt status from the Internal Revenue Service.

Along the way there were some occasional chuckles, such as when charter member number 63, who had described himself as president of an Arizona university bearing his name, was found to be 13 years old. He was dropped forthwith.

Among the more well-to-do members were Ted Naftzger and Robinson S. Brown Jr., the latter the chief executive officer of Brown-Forman Distilleries in Kentucky, and a collector in many fields. R. Tettenhorst, active today, is in the same category. At EAC meetings they mingled comfortably with the latest new members, including junior members and many for whom the ownership of a Mint State early cent was an impossible dream.

The catalog of the John W. Adams Collection of 1794 cents, published in 1982, included this note about EAC:

> Numbering over one thousand members who are interested in early United States copper coins, particularly large cents, the group is small enough to maintain an enthusiasm and feeling of fraternity, but large enough to engage in serious research and study. Membership is open to anyone interested in the field. A periodical, *Penny-Wise*, is edited by Dr. Warren A. Lapp, and contains news of discoveries, meetings, history, and other items of interest to early copper enthusiasts.

Adams, who seemed to enjoy the lore of history and tradition as much as the coins themselves, was a frequent contributor to *Penny-Wise*, including such submissions as "The American Numismatic Society and Mr. Clapp," "Thomas Harrison Garrett 1849–1888," "The Hall-Brand Saga," "Rarity and Value of Large Cent Literature," and "The Henry Hines Collection."

Other writers for *Penny-Wise* emphasized grading, in particular of certain cents described in auction sales. Bill Noyes and Del Bland were especially important contributors in this respect. Bill Eckberg, Richard Coleman, Walter Breen, Ron Manley, Bob Grellman, and others were apt to focus on die varieties. Pete Smith discoursed on popular figures of the specialty; Tom Reynolds, on market appearances of certain varieties. John D. Wright's scholarship contributed much on the technical aspects of coppers. Mint history and procedures were Craig Sholley's interests. Denis Loring wrote about everything under the sun. His wife Donna, a constructor of crossword puzzles, once created one with answers such as CHAIN AMERI and WHEELSPOKE, terms foreign to a *New York Times* puzzle enthusiast, perhaps, but second nature to any reader of Sheldon's book. A complete list of contributors and articles would fill many pages.

Members voted that Hard Times tokens and colonials could be part of EAC's coverage, as these were indeed "early coppers." Some articles and coverage resulted, but half cents and large cents remained the prime focus of interest.

Lapp remained in the editor's chair through issue number 113, in the meantime contributing many articles, some signed, but many unattributed. He was a fine friend, and every so often a little package from him would arrive in my mailbox with a gift of some counterstamped cents. Going outside of *Penny-Wise*, he contributed an article to the April 1971 issue of *The Numismatist*, "The Yellow Fever Epidemics in Philadelphia and Their Effect on the First U.S. Mint." This won a Heath Literary Award.

In May 1986, Harry E. Salyards, of Hastings, Nebraska, was appointed as editor of *Penny-Wise*. The shoes of the kind, erudite, and sociable Lapp were expected to be hard to fill, but Salyards's editorship has been a great asset to EAC. His style has been unique for any numismatic publication, his message in each issue apt to be completely varied from the last—touching on the psychology of collecting, the vagaries of the marketplace, the latest market fad, and more. Always a delight to read, his message guarantees that when *Penny-Wise* arrives in a pile of mail, it will be the first item opened.

With knowledge that spans many fields, Salyards was the first person I asked what *regula* means, as used in 1916 by Ebenezer Gilbert to describe a certain feature of an 1803 half cent. Nothing from *Merriam-Webster's Collegiate Dictionary*, the *Encyclopedia Americana*, or the Wikipedia site on the Internet offered any clue. "*Regula* is Latin for 'a straight length,' so maybe the fraction bar itself?" was his matter-of-fact reply![2] Next question, please! Really, this was not a surprise to me, as in the past he has copyedited several of my books (a tradition continued with the present text).

Today, EAC remains the focal point of social and information exchange in the hobby and is one of the most accomplished groups in numismatics.

COLLECTING HALF CENTS
THE SMALLEST U.S. DENOMINATION

Copper half cents, the smallest denomination ever made in the United States, were first struck in the summer of 1793, under the provisions of the Mint Act of April 2, 1792. For the first several years, production was extensive—as the Treasury department envisioned that the half cent would become a very useful coin on the American scene. However, demand proved to be less than was anticipated, and after 1795 production fell off sharply. The production of copper coins was a profitable operation for the Mint, unlike silver and gold coinage, which was mainly an accommodation to depositors. In making coppers for its own account, striking a single cent instead of two half cents represented an efficiency. Until 1857 the half cent remained part of the American coinage scene, but production was intermittent, and today many varieties are very scarce.

Indeed, there were many dates that never appeared on half cents: 1798, 1799, 1801, 1812 to 1824, 1827, 1830, and 1837 to 1839. Sometimes, half cents were coined in calendar years, such as a delivery of 12,170 in 1799, but from dies bearing earlier dates.[1] The mintage was limited solely to Proofs for collectors in the years 1836, 1840 to 1848, and 1852. Only 2,200 half cents dated 1831 were struck; all of them seem to have mirrored surfaces but were not specifically intended for numismatists, who in any event were small in number at that early time.

LIMITED USE IN COMMERCE

During the era that half cents were coined, many products and services were priced in figures that ended in a half cent, such as 12-1/2¢, or 37-1/2¢. This was not due to the availability of half cent coins but, instead, was a result of the *silver* coinage of the era: the Spanish-American real or *bit*, valued at 12-1/2¢, was a popular coinage unit, and the quarter dollar or *two-bits* (which became a nickname for the federal quarter dollar as well) was seen more often than were Uncle Sam's 25¢ pieces. A storefront museum in New York City charging 12-1/2¢ admission expected patrons to tender a silver bit worth that amount, not, for example, a United States dime, two copper cents, and a half cent.

Now and again the Mint would get special requests for half cents, most notably an order on May 11, 1832, by Washington Cilley, of New York City, for the immense quantity of 400,000.[2] It could be that this spurred additional coinages for the next several years, but if that order was filled, a large inventory remained.

As was true of most other federal coins, half cents were familiar to citizens in their time of production (1793 to 1857) and were so ordinary that few people stopped to record them. Accordingly, you can read hundreds if not thousands of newspaper articles, scenes of everyday American life, and more, and not come across a single mention of a half cent coin being in a change drawer or purse, or being spent in circulation. What was everybody's business in, say, 1804, is nobody's business now, for contemporary writers ignored the commonplace.

Examples of half cents in existence today tell us that these pieces were indeed used, and used intensely, especially for pieces dated from 1793 through 1811 (after which there was a long gap in which none were made), as today grades such as Good, Very Good, and Fine are normal for such years. However, in comparison to cents, mintages were small.

Half cents of later decades (starting with 1825, when coinage resumed) tended to circulate very little, and today examples dated from the 1820s most often seen in grades such as Extremely Fine or About Uncirculated. Finally, in January 1857, half cents were produced for the last time. However, James Ross Snowden, the director of the Mint, noted a few years later in his book *A Description of Ancient and Modern Coins in the Cabinet of the Mint of the United States* that most 1857-dated coins were held back at the Mint and melted.[3]

DESIGNS OF HALF CENTS

Half cents were produced in a variety of designs, more or less following those used on large copper cents (except for the first year, 1793) and often lagging behind the year in which a given motif was first used on the cent. For example, the Draped Bust obverse made its debut on cent pieces in 1796, but it was not until 1800 that this style of half cent appeared. On the half cent the Classic Head motif was used as late as 1836, but in the cent series the last year it was employed was 1814.

The designs of half cents included these, listed here with a comparison of their dates of use on cent pieces:

> 1793: Liberty Cap, Head Facing Left (not used on cents)
>
> 1794: Liberty Cap, Head Facing Right, Large Head (used on cents from 1793 to 1796)
>
> 1795–1797: Liberty Cap, Head Facing Right, Small Head (similar in style to cents of 1795)
>
> 1800–1808: Draped Bust (used on cents from 1796 to 1807)
>
> 1809–1836: Classic Head (used on cents from 1808 to 1814)
>
> 1840–1857: Braided Hair (used on cents from 1839 to 1857)

WAYS TO COLLECT

While over the years the half cent has been a focus of attention for many serious numismatists, the denomination has never been in the mainstream of popularity. The main reason is probably the presence of many formidable rarities, including the famous 1796 half cent (which exists in two die varieties—with pole to the liberty cap and without pole, the latter an engraving error), the 1831 and 1836 half cents, and the string of Proofs produced from 1840 through 1848 and again in 1852, with no related circulation strikes. The passion of American numismatists to acquire long sequences of dates is thwarted by the many interruptions in the series. The unintended benefit for numismatists is that in many instances high-grade and very rare half cents can be purchased today at prices much lower than those for copper cents of comparable rarity or, for that matter, for contemporary silver coins.

Today, the main market of half cents is from collectors who desire one nice example of each major *design type*. This is a very doable challenge, as all are readily available except for the 1793 half cent, which stands alone as the only year of its design and is somewhat scarce and expensive.

Beyond that, other numismatists aspire to collect half cents by basic dates and major varieties, such as those listed in the regular edition of *A Guide Book of United States Coins* (the Red Book). Still beyond that, specialists endeavor to collect by die varieties as listed by Roger S. Cohen Jr. and Walter Breen in their texts. Some collectors concentrate on a specific era of coinage, such as early issues, or, in some instances, on a particular year— 1804, for example, which yields a dozen die combinations and many die states (showing development and progression of cracks, breaks, relapping, and die deterioration). In addition, there are a few collectors who specialize in collecting error half cents or even varieties by different die rotation positions or die states—1804, Crosslet 4 "Spiked Chin," Stems to Wreath (BW-4), has a nearly unlimited number of die states, for example. Misstruck coins and other mint errors are widely desired.

BOOKS ABOUT HALF CENTS

The die varieties and characteristics of half cents have commanded the attention of several scholars and writers who have published articles and a handful of books about them. In the latter category is Édouard Frossard's *United States Cents and Half Cents Issued Between the Years of 1793 and 1857*, published in 1879. The next notable comprehensive study of die varieties was Ebenezer Gilbert's 1916 book *United States Half Cents*, which was used by several generations of numismatists, who attributed varieties by "G" numbers, such as 1793 G-2, for a particular die variety struck during the first year of issue, G-2 being one of four varieties known of that date. Some old-time collectors still use Gilbert numbers today.

Quietly, a Maryland accountant named Roger S. Cohen Jr. enjoyed collecting and studying this denomination over a long period of years. In 1971 his book *American Half Cents: "The Little Half Sisters"* reached print to the extent of about 2,000 copies, followed by a second edition in 1982.[4] Cohen concentrated mainly on issues made for circulation, although he gave light treatment to the large panorama of Proofs produced for collectors, most notably for the dates 1831, 1836, 1840 to 1848, and 1852. These are classified in the back of the book under "Other Half Cents." Moreover, Cohen sought to illustrate his study with worn examples, often lacking detail, with the rationale that these were what the typical person might collect. This, in effect, was an everyman's guide to half cents. Cohen designations or "C" numbers began to be used, often supplanting the Gilbert numbers that had been popular for such a long time, as the Gilbert book was long out of print. Today, the Gilbert numbers have all but disappeared in use, although sometimes they are cross-referenced.

Jack H. Robinson's popular *Copper Quotes by Robinson*, launched in 1982, and now in its 19th edition, does not list Proofs. The rationale for this is that Proof-only half cents are all very rare, and a nice collection can be formed by concentrating on circulation issues. As Proofs represent a different method of manufacture, this can be an additional rationale. However, in other series, Proof-only dates are collected as part of a complete set. One of many examples is the Shield nickel type from 1866 to 1883, in which the 1877 and 1878 were made only in Proof format.

After losing his original manuscript, Walter Breen was forced to start over from scratch and eventually compiled a masterpiece published in 1983 under the direction of Jack Collins and with the help of Alan Meghrig: *Walter Breen's Encyclopedia of United States Half Cents 1793–1857*. For this book—a magnificent tome of more than 500 pages in length, with superb illustrations and on coated paper—Breen outdid himself, including more minutiae than most readers thought existed! Breen's text introduced "B" numbers.

Almost immediately after Breen's book was produced, many collectors felt compelled to declare their allegiance to either the older Cohen text, viewed as very easy to use, or the almost overwhelming new effort by Breen. Some dealers and collectors refused to use the new Breen numbers. However, in time these feelings faded, and today most people who are deeply involved in the half cent series find both books to be very useful. For the specialist interested in such arcane but interesting byways as striking methods, planchet sources and characteristics, and extensive descriptions of particularly notable individual examples, the Breen book is foundational. The politics of the matter are beyond the purview of the present book.

A later addition to the literature is the grand opus of Ronald P. Manley, *The Half Cent Die State Book 1793–1857*, published in 1998. This text goes beyond Breen and Cohen and concentrates on the various *states* of the dies, including cracks, buckling, breakage, and more, with sage comments on what the author observed. The entire work is illustrated with enlarged photographs. Circulation strikes, not Proofs, are discussed, and for this reason the Cohen numbers are given precedence in the text, with Breen numbers mentioned in a subsidiary role. This essential book was meant to be used with the Cohen and Breen books, not to supersede them.

EARLY AMERICAN COPPERS AND FELLOWSHIP

The bimonthly journal *Penny-Wise*, published by the numismatic society Early American Coppers, serves as a forum for critiques of past studies (the Breen book in particular), announcements of new discoveries, market updates, and various commentaries and articles on half cents, including much information not available elsewhere. In recent years the editor has been Harry E. Salyards, a man who combines intellectual depth with an appreciation for what the public enjoys to create an editorial mix somewhat reminiscent of another physician, George F. Heath, who founded the *Numismatist* in 1888 and remained with the journal through his death in 1908.

The pleasure of collecting is always enhanced by having good friends engaged in the same pursuit. Although the number of half cent specialists is small in comparison to those collecting large copper cents, there are still enough enthusiasts that there is no lack of opportunity to share a prized new acquisition, inquire about a die variety, or simply "talk coins."

9

HALF CENTS, 1793–1857
Varieties, Populations, Values
LIBERTY CAP, HEAD FACING LEFT (1793)

1793 (Bowers-Whitman–4, Cohen-4, Breen-4).

Designer: *Henry Voigt.* **Weight:** *104 grains (6.74 grams).* **Composition:** *Copper.*
Diameter: *21.2 to 24.6 mm.* **Edge:** *Lettered TWO HUNDRED FOR A DOLLAR.*

The 1793 half cent, the key issue of the six major half cent types, is the only year of its design, with Miss Liberty facing left and a liberty cap on a pole behind her head, this cap being the ancient *pilaeus*, or symbol of freedom. The motif was adapted from Augustin Dupré's Libertas Americana medal, created in Paris in 1782 by commission from Benjamin Franklin. Soon after these half cents were struck, with the first delivery being on July 20, the Liberty Cap design was employed on the large copper cent, but with Miss Liberty facing to the right.

Augustin Dupré's famous Libertas Americana, struck in France under a commission given by Benjamin Franklin. This inspired the Liberty Cap motif used on half cents and cents beginning in 1793. This impression is in silver.

The Liberté Françoise medal by Andre Galle, struck in bell metal and issued in 1792 for a reunion of French artists held in Lyon, has a similar motif, obviously adapted from the preceding, on which Miss Liberty faces to the left (as on the half cent).

Coiner Henry Voigt cut the dies for the 1793 half cents. The same motif, but slightly differently styled and with the head facing the other way, is thought to have been used by Joseph Wright for the 1793 Liberty Cap cents.

Not only is the 1793 half cent one of a kind as a design type, but it has the further cachet of being the first year of the denomination and a key date as well—it is elusive in all grades. Accordingly, the possession of an attractive 1793 half cent has been a badge of distinction for many accomplished numismatists.

DESIGN DETAILS

As noted, the obverse features the head of Miss Liberty, facing left, with a liberty cap on a pole behind her head. LIBERTY is above, curved along the border. The date 1793 is between the neck truncation and the border. A circle of raised beads is around the border on both sides a short distance in from the rim. Such beads were not used on half cents of later years.

The reverse displays a wreath open at the top and tied with a ribbon bow below. Among the wreath leaves are *sprays of berries*, the only use of this feature in the series. Around the border is the inscription UNITED STATES OF AMERICA. At the center in two lines is HALF / CENT. The fraction 1/200 is below the ribbon bow.

The 1793 half cent gives the denomination *three times:* as HALF / CENT and 1/200 on the reverse and as TWO HUNDRED FOR A DOLLAR on the edge. The same triple denomination feature is found on several other early copper types. Interestingly, during this decade no mark of value at all is found on certain other denominations—such as the silver half dime, dime, and quarter, and all gold coins!

1793, Liberty Cap, Head Facing Left
Mintage (per Mint Report*): 35,334.*

The 1793 half cent is among the most famous of United States design types, as the Liberty Cap, Head Facing Left motif was made only in this year. Accordingly, there has always been a strong demand for them. The appearance of a high-grade example is always a notable occasion.

Most 1793 half cents are fairly decent in appearance, although some, particularly of Bowers-Whitman–1, have light striking, due to the die, of the words HALF / CENT on the reverse. For BW-1 it is not unusual for a piece to be in, say, Fine grade with all features distinct, except with scarcely a trace of the denomination. Such pieces should be avoided if you are seeking a single coin for type, as enough examples of other varieties occur with full lettering. Planchet quality is another aspect, and sometimes rifts and fissures are encountered. Other half cents may have rim bruises. The use of "BW" numbers is a convenience to readers in cross-referencing half cents within each year-by-year section of the text, as they do not run in continuous order throughout the text.

Somewhat more than 1,000 1793 half cents are estimated to exist, most of which are in grades from AG-3 to F-12. At these levels, many are dark and porous. Cherrypicking of quality is advised. At the VF and EF levels the 1793 is scarce, but enough exist that market appearances occur often. Eye appeal tends to be higher, but there are many exceptions. True AU and Mint State coins range from scarce to very rare. Most of these are very attractive.

The copper for the 1793 half cent was of good quality, giving a pleasing, light-brown, smooth planchet to nearly all examples (in sharp contrast with the next year). Over the years a number of pieces have been variously described as AU or Uncirculated, and some of these are truly beautiful to behold and, better yet, to own. As a general rule, high-grade pieces typically have lustrous light-brown surfaces but little if anything in way of *original* mint red.

There are four die combinations of the 1793 half cent which are of interest to dedicated specialists. These combine two different obverse dies with three different reverses. All are collectible and of about the same rarity and market value, although availability varies in certain grades.

Typical values for 1793 half cents.

1793		Cert	Avg	%MS
		162	32.9	9%

AG-3	G-4	VG-8	F-12	VF-20	EF-40	AU-50	MS-60BN	MS-63BN
$1,250	$3,000	$5,750	$9,500	$14,000	$25,500	$40,000	$67,500	$100,000

1793 • Bowers-Whitman–1, Cohen-1, Breen-1. *Breen dies:* 1-A. **Estimated population:** 250 to 300.

1793 (Bowers-Whitman–1, Cohen-1, Breen-1).

Detail of period after AMERICA.

Obverse: L in LIBERTY on same level as I; L over forehead. Bottom of 7 closer to rim than bottom of 9. No center dot. The bottom edge of the bust is smoothly curved on this variety. *Points of distinction:* The obverse develops rust streaks, but no cracks or breaks.

Reverse: Left branch: 15 leaves, 10 sprays of berries. *Right branch:* 16 leaves, 10 sprays of berries. Period after AMERICA. The center of the reverse was cut shallowly in the die, with the result that even high-grade examples are apt to show HALF / CENT lightly defined, and once wear took place, the inscription often partially or completely disappeared. *Points of distinction:* The reverse in its latest and very rare state has a rim cud over F AME extending only into the denticles.

Notes: This variety exists in Mint State, but it is very rare as such. *Gilbert* (1916) G-4 "Letter L entirely over forehead / 15 leaves on left branch, 16 leaves on right." This is considered by some to be the rarest of the four varieties of the year. However, Bill Eckberg and Tom Reynolds studied the matter and found all four varieties of the year to be about the same rarity, averaging an estimated 300 or so of each.[1] Usually seen in lower grades, although a few EF and AU coins appear now and again. This is the first 1793 half cent variety struck, a variety desired by type collectors who seek first-year-of-issue pieces.

1793 • BW-2, C-2, B-2. *Breen dies:* 1-B. *Estimated population:* 275 to 350.

1793 (BW-2, C-2, B-2).

Obverse: Same die as preceding. *Points of distinction:* A little spur or die defect develops at the upper left of the 9.

Reverse: Left branch: 15 leaves, 8 sprays of berries. *Right branch:* 15 leaves, 9 sprays of berries. Heavy center dot above left upright of N in CENT. Ribbon ends crowd fraction; bar curved downward; 2 high.

Notes: This variety exists in Mint State, but it is very rare as such. *Gilbert* (1916) G-3 "Letter L entirely over forehead / 15 leaves on each branch." The dies are often misaligned.

1793 • BW-3, C-3, B-3. *Breen dies:* 2-B. *Estimated population:* 275 to 350.

1793 (BW-3, C-3, B-3).

Obverse: L lower than I; L over junction of forehead and hair. Bottom of 9 closer to rim than bottom of 7. The bottom edge of the bust is sharply "hooked."

Reverse: Same die as preceding.

Notes: This variety exists in Mint State, but it is rare as such. *Gilbert* (1916) G-1 "Low L partly over hair / 15 leaves on each branch of wreath."

1793 • BW-4, C-4, B-4. *Breen dies:* 2-C. *Estimated population:* 275 to 350.

1793 (BW-4, C-4, B-4).

Obverse: Same die as preceding. *Points of distinction:* Clash marks develop as the die is used.

Reverse: Left branch: 13 leaves, 9 sprays of berries. *Right branch:* 14 leaves, 10 sprays

of berries. Light center dot above upper left of N. *Points of distinction:* Light clash marks develop.

Notes: This variety exists in Mint State, but it is rare as such. *Gilbert* (1916) G-2 "Low L partly over hair / 13 leaves on left branch, 14 on right." This is the most often seen die combination and also the variety most often seen in grades of AU and above. Sometimes on planchets that are slightly wider than normal. Walter Breen writes of "presentation pieces," but elsewhere no information is found about this.

LIBERTY CAP, HEAD
FACING RIGHT (1794–1797)

1794, High Relief Head (BW-9, C-9, B-9).

Designer: *Robert Scot.* **Weight:** *104 grains (6.74 grams) for thick planchet, lettered edge varieties (including all of 1794 and two of 1795); variable weights for other examples struck on planchets cut down from misstruck large cents or Talbot, Allum & Lee tokens (each bearing the denomination states as "one cent"); 84 grains (5.44 grams) for plain edge varieties as well as the lettered edge 1797 variety. The figures given are statutory weights. Actual weights usually vary.* **Composition:** *Copper.* **Diameter:** *23.5 mm.* **Edge:** *Lettered TWO HUNDRED FOR A DOLLAR on all of 1794, some of 1795, and one variety of 1797; plain edge on some of 1795, all of 1796, and most of 1797. One variety of 1797 has a gripped edge with indentations.*

Half cents of this type are remarkably diverse. The portraits are in two distinctive sizes, and planchets are of two different formats, plus some variations. As a general type such coins are readily available, the most often seen being pieces dated 1795. The quality of striking and the appearance of surviving pieces is subject to wide variation. Overall, these factors create a very interesting section within the half cent denomination.

TALBOT, ALLUM & LEE

In 1795 the Mint experienced a shortage of copper, and to satisfy the demand the Mint purchased many thousands of undistributed cent-size advertising tokens minted by Peter Kempson & Co., Birmingham, England, and imported them into America by the New York City firm of Talbot, Allum & Lee. Dated 1794 and 1795, these bore the image of the standing goddess of Commerce on the obverse and a fully rigged sailing ship on the reverse. Each was denominated "ONE CENT."

At the Mint, half cent planchets were cut from them, much as a cookie cutter might take a circle of dough from a larger piece. Fed into the coining press, the planchets became half cents, but in many instances the parts of the original design of the token can still be seen in the fields or even on the edges, creating interesting undertypes for collectors. Some half cents of 1795 and 1797 show this feature.

DESIGN DETAILS

The type of 1794 with *Large* Liberty Head Facing Right, Liberty Cap behind head, is very distinctive. As to whether it should be considered as a basic type, or simply as a sub-type to be included with the issues from 1795 to 1797, as here, is a matter of opinion, and you can make your own decision.

The obverse of the 1794 half cent features Miss Liberty with a *large* Liberty Head facing right, with a liberty cap on a pole behind her head. LIBERTY is above, curved along the border. The date is between the neck truncation and the border. Portrait styles vary, and the regular-edition *Guide Book of United States Coins* lists a "High Relief" head and a "Normal Head" for 1794. These are considered distinctive styles within the present type. It is thought that Robert Scot was the engraver of the portrait and wreath hubs.

The half cents 1795 to 1797 have a *small* Liberty Head facing right, but are otherwise similar in general style to the 1794. Unlike the type of 1794, half cents of the years 1795 to 1797, with small head, have a cameo-like appearance, with the portrait surrounded by an especially large area of open field. On certain varieties, the denticles are especially large and prominent, nicely framing the interior features. Engraving may have been by John Smith Gardner, an assistant to Robert Scot, or may have been by or shared with Scot.

1794, Liberty Cap, Large Head Facing Right
Mintage (per Mint Report): 81,600.

Half cents of this date are a distinct type, Liberty Cap, Large Head Facing Right. The key is *Large*, as the later years of this general style (1795 to 1797) all have a Small Head. Five different obverse dies and a like number of reverse dies were made, yielding nine different combinations. The obverse dies can vary widely in their appearance, some with the head in high relief, others with a low-relief portrait. The use of hub punches was in its beginning stages. The boldness of the letters and numerals can vary as well.

The reverse wreaths fall into two main categories: What Walter Breen calls the Heavy Wreath is the earlier style and is more "solid" in its appearance. The Cent Type Wreath is lighter and somewhat delicate; berries and stems were added by hand, as were some leaves, giving differences in placement among the various dies. Lettering was punched in by hand as well, as were the fraction details.

Certain varieties exist with both large and small edge letters, designated respectively as "a" and "b" in the text below, following the method of Roger S. Cohen Jr. This does not necessarily reflect the order in which they were struck.

Half cents of 1794 have a personality all of their own. Generally, they were struck on rough planchets, granular, and—if not dark and spotted at the time of use—certainly with enough metallic imperfections that such pieces quickly toned to gray or even black. Although there are some exceptions, the typical half cent of 1794 is rather rustic in its appearance, not particularly well struck, and somewhat porous. Finding one with nice eye appeal can be a challenge—much more so than for the 1793.

Not many 1794 half cents have survived in higher grades. Typically encountered are pieces in Good, VG, and Fine, not often VF, and hardly ever EF or finer. No matter what the grade, aesthetic appeal is apt to be low—a factor that numismatists have to live with, although some examples are nicer than others. However, you do have the market advantage that not everyone considers the 1794 to be a separate type, and, beyond that, relatively few non-specialists are aware of the rarity of pieces with good eye appeal.

Mint State coins are exceedingly rare—far rarer than the famous 1793, although this is not well known. Grading is apt to be liberal.

Typical values for 1794 half cents.
Rare varieties may be worth more.

1794		Cert	Avg	%MS
		195	34.4	10%

AG-3	G-4	VG-8	F-12	VF-20	EF-40	AU-50	MS-60BN	MS-63BN
$300	$500	$825	$1,550	$2,750	$6,100	$14,250	$24,000	$46,250

1794 • BW-1a and b, C-1a and b, B-1a and b. *Breen dies:* 1-A. **Estimated population:** BW-1a: 350 to 500; BW-1b: 23 to 30.

1794 (BW-1a, C-1a, B-1a).

Detail of widely spaced date.

Obverse: Date low, double punched, and very widely spaced, far below neck, giving this die a very distinctive appearance. The 4 much closer to denticles than to portrait. The pole is weak and is distant from denticles. Head high in field, especially the bottom of the hair.

Reverse: Heavy Wreath. 15 leaves on each branch. 4 berries on left branch and 4 on the right. *Points of distinction:* On a few pieces swelling is seen at the top of the wreath.

Notes: BW-1a occurs in Mint State, and is rare as such. VF or so is the highest grade known for BW-1b. *Gilbert* (1916) G-9 (without reference to edge lettering) "Head large and high—date very low / 8 berry reverse. . . . In Dr. Maris' description of half cents of this year he includes one variety that would be a combination of my Obverse No. 6 with Reverse of No. 9. Neither Steigerwalt nor Frossard mention this variety, and it is unknown to me." Large or small edge letters, designated a or b. R. Tettenhorst found that the space between the R and E of HUNDRED is much greater on the small letters issues than on the large.[2] It is not unusual for this variety to be dark or to be slightly greenish. Most are in lower grades.

1794 • BW-2a and b, C-2a and b, B-2a and b. *Breen dies:* 2-B. **Estimated population:** BW-2a: 16 to 20; BW-2b: 400 to 700.

1794 (BW-2, C-2, B-2).

Obverse: Date low and closely spaced with 94 closer than the other numerals; 1 below neck (on all other dies it is below hair); 4 slightly closer to denticles than to portrait. Pole bold and nearly touches a denticle. Portrait centered in the field. *Points of distinction:* A faint crack is seen at the tops of ERTY. Clash marks later develop, then multiply as their intensity increases.

Reverse: Heavy Wreath. 15 leaves on each branch, or 16 if you include the merest trace of leaves at each side of HALF. 5 berries on left branch and 4 on the right, or 5 if you include the merest trace of one protruding slightly from a leaf below the first A of AMERICA.

Notes: VF and EF are the highest grades known for BW-2a, and rare so fine. EF and AU are the highest grades known for BW-2b. *Gilbert* (1916) G-5 (without reference to edge lettering) "Large head, 7 of date low / 9 berry reverse." Large or small edge letters, designated a or b. This variety has a bold, pleasing portrait, well placed in the field. On later die states (Manley 2.0 and 3.0) prominent clash marks are seen in the field in front of the portrait, showing leaves from the wreath on the reverse.

1794 • BW-3a and b, C-5, B-3a and b. *Breen dies:* 3-C. **Estimated population:** BW-3a: 6 to 10;[3] BW-3b: 110 to 140.

1794 (BW-3b, C-5, B-3b).

Obverse: Date distinctively spaced as 1 79 4; low and closely spaced with 79 closer than the other numerals; 4 slightly closer to denticles than to portrait. Pole bold and nearly touches a denticle. Portrait centered in the field. (Compare to BW-1) *Points of distinction:* Perfect die examples are followed by examples with clash marks beneath the chin and in front of the throat.

Reverse: Heavy Wreath. 16 leaves on each branch. 5 berries on left branch (including one hardly visible at the first T in STATES) and 6 on the right.

Notes: Fine or so is the highest grade known for BW-3a. AU is the highest grade known for BW-3b. *Gilbert* (1916) G-8 (without reference to edge lettering) "Large head, 79 about level at top and close together / 11 berries." Large or small edge letters, designated a or b. On this variety the portrait is in especially high relief with luxuriant waves of hair and a rounded cheek, very attractive. The reverse is equally nicely styled, with a bold wreath enclosing and also within delicate letters.

1794 • BW-4a and b, C-6, B-4a and b. *Breen dies:* 3-D. **Recorded population:** BW-4a: 1. **Estimated population:** BW-4b: 30 to 40.

1794 (BW-4b, C-6, B-4b).

Obverse: Same die as preceding. *Points of distinction:* Clash marks are present, as with the earlier use.

Reverse: Cent Type Wreath. 14 leaves on left branch, 18 on the right. Leaves at apex of wreath are distant from each other. Tip of second highest leaf on left is under A.

Notes: Gilbert (1916) G-6 (without reference to edge lettering) "Large head, 79 about level at top and close together / 12 berries, leaf touching left stand of H." Large or small edge letters, designated a or b. The only known example of BW-4a has been graded from VG cleaned to simply Fine. It is believed to have first appeared in Abe Kosoff's sale of the Lehrman Collection, 1963, lot 50. In the sale of the Roger S. Cohen, Jr. Collection by Superior, 1992, it was graded VG-8. The piece has been cleaned and shows extensive friction marks.[4] The highest grade known for BW-4b is EF.

1794 • BW-5a and b, C-3a and b, B-5a and b. *Breen dies:* 3-E. **Estimated population:** BW-5a: 5 to 8; BW-5b: 55 to 70.

1794 (BW-5a, C-3a, B-5a).

Detail of clash marks in front of the neck and mouth, showing outlined leaves from the wreath on the reverse.

Obverse: Same die as preceding.

Reverse: Cent Type Wreath. 14 leaves on left branch, 18 on the right. Leaves at apex of wreath touch or nearly touch. Second-highest leaf on left is under T. *Points of distinction:* The obverse is first seen with clash marks around the portrait, most notably in front of the neck. Later, mounding is seen to the right of 4.

Notes: AU is the highest grade known for BW-5a. VF is the highest grade known for BW-5b. *Gilbert* (1916) G-7 (without reference to edge lettering) "Large head, 79 about level at top and close together / 12 berries—Leaf nearly touching top of H and another the top of T." Large or small edge letters, designated a or b.

1794 • BW-6a and b, C-4a and b, B-6a and b. *Breen dies:* 4-E. **Estimated population:** BW-6a: 10 to 12; BW-6b: 900 to 1,100.

1794 (BW-6b, C-4b, B-6b).

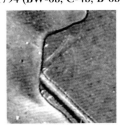

Detail of clash marks below the chin and in front of the neck.

Obverse: Date high and heavy, 9 low and leans left, 4 close to neck. Cap very close to denticles. Pole heavy and touches denticles. *Points of distinction:* Clash marks are seen below the chin and in front of the neck. Later, mounding begins from the left of the date.

Reverse: Same die as preceding. *Points of distinction:* There is a crack from the denticles between TE of UNITED and to the leaves. Later, another crack is seen through M of AMERICA.

Notes: Fine is the highest grade known for BW-6a. BW-6b exists in Mint State, but is very rare as such. *Gilbert* (1916) G-4 (without reference to edge lettering) "Large head—9 low / 12 berries with a leaf nearly touching top of H." Large or small edge letters, designated a or b. Concerning the "a" variety: eight are known to Ronald P. Manley. This variety was discovered by Commodore W.C. Eaton in 1921, after which the next was publicized by W.K. Raymond in 1973.[5] The finest is Fine. BW-6b is considered the second most common variety of the year.[6]

1794, High Relief Head • BW-7, C-7, B-7. *Breen dies:* 5-D. **Estimated population:** 35 to 50.

1794, High Relief Head (BW-7, C-7, B-7).

Detail of the date.

Obverse: Head in high relief, more so than for any other obverse die. This is Breen's *High Relief Head.* The cap is spaced away from the denticles. The 4 very nearly touches the neck. The pole is distant from denticles and terminates about even with the neck tip. *Points of distinction:* Because of the high relief, the highest details are sometimes weakly struck. Light clash marks are seen.

Reverse: Same as reverse of BW-4. *Points of distinction:* A crack is seen from the denticles through the right side of E of UNITED into the wreaths, causing a bulging at the same time.

Notes: Two are in Mint State, one of which is in the British Museum. *Gilbert* (1916) G-2 (without reference to edge lettering) "Small head, 4 nearly touching bust / 12 berries—Leaf touches left stand of H." Small edge letters. Most are in lower grades.

1794, High Relief Head • BW-8, C-8, B-8. *Breen dies:* 5-C. **Estimated population:** 45 to 60.

1794, High Relief Head (BW-8, C-8, B-8).

Obverse: Same die as preceding. *Points of distinction:* Delicate clash marks can be seen, mainly between the Liberty Cap and the hair.

Reverse: Same as reverse of BW-3. *Points of distinction:* Clash marks at the left. Later, on the reverse a crack develops from the denticles through the second T of STATES to the wreath, later still going farther to the right.

Notes: EF is the highest grade known, but examples are very rare at this level. *Gilbert* (1916) G-3 "Small head, 4 nearly touching bust / 11 berry reverse." Small edge letters. Most are in lower grades. An EF coin is exceptional.

1794, High Relief Head • BW-9, C-9, B-9. *Breen dies:* 5-B. **Estimated population:** 700 to 900.

1794, High Relief Head (BW-9, C-9, B-9).

Obverse: Same die as preceding. *Points of distinction:* The pole is usually rather light. First seen with no crack, but with light clash marks. In a slightly later state a crack is seen through the top of IBERTY. Another crack develops from the rim at the lower left, extending to the hair.

Reverse: Same as reverse of BW-4. *Points of distinction:* On the reverse a rim cud affecting only the denticles is to the lower left of the fraction.

Notes: Rare in Mint State, but among 1794 half cents this is the variety most often seen at this level. *Gilbert* (1916) G-1 "Small head—4 nearly touches bust / 9 berry reverse." Small edge letters. Comment from R. Tettenhorst: "Among the 1794, High Relief Head (BW-9), and 1795, Pole to Cap, Lettered Edge (BW-1), and 'Punctuated Date' (1,795), Lettered Edge (BW-2), half cents there exist a few thin-planchet lettered-edge specimens. I have a speculation that these may have been test strikings to see if the appearance of the new thinner coins was satisfactory. What led to my thought was the observation that these thinner-planchet lettered-edge specimens exist only on the varieties struck after Congress approved the reduction in weight. Some 1794 BW-9s are believed to have been struck in 1795, after the approval. I do not know of any thin-planchet specimens of other 1794-dated varieties. This likely led to the Mint finding that the obverse and reverse impressions were quite acceptable, but the edge was too thin to support the lettering without running into the top and bottom of the rim to create unsightly nicks."[7] BW-9 is the most often seen variety of the year. The high relief of the head has made this an especially popular coin. Most are in lower grades. Any coin AU or finer is a rarity.

1795, Liberty Cap, Small Head Facing Right
Mintage (per Mint Report*): 139,690.*

Half cents of 1795 feature the new small Liberty Head. The engraver is unknown. It may have been Robert Scot, or there is the possibility (per Walter Breen) that an assistant, John Smith Gardner, did the work. The result was very pleasing, yielding a small portrait surrounded by a wide field and framed by prominent denticles. This style was continued through 1797.

The reported circulation-strike mintage of 139,690 for *all* 1795 half cents (lettered and plain edge varieties) may include some coins of earlier dates. It is thought that the mintage of the lettered edge pieces was 25,600. The numismatic availability of the 1795 Lettered Edge half cents is probably about a third of the total, with the Plain Edge varieties accounting for the remaining two-thirds.

The first half cents of this year were struck on thick planchets, with lettered a edge, and an authorized weight of 104 grains. Soon, the standard was changed to 84 grains, resulting in a thinner planchet, now with plain edge. However, some plain-edge half cents were struck on thick, heavy planchets cut down from misstruck large cents. Accordingly, 1795-dated half cents can be quickly grouped into two major categories: Lettered Edge and Plain Edge. Within these categories are die varieties including the popular "Punctuated Date," which has a small, comma-like die flaw after the 1, giving the fanciful appearance of 1,795.

As a rule of thumb, the Lettered Edge half cents, the rarer of the two styles, are much harder to find well struck and on smooth planchets. Many are porous and rough. In contrast, the Pole to Cap and Punctuated Date varieties of Plain Edge are often seen with superb eye appeal. The No Pole to Cap variety is from a ground-down or resurfaced die that originally had a pole. These are often poorly struck regarding details of the design or have other problems, including off-center and double impressions.

Finding a high quality 1795, Lettered Edge, will be a challenge. In contrast, enough high-grade Plain Edge examples have survived that EF, AU, or even Mint State pieces can be found with some looking.

1795, Pole to Cap, Lettered Edge • BW-1, C-1, B-1. *Breen dies:* 1-A. *Estimated population:* 1,000 to 1,500.

1795, Pole to Cap, Lettered
Edge (BW-1, C-1, B-1).

Detail of erroneous I in date.

Obverse: Date as I795 with I instead of 1 punch used for date, an engraving error unique among early copper coins.

Reverse: 17 leaves on left branch, 16 on the right. 4 berries on left branch, 4 on the right, with berries to each side of the ribbon bow. Tip of lowest outside-left leaf opposite bottom of U of UNITED. Leaf tip under upright of second T in STATES. *Points of distinction:* On later states there is slight mounding at AME.

Notes: This variety exists in Mint State, but is very rare at this level. *Gilbert* (1916) G-1 "Lettered edge with pole / 8 berries, 4 on each branch" Gilbert inadvertently lists the same variety as G-2, as preceding, but with a *plain* edge. Comment by R. Tettenhorst: "He is wrong about this, since all examples are simply specimens of BW-1 with the edge lettering ground off, outside of the Mint, possibly to be passed off as specimens of G-2."[8] Regarding thick (usual) and thin planchets for BW-1, see commentary by R. Tettenhorst under 1794, High Relief Head (BW-9). This variety is usually seen in lower grades, but AU and Mint State coins are occasionally offered.

1795, Pole to Cap, Lettered Edge		Cert	Avg	%MS
		56	32.7	13%

AG-3	G-4	VG-8	F-12	VF-20
$290	$490	$800	$1,500	$2,750

EF-40	AU-50	MS-60BN	MS-63BN
$6,000	$12,000	$17,000	$24,000

1795, "Punctuated Date" (1,795), Lettered Edge • BW-2a and b, C-2a, B-2a. *Breen dies:* 2-A. *Estimated population:* 400 to 600.

1795, "Punctuated Date" (1,795),
Lettered Edge (BW-2, C-2a, B-2a).

Obverse: Die flaw between 1 and 9 gives the appearance of 1,795. *Points of distinction:* A slight mounding is seen.

Reverse: Same die as preceding. *Points of distinction:* A slight mounding at AME is present. Later mounding occurs at ER of AMERICA, and clash marks are added near the top.

Notes: This variety exists in Mint State, but is extremely rare at this level. *Gilbert* (1916) G-3 "Lettered edge with pole, punctuated date / 8 berry reverse." Large (a) and small (b) edge lettering. Regarding thick (usual) and thin planchets for BW-2, see commentary by R. Tettenhorst under 1794, High Relief Head (BW-9). Most are in lower grades.

1795, "Punctuated Date" (1,795), Lettered Edge		Cert	Avg	%MS
		5	19.2	0%

AG-3	G-4	VG-8	F-12
$360	$540	$800	$1,500

VF-20	EF-40	AU-50	MS-60BN
$3,000	$6,500	$12,000	$25,000

1795, "Punctuated Date" (1,795), Plain Edge • BW-3, C-2b, B-2b. *Breen dies:* 2-A. **Estimated population:** 18 to 24.

Obverse: Same die as preceding.

Reverse: Same die as preceding.

Notes: This variety exists in AU and Mint State, though both are exceedingly rare. *Gilbert* (1916) G-8 "Plain edge with pole, punc-tuated date / 8 berry reverse. . . . Struck on thin planchet with *plain* edge. It is believed to be excessively rare as but one specimen is known." Typical grades are About Good to Very Good. Priced after BW-5.

1795, "Punctuated Date" (1,795), Plain Edge • BW-4, C-3, B-3. *Breen dies:* 2-B. **Estimated population:** 40 to 55.

1795, "Punctuated Date" (1,795),
Plain Edge (BW-4, C-3, B-3).

Detail of the comma-like flaw in the date. Also
note that the 5 is from a much smaller font.
Often, matching the sizes of numerals was
overlooked in making dies for early half cents.

Obverse: Same die as preceding.

Reverse: 17 leaves on left branch, 16 on the right. 5 berries on left branch, 4 on the right, with berries to each side of the ribbon bow. Tip of lowest outside-left leaf opposite bottom of U of UNITED. No leaf tip under upright of second T of STATES. *Points of distinction:* This variety can be found with a perfect die, but mounding develops at the center, causing the letters AL and EN to become weak.

Notes: VF and EF are the highest grades known, the latter extremely rare. *Gilbert* (1916) G-7 "Plain edge with pole, punctu-ated date / 2 leaves and 2 berries under first A in AMERICA. . . . Excessively rare variety, but two specimens actually known." Walter Breen observed that "Gilbert's description was confusing." Low grades are par for this variety, About Good to Fine, although a few exist in higher grades. Priced after BW-5.

1795, "Punctuated Date" (1,795), Plain Edge • BW-5, C-4, B-4. *Breen dies:* 2-C. **Estimated population:** 300 to 500.

1795, "Punctuated Date" (1,795), Plain Edge
(BW-5, C-4, B-4). Overly long dentils are
a characteristic of certain half cent dies of
1795 to 1797. On this example, HALF CENT
is lightly struck due to the requirement for
metal flow to fill the obverse portrait.

Obverse: Same die as preceding. *Points of distinction:* There is a slight mounding in the right field. This increases as the die continues in use.

Reverse: 17 leaves on left branch, 16 on the right. 3 berries on left branch, 4 on the right, none to each side of the ribbon bow. Tip of lowest outside-left leaf opposite center of N of UNITED. Lowest outside leaf on right is opposite C of AMERICA. *Points of distinction:* At first the die is bulged, then a diagonal crack develops. Usually weakly struck at the center.

Notes: This variety exists in Mint State, but is very rare at this level. *Gilbert* (1916) G-4 "Plain edge with pole—punctuated dates / 7 berry reverse." This variety exists across the board grade-wise. AU and Mint State coins are usually very attractive.

1795, "Punctuated Date" (1,795), Plain Edge		Cert	Avg	%MS
		6	32.2	17%

AG-3	G-4	VG-8	F-12	VF-20
$250	$400	$625	$1,200	$1,900

EF-40	AU-50	MS-60BN	MS-63BN
$4,800	$9,500	$14,000	$23,000

1795, No Pole to Cap, Plain Edge • BW-6a and b, C-5a and b, B-5a and b

(thin and thick planchets). *Breen dies:* 3-C. *Estimated population:* BW-6a: 500 to 800; BW-6b: 80 to 120.

1795, No Pole to Cap, Plain Edge (BW-6a, C-5a, B-5a).

1795, No Pole to Cap, Plain Edge (BW-6a, C-5a, B-5a), detail of another coin with part of a Talbot, Allum & Lee token inscription visible in an inverted position at the left of and below the date.

Obverse: Obverse of BW-1, but ground down so as to remove the pole.

Reverse: Same die as preceding. Advanced state with diagonal crack and some bulging. *Points of distinction:* In its final state, cracks are major, causing the die to fail, resulting in somewhat lower relief of the lower two-thirds of the coin, as compared to the upper third.

Notes: This variety exists in Mint State, but is very rare at this level. *Gilbert* (1916) G-6 "Plain edge without pole / 7 berry reverse, 3 on left branch and 4 on right. . . . Sometimes found struck on a thick planchet." Valued slightly higher if significant traces of a Talbot, Allum & Lee undertype can be seen. Some on thick planchets cut down from misstruck large cents; worth a strong premium if significant traces of the cent are still discernible. On thick planchet examples the date can be weak on the obverse, and the denomination can be weak at the center of the reverse. Priced after BW-7.

1795, No Pole to Cap, Plain Edge • BW-7; C-6a and b; B-6a, 6b, and 6c.

Breen dies: 3-D. *Estimated population:* Thin (normal) planchet: 1,000 to 1,500; thick planchet: 500 to 750.

1795, No Pole to Cap, Plain Edge (BW-7, C-6a, B-6a).

Obverse: Obverse of BW-1, but ground down so as to remove the pole, in this state also used for BW-6. *Points of distinction:* Early impressions are from a perfect die. Later there is a slight mounding to the right of Y.

Reverse: 18 leaves on left branch, 16 on the right. 3 berries on left branch, 6 on the right. Tip of lowest outside-left leaf opposite left part of N of UNITED. Lowest outside leaf on right opposite second A of AMERICA.

Notes: Mint State is seen. Examples are rare so fine, but this is the 1795 variety most often seen at this level. *Gilbert* (1916) G-5 "Plain edge without pole / Triple leaf under IT. 3 berries on left branch and 6 on right. . . . This variety is often found struck over Talbot, Allum & Lee cents of 1794." Valued considerably higher if inscriptions from an undertype large cent are legible. Valued slightly higher if significant traces of the Talbot, Allum & Lee undertype can be seen. On a few there are some traces of the original T.A.&L. edge lettering; these are worth even more. Three examples are known struck on planchets cut out from

copper trial pieces for half dollars, including 1794 Overton-104 and 105 and 1795 Overton-117, according to Manley (*Half Cent Die States*, page 63). These are of exceptional value. R. Tettenhorst: "There is an unusually large number of double strikes, including flip-over double strikes, for this particular variety. What was going on at the Mint to create these anomalies is unknown."[9] The date is usually weak on thick-planchet half cents.

1795, No Pole to Cap, Plain Edge		Cert	Avg	%MS
		32	27.4	0%

AG-3	G-4	VG-8	F-12	VF-20
$250	$400	$625	$1,200	$1,900

EF-40	AU-50	MS-60BN	MS-63BN
$4,800	$9,500	$14,000	$23,000

1796, Liberty Cap, Small Head Facing Right
Circulation mintage (popular estimate): 1,390.

The 1796 half cent is one of America's "trophy" rarities, a classic. For this coinage two obverse dies were prepared. The first lacked the pole to the cap, not because of grinding (as with 1795), but due to forgetfulness on the part of the die cutter, a true engraving error. This die developed a horizontal crack at an early stage, and relatively few were made.

In the *American Numismatical Manual*, 1859, Montroville W. Dickeson commented about the 1796 half cents:

> In our very extensive researches, though were 115,480 pieces of this design and denomination issued in this year, we have only been able to find 10 pieces in the whole; and our investigations have resulted in but one type and two varieties. There may be more, but we have not been able to discover them.
>
> Taking into view the number coined, it is difficult to account for this scarcity. But, probably being defective, from the imperfect tempering of the dies, as the greater number of the very few pieces we have found indicate, they may have been deemed unworthy of care or preservation. But three cabinets in Philadelphia contain a specimen of this coin; they are consequently both rare and valuable.

The Dickeson text, the first comprehensive book on American rare coins, necessarily had many errors, as the author had little to draw upon in this early era. However, the account is reflective of the rarity of the date. That there was another variety, the No Pole variety, was not known at the time. Walter Breen writes that the first publication of the No Pole was by David Proskey in 1880.

Modern standard references usually state the total production of 1796-dated half cents to have been 1,390, the figure quoted above, but this is a guess, representing the smallest of several deliveries of half cents this year. Moreover, even for this delivery there is no evidence that the coins were from 1796-dated dies. The truth is that except for calendar year 1793, when all half cents in the first year necessarily bore that date, we have no precise figures for *any* mintage of early half cents bearing a particular date. Even for 1793-dated half cents, some may have been made in 1794, adding to the 1793 calendar-year figure.

In his Mint history, Stewart wrote, "For 1796 half cents, in calendar year 1796, 60,000 were delivered on March 12, 49,000 on March 31st, then 5,090 in the second quarter, and 1,390 in the third and fourth quarters combined."

Stewart contemplated the situation and continued, "It is probable that the half cents delivered in March were dated 1796, which, if true, should make the half cents of 1796 common, but the fact remains they are very rare. If the half cents of March were dated 1795 this would account for the rarity of the 1796 half cent."

This open conjecture by Stewart was later translated into *fact*, and today the figure of 1,390 1796 half cents is usually given without question. In actuality, no one knows how many were made. It is possible that some but not all were made earlier than the third and fourth quarters. It is also possible that some were made in 1797.[10]

Certainly, the production of 1796 half cents was low, whatever the figure. In proportion to surviving examples the popular estimate given above is probably in the right ballpark. Likely, about 20 percent of these were of the No Pole variety.

In the *Numismatist*, July 1916, Commodore W.C. Eaton, an early student of die varieties in several series, including current Lincoln cents, suggested that the publication:

> [s]tart an investigation as to how many collectors have specimens of the 1796 half cent? In my belief, considering the prices even poor copies bring, this is one of the most overrated coins in the whole United States series. I have nearly a dozen half cents in my collection that I consider rarer than the 1796, bought at prices very far less than that half cent brings, though, to be sure, there are only types that are rare and not the entire date, as in the case of the 1796.
>
> But the securing of a 1796 is only a question of money, for they appear in auctions every little while, when an unlimited bid will secure them, while those I have in mind, money could not buy, because they could not be found. I venture to say that if collectors will come forward and own up to the possession of a 1796, the number found will surprise one who judges only by the price they bring. To be sure, the fear of lessening the value of the coin in their possession may deter collectors from so coming forward, but we must depend on their interest in true numismatic knowledge to urge them on.

Nothing worthwhile came of the proposal, although a few responses were received.

The second variety of 1796 half cent is from a different die, with prominent pole, and is that most often seen, although on an absolute basis it is also rare. Today, perhaps as many as two dozen of the 1796, No Pole, half cents exist, mostly in low grades in about Good to Fine, often porous, but with several high-grade and notable examples to delight connoisseurs who can afford them. For the 1796, With Pole, the population is likely in the range of 100 to 120 or so pieces, again mostly in lower grades, although the number of pieces in AU or Mint State is around a dozen.

Some of the highest-grade half cents of both types for 1796 were located in England, where in the late 1700s such pieces were collected, during an era in which numismatics had not yet become popular in the United States. Thomas L. Elder, leading New York City coin dealer and auctioneer, reminisced about an English find by well-known numismatist Henry C. Miller.

He sold out his fine cent collection and some other items in 1916, I think it was, and we got fine results for him. Sometime prior to that he had secured a pair of Proof 1796 half cents from a dealer in London for something less than $50 for the two. As he collected no half cents, he turned them over to me, and in a sale on East 23rd Street we got $300 for one of the half cents, which to that time seemed a world's record. In the cent sale just mentioned, however the second half cent made the great record of over $700, going into the cabinet of a leading Detroit collector, now retired.[11]

Today the 1796 is recognized as a formidable rarity, and either of the 1796 half cent varieties in *any* grade at all can be called a landmark and causes a ripple of excitement when appearing in an auction presentation.

1796, No Pole to Cap • BW-1, C-1, B-1a. *Breen dies:* 1-A. ***Estimated population:*** 20 to 24, although estimates vary, some as low as 17.

1796, No Pole to Cap (BW-1, C-1, B-1a). This is the most famous rarity in the half cent series. All known examples have a die crack bisecting the obverse.

Obverse: No pole to cap, an engraving error.

Reverse: Continuing the style of the preceding year. On this die, 4 berries on the left side, 3 on the right.

Notes: Gilbert (1916) G-2 "Plain edge without pole." All known examples have a nearly horizontal die crack bisecting the obverse, no doubt accounting for the short use of this die and the consequent rarity of coins today. Some pieces have reflective surfaces and have been cataloged as *Proof* in the past. Examples of the 1796, No Pole, change hands infrequently, and thus the market value is subject to differing opinions.

About four are known in Mint State. The finest two are believed to be one in a Missouri collection (illustrated here; ex John Murdoch Collection, London, 1904) and the Louis E. Eliasberg Collection example (ex Richard Winsor Collection, 1895), the latter certified as MS-67, which is perhaps generous, but the coin is wonderful.[12]

Numismatic Notes: *A Proof 1796, No Pole, half cent?:* The Louis E. Eliasberg Collection sale in 1996 offered a remarkable example of this rarity (one of three there), cataloged as, "MS-65 or better, red and brown. Superb, sharp strike and well centered with excellent definition of all denticles. Square edge. Fully prooflike and most probably a presentation or specimen coin; just as easily called Proof-65 or finer. Mirrorlike characteristics in every aspect of obverse and reverse. Mostly light brown with significant areas of original mint red, especially in protected areas such as the date numerals, LIBERTY, and, on the reverse, within the wreath and letters," followed by extensive additional information.

The pedigree was given as:

> Richard B. Winsor; S.H. and Henry Chapman, December 16–17, 1895, Lot 1012 $300; George H. Earle, Jr.; Henry Chapman, June 25–29, 1912, Lot 3609 $400; Col. James W. Ellsworth; Wayte Raymond, privately; William Cutler Atwater, Sr.; Atwater Estate; B. Max Mehl, June 11, 1946, Lot 129 $1,125; Louis E. Eliasberg, Sr.

In his 1946 offering of the Atwater coin, B. Max Mehl called this a "Brilliant semi-Proof," and went on to say:

I really believe the coin is and was struck as a Proof. It has a brilliant light olive surface with traces of the original mint red nicely blended in. It is magnificently struck and centered with deep milled borders and sharp edge. While I am endeavoring to be conservative in both my description of condition of these coins, and also the use of superlative adjectives, but this gem is simply too much for me to overcome.

Indeed, Henry Chapman described this coin as a "Proof" while cataloging the Earle Collection in 1912.

It is sometimes fashionable to call early prooflike coins "Proofs," and in some instances they may have been intended as presentation pieces in this regard. However, there is no documentation of any Proofs in any series being made by a special proofing process prior the early 1820s (the Smithsonian Institution has a full 1821 Proof set, ex the Mint Cabinet, the earliest such set). Even after the early 1820s there are few records available until the late 1850s. Should a coin be called a Proof because it looks like one, or should there be surrounding evidence or documentation or at least long-standing tradition that it was made as a Proof? This point has not been completely resolved.

1796, No Pole to Cap		Cert	Avg	%MS
		1	62.0	100%

AG-3	G-4	VG-8	F-12
$18,750	$42,500	$65,000	$125,000

VF-20	EF-40	AU-50	MS-60BN
$180,000	—	—	$500,000

1796, With Pole to Cap • BW-2, C-2, B-2a and b. *Breen dies: 2-A.* **Estimated population:** 100 to 120.

1796, With Pole to Cap (BW-2, C-2, B-2). A famous rarity.

Obverse: With pole to cap. LIBERTY positioned slightly more to the right than on BW-1.

Reverse: Same die as preceding.

Notes: Gilbert (1916) G-1 "Plain edge with pole." Despite the absolute rarity of this issue, nearly 10 different examples have been graded as Mint State, with Europe as the main source (see BW-1 and also Numismatic Notes). R. Tettenhorst note: "It is interesting that more Mint States or nearly Mint State specimens of 1796 exist than for any other Liberty Cap half cent, despite the overall rarity of these two varieties. This would seem to indicate that

there was some early activity by collectors who recognized the rarity of the date."[13] About 10 to 12 are known in Mint State.[14]

The Edwards 1796 half cent copy.

Numismatic Notes: Edwards copies: Sometime before 1866, Francis S. Edwards issued a copy of the 1796, With Pole, half cent from new dies. The copy has many minute differences from the original. On the copy the leaf below O in OF extends significantly to its left; on the original the leaf ends below the left edge of the O. Both dies were rusted. Reportedly, after his death the dies were destroyed as were all but 12 remaining coins. The number actually struck is not known. These are collectible in their own right today.

Such a coin was mentioned in a January 5, 1866, address by Dr. Winslow Lewis to the Boston Numismatic Society.

> As an association we have endeavored to caution collectors against the unjustifiable practice, now too palpably restored to, of issuing facsimiles of rare coins and medals. Of the funeral gold medal of Washington, we are cognizant of at least two struck recently in New York, and we know, also, that the rare half cent, which has brought $96, has been imitated and the counterfeits circulated.[15]

On November 7, 1907, H.O. Granberg, of Oshkosh, Wisconsin, a wealthy collector and coin trader of the era, made an offer to Theophile E. Leon, of Chicago, who was the main buying agent for Virgil M. Brand: "Smith's re-strike half cents $100.00." It is not known if Granberg had more than one.

As to Dr. Edwards, he is famous, or perhaps notorious, as an issuer of copies that seemed to have been marketed without disclosing their true nature. This included the Charles Carroll of Carrollton medal (the original was from dies by Christian Gobrecht), gold Washington funeral medals (in imitation of the Jacob Perkins dies), reissues of Bolen copies from dies acquired from Bolen (these are widely chronicled in specialized numismatic literature), and unknown others.

His collection was cataloged by Edward D. Cogan at the sale room of Bangs, Merwin & Co., New York City, on October 16–20, 1865, under the title of *Catalogue of a Very Extensive and Valuable Collection of American and Foreign Gold, Silver, Copper Coins and Medals, also Colonial, Pattern, Washington, and Presidential and Political Pieces. The property of the late Dr. F.S. Edwards of New York.* Emmanuel Attinelli commented:

> Dr. Francis S. Edwards, whose decease brought his large and valuable collection under the hammer, was an Englishman by birth, by profession a physician. To him was attributed the appearance of several counterfeit pieces of rare American coins and medals, which, though extremely well executed, were quickly detected.[16]

R. Tettenhorst comments:

> An interesting fact about the Edwards copy is the enormous variation in weight. I have a specimen weighing 59.4 grains and another weighing 91.8 grains, and have seen others with in-between weights, for example, 63.3 grains and 73.8 grains. No two seem to have the same weight.[17]

1796, With Pole to Cap			Cert	Avg	%MS
			22	38.3	45%

AG-3	G-4	VG-8	F-12	VF-20
$14,000	$21,500	$27,500	$37,500	$60,000

EF-40	AU-50	MS-60BN	MS-63BN
$85,000	$110,000	$200,000	$362,500

Edwards Copy			Cert	Avg	%MS
			0	n/a	

MS-60BN	MS-63BN	MS-63RB	MS-65BN	MS-65RB
$16,250	$20,000	$31,250	$37,500	$45,000

1797, Liberty Cap, Small Head Facing Right
Mintage (per Mint Report): 27,525.

Half cents of 1797 continue the small portrait style initiated in 1795, but are apt to be casually struck, sometimes on rough planchets, and sometimes lacking detail in certain areas. The planchets for some of these are believed to have been cut from misstruck cents. Of course, this is part of the charm and fascination of early coppers—the numismatic equivalent of being *rustic* or *naïve*, to pick up terms from folk art. Perhaps the most rustic is the so called Low Head, in which the portrait of Miss Liberty is quite low on the die, with the date crowded below it. Some of the Low Head half cents have lettered edges, incompletely fitting on the thin planchet, with the result that the letters are not fully visible. Why these were made is anyone's guess. Nearly all examples in existence today are in low grades. Planchets cut from Talbot, Allum & Lee cents were extensively used this year. Many surviving coins show traces of the T.A.&L. lettering or motifs.

Half cents of 1797 were extensively used in circulation, to which the abundance of worn examples attests. After 1797 there was no call for the denomination, and none were struck with the dates 1798 or 1799.

1797, 1 Above 1 in Date • BW-1; C-1; B-1a, 1b, and 1c. *Breen dies:* 1-A. *Estimated population:* Thin planchet: 400 to 600; thick planchet: 900 to 1,200.

1797, 1 Above 1 in Date (BW-1, C-1, B-1).

Detail of 1 above 1.

Obverse: Erroneous 1 over regular 1 in date. The engraver started the date too high, abandoned the 1, and punched 1797 below it. Slight traces of other earlier digits can be seen above the date on high-grade examples. Bottom of 9 with knob. *Points of distinction:* Perfect die in early impressions. Then a crack develops at the rim by the end of the pole, followed by a mounding at L of LIBERTY, other bulges, and more cracks, culminating in a shattered die (Manley State 5.0).

Reverse: 5 berries to the left, 3 to the right. Pair of leaves under ME of AMERICA. *Points of distinction:* In late states a crack starts below the 2 in the fraction, and later mounding develops, actually a result of metal displacement due to problems on the obverse, resulting in ICA being indistinct or absent.

Notes: Perhaps 10 to 12 exist in Mint State. *Gilbert* (1916) G-4 "Plain edge with pole, 1 over date." Breen's a, b, and c are for thin planchets, thick planchets cut down from large cents, and thick planchets cut down from T.A.&L. cents. If with significant traces of a T.A.&L. undertype this variety is worth a slight premium. This is a very popular and widely available variety. Quite a few are in grades of EF or finer, usually showing die cracks.

1797, 1 Above 1 in Date	Cert	Avg	%MS
	60	31.7	0%

AG-3	G-4	VG-8	F-12	VF-20
$190	$375	$650	$1,100	$1,800

EF-40	AU-50	MS-60BN	MS-63BN
$4,100	$7,200	$16,000	$32,500

1797, Regular Head, Plain Edge • BW-2; C-2; B-2a, 2b, and 2c. *Breen dies:* 2-A. *Estimated population:* Thin planchet: 250 to 400; thick planchet with traces of cent undertype: 8 to 12; thick planchet with no traces of undertype: 50 to 75.

1797, Regular Head, Plain
Edge (BW-2, C-2, B-2).

Detail of knobbed nine.

Obverse: Head centered on the die. Date low. Bottom of 9 with knob. *Points of distinction:* Perfect die.

Reverse: Same die as preceding.

Notes: 8 to 10 are in Mint State. *Gilbert* (1916) G-3 "Plain edge with pole, date distant from bust." Breen's a, b, and c are for thin planchets, thick planchets cut down from large cents, and thick planchets cut down from T.A.&L. cents. If with significant traces of a T.A.&L. undertype this variety is worth a slight premium. Most are in lower grades.

1797, Regular Head, Plain Edge		Cert	Avg	%MS
		59	24.2	7%

AG-3	G-4	VG-8	F-12
$200	$425	$700	$1,250

VF-20	EF-40	AU-50	MS-60BN
$3,000	$6,000	$8,100	$16,000

1797, Low Head, Lettered Edge • BW-3, C-3b, B-3a. *Breen dies:* 3-B. *Estimated population:* 75 to 100.

1797, Low Head, Lettered
Edge (BW-3, C-3b, B-3a).

Obverse: Head very low. 1 of 1797 nearly touches hair. Bottom of 9 sharply pointed. *Points of distinction:* A light crack develops in the right obverse field, with accompanying mounding. This becomes larger as the use of the die continues.

Reverse: 4 berries to the left, 3 to the right. Cluster of three leaves under ME of AMERICA. *Points of distinction:* There is a crack from the denticles through E of UNITED into the interior of the wreath.

Notes: EF is the highest grade known. *Gilbert* (1916) G-1 "Lettered edge with pole." The Low Head varieties are presented here in the same order that they appeared in Breen: Lettered Edge, Gripped Edge, and Plain edge. Ronald P. Manley studied the die states and came to the same conclusion as Breen, writing "it appears to me that most (or perhaps all) 1797 C-3c specimens were minted after the lettered edge coins, but before the plain edge coins."[18] All are on thick planchets, presumably from cut-down large cents. Often seen on a dark and porous planchet and with extensive wear. With its unusual obverse die and the anachronistic edge lettering, this is one of the great curiosities among early American copper coins. Demand is insatiable, and the typical coin in Good or VG grade with surfaces as mentioned will inevitably draw many bids at an auction.

1797, Low Head, Lettered Edge			Cert	Avg	%MS
			4	14.3	0%

AG-3	G-4	VG-8	F-12	VF-20	EF-40
$1,200	$1,875	$2,950	$6,000	$15,000	$30,000

1797, Low Head, Gripped Edge • BW-4, C-3c, B-3b. *Breen dies:* 3-B. **Estimated population:** 12 to 15.

Obverse: Same die as preceding.

Reverse: Same die as preceding.

Notes: VG is the highest grade known. Edge with widely and irregularly incised vertical and curved lines, the "gripped" edge.[19] All known are in low grades.

1797, Low Head, Gripped Edge	Cert	Avg	%MS
	0	n/a	

AG-3	G-4	VG-8
$32,500	$48,750	$65,000

1797, Low Head, Plain Edge • BW-5, C-3a, B-3c. *Breen dies:* 3-B. **Estimated population:** 400 to 600.

1797, Low Head, Plain Edge (BW-5, C-3a, B-3c).

Obverse: Same die as preceding.

Reverse: Same die as preceding.

Notes: EF and AU are the highest grades known, and examples are rare as such. *Gil-*

bert (1916) G-2 "Plain edge with pole, date close to bust." Thick and thin planchet varieties. Low grades are the rule, but the Plain Edge is found in higher average grades, by far, than the Lettered Edge variety from the same dies.

1797, Low Head, Plain Edge	Cert	Avg	%MS
	6	11.7	0%

AG-3	G-4	VG-8	F-12	VF-20	EF-40
$300	$625	$975	$2,250	$4,500	$13,500

DRAPED BUST (1800–1808)

1806, Small 6, Stems to Wreath (BW-1, C-2, B-1); a well-known rarity.

Designer: *Robert Scot.* **Weight:** *84 grains (5.44 grams).* **Composition:** *Copper. Most planchets were imported from Boulton & Watt of Birmingham, England. These were of exceptionally high quality, in contrast to the variable stock made at the Mint from scrap copper and other sources. There were exceptions, and it is thought that the half cents of 1802 were made from domestic sources.* **Diameter:** *23.5 mm.* **Edge:** *Plain.*

For purposes of finding a nice example to include in a type set, Draped Bust half cents are readily available in most any desired grade, up through and including Mint State, the latter being somewhat elusive in proportion to the demand for them. Many pieces have a generous measure of eye appeal. Examples from old-time hoards are sometimes available for the 1800 and 1806 varieties, especially the latter date. These are usually highly lustrous, attractive, and have original mint orange blended with natural light-brown toning. The reverses typically have areas of light striking, particularly on the upper leaves.

Within this type the 1802, 2 Over 0, is an exception to the above rule, is scarce, and is often seen in low grades or with rough surfaces. Those dated 1804 exist in a wide and fascinating panorama of obverses with Plain 4 and Crosslet 4, and reverses With Stem to Wreath and Without Stem, in various combinations. The half cents of 1808, 8 Over 7, and 1808 are rare in high grades.

DESIGN DETAILS

On the obverse the head of Miss Liberty faces to the right, her hair behind, some tied with a ribbon at the back and with other tresses falling to her shoulder. Her bosom at the lower right is draped in cloth. The letters of LIBERTY are above her head, and the date is between the bust and the bottom border. The image was from a drawing by Gilbert Stuart, said to have been of a society lady. John Eckstein was paid $30 on September 9, 1795, to take the Stuart image and make a model from it, from which a punch or hub could be made for coinage. The dies were made by Robert Scot, chief engraver at the Mint. The Draped Bust motif was first used on certain silver dollars of 1795, then on copper cents and silver half dimes, dimes, quarter dollars, and half dollars of 1796.

The reverse is of the same general style as the 1794 through 1797 type, but more carefully executed in the dies and, accordingly, more standardized. The wreath is open at the top and tied with a ribbon bow below. Around the border is the inscription UNITED STATES OF AMERICA. At the center in two lines is HALF / CENT. The fraction 1/200 is below the ribbon bow. All half cents of 1800 and some of 1802 have a single leaf at each side of the wreath apex. This style is called the Reverse of 1800. Most of the 1802 half cents and all later coins through 1808 have one leaf at the top left and a pair of leaves at the top right, called the Reverse of 1802. The left side of the wreath has 16 leaves and the right has 19 leaves. The berries and stems were added by hand, as was the lettering, resulting in discernible variations.

1800, Draped Bust
Mintage (per **Mint Report***): 202,908.*

Half cents dated 1800, known from just a single pair of dies, are from a mintage reported to be 202,908 pieces. This high figure probably represents the use of improved-quality steel in the dies, although some coins of earlier dates could have been included in the figure. Proportionally, the mintage seems reasonable in relation to surviving examples of the year.

Most 1800-dated half cents are fairly well struck on pleasing, smooth planchets. Today, examples are apt to be very attractive in appearance. Examples are readily available in just about any desired grade.

In the 1930s a hoard of several dozen or more 1800 half cents was discovered in Boston. Examples from this holding display mint red, but are usually spotted. Estimates that the hoard was of 30 to 100 pieces have reached print. Other 1800-dated half cents of the same variety, typically with lustrous brown surfaces, are said to have come from another hoard discovered in New England. This other cache is believed to have been found before 1910 and to have contained "hundreds of pieces."[20] These no doubt account for the Mint State coins seen with some frequency in the marketplace today.

Typical values for 1800 half cents.

1800				Cert	Avg	%MS
				195	46.0	31%

G-4	VG-8	F-12	VF-20	EF-40	AU-50	MS-60BN	MS-63BN	MS-63RB	MS-65BN
$55	$100	$190	$300	$700	$1,000	$2,100	$4,050	$6,750	$14,000

1800 • BW-1, C-1, B-1a and b. *Breen dies:* 1-A. **Estimated population:** 1,200 to 1,600.

1800 (BW-1, C-1, B-1).

Obverse: Draped Bust type, 1800 date.

Reverse: Reverse of 1800 with a single leaf at each side of the wreath apex. *Points of distinction:* The die goes through several states, from perfect to relapped. Perfect die specimens are relatively rare and usually command a premium. In late impressions a crack is seen through at the tops of NITE, expanding slightly on very late impressions.

Notes: Some were struck on planchets made from cut-down large cents. Light striking at the top of the wreath is typical. Early die state pieces with complete and bold obverse and reverse border dentilation are extremely rare and highly prized among specialists. Mint State coins are plentiful. Pristine (untreated and with original surfaces) coins are usually a glossy red-and-brown color.

Numismatic Notes: Walter Breen, in his *Encyclopedia*, states that 20,978 of the 1800-dated half cents were from planchets made at the Mint, and that 190,552, representing higher quality, were imported. In actuality, there is no way of knowing this. R.W. Julian suggests that the 20,978 figure probably includes coins dated 1797.[21]

1802, 2 Over 0, Draped Bust
Mintage (per Mint Report*): 14,366.*

The 1802 half cents are quite curious. The die was overdated from an unused 1800 die, creating 1802, 2 Over 0. Two reverse varieties are known, the extremely rare early style with one leaf at each side of the wreath apex (Reverse of 1800), and the scarce but available second reverse with one leaf at the left of the wreath and two leaves at the upper right (Reverse of 1802).

As to whether the *Mint Report* coinage figure of 14,366 is correct, this cannot be determined. In any event, half cents dated 1802 are sufficiently rare to support a figure in this range. If so, an estimate might be 500 of the Reverse of 1800 style and 13,866 of the Reverse of 1802.

Most half cents of 1802, 2 Over 0, were struck on poor planchets and when seen today are apt to be porous and rough. All or nearly all were struck on planchets cut down from misstruck large cents. Any example showing significant traces of the undertype lettering or other features is worth a sharp premium.

Nearly all are in low grades, with Good and VG being about normal; some are even lower quality, and only a few can be legitimately called Fine. At the VF level the 1802, 2 Over 0, is rare. Any coin that can reasonably be designated EF is an extreme rarity. No AU or Mint State examples are known of either variety.

The 1802, 2 Over 0, with Reverse of 1800 is more than just a rare die variety of interest to advanced specialists. It is rare as a *basic* variety, listed in the regular edition of the *Guide Book of United States Coins*, and widely desired. All known examples show extensive wear. The auction offering of an example in any grade is traditionally the cause for a lot of excitement.

1802, 2 Over 0, Reverse of 1800, 1 Leaf Each Side of Wreath Apex •
BW-1, C-1, B-1. *Breen dies:* 1-A. *Estimated population:* 20 to 25.[22]

1802, 2 Over 0, Reverse of 1800,
1 Leaf Each Side of Wreath Apex
(BW-1, C-1, B-1); a classic rarity.

Obverse: 1802 Over 0 die.

Reverse: Reverse of 1800.

Notes: Fine is the highest grade known, to the extent of just 3 or 4 coins. *Gilbert* (1916) G-2 "This combination is exceedingly rare." All known pieces are in low grades, and a nice VG would be a prize. Most were struck after the coins of the BW-2, C-2, variety were coined.

1802, 2 Over 0, Reverse of 1800		Cert	Avg	%MS
		2	0.0	0%

AG-3	G-4	VG-8	F-12
$13,750	$24,500	$35,000	$50,000

1802, 2 Over 0, Reverse of 1802, 1 Leaf Left, 2 Leaves Right at Wreath Apex • BW-2, C-2, B-2. *Breen dies:* 1-B. *Estimated population:* 500 to 800.

1802, 2 Over 0, Reverse of 1802,
1 Leaf Left, 2 Leaves Right at Wreath
Apex (BW-2, C-2, B-2). Rare in any grade.

Detail of overdate.

Obverse: Same die as preceding.

Reverse: Reverse of 1802.

Notes: Two EF coins are the highest-graded examples known, followed by several VF coins. *Gilbert* (1916) G-1 "This reverse is usually found in poor condition, and sometimes with slight die breaks from end of stems extending toward A and U."

Nearly all are in low grades with dark or porous surfaces.

Numismatic Notes: Mintage figures: The original mintage of 1802 half cents is subject to debate. The regular edition of the *Guide Book of United States Coins* reports a total of 20,266 coins, this being the total of deliveries dated August 8, 1802; October 4, 1802; and August 8, 1803. Others believe the mintage should be recorded as just 14,366 coins, with the 5,900 of August 1803 being coins actually dated 1803.

Contemporary records state that those of August 1803 were struck on planchets made from *spoiled cents* or *mint errors*, using today's terminology. The reason for assuming these to be dated 1802 is simple: a few 1802 half cents show traces of undertype from large cents, while not a single example dated 1803 shows any undertype.

An early comment: In the *American Numismatical Manual*, 1859, Montroville W. Dickeson commented about the 1802 half cents:

[There are but] one type and three varieties, and the number coined very small, being but 14,366, which has rendered them very rare. One of the varieties is from the die of 1800 altered, and portions of the naught are perceptible around the figure 2, which is smaller than the other figures. They command a good price when perfect, which is rarely the case.

As noted earlier (under 1796), Dickeson's comments are often inaccurate, but are interesting to read today. Only two varieties are known to modern numismatists.

1802, 2 Over 0, Reverse of 1802			Cert	Avg	%MS
			47	9.0	0%

AG-3	G-4	VG-8	F-12	VF-20	EF-40
$475	$850	$2,000	$4,500	$14,000	$35,000

1803, Draped Bust

Mintage (per Mint Report): 97,000.

Although the number of 1803-dated half cents is not known for certain, as Mint records reflect quantities minted during a *calendar year*, which can be quite different from the *dates on the dies actually used*, the figure 97,200 appears in the regular edition of the *Guide Book of United States Coins* and other places. Most likely, the actual mintage of pieces dated 1803 was several times that figure, from coins struck in 1804 and 1805, but with the 1803 date.

Most pieces are quite attractive, are on nice planchets, and are seen in grades from Good to VF, although occasional EF or finer pieces are encountered. Any true Uncirculated coin is a first-class rarity. It is not unusual for there to be some light striking at the center of the reverse, particularly at the A of HALF and the E of CENT.

This particular year did not turn up in hoards, and thus Mint State coins are very rare. The typical showing for a high-grade collection of half cents is AU.

Two obverse dies and four reverse dies were combined to create four different varieties. All are collectible, but BW-2 and BW-3 are scarcer than the others, with BW-2 being the scarcest.

Typical values for 1803 half cents.
Rare varieties may be worth more.

1803	Cert	Avg	%MS
	197	32.7	11%

G-4	VG-8	F-12	VF-20	EF-40	AU-50	MS-60BN	MS-63BN
$38	$75	$190	$300	$800	$1,300	$3,200	$6,500

1803 • BW-1, C-1, B-1. *Breen dies:* 1-A. ***Estimated population:*** 3,000 to 4,000.

1803 (BW-1, C-1, B-1).

Detail of the engraver's scratch joining the fraction bar to the right ribbon.

Obverse: 03 very close. TY of LIBERTY close. 3 close to drapery.

Reverse: 5 berries at left and right. A bold engraver's scratch in the form of a line joins the right side of the fraction bar to the ribbon. An artifact from an earlier punch is seen as a raised area at the top inside of U of UNITED.

Notes: This variety exists in Mint State, but is scarce at this level. *Gilbert* (1916) G-2 "Large 1/200 with imperfect regula." A *regula* is a fraction bar. This is the most available variety of the year.

1803 • BW-2, C-2, B-2. *Breen dies:* 1-B. *Estimated population:* 80 to 120.

1803 (BW-2, C-2, B-2).

Obverse: Same die as preceding.

Reverse: 5 berries at left and right. No artifact inside of U of UNITED. No engraver's scratch at fraction bar. In

denominator, 200 properly spaced. *Points of distinction:* At a late state there is a rim cud over TAT on the reverse. This expands to cover STAT.

Notes: EF examples occur, but the variety is very rare at this level. *Gilbert* (1916) G-4 "Large 1/200 variety with no imperfection in the regula." This is the most elusive variety of the year, and by a wide margin. Choice examples are particularly desirable. The highest grade known to Walter Breen was EF, with the next finest being VF.

1803 • BW-3, C-4, B-4. *Breen dies:* 1-D. *Estimated population:* 250 to 300.

1803 (BW-3, C-4, B-4).

Obverse: Same die as preceding.

Reverse: 6 berries to the left, 5 to the right (only reverse with this count). F of HALF leans right and touches L at left and berry at right. This die was probably made in

1805 and combined with an 1803 obverse still on hand to strike coins. *Points of distinction:* This die was used to coin 1803 (BW-3); 1805, Small 5, Stems to Wreath (BW-2); 1805, Small 5, Stems to Wreath (BW-3); and 1805, Large 5, Stems to Wreath (BW-4).

Notes: Mint State is known in this variety, but AU is a more practical objective. *Gilbert* (1916) G-1 "The only 11 berry variety." This variety was actually struck in 1805. Accordingly, a listing by emission sequence (which this is not) would have this as the last variety of the year.

1803 • BW-4, C-3, B-3. *Breen dies:* 2-C. *Estimated population:* 1,250 to 1,750.

1803 (BW-4, C-3, B-3).

Obverse: 0 and 3 distant from each other, as 180 3. TY of LIBERTY wide. 3 not close to drapery.

Reverse: 5 berries at left and right. No artifact inside of U of UNITED. No engraver's scratch at fraction bar. In denominator 200 the 2 and 0 are properly spaced, but 00 almost touch; fraction bar is long and extends to nearly halfway over the top of 2. Berry under left upright of M of AMERICA, point of leaf under right upright of M. *Points of distinction:* This die was used to coin 1803 (BW-4) and 1804, Crosslet 4, Stems to Wreath (BW-1).

Notes: Mint State is known for this variety, but examples are very scarce as such. How-

ever, among the Mint State 1803 half cents that exist, nearly all with lustrous brown surfaces, most are of the BW-4 variety. *Gilbert* (1916) G-3 "Figure 3 in date distant from 0 / Ciphers in denominator nearly connect." [Ciphers = 00] "But few coins of this variety are without die imperfections."

1804, Draped Bust

Mintage (per Mint Report*): 1,055,312.*

The *Mint Report* gives 1,055,312 as the coinage for this calendar year. It is likely that 200,000 or more were from 1803-dated dies. Still, if 800,000 dated 1804 were struck, this is still the most generous figure of the half cent denomination up to this point in time, a figure later exceeded only by the 1809 half cent. Interestingly, these year-date productions are the converse of the total production quantities of cents of these two years, which were made in relatively low quantities. Further, certain 1804-dated half cents are believed to have been struck in calendar year 1805.

Such a large production necessarily called for many half-cent dies to be made. The result created a playground for numismatists of a later era. Walter Breen states it well: "The date 1804 is the commonest of all the Draped Bust half cents. It is also the date with the largest number of varieties, and it is rich in rare dies and bizarre or extreme die breaks; dies were used long after they would otherwise have been discarded."[23]

Popular varieties exist of various combinations of the obverse with Plain 4 in date, with Crosslet (Serif) at the right side of the 4, With Stems in the reverse wreath (normal), and Stemless (an engraving error). In addition, certain 1804 half cents have a so-called "Spiked Chin," a little thorn protruding from Miss Liberty's chin, and a series of fingerprint-like lines in the right field. These are marks from a piece of a screw that fell into the press after the die had been used to strike "perfect" coins. It became trapped between a planchet and the obverse die, leaving telltale marks on the die.[24] Mint errors such as double strikes are rare for the earlier varieties of 1804, but become fairly plentiful among the later ones, extending to 1805, Medium 5, Stemless Wreath (BW-1).[25]

Adding to the collecting possibilities in the field of 1804 half cents, many coins show varying degrees of die cracks, and some have "cud" breaks from a piece falling out of the die at the rim. As if this were not enough, some coins were struck with dies aligned other than the normal 180 degrees apart. *The Half Cent Die State Book 1792–1857,* by Ronald P. Manley, is the definitive guide to these specialties.

As a general rule, half cents of 1804 are usually found on attractive planchets, with nice surfaces, often medium to dark brown, sometimes lighter. AU coins are seen with frequency, although Mint State pieces are very scarce. There were no hoards found of this date, as were found for half cents of 1800 and 1806.

1804, Crosslet 4, Stems to Wreath • BW-1, C-1, B-1. *Breen dies:* 1-A. **Estimated population:** 250 to 400.

1804, Crosslet 4, Stems to Wreath (BW-1, C-1, B-1).

Obverse: 4 high; crossbar points to center of 0. 1 slightly nearer to denticles than is the 4.

Reverse: 5 berries at left and right. In denominator 200 the 2 and 0 are properly spaced, but 00 almost touch; fraction bar long and extends to nearly halfway over the top of 2. Berry under left upright of M of AMERICA, point of leaf under right upright of M. *Points of distinction:* This die was used to coin 1803 (BW-4) and 1804,

Crosslet 4, Stems to Wreath (BW-1). A crack develops at the right side of the second T of STATES.

Notes: Mint State is known, but examples are exceedingly rare at this level. This variety is also rare in AU. *Gilbert* (1916) G-6 "Figure 4 of date touches bust / Ciphers of denominator nearly touch each other." Nearly all of this variety are found in worn grades, with Very Fine being about the best that normally can be obtained.

1804, Crosslet 4, Stems to Wreath (BW-1)	Cert	Avg	%MS
	(a)		

G-4	VG-8	F-12	VF-20	EF-40
$45	$85	$110	$225	$900

(a) Included in certified population for 1804, Crosslet 4, Stems to Wreath (BW-6 to BW-9).

1804, Crosslet 4, Stems to Wreath • BW-2a, C-delisted, B-4. *Breen dies:* 1-B. **Estimated population:** 12 to 14.

Obverse: Same die as preceding.

Reverse: 5 berries at left and right. Berry slightly right of the middle of M of AMERICA. No leaf point under F in OF.

Notes: Not known to Gilbert. This variety is an earlier state of the following and struck from the same die pair.[26] VG is the highest grade known.

1804, Crosslet 4 "Spiked Chin," Stems to Wreath (Later die state of the preceding) • BW-2b, C-5, B-4a. *Breen dies:* 1a-B. **Estimated population:** 150 to 250.

1804, Crosslet 4 "Spiked Chin," Stems to Wreath (BW-2b, C-5, B-4a).

Obverse: Same as obverse of BW-1 and BW-2, but die now injured, with a thorn or "spike" protruding to the right from the

chin and grooves (threads from a bolt segment that was mistakenly left in the press) in the field below the chin.

Reverse: Same die as preceding.

Notes: Gilbert (1916) G-11 "Spiked chin / Outer figures of the denominator under ribbon ends." Later state of the BW-2 die combination. Two or three Mint State examples have been reported. Most are VF or graded lower. Priced after BW-5.

1804, Crosslet 4 "Spiked Chin," Stems to Wreath • BW-3, C-7, B-5.

Breen dies: 1a-C. ***Estimated total population:*** 125 to 175.

**1804, Crosslet 4 "Spiked Chin,"
Stems to Wreath (BW-3, C-7, B-5).**

Obverse: Same die and state as preceding. *Points of distinction:* The die in this combination always has a light crack through the top of LIBERTY. In its latest state a spectacular die cud exists from 1 o'clock clockwise to 4 o'clock.

Reverse: 5 berries at left and right. Berry slightly right of the middle of M of AMERICA. Point of a leaf ends below bottom-left serif of F in OF. *Points of distinction:* In its latest state there is a die cud from 1 o'clock clockwise to 4 o'clock, and another over TES of STATES.

Notes: AU examples exist, but are rare so fine. *Gilbert* (1916) G-9 "Spiked chin / With triple leaves under the left stand of F in OF. . . . Excessively rare—but two specimens now known." Priced after BW-5.

1804, Crosslet 4 "Spiked Chin," Stems to Wreath • BW-4, C-6, B-6.

Breen dies: 1a-D. ***Estimated total population:*** 1,200 to 1,500.

**1804, Crosslet 4 "Spiked Chin,"
Stems to Wreath (BW-4, C-6, B-6).**

Detail of "spiked" chin.

Obverse: Same die and state as preceding.

Reverse: 5 berries at left and right. Fraction bar long and extends to nearly halfway over the top of 2. Berry nearly opposite center of M of AMERICA. *Points of distinction:* Cracks develop, and in the latest state the reverse has spectacular rim cuds comprising most of the area from half past 2 o'clock at the right, continuing clockwise until about 8 o'clock on the left. The Manley text gives illustrations of the die as it deteriorates.

Notes: *Gilbert* (1916) G-8 "Spiked chin / With slight break from right stem end." According to Ronald P. Manley, fewer than six Mint State examples are known. Priced after BW-5.

1804, Crosslet 4 "Spiked Chin," Stems to Wreath • BW-5, C-8, B-7.
Breen dies: 1a-E. **Estimated population:** 2,200 to 3,000.

1804, Crosslet 4 "Spiked Chin,"
Stems to Wreath (BW-5, C-8, B-7).

Obverse: Same die and state as preceding. *Points of distinction:* The die crack at the top of LIBERTY expands. This develops into what is called a "retained cud" above LIBE, a broken section of the die at a different level, but still in the coining press, therefore not creating a cud.

Reverse: 5 berries at left and right. Second A of AMERICA very close to and nearly touches ribbon; tip of outermost leaf in pair is below right upright of M.

Notes: Gilbert (1916) G-7 "Spiked chin and protruding tongue / Crack connects R in AMERICA to border." Known in Mint State.

Typical values for 1804, "Spiked Chin". Rare varieties may be worth more.

1804, Crosslet 4 "Spiked Chin," Stems to Wreath	Cert	Avg	%MS
	368	43.9	14%

G-4	VG-8	F-12	VF-20
$45	$85	$110	$250

EF-40	AU-50	MS-60BN	MS-63BN
$425	$800	$1,700	$3,200

1804, Crosslet 4, Stems to Wreath • BW-6, C-4, B-2. *Breen dies:* 2-B. **Estimated population:** 40 to 70.

1804, Crosslet 4, Stems to
Wreath (BW-6, C-4, B-2).

Obverse: 4 of 1804 slightly closer to the rim than to the drapery.

Reverse: Same as reverse of BW-2.

Notes: AU is the highest grade known. *Gilbert* (1916) G-10 "4 of date low / Outer figures of denominator under ribbon ends." Cracks develop in both obverse and reverse in a later state. Ronald P. Manley believes this to be the first variety issued among half cents dated 1804. Most are in lower grades. Priced after BW-9.

1804, Crosslet 4, Stems to Wreath • BW-7, C-2, B-3. *Breen dies:* 2-A. **Estimated population:** 15 to 20.

1804, Crosslet 4, Stems to
Wreath (BW-7, C-2, B-3).

Obverse: Same die as preceding. *Points of distinction:* A crack develops into a rim cud over RTY.

Reverse: Same as reverse of BW-1.

Notes: Not known to Gilbert. The finest recorded is Fine-15. Priced after BW-9.

1804, Crosslet 4, Stems to Wreath • BW-8, C-9, B-8. *Breen dies:* 3-E. **Estimated population:** 1,200 to 1,700.

1804, Crosslet 4, Stems to Wreath (BW-8, C-9, B-8).

Obverse: Date widely spaced. Crossbar of 4 points to below center of 0. 4 with ample space separating it from the drapery and the denticles, but slightly closer to the drapery. *Points of distinction:* In its latest state there is a heavy die crack through IBER and a cud above RTY.

Reverse: Same as reverse of BW-6.

Notes: Gilbert (1916) G-5 "Crosslet 4 With Stems, 4 distant from 0 in date." Most examples are VF or lower. A few Mint State coins have been reported. Priced after BW-9.

1804, Crosslet 4, Stems to Wreath • BW-9, C-10, B-9. *Breen dies:* 4-E. *Estimated population:* 2,000 to 3,500.

1804, Crosslet 4, Stems to Wreath (BW-9, C-10, B-9).

Obverse: 4 high; crossbar points to slightly below center of 0. 1 and 4 about the same distance above the denticles.

Reverse: Same die as preceding. Die crack through R is heavier.

Notes: Gilbert (1916) G-4 "Crosslet 4 nearly touching 0 in date / With stems." Mint State examples appear regularly, one of relatively few of 1804 for which this can be said.

Typical values for 1804, Crosslet 4, Stems to Wreath. Rare varieties may be worth more.

1804, Crosslet 4, Stems to Wreath (BW-6 to BW-9)		Cert	Avg	%MS
		113	45.9	18%

G-4	VG-8	F-12	VF-20
$40	$75	$100	$200

EF-40	AU-50	MS-60BN	MS-63BN
$375	$675	$1,300	$2,800

1804, Crosslet 4, Stemless Wreath • BW-10, C-12, B-11. *Breen dies:* 4-F. *Estimated population:* 1,600 to 2,000.

1804, Crosslet 4, Stemless Wreath (BW-10, C-12, B-11).

Obverse: Same die as preceding.

Reverse: Stemless Wreath. 6 berries on left branch, 5 on the right. *Points of distinction:* This durable die was used to coin 1804, Crosslet 4, Stemless Wreath (BW-10); 1804, Plain 4, Stemless Wreath (BW-11); 1805, Medium 5, Stemless Wreath (BW-1); and 1806, Small 6, Stemless Wreath (BW-3).

Notes: Gilbert (1916) G-3 "Crosslet 4 nearly touching 0 of date / With stemless wreath." Walter Breen wrote: "Prior to about 1965 this was a rarity in Mint State. Since then, many have turned up, mostly brown or strangely mottled, possibly representing a hoard. Weak, uneven strikings are common."[27]

1804, Crosslet 4, Stemless Wreath		Cert	Avg	%MS
		54	54.9	46%

G-4	VG-8	F-12	VF-20	EF-40
$45	$85	$110	$200	$365

AU-50	MS-60BN	MS-63BN	MS-63RB	MS-65BN
$675	$1,300	$2,800	$4,000	$9,000

1804, Plain 4, Stemless Wreath • BW-11, C-13, B-10. *Breen dies:* 5-F. *Estimated population:* 6,000 to 9,000.

1804, Plain 4, Stemless Wreath (BW-11, C-13, B-10).

Obverse: Plain 4 (without crosslet), unique for this year.

Reverse: Same die as preceding. *Points of distinction:* In later stages a rim cud develops in the denticles over MER.

Notes: Gilbert (1916) G-2 "Plain 4 / Without stems." Readily available in Mint State, usually with attractive brown surfaces.

1804, Plain 4, Stemless Wreath		Cert	Avg	%MS
		187	44.2	18%

G-4	VG-8	F-12	VF-20	EF-40
$40	$75	$100	$200	$350

AU-50	MS-60BN	MS-63BN	MS-63RB	MS-65BN
$650	$1,300	$2,800	—	$8,500

1804, Plain 4, Stems to Wreath • BW-12, C-11, B-12. *Breen dies:* 5-G. *Estimated population:* 500 to 750.

1804, Plain 4, Stems to Wreath (BW-12, C-11, B-12).

Obverse: Same die as preceding.

Reverse: Stems to Wreath. 6 berries on left branch, 5 on the right. *Points of distinction:* On the latest state the reverse die sinks, creating bulges in coins struck, essentially obliterating the center of the coins on examples that survive today in worn grades.

Notes: Gilbert (1916) G-1 "Plain 4 / With stems." Although this variety is not at all hard to find, lower grades are the rule. Walter Breen commented, "Very rare above Very Fine." Known in Mint State, but rare so fine.

1804, Plain 4, Stems to Wreath		Cert	Avg	%MS
		11	31.4	0%

G-4	VG-8	F-12	VF-20	EF-40
$50	$100	$150	$475	$1,250

1805, Draped Bust

Mintage (per Mint Report*): 814,464.*

Although the reported coinage for the calendar year 1805 is generous, it is likely that many within that figure were from earlier-dated dies, specifically 1804.

Half cents of 1805 fall neatly into two major categories (with four die combinations): Small 5 with Stemless Wreath (with two die varieties) and Large 5 with Stems to Wreath. The four die combinations are Medium 5 with Stemless Wreath, Small 5 with Stems to Wreath (with two Small 5 die varieties), and Large 5 with Stems to Wreath. Two of these varieties are readily available, the other two are elusive. Although the sizes of the 5 numeral are popularly called Small, Medium, and Large, the difference is not great and is sometimes difficult to tell if a reference coin or photograph is not handy. However, as the Medium 5 obverse is only combined with the Stemless Wreath reverse (the same die used in 1804), this makes identification of the Stems to Wreath coins easier.

Generally, half cents of this date are attractive and on nice planchets, somewhat similar to 1804 in this regard. In the absence of any known hoards, high-grade examples of BW-1 and BW-4, the usually seen varieties, are very scarce. The Small 5, Stems to Wreath, varieties—BW-2 and BW-3—are found only in lower grades. These are very well known, due to wide listings, such as in the regular edition of the *Guide Book of United States Coins.*

1805, Medium 5, Stemless Wreath • BW-1, C-1, B-1. *Breen dies:* 1-A. **Estimated population:** 1,600 to 1,900.

1805, Medium 5, Stemless Wreath (BW-1, C-1, B-1).

Obverse: Medium 5 closer to the drapery than to the denticles; top of 5 double punched. The vertical stroke of the 5 is longer than the flag at the top.

Reverse: Stemless Wreath, the die used in 1804. *Points of distinction:* This durable die was used to coin 1804, Crosslet 4, Stemless Wreath (BW-10); 1804, Plain 4, Stemless

Wreath (BW-11); 1805, Medium 5, Stemless Wreath (BW-1); and 1806, Small 6, Stemless Wreath (BW-3). Most are in worn grades. Mint State coins occasionally come on the market, but these cannot be traced to any particular hoard.

Notes: *Gilbert* (1916) G-1 "Small 5 / Stemless wreath." Known in Mint State, but uncommon at this grade.

1805, Medium 5, Stemless Wreath	Cert	Avg	%MS
	43	39.7	12%

G-4	VG-8	F-12	VF-20	EF-40
$45	$75	$135	$200	$400

AU-50	MS-60BN	MS-63BN	MS-63RB
$750	$1,350	$3,000	$4,000

1805, Small 5, Stems to Wreath • BW-2, C-2, B-2. *Breen dies:* 2-B. **Estimated population:** 35 to 50.

**1805, Small 5, Stems to Wreath
(BW-2, C-2, B-2); a classic rarity.**

Obverse: 5 small and about equidistant from the denticles and the drapery. The vertical stroke of the 5 is shorter than the flag at the top.

Reverse: Top of T of CENT clearly separated from leaf; tip of lower-right serif in leaf. Tip of leaf between A and T of STATES. Tip of rightmost leaf in cluster under center of O in OF. *Points of distinction:* This die was used to coin 1803 (BW-3); 1805, Small 5, Stems to Wreath (BW-2);

1805, Small 5, Stems to Wreath (BW-3); and 1805, Large 5, Stems to Wreath (BW-4).

Notes: Gilbert (1916) G-4 "Small 5 / With stems; with a berry touching F. . . . Excessively rare—but two specimens now known." *Points of distinction:* Nearly all are in very weak or low grades. On most, HALF / CENT is very weak. EF is the highest grade known, but examples are seldom seen at this level. VF coins are very rare as well.

1805, Small 5, Stems to Wreath (BW-2)		Cert	Avg	%MS
		(a)		

AG-3	G-4	VG-8	F-12	VF-20
$3,750	$6,500	$10,000	$20,000	$50,000

(a) Included in certified population for 1805, Small 5, Stems to Wreath (BW-3).

1805, Small 5, Stems to Wreath • BW-3, C-3, B-3. *Breen dies:* 2-C. **Estimated population:** 140 to 180.

**1805, Small 5, Stems to
Wreath (BW-3, C-3, B-3).**

Obverse: As preceding. Later use of the die, now with a prominent bulge before the face.

Reverse: Same 5 berries to the left, 6 to the right. F of HALF leans right and touches L at left and berry at right. *Points of distinction:*

This die was used to coin 1803 (BW-3); 1805, Small 5, Stems to Wreath (BW-2); 1805, Small 5, Stems to Wreath (BW-3); and 1805, Large 5, Stems to Wreath (BW-4).

Notes: Gilbert (1916) G-3 "Small 5 / With stems; a berry above F in HALF. . . . Very rare." Usually found in lower grades. EF is the highest grade known, but examples are very rare at this level.

1805, Small 5, Stems to Wreath (BW-3)		Cert	Avg	%MS
		7	13.9	0%

AG-3	G-4	VG-8	F-12	VF-20
$250	$525	$1,000	$3,875	$14,000

1805, Large 5, Stems to Wreath • BW-4, C-4, B-4. *Breen dies:* 3-C. **Estimated population:** 1,300 to 1,600.

1805, Large 5, Stems to Wreath (BW-4, C-4, B-4).

Obverse: 5 large and touches the drapery. The vertical strike of the 5 is about the same length as the flag at the top.

Reverse: Same die as preceding, but a later state. *Points of distinction:* This die was used to coin 1803 (BW-3); 1805, Small 5, Stems to Wreath (BW-2); 1805, Small 5, Stems to Wreath (BW-3); and 1805, Large 5, Stems to Wreath (BW-4). Light cracks develop

on the obverse. Ronald P. Manley reports that, comments in the Breen *Encyclopedia* notwithstanding, no examples have been found without cracks. It could be that the cracks were created during the hardening of the die, which would mean that all states have this characteristic.

Notes: Gilbert (1916) G-2 "Large 5 / With stems." Despite a relatively high population, this variety is nearly always seen in lower grades. Mint State is known, but examples are rare at this level.

1805, Large 5, Stems to Wreath		Cert	Avg	%MS
		27	33.4	0%

G-4	VG-8	F-12	VF-20	EF-40	AU-50
$55	$85	$150	$225	$415	$850

1806, Draped Bust
Mintage (per Mint Report): 356,000.

The mintage figure of 356,000 for the calendar year was probably augmented greatly by additional production of 1806-dated half cents in calendar years 1807 and 1808. Today the date is easily available, although one of the four die varieties is scarce and another is rare.

Half cents of 1806 are popularly classified as 1806, Small 6, Stems to Wreath (a rarity); 1806, Small 6, Stemless Wreath; and 1806, Large 6, Stems to Wreath. The later two are readily available in high grades, this being especially true for 1806, Large 6, Stems to Wreath (BW-4).

It is said that sometime around 1906 Philadelphia dealer Henry Chapman found a hoard of 1806 half cents (BW-4) variously estimated to contain from about 200 pieces up to "many hundreds." Certainly, the latter comment is closer to the truth, as these are seen with some frequency today. Many of these have generous areas of original mint red, but are spotted. They are almost always weakly struck at the drapery and the upper part of the wreath.[28]

1806, Small 6, Stems to Wreath • BW-1, C-2, B-1. *Breen dies:* 1-A. **Estimated population:** 175 to 225.

1806, Small 6, Stems to Wreath (BW-1, C-2, B-1); a well-known rarity.

Obverse: Small 6, positioned lower than the following; bottom about level with bases of 180. *Points of distinction:* Light clash marks are always seen.

Reverse: 6 berries left (lowest outside berry has no stem and is attached to a leaf point), 5 to the right. Lowest outside berry on left has no stem and is at the point of a leaf. Fraction bar short.

Notes: Gilbert (1916) G-2 "Small 6 / With stems. R and I in AMERICA connect. . . . A rare variety." Several AU pieces are known, but only one Mint State. The die faces do not seem to have been parallel with each other, with the result that the left side is often lighter in detail than the right.

1806, Small 6, Stems to Wreath (BW-1)	Cert	Avg	%MS
	19	29.1	0%

G-4	VG-8	F-12	VF-20	EF-40	AU-50
$240	$390	$775	$1,450	$3,375	$7,750

1806, Small 6, Stems to Wreath • BW-2, C-3, B-2. *Breen dies:* 2-A. *Estimated total population:* 20 to 30.

1806, Small 6, Stems to Wreath (BW-2, C-3, B-2); the key variety of this year.

Detail of the date.

Obverse: Small 6, higher than the previous; bottom higher than bases of 180.

Reverse: Same die as preceding. *Points of distinction:* Late die states have a rim cud over ICA.

Notes: This is a very famous and highly desired rarity. Unknown to Gilbert. Ronald P. Manley: "The rarest variety for the date. Unknown in grades higher than Fine. Almost always found with the obverse die misaligned–off center, with an unusually broad rim at 6 o'clock. The reverse is typically well centered."

1806, Small 6, Stems to Wreath (BW-2)	Cert	Avg	%MS
	(a)		

AG-3	G-4	VG-8	F-12
$3,750	$7,750	$19,000	$35,000

(a) Included in certified population for 1806, Small 6, Stems to Wreath (BW-1).

1806, Small 6, Stemless Wreath • BW-3, C-1, B-3. *Breen dies:* 2-B. *Estimated population:* 4,500 to 6,000.

1806, Small 6, Stemless Wreath (BW-3, C-1, B-3).

Obverse: Same die as preceding.

Reverse: Stemless wreath. *Points of distinction:* This durable die was used to coin 1804, Crosslet 4, Stemless Wreath (BW-10); 1804, Plain 4, Stemless Wreath (BW-11); 1805, Medium 5, Stemless Wreath (BW-1);

and 1806, Small 6, Stemless Wreath (BW-3).

Notes: Gilbert (1916) G-1 "Small 6 / Without stems." This variety exists in Mint State.

1806, Small 6, Stemless Wreath	Cert	Avg	%MS
	115	46.3	20%

G-4	VG-8	F-12	VF-20	EF-40
$40	$75	$100	$175	$300

AU-50	MS-60BN	MS-63BN	MS-63RB
$675	$1,200	$2,900	$3,800

1806, Large 6, Stems to Wreath • BW-4, C-4, B-4. *Breen dies:* 3-C. **Estimated population:** 2,000 to 3,000.

1806, Large 6, Stems to Wreath (BW-4, C-4, B-4).

Obverse: Large 6 with tip into the drapery. *Points of distinction:* Early impressions show repunching at the top of the 6, which is thin; later impressions show the 6 heavier and without traces of repunching.

Reverse: 5 berries left, 5 berries right. Fraction bar lengthened with a spine to the right that ends close to the ribbon.

Points of distinction: This die was also used to coin 1807 (BW-1).

Notes: Mint State is known for this variety. *Gilbert* (1916) G-3 "Large 6 with 6 touching bust / With stems." Many Uncirculated coins exist from the hoard described above. Most have a generous amount of original mint red-orange. Usually lightly struck at the top of the wreath.

1806, Large 6, Stems to Wreath			Cert	Avg	%MS
			80	51.6	45%

G-4	VG-8	F-12	VF-20	EF-40
$40	$80	$125	$180	$325

AU-50	MS-60BN	MS-63BN	MS-63RB
$675	$1,100	$2,750	$3,600

1807, Draped Bust
Mintage (per Mint Report*): 476,000.*

The number of 1807-dated half cents is not known, but the figure 476,000 represents the number of coins struck during the calendar year, probably with many from earlier-dated dies. There is only one die variety of the 1807. Many of the 1807-dated coins were likely struck in 1808.

No hoards contained 1807 half cents to any degree, and today most pieces are encountered in worn grades, mostly VG to EF, with AU or better falling into the scarce category. A true Mint State 1807 is *very* rare. Surfaces are often dark and/or porous, as is also the case for 1808 half cents.

Typical values for 1807 half cents.

1807		Cert	Avg	%MS
		258	38.0	7%

G-4	VG-8	F-12	VF-20	EF-40	AU-50	MS-60BN	MS-63BN
$45	$95	$145	$200	$500	$1,000	$2,000	$3,750

1807 • BW-1, C-1, B-1. *Breen dies:* 1-A. **Estimated population:** 4,000 to 5,000.

1807 (BW-1, C-1, B-1).

Obverse: 180 close to border, 7 overly large and close to border and to drapery. The only die of the year.

Reverse: The same die used to coin 1806, Large 6, Stems to Wreath (BW-4). Now the die is relapped, removing many denticles.

Notes: Mint State is known, but examples are very rare at this level. *Gilbert* (1916) G-1 "Many specimens of this date have the entire border on both obverse and reverse milled [with denticles prominent], while on others the milling is on a portion of the circumference only, or entirely absent." Early die state pieces with full obverse and reverse border denticles exist, but they are extremely rare. These are highly prized by specialists.

1808, 8 Over 7, Draped Bust
Circulation mintage (estimate): Fewer than 50,000.

The *Mint Report* of 400,000 half cents struck in calendar year 1808 may have comprised some half cents of earlier dates, most likely 1804 to 1806. Half cents dated 1808, 8 Over 7, as here, and 1808 are quite scarce in comparison to these earlier dates.

One overdated obverse die was combined with two reverses, creating two varieties for the year. BW-1, discovered by Roger S. Cohen Jr. in 1952, is sufficiently rare that Walter Breen knew of only four by the time he created his work on half cents in 1983. Today there are perhaps a dozen known, the finest VF.

Surfaces are often dark and/or porous, similar to 1807.

As for BW-2, examples are scarce in any grade. Breen knew of only one Uncirculated coin, in a Missouri collection, tracing its pedigree to Philadelphia pharmacist Robert Coulton Davis. The Eliasberg specimen of BW-2, graded EF-40, was accompanied by the note, "Fewer than ten examples are known in grades equal or better than this."[29]

1808, 8 Over 7 • BW-1, C-1, B-1. *Breen dies:* 1-A. ***Estimated population:*** 12 to 15.

1808, 8 Over 7 (BW-1, C-1, B-1); a classic rarity.

Obverse: Overdated die, 1808 Over 7.

Reverse: Berry opposite and slightly higher than center of T of CENT. In fraction, 20 closer than 00. Stem tip is distant from base of second A of AMERICA. *Points of distinction:* In late states a die crack develops through the tops of STATES, and others are seen as well.

Notes: This variety is a major rarity. Nearly all are in low grades, an exception being a VF coin. VG and Fine are about the highest grades available from a practical viewpoint. Unknown to Gilbert. This variety was discovered in 1952 by Roger S. Cohen Jr. A Good-4 coin in Superior's February 1992 sale of the Cohen Collection brought $18,150.

1808, 8 Over 7 (BW-1)	Cert	Avg	%MS
	(a)		

G-4	VG-8	F-12	VF-20
$38,750	$52,500	$100,000	$157,500

(a) Included in certified population for 1808, 8 Over 7 (BW-2).

1808, 8 Over 7 • BW-2, C-2, B-2. *Breen dies:* 1-B. **Estimated population:** 600 to 900.

1808, 8 Over 7 (BW-2, C-2, B-2).

Obverse: Same die as preceding.

Reverse: Berry opposite upper serif of T of CENT. In fraction, 20 wider than 00. Stem tip has thorn-like projection extending to nearly touch the base of second A of AMERICA. *Points of distinction:* This die was used to coin 1808, 8 Over 7 (BW-2),

and 1808 (BW-1). On later states a rim cud is seen above TY, extending to the right. Still later, another cud over BE develops, then in the latest stages, the cud is continuous from BE to the right, past the final Y.

Notes: Gilbert (1916) G-1 "Small 8 over 7." Rare VF or better, very rare at any higher level. Unique in Mint State. AU coins are extremely rare.

1808, 8 Over 7 (BW-2)	Cert	Avg	%MS
	44	21.0	0%

G-4	VG-8	F-12	VF-20	EF-40	AU-50
$240	$390	$725	$2,000	$5,000	$11,750

1808, Draped Bust
Mintage (per Mint Report): 400,000.

The 1808 regular half cents, not overdated, are somewhat scarce. Very curiously, the *second* 8, but not the first, was made by taking the small 0 punch used to create the fraction 1/200 and punching it twice, one impression over the other![30] This would likely indicate that the die was first made with a partial date, and with a regular 8 punch, reading 180, but when completed an 8 punch was not readily at hand.

Typical grades range from Good to VF, with anything higher ranging from scarce to rare. Surfaces are often dark and/or porous, similar to 1807.

Similar to the comment for 1807, the mintage figure has no real meaning. The actual production of the 1808 perfect date half cents was probably less than 100,000.

Typical values for 1808 half cents.

1808	Cert	Avg	%MS
	119	30.8	2%

G-4	VG-8	F-12	VF-20	EF-40	AU-50	MS-60BN	MS-63BN
$45	$85	$145	$220	$525	$1,300	$2,500	$5,000

1808 • BW-1, C-3, B-3. *Breen dies:* 2-B. **Estimated population:** 3,000 to 4,000.

1808 (BW-1, C-3, B-3).

Detail of the date showing the second 8 improvised by using a small 0 punch twice.

Obverse: 1808 die with curious second 8 made by using a small 0 punch twice (the same punch that made the 00 in the fraction denominator).

Reverse: Berry opposite center of T of CENT. In fraction, 20 wider than 00. Stem tip has thorn-like projection extending to nearly touch the base of second A of AMERICA. *Points of distinction:* This die was used to coin 1808, 8 Over 7 (BW-2), and 1808 (BW-1).

Notes: Gilbert (1916) G-2 "High 8 touching bust." Gilbert also listed his No. 3, with relapped obverse "to eliminate a slight accidental defect at the top of the head." Very rare in Mint State with slightly more than a half dozen reported, mostly at lower levels. AU coins are rare.

CLASSIC HEAD (1809–1836)

1835 (BW-1, C-1, B-1).

Designer: *John Reich.* **Weight:** *84 grains (5.44 grams).*
Composition: *Copper.* **Diameter:** *23.5 mm.* **Edge:** *Plain.*

The Classic Head half cent design was first used in 1809 and was continued intermittently until 1836. Large quantities were struck of certain years (especially 1809) and for certain dates in the 1820s and 1830s. This type is quite unusual within American numismatics, as there was a flurry of coinage activity from 1809 to 1811, and after that, nothing until 1825. The final shipment of copper planchets prior to the War of 1812 arrived from Boulton & Watt on April 15, 1812, and contained cents only, as the Mint had not ordered any for half cents. On April 27, 1829, Director Moore wrote to Senator Sanford of New York stating that half cents were not popular, and banks, post offices, and others did not order them often. If half cents were shipped in lieu of cents, complaints arose.[31] Once the Mint resumed making half cents in 1825, demand remained erratic. By 1829, coinage outstripped demand to the point that a large surplus was built up, and remained in the vaults until 1833. In addition, as copper coins were a profit center for the Mint, it was inefficient to coin copper into half cents instead of cents, as it took twice as much effort.

The worn appearance of most early half cents is testimony that they found extensive use in commerce, in spite of their unpopularity. Typical grades seen today in the marketplace range from Good to VF, but with enough EF and AU coins that finding one will not be a problem. Most of the higher-grade coins of the first three years are of the 1809 date. Occasional coins of Mint State are encountered for the early dates, again nearly always of 1809, and never with significant original orange-red mint color.

After 1811 there was a long span in which no half cents were coined, until 1825, when production recommenced with 63,000 in that calendar year; followed by 234,000 in 1826; none in 1827; 606,000 in 1828; and 487,000 in 1829. Again these are calendar-year figures. Actual dating of the coins may have varied. One curious variety among 1828 half cents is the variety with 12 instead of 13 stars on the obverse, an engraving error. This variety is scarcer than the 13-star issue, particularly in higher grades. Most examples show signs of wear. Ronald P. Manley in his essential *Half Cent Die State Book* comments that the obverse die for Classic Head half cents of 1825 to 1836 was made from a new hub created from the master hub of 1809. The new dies lacked the crack-like defect across Miss Liberty's neck and the hair that was so characteristic of early Classic Head dies. Deterioration resulted in a defective L in LIBERTY.

After 1829 there was again a gap in coinage, until 1831, when Mint records suggest that just 2,200 were struck, creating a great rarity. Today, very few are known. However, at a later time the Mint stepped into the breach and supplied collectors by creating restrikes, not carefully matching the dies, with the result that among restrikes, one variety has a die originally used in 1836, and another 1831-dated restrike has a die from the era of 1840 to 1857. Such technical niceties were not widely known when such pieces were restruck, but later generations of collectors used them as forensic evidence to endeavor to decipher what happened.

Although the term *restrike* has a negative connotation, in the half cent series this has had little effect on the demand for the rare issues. These commence with the curious 1811 restrike and continue into the 1850s. Many are the instances in which restrikes of certain dates have brought far more money than have originals. Walter Breen's 1983 text on half cents devotes many pages to the technical aspects of restrikes of various sorts, and the present reader is referred to that text for additional data.

From 1832 through 1835, more half cents were struck. It is not known if the dates on the coins matched the calendar years, and some questions have been raised. Half cents of this era were not popular with the public. Many were stored by banks and others, and some coins found their way into hoards that were later distributed into numismatic circles. Today, half cents of this era are available in Mint State with some frequency, often with significant amounts of mint red (actually orange), but usually with flecks or spots. Half cents of the year 1833 are sometimes highly prooflike, and now and again they are listed as Proofs in catalogs, this being more the policy of generations ago than of collectors today.

The Classic Head half cent rounded out its existence with those dated 1836, struck only in Proof format for cabinet or collecting purposes, with none made for general circulation. Today, only a few dozen 1836-dated half cents are known, the so-called originals, with the correct reverse of the year; restrikes with the correct reverse; and restrikes with a mismatched reverse of the general style used from 1840 to 1857 (and lacking the line under the word CENT).

While rarities such as 1831 and 1836 are highly admired by those who can afford them, the elite and generally unavailable status of these has turned some away from collecting half cents in general. Roger Cohen, in the first edition of his book, elected not to study them, preferring to concentrate only on pieces made for general circulation. Proofs were given light treatment in his second edition. Note that the Cohen or "C" cross references for Proofs are cumbersome and hardly ever cited today.

There were no half cents struck in 1837, 1838, or 1839. Sometimes a popular Hard Times Token with the inscription HALF CENT WORTH OF PURE COPPER of a completely different design, has been collected along with the half cent series, simply because in the 1930s Wayte Raymond—realizing there were no federal half cents of this date—included a space for the token in his "National" brand albums. A tradition was created, and today such pieces jump out from a page of the *Guide Book of United States Coins*. Properly the piece belongs in the Hard Times tokens series.

Half cents of 1825 and later are available in higher average grades such as EF and AU, as these did not circulate widely. Mint State coins from old-time hoards are available of certain dates in the 1820s and 1830s, particularly 1828, 1833, and 1835. Such coins may have generous amounts of original mint-orange color (incorrectly called "red"), but usually with flecks or spots. There are *many* retoned and artificially colored pieces on the market, including in certified holders. Cherrypicking is strongly recommended, and you may have to consider several or more possibilities before finding one with excellent aesthetic appeal. A trustworthy dealer can be a good counsel in your search, until you gain sufficient knowledge.

Proofs were struck of various years in the 1820s per "conventional wisdom," but this is open to serious question. Ronald P. Manley states, "No unequivocal Proof half-cent from the 1820s is known to me."[32] PCGS has certified no Proof half cent dated before 1831.[33] Q. David Bowers and several half cent and large cent experts have agreed that no Proofs of the 1820s, at least through and including 1828, can be confirmed to be true mirror Proofs, sharply struck, and with mirror edges (when viewed edge-on). This is in contravention to Walter Breen's texts, which list *many* Proofs from that decade.

Proofs were definitely made in the 1830s, with the well-known 1831 and 1836 being great rarities (these dates were also restruck at the Mint circa 1859 and later). Some prooflike coins (especially of the 1833 date) have been sold as Proofs. Finding a choice Proof with excellent appeal is a daunting task.

DESIGN DETAILS

The Classic Head design was created by John Reich, a German immigrant who worked as an assistant engraver at the Mint. The motif was created in 1808 for the large copper cent, but first used in the half cent series in 1809.

On the obverse the head of Miss Liberty faces to the left, her hair in curls close to her head and secured by a band on which is lettered LIBERTY. The date is below the head. Seven stars are at the left border and six are to the right. All numerals were entered individually into the die by separate punches. This design was essentially swiped by Chief Engraver William Kneass in 1834 for use on the Classic Head $2.50 gold coins and $5 gold pieces.

In 1809 a crack developed in the obverse hub midway between the bottom of the ear and the top of the curl that rests completely on the neck. This crack is seen on all dies of 1810 and 1811. In 1825 a new hub was introduced with some slight differences in the hair and ribbon ends to the right.

The wreath is a departure from earlier times and now features a continuous wreath of leaves and berries decorated with a ribbon bow at the bottom. Within is the denomination HALF / CENT. Around the border is UNITED STATES OF AMERICA.

1809, Classic Head
Mintage (per Mint Report): *1,154,572.*

The production of the first year, 1809 was very generous at 1,154,572, presumably all from 1809-dated dies, based on the ratio of surviving examples. This production figure takes its place as the highest quantity produced for any half cent from 1793 to 1857.

Today, half cents of 1809 are among the more plentiful in the marketplace. Several die varieties exist of 1809, including one with a small 0 figure inside the larger regular 0 and the 1809, Triple Punched 9 (earlier called 1809 over inverted 6, but now with that status debunked).

Half cents dated 1809 are seen in a wide variety of grades, including more than a few in EF, AU, or even in lustrous brown Mint State. Planchets tend to be somewhat on the dark side.

Typical values for 1809, Normal Date,
half cents. Rare varieties may be worth more.

1809, Normal Date	Cert	Avg	%MS
	379	45.8	26%

G-4	VG-8	F-12	VF-20	EF-40	AU-50	MS-60BN	MS-63BN	MS-63RB
$30	$60	$100	$150	$375	$750	$1,300	$2,200	$3,500

1809, Normal Date • BW-1, C-1, B-2. *Breen dies: 2-B. Estimated population: 50 to 100.*

1809, Normal Date (BW-1, C-1, B-2).

Obverse: Left edge of curl is slightly to the left of the center of the 0. *Points of distinction:* In its latest state in the present combination a faint crack connects stars 11 and 12.

Reverse: Tip of highest leaf directly below right edge of second S of STATES. Berry directly opposite upright of T of UNITED. Berry directly opposite right foot of R of AMERICA. *Points of distinction:* A rim cud is seen from M through slightly past I of AMERICA.

Notes: This variety, unknown to Gilbert, was discovered by Richard Picker in 1954. That several dozen have been found since that time is testimony to the popularity of Roger S. Cohen Jr.'s book, which came into wide use in an era in which very few collectors had a copy of the Gilbert text. EF is the highest grade known.

1809, Normal Date • BW-2, C-2, B-3. *Breen dies: 2-C. Estimated population: 200 to 350.*

1809, Normal Date (BW-2, C-2, B-3).

Obverse: Same die as preceding. *Points of distinction:* The tiny crack at stars 11 and 12 expands.

Reverse: Tip of highest leaf slightly past right edge of second S of STATES. Berry slightly to the right of the upright of T of UNITED. Tip of leaf opposite tip of lower-right serif of F in OF. *Points of distinction:* In time a tiny cud break appears above the space between D and S.

Notes: Gilbert (1916) G-3 "The cipher of date without the inner circle / High leaf ending before the front of S." Known in Mint State, but very rare as such.

1809, Normal Date • BW-3, C-3, B-4. *Breen dies:* 3-C. **Estimated population: 800 to 1,200.**

1809, Normal Date (BW-3, C-3, B-4).

Obverse: Star 13 close to 9 of 1809. Left edge of curl is above center of 0. *Points of distinction:* Cracks are seen at the stars.

Reverse: Same die as preceding. *Points of distinction:* The die in a late state shows deterioration of the denticles.

Notes: Known in Mint State. *Gilbert* (1916) G-4 "Close star variety / High leaf below front of S and another below right stand of F in OF. . . . First star to the right is but 1-1/4 mm from the 9."

1809, Normal Date • BW-4, C-6, B-6. *Breen dies:* 5-E. **Estimated population: 3,000 to 5,000.**

1809, Normal Date (BW-4, C-6, B-6).

Obverse: Star 13 distant from 9 of 1809; the 9 is about the same distance from the 8 in the date as from Star 13. Star 1 is closer to the denticles than to the bust.

Left edge of curl is above and slightly to the right of the center of 0.

Reverse: Tip of highest leaf far past right edge of second S of STATES, but not quite halfway to O in OF.

Notes: This variety exists in Mint State. *Gilbert* (1916) G-2 "Perfect date variety / High leaf ending midway between S and O." The dies deteriorate with use, with rim breaks developing on the obverse, and with relapping and deterioration of the reverse.

1809, Small o Within 0 of Date • BW-5, C-4, B-1. *Breen dies:* 1-A. **Estimated population: 700 to 1,000.**

1809, Small o Within 0 of Date (BW-5, C-4, B-1).

Detail of the date, showing a large 0 punched over a smaller o.

Obverse: 0 in date punched over earlier smaller 0 digit.

Reverse: Tip of highest leaf below left edge of O in OF.

Notes: Mint State is known, but examples are seldom seen at this level. *Gilbert* (1916) G-1 "In date the cipher has an inner circle / High leaf ending near letter O." Most show extensive circulation. The obverse and reverse dies seem to have been relapped (details in Ronald P. Manley, *The Half Cent Die State Book 1793–1857*, a source generally valuable for all of the half cent varieties).

1809, Small o Within 0 of Date		Cert	Avg	%MS
		16	36.8	0%

G-4	VG-8	F-12	VF-20	EF-40	AU-50
$45	$70	$120	$275	$650	$1,350

1809, Repunched 9 • BW-6, C-5, B-5. *Breen dies:* 4-D. **Estimated population:** 2,000 to 3,000.

1809, Repunched 9 (BW-6, C-5, B-5).

Detail of the date, showing the repunched 9.

Obverse: With repunched date, formerly called "9 over inverted 9," but now known not to have an inverted digit.[34]

Reverse: Tip of highest leaf slightly past right edge of second S of STATES. Berry slightly to the right of the upright of T of UNITED. Tip of leaf past tip of lower-right serif of F in OF.

Notes: This variety exists in Mint State. *Gilbert* (1916) G-5 "Very close star variety / High leaf past front of S and another ending to the right of F. . . . Date measures 7-1/2 mm wide, with first star to the right 1 mm. distant." Gilbert made no mention of any date punch anomaly. Both dies deteriorate with use, mainly affecting the denticles, which become increasingly blurry. Relapping removes some low relief details.

1809, Repunched 9		Cert	Avg	%MS
		214	49.8	18%

G-4	VG-8	F-12	VF-20	EF-40	AU-50
$37	$70	$100	$150	$375	$750

MS-60BN	MS-63BN	MS-63RB	MS-65BN	MS-65RB
$1,300	$2,200	$3,250	$10,000	$20,000

1810, Classic Head
Mintage (per Mint Report): 215,000.

Among early Classic Head half cents the 1810 is considered to be slightly scarce, but not quite in the same league of scarcity as the 1811. Only one pair of dies was used. Most are seen with extensive wear. Always seen with some areas of light striking on the obverse stars on the right, as the die faces were not parallel. Mint State examples are rare and are unknown with significant original red-orange mint color.

Typical values for 1810 half cents.

1810		Cert	Avg	%MS
		94	41.6	19%

G-4	VG-8	F-12	VF-20	EF-40	AU-50	MS-60BN	MS-63BN	MS-63RB
$40	$75	$125	$260	$540	$1,000	$2,000	$3,200	$6,750

1810 • BW-1, C-1, B-1. *Breen dies:* 1-A. ***Estimated population:*** 2,000 to 3,000.

1810 (BW-1, C-1, B-1).

Obverse: 0 of 1810 slightly repunched. *Points of distinction:* A crack is seen through stars 5 to 7, continuing to the top of the hair.

Reverse: Standard design of the type.

Notes: Mint State is known for this variety. Examples grading better than EF are scarce.

1811, Classic Head
Mintage (per Mint Report): 63,140.

The 1811 is the key date among early half cents of the Classic Head type. The mintage is given as 63,140, which is likely in the ballpark, at least. Two different die varieties are known, sometimes called Wide Date and Close Date, although the difference is not particularly noticeable. In the marketplace, VF is a high grade for either of the two varieties, and a sharp EF is exceptional. True Mint State coins are rare, with perhaps a half dozen or so different examples known, with maybe the finest being the BW-2 in the Eliasberg Collection, 1996, graded as MS-63.

The so-called 1811 restrike, actually a numismatic fantasy or novodel (as the die combination was never originally struck, so it cannot be restruck), is an interesting addition to the coinage of this year. These are very rare and always attract attention when offered.

1811 • BW-1, C-1, B-1. *Breen dies:* 1-A. ***Estimated population:*** 150 to 225.

1811 (BW-1, C-1, B-1); this is by far the rarer of two varieties of this year.

Obverse: Wide Date. Spaced as 1 81 1 with 81 closer than 18 or 11. Star 1 about equidistant from denticles and neck. Star 13 is equidistant between the curl and border (a quick reference point). *Points of distinction:* The die developed a crack to the left of the date, which progressively enlarges, eventually resulting in a large piece falling from the left obverse rim, extending to include part of two stars, and later consuming part of four stars. Examples with the break involving two stars are extremely rare, with only a half dozen known, and those always in low grades. Those showing the break through all four stars are rare, although much more available than the two-star break pieces.

Reverse: Only one die. Berry opposite upright of R of AMERICA, unlike any other dies to this point in time. *Points of distinction:* The die develops a light crack which expands along the rim.

Notes: *Gilbert* (1916) G-2 "Distant 18 in date." Mint State is known, and examples are rare so fine. AU coins occasionally come on the market and are also rare.

1811 (BW-1)			Cert	Avg	%MS
			3	18.3	0%

G-4	VG-8	F-12	VF-20	EF-40
$390	$875	$1,650	$2,750	$6,500

1811 • BW-2, C-2, B-2. *Breen dies:* 2-A. **Estimated population:** 1,000 to 1,400.

1811 (BW-2, C-2, B-2).

Detail of star 13, nearly touching the border.

Obverse: Close Date. Spaced as 181 1 with second 1 farther away. Star 1 much closer to denticles than to neck. Star 13 nearly touches the border (a quick reference point).

Reverse: Same die as preceding.

Notes: *Gilbert* (1916) G-1 "Close 18 in date." Mint State is known for this variety, and examples are very rare as such. AU and EF are practical goals.

1811 (BW-2)			Cert	Avg	%MS
			5	23.4	0%

G-4	VG-8	F-12	VF-20	EF-40	AU-50
$375	$850	$1,550	$2,500	$6,000	$7,500

1811, "Restrike" with Reverse of 1802, Mismatched Dies • BW-3.
Breen dies: 1811, 2-1802, B. **Estimated population:** 10 to 12.

1811, "Restrike" with Reverse of 1802, Mismatched Dies (BW-3).

Obverse: Same as BW-2.

Reverse: Die used to coin 1802 Over 0, Reverse of 1802, 1 Leaf Left, 2 Leaves Right at Wreath Apex (BW-2), open wreath.

Notes: Exists in Mint State. All such examples are about the same, although some have mint color. A numismatic fantasy or novodel pairing two dies never originally used together. All are in Mint State, usually brown with some traces of red-orange, from rusted dies yielding rough surfaces. Walter Breen in his 1983 work listed 10 "demonstrably different" specimens.

Numismatic Notes: *The 1811 restrike:* This curious coin was privately struck in the mid-1800s using dies discarded as scrap iron by the Mint. The obverse is that of 1811 (BW-2), and the reverse is a mismatched type used to coin 1802 Over 0, Reverse of 1802, 1 Leaf Left, 2 Leaves Right at Wreath Apex (BW-2). This is popularly known as the "Mickley Restrike," but evidence specifically linking the *production* to that old-time Philadelphia collector is circumstantial at best, seemingly based on this posthumous listing by Édouard Frossard in his 16th Sale:

> Lot 1246: 1811 Very fine impression; struck from the dies while in the possession of the late Mr. Mickley. It will be remembered that the reverse of this half cent is the same as reverse of a 'draped bust' half cent, and that both obverse and reverse dies have since been destroyed. Extremely rare.

However, Mickley did own the obverse die at one time, as it was included in the catalog of his estate.

The first auction appearance was likely in a sale by Edward Cogan in 1859, when an 1811 half cent was described as having a "Different reverse, very rare type." Later, it became popular to state that 12 specimens were coined, but there seems to be no doc-umentation at all as to when it was struck, or by whom, or how many were made.

1811, "Restrike" with Reverse of 1802, Mismatched Dies	Cert	Avg	%MS
	5	63.8	100%

MS-60BN	MS-63BN	MS-63RB	MS-64BN	MS-64RB
$18,750	$24,500	$30,000	$37,500	$50,000

QUALITY AMONG LATER-DATE HALF CENTS

Half cents from 1825 onward are generally found with good eye appeal and on good planchets. Striking is usually quite good. Prices listed are for such coins. Examples with flat stars, mushy denticles, or other problems should be worth slightly less, but the market hardly notices. Among Mint State coins, recolored, stained, or blotchy coins are worth less (again, in the marketplace such coins are usually not identified as such). There are opportunities for cherrypicking for quality, but not to the extent found on earlier half cent issues.

1825, Classic Head
Mintage (per Mint Report): 63,000.

The idea of resuming coinage of half cents occurred by August 10, 1824, when Mint Director Samuel Moore wrote to Matthew Boulton on August 10, to ask about prices of half cent planchets. None had been struck for many years. Planchets were obtained from Boulton, who was supplying *cent* planchets to the Mint at the time. John Reich's Classic Head motif was dusted off for the new coinage.

Mintage began in December 1825 in response to a significant order placed in November by Jonathan Elliott & Sons of Baltimore. The Mint Treasurer informed the Elliott company on November 23 that no half cents were on hand at the time, but they perhaps would be in January. Mint records, however, indicate that none were paid out until the second quarter of 1826.[35] By that time, the Classic Head motif had been discontinued years earlier on the *cent* pieces and had been replaced in 1816 with what Ken Bressett designated in modern times (for use in the regular edition of the *Guide Book of United States Coins*) as the Matron Head.

Half cents were not called for in commerce, and none had been made for a long period of time. In 1859 Dr. Montroville W. Dickeson noted that by 1825 "people had acquired the habit of disregarding fractions, and had no disposition to renew them for making change. We can recollect, however, when in some portions of our country the half cent was rigidly exacted, and where many a war of words, and sometimes of fists, grew out of such a controversy."[36]

The mintage figure is for the calendar year. The availability of this date suggests that additional coins were struck in 1826 and recorded in that calendar year.

Examples are easy enough to find, and are usually in higher grades, VF upward. Mint State coins appear with frequency, but are usually in lower MS ranges.

Proofs: None.

1825 • BW-1, C-1, B-1. *Breen dies:* 1-A. ***Estimated population:*** 300 to 500.

1825 (BW-1, C-1, B-1).

Obverse: Center of curl over the center of the 5. Stars 4 and 5, 8 and 9, and 11 and 12 are more widely spaced than the others. *Points of distinction:* The die develops light cracks in its latest state.

Reverse: Only one die. Standard type of the period.

Notes: *Gilbert* (1916) G-2 "Curl over 5 of date." Examples exist in Mint State, typically brown.

1825 • BW-2, C-2, B-2. *Breen dies:* 2-A. ***Estimated population:*** 3,500 to 4,500.

1825 (BW-2, C-2, B-2).

Obverse: Center of the curl over the left edge of the 5. Stars 1 through 3 and 11 to 12 more widely spaced than are the others.

Reverse: Same die as preceding.

Notes: *Gilbert* (1916) G-1 "Curl over 25 of date." Some coins have prooflike surfaces. Examples exist in Mint State, typically brown.

Typical values for BW-2. BW-1 is worth more.

1825 (BW-2)		Cert	Avg	%MS
		262	49.7	26%

G-4	VG-8	F-12	VF-20	EF-40	AU-50
$35	$55	$75	$100	$200	$325

MS-60BN	MS-63BN	MS-63RB	MS-65BN	MS-65RB
$800	$1,750	$3,000	$6,000	$15,000

1826, Classic Head
Mintage (per Mint Report): 234,000.

It is likely that the mintage figure for calendar year 1826 included many from 1825-dated dies. Half cents of 1826 are characteristically lightly struck at the highest stars on each side of the head. Examples are easy enough to find in circulated grades, VF and upward, with EF and AU being typical. Mint State coins are fairly scarce and are usually in lower MS ranges.

 Proofs: None.

1826 • BW-1, C-1, B-1. *Breen dies:* 1-A. ***Estimated population:*** 3,500 to 4,500.

1826 (BW-1, C-1, B-1).

Obverse: Stars 1 and 2 are widely separated in comparison to stars 2 and 3, which are closer together. Star 13 points to a denticle slightly below its center. Crosshatching of raised file marks to the right of the 6. *Points of distinction:* Light cracks develop on later states.

Reverse: Leaf tip ends far past second S of STATES. Stray part of serif between tops of E and D of UNITED.

Notes: Gilbert (1916) G-1 "High leaf past S." Examples exist in Mint State, typically brown.

Typical values for BW-1. BW-2 is worth more.

1826 (BW-1)		Cert	Avg	%MS
		344	50.0	32%

G-4	VG-8	F-12	VF-20	EF-40	AU-50
$30	$50	$75	$90	$150	$300

MS-60BN	MS-63BN	MS-63RB	MS-65BN	MS-65RB
$600	$1,000	$1,500	$2,875	$5,000

1826 • BW-2, C-2, B-2. *Breen dies:* 2-B. **Estimated population:** 200 to 275.

1826 (BW-2, C-2, B-2).

Obverse: Stars 1 and 2 are close together in comparison to stars 2 and 3, which are more widely separated. Star 13 points to a space between denticles. *Points of distinction:* At the date tiny remnants of a horizontal 6 are visible. Lower-grade examples do not show this. In the extreme-latest state there is a rim cud on the left, consuming parts of stars 4 and 5, creating a much-sought variety. Just seven are known according to Ronald P. Manley.

Reverse: Leaf tip ends under second S of STATES, slightly to the right of its center. *Points of distinction:* This die was also used to coin 1828, 13 Stars (BW-1). Was it also used for 1828, 12 Stars (BW-3)? (See that listing for Gilbert comment.)

Notes: Gilbert (1916) G-2 "High leaf under S." Mint State is known, and examples are very rare as such.

1828, Classic Head

Mintage (per Mint Report*): 606,000.*

The 1828 half cent is found with three die varieties. Two of these have the normal 13 stars on the obverse, but the third has just 12. Interestingly, coins of this date consist of three different obverses combined with three different reverses, with no overlapping. As the dies do not show signs of significant breakage, dies in each pair must have been retired from the press at the same time.

The 12-star variety is a remarkable die-cutting error with relatively few equivalents in American coinage (others include the 1817 cent with 15 instead of 13 stars and the 1832 half eagle with only 12 stars). It is likely that many coins from the large mintage of 606,000 were never released.

Today, the 13-star coins, which exist in two die varieties, are plentiful in the marketplace. The typical coin is EF or AU with light-brown surfaces. Mint State coins are easily found, most no doubt from the Collins Find (see page 241). These hoard coins are often seen with much or most original orange-red mint color, but nearly always with flecks or spots. Cherrypicking will yield a very eye-pleasing coin.

The 12-star variety is readily found, usually at the VF or EF level. AU coins are scarce, and true Mint State coins are slightly rare. None were in the Collins Find. These typically have lustrous brown surfaces. The Eliasberg coin, a notable specimen, was graded MS-63 with about 10 percent original mint red. We have never seen one with full *original* mint color. The demand for this variety, in any and all grades, has always been very strong. This is a "must have!" coin for many buyers who do not otherwise seek die varieties, with the listing in the perennially popular *Guide Book of United States Coins* making it known to millions of readers.

Proofs: None.

1828, 13 Stars • BW-1, C-1, B-1. *Breen dies:* 1-A. *Estimated population:* 1,000 to 1,500.[37]

1828, 13 Stars (BW-1, C-1, B-1).

Obverse: 13 stars. Rays of Star 7 point to slightly above and slightly below the outline of the ribbon. Star 13 points to between two denticles.

Reverse: Berry under upright of T of UNITED just slightly above its center. Tip of leaf under second S of STATES slightly right of its center. *Points of distinction:* This die was also used to coin 1826 (BW-2).

Notes: Gilbert (1916) G-2 "High leaf under S." There is not much price differentiation in the marketplace between BW-1 and BW-2. In Mint State the BW-1 is *far rarer* than BW-2. Mint State examples are typically brown. Priced after BW-2.

1828, 13 Stars • BW-2, C-3, B-2. *Breen dies:* 2-B. *Estimated population:* 5,000 to 7,000.

1828, 13 Stars (BW-2, C-3, B-2).

Detail of date with 2 slightly out of alignment.

Obverse: 13 stars. Rays of Star 7 point to the top corner of the ribbon frame and to the curl on the forehead. 2 of 1828 leans forward so that the lower left is out of alignment with the first 8. Star 13 points to a denticle.

Reverse: Berry under upright of lower-left serif of E of UNITED just slightly above its center. Tip of leaf past right edge of second S of STATES. Tip of leaf under C of AMERICA just slightly right of its center.

Notes: Gilbert (1916) G-1 "High leaf extending beyond S." This is the variety found in the Collins Hoard. Such coins are plentiful in the marketplace today. As such, Mint State is known, often with significant original color.

Typical values for 1828, 13 Stars. BW-1 is worth slightly more, and BW-2, slightly less.

1828, 13 Stars			Cert	Avg	%MS
			132	49.0	38%

VG-8	F-12	VF-20	EF-40	AU-50	MS-60BN
$50	$70	$95	$125	$225	$350

MS-63BN	MS-63RB	MS-65BN	MS-65RB	MS-65RD
$600	$1,000	$1,875	$3,500	$6,000

1828, 12 Stars • BW-3, C-2, B-3. *Breen dies:* 3-C. **Estimated population:** 3,000 to 4,000.

1828, 12 Stars (BW-3, C-2, B-3); the curious variety with 12 obverse stars.

Obverse: 12 stars. The date is farther to the right than usual for the type.

Reverse: Berry under lower-right serif of upright of T of UNITED just slightly above its center. Tip of leaf slightly farther past second S of STATES than on BW-2. Tip of leaf under right edge of C of AMERICA.

Notes: Mint State exists in this variety, typically brown. *Gilbert* (1916) G-3 "12 star variety." Gilbert also noted—upon close examination of the die state of "a coin struck from practically a perfect die"—that *in a later state* this reverse was combined with an 1826 obverse die. However, this 1828 reverse die does not match that used on either of the 1826 half cents described here or in the Breen *Encyclopedia*. Meanwhile, *another* 1828 reverse (BW-1) was combined with 1826 (BW-2). This 1828 use seems to have occurred later.

Numismatic Notes: The 1828 with 12 stars: In the *Historical Magazine*, May 1860, a reader's query was published from W. West, of Haverford, Pennsylvania: "Half cent of 1828. Can you, or any of the knowing ones among your correspondents, tell why there are only twelve, instead of thirteen, stars on the half cents of 1828? I have often asked coin collectors, but they professed ignorance."

1828, 12 Stars			Cert	Avg	%MS
			213	50.8	25%

G-4	VG-8	F-12	VF-20	EF-40
$35	$55	$75	$120	$250

AU-50	MS-60BN	MS-63BN	MS-63RB
$425	$1,300	$1,850	$3,500

THE COLLINS FIND OF 1828 HALF CENTS (WITH 13 STARS)

In his catalog of the Allison W. Jackman Collection, June 28–29, 1918, Philadelphia dealer Henry Chapman inserted this commentary after lot 879, a rare *1811* half cent, to shed light on the ready availability in Uncirculated grade of 1828-dated half cents, the variety with 13 obverse stars:

> This [1811] coin was discovered in 1884, being brought by an old colored woman of Alexandria, Va., to Mr. Benjamin H. Collins of Washington, to whom she stated she had a bag of them! He, thinking there was not any mistake about the hoard, sold it [*i.e.*, the 1811] to S.H. & H. Chapman for $3! With the remark, 'How many more will you take?'
>
> We said the lot.
>
> The woman subsequently brought him the bag, but to his astonishment they were all 1828 13 stars! And it has always been a mystery to me that an 1811 equally fine as the 1828s should have been in with the later date, and that her pick at random should have alighted on the only 1811 in the bag! It was subsequently sold in the Warner Sale, $67, and there bought by Mr. Jackman.

The preceding account has a number of inaccuracies and requires some amplification and modification including the following information:

B.H. Collins of Washington, D.C., specialized in early copper coins, especially cents, and was known for the fine specimens he handled, including several notable pieces imported from Europe. However, in 1884 he was an employee of the Treasury department. It was not until the 1890s that he became a rare coin dealer. Thus, the date of the hoard is moved up a decade to 1894. The 1811 half cent was sold by Collins to Chapman for $18, not $3. Further, the Warner and Jackman specimens were two different coins. The number of 1828 half cents in the hoard was stated to be 50 by Collins in a conversation with John F. Jones in December 1899.

It is not known how many 1828 13-stars half cents were in the Collins Find, and the figure of 50 may be correct, but probably it is not. Many more than that are known today. In 1988 Walter Breen commented that the hoard "apparently originally numbered 1,000; as late as 1955 a remnant containing several hundred pieces was in the holdings of F.C.C. Boyd."[38]

In confirmation of the preceding, in 1996 John J. Ford Jr. stated that many of these pieces were owned by David U. Proskey, who sold them to Boyd along with other material. In the early 1950s about 200 to 300 bright red coins were sold by Boyd to New Netherlands Coin Co.[39]

Fact-finding concerning hoards is never an easy task, and absolute definition is often impossible. The typical Collins Find specimen seen today is bright orange-red with spotting.[40]

1829, Classic Head

Mintage (per Mint Report*): 487,000.*

The reported coinage of 487,000 for the calendar year probably includes some of earlier dates. There is only one die pair known for the 1829 half cents. Alternatively, more than one pair of dies may have been used, but production from the other dies was never released. Mintage figures for half cents of this era do not usually correlate with the availability of coins in the marketplace today.

On December 31, 1829, the Mint had 43 kegs of half cents on hand, comprising 848,000 coins—including the undistributed production of that year plus many from the year previous; this represents an average of 19,721 coins per keg.[41] The Mint shipped coins in wooden kegs as a heavy keg could be rolled easily, whereas if the coins had been boxed, a wheeled cart would have been required.

Today, the 1829 half cent is common in grades such as EF or AU. As to Mint State coins, they are scarce, but enough exist that finding one will be no problem. Most are lustrous brown or with some tinges of mint red (orange-red)—scarcely ever with much original mint red.

Proofs: A few meeting the qualification for this attribution exist, including the Philip Showers coin now in a Missouri collection.

1829	Cert	Avg	%MS
	335	51.9	47%

G-4	VG-8	F-12	VF-20	EF-40	AU-50	MS-60BN	MS-63BN	MS-63RB	MS-65BN	MS-65RB
$30	$50	$70	$100	$140	$235	$400	$700	$1,175	$2,000	$3,750

1829 • BW-1, C-1, B-1. *Breen dies:* 1-A. **Estimated population:** 3,000 to 5,000.

1829 (BW-1, C-1, B-1).

Obverse: Date low and close to border, 1 and 2 slightly high. Stars 1 and 2 and 11 and 12 closely spaced.

Reverse: Berry opposite lower-left serif of E of UNITED. Tip of leaf ends slightly past second S of STATES.

Notes: None known to have been in any hoard. Mint State exists in this variety, typically brown.

1831, Classic Head
Mintage (per Mint Report): 2,200.

This year introduced a modification of the rims. The denticles are in the form of beads set inside a flat rim, the equivalent of what has been called a "closed collar" in the new style of certain silver coins of the era, beginning in 1828.

Although hundreds of thousands of undistributed half cents of earlier years were in storage at the Mint, coinage in 1831 was reported as 2,200 pieces. No examples are known with mint luster or frost. Whether the circulated coins that are recorded are circulation strikes or Proofs that were spent has been a matter of debate in the pages of *Penny-Wise.* Ronald P. Manley, for instance, took up the subject in "A Case for Proof-Only 1831 Half Cents," May 15, 1996. Just one obverse die was made, and this was used to coin Proofs as well as circulation strikes. R.W. Julian cites convincing evidence that 2,200 half cents were struck in this year, although the documents do not mention the date(s) on the coins. It is Q. David Bowers's view that 2,200 1831-dated half cents were struck as representatives of the new technology. These seem to have been struck from a single die pair that had prooflike or full Proof surfaces. Whether all were released is an open question, as the coins today are even rarer than a typical surviving percentage of the mintage might suggest.

Regarding the surface, an analogy can be drawn to the 1836-dated Gobrecht silver dollars struck at the Mint in 1836 and early 1837 to the extent of 1,600 pieces—all with mirrored surfaces. Nearly all of these dollars were simply listed as coinage in the *Mint Reports* (no mention of mirror surfaces), and nearly all were placed into circulation for face value at the time. Thus, the answer seems to be: all were Proofs or had mirrored surfaces.

Original 1831 half cents were made in the year indicated, in small numbers for inclusion in Proof sets as well as for any interested numismatists (the Mint was very accommodating for such requests, but the population of collectors was very small), as well as in larger amounts for circulation (but from the same dies). Sometime after 1836, the so-called First Restrikes were coined, combining the single obverse die with a Proof die used to make 1836-dated Proof half cents. Still later, Second Restrikes were made, with the new reverse style (probably not before spring 1859, smaller wreath, no line below CENT) introduced in 1840, but on a Proof die with parallel die scratches over RICA (the "Second Restrike" reverse, used with dies 1840 through 1849 and again in 1852).

1831, Original • BW-1, C-1 (for Proof, EO-5), B-1. *Breen dies:* 1-A. **Estimated population:** Circulated Proofs: 20 to 30; Proof-60 and upward: 10 to 15.

1831, Original (BW-1, C-1, B-1).

Obverse: Small date placed low on the coin. 8 smaller and with base higher than other numerals.

Reverse: Large Berries. Tip of leaf under right edge of second S of STATES. Tiny artifact remainder of an accidental stray serif at inside leaf and field below E of STATES. *Points of distinction:* Also used to coin 1832 (BW-1).

Notes: Proofs for numismatic purposes were made in two styles: with bright, mirrorlike surface and with matte-like bronzed surface. Today, perhaps two-thirds or so of the known pieces are mirrorlike and one-third are bronzed. The bronzed Proofs were made by a special process involving bronzing powder, a popular format for Mint *medals,* but not often employed for coins. Otherwise, all had mirrored surfaces.

1831, Original (Proofs and circulated coins)		Cert	Avg	%MS
		6	54.7	

PF-40	PF-50	PF-60	PF-63BN	PF-63RB
$50,000	$60,000	$77,500	$150,000	$200,000

1831, Restrike From the Same Obverse Die, Reverse of 1836 • BW-1a, C-PR-2, B-2. *Breen dies:* 1-B. **Estimated population:** Proofs: 35 to 50.

1831, Restrike From the Same Obverse Die, Reverse of 1836 (BW-1a, C-PR-2, B-2).

Obverse: Same die as preceding. Now repolished.

Reverse: Large Berries. Tip of leaf under lower-left serif of second S of STATES.

Later use of the reverse of 1836, Proof (BW-1). Cracks eventually develop.

Notes: Breen's "First Restrike," but not called that here, to avoid confusion—as elsewhere, that nomenclature refers to a style of 1840 die with Small Berries.

1831, Restrike From the Same Dies		Cert	Avg	%MS
		(a)		

PF-60	PF-63BN	PF-63RB	PF-65BN	PF-65RB
$10,000	$15,000	$20,000	$23,000	$37,500

(a) Included in certified population for 1831, Original.

1831, Second Restrike Die, Reverse of 1840 • BW-2, C-SR-25, B-3. *Breen dies:* 1-C. **Estimated population:** Proofs: 7 to 11.

1831, Second Restrike Die, Reverse of 1840 (BW-2, C-SR-25, B-3).

Obverse: Same die as preceding. Further polished, now with slight bulging in field.

Reverse: Small Berries. Wreath type by Christian Gobrecht, introduced in 1840; later Proof die with diagonal raised lines over RICA ("Second Restrike" die).

Notes: Usually well struck, but at least one is known with flat striking.[42]

Numismatic Notes: Levick commentary (1866): J.N.T. Levick, in his copy of W. Elliot Woodward's auction catalog of the Francis S. Hoffman Collection, offered in April 1866, provided a marginal note helping to pinpoint the time of issue. For an 1831, Large Berries, Proof, half cent Levick noted, "These were restruck at the Mint in quantity in 1860."

This was probably a reference to restriking 1831 half cents in general, not to the specific example being sold in the Hoffman sale. Levick's comment is one of the earliest to address restrikes of the 1831 year. The Second Restrikes were known at the time and were called "Small Berries."

Frossard commentary (1879): Édouard Frossard, in his 1879 *Monograph of United States Cents and Half Cents issued between the years 1793 and 1857*, stated:

The obverse dies of 1831 and 1836 were at some subsequent date combined with the reverse of probably the 1856 half cent, forming a combination known among collectors as the 1831 and 1836 Mint Restrikes. Only 12 of the 1831 and possibly less of the 1836 are said to have been issued.

However, the Mint did not release production figures for such restrikes, which are thought to have been a private venture to enrich Mint personnel, and thus Frossard's estimate is a guess. The reverse of 1856—small berries and with doubling of NT of CENT and of the wreath ribbon, as used on restrikes of half cents dated in the 1840s—is a different die.

1831, Second Restrike Die	Cert	Avg	%MS
	10	65.6	

PF-60	PF-63BN	PF-63RB	PF-65BN	PF-65RB
$14,500	$22,000	$33,750	$45,000	$65,000

1832, Classic Head
Circulation mintage (estimate): 51,000.

The *Mint Report* data for 1832 to 1835 are patently incorrect and, in any event are given for *1833 to 1836* (in fact, there were no circulation strikes *dated* 1836). The estimated figures given here are moved back a year, to reflect 1832 to 1835, and are still probably off the mark. These are calendar-year production numbers and do not necessarily reflect the dates on the coins.

Half cents of this year are readily available. Most are well struck. Typical grades are EF and AU. Mint State coins are scarcer. These are generally seen in grades from MS-60 to MS-63 with brown color.

Typical values for 1832 half cents.

1832	Cert	Avg	%MS
	397	53.3	39%

F-12	VF-20	EF-40	AU-50	MS-60BN
$70	$100	$140	$200	$325

MS-63BN	MS-63RB	MS-65BN	MS-65RB
$475	$875	$1,450	$4,000

1832, Proof	Cert	Avg	%MS
	1	64.0	100%

PF-60	PF-63BN	PF-63RB	PF-65BN	PF-65RB
$7,000	$10,000	$13,500	$20,000	$32,500

1832 • BW-1, C-1, B-1. *Breen dies:* 1-A. ***Estimated population:*** Circulation strikes: 1,250 to 1,750; Proofs: 4 to 8.

1832 (BW-1, C-1, B-1).

Obverse: Small date close to border. 1 slightly high.

Reverse: Tip of leaf under right edge of second S of STATES. Tiny artifact remainder of an accidental stray serif at inside leaf and field below E of STATES. Berry opposite space between T and E of UNITED.

Notes: *Gilbert* (1916) G-2 "High leaves terminate at end of S and under upright of F." Many Mint State examples are known, usually with brown surfaces, rarely with some mint color.

1832 • BW-2, C-2, B-2. *Breen dies:* 1-B. ***Estimated population:*** 1,250 to 1,750.

1832 (BW-2, C-2, B-2).

Obverse: Same die as preceding. *Points of distinction:* A light crack develops in later states.

Reverse: Tip of leaf under E of STATES. Berry opposite lower-left serif of T of UNITED. *Points of distinction:* A light crack develops into a heavy crack.

Notes: *Gilbert* (1916) G-1 "High leaves end under E and F." Proofs were struck from these dies. Mint State is known, brown being usual, occasionally with some mint color.

1832 • BW-3, C-3, B-3. *Breen dies:* 1-C. ***Estimated population:*** 1,250 to 1,750.

1832 (BW-3, C-3, B-3).

Obverse: Same die as preceding.

Reverse: Tip of leaf under right edge of second S of STATES. Berry opposite upright of T of UNITED. Tip of leaf slightly past C of AMERICA.

Notes: *Gilbert* (1916) G-3 "High leaves terminate at ends of S and F." Walter Breen states a few Proofs were struck of this variety. Mint State is known, brown being usual, occasionally with some mint color.

1833, Classic Head
Circulation mintage (estimate): 103,000.

Only one die pair is known for the 1833 half cents. The number of coins minted with the date 1833 is not known, but the production must have been into six figures. Today, most pieces in the marketplace are EF or AU. Mint State coins are plentiful. These are often highly prooflike, thus making the differentiation between a prooflike Mint State coin and a full Proof coin controversial and very difficult to determine. Many of these are hoard coins (see Numismatic Notes below). As late as the mid-1950s, it was not unusual for old-time dealers to have a nice supply of these in stock. Today, they are widely dispersed. Many have been cleaned and recolored, giving them an orangish hue. Undipped coins are *light* yellow-orange with some black toning flecks. Most are well struck.

Half cents had piled up in storage at the Mint after coinage of the denomination resumed in the 1820s (see information under 1829). Between 1829 and a report of June 19, 1833, 12 kegs with $1,170 face value, or 234,000 half cents, had been melted for use as alloy in the silver and copper coinage. Nine kegs (141,000 coins) were still at the Mint as of June 19.[43]

Proofs: Many if not *most* 1833 "Proof" half cents are really prooflike circulation strikes, in Q. David Bowers's opinion. This yields a large population far exceeding any true Proof mintage of the era, and far exceeding the number of numismatists interested in such pieces at that time.

Typical values for 1833 half cents.

1833			Cert	Avg	%MS
			588	58.6	68%

F-12	VF-20	EF-40	AU-50	MS-60BN
$70	$100	$140	$200	$325

MS-63BN	MS-63RB	MS-65BN	MS-65RB	MS-65RD
$450	$750	$1,250	$3,500	$7,250

1833, Proof			Cert	Avg	%MS
			15	64.1	

PF-60	PF-63BN	PF-63RB	PF-65BN	PF-65RB
$4,750	$5,750	$8,500	$10,500	$13,000

1833 • BW-1, C-1, B-1. *Breen dies:* 1-A. ***Estimated population:*** Circulation strikes: 3,500 to 5,000; Proofs: 25 to 50.

1833 (BW-1, C-1, B-1).

Obverse: Only one die. Date widely spaced, 83 closer than are the other numerals.

Reverse: Only one die. *Points of distinction:* Also used to coin all half cents of 1834 and some of 1835.

Notes: Gilbert (1916) B G-1 "High leaves terminate under S and upright of F." Mint State exists with much original color, usually with flecks.

Numismatic Notes: *The Guttag Hoard:* In the 1930s the Guttag Brothers, New York City securities brokers and rare coin dealers, discovered a large hoard of 1833 half cents.[44] The number was never published, but likely was well over 1,000 pieces, perhaps over 2,000. Most were bright red, usually with some tiny black flecks. During the 1930s, these sold for about 25¢ each on the market. In the mid-1950s the remainder coins were distributed in New York and sold for several dollars apiece. Many of the 1833 half cents were prooflike and more than just a few were offered as Proofs.[45]

1834, Classic Head
Circulation mintage (estimate): 141,000.

The 1834 half cent is similar to the 1833 in several ways. There is only one die pair this year. The actual coinage of pieces bearing this date is not known, but must have been generous. Circulated examples are plentiful and are typically EF or AU. Mint State coins are easy to find as well, but they are not nearly as plentiful as those of 1833 and 1835. Relatively few display original mint color.

Proofs: Proofs were struck from this die pair. Some prooflike circulation strikes have been classified as Proofs, but the problem is not nearly as acute as for 1833.

Typical values for 1834 half cents.

1834			Cert	Avg	%MS
			603	56.4	53%

F-12	VF-20	EF-40	AU-50	MS-60BN
$70	$100	$140	$200	$325

MS-63BN	MS-63RB	MS-65BN	MS-65RB	MS-65RD
$450	$750	$1,250	$3,500	$5,250

1834, Proof			Cert	Avg	%MS
			13	65.0	

PF-60	PF-63BN	PF-63RB	PF-65BN	PF-65RB
$5,000	$6,000	$9,000	$13,750	$17,500

1834 • BW-1, C-1, B-1. *Breen dies:* 1-A. **Estimated population:** Circulation strikes: 3,500 to 5,000; Proofs: 20 to 30.

1834 (BW-1, C-1, B-1).

Obverse: Only one die. Date widely spaced, 8 slightly high, 4 larger than the other numerals.

Reverse: Only one die. *Points of distinction:* Also used to coin half cents of 1833 and 1835.

Notes: Mint State with brown surfaces can be found, sometimes with a small amount of original color.

1835, Classic Head
Circulation mintage (estimate): 398,000.

Why the Mint struck more half cents in 1835—when several hundred thousand were still on hand from earlier years—is a mystery. Today, the 1835, known in two varieties, is a common date. Most in the marketplace are EF or AU, although many Mint State coins exist, mostly from the Elmer Sears hoard (see Numismatic Notes for BW-2).

Proofs: Proofs were struck from the BW-2 die combination and are rare today.

Typical values for 1835 half cents.

1835			Cert	Avg	%MS
			1,126	56.1	56%

F-12	VF-20	EF-40	AU-50	MS-60BN
$70	$100	$140	$200	$325

MS-63BN	MS-63RB	MS-65BN	MS-65RB
$450	$750	$1,250	$3,500

1835, Proof			Cert	Avg	%MS
			2	64.0	

PF-60	PF-63BN	PF-63RB	PF-65BN	PF-65RB
$5,000	$6,000	$8,500	$10,500	$13,000

1835 • BW-1, C-1, B-1. *Breen dies:* 1-A. *Estimated population:* 4,500 to 6,000.

1835 (BW-1, C-1, B-1).

Detail of wide ST of STATES.

Obverse: Small date placed well above the border. The 3 is slightly smaller than the other numerals.

Reverse: Berry opposite lower-right serif of T of UNITED. ST of STATES widely spaced. *Points of distinction:* This die was also used to coin half cents of 1833 and 1834.

Notes: Gilbert (1916) G-2 "A wide space between S and T in STATES." Mint State with red and brown surfaces can be found.

Numismatic Notes: See BW-2.

1835 • BW-2, C-2, B-2. *Breen dies:* 1-B. *Estimated population:* Circulation strikes: 4,000 to 5,000. Proofs: 15 to 20.

1835 (BW-2, C-2, B-2).

Obverse: Same die as preceding.

Reverse: Berry opposite upright of T of UNITED. ST of STATES closely spaced. *Points of distinction:* Cracks develop in the later state.

Notes: Gilbert (1916) G-1 "Little space between S and T in STATES." Proofs were struck from this die combination. Mint State with red and brown surfaces can be found.

Numismatic Notes: The Sears Hoard: In the 1930s dealer Elmer Sears is said to have found a hoard of 1835 half cents, "probably a bag of 1,000 pieces, possibly more than that. They were in spotty mint red Uncirculated state."[46] It was not unusual to see groups of these coins as late as the 1950s.[47]

1836, Classic Head
Proof mintage (estimate): 140 to 240.

As there was no need for more half cents in 1836, no circulation strikes were made. Proofs were struck in small numbers for inclusion in sets and for anyone else interested. The *original* coinage was very small, probably fewer than 50.

Sometime later, this same die pair was taken out of a vault, repolished, and used to strike more 1836-dated Proofs. These are designated as "First Restrikes." These tend to have squarer rims and edges than do originals. It is not known when these restrikes were made, but it may have been in the 1840s and 1850s, when the 1836 was found to be rare as a date by numismatists, and requests for more were made. The curators of the Mint Cabinet (established in June 1838), Jacob Reese Eckfeldt and William E. DuBois, were very interested in numismatics and were accommodating to collectors.

At a later date, possibly beginning in the spring of 1859, the Second Restrike coins were made, perhaps initiating a production that extended over the next decade or so.

These have the style introduced in 1840, with smaller wreath and other modifications. This particular die is distinguished by having four diagonal die lines over RICA. The same die was paired with other Proof obverses of various dates from 1840 onward as well as the earlier 1831 obverse.

1836, Early Die State, Original, Proof • BW-1, C-EO-12, B-1. *Estimated population:* Proofs: 30 to 40.

1836, Early Dies State, Original, Proof (BW-1, C-EO-12, B-1).

Obverse: Small date fairly high from the border. 3 low.

Reverse: Large Berries. Tip of leaf under lower-left serif of second S of STATES.

Notes: Compare to the following.

1836, Early Die State, Original, Proof		Cert	Avg	%MS
		13	63.8	

PF-60	PF-63BN	PF-63RB	PF-65BN	PF-65RB
$6,000	$8,000	$10,000	$12,500	$17,500

1836, Later Die State, Restrike from the Same Dies, Proof • BW-1a, C-PR-1, B-1a. *Estimated population:* Proofs: 10 to 15.

1836, Later Die State, Restrike from the Same Dies, Proof (BW-1a, C-PR-1, B-1a).

Obverse: Same die as preceding. Slightly bulged or buckled at the center.

Reverse: Same die as preceding. Now repolished.

Notes: Walter Breen gives these separate numbers, but as the dies are identical, the BW-1 designation covers both here, with the additional notation.

1836, Later Die State, First Restrike, Proof		Cert	Avg	%MS
		(a)		

PF-60	PF-63BN	PF-63RB	PF-65BN	PF-65RB
$5,000	$7,000	$10,500	$13,500	$17,500

(a) Included in certified population for 1836, Early Die State, Original, Proof.

1836, Second Restrike, Proof • BW-2, C-SR-16, B-2. *Breen dies:* 1-C. *Estimated population:* Proofs: 6 to 10.

1836, Second Restrike, Proof (BW-2, C-SR-16, B-2).

Obverse: Same die as preceding. Further bulging, especially in the right field, causing some weakness to the stars.

Reverse: Small Berries. Wreath type by Christian Gobrecht, introduced in 1840s; later Proof die with diagonal raised lines over RICA ("Second Restrike" die).

Notes: Wide rims on both sides. The illustrated coin, from a Missouri collection, is struck off center. This is a late restrike, probably from the 1860s or perhaps early 1870s. This issue is a classic rarity.

1836, Second Restrike, Proof	Cert	Avg	%MS
	2	64.5	

PF-60	PF-63BN	PF-63RB	PF-65BN	PF-65RB
$15,000	$20,000	$26,250	$32,500	$42,500

The 1837 Half Cent Token (Not a Mint Issue)

No half cents were struck with the date of 1837. After 1836, the next circulation-strike mintage was in 1849. In the meantime, Proofs were struck for each year from 1840 onward. During the Hard Times era, which began in 1837, several hundred different varieties of copper cent-sized tokens were issued. Some bore political or satirical devices and inscriptions, while others advertised merchants or products.

Among all of these was a single variety of the *half cent* denomination. Struck from dies believed to have been made by New York City engraver Edward Hulseman, the token bears on the obverse a perched eagle, copied from the motif used on contemporary quarter dollars, with the inscription STANDARD WEIGHT AND VALUE, 1837. The reverse has a wreath enclosing the inscription HALF / CENT / WORTH / OF with the additional inscription PURE COPPER and stars on the outside of the wreath.

An early mention of it by J.N.T. Levick was published in the *American Journal of Numismatics*, April 1870, as part of "Description of the 'Hard Times Tokens' of '37": "Many collectors regard this piece as a pattern; but why, I can not explain. I should more readily assume it to be a satirical piece. Other collectors place it among their half cents of that year, there being no half cents issued in 1837, '8, and '9."

Likely, the dies made by Hulseman at his shop at 80 Nassau Street were for the account of one of the token manufacturers in New England. Cent-sized tokens were typically wholesaled at $6 per thousand to merchants and others, who gave them out in change at the value of a cent. Perhaps these half-cent tokens wholesaled for $3 per thousand.

Later, this token became well known and was listed in Lyman H. Low's definitive text, *Hard Times Tokens,* and still later elsewhere, as in Russell Rulau's *Standard Catalog of United States Tokens 1700–1900.* Wayte Raymond's "National" album for half cents included a space for it.

Examples are readily collectible today. Typical grades are VF and EF, with AU being scarcer. Mint State coins are scarcer yet and invariably are lustrous brown.

1837 "Hard Times" Token	Cert	Avg	%MS
	0	n/a	

VF-20	EF-40	AU-50	MS-60BN	MS-63BN
$145	$250	$350	$725	$1,250

1837, Half Cent Token (Hard Times Token) • *Estimated Population:* 400 to 600.

Notes: Mint State with brown surfaces can be found.

1837, Half Cent Token (Hard Times Token).

BRAIDED HAIR (1840–1857)

1853 (BW-1, C-1, B-1).

Designer: *Christian Gobrecht.* **Weight:** *84 grains (5.44 grams).*
Composition: *Copper.* **Diameter:** *23.5 mm.* **Edge:** *Plain.*

The Braided Hair half cent type was introduced in 1840, a year after it was inaugurated in the copper cent series. At the time there was little market demand for the denomination, and quantities of earlier dates were on hand at banks and at the Mint. Accordingly, the half cents of the years 1840 through 1848 were made only in small numbers, in Proof format, for sale to collectors and for inclusion in Proof sets.

To be specific, Mint inventory figures show these earlier-dated half cents on hand:

> December 31, 1840: 402,200 • September 22, 1841: 371,710 • December 31, 1842: 330,400 • September 30, 1843: 267,100 • December 31, 1844: 174,952 • December 31, 1845: 149,594 • June 30, 1846: 135,560 • September 30, 1847: 102,956 • March 31, 1848: 95,844 • June 30, 1848: 88,848 • September 30, 1848: 7,258.[48]

As the inventory was depleted, circulation strikes of the Braided Hair design were first made in 1849 (of the Large Date variety first) and were produced through 1857, with the exception of 1852 (for which only Proofs were made). These circulation issues are easily enough collected today.

The 1840 to 1848; 1849, Small Date; and 1852 issues are referred to as "Proof only" in listings. Proofs of the years 1854 to 1857 can be found with some searching, as they appear on the market with regularity. For these dates, circulation strikes are plentiful. Some earlier Proofs were made, including for the 1849, Large Date, and are extremely rare.

Philadelphia dealer E.B. Mason Jr. contributed this to the *American Journal of Numismatics* in January 1871:

> *Re-Struck Half Cents Distinguishable from Originals, Hub of 1841.* Scarcer half cents, comprising amongst others, those from 1840 to 1849 inclusive, were re-struck at the U.S. Mint some years subsequently to the date of their issue. By one formerly employed in the Mint I have been told that all these dates were re-coined excepting two, the dies of which he understood could not be found.

He apprehended there was no way by which they could be distinguished from originals, unless the latter could be traced to a time prior to the year of re-coinage. Another person who had, as I supposed, unusual facilities for acquaintance with the subject, stated that there were re-strikes of all the forties, but not more to the best of his knowledge than three complete sets.

These representations not being satisfactory to my mind, I have endeavored to find out what I could learn from a careful examination of the coins themselves. In the effort to obtain a complete set of the Half Cents, a '46 and a '43 came into my hands. I found they had reverses that were not products of the same die. The former had ten large round berries, prominently adorning its wreath. The other had eleven berries of much smaller size, some of them even rudimentary, and mostly rather elongated. They also differed in the arrangement of the ribbon which fastens the ends of the wreath. On the '46, it was turned, at the upper part, *behind the first leaf* to the observer's left. On the '43, it was turned back upon itself at an acute angle, *leaving the corresponding leaf in its entirety* resting upon the field.

Further investigation showed there was a '46, having a like reverse with my '43, and a '43 with a reverse like my '46; and not only so, but eventually I found half cents from 1840 to 1849, inclusive, having each of the reverses. The small berry and sharp-angled-ribbon reverse, proved to be precisely that of all the common halves of '49, and later dates.

The inference was irresistible, either that two dies were employed each year during the decade under consideration—which is highly improbable, considering the exceedingly limited number coined—or else that those with a reverse like that of the late dates, were made with one or more of the late dies. This last supposition has been confirmed by an inspection of the Mint Cabinet, an opportunity for which was recently given me by the Director, where I found all these halves to be products of what is concluded by considerations presented above, to have been original dies.

The reader may be assured that more than three complete sets were made, true though it be that they, as well as the originals, on account of the chain of which they form an important part, as well as their great scarcity, will always be desirable, and only to be obtained at a large premium.

It may be interesting to mention a slight accidental depression which can be traced on all half cents of the '40s and '50s, excepting 1840. This depression runs across the hair, below the ear, in the direction of the fourth star to the right of the date. It shows that the hub of 1841 was ever after employed on the half cents, and is another instance of the light which minute examination throws upon the science of numismatics.

E.M., Philadelphia, October 1870.

In *Numisma*, in January 1883, Édouard Frossard included this under "Numismatic Correspondence":

We lay no claim to the discovery of differences in half cents. These have always been known and recognized among well posted coin dealers and collectors. The greater part of the half cents were restruck at the Mint at a time when the governing officers desired to increase the collection of Washington medals at the Mint by exchange, and were coined with that object in view, not as is generally supposed for speculative purposes.

It was not until Breen's monograph, *Proof Coins Struck by the United States Mint,* was published by Wayte Raymond in 1953, that the "First Restrike" and "Second Restrike" terms were used by specialists, and even then the interest was not widespread. New Netherlands

Coin Company catalogs that were written in that decade by Breen and John J. Ford Jr. used the nomenclature. Since then, such listings have been widespread. Earlier, they were typically called Originals and Restrikes, or Large Berries and Small Berries.

Although there are no records of coinage, as the rarity of various First Restrike and Second Restrike half cents can vary widely, it may be that the Mint kept a small stock of originals (possibly) and restrikes on hand (not differentiating the two reverse varieties of the restrikes), and from time to time struck more as needed. Certainly, they were never made in sets.

As to Proofs in the marketplace today, the traditional way to collect them—for collectors desiring more than one of each date—is to acquire them by Large Berries (Original) and Small Berries (Restrike) varieties, often ignoring that within the restrikes there are two reverse dies. The first person to collect all three reverses was probably Emery May Holden Norweb, who sought them as early as the mid-1950s.[49] Somewhat later, R. Tettenhorst collected these three, plus a later-identified fourth variant, the Second Restrike on 96.1 grain planchets—struck after the regular Second Restrikes.

Today, most Proofs are in grades from Proof-60 to 63 or 64. True Proof-65 and higher coins are rare. Many have been cleaned and later retoned (any coin with hairlines has been dipped or cleaned at one time). This is not necessarily important, as it is the overall eye appeal that counts the most.

As to circulation strikes, most Braided Hair half cents on the market are well struck and of pleasing appearance. Grades range from VF to AU for most seen, although Mint State coins appear with frequency. Full or nearly full-bright mint-orange examples can be found for 1854 and 1855. The 1849, Large Date, 1850, and the 1853 are usually seen toned. Half cents of 1850, 1856, and 1857 are usually brown or, sometimes, red and brown. Many recolored pieces are on the market, and others have spots, etc. Connoisseurship is needed to acquire choice examples, and it is worthwhile to pay a premium for such.

Design Details

Christian Gobrecht, a highly accomplished artist and engraver, created the motif. The head of Miss Liberty is compact, faces left, with a tiara or diadem inscribed LIBERTY, and with her hair in a knot at the back, circled with beads. Thirteen stars surround most of the periphery. The date is below. In 1840 the half cent series began entering the date into the die by a four-digit logotype. Throughout the rest of the design's tenure, which continued to 1857, the same date logotype was used on all dies made for a given year, with the solitary exception of 1849, which occurs in Large Date and Small Date styles.

The reverse design of the 1840 to 1857 half cents is somewhat similar to the preceding type, except no line appears under CENT, the wreath is smaller, and the rim is flat and more prominent.

Originals among the Proof-only dates have Large Berries in the wreath. This is the style used to strike half cents in the year indicated on the dies, for inclusion in Proof sets or for sale to numismatists. Until First Restrikes were made—circa 1856—Original die pairs for some dates were used to make a small number of restrikes. Some of these probably cannot be differentiated today from Original strikings.

First Restrike half cents among the Proof-only dates have Small Berries, and the NT of CENT is slightly doubled, and there is also doubling of the wreath ribbon. This was the die used to strike Proof 1856 half cents for inclusion in sets of that year. Accordingly, it is sometimes called the Reverse of 1856.

Second Restrike half cents among the Proof-only dates have Small Berries, and diagonal file marks over RICA of AMERICA. Likely, these were made from about the spring of 1859, or later, and continued in production in occasional batches for a decade or more. These are on planchets that are more or less within range of the normal weight of 84 grains.

Second Restrike half cents on heavy planchets, averaging 96.1 grains, are known for all dates from 1840 to 1848 and are very rare as a class. The collection of R. Tettenhorst includes one of each of these.

As *Walter Breen's Encyclopedia of United States Half Cents 1793–1857* delineates, there are occasional exceptions, such as Large Berry pieces being made as restrikes, etc., such technicalities being beyond the scope of the discussion here.

1840, Braided Hair
Proof mintage (estimate): 125 to 200.

Production was limited only to Proofs. Originals struck for inclusion in sets this year and for sale to numismatists have large berries. First Restrikes were coined beginning in 1856 or later, and Second Restrikes were likely coined commencing in or after the spring of 1859, as noted in the overview of this type.

1840, Original, Large Berries, Proof • BW-1, C-PO-1, B-1a. *Breen dies:* 1-A. *Estimated population:* Proof: 20 to 25.

1840, Original, Large Berries, Proof (BW-1, C-PO-1, B-1a).

Obverse: 1840, only die of the year.

Reverse: Large Berries in wreath.

Notes: Some show traces of flattened reeding or reeding-like vertical lines. According to Walter Breen, "Blanks were experimentally reeded, then coined in a plain collar, obliterating the reeding, but leaving a knurled effect at the junction between outer rim and edge. Reason unknown." Robert Schonwalter suggested that the Mint used an old collar for the half eagle denomination which was 22.5 mm diameter.[50] He continues on to theorize that they reamed out the collar to the proper 23 mm diameter, leaving only traces of the edge reeding. Some 1840 half cents were made from these dies at a slightly later date (Breen-1b).

1840, Original, Large Berries, Proof		Cert	Avg	%MS
		11	63.8	

PF-60	PF-63BN	PF-63RB	PF-65BN	PF-65RB
$5,500	$6,500	$8,000	$10,000	$15,000

1840, First Restrike, Small Berries, Proof • BW-2, C-SR-2, B-2. *Breen dies:* 1-B. **Estimated population:** Proof: 7 to 9.

1840, First Restrike, Small Berries,
Proof (BW-2, C-SR-2, B-2).

Obverse: Same die as preceding.

Reverse: Small Berries in wreath. Slight doubling at NT of CENT and wreath ribbon.

1840, First Restrike, Small Berries, Proof	Cert	Avg	%MS
	(a)		

PF-60	PF-63BN	PF-63RB	PF-65BN	PF-65RB
$4,750	$5,750	$7,500	$10,500	$15,000

(a) Included in certified population for 1840, Second Restrike, Small Berries, Proof.

1840, Second Restrike, Small Berries, Proof • BW-3, C-SR-17, B-3. *Breen dies:* 1-C. **Estimated population:** Proof: 14 to 17.

1840, Second Restrike, Small Berries,
Proof (BW-3, C-SR-17, B-3).

Notes: Some have high wire rims. Some were restruck on heavy (96.1 grains average) planchets and are exceedingly rare (the suffix "a" can be added after the BW number to describe these).

1840, Second Restrike, Small Berries, Proof	Cert	Avg	%MS
	8	64.5	

PF-60	PF-63BN	PF-63RB	PF-65BN	PF-65RB
$5,300	$6,375	$7,500	$9,375	$14,000

Obverse: Same die as preceding.

Reverse: Small Berries in wreath. Diagonal die lines over RICA.

1841, Braided Hair
Proof mintage (estimate): 150 to 250.

Production was limited only to Proofs. Originals struck for inclusion in sets this year and for sale to numismatists have Large Berries. First Restrikes were coined beginning in 1856 or later, and Second Restrikes were likely coined commencing in or after the spring of 1859, as noted in the overview of this type.

The 1841 seems to be the most available of all the Original-Proof half cents of the years 1840 to 1849; Proof *cents* of this year are also plentiful in comparison to others of the era. Remarkably, six were in the Chapman brothers' sale of the George Eavenson Collection, April 16–17, 1903.[51]

The color is sometimes an especially bright orange-red. All examples seen by the author have a die crack beginning at the rim, extending close to—but not touching—star 7, through stars 3 to 5, to the border. This crack occurred at a very early time. (Breen notes one perfect die piece was reported to him, though he did not see it.) The Eliasberg coin and a number of others have what can be called a crushed reeded edge (alternatively, reamed collar) similar to the 1840, Original.

This year the obverse hub sustained a dent or injury to the thick strand of hair that extends from under the back of the earlobe downward. Now, there is a gap in the strand, which is seen on all 1841 and later obverses of the Braided Hair type.

1841, Original, Large Berries, Proof • BW-1, C-PO-2, B-1. *Breen dies:* 1-A. **Estimated population:** Proof: 35 to 50.

1841, Original, Large Berries, Proof (BW-1, C-PO-2, B-1).

Obverse: 1841, only die of the year.

Reverse: Large Berries in wreath.

Notes: Some have crushed "reeding" on the edge (as viewed edge-on). All seen have a cracked obverse die.

1841, Original, Large Berries, Proof	Cert	Avg	%MS
	18	64.2	

PF-60	PF-63BN	PF-63RB	PF-65BN	PF-65RB
$4,350	$5,500	$7,500	$8,750	$13,000

1841, First Restrike, Small Berries, Proof • BW-2, C-SR-3, B-2. *Breen dies:* 1-B. **Estimated population:** Proof: 5 to 7.

1841, First Restrike, Small Berries, Proof (BW-2, C-SR-3, B-2).

Obverse: Same die as preceding.

Reverse: Small Berries in wreath. Slight doubling at NT of CENT and wreath ribbon.

1841, First Restrike, Small Berries, Proof	Cert	Avg	%MS
	(a)		

PF-60	PF-63BN	PF-63RB	PF-65BN	PF-65RB
$5,500	$6,500	$8,000	$11,000	$15,000

(a) Included in certified population for 1841, Second Restrike, Small Berries, Proof.

1841, Second Restrike, Small Berries, Proof • BW-3, C-SR-18, B-3. *Breen dies:* 1-C. **Estimated population:** Proof: 10 to 12.

1841, Second Restrike, Small Berries, Proof (BW-3, C-SR-18, B-3).

Obverse: Same die as preceding.

Reverse: Small Berries in wreath. Diagonal die lines over RICA.

Notes: Most advanced stage of the obverse crack, heavier at and near stars 2 and 3. Sometimes seen with a high wire rim. Some were restruck on heavy planchets (96.1 grains average) and are exceedingly rare (the suffix "a" can be added after the BW number to describe these).

1841, Second Restrike, Small Berries, Proof	Cert	Avg	%MS
	8	64.6	

PF-60	PF-63BN	PF-63RB	PF-65BN	PF-65RB
$4,500	$5,500	$7,500	$9,000	$13,000

1842, Braided Hair

Proof mintage (estimate): 120 to 180.

Similar to other half cents of the era, production of the 1842 was limited only to Proofs. Originals struck for inclusion in sets this year and for sale to numismatists have large berries. First Restrikes were coined beginning in 1856 or later, and Second Restrikes were likely coined commencing in or after the spring of 1859, as noted in the overview of this type.

The 1842 is one of the rarest Originals of the decade. Examples come on the market at widely spaced intervals, and usually only when advanced collections of half cents are sold—although, in the market since the 1990s, some have been bought by "trophy coin" enthusiasts, who are not otherwise interested in half cents. It is difficult to determine the population of *any* half cent, except for a handful of famous pedigreed rarities. Often, the same coin will appear in multiple catalog listings or be represented more than once in certification service reports. Some of these were distributed as part of full 1842 Proof sets, which contained the famous 1842, Small Date, quarter dollar.

1842, Original, Large Berries, Proof • BW-1, C-PO-3, B-1. *Breen dies:* 1-A. **Estimated population:** Proof: 15 to 20.

1842, Original, Large Berries, Proof (BW-1, C-PO-3, B -1).

Obverse: 1842, only die of the year.

Reverse: Large Berries in wreath.

1842, Original, Large Berries, Proof	Cert	Avg	%MS
	5	63.4	

PF-60	PF-63BN	PF-63RB	PF-65BN	PF-65RB
$5,925	$7,000	$9,000	$10,000	$15,000

1842, First Restrike, Small Berries, Proof • BW-2, C-SR-4, B-2. *Breen dies:* 1-B. **Estimated population:** Proof: 15 to 20.

1842, First Restrike, Small Berries, Proof (BW-2, C-SR-4, B-2).

Obverse: Same die as preceding.

Reverse: Small Berries in wreath. Slight doubling at NT of CENT and wreath ribbon.

Notes: Often seen with a high wire rim.

1842, First Restrike, Small Berries, Proof	Cert	Avg	%MS
	(a)		

PF-60	PF-63BN	PF-63RB	PF-65BN	PF-65RB
$5,000	$6,000	$7,500	$9,000	$13,000

(a) Included in certified population for 1842, Second Restrike, Small Berries, Proof.

1842, Second Restrike, Small Berries, Proof • BW-3, C-SR-19, B-3.
Breen dies: 1-C. ***Estimated population:*** Proof: 20 to 25.

1842, Second Restrike, Small Berries,
Proof (BW-3, C-SR-19, B-3).

Obverse: Same die as preceding.

Reverse: Small Berries in wreath. Diagonal die lines over RICA.

Notes: Some were restruck on heavy planchets (96.1 grains average) and are exceedingly rare (the suffix "a" can be added after the BW number to describe these).

1842, Second Restrike, Small Berries, Proof		Cert	Avg	%MS
		10	64.7	

PF-60	PF-63BN	PF-63RB	PF-65BN	PF-65RB
$5,500	$6,500	$8,000	$10,000	$14,000

1843, Braided Hair
Proof mintage (estimate): 125 to 200.

The story of the 1843 half cent is similar to that of the other Proof-only issues of the decade. Originals struck for inclusion in sets this year and for sale to numismatists have large berries. First Restrikes were coined beginning in 1856 or later, and Second Restrikes were likely coined commencing in or after the spring of 1859, as noted in the overview of this type.

In the midst of this listing of the "rarest of the rare" in the half cent series it is easy to lose sight of the absolute rarity of these pieces—an experience similar to being in the room full of Rembrandt oils at the Metropolitan Museum. However, *any single specimen* from the lineup of 1840 to 1849 Proofs, originals as well as restrikes, can be incredibly difficult to find in the first place, and even more so for an eye-appealing example.

The 1843, Second Restrike, is one of the great rarities of the decade, with fewer than a dozen estimated to exist, perhaps only slightly more than a half dozen. As First Restrikes exist in much larger numbers, this may reinforce the idea of the Mint keeping an inventory of restrikes, and making only a few Second Restrikes, as the supply of First Restrikes was generous. However, it is often unwise to theorize.

1843, Original, Large Berries, Proof • BW-1, C-PO-4, B-1a. *Breen dies:* 1-A. ***Estimated population:*** Proof: 25 to 35.

1843, Original, Large Berries,
Proof (BW-1, C-PO-4, B-1a).

Obverse: 1843, only die of the year.

Reverse: Large Berries in wreath.

1843, Original, Large Berries, Proof		Cert	Avg	%MS
		6	62.7	

PF-60	PF-63BN	PF-63RB	PF-65BN	PF-65RB
$5,175	$6,250	$8,250	$9,375	$14,000

1843, First Restrike, Small Berries, Proof • BW-2, C-SR-5, B-2. *Breen dies:* 1-B. **Estimated population:** Proof: 30 to 35.

1843, First Restrike, Small Berries,
Proof (BW-2, C-SR-5, B-2).

Obverse: Same die as preceding.

Reverse: Small Berries in wreath. Slight doubling at NT of CENT and wreath ribbon.

Notes: Some have high wire rims. Sometimes with striking weakness at the center of the reverse.

1843, First Restrike, Small Berries, Proof	Cert	Avg	%MS
	(a)		

PF-60	PF-63BN	PF-63RB	PF-65BN	PF-65RB
$5,000	$6,500	$7,750	$9,500	$14,000

(a) Included in certified population for 1843, Second Restrike, Small Berries, Proof.

1843, Second Restrike, Small Berries, Proof • BW-3, C-SR-20, B-3. *Breen dies:* 1-C. **Estimated population:** Proof: 7 to 9.

1843, Second Restrike, Small Berries,
Proof (BW-3, C-SR-20, B-3).

Obverse: Same die as preceding.

Reverse: Small Berries in wreath. Diagonal die lines over RICA.

Notes: Some were restruck on heavy planchets (96.1 grains average) and are exceedingly rare (the suffix "a" can be added after the BW number to describe these).

1843, Second Restrike, Small Berries, Proof	Cert	Avg	%MS
	7	64.7	

PF-60	PF-63BN	PF-63RB	PF-65BN	PF-65RB
$5,250	$6,750	$8,000	$9,750	$14,500

1844, Braided Hair
Proof mintage (estimate): 120 to 180.

Half cents of 1844 continue the pace of Proof-only dates. Originals struck for inclusion in sets this year and for sale to numismatists have large berries. First Restrikes were coined beginning in 1856 or later, and Second Restrikes were likely coined commencing in or after the spring of 1859, as noted in the overview of this type.

The 1844, First Restrike, is a prime rarity for the specialist, possibly because the Mint had a supply of Originals on hand to satisfy the numismatic demand. Often a span of many years will elapse between auction appearances for the First Restrike. It should be noted that for nearly all auction appearances before 1950 there is no way to determine whether a given "Small Berries" half cent is a First Restrike or a Second Restrike, unless its later pedigree can be traced. The differences are too minute to show up in halftone photographs, and collectors and dealers were not aware of such distinctions.

1844, Original, Large Berries, Proof • BW-1, C-PO-5, B-1. *Breen dies:* 1-A. *Estimated population:* Proof: 19 to 24.

1844, Original, Large Berries, Proof (BW-1, C-PO-5, B-1).

Obverse: 1844, only die of the year.

Reverse: Large Berries in wreath.

1844, Original, Large Berries, Proof			Cert	Avg	%MS
			9	62.9	

PF-60	PF-63BN	PF-63RB	PF-65BN	PF-65RB
$5,550	$6,500	$8,750	$9,500	$14,750

1844, First Restrike, Small Berries, Proof • BW-2, C-SR-6, B-2. *Breen dies:* 1-B. *Estimated population:* Proof: 7 to 9.

1844, First Restrike, Small Berries, Proof (BW-2, C-SR-6, B-2).

Reverse: Small Berries in wreath. Slight doubling at NT of CENT and wreath ribbon.

Notes: Most are toned brown with little or no orange-red mint color.

Obverse: Same die as preceding.

1844, First Restrike, Small Berries, Proof			Cert	Avg	%MS
			(a)		

PF-60	PF-63BN	PF-63RB	PF-65BN	PF-65RB
$5,750	$6,750	$8,500	$10,000	$17,500

(a) Included in certified population for 1844, Second Restrike, Small Berries, Proof.

1844, Second Restrike, Small Berries, Proof • BW-3, C-SR-21, B-3. *Breen dies:* 1-C. *Estimated population:* Proof: 14 to 17.

1844, Second Restrike, Small Berries, Proof (BW-3, C-SR-21, B-3).

Obverse: Same die as preceding.

Reverse: Small Berries in wreath. Diagonal die lines over RICA.

Notes: Some have high wire rims. Some were restruck on heavy planchets (96.1 grains average) and are exceedingly rare (the suffix "a" can be added after the BW number to describe these).

1844, Second Restrike, Small Berries, Proof			Cert	Avg	%MS
			2	65.5	

PF-60	PF-63BN	PF-63RB	PF-65BN	PF-65RB
$5,000	$6,000	$7,500	$9,000	$14,000

1845, Braided Hair
Proof mintage (estimate): 110 to 170.

Half cents of 1845 are next in the lineup of Proof-only dates. Originals struck for inclusion in sets this year and for sale to numismatists have large berries. First Restrikes were coined beginning in 1856 or later, and Second Restrikes were likely coined commencing in or after the spring of 1859, as noted in the overview of this type.

Original 1845 half cents have been cataloged in the past as the rarest date among the Proof-only dates in the 1840s. However, it is likely that the 1842 and the 1849, Small Date, are rarer. The distinction is largely academic, for rarity-wise each of these three Proofs is more or less in the league of such classics as the 1876-CC twenty-cent piece, 1838-O half dollar, and 1804 silver dollar.

1845, Original, Large Berries, Proof • BW-1, C-PO-6, B-1a. *Breen dies:* 1-A. *Estimated population:* Proof: 16 to 20.

1845, Original, Large Berries, Proof (BW-1, C-PO-6, B-1a).

Obverse: 1845, only die of the year.

Reverse: Large Berries in wreath.

Notes: Walter Breen reported one example from this die pair from dies later repolished.

1845, Original, Large Berries, Proof		Cert	Avg	%MS
		3	65.0	

PF-60	PF-63BN	PF-63RB	PF-65BN	PF-65RB
$5,425	$6,500	$8,750	$11,000	$17,500

1845, First Restrike, Small Berries, Proof • BW-2, C-SR-7, B-2. *Breen dies:* 1-B. *Estimated population:* Proof: 8 to 10.

1845, First Restrike, Small Berries, Proof (BW-2, C-SR-7, B-2).

Obverse: Same die as preceding.

Reverse: Small Berries in wreath. Slight doubling at NT of CENT and wreath ribbon.

1845, First Restrike, Small Berries, Proof		Cert	Avg	%MS
		(a)		

PF-60	PF-63BN	PF-63RB	PF-65BN	PF-65RB
$5,750	$6,750	$8,500	$10,000	$16,000

(a) Included in certified population for 1845, Second Restrike, Small Berries, Proof.

1845, Second Restrike, Small Berries, Proof • BW-3, C-SR-22, B-3. *Breen dies:* 1-C. *Estimated population:* Proof: 12 to 14.

1845, Second Restrike, Small Berries, Proof (BW-3, C-SR-22, B-3).

Obverse: Same die as preceding.

Reverse: Small Berries in wreath. Diagonal die lines over RICA.

Notes: Some were restruck on heavy planchets (96.1 grains average) and are exceedingly rare (the suffix "a" can be added after the BW number to describe these).

1845, Second Restrike, Small Berries, Proof		Cert	Avg	%MS
		9	64.4	

PF-60	PF-63BN	PF-63RB	PF-65BN	PF-65RB
$5,000	$6,000	$8,000	$9,000	$14,000

1846, Braided Hair
Proof mintage (estimate): 125 to 200.

Half cents of 1846 are similar in concept to other Proof-only issues of the era. Originals struck for inclusion in sets this year and for sale to numismatists have large berries. First Restrikes were coined beginning in 1856 or later, and Second Restrikes were likely coined commencing in or after the spring of 1859, as noted in the overview of this type.

Curiously, the numerals in the date of the 1846 die are very rustic and not from normal punches of the era. This anomaly, vividly evident when the digits are viewed under magnification, is unexplained. Perhaps an amateur cut certain of the punches, with the "8" in particular being crude in comparison to other "8" digits of the era and also in the "script" style (as opposed to the "block" style used elsewhere on coppers of the decade).

The First Restrike is one of the great rarities of the series. Walter Breen knew of only six examples.

Detail of the 1846 date with script-style 8.

1846, Original, Large Berries, Proof • BW-1, C-PO-7, B-1. *Breen dies: 1-A. Estimated population:* Proof: 20 to 25.

1846, Original, Large Berries, Proof (BW-1, C-PO-7, B-1).

Obverse: 1846, only die of the year.

Reverse: Large Berries in wreath.

1846, Original, Large Berries, Proof		Cert	Avg	%MS
		8	64.0	

PF-60	PF-63BN	PF-63RB	PF-65BN	PF-65RB
$5,550	$6,500	$8,500	$9,500	$14,750

1846, First Restrike, Small Berries, Proof • BW-2, C-SR-8, B-2. *Breen dies:* 1-B. *Estimated population:* Proof: 5 to 7.

1846, First Restrike, Small Berries, Proof (BW-2, C-SR-8, B-2).

Obverse: Same die as preceding.

Reverse: Small Berries in wreath. Slight doubling at NT of CENT and wreath ribbon.

Notes: A great rarity.

1846, First Restrike, Small Berries, Proof		Cert	Avg	%MS
		(a)		

PF-60	PF-63BN	PF-63RB	PF-65BN	PF-65RB
$8,000	$10,000	$12,500	$15,000	$20,000

(a) Included in certified population for 1846, Second Restrike, Small Berries, Proof.

1846, Second Restrike, Small Berries, Proof • BW-3, C-SR-23, B-3.

Breen dies: 1-C. ***Estimated population:*** Proof: 14 to 17.

1846, Second Restrike, Small Berries, Proof (BW-3, C-SR-23, B-3).

Obverse: Same die as preceding.

Reverse: Small Berries in wreath. Diagonal die lines over RICA.

Notes: Some were restruck on heavy planchets (96.1 grains average) and are exceedingly rare (the suffix "a" can be added after the BW number to describe these).

1846, Second Restrike, Small Berries, Proof			Cert	Avg	%MS
			7	65.1	

PF-60	PF-63BN	PF-63RB	PF-65BN	PF-65RB
$5,000	$6,000	$8,000	$9,000	$14,000

1847, Braided Hair
Proof mintage (estimate): 200 to 300.

The Proof-only half cents of 1847 mirror the other issues of the era. Originals struck for inclusion in sets this year and for sale to numismatists have large berries. First Restrikes were coined beginning in 1856 or later, and Second Restrikes were likely coined commencing in or after the spring of 1859, as noted in the overview of this type.

The date logotype of this year is large in relation to the space provided for it, this also being true for 1848. The First Restrike is one of the great rarities in the series. Walter Breen knew of three pieces and commented, "It is still the rarest of all die combinations among the Proof-only dates, being rarer than the 1831 or 1836 with Small Berries or the 1852 with Large Berries." This probably precipitated a generous production of Second Restrikes, which today are among the most available Proofs of the era.

1847, Original, Large Berries, Proof • BW-1, C-PO-8, B-1a. *Breen dies:* 1-A. ***Estimated population:*** Proof: 20 to 25.

1847, Original, Large Berries, Proof (BW-1, C-PO-8, B-1a).

Obverse: 1847, only die of the year.

Reverse: Large Berries in wreath.

Notes: Some seem to have been restruck from this die pair, but probably sparingly.

1847, Original, Large Berries, Proof			Cert	Avg	%MS
			10	64.4	

PF-60	PF-63BN	PF-63RB	PF-65BN	PF-65RB
$10,000	$12,500	$17,500	$25,000	$40,000

1847, First Restrike, Small Berries, Proof • BW-2, C-SR-9, B-2. *Breen dies:* 1-B. **Estimated population:** Proof: 3 or 4.

1847, First Restrike, Small Berries, Proof (BW-2, C-SR-9, B-2).

Obverse: Same die as preceding.

Reverse: Small Berries in wreath. Slight doubling at NT of CENT and wreath ribbon.

1847, First Restrike, Small Berries, Proof	Cert	Avg	%MS
	(a)		

PF-60	PF-63BN	PF-63RB	PF-65BN	PF-65RB
$40,000	$50,000	$77,500	$97,500	$110,000

(a) Included in certified population for 1847, Second Restrike, Small Berries, Proof.

1847, Second Restrike, Small Berries, Proof • BW-3, C-SR-24, B-3. *Breen dies:* 1-C. **Estimated population:** Proof: 30 to 40.

1847, Second Restrike, Small Berries, Proof (BW-3, C-SR-24, B-3).

Obverse: Same die as preceding.

Reverse: Small Berries in wreath. Diagonal die lines over RICA.

Notes: Some were restruck on heavy planchets (96.1 grains average) and are exceedingly rare (the suffix "a" can be added after the BW number to describe these).

1847, Second Restrike, Small Berries, Proof	Cert	Avg	%MS
	15	64.7	

PF-60	PF-63BN	PF-63RB	PF-65BN	PF-65RB
$5,000	$6,000	$8,000	$9,000	$14,000

1848, Braided Hair
Proof mintage (estimate): 150 to 225.

The 1848 winds down the Proof-only run of this decade, as the next year, 1849, did include circulation strikes in addition to Proofs. Originals struck for inclusion in sets in 1848 and for sale to numismatists have large berries. First Restrikes were coined beginning in 1856 or later, and Second Restrikes were likely coined commencing in or after the spring of 1859, as noted in the overview of this type.

The date is too large for the space provided and crowds the base of the portrait of Miss Liberty. The Mint had a similar problem with the overly large dates on certain 1848 half dimes. Originals are on the rare side. In contrast, in the context of Proof-only half cents the First Restrike is plentiful.

1848, Original, Large Berries, Proof • BW-1, C-PO-9, B-1a. *Breen dies:* 1-A. *Estimated population:* Proof: 15 to 20.

1848, Original, Large Berries, Proof (BW-1, C-PO-9, B-1a).

Obverse: 1848, only die of the year.

Reverse: Large Berries in wreath.

Notes: Several known examples seem to have been restruck at a later date (see Breen).

1848, Original, Large Berries, Proof	Cert	Avg	%MS
	4	64.0	

PF-60	PF-63BN	PF-63RB	PF-65BN	PF-65RB
$6,000	$7,000	$9,000	$10,000	$14,000

1848, First Restrike, Small Berries, Proof • BW-2, C-SR-10, B-2. *Breen dies:* 1-B. *Estimated population:* Proof: 30 to 35.

1848, First Restrike, Small Berries, Proof (BW-2, C-SR-10, B-2).

Obverse: Same die as preceding.

Reverse: Small Berries in wreath. Slight doubling at NT of CENT and wreath ribbon.

Notes: Walter Breen considered this to be the most available of all First Restrike dates.

1848, First Restrike, Small Berries, Proof	Cert	Avg	%MS
	(a)		

PF-60	PF-63BN	PF-63RB	PF-65BN	PF-65RB
$5,000	$6,000	$8,000	$9,000	$14,000

(a) Included in certified population for 1848, Second Restrike, Small Berries, Proof.

1848, Second Restrike, Small Berries, Proof • BW-3, C-SR-25, B-3. *Breen dies:* 1-C. *Estimated population:* Proof: 10 to 12.

1848, Second Restrike, Small Berries, Proof (BW-3, C-SR-25, B-3).

Obverse: Same die as preceding.

Reverse: Small Berries in wreath. Diagonal die lines over RICA.

Notes: Some were restruck on heavy planchets (96.1 grains average) and are exceedingly rare (the suffix "a" can be added after the BW number to describe these).

1848, Second Restrike, Small Berries, Proof	Cert	Avg	%MS
	12	64.5	

PF-60	PF-63BN	PF-63RB	PF-65BN	PF-65RB
$6,000	$7,500	$9,500	$11,000	$15,500

1849, Braided Hair

Proof mintage, Small Date (estimate): 70 to 90.
Circulation mintage, Large Date: 39,864.

Half cents of 1849 are classified by two major varieties: Small Date, made early in the year and only in Proof format, and Large Date, made for circulation, with a few Proofs.

The Proof 1849, Small Date, was made for sets of this year and to supply numismatists who desired a Proof of the date. The estimated Proof mintage for this date size reflects its scarcity. Probably, some collectors of the 1850s and 1860s who had a Large Date did not desire a Small Date, as the year 1849 was already represented.

Originals of the Small Date variety have large berries. This is the rarest of the Proof-only Original half cents of the 1840s. In 1879 in his *Monograph of United States Cents and Half Cents Issued Between the Years 1793 and 1857*, Édouard Frossard stated that he had never seen the one that Dr. Edward Maris had. For many years the Chapman brothers stated that only five were known. In recent decades the census has expanded, but any larger figure probably contains some duplication. In the era of the Chapmans—roughly from the late 1870s to the late 1920s—only a few dealers handled most of the major rarities, and it was easier to keep track of them. Today, in the early 21st century, coins are much more widespread in their distribution, and there are probably a couple hundred dealers or more who handle American rarities, most of whom keep little record of pedigrees.

First Restrikes of the Small Date variety were coined beginning in 1856 or later. The production seems to have been modest, no doubt as circulation-strike Large Date coins filled the demand for half cents of the 1849 year. No Second Restrikes have been reported for this issue. The Small Date is from a small logotype punch similar to that used for half cents prior to 1847.

In summary, the Proof 1849, Small Date, half cent with large berries may be rarer than presently thought, and more in line with the Chapmans' account than later tabulations. Breen forthrightly states, "12 known." The status of the 1849, Large Berries, half cent as "Original" or "Restrike" has been debated over the years, although the "large berries = original" rule of thumb is usually applied for half cents of the 1840s, never mind that there are occasional exceptions.

You may want to review Breen's comments on pages 426 and 427 of his *Encyclopedia of United States Half Cents 1793–1857*. In brief, 1849, Small Date, half cents with the large berries reverse style have long been called originals. As there is only one variety and one die state of the 1849, Small Date, half cent with Large Berries reverse, it is presumed that they were all made at the same time. It is not known for certain whether that time was 1849, or whether it was later. Further, as Breen states, "Should it later prove that all of them were made in 1859 or 1860, their status would not affect their rarity and should not affect their value."

Another obverse die was made with a Large Date logotype and used to produce circulation strikes, the first in this format since 1835. Such format is exceedingly rare. Demand for the denomination remained low, and the mintage was modest. The reverse is of the Small Berries style. Only one die variety is known. Examples are fairly scarce, but are easily obtainable in relation to the demand for them. EF and AU are typical grades. Mint State coins are seen now and again, and usually are well struck with lustrous brown surfaces. One Proof is reported by R. Tettenhorst.

1849, Small Date, Original, Large Berries, Proof • BW-1, C-PO-10, B-1. *Breen dies:* 1-A. *Estimated population:* Proof: 12 to 14.

Obverse: 1849, small numerals in date.

Reverse: Large Berries in wreath.

1849, Small Date, Original, Large Berries, Proof (BW-1, C-PO-10, B-1).

1849, Small Date, Original, Large Berries, Proof	Cert	Avg	%MS
	4	59.0	

PF-60	PF-63BN	PF-63RB	PF-65BN	PF-65RB
$4,700	$6,000	$7,750	$10,500	$22,500

1849, Small Date, First Restrike, Small Berries, Proof • BW-2, C-SR-11, B-2. *Breen dies:* 1-B. *Estimated population:* Proof: 18 to 22.

Reverse: Small Berries in wreath. Slight doubling at NT of CENT and wreath ribbon.

1849, Small Date, First Restrike, Small Berries, Proof (BW-2, C-SR-11, B-2).

1849, Small Date, First Restrike, Small Berries, Proof	Cert	Avg	%MS
	5	64.4	

PF-60	PF-63BN	PF-63RB	PF-65BN	PF-65RB
$4,850	$5,750	$9,250	$9,750	$15,000

Obverse: Same die as preceding.

1849, Large Date • BW-3, C-1 (Proof, PO-11), B-4. *Breen dies:* 2-D. *Estimated population:* Circulation strikes: 1,750 to 2,250; Proofs: 2 to 4.

with partial original color. One Proof was reported by R. Tettenhorst. Jim McGuigan suggests a population of 2 to 4 Proofs.

1849, Large Date (BW-3, C-1, B-4).

1849, Large Date	Cert	Avg	%MS
	276	58.4	63%

VF-20	EF-40	AU-50	MS-60BN
$100	$150	$240	$500

MS-63BN	MS-63RB	MS-65BN	MS-65RB
$700	$1,500	$2,550	$3,500

Obverse: Date in large numerals.

Reverse: Small berries in wreath.

Notes: Mint State is the highest grade for this variety, usually brown, sometimes

1850, Braided Hair

Circulation mintage: 39,812.

The 1850 is the scarcest date of the 1849 to 1857 circulating issues, but enough exist that finding one will be no problem. EF and AU grades are the rule. Mint State coins are scarce. When seen, they typically have lustrous brown surfaces. Coins with significant original color are rare.

Proofs: Proofs were struck from the same die pair used for circulation, which always causes problems in attribution. The numismatic tradition on what is an early Proof and what is a prooflike circulation strike still is not definitive or complete, and thus population estimates, which are based on the literature (in combination with personal experience), must be taken with a grain of salt. In general, for all 1850 denominations, few Proofs were struck.

Typical values for 1850 half cents.

1850			Cert	Avg	%MS
			226	57.8	60%

VF-20	EF-40	AU-50	MS-60BN	MS-63BN
$100	$150	$240	$500	$575

MS-63BN	MS-63RB	MS-65BN	MS-65RB
$750	$1,425	$2,400	$3,500

1850, Proof			Cert	Avg	%MS
			8	62.8	88%

PF-60	PF-63BN	PF-63RB	PF-65BN	PF-65RB
$5,000	$7,000	$10,000	$13,000	$17,000

1850 • BW-1, C-1 (Proof, PO-12), B-1. *Breen dies:* 1-A. **Estimated population:** Circulation strikes: 1,750 to 2,250; Proofs: 10 to 12.

1850 (BW-1, C-1, B-1).

Obverse: Four-digit 1850 logotype impressed shallowly into the single working die, thus the date is never bold. This die was used to make circulation strikes as well as Proofs.

Reverse: Small Berries. Tiny line connects bases of A and T of STATES.

Notes: This variety exists in Mint State, usually with brown surfaces, and is elusive as such.

1851, Braided Hair
Circulation mintage: 147,672.

Mint records note that two obverse dies were prepared for the 1851 half cent, but a second has never been identified. Circulated coins are plentiful in the context of the series. EF and AU are typical grades. Uncirculated coins are plentiful in the marketplace, many with some pale mint red. Luster is usually "shallow," rather than deep and frosty.

Proofs: Although Walter Breen has stated that "at least 20 exist," the attribution of prooflike circulation strikes vis-à-vis Proofs is not always certain. True Proofs are very rare.

Typical values for 1851 half cents.

1851			Cert	Avg	%MS
			754	58.5	64%

VF-20	EF-40	AU-50	MS-60BN	MS-63BN
$80	$100	$175	$275	$550

MS-63RB	MS-65BN	MS-65RB	MS-65RD
$650	$1,000	$2,000	$3,500

1851, Proof			Cert	Avg	%MS
			0	n/a	

PF-60	PF-63BN	PF-63RB	PF-65BN	PF-65RB
$7,000	$8,000	$15,000	$20,000	$25,000

1851 • BW-1, C-1 (Proof, PO-13), B-1. *Breen dies:* 1-A. **Estimated population:** Circulation strikes: 5,500 to 7,500. Proofs: 3 to 5.

1851 (BW-1, C-1, B-1).

Obverse: Four-digit 1851 logotype in small digits, well placed between the por-trait and the denticles, and deeply punched into the die. Traces of an earlier 1 to the right of the final digit. *Points of distinction:* Only one die this year—used to make circulation strikes as well as Proofs.

Reverse: Small Berries. Top of crosslet of E of CENT joined to top of letter. Tiny line connects bases of A and T of STATES.

Notes: Mint State can be found, brown or with some original color.

1852, Braided Hair
Proof mintage (estimate): 225 to 325.

The 1852 half cent was made only in Proof format. These can be classified as Originals with Large Berries accompanied by First Restrikes and Second Restrikes with small berries.

The situation, however, is more complex, especially if the extensive commentary in Walter Breen's 1983 *Encyclopedia of United States Half Cents 1793–1857* is followed. He suggests that Large Berries coins are restrikes, devoting nearly three pages to his discussion (hinting that he could have spent more: "There is no point in devoting 20-odd pages. . . ."), concluding that the 1852 B-4 is struck from the Large Berries reverse used on Originals of the 1840s, but with the 1852 obverse die repolished and *in a later state than 1852 B-2* (First Restrike die), which, if characteristic of all Large Berries examples, would seem to support his restrike view. As to what constituted an Original, Breen suggested that a Small Berries die, but not either of the First Restrike or Second Restrike dies, was likely, but he had never encountered one.

This view seems more likely: Richard T. Coleman Jr., in "Series VII Restrikes: The Breen Effect," *Penny-Wise*, November 15, 1998, states, "The entire concept of Series VII restrikes seems to have been fabricated by Mr. Breen in order to support his theory that 1852 Large Berry reverse half cents are 'restrikes' not originals."

In the present text we list the Large Berries first, then the two restrikes, following the order of 1840 to 1848 and 1849, Small Date, Proofs.

1852, Original, Large Berries, Proof • BW-1, C-SR-1, B-4. *Breen dies:* 1-A. **Population:** Proof: 5 recorded (see Eliasberg Collection, 1996).

1852, Original, Large Berries, Proof (BW-1, C-SR-1, B-4).

Obverse: 1852, only die of the year.

Reverse: Large Berries in wreath.

Notes: Called a restrike by Walter Breen and Roger Cohen Jr. (who listed this variety as Original in the first edition of his book, but a Restrike in the second edition). Emery May Holden Norweb spent several decades in the search for one.

1852, Original, Large Berries, Proof	Cert	Avg	%MS
	1	65.0	

PF-60	PF-63BN	PF-63RB	PF-65BN	PF-65RB
$200,000	$200,000	$200,000	$400,000	$400,000

1852, First Restrike, Small Berries, Proof • BW-2, C-SR-12, B-2. *Breen dies:* 1-B. *Estimated population:* Proof: 100 to 125.

1852, First Restrike, Small Berries, Proof (BW-2, C-SR-12, B-2).

Obverse: Same die as preceding.

Reverse: Small Berries in wreath. Slight doubling at NT of CENT and wreath ribbon.

Notes: This is the variety usually seen.

1852, First Restrike, Small Berries, Proof	Cert	Avg	%MS
	(a)		

PF-60	PF-63BN	PF-63RB	PF-65BN	PF-65RB
$4,000	$5,875	$8,750	$10,000	$15,000

(a) Included in certified population for 1852, Second Restrike, Small Berries, Proof.

1852, Second Restrike, Small Berries, Proof • BW-3 C-SR-26, B-3. *Breen dies:* 1-C. *Estimated population:* Proof: 10 to 15.

1852, Second Restrike, Small Berries, Proof (BW-3, C-SR-26, B-3).

Obverse: Same die as preceding.

Reverse: Small Berries in wreath. Diagonal die lines over RICA.

Notes: The Small Berries half cents of this year have been described by die varieties only rarely, and thus estimates are more tentative than among other Proof-only years.

1852, Second Restrike, Small Berries, Proof	Cert	Avg	%MS
	34	64.3	

PF-60	PF-63BN	PF-63RB	PF-65BN	PF-65RB
$5,000	$7,250	$12,000	$15,000	$20,000

1853, Braided Hair
Circulation mintage: 129,694.

The 1853 half cent is available in high grades. All Mint State coins are brown or, less often, brown with traces of red. No full orange-red example is known, except for cleaned pieces. No Proofs are known. Circulated coins are typically EF or AU.

Typical values for 1853 half cents.

1853	Cert	Avg	%MS
	947	61.0	80%

VF-20	EF-40	AU-50	MS-60BN	MS-63BN	MS-63RB	MS-65BN	MS-65RB
$80	$100	$175	$275	$550	$650	$1,000	$1,700

1853 • BW-1, C-1, B-1. *Breen dies:* 1-A. **Estimated population:** 5,500 to 7,500.

1853 (BW-1, C-1, B-1).

Detail of crowded date.

Obverse: Date in a large logotype is boldly impressed into the die. It is too large for the allotted space and appears crowded.

Reverse: Small Berries.

Notes: Mint State with brown surfaces or some mint color are common.

1854, Braided Hair
Circulation mintage: 55,358.
Proof mintage (estimate): 40 to 60.

A single obverse and two reverse dies were used to coin 1854 half cents. Circulation strikes are fairly scarce and are typically in grades of EF or AU. Hundreds of Mint State coins exist, mostly from the A.C. Gies hoard (see Numismatic Notes on page 273).

Proofs: Proofs are very rare in proportion to later half cent Proofs of the decade.

Typical values for 1854 half cents.

1854		Cert	Avg	%MS
		698	61.6	84%

VF-20	EF-40	AU-50	MS-60BN	MS-63BN
$90	$105	$175	$290	$560

MS-63RB	MS-65BN	MS-65RB	MS-65RD
$675	$1,050	$1,750	$3,000

1854, Proof		Cert	Avg	%MS
		4	64.3	

PF-60	PF-63BN	PF-63RB	PF-65BN	PF-65RB
$3,825	$4,750	$7,500	$7,750	$12,000

1854 • BW-1a and b, C-1 (Proof, PO-14), B-1 and 2. *Breen dies:* 1-A and B. **Estimated population:** Circulation strikes: 2,500 to 3,500. Proofs: 25 to 30.

1854 (BW-1a, C-1, B-1).

Obverse: Medium-size logotype positioned slightly high in the die. *Points of distinction:* Only one die this year—used to make circulation strikes as well as Proofs.

Reverse: The Breen text describes these two dies, here with Bowers-Whitman numbers assigned:

BW-1a: Heavily impressed; no rust pit on I of United; Stem right of T forms a loop, though it is very thin; both A's in AMERICA closed; base arc line joins AT in STATES.

BW-1b: Rust pit on I in UNITED at top and extending down a little into upright; steams right of T in CENT do not form a loop; A's in AMERICA open at their bases. The scarcer of the two varieties by far, although most in the marketplace have not been attributed. Mirror Proofs were also struck from this die pair.

Notes: This variety exists in Mint State.

Numismatic Notes: The A.C. Gies hoard: August C. Gies, a jeweler and numismatist of Pittsburgh, Pennsylvania, was said to be a hoarder par excellence, and it is has been related that he had bank-wrapped rolls of most bronze, nickel, and silver coins after about 1900. Apparently he did have some, but they were nearly all of smaller denominations. An example of a story that grew in the telling, he is traditionally assigned the ownership of one roll each of such rarities as the 1901-S and 1913-S quarter dollars. After a few more retellings he was said to have quantities of just about everything.[52]

Circa 1935 Gies happened upon a marvelous group of 1,000 half cents dated 1854, each coin being a bright orange-red, typically with some minor spotting. The 1930s seemed to be a good decade for finding such things, as other half cents came to light elsewhere. These 1854 half cents were distributed in numismatic channels in due course and provide the source for most pieces seen today.

In 1941, as his first job when working for Joe and Morton Stack, young John J. Ford Jr. had to catalog cents and other coins from the Gies holdings. Thomas L. Elder may have been involved in the transaction as well. At the time Ford was given the opportunity to buy some bright red 1854 half cents for $1 each, which he did. Ford later stated that accounts of Gies putting away rare rolls of higher denominations were "pure hogwash."[53]

Gies was born on January 29, 1855, and spent his life in the Pittsburgh area. In 1879 he moved to East Liberty and gained employment with a jeweler. In 1883 he opened his own jewelry business, and remained active in the trade until 1941. Along the way he collected coins and saved bank-wrapped rolls of coins of smaller denominations. He died in 1944.

1855, Braided Hair

Circulation mintage: 56,500.
Proof mintage (estimate): 90 to 110.

Half cents of 1855 were struck from a single die pair. Circulated examples are slightly scarce and are usually EF or AU. Mint State coins are seen often and are mostly from hoards (see Numismatic Notes below). These usually have some light spotting.

Proofs: Proofs were made from the same die pair, for inclusion in sets as well as single sales.

Typical values for 1855 half cents.

1855		Cert	Avg	%MS
		1,007	62.1	87%

VF-20	EF-40	AU-50	MS-60BN	MS-63BN
$80	$100	$170	$275	$550

MS-63RB	MS-65BN	MS-65RB	MS-65RD
$650	$1,000	$1,600	$3,000

1855, Proof		Cert	Avg	%MS
		19	64.3	

PF-60	PF-63BN	PF-63RB	PF-65BN	PF-65RB
$3,500	$4,500	$7,500	$7,500	$10,000

1855 • BW-1, C-1 (Proof, SO-1), B-1. *Breen dies:* 1-A. **Estimated population:** Circulation strikes: 4,000 to 5,000; Proofs: 40 to 60.

1855 (BW-1, C-1, B-1).

Obverse: Date small logotype with italic 5s. *Points of distinction:* Only one die this year—used to make circulation strikes as well as Proofs.

Reverse: Small Berries. Raised line from denticle above E of AMERICA.

Notes: Very common in Mint State with much original color. There are more "RD" half cents of this date than for all others combined.[54]

Numismatic Notes: The Judge Putnam hoard: In 1864 and again in 1868, 1871, and 1877, Judge J.P. Putnam of Boston journeyed to Philadelphia to participate in the annual Assay Commission ritual. Putnam was a numismatist and a personal friend of Roxbury, Massachusetts, dealer W. Elliot Woodward.[55] Under the Assay Commission procedure, the various mints (at the time these being Philadelphia, Carson City,[56] and San Francisco) set aside samples of coins struck from silver and gold (but not copper). These were sent to the Philadelphia Mint and reserved for the Assay Commission, which met early the following year to review the preceding year's precious-metal coinage. Thus, on Monday, February 8, 1864, the commission members gathered to review coins bearing the date 1863.[57]

Undoubtedly, Judge Putnam enjoyed being a part of the 1864 ceremony, for it was considered an honor to be named to the select group. Apparently, while he was there he sought to acquire some souvenirs of his visit, and obtained a few bright Uncirculated copper half cents bearing the date 1855, which were left over from that year. Coins of this denomination had not been made at the Mint since early 1857, and almost all supplies on hand had been melted shortly afterward.[58] Nearly 20 years later, on December 16–18, 1885, W. Elliot Woodward offered for sale the A.W. Matthews Collection and other properties, to which certain coins from the former holdings of Putnam, now deceased, had been consigned.[59] Lot 1761 was described as:

> 1855 [half cents] Bright red Uncirculated. In 1855 Judge J.P. Putnam, of Boston, was a member of the Mint Assay Commission; he bought these half cents from the Mint, and parted with them only just before his death. All are perfect, and nearly all are selected for fineness of impression, as well as other qualities. Another lot so fine probably does not exist. 10 pieces.

A further 18 pieces were described as being from the same source and of the same quality, followed by 47 more with no attribution, but likely from the same group. The same sale continued with quantities of 1856 and 1857 half cents, including 19 Uncirculated examples of the last date of the denomination.

The Charles French hoard: In the 1940s Charles French (born Lehrenkraus), a hobby-shop operator and rare-coin dealer in Troy, New York, purchased a small cloth bag containing 500 bright-red half cents, each bearing the date 1855. The coins had been found in a small metal safe, of the type painted black with a scene on the front, as were commonly used in the late 1800s and early 1900s.

Fearing a reduction in their numismatic market value, French said little about the coins at the time, but parceled them out to clients and in small groups to dealers. By about 1960 most or all were gone.[60]

1856, Braided Hair
Circulation mintage: 40,230.
Proof mintage (estimate): 110 to 130.

One obverse die and three reverse dies were used to coin 1856 half cents. Circulation strikes are fairly scarce and are usually EF or AU.[61] Mint State examples are scarcer yet. Most are brown or have some tinges of red. Full original mint red coins, uncleaned and unspotted, are exceedingly rare.

Proofs: These were made in fair quantity and are mostly from the die with doubling at NT and the ribbon, used to make First Restrike Proofs of earlier dates. Some copper-nickel strikings were made from Proof dies (Judd-177), as patterns to test alloy variations.

Typical values for 1855 half cents.

1856			Cert	Avg	%MS
			368	60.3	74%

VF-20	EF-40	AU-50	MS-60BN	MS-63BN
$100	$125	$185	$325	$575

MS-63RB	MS-65BN	MS-65RB	MS-65RD
$690	$1,250	$2,000	$3,750

1856, Proof			Cert	Avg	%MS
			24	64.2	

PF-60	PF-63BN	PF-63RB	PF-65BN	PF-65RB
$3,500	$4,500	$7,500	$7,500	$11,500

1856 • BW-1a, b, and c; C-1 (Proof, SO-2 from BW-1a, SR-13 for BW-1c); B-1 to 3. *Breen dies:* 1-A, B, and C. **Estimated population:** Circulation strikes: 1,400 to 1,800; Proofs: 70 to 90 (typically Breen dies 1-C).

1856 (BW-1c, C-1, B-3).

Obverse: Medium logotype punched deeply into the die, a bit deeper on the right, giving the 56 digits a bolder appearance. *Points of distinction:* Only one die this year—used to make circulation strikes as well as Proofs.

Reverse: The Breen text describes these three dies, here with Bowers-Whitman numbers assigned. *BW-1a:* Rust pit on I in UNITED. *BW-1b:* No rust pit on I in UNITED. Only used to strike *patterns,* Judd-177. Fewer than 25 known. *BW-1c:* Doubled NT in CENT, this being the same die used to make First Restrike half cents of the 1840s. So called "Reverse of 1856," the regular reverse thought to have been first used this year (earlier-dated half cents from this die are considered to be restrikes).

Notes: Mint State, brown, can be found—sometimes with hints of red.

1857, Braided Hair
Circulation mintage: 35,180.
Proof mintage (estimate): 170 to 220.

Although 35,180 half cents were struck in 1857 (delivered on January 14), Mint records seem to indicate that only 10,000 were shipped. It is not known if all were dated 1857. Requests for coins, including from collectors, were honored by the director until February 28, 1857, after which the remaining coins were melted.[62]

Today, examples of the 1857 half cent are scarce. Most are EF or AU, but probably as many as 500 Mint State coins exist, most of which are brown, sometimes with tinges of red, often mottled. Full-red pieces exist and are usually a pale hue. There are two die varieties, but in the marketplace little notice is taken of the differences.[63]

Proofs: Proofs are known from two die pairs, most being of the BW-2 variety. This is the most available Proof year in the half cent series.

Typical values for 1857, Proof, half cents.

1857, Proof		Cert	Avg	%MS
		39	63.9	

PF-60	PF-63BN	PF-63RB	PF-65BN	PF-65RB
$3,400	$4,500	$7,500	$7,500	$12,000

1857 • BW-1, C-1 (Proof, SO-3 for BW-1a, SR-14 for BW-1b), B-1. *Breen dies:* 1-A. **Estimated population:** Circulation strikes: 1,600 to 3,200; Proofs: 5 to 7.

1857 (BW-1, C-1, B-1).

Obverse: Standard design.

Reverse: Breen: "Plain dot on right side of first A in AMERICA, about mid-high, noticeable even on worn examples."

Notes: Uncirculated examples are easily found, usually brown, but often with traces of mint red. Mint State coins are seen more often than are circulated examples.

1857 (BW-1)		Cert	Avg	%MS
		567	61.0	81%

VF-20	EF-40	AU-50	MS-60BN	MS-63BN
$140	$180	$260	$400	$650

MS-63RB	MS-65BN	MS-65RB	MS-65RD
$800	$1,750	$2,750	$5,000

1857 • BW-2, C-1, B-2. *Breen dies:* 1-B. **Estimated population:** Circulation strikes: 50 to 80. Proofs: 120 to 150.

1857 (BW-2, C-1, B-2).

Obverse: Same as preceding.

Reverse: With doubling at NT of CENT and wreath ribbon. The "First Restrike" die.

Notes: This variety exists in Mint State, usually brown.

COLLECTING LARGE CENTS

THE MOST POPULAR AMERICAN DENOMINATION

Large copper cents were made in larger quantities than any other denomination during their era, from 1793 to 1857. Produced under the provisions of the Mint Act of April 2, 1792, the first coins were delivered in March 1792. Excepting 1,500 silver half dismes struck in July 1792, before the Mint was built, these were the first federal coins coined for general circulation under that legislation.

Cents and half cents were struck for the Mint's own account. Any difference between the cost of copper and the production of the coins went to the bottom line. In contrast, silver coins and gold coins, first made in 1794 and 1795, respectively, were produced as an accommodation to depositors of those metals, and the Mint's service charge yielded a negligible return. This profit policy translated into a desire for the Mint to produce copper coins year in and year out, resulting in a fairly steady output of copper cents.

The *Annual Report of the Director of the Mint* stated that copper cents were delivered from the coiner to the treasurer for every calendar year except 1815 and 1823. However, in the waning days of 1815 some cents were indeed struck, but from dies dated 1816, as evidenced by a January 1, 1816, report that coinage was already underway. Regarding 1823-dated cents, examples exist, but are scarce, of 1823, 3 Over 2, and 1823—no doubt struck in calendar year 1824. Until Robert Maskell Patterson became Mint director in July 1835, it seems to have been standard practice to use dies until they were well worn or cracked, even after the expiration of the date on the die. There were exceptions, such as when existing dies were overdated, including 1799, 9 Over 8; 1800, 180 Over 179; 1800, 1800 Over 1798; 1810, 10 Over 09; 1811, 1 Over 0; 1823, 3 Over 2; 1824, 4 Over 2; 1826, 6 Over 5; and 1839, 9 Over 6.

USE IN COMMERCE

During the era that large cents were coined, they were widely used, but only in certain regions. Reports reveal that they were very popular in the Northeast, continuing down to about Virginia, but were not as often seen south of that point. To the west, they were in wide use to the western border of Pennsylvania in the early years; then they came into use in certain of the prairie states. Otherwise, the lowest-value coins in circulation in the deep South and the West were the silver half dime and the Spanish-American half real, or *medio*, worth 6-1/4¢. Cents were often shipped in wooden kegs, some with an estimated 14,000 coins. Kegs were easier to handle than crates, as they could be rolled on the ground or floor. At least two accounts tell of unopened kegs of cents being shipped back to the North years after they had come to the South: one, of 1811-dated cents, sent back to the Mint; another, of mixed-date 1816 to 1820 coins, shipped from Georgia to New York City after the Civil War.

In the areas of their popularity, cents circulated actively, as evidenced by the worn condition of early dates surviving today. These were everybody's coins. A pocketful of "pennies" would buy breakfast, lunch, or dinner; a glass of beer; permission to use a turnpike; or admission to a museum.

More than a few were counterstamped as advertisements or souvenirs by merchants and others. In Pittsfield, New Hampshire, dentist and saloon operator Dr. G.G. Wilkins stamped his name on thousands of large cents. When the Marquis de LaFayette revisited America in 1824 and 1825, many copper cents were stamped with his portrait on one side and Washington's on the other. Federal cents were not alone in circulation, as cent-sized copper coins dating back to the 1780s, Hard Times tokens, and various foreign coppers were plentiful as well.

A 1793, Wreath, cent, a numismatic classic in its own right, counterstamped "BRADBURY" in a hallmark punch, by Theophilus Bradbury, a Newburyport, Massachusetts, silversmith and jeweler. The coin is also stamped with a punch depicting an eagle in a vertical oval.

An 1825 cent advertising MESCHUTT'S / METROPOLITAN / COFFEE ROOM / 433. BdWAY. The stamper, proprietor Frederick Meschutt, found that the logotype punch was best impressed upon well-worn large cents with fairly smooth surfaces, as is evidenced by surviving pieces. Most coins observed have the counterstamp sharp, but the host coin worn nearly smooth, indicating that the stamp was applied to a well-worn coin.

Dr. G.G. Wilkins of Pittsfield, New Hampshire, practiced dentistry in addition to other activities, including operating a restaurant and compounding patent medicine. On the main street of Pittsfield he displayed a live bear in a cage. He seems to have been a rascal of sorts: he was accused of burning down the barn of someone who had crossed him, and of passing counterfeit money. He was America's most prolific counterstamper of copper cents.

An 1841 cent stamped VOTE THE LAND FREE, for use in the presidential campaign of 1844.

A counterstamp of an 1851 cent advertising Goodwin's Grand Greasejuice (G.G.G.) and Goodwin's Grand Glittering Globules (G.G.G.G.)—products of Charles H. Goodwin of Exeter, New Hampshire.

CHARLES H. GOODWIN,
DRUGGIST & MANUFACTURING CHEMIST,
DEALER IN
Drugs, Medicines, Dye Stuffs, Perfumery and Fancy Goods.
Inventor, Manufacturer, and Proprietor of the following Preparations:
G. G. G., or Q. of F, GOODWIN'S GRAND GREASEJUICE, OR QUINTESSENCE OF FAT,
The great AMERICAN Compound for the embellishment, preservation, growth, and beauty of the Human Hair.
The unrivalled Breath Perfume,
G. G. G. G., GOODWIN'S GRAND GLITTERING GLOBULES, or AMBROSIAL AROMATIC YANKEE CACHOUS.
G. G. T., and Q. of Q., Goodwin's Grand Tobaccojuice, and Quintessence of Quicksilver,
The great American Remedy for the *Cimex Lectularius*, or common Bed Bug.
Also of **Goodwin's Flavoring Extracts,** and **Madame Delectable's Handkerchief Perfume.**
All orders to be addressed to CHARLES H. GOODWIN, Chemist, at
GOODWIN'S GRAND GREASEJUICE DEPOT,
No. 49 Water Street, Exeter, N. H.

A Charles H. Goodwin directory advertisement featuring the G.G.G.G. and related products. (*New England Business Directory*, 1856).

Large cents remained in use until after the passage of the Act of February 21, 1857, which changed the standard to the small copper-nickel cent. A two-year period was allowed to exchange Spanish-American silver coins for the new cents, followed by an extension of six months. Millions of copper cents were exchanged at the same time. Early in the Civil War, all coins disappeared from circulation. However, in Canada these coins remained in wide use throughout the 1860s (Canada did not mint its own cents until 1858).

IF A CENT COULD SPEAK

In 1861 Harper & Brothers published W.C. Prime's guide to numismatics, *Coins, Medals, and Seals, Ancient and Modern*, which was copyrighted 1860. Prime included this contemplation, relevant to early coppers:

> It is a trite, but by no means a worn-out idea, that a coin, could it speak, would be able to relate a stranger story than any other article to which imagination might give a voice. Such a thought can never be worn out, for it is inexhaustible in its richness. Human fancy fails utterly to trace the possible adventures of a copper that was coined even last year; and for every month that a coin has been in circulation a lifetime must needs be added to the years that would be required to sum up the incidents in which one can conjecture that coin as an actor.

The idea that a copper's own story could be interesting was hardly new, and seems to have been included as a writing exercise in formal instruction in English composition, as in this paper written by a student at a Massachusetts preparatory school in 1858:

Autobiography of a Cent

> I am one of the humblest of a large class of beings who have made some stir in the world.
>
> There are others that can boast of far greater value and higher pretentions. I have not the brilliancy of an eagle nor yet the lustre of the dollar, all we lay claim to as a race is good common sense. I do not wish to boast but in my sphere, I am as useful as those who take a higher rank in society.
>
> I was born in the year 1800 in the city of Philadelphia, when with thousands of others I was cast-forth upon the tender mercies of this selfish world. Then I had not the sad and dull aspect I now wear but was bright and cheerful. The world was all before me and on my mission for good or for evil I went forth. I would here say that I have always been the slave of others to come and to go at their bidding.
>
> My pleasing looks caught the notice of a lovely boy and I was laid aside as a keep-sake, but my beauty soon faded. I became dim and it was not long before I passed into the possession of the confectioner where I met many of my companions. With the candy merchants I have always been a great favorite, but my stay here was short.
>
> I cannot now give a detailed account of my life and adventures but it must be reserved for another time. Mine has been an active life. I have done some good in my day, have been the humble instrument of feeding the hungry and clothing the naked. To man I have been a friend indeed.
>
> I have mingled in all kinds of society, have been in the mansion of the sick and the cottage of the poor and everywhere have I been welcomed as a friend. I have grasped the hand of the miser and pressed the trembling finger of the beggar. With children I have ever been deemed a great favorite.

I have resided for the most of my life in the New England states; have made occasional visits to the middle states; and have been over as far as the Mississippi River; and I once went down to New Orleans. We meet with but little favor in the South, and my owner could not dispose of me until his return to the North.

About a year since an event took place which I fear will prove fatal to many of my companions if not to myself. Another race has taken our good name with no more merit and even less show but the public are always caught with new things and they are now the favorites.[1]

I am at present now quietly resting from my labors, what is before me I cannot tell. Like the race of the red man we may be destined to become extinct and be found only here and there wanderers on the earth or carefully preserved on the shelves of the museum.

A.A. Ingersoll.
Merrimac Academy
June 14, 1858.
Composition No. 4.[2]

Designs of Large Copper Cents

Cents were produced in a variety of designs, mostly of distinctive motifs used only on this denomination and the copper half cent. Exceptions were the obverse designs of Draped Bust coins, which were also used on silver issues, and Braided Hair cents, which were also used on gold. In both instances, their appearance on higher denomination coins antedated their use on copper.

The designs of cents included these, listed here with a comparison of their dates of use on half cents and higher-denomination coins:

> 1793: Flowing Hair obverse, Chain reverse (not used on other coins)
>
> 1793: Flowing Hair obverse, Wreath reverse (not used on other coins)
>
> 1793–1796: Liberty Cap, Head Facing Right (used on half cents 1794–1797)
>
> 1796–1807: Draped Bust (used on half cents 1800–1808, silver coins 1795–1807)
>
> 1808–1814: Classic Head (used on half cents 1809–1836)
>
> 1816–1839: Matron Head and variations (not used on other coins)
>
> 1839–1857: Braided Hair (used on half cents 1840–1857, gold coins 1838–1908)

Ways to Collect

Large copper cents have been a foundation stone of American numismatics ever since the 1850s. The completion of a date set from 1793 to 1857 (except 1815) with one of each, plus important varieties, has been a goal of thousands of collectors, from the casual to those serious enough to make it a lifetime pursuit. Fortunately, all are available in the marketplace, although 1793, 1799 in particular, and 1804 are rare. Among later dates, the 1823 is the key issue, although thousands exist.

Collecting cents by basic design types, rather than by years, is a popular pursuit, often done in connection with obtaining one of each motif in other series from half cents to gold double eagles. Those who concentrate on cents usually desire not just dates, but major varieties, such as those listed in the regular edition of *A Guide Book of United States Coins.* Still beyond that, specialists endeavor to collect these cents by die varieties as listed in the book on cents of 1793 to 1814 by Dr. William H. Sheldon and the later cents of 1816 to 1857 in Howard R. Newcomb's study. For certain years, such as 1794 and some of the later Braided Hair dates, there are dozens of varieties. Other years, such as 1806 and 1809, have just one die combination.

To know large cents is to love them, it has been said. They possess a quintessence that is elusive of definition. In *Early American Cents*, Dr. William H. Sheldon discussed their appeal, including this:

> Old copper, like beauty, appears to possess a certain intrinsic quality or charm which for many people is irresistible. An experienced dealer in American numismatic materials recently wrote as follows: "Sooner or later, if a collector stays at the business long enough, it is three to one his interest in all the other series will flag and he will focus his attention on the early cents."
>
> Gold, silver, and even bronze appear to be very much the same wherever you see them. Coins made of these metals become "old money" and "interesting," like the stuff seen in museums, but copper seems to possess an almost living warmth and a personality not encountered in any other metal. The big cent is something more than old money. Look at a handful of the cents dated before 1815, when they contained relatively pure copper. You see rich shades of green, red, brown, yellow, and even deep ebony; together with blendings of these not elsewhere matched in nature save perhaps in autumn leaves. If the light is good (direct sunlight is preferable) you will possibly observe that no two of the coins are of quite the same color.
>
> Copper oxidizes differently in different atmospheres, and the way it colors and weathers depends also upon the impurities and traces of other metals which it may contain. The copper that went into the early cents must have been of highly variable assay, recruited as it was from almost every possible source. Some came from Sweden, some from England, some was obtained by melting up copper nails, spikes, and copper finishings from wrecked ships (including both British and American men-of-war). Some of it came from kitchen and other household utensils donated or sold to the Mint in response to urgent appeals. George Washington is said to have donated 'an excellent copper tea-kettle as well as two pairs of tongs' early in 1793 for the first cents. It is not surprising, therefore, that to some extent the different early die varieties are recognizable by characteristic color and surface texture, as well as by die breaks, peculiarities of the planchets, and so on. Every early cent has a character of its own.

This is, indeed, the quintessential part. It has no equivalent in the collecting of contemporary gold and silver coins. A VF-20 example of scarce die variety of a 1795 half eagle, a date made in many different obverse and reverse combinations, would stir very little interest even at a gathering of gold specialists. A VF-20 copper cent of 1795, a variety of equal rarity, would be a pass-around-and-examine coin at a meeting of cent enthusiasts.

Another appeal of large cents is that the market for large copper cents is remarkably steady over the years. In *Early American Cents*, Dr. William H. Sheldon singled out a particular date, 1794, as being a bellwether of the coin market as a whole, and this is not inaccurate. Beyond that, a newcomer to large cents may wish to take a quick glance at several large copper cents, listed common to rare, by dates, but not die varieties—such as those listed in the *Guide Book of United States Coins*—and note the prices over a period of years. From the first edition of the *Guide Book of United States Coins*, which was published in 1946 (with a cover date of 1947) down to the latest, the "profit march" for these coins has been upward. Few people seeking to buy rare coins as an investment would investigate large copper cents, as "investment quality" coins are supposed to be in silver or gold and in grades of MS-65 and higher. However, a well-worn 1793, Chain, cent, or a Mint State 1820 from the Randall Hoard, or the curious 1839, 9 Over 6, in Fine-12 grade have all done very well over the years, as have most others.

Books About Cents

Today, varieties of the 1793 to 1814 cents are generally collected by the Sheldon numbers (S-1, S-2, etc.) first given in *Early American Cents*, 1949, and its revision, *Penny Whimsy*, 1958. Building upon this foundation, *Walter Breen's Encyclopedia of Early United States Cents 1793–1814*, edited by Mark Borckardt, gives more information than available in any other single source, along with Breen numbers (B-1, B-2, etc.).[3]

For later issues, *United States Copper Cents 1816–1857*, by Howard R. Newcomb, 1944, remains the standard reference, with Newcomb numbers (N-1, N-2, etc.), which include numerous additions by later scholars. *United States Large Cents 1816–1839*, by William C. Noyes, 1991, and *The Cent Book, 1816–1839*, by John D. Wright, 1992, each offer large illustrations of varieties in combination with useful information. The *Attribution Guide for United States Large Cents 1840–1857*, by J.R. (Bob) Grellman Jr., 1987, is useful for these later issues, for which die-variety differences are often very tiny.

Studies of the availability of various cents in different grades include the popular *Copper Quotes by Robinson* (Jack H. Robinson) and various censuses created by EAC members Del Bland, William C. Noyes, and others. Population reports published by the Numismatic Guaranty Corporation of America (NGC) and the Professional Coin Grading Service (PCGS) are useful for general information, but are usually organized by dates and/or (use is inconsistent) the major varieties listed in the regular edition of the *Guide Book of United States Coins*. Sheldon and Newcomb–listed die combinations are not treated.

In addition to the preceding works, much pleasure can be derived from collecting older texts on cents by Sylvester S. Crosby, Edward Maris, Édouard Frossard, Frank D. Andrews, George Clapp, and others. Auction catalogs with descriptions and illustrations of important collections of large cents furnish a challenge to collect, with certain early sales—such as those by the Chapman brothers and issued with photograph plates—rare and in strong demand. In modern times, many fine collections have been brought to market by auction companies via memorable catalogs.

Two books by John W. Adams, *United States Numismatic Literature. Volume I. Nineteenth Century Auction Catalogues* (1982) and *United States Numismatic Literature. Volume II. Twentieth Century Auction Catalogues* (1990), listed catalogs and rated them by content on an alphabetical scale. Those with large copper cents earning an A+ rating are especially important.

Early American Coppers and Fellowship

The bimonthly journal *Penny-Wise*, published by Early American Coppers, serves as a forum for critiques of past studies, the announcement of new discoveries, market updates, and various commentaries and articles on cents as well. The group is dynamic and has sustained and developed interest in copper cents for more than 40 years. It has attracted the "brightest and the best" of the numismatic community. Many are the Ph.D. and M.D. degrees attached to members' names.

The basic appeal of EAC is that, while a checkbook and a good bank account are nice to have, neither is at all essential to the enjoyment of EAC membership, and the possession of such is not even a consideration of camaraderie. To enjoy copper cents it is necessary to add investigation, study, and connoisseurship to the equation. The field is always changing, new ideas and theories are constantly presented, and new discoveries made. Thanks to this dynamism, facilitated in part by EAC, copper cents remain as appealing to collect today as they were in the 1850s.

Large Cents, 1793–1857

Varieties, Populations, Values

Flowing Hair, Chain Reverse (1793)

1793, Chain AMERICA (Bowers-Whitman–4, Sheldon-3, Breen-4).

Designer: *Henry Voigt.* **Weight:** *208 grains (13.48 grams).* **Composition:** *Copper.*
Diameter: *Average 26 to 27 mm.* **Edge:** *Vine and bars design.*

The first federal cents for circulation were struck at the Mint from February 27 through March 12, 1793. These were of the Chain motif and were made to the extent of 36,103 pieces. The first of these issues bore the abbreviated inscription UNITED STATES OF AMERI. Perhaps 5,000 to 10,000 were made of this style, judging from the ratio of surviving examples. The rest of the 36,103 pieces of the Chain type were of the AMERICA type.

Today Chain AMERI. cents are scarce in all grades. These can be considered a separate type, but most collectors opt to acquire just one Chain cent, with either the AMERI. or AMERICA spelling.

Design Details

The obverse depicts the head of Miss Liberty facing right, her hair loosely arranged. LIBERTY is lettered at the border above. The date 1793 is between the head and the bottom border.

On the reverse a chain of 15 elongated links forms a circle enclosing ONE / CENT and the fraction 1/100. At the time there were 15 states in the Union (the most recent additions being Vermont in 1791 and Kentucky in 1792). The links were intended to symbolize unity, a similar gesture to the interlocked rings that appeared on the 1776, Continental Currency, pewter dollar and certain paper money. As noted, around the outer border is the inscription UNITED STATES OF AMERI. On the second type the inscription is spelled out fully as UNITED STATES OF AMERICA.

Both obverse and reverse borders are plain (without beads or denticles). The edges have a design of vines and vertical bars.

Design featuring vines and vertical bars on the edge of a 1793 cent.

Historical Magazine, founded in 1857, was the first American periodical to regularly include numismatic items. The February 1859 issue included a submission by L.C. of Hartford, Connecticut, who sent in a notice from the *Argus*, which had been published in Boston on March 26, 1793. This quoted an account from Newark, New Jersey, criticizing America's first cent from the Philadelphia Mint:

> The American *cents* (says a letter from Newark) do not answer our expectations. The chain on the reverse is but a bad omen for liberty, and liberty herself appears to be in a fright. May she not justly cry out in the words of the apostle, *"Alexander the coppersmith has done me much harm; the Lord reward him according to his works!"*

It will be remembered that *Alexander* Hamilton was at that time secretary of the Treasury. At the time newspapers often acquired information by clipping items from other periodicals. Earlier, on March 18, essentially the same observation had been printed in Philadelphia in the *Mail, or Claypoole's Daily Advertiser*.

Comments such as this were undoubtedly responsible for the motifs being changed to a fuller portrait of Miss Liberty on the obverse and a wreath design in place of the chain motif on the reverse.

1793, Chain Reverse
Circulation mintage (assumed): 36,103.

The first delivery of cents from the coiner (Henry Voigt) to the Mint treasurer was on March 1, 1793, and consisted of 11,178 pieces—these representing the first copper coins of the new Mint.[1] Frank H. Stewart, in *History of the First United States Mint, Its People and Its Operations*, suggested that the 110,512 cents struck during calendar year 1793 included 36,103 of the Chain type, made from March 1 to 12; 63,353 Wreath cents, struck from April 9 to July 17; and 11,056 Liberty Cap cents, delivered from the coiner to the treasurer on September 18. While the delivery figures are correct, there are no hard facts to back up the assignment of specific designs to the deliveries. It is not necessarily true that different deliveries represent abandonment of earlier dies—in fact it is improbable! This is a *very important* concept as it applies across the board to all early delivery figures for half cents and large cents.

Perhaps the September 18 shipment included some of the Wreath type? In such situations, certain figures can be no more than estimates. Nevertheless, they can be useful, if backed up by surveys of existing coins, to determine relative population. At least with the 1793 cents we know they were all dated that year. It would not be surprising if certain 1793 cents (of the later Liberty Cap type) were also struck in calendar year 1794, but we will never know.

There were four different obverse dies cut for the Chain cents, one of them having a period after LIBERTY and another after the date. Just two reverses were made, one with AMERI. and the other with AMERICA. R.W. Julian has provided a Mint record stating that coiner Henry Voigt cut the dies.[2]

The details of Miss Liberty's hair are often indistinct or missing, even on many higher-grade examples. For all grades, the reverse is often sharper than the obverse.

Hence, if split grading were popular today (as it once was), a Chain AMERI. cent might be correctly graded as VG-8/F-12, or similarly.

The Chain cents remained in circulation for many years. In 1859 Dr. Montroville W. Dickeson wrote in the *American Numismatical Manual* that he had found several different varieties by pulling them from circulation. In the cradle days of numismatic popularity, beginning in a large way in 1858 and 1859, any 1793 cent attracted attention, and a particularly nice one was apt to cost several dollars.

Most 1793, Chain, cents known today are well worn, as might be expected from their first having attracted widespread notice in the 1850s. Today, even in Fair-2 or About Good-3 grades, they are collectible and in strong demand. Some of the lowest grades have nearly everything worn away except a shadow or outline of the chain—enough to identify the type, but not to reveal much else. Such a coin is still very desirable as a filler and will find many buyers in the marketplace.

Grades from G-4 through F-12 constitute most of the Chain cents in the marketplace. VF coins are scarcer, and EF scarcer yet. Offerings at the AU level, punctuated by the occasional Mint State example, draw a lot of attention and are usually showcased as prime attractions when offered at auction.

Scratches, edge bumps, and porosity are common among 1793 cents. The answer is to cherrypick for quality.

Several collectors have found cents of the 1793 year (all three types) to be an interesting specialty, none more so than Charles Ruby, a California college professor who was prominent in the large cent field for many years. Kenneth Rendell and Q. David Bowers were overnight guests at his home in 1958, and were treated to seeing multiple custom plastic holders filled with 1793 cents, most of which were in low grades, but each with its own charm.

1793, Chain AMERI. • Bowers-Whitman–1, Sheldon-1, Breen-1. Crosby 1-A.[3] *Breen dies:* 1-A. *Estimated population:* 120 to 160.

1793, Chain AMERI. (Bowers-Whitman–1, Sheldon-1, Breen-1).

Detail of the finely delineated hair strands and widely spaced date.

AMERI. abbreviation and part of chain.

Obverse: Y of LIBERTY opposite lower forehead. Date widely spaced with widest space between 7 and 9. *Points of distinction:* Clash marks develop from the chain on the reverse, and can be seen near the center of the coin. On most examples there is a bulge under the 1 of the date. The obverse die was slightly misaligned in the coin press. This causes the date to be weak and LIBERTY to be strong. This is especially noticeable on lower-grade examples on which the date can be completely worn away. This also happens on the BW-24 obverse.

Reverse: AMERI. abbreviation. *Points of distinction:* The reverse is found either perfect or with a bulge under the U of UNITED. The next die state has a crack over TAT of STATES. The rarest die state is terminal because this crack has become a heavy cud that extends to the rim. It is the failure of this die that is the cause of the creation of the next variety that now spells AMERICA in full.

Notes: Mintage estimated as 4,500.[4] This variety occurs in Mint State occasionally. EF and AU are more practical possibilities for collectors.

Numismatic Notes: 1889 comment on the desirability of BW-1, suggesting this variety had been popular since about 1839: W.E. Woodward's January 21–22, 1889, sale of the Charles Stetson Collection included lot 4: "1793 Reverse has the abbreviated legend 'Ameri.' this cent is Uncirculated and almost bright; it is the finest cent of this kind known, except that of Mr. Mickley's, which is a brilliant Proof, and has sold several times for about $175. . . . As collectors have been looking for this cent for about 50 years, that another perfect specimen should turn up is hardly to be expected."[5]

1793, Chain AMERI.	Cert	Avg	%MS
	36	23.9	8%

AG-3	G-4	VG-8	F-12
$6,300	$11,250	$17,625	$28,500

VF-20	EF-40	AU-50	MS-60BN
$49,250	$87,500	$200,000	$318,750

1793, Chain AMERICA • BW-2, S-2, B-2. Crosby 1-C. *Breen dies:* 1-B.

Estimated population: 75 to 120.

1793, Chain AMERICA (BW-2, S-2, B-2).

Obverse: Same die as preceding. *Points of distinction:* Clash marks develop near the center. There is a bulging beneath the last three date numerals.

Reverse: AMERICA spelled out in full.

Notes: Mintage estimated as 6,500. This variety can be found in Mint State, but it is very rare as such. AU coins appear now and again.

1793, Chain AMERICA (BW-2)	Cert	Avg	%MS
	(a)		

AG-3	G-4	VG-8	F-12
$4,650	$7,750	$13,625	$19,250

VF-20	EF-40		AU-50
$36,125	$61,500		$111,000

a. Included in certified population for 1793, Chain AMERICA (BW-4).

1793, Chain AMERICA • BW-3, S-NC-1, B-3. Crosby 2-C. *Breen dies:* 2-B.

Recorded population: 2.

1793, Chain AMERICA (BW-3, S-NC-1, B-3).

Obverse: Widest LIBERTY, with the Y opposite the eye. LIBERTY is also farther away from the rim than on any other Chain variety. *Points of distinction:* A crack develops at the rim below 7, continuing up to the left. This probably happened very early in the life of the die, accounting for the extreme rarity of impressions today.

Reverse: Same die as preceding.

Notes: Mintage estimated as 100. Two known: EF-45, American Numismatic Society; and Poor-1, found in 1967, in the Daniel W. Holmes Jr. Collection 1996–2008. The EF coin shows a small crack from the border through 1 of 1793, which may have quickly developed so as to render the die useless, accounting for the rarity.

1793, Chain AMERICA • BW-4, S-3, B-4. Crosby 3-C. *Breen dies:* 3-B. *Estimated population:* 400 to 500.

1793, Chain AMERICA (BW-4, S-3, B-4).

Obverse: Y of LIBERTY opposite eyebrow. 179 spaced about the same distance apart; 93 very close, 3 slightly low. The R is overly large and tilts to the right. Clash marks from the reverse often seen in front of the mouth and throat and under the neck. *Points of distinction:* The planchets used for this variety are approximately 1 mm larger than those used on the other Chain cents.

Reverse: Same die as preceding. *Points of distinction:* The late die state exhibits a crack through the bottom of UNITED.

Notes: Mintage estimated as 16,000. This variety is available in Mint State, but it is exceedingly rare as such. EF and AU coins are more practical possibilities.

1793, Chain AMERICA (BW-4)	Cert	Avg	%MS
	113	24.0	6%

AG-3	G-4	VG-8	F-12
$4,650	$7,750	$13,625	$19,250

VF-20	EF-40	AU-50	MS-60BN
$36,125	$61,500	$111,000	$250,000

1793, Chain AMERICA, Period After LIBERTY and Date • BW-5, S-4, B-5. Crosby 4-C. *Breen dies:* 4-B. *Estimated population:* 200 to 300.

1793, Chain AMERICA, Period After LIBERTY and Date (BW-5, S-4, B-5).

Obverse: With a period after LIBERTY and another after the date. The hair detail is more attractive than on the preceding dies and somewhat differently styled. *Points of distinction:* Early-die-state coins usually have a bulge between the lower hair and the rim. This bulge develops into a tiny crack, which is joined by a second crack that goes toward the date. There is also a small rim break at 8 o'clock.

Reverse: Same die as preceding.

Notes: Mintage estimated as 9,000. This variety can be found in Mint State, but it is exceedingly rare as such. EF and AU coins are more practical possibilities. An MS-66BN example of this coin sold at auction for $2,350,000 in January 2015.

1793, Chain AMERICA, Period After LIBERTY and Date	Cert	Avg	%MS
	13	26.6	0%

AG-3	G-4	VG-8	F-12
$5,075	$8,125	$14,500	$20,500

VF-20	EF-40	AU-50
$38,750	$66,250	$123,750

Flowing Hair, Wreath Reverse (1793)

1793, Sprung Die, Wreath Type, Vine and Bars Edge (BW-12, S-6, B-7).

Designer: *Henry Voigt.* **Weight:** *208 grains (13.48 grams).* **Composition:** *Copper.*
Diameter: *26 to 28 mm.* **Edge:** *Vine and Bars design, or lettered ONE HUNDRED FOR A DOLLAR. The varieties with lettered edge give the denomination three times: as ONE / CENT and 1/100 on the reverse and as ONE HUNDRED FOR A DOLLAR on the edge. The same triple denomination feature is found on several other early copper types.*

Mint records (from coiner Voigt's account book) show that coining of the Wreath cents commenced on April 4. Between April 9 and July 17, 1793, there were 63,353 large copper cents delivered. Conventional wisdom is that all of these were of the Wreath type, although whether the division is clear cut between the ending of the Chain type and the beginning of the Wreath type is subject to question, as noted above in the narrative concerning Chain cents.

The Wreath cent, named for the reverse, reflected a great change in the cent motif—now with a restyled portrait in high relief and with the reverse chain eliminated. Both obverse and reverse were given a beaded border, at once protective and attractive. The present author has said that the elegance of this issue has no equivalents earlier or later in the large cent series.

Eleven different die combinations were used to accomplish the coinage. All but the final combination has the vine and bars edge treatment. The BW-21 and BW-22 edge devices are split between the vine and bars (scarcer) and those lettered ONE HUNDRED FOR A DOLLAR.

Today, Wreath cents are at once rare and popular, serving as foundation stones in American numismatics. Such coins are in continual demand, and there has never been a time in which the market for them has been slow. Typical grades range from Good to Fine, or so. Many pieces have problems, and cherrypicking is needed to find one that is just right.

Design Details

As with the Chain cents, R.W. Julian has located documentation that the dies of the Wreath cents were cut by coiner Voigt.[6] On the obverse the head of Miss Liberty faces to the right, in bold relief, with prominent hair tresses flowing back. Above, is LIBERTY; below, a three-leaf sprig, and below that the date 1793. The border is beaded. The entire arrangement is very elegant. The botanical nature of the sprig and its variations have furnished the subject for many numismatic commentaries. For the usually seen sprig, laurel has been suggested. Writing in the *New-York Dispatch*, April 19, 1857, Augustus B. Sage offered this possibility. "The palm leaf cent of 1793 [has] the addition of three small palm leaves under the bust, and the olive wreath, taking the place of the chain around 'one cent, 1-100.'" Although palm leaves may have been used on other coins (most notably the $5 and $10 issues of 1795), they do not seem to be a candidate for the foliage on the 1793 cent.

The most famous sprig is that of the 1793, Strawberry Leaf, cent, as it has been called by generations of numismatists. This motif has been called a *pattern* by some, but there seems to be little support for that, as all examples show evidence of circulation. John Kleeberg suggested it may be a contemporary counterfeit.[7] Walter Breen in his *Encyclopedia* discussed such theories and concluded, "What punches are clear enough for certainty leave no doubt of its Mint origin, and the edge ornamentation is as on the other genuine 1793 cents." As this variety is front-row center in the numismatic annals of 1793 cents, it is worthwhile to devote space here for a detailed discussion.

Sylvester Sage Crosby included this in *The United States Coinage of 1793—Cents and Half Cents*, 1897:

> This is the obverse . . . having been first known as the "Clover leaf" Cent, but which I think may properly be called the Cotton leaf Cent, and is the greatest rarity of its class, only three specimens being known to collectors, one having reverse D, and two, reverse E. It bears upon a stem rising from near the angle of the 7, three trefoil leaves and a blossom, or boll of cotton.
>
> The legend and date are in small characters, the R larger and higher than the other letters and placed over the hair, close above the forehead. The date is less than two millimeters from the hair at the left, and more than four from the point of the bust, which is longer and more rounded at its tip than in any other known die. The double curl under the neck is rather heavy.
>
> It is difficult to account for the scarcity of specimens from this die, as it appears to have been thought worthy of two reverse dies, neither it, or either of its reverses showing any signs of deterioration, and neither reverse being known to have been used with any other obverse. It is hoped that better specimens of these may yet be discovered.

In *The Numismatist*, May 1912, Edgar H. Adams in his "Live American Numismatic Items" column, included mention of the auction offering of such a cent, when Lyman H. Low called the cataloger of the coin, Édouard Frossard, a "liar":

> At one of Frossard's sales at Kennedy's Fifth Avenue Auction Rooms, on December 20th, 1894 a specimen described as "Very Fair" for $120. It was this cent that incidentally caused the historic fight when Frossard and another prominent dealer, both veterans, rolled around the floor of the auction room, trying to kick each other, and the late H.P. Smith lost a diamond pin in the confusion incidental to separating them.

Adams went on to discuss the "rare variety of the clover, strawberry, or whatever kind of leaf one may choose," noting that an article in the current issue of *Steigerwalt's Messenger* was confused and contained several errors.

Jim Neiswinter, well-known specialist in the study of cents of the 1793 year, provided this comment in connection with the present book:

> In December 2004 Bob Grellman, Dan Holmes, John Kleeberg, Bob Hoge, and I met at the American Numismatic Society. Dan brought his two Strawberry Leafs plus some of his other Wreath cents. We spent the day comparing them to the ANS Strawberry and Wreath cents. At the end of the day we all agreed that the Strawberries were all Mint products. This was later delineated in the *Penny Whimsy* article of March 2005. We also discovered that there are two varieties of the Vine and Bars edge device—the first is on all the Chains, plus the Sheldon-8 and 9.[8]

In *Coin World,* January 17, 2005, this commentary by Andrew W. Pollock III appeared, and is probably the last word on the subject:

The 1793 Flowing Hair, Wreath, "Strawberry Leaf" cent has been one of the most celebrated varieties in American numismatics since the 19th century. Although the "Strawberry leaf" moniker has been a popular designation for many decades, some numismatists over the years have conjectured that the intended design of the sprig beneath Miss Liberty's head is either from a cotton plant or clover plant.

The suggestion that the design represents cotton is supported not only by the shape of the leaves, which is very similar to the shape of the leaves of certain varieties of cotton plants that can be found illustrated on the Internet and in agricultural text-books, but also from the fact that Eli Whitney's cotton gin was invented in 1793, something brought to my attention by John Pack.

The recent auction of the finest known example of the "Strawberry Leaf" cent (American Numismatic Rarities, Nov. 30, Lot 130) resulted in my having an oppor-tunity to examine the coin, whereupon I suspected that the sprig was actually intended to be that of a grape plant, having three leaves; a poorly defined cluster of grapes; and possibly a vestigial tendril. It could be argued that the "cluster" element might have been intended as a cotton boll. However, I'm inclined to the view that an open cotton boll would have been depicted as having a more uniform periphery and perhaps with the open boll projecting upward as is represented in drawings and pho-tographs of cotton plants having ripe cotton ready to be harvested. I have found an example of a grape ornamentation on a piece of silverware made in Great Britain in the first quarter of the 19th century. The ornamentation depicts grape leaves, grape clusters and tendrils. The similarity of the grape leaves depicted in the ornamenta-tion with the leaves featured on the 1793 Flowing Hair cent is striking. It is also worth mentioning that the grape clusters in the ornamentation are not all of a uniform inverted pear shape, which seems to be characteristic of modern depictions seen in still life paintings and advertisements.

I also found at chartingnature.com another rendering of a grape leaf that is similar titled *Wine-Grape-Raisin Precoce de Montreuil.* The Internet has provided numisma-tists and other students of the humanities with vast resources by which they can pur-sue their scholarly investigations. In connection with the inquiry to ascertain if the 1793 Flowing Hair, "Strawberry Leaf" cent may have actually been intended as a "Grape Leaves and Cluster" cent, I conducted a Google search to determine if any events occurred in America in 1793 pertaining to grapes or vineyards.

I learned that according to some unattributed lecture notes posted on the Purdue University website pertaining to the topic of "Wine Appreciation" that "America's first commercial winery, the Pennsylvania Vine Company, [was] founded in 1793 near Philadelphia by Pierre Legaux." At the web site of the American Philosophical Society in Philadelphia, an archival finding aid presents the background story of Peter Legaux and the Pennsylvania Vine Co.:

"In January 1793, Peter Legaux submitted a plan to the American Philosophical Society for 'the establishment of the Vine culture in Pennsylvania by means of public subscription, authorized and protected by Government.'"

Following Legaux's proposal to the APS, the Pennsylvania Legislature passed an act authorizing the incorporation of a company for promoting culture of the vine. A subscription was raised and shares issued to some of Philadelphia's most important merchants and friends of improvement. . . . It should be noted that the president of the American Philosophical Society at the time of Legaux's proposal was David Rittenhouse, who also at that time was the director of the Mint. Production of the coin variety may have simply been intended to signify Rittenhouse's approbation of the project. Although this evidence in no way constitutes proof that the 1793 Flowing Hair, "Strawberry Leaf" cent is indeed a Pennsylvania vineyard commemorative, nonetheless, the information provides what seems to be a plausible context for the creation of a fascinating and enigmatic variety.

The reverse displays an open wreath with sprays of berries among the leaves (the only year with this feature), tied with a single ribbon bow at the bottom, enclosing the two-line inscription, ONE / CENT. Around the border is UNITED STATES OF AMERICA. Below the bow is 1/100. The border is beaded. The wreath is *extremely curious* from a botanical viewpoint, and what the engraver had in mind is anybody's guess. The sprays of berries are among olive or, most likely, laurel leaves, or whatever (the same type of leaves had different berries on later reverses), with the same branches also yielding *tiny maple leaves.* The reverse is very attractive and closely matches the style used on all half cents of the 1793 year.

1793, Wreath Reverse
Circulation mintage (assumed): 63,353.

Cents of the Wreath design are often acquired singly for inclusion in a type set. Collecting by varieties has also been popular, this including varieties created by the two edge types. The final die pair, which created BW-21, with Vine and Bars edge, was the only pair used for Lettered Edge coins, with either two leaves or one on the edge, as on BW-22 and BW-23.

The most famous of all Wreath cents is the so-called Strawberry Leaf, as discussed in the introductory material for this type. These are very rare and are always seen with extensive wear. There are two varieties, with one obverse die combined with two reverses.

Extensive wear is the rule for all varieties. Similar to the situation for Chain cents, the Wreath cents did not attract much attention until the rise of numismatics as a popular hobby in the 1850s, by which time the typical coin had spent many decades in commercial use.

Grades of surviving coins ranging from About Good-3 upward are collectible and highly prized. Most in the marketplace range from G-4 to Fine-12 or so, although Very Fine and Extremely Fine coins cross the auction block with regularity. Mint State examples exist for the Vine and Bars edge type, some of which are rather liberally graded, and these always attract a lot of attention. The Lettered Edge type is exceedingly rare if better than AU.

The dies were cut by hand and have many distinctive differences from one to another. The descriptions given below can be used quickly and simply. Other features can be discerned from the photographs.

Every 1793, Wreath, cent has its own personality. Use the grading number as a start, and then seek a coin with minimal or no edge bumps, planchet rifts, porosity, or heavy marks. Choice-appearing cents may be more expensive, and it may be necessary to view several coins to find one that is just right, but the search will be worth it. A smooth, attractive 1793, Wreath, cent is an item of rare beauty in any grade.

Most 1793, Wreath, cents are fairly well struck, although high-grade pieces may exhibit some weakness on the highest hair tresses and on the leaf details. On lower-grade pieces these areas are worn, so the point is moot.

It has been estimated that more than 2,000 1793, Wreath, cents with Vine and Bars edge exist and 500 or so of the Lettered Edge. As is true of many other American coins with interesting or unusual edge devices, the encasing of examples in certain types of certified holders prevents study and numismatic enjoyment of this feature.

1793, Wreath Type, Vine and Bars Edge • BW-11, S-5, B-6. Crosby 6-F.
Breen dies: 5-C. **Estimated population:** 120 to 160.

1793, Wreath Type, Vine and Bars Edge (BW-11, S-5, B-6).

Detail of the date area.

Detail of part of the wreath, including sprays of berries, beaded border, tiny maple leaves ("trefoils").

Obverse: Stem slanted, distant from 9, points to upper right of 7 and is about on the same slant as the upright of the 7. The date and LIBERTY are larger on this die than on any other of the type. The sizes of

LIBERTY and the date are the same size as those found on all the Chain varieties. That is why this is considered the first Wreath variety. Found perfect and also in a very rare late state with the die broken over LI and BER.

Reverse: Outside maple leaves (a.k.a. trefoils) under N and D of UNITED. Bow small and heavy. *Points of distinction:* A couple of tiny bulges are seen on later states.

Notes: This variety is available in Mint State, but rare so fine. Several exist. EF and AU pieces are seen with some regularity and are highly prized.

1793, Wreath Type, Vine and Bars Edge (BW-11)		Cert	Avg	%MS
		(a)		

AG-3	G-4	VG-8	F-12	VF-20
$700	$2,380	$4,700	$7,400	$14,500

EF-40	AU-50	MS-60BN	MS-63BN
$28,000	$40,625	$65,000	$117,500

a. Included in certified population for 1793, Wreath Type, Vine and Bars Edge (BW-17).

1793, Sprung Die, Wreath Type, Vine and Bars Edge • BW-12, S-6, B-7.
Crosby 7-F. *Breen dies:* 6-C. *Estimated population:* 300 to 400.

1793, Sprung Die, Wreath Type, Vine and Bars Edge (BW-12, S-6, B-7).

Obverse: Leaves meet above 9, stem is close to 9 and points at upper right of 7. Rightmost leaf extends far beyond 3 and points to the tip of the neck. Leftmost leaf ends below curl. B of LIBERTY low. *Points of distinction:* First called the "Sprung Die" by Sylvester Crosby because there is always a bulge or convexity on the obverse running from the back of the hair to the rim.

The latest die state has a crack from the lower lip to the right rim, and another short horizontal crack hidden in the hair below the bulge.

Reverse: Same die as preceding. *Points of distinction:* On some examples, on the back there is a short crack through TE of UNITED.

Notes: This coin can be found in Mint State, but is very rare as such.

1793, Sprung Die, Wreath Type, Vine and Bars Edge		Cert	Avg	%MS
		(a)		

AG-3	G-4	VG-8	F-12
$675	$2,200	$4,370	$6,930

VF-20	EF-40	AU-50
$13,500	$24,670	$36,170

a. Included in certified population for 1793, Wreath Type, Vine and Bars Edge (BW-17).

1793, Wreath Type, Vine and Bars Edge • BW-13, S-7, B-8. Crosby 8-F.
Breen dies: 7-C. **Estimated population:** 25 to 30.

1793, Wreath Type, Vine and Bars Edge (BW-13, S-7, B-8).

Detail of LIBERTY with dots above I.

Obverse: Stem ends above left edge of 9 and not close to it; right leaf very small. *Points of distinction:* Charles Ruby's famous double dot cent is considered by some to be the only known example of the earliest die state. This coin has two beads, one on top of the other, above the I of LIBERTY and does not exhibit any die sinking at the date. On most other examples there is some degree of die sinking at 1793 that leaves a swelling or raised area which tends to weaken the last three figures. In the latest state there is a crack from the top border from above R, through the base of T, to the front part of the hair, and the swelling at the date has developed into a crack from the rim, through the 9, and to the top part of the 7.

Reverse: Same die as preceding. There is usually a light crack through TE of UNITED. See notes below concerning the discovery of this variety.

Notes: Only two examples are known above VF, one of which is held by the American Numismatic Society.

Numismatic Notes: From Sylvester Sage Crosby, *The United States Coinage of 1793—Cents and Half Cents,* 1897:

> The discovery of this obverse was a curious instance of the appearance of a new die after a search of many years over a large field. Nearly ten years after the publication of the article on these cents in the *Journal of Numismatics,* in 1869, when we had most of the important collections at our service, and a thorough search had been made in all directions, a lot of about seventy-five worn-out 1793 Cents was sent to me from Philadelphia, for examination. Among these I found two pieces from a die hitherto unnoticed, the only feature sufficiently preserved to distinguish them being the sprig under the bust.
>
> I learned of no similar pieces for another ten years, when a better specimen was shown to me, belonging to Mr. Henry Phelps, of Worcester, Mass.; but in the Winsor sale of 1895, a fine and well-preserved specimen was discovered and purchased by its present owner, Dr. Thomas Hall, of Boston, and was by him alone recognized as from this rare die. This is the piece represented upon the plate. The two worn pieces first found are still in my

possession, but are in so poor condition that they should not be considered as affecting its rarity, which should be estimated as only short of unique.

[This variety was discovered in 1878, just in time to be noted in Édouard Frossard's 1879 *Monograph of United States Cents and Half Cents*.]

1793, Wreath Type, Vine and Bars Edge (BW-13)	Cert	Avg	%MS
	(a)		

AG-3	G-4	VG-8	F-12	VF-20
$7,125	$10,250	$19,000	$33,750	$50,000

a. Included in certified population for 1793, Wreath Type, Vine and Bars Edge (BW-17).

1793, Wreath Type, Vine and Bars Edge • BW-14, S-NC-5, B-9. Crosby 10-F. *Breen dies:* 8-C. *Recorded population:* 1.

1793, Wreath Type, Vine and Bars Edge (BW-14, S-NC-5, B-9).

Obverse: Stem end is thick, points down past the right side of 7 and ends near the upper right of 7.

Reverse: Same die as preceding. *Points of distinction:* On the only known example there is a short break through TE of STATES, more advanced than on any other use of this reverse.

Notes: Unique. In the collection of the American Numismatic Society. EF-45.

1793, Wreath Type, Vine and Bars Edge, "Injured Rim" • BW-15, S-10, B-10. Crosby 10-I. *Breen dies:* 8-D. *Estimated population:* 120 to 160.

1793, Wreath Type, Vine and Bars Edge, "Injured Rim" (BW-15, S-10, B-10).

Detail of the injured rim.

Obverse: Same die as preceding. *Points of distinction:* Known as the "Injured Rim" variety because the obverse die has been injured at the 3 o'clock position on the coin, opposite Liberty's nose. This has caused the edge of the die to become slightly indented, which causes the beads on the coin to become somewhat raised and form a straight line for about 6 mm.

Reverse: Outside maple leaf under E of UNITED. Between S and the O in OF one spray of berries, ends below left side of O. *Points of distinction:* Early die state coins have a rim crack or break over NIT in UNITED. On the latest state this break extends from the end of the U to the beginning of the E.

Notes: This variety appears in Mint State, but is rare at this level. The finest is held by the ANS.

1793, Wreath Type, Vine and Bars Edge (BW-15)	Cert	Avg	%MS
	(a)		

AG-3	G-4	VG-8	F-12
$675	$2,430	$4,675	$7,350

VF-20	EF-40	AU-50
$14,625	$28,250	$42,500

a. Included in certified population for 1793, Wreath Type, Vine and Bars Edge (BW-17).

1793, Wreath Type, Vine and Bars Edge • BW-16, S-NC-4, B-11. Crosby 9-I. *Breen dies:* 9-D. **Recorded population:** 5.

1793, Wreath Type, Vine and
Bars Edge (BW-16, S-NC-4, B-11).

Obverse: Horizontal stem over 79, only die with this feature.

Reverse: Same die as preceding. *Points of distinction:* The rim break now extends from the middle of the U to the end of E of UNITED.

Notes: Of the five recorded examples, the most recent was discovered by Chris Young in 2000. The highest-graded pieces are G-4 to VG-8. The finest is owned by Yale University.

1793, Wreath Type, Vine and Bars Edge, Widest Ribbon Bow • BW-17, S-9, B-12. Crosby 9-H. *Breen dies:* 9-E. **Estimated population:** 750 to 1,000.

1793, Wreath Type, Vine and Bars Edge,
Widest Ribbon Bow (BW-17, S-9, B-12).

Obverse: Same die as preceding. *Points of distinction:* Eventually cracks develop on the portrait.

Reverse: Widest ribbon bow extends from C to T of CENT. Outside maple leaf under E of UNITED. Between S and O in OF two sprays of berries end, each at a different angle. *Points of distinction:* The reverse is sometimes found perfect but also with several progressions of short cracks. One starts at the top of C in AMERICA and crosses the second A and the ends of

the ribbon. Another runs from R of AMERICA to the lower leaves on the right. A light crack is sometimes found running through UNITED. The latest die state has severe die failure between CA of AMERICA and the right ribbon.

Notes: The most often encountered 1793 variety. Mint State examples come on the market now and again and are the Wreath cents most often seen at this level. An MS-66BN+ example of this coin sold at auction for $528,750 in August 2014.

1793, Wreath Type, Vine and Bars Edge (BW-17)	Cert	Avg	%MS
	186	33.0	12%

AG-3	G-4	VG-8	F-12	VF-20
$675	$2,300	$4,460	$7,075	$13,875

EF-40	AU-50	MS-60BN	MS-63BN
$25,375	$36,170	$59,375	$106,250

1793, Wreath Type, Vine and Bars Edge, Triangular Ribbon Bow, ONE / CENT High • BW-18, S-8, B-13. Crosby 9-G. *Breen dies:* 9-F. *Estimated population:* 400 to 500.

1793, Wreath Type, Vine and Bars Edge, Triangular Ribbon Bow, ONE / CENT High (BW-18, S-8, B-13).

Obverse: Same die as preceding. *Points of distinction:* A faint die crack is usually seen from the point of the bust to the border. Sometimes a short crack runs from the left top of the Y to the border, another from the top of the R, and still another from the top of the B to the border. The 9 and the 3 are sometimes poorly formed due to clash marks.

Reverse: The ribbon bow is triangular and ONE / CENT is high. Outside maple leaf under T of UNITED. *Points of distinction:* The reverse is always found with a delicate break and sometimes a sort of bulge extending almost straight across the coin from the first T of STATES to the second A of AMERICA, running through the center dot.

Notes: This variety can be found in Mint State, but it is quite rare as such.

1793, Wreath Type, Vine and Bars Edge (BW-18)		Cert	Avg	%MS
		(a)		

AG-3	G-4	VG-8	F-12
$675	$2,300	$4,460	$7,075

VF-20	EF-40	AU-50
$13,875	$25,375	$36,170

a. Included in certified population for 1793, Wreath Type, Vine and Bars Edge (BW-17).

1793, Wreath Type, Strawberry Leaf, Vine and Bars Edge • BW-19, S-NC-2, B-14. Crosby 5-D. *Breen dies:* 10-G. *Recorded population:* 1.

1793, Wreath Type, Strawberry Leaf, Vine and Bars Edge (BW-19, S-NC-2, B-14). For detail of "Strawberry" leaf, see BW-20.

Obverse: "Strawberry" or other variant twig.

Reverse: ONE / CENT is centered in the wreath. Second A of AMERICA very close to ribbon.

Notes: The only recorded example of this variety has been graded as Fair-2 or finer. One expert suggested VG-8. It is in the Daniel W. Holmes Jr. Collection. It was found in circulation in 1845 by John Meader, a grocer in Providence, Rhode Island.

1793, Wreath type. Strawberry Leaf, Vine and Bars Edge • BW-20, S-NC-3, B-15. Crosby 5-E. *Breen dies:* 10-H. **Recorded population:** 3.

1793, Wreath Type, Strawberry Leaf, Vine and Bars Edge (BW-20, S-NC-3, B-15). This is the Parmelee coin, the finest known.

Detail of strawberry leaf.

Obverse: Same die as preceding.

Reverse: ONE / CENT high in wreath. Second A of AMERICA distant from ribbon.

Notes: The finest example is VG-7 by conservative grading (or VG-10 or F-12, opinions vary). It was housed in the Lorin G. Parmelee Collection (1890), years later in an old-time Maine estate, then with Republic Jewelry and Coins, and subsequently it was auctioned by American Numismatic Rarities, then by Stack's in January 2009 for $862,500. The other two examples are AG-3.

Numismatic Notes: An early auction offering: On October 23–24, 1877, J.W. Scott & Co. held its first auction. The venue was the sale room of Bangs & Co. This 62-page offering, *Catalogue of a Fine Collection of Gold, Silver & Copper Coins and a Very Complete Collection of Centennial Medals*, included publicity about the curious and rare 1793, Strawberry Leaf, large cent. Cataloged by Scott himself according to some accounts (alternatively, David Proskey may have done the work), the effort was later criticized by Scott's jealous competitor and former employee, Édouard Frossard, in *Numisma*, who wrote that he expected better of Scott. Frossard called the sale an event of little numismatic importance and for good measure noted:

> There is no method in the arrangement, the descriptions are for the better part crude, and mostly faulty, especially in the estimates of degree of preservation, most of the silver looking as if it had been polished or burnished. . . . The work of a numismatist is the result of close and undisturbed application, attention, and training; it can never be satisfactorily accomplished by hurried consultations with chance visitors during the bustle and hurry incidental to a miscellaneous publishing business and the retailing of postage stamps.[9]

1793, Wreath Type, Vine and Bars Edge • BW-21, S-11a, B-16a. Crosby 11-J Vine and Bars. *Breen dies:* 11-I. **Estimated population:** 75 to 120.

Obverse: Stem points to, and ends above, the top of 9. First leaf points straight up, next two point right. *Points of distinction:* Clash marks from the wreath are usually seen below the chin.

Reverse: Outside maple leaf under IT of UNITED. *Points of distinction:* A faint crack is often seen crossing the left ribbon and stem, the bottom of the numerator, and the fraction bar, reaching the end of the right ribbon.

Notes: This variety can be found in Mint State, but is exceedingly rare as such.

1793, Wreath Type, Vine and Bars Edge (BW-21)	Cert	Avg	%MS
	(a)		

AG-3	G-4	VG-8	F-12
$775	$2,850	$5,375	$8,440

VF-20	EF-40	AU-50
$16,875	$35,000	$48,330

a. Included in certified population for 1793, Wreath Type, Vine and Bars Edge (BW-17).

1793, Wreath Type, Lettered Edge With 2 Leaves • BW-22, S-11b, B-16b. Crosby 11-A Lettered Edge, 2 Leaves. *Breen dies:* 11-I. *Estimated population:* 120 to 160.

Obverse: Same die as preceding. *Points of distinction:* Clash marks develop, including AMERICA incused in front of Liberty's face, then are removed from the die.

Reverse: Same die as preceding.

Notes: The highest-known grade for a piece of this variety is AU.

1793, Wreath Type, Lettered Edge With 2 Leaves	Cert	Avg	%MS
	(a)		

AG-3	G-4	VG-8	F-12	VF-20	EF-40
$875	$3,100	$5,625	$8,940	$18,750	$37,500

a. Included in certified population for 1793, Wreath Type, Lettered Edge With 1 Leaf.

1793, Wreath Type, Lettered Edge With 1 Leaf • BW-23, S-11c, B-16c. Crosby 11-J Lettered Edge, 1 Leaf. *Breen dies:* 11-I. *Estimated population:* 400 to 500.

1793, Wreath Type, Lettered Edge With 1 Leaf (BW-23, S-11c, B-16c).

Obverse: Same die as preceding.

Reverse: Same die as preceding.

Notes: These Lettered Edge cents are often seen on defective planchets. This variety exists in Mint State, but for all practical purposes is unobtainable. AU coins come on the market now and then.

1793, Wreath Type, Lettered Edge With 1 Leaf	Cert	Avg	%MS
	36	26.5	6%

AG-3	G-4	VG-8	F-12
$775	$2,680	$4,940	$7,940

VF-20	EF-40	AU-50
$15,625	$30,875	$48,250

Liberty Cap (1793–1796)

1794, Buckled Obverse, No Protruding Leaf Under I of AMERICA (BW-17, S-27, B-9).

Designer: *Probably Joseph Wright.* **Weight:** *208 grains (13.48 grams)*
for the thick planchet, 168 grains (10.89 grams) for the thin planchet.
Composition: *Copper.* **Diameter:** *Average 29 mm.* **Edge:** *Early pieces*
lettered ONE HUNDRED FOR A DOLLAR; the later pieces have plain edges.

The Liberty Cap cent was created in the summer of 1793, probably by Joseph Wright, whom the Mint had intended to be staff engraver. The records show that Wright unfortunately fell ill from yellow fever before he could officially take office, and he passed away sometime in mid-September, although the exact death date has not been found. An accomplished portrait artist, he had earlier engraved some dies for the Mint, including the 1792 eagle-on-globe pattern quarter dollar.

The motif of the Liberty Cap cent followed the obverse design of Augustin Dupré's Libertas Americana medal—which was produced in Paris in 1782 at the suggestion of Benjamin Franklin—except that on the cent the head faces to the right rather than to the left. This was the second use of the motif at the Mint, as, in July, half cents were made of the Liberty Cap design (with Miss Liberty facing to the left, as on Dupré's original).

After Wright's passing, the duty of making new dies fell to Robert Scot. This he did in fine style, although he lowered the relief of the Liberty Cap motif in 1794, after which the design lost some of its charm. Walter Breen, seemingly acting on presumption rather than facts, specifically attributed various Liberty Cap obverse portraits and reverse wreath styles to John Smith Gardner, who was hired as an assistant to Scot in November of that year. In 1795 Gardner's annual salary was $936. Gardner, a seal engraver by profession, left the Mint in early 1796, but returned for a time that summer. It is likely that various people, ranging from talented engravers such as Gardner to mechanics and other employees, made certain dies using portrait punches created by Scot. Although the die sinking was well done, the workmanship of the *finish punching* (alignment of separately entered letters and numerals) of the dies of 1794 cents ranges from expert, these being the majority, to amateur. The Liberty Cap cents of 1795 and 1796 are more uniform in their appearance.

While Liberty Cap cents dated 1793 are major rarities, during 1794, 1795, and part of 1796, far more than a million were made, offering an example of an affordable type set. Those of 1794 and some of 1795 have the edge lettered ONE HUNDRED FOR A DOLLAR, while those made later in 1795 and in 1796 are on thinner planchets and have a plain edge.

Cents of this type are from hand-made dies and have many interesting variations. On the obverse the letters in LIBERTY and the numerals in the date vary in their placement. On the reverse the letters, fraction details, and berries were added by hand, creating many differences. Denticles range from short to long, closely or widely spaced, and with rounded or pointed tips.

As a basic type, the Liberty Cap cent is sufficiently plentiful that there is a wide selection in the marketplace for almost any grade desired up to VF, although offerings are scarce in higher grades. Liberty Cap cents of 1793 are rare in any grade, but especially so if VF and EF, and of pleasing appearance. Cents of 1794 can be found in grades from well worn to EF and AU, with occasional appearances of Mint State coins. Cents of 1795 of the Plain Edge type are readily available in all grades, including AU and, to a lesser extent, Mint State, although there are not many Mint State coins in existence. Cents of 1796 are elusive in high grades, although some Mint State coins come on the market now and again.

While there are many variations, in general the Liberty Cap cents of 1793 are found with dark surfaces and in lower grades. High quality is elusory. Cents of 1794 vary widely, but most are one or another shade of brown. The cents of 1795 and 1796 are more uniform in appearance and are found in higher average grades. Striking varies depending upon the die combination.

As is true of other early coppers, many Liberty Cap cents have scratches, edge bumps, discoloration, porosity, and other detriments. The manner of describing these varies widely. For certified coins, a number such as VF-20 is all the information given. Specialists, the better auction houses, and others sophisticated in the field usually describe the appearance and any negatives with an accompanying narrative.

Dr. Sheldon particularly enjoyed the Liberty Cap issues, and in *Penny Whimsy* wrote this:

> Considered as a whole, the Liberty Cap cents possess a charm not often exceeded among the things made by man. To no small degree the charm inheres in the great variability and individuality of these dies, of which there are no less than 105 [*sic*, should be 106]—53 obverses and 52 [*sic*, should be 53] reverses (in 1793, 3 obverses and 2 reverses; in 1794, 39 obverses and 38 reverses; in 1795, 5 obverses and 6 reverses; in 1796, 6 obverses and 7 reverses).
>
> About three-fourths of the Liberty Caps are dated 1794, and among these nearly all of the variation occurs, since the first of the 1794s are practically duplicates of the 1793s, and the last of them are virtually duplicates of the 1795s and 1796s. A collection of 1794 cents reflects much of the story of one of the most pioneering and romantic struggles in American history. In the little Mint building on 7th Street in Philadelphia, during the middle of the last decade of the 18th century, history seems to have almost held her breath for a time, and we find the marks of her desperately clenched teeth engraved deeply on the soft copper pennies of those years. . . .

DESIGN DETAILS

The obverse features the head of Miss Liberty facing right, her hair flowing downward in tresses behind. A liberty cap is behind her head, and the pole to the cap is partially visible behind her head and above her neck to the right. LIBERTY is above. The date is below her neck. Issues of 1793 have a beaded border on both sides, adding a special elegance. Issues of 1794 to 1796 have denticles around the border of the obverse and reverse.

The portrait was modified slightly during this span, with the Head of 1793 (used on some 1794 cents as well) being more delicate, the Head of 1794 describing most for that year, and the Head of 1795 describing the final issues.

The reverse features an open wreath of olive (presumably) leaves, tied with a ribbon bow (that now has two loops) at the bottom and enclosing ONE / CENT. It is somewhat similar to the reverse used on 1793, Wreath, cents, except no longer with sprays of berries or maple leaves (trefoils). Numismatists usually refer to *berries* on Wreath cents, not to *olives.* Around the border is UNITED STATES OF AMERICA. The fraction 1/100 is below the bow.

The earlier varieties, those minted in 1794 and in early 1795, with lettered edge give the denomination *three times:* as ONE / CENT and 1/100 on the reverse and as ONE HUNDRED FOR A DOLLAR on the edge. The same triple denomination feature is found on several other early copper types.

1793, Liberty Cap
Circulation mintage (assumed): 11,056.

In terms of artistic beauty, many numismatists agree that the 1793, Liberty Cap, cents represent the best vintage for the design, being more attractive than the cents of late 1794 continuing through 1796. The 1793 cents were struck on broad planchets, providing ample field area between the border of raised beads and the rim and highlighting the beads, which seem to have been fully struck on all examples. It is thought that 1793-dated Liberty Cap cents were made from September 1793 to January 1794, although no specific records exist. Beads were not used on later cents of this design.

1793, Liberty Cap, cents are usually seen in low grades, Good or Very Good, often with dark and porous surfaces. Smooth, evenly worn pieces with attractive surfaces are in the distinct minority, probably on the order of about one coin in five. Thus, cherrypicking is essential to achieve quality—this being more true for the 1793, Liberty Cap, than for any other single cent type. If offered two examples, each Fine-15, one ordinary (dark and/or porous) coin priced at "market" per listings in standard guides, and the other with a pleasing surface and offered at 50% over market, it would be best, according to the advice of Q. David Bowers, to buy the more expensive one. Similarly, a smooth, pleasing VG-8 coin would be better to own than a dark and porous VF-20.

An estimated several hundred exist today, all save a handful being in lower grades as noted above. AU examples are exceedingly rare, and anything higher is in the "impossible" category.

The finest known example is the piece, BW-27, described as MS-64 or finer by Mark Borckardt in the sale of the Louis E. Eliasberg Sr. Collection, 1996, which is also the only known 1793, Liberty Cap, cent of any variety in Mint State. It now reposes in a fine Southern collection. Here is the pedigree chain, along with excerpts from certain of the descriptions:

Édouard Frossard sale #21, May 1882, lot 627 $181.

William H. Cottier; S.H. and H. Chapman, June 1885, lot 655 $90. "Uncirculated. Magnificent, strong even impression. Brilliant light olive, partly red color. The finest example known of this, the rarest U.S. cent."

Thomas Cleneay; S.H. and H. Chapman, December 1890, lot 1800 $200, to Peter Mougey.

Thomas L. Elder sale #43, Mougey Collection, September 1910, lot 1 $340, to Clarence S. Bement:

> 1793 Liberty Cap variety. Crosby 12-L. Perfectly centered, even impression, sharp, Uncirculated, and partly red. From the Cleneay Sale, Lot No. 1800. Mr. Mougey journeyed from Cincinnati to Philadelphia for the sole purpose of securing this prize, which is the finest known specimen of this variety, and as such, its actual value is practically unlimited.

Henry Chapman, Bement Collection, May 1916, lot 291 $720, to Col. James W. Ellsworth:

> Uncirculated, and might easily be called a Proof. Superb, even, sharp impression. Most beautiful light olive with traces of the original color, and acknowledged by everyone to be the finest example known to exist. It is a gem of the highest class, and unique in this state of preservation. This cent cost Mr. Bement $500, the greatest price a U.S. cent has ever sold for, and I predict that it will now bring a greater sum.

Wayte Raymond and John Work Garrett, 1923, as part of their purchase for $100,000 of the Ellsworth Collection. The collection was divided, Raymond got the cent, and in the same year sold it to William Cutler Atwater.

B. Max Mehl, June 11, 1946, Atwater Collection, lot 14 $2,000, to Louis E. Eliasberg Sr.:

> Truly the possession of this cent will pay great dividends not only in dollars and cents, but in the satisfaction, joy and pride of ownership. I do not recall during my forty-five years of numismatic experience, during which time I have handled a very goodly portion of the finest collections of American coins offered, of having pass through my hands such a thrilling coin!

Bowers and Merena Galleries, May 1996, Eliasberg Collection. $319,000 to a Southern numismatist:

> 1793 Liberty Cap. S-13. High Rarity-3. MS-64 or finer, brown. *Strike:* On a broad planchet thus providing field area between the beads and the rim, showcasing the beads, which in all instances are sharply struck. An early striking and quite possibly a presentation or specimen striking as indicated by Walter Breen in his *Encyclopedia of United States and Colonial Proof Coins.* The edge is lettered ONE HUNDRED FOR A DOLLAR with this lettering boldly defined. *Surfaces:* Light brown with ample tinges of red mint color. Very faint planchet roughness is noted inside the wreath. *Narrative:* An American numismatic landmark, and certainly one of the foremost highlights in the entire field of extant large cents 1793 to 1857. The only fully Mint State example of 1793 Liberty Cap coinage known—of any die variety. . . .

1793, Bisecting Obverse Crack, Liberty Cap • BW-24, S-14, B-17.

Crosby 13-L. *Breen dies:* 12-J. ***Estimated population:*** 60 to 75.

1793, Bisecting Obverse Crack, Liberty Cap (BW-24, S-14, B-17).

examples have a prominent die crack vertically bisecting the die. The obverse die was slightly misaligned in the coin press. This caused the date to be weak and LIBERTY to be strong. This is especially noticeable on lower-grade examples. This also happened on the 1793, Chain AMERI. (BW-1).

Obverse: Space between two beads is over upright of I of LIBERTY; ample space between top of L and bead. The border has 95 beads. *Points of distinction:* All known

Reverse: Upper-left leaf at wreath top nearly touches bottom leaf in pair to the right. Heavy cluster of three leaves below O in OF. The leaf opposite the M of AMERICA points towards the first A. The right ribbon is squared off and ends just below the fraction bar, which it touches. *Points of distinction:* Die used on BW-26, BW-27, BW-29, BW-30. This reverse die was reworked to create 1794, Fallen 4 in Date (Also with Button on Cap) (BW-84).[10]

Notes: The highest-graded examples of this variety are AU. More practically, a collector should seek EF and VF examples.

1793, Bisecting Obverse Crack, Liberty Cap	Cert	Avg	%MS
	(a)		

AG-3	G-4	VG-8	F-12	VF-20	EF-40
$6,330	$10,500	$14,500	$29,500	$49,375	$90,000

a. Included in certified population for 1793, Liberty Cap (BW-27).

1793, Liberty Cap • BW-25, S-NC-6, B-18. Crosby unlisted. *Breen dies:* 13-J. *Recorded population:* 2.

1793, Liberty Cap (BW-25, S-NC-6, B-18).

Obverse: One bead is centered above R of LIBERTY, both pole and bottom of 7 point directly at a bead. There is a space between the 2 beads over the upright of T. *Points of distinction:* A bulging develops at the left side of the obverse, apparently causing failure and quick retirement of this die, explaining its rarity.

Reverse: Same die as preceding.

Notes: The known examples grade VG-8 and G-4. Discovered by R.E. Naftzger Jr. in February 1978.

1793, Liberty Cap • BW-26, S-16, B-19. Crosby 14-L. *Breen dies:* 14-J. *Estimated population:* 20 to 25.

1793, Liberty Cap (BW-26, S-16, B-19).

Obverse: Bead over upright of I of LIBERTY; bead over upright of T. The lowest lock of hair has a short, heavy hook at the end in contrast with its delicate termination on the other two obverses. The border has 97 beads. *Points of distinction:* A faint crack is seen from the rim, through Y, and to the forehead. Another crack develops at the lower left and extends to the lowest curl. The obverse, plated by Sheldon— listed as S-16 by Sheldon—in *Early American Cents* and *Penny Whimsy*, is described as having a "heavy die break." This break has proven to be a lamination defect in the planchet.[11] Also used on BW-28.

Reverse: Same die as preceding.

Notes: The reverse is usually rotated 135° instead of the normal 180°. The highest-graded examples are Fine and VF.

1793, Liberty Cap (BW-26)	Cert	Avg	%MS
	(a)		

AG-3	G-4	VG-8	F-12
$11,000	$16,660	$28,125	$52,500

a. Included in certified population for 1793, Liberty Cap (BW-27).

1793, Liberty Cap • BW-27, S-13, B-20. Crosby 12-L. *Breen dies:* 15-J. *Estimated population:* 160 to 200.

1793, Liberty Cap (BW-27, S-13, B-20).

Obverse: Space between two beads is over upright of I of LIBERTY; L extremely close to bead. The border has 95 beads. Also used on BW-29.

Reverse: Same die as preceding. *Points of distinction:* A slight bulge develops at the center.

Notes: The finest example is the spectacular Atwater-Eliasberg Mint State coin, unique at that level. Several AU examples exist.

1793, Liberty Cap (BW-27)	Cert	Avg	%MS
	21	13.2	0%

AG-3	G-4	VG-8	F-12
$5,830	$9,670	$13,375	$25,750

VF-20	EF-40	AU-50
$45,500	$85,000	$200,000

1793, Liberty Cap • BW-28, S-15, B-22. Crosby 14-K. *Breen dies:* 14-K. *Recorded population:* 12.

1793, Liberty Cap (BW-28, S-15, B-22).

Obverse: Same as used for BW-26, except for the top of the L of LIBERTY not being fully struck up. This is probably due to that part of the die being filled. This does not occur on the BW-26.

Reverse: One leaf under O in OF. Another leaf points directly at, and almost touches, the center stem of the M of AMERICA. The right ribbon is pointed and ends below the fraction bar next to the denominator.

Notes: The highest-graded example is Fine.

1793, Liberty Cap • BW-29, S-12, B-21. Crosby 12-K. *Breen dies:* 15-K. *Estimated population:* 25 to 30.

1793, Liberty Cap (BW-29, S-12, B-21).

Obverse: Same die as used for BW-27. *Points of distinction:* A slight bulge develops in the left field.

Reverse: Same as the preceding. *Points of distinction:* The die sunk at the center, causing the coins to bulge and the central features to wear away quickly.

Notes: The highest-graded example is VF.

Numismatic Notes: Sylvester Crosby discovered this variety in the collection of William Fewsmith of Camden, New Jersey, in October 1869. This was just six months after J.N.T. Levick's plate of 1793 cents was published in the *American Jour-nal of Numismatics.* Remarkably, Levick and Crosby missed only two collectable varieties of 1793—this one and the BW-13.

1793, Liberty Cap (BW-29)	Cert	Avg	%MS
	(a)		

AG-3	G-4	VG-8	F-12	VF-20
$9,500	$14,330	$20,375	$40,000	$61,670

a. Included in certified population for 1793, Liberty Cap (BW-27).

1794, Liberty Cap
Circulation mintage (assumed): 918,521.

Among all early American coins there is no numismatic panorama of die varieties more interesting and extensive than the copper cents of 1794. These have been a specialty for many collectors over the years, forming collections exemplified most notably, in recent generations, by the John W. Adams Collection (sold by Bowers and Merena Galleries, 1982), a 1794 copper cent exhibit that took the Best of Show award at the ANA convention in the summer of 1982, and the Walter Husak Collection (auctioned by Heritage, 2008).[12] Cents of this date display many interesting differences in die arrangement and are particularly fascinating to collect. Within EAC, the "Boys of '94" take special interest in these issues. Jon Alan Boka treated the topic in his 2005 book, *Provenance Gallery of the Year 1794, United States Large Cents.*

The appeal of cents of this date has a particularly rich numismatic history, beginning in a significant way with the monograph, *Varieties of the Copper Issues of the United States Mint in the Year 1794,* published by Dr. Edward E. Maris in 1869, with a second edition in 1870. By any account, Maris was one of the greats in the early years of the hobby. He is still remembered for his attribution of New Jersey state coppers of the years 1786 through 1788, for which numismatists still use the Maris variety designations today. In the early 1870s he seems to have been the discoverer of the hitherto numismatically unknown 1861, Confederate States of America, cent, which was struck from dies by Robert Lovett Jr. To tell all about Maris would require many pages and would still be abbreviated.

His 1869 work and the 1870 second edition described the dies and assigned names for the cents, some of which were derived from medicine and mythology. Examples include varieties such as *Double Chin, Sans Milling, Tilted 4, Young Head, The Coquette, Crooked 7, Pyramidal Head, Mint Marked Head, Scarred Head, Standless 4, Abrupt Hair, Severed Hairs, The Ornate, Venus Marina, Fallen 4, Short Bust, Patagonian, Nondescript, Amatory Face, Large Planchet, Marred Field, Distant 1, Shielded Hair, Separated Date, The Plicae* (for a group of varieties), *Roman Plica* and *'95 Head,* among a few others.

His preface included this:

> As far as our means of information enable us to arrive at a conclusion, the only copper coins made at our Mint in 1794, were of the denomination of Cent and Half Cent. Of the former, the record says 918,521 were issued, and 81,600 of the latter.
>
> The interest excited in the minds of collectors by their variety—a consequence probably of the breakage of dies—is shared by the writer, and has resulted in this attempt to describe the most noticeable peculiarity of each with sufficient accuracy to enable the careful examiner to recognize any given specimen, in a condition not below fair.

This has been no easy work, as the close general resemblance which many of them bear to each other, makes it difficult to convey by the pen, points of difference readily detected by the eye. It is not claimed that every existing variety has come under examination. A pioneer work should not be expected to be thorough. On the other hand, the descriptions given were made from personal inspection of pieces now in his cabinet.

Significantly, Maris observed that cents of this year are so diverse they can be attributed in any condition "not below fair." This probably translates to Good-4 today. The point remains well taken, as today as in 1869, a nice collection of this year can be assembled in lower grades without losing any of the coins' numismatic desirability and significance.

Modern numismatists with a sense of tradition and history occasionally use Maris's designations in catalog descriptions. Later students of the series, including Dr. William H. Sheldon, added more nicknames, including *Apple Cheek*, *Wheel Spoke Reverse*, etc. Beyond these, such appellations as *Starred Reverse* and *Missing Fraction Bar* are self-explanatory.

Édouard Frossard, W.W. Hays, Francis Worcester Doughty, and others studied cents of this year and wrote about them, occasionally adding new varieties and redescribing previously known ones.

In 1923 S. Hudson Chapman published *United States Cents of the Year 1794*. In 1982 John W. Adams, specialist in cents of that year, wrote:

> Chapman added two more 1794 varieties which had been discovered in the interim, thus raising the number to 59. He also rearranged the listing of the varieties, substituting new numbers for the Hays numbers. The Chapman monograph is illustrated by excellent plates, and it is perhaps the most generally adequate presentation of the subject. However, the older Hays numbers seem to have taken deep root in the affections of coin collectors and it now appears likely that the name Hays will long be associated with this, the most extensive one-date series of American coins.[13]

Curiously, Chapman had some difficulty photographing the cents, and one of his experiments involved placing the coins underwater in front of a camera lens peering downward.

Other studies could be mentioned, but the most comprehensive was that created by Dr. William H. Sheldon for *Early American Cents*, 1949, followed by the updated *Penny Whimsy* in 1958. *United States Large Cents 1793–1814*, by William C. Noyes, is particularly valuable for its photographs. The last word in terms of detail is provided by *Walter Breen's Encyclopedia of Early United States Cents 1793–1814*, 2000. Much in terms of the spirit and enjoyment of these cents can be found in various issues of *Penny-Wise*, a journal of Early American Coppers.

Amidst everyday cares, 1794 large cents remain an island of refuge—an escape perhaps from present-day reality to the times of long ago when, at least in retrospect, the surroundings were incredibly nostalgic and romantic.

The appeal that 1794 cents possess has prompted hours of discussion among collectors of the series and has motivated otherwise busy individuals to travel tens of thousands of miles, write innumerable letters, and spend tens of thousands of dollars in their quest for needed varieties. What is the quintessence that has caused the owners of such coins to experience a deep joy unsurpassed elsewhere in American numismatics?

In addition to the obvious characteristics—rich surface coloration, interesting and varied dies, curious and unexplained varieties, elusive rarities, and the like—there seems to be a special aura surrounding the pieces, a quality which has aroused a fierce desire on the part of those who lack certain varieties and a pride of possession for those who own them. Dr. Sheldon has touched upon this in his writings, as have John Adams and others. As you review the variety descriptions and illustrations to follow, perhaps you will capture some of the spirit. It can be said that to know 1794 cents is to love them.

Thousands of cents of this date exist, and appearances in the marketplace are frequent. While specialists have attributed them by die varieties for many years, especially since the appearance of Sheldon's *Early American Cents*, most collectors and dealers have simply called them 1794 cents, or used one of the several styles listed in the regular edition of the *Guide Book of United States Coins*. For many years neither PCGS nor NGC cited variety attributions, but this has changed in recent times. The result is that today there is ample opportunity to examine "generic" 1794 cents and find scarce or even rare die combinations. This has been a sport for users of eBay, where photographs permit identification while sitting in a comfortable chair and browsing on a laptop computer.

Per *Penny Whimsy*, there are 58 collectible varieties for cents of this year, plus Dr. Sheldon's non-collectibles. The pursuit of a complete set of the "collectibles" is both possible and relatively affordable, though the fugitive element of timing has a role in the accomplishment. The acquisition of certain rare varieties may involve waiting until a desirable one appears on the market and being the highest bidder. Throughout numismatic history, approximately 30 individuals have been able to assemble all 58, two of them doing it twice (Robinson S. Brown Jr. and Denis W. Loring). One collector, George H. Clapp, donated his complete set to the American Numismatic Society. Daniel W. Holmes Jr. did the "impossible" by obtaining all of the non-collectible varieties as well!

Most 1794 cents show extensive wear, with typical grades ranging from Good to Fine. In proportion to demand, VF examples are scarce, EF coins are rare, and AU cents are rarer yet. Mint State coins are encountered only infrequently, such as when notable collections cross the auction block. While the planchet quality for 1794 cents is generally good, the experience of circulation in commerce has resulted in many receiving rim bumps, nicks, scratches, corrosion, and other problems. Accordingly, cherrypicking is a very worthwhile pursuit. Striking sharpness ranges from weak to strong, and generally is dependent on the die variety. A given variety usually has the same striking characteristics.

Although much ink is usually spent when a high-grade or rare 1794 cent crosses the auction block for tens of thousands of dollars, a very nice set with most of the varieties can be assembled in lesser grades. These are sharp enough to reveal enough detail needed to identify the varieties, and for the most part they may be quite affordable.

Today, building a representative collection of 1794-dated cents is an enjoyable pursuit. Within such grades as Good to Fine, most of the varieties can be acquired, and for a modest cost. Even the famous Starred Reverse, with slightly more than 60 examples known, comes on the market regularly, usually in lower grades, but with a number of the definitive stars visible around the border on the opposite side.

1794, Head Style of 1793

BW-1 to BW-4 are in the style Early Head, or Head of 1793. Hair is heavy, particularly behind the ear. The lowest lock ends in a short, small hook (except BW-1). These are from the same obverse portrait punch cut by Joseph Wright for the 1793, Liberty Cap, cents. Hair details were modified by hand, resulting in some differences, especially in their tips to the lower left.

There are three obverse dies. Check the thickness of the hair and lower lock first to be sure that a coin is a member of this class. Then check the obverse features, then verify by checking the reverse possibilities, for which there are only two.

There are two edge styles, the "a" having the point and stem of the leaf after DOLLAR pointing down, and "b" with these features pointing up.

1794, Head of 1793, Wide Straight Date • BW-1a and b, S-17a and b, B-1a and b. *Breen dies:* 1-A. **Estimated population:** BW-1a: 60 to 75; BW-1b: 2 known.

1794, Head of 1793, Wide
Straight Date (BW-1a, S-17a, B-1a).

Detail of the "Wide Straight
Date" and surrounding area.

Obverse: Date: In line rather than curved; 9 high. *Tip of pole points to:* Denticle, slightly right of its center. Pole heavy. *LIBERTY:* B slightly low; I opposite denticle. *Points of distinction:* Hook on lowest curl not fully formed. Many show a swelling and a tiny crack from L to the head and a small crack from the end of the pole to the border. In the very rare latest stage a crack

bisects the die. *Maris designation:* Tilted 4. *Sheldon designation:* Wide Straight Date.

Reverse: Berries left and right: 8-7. Berries are small. *Upright of second T of STATES opposite:* Denticle. *Fraction:* Numerator high and truncated at lower left. Bar slightly curved, extends from upper left of 1 to slightly past center of second 0. *Points of distinction:* UNITED STATES distant from denticles. TE of STATES wide. Stem is boldly visible below the ribbon knot, between the sides of the ribbon. Branch on left is out of alignment with its continuation as the stem to lower right. N of CENT first punched upside down, then corrected, leaving an irrelevant serif visible at lower right. Denticles smaller than on next reverse.

Notes: The highest grades that BW-1a—point and stem of leaf after DOLLAR point downward—is known in are EF and AU. For BW-1b—point and stem of leaf after DOLLAR point upward—the highest-known grade is AG-3.

1794, Head of 1793, Double Chin • BW-2a and b, S-18a and b, B-2a and b. *Breen dies:* 2-A. **Estimated population:** BW-2a: 15 to 20; BW-2b: 120 to 160.

1794, Head of 1793, Double
Chin (BW-2b, S-18b, B-2b).

Obverse: Date: Date curved along border with each digit being about the same distance from the border. 1 centered. 4 slightly low. *Tip of pole points to:* Denticle, slightly right of its center. Pole lighter toward its end. *LIBERTY:* LIB and TY wide; I opposite denticle. *Points of distinction:* Slight double chin. A tiny crack is usually seen on the 12th denticle to the left of the 1 in the date. *Sheldon designation:* Double Chin.

Reverse: Same die as preceding. *Points of distinction:* The die is lightly lapped or polished to remove clash marks. The die was polished again, after which there were more clash marks—one of many dies that were subjected to repeated abuse through operator carelessness. On about half the examples there is a bulge at and near TED of UNITED.

Notes: The highest grade that BW-2a—point and stem of leaf after DOLLAR point downward—is known in is VF. Mint State examples exist for BW-2b—point and stem of leaf after DOLLAR point upward.

Typical values for BW-2b only. BW-2a is worth much more.

1794, Head of 1793, Double Chin (BW-2b)	Cert	Avg	%MS
	17	13.5	6%

AG-3	G-4	VG-8	F-12
$900	$1,630	$2,800	$5,250

VF-20	EF-40	AU-50	MS-60BN
$13,125	$29,750	$58,125	$128,330

1794, Head of 1793, Double Chin, Reverse Letters Close to Denticles
• BW-3a and b, S-19a and b, B-3a and b. *Breen dies:* 2-B. **Estimated population:** BW-3a: 30 to 45; BW-3b: 120 to 160.

1794, Head of 1793, Double Chin, Reverse Letters Close to Denticles (BW-3a, S-19a, B-3a).

Obverse: Same die as preceding. *Points of distinction:* Bulge from below the cap to a curl. All have a tiny crack at the 12th denticle to the left of the first digit of the date.

Reverse: Berries left and right: 8-7. One berry detached in field beyond fourth berry on right. *Upright of second T of STATES opposite:* Denticle. *Fraction:* Numerator right of center and leans left. Bar slightly curved; extends from near upper left of 1 to center of second 0; 1 slightly low. *Points of distinction:* UNITED STATES very close to denticles. Right stem ends near rightmost serif of A. No stems between ribbon ends below knot. Denticles heavy and pointed.

Notes: The highest grade that BW-3a—point and stem of leaf after DOLLAR point downward—is found in is VF. BW-3b—point and stem of leaf after DOLLAR point upward—can be found in EF.

Typical values for BW-3b only. BW-3a is worth more.

1794, Head of 1793, Double Chin (BW-3b)	Cert	Avg	%MS
	(a)		

AG-3	G-4	VG-8	F-12	VF-20	EF-40
$950	$1,920	$3,360	$6,375	$16,875	$43,330

a. Included in certified population for 1794, Head of 1793, Double Chin (BW-2b).

1794, Head of 1793, Close Straight Date, Reverse Letters Close to Denticles • BW-4a and b, S-20, and B-4a and b. *Breen dies:* 3-B. **Estimated population:** BW-4a: 1 known; BW-4b: 75 to 120.

1794, Head of 1793, Close Straight Date, Reverse Letters Close to Denticles (BW-4b, S-20, B-4b).

Detail of the "Close Straight Date" and surrounding area.

Obverse: *Date:* In line rather than curved; 94 slightly low; 94 wide. *Tip of pole points to:* Space between denticles. *LIBERTY:* RT slightly wide; I opposite space between denticles. *Maris designation:* Exact Head of 1793. *Sheldon designation:* Close Straight Date.

Reverse: Same die as preceding.

Notes: George Clapp considered his example of this variety to be the very finest coin he owned (see Sheldon). With the "a" edge—point and stem of leaf after DOLLAR point downward—the highest-known grade is Good. With "b" edge—point and stem of leaf after DOLLAR point upward—the highest-known grade is AU (American Numismatic Society), but VF is a more realistic objective for collectors.

Typical values for BW-4b only. BW-4a is unique.

1794, Head of 1793, Close Straight Date (BW-4b)	Cert	Avg	%MS
	(a)		

AG-3	G-4	VG-8	F-12	VF-20
$1,430	$2,580	$4,420	$9,750	$24,250

a. Included in certified population for 1794, Head of 1793, Double Chin (BW-2b).

1794, Head Style of 1794

For all varieties listed in this style (except BW-45 to BW-48) the tip of the lower lock forms a hook.

Typical values for 1794, Head of 1794.
Rare varieties may be worth more.
Some varieties are priced individually, as follows.

1794, Head of 1794	Cert	Avg	%MS
	264	32.1	4%

AG-3	G-4	VG-8	F-12	VF-20	EF-40	AU-50	MS-60BN	MS-63BN
$275	$410	$600	$950	$1,925	$4,625	$7,150	$15,750	$34,625

1794, Flat Pole, Reverse Letters Close to Denticles • BW-10, S-21, B-5. *Breen dies:* 4-B. *Estimated population:* 300 to 400.

1794, Flat Pole, Reverse Letters
Close to Denticles (BW-10, S-21, B-5).

Detail of the date and flat pole. Note the
hook at the bottom of the lowest lock,
characteristic of most of the Head of
1794 cents. The missing denticles at
the right are due to a planchet clip.

Obverse: *Date:* 1 centered. 4 slightly low. *Tip of pole points to:* Space between denticles; recut and broad and flat at its end (very distinctive). *LIBERTY:* RTY wide; I opposite denticle slightly to right of its center. *Points of distinction:* Sixth lock (counting from bottom) bent downward and nearly touching the fifth. Most have a tiny crack from the border to the top of the cap. Some have other cracks at and near the cap. *Maris designation:* Sans Milling. *Sheldon designation:* Flat Pole.

Reverse: Same die as preceding. Usually with two tiny cracks at the border at the second S of STATES and left of E of AMERICA.

Notes: Édouard Frossard's description (*Monograph*, 1879): "Date wide. Liberty staff expanded and flattened at the end. There is not the slightest trace of milling on obverse, thus contrasting with the reverse, which is protected by a bold and serrated elevation around the edge." This variety occurs in Mint State, but it is very rare as such.

1794, Bent Hair Lock, Mounded Reverse • BW-12, S-22, B-6. *Breen dies:* 5-C. *Estimated population:* Thousands.

1794, Bent Hair Lock, Mounded Reverse
(BW-12, S-22, B-6), die cracks from B to head,
from Y to head, and to the right of the pole.

Detail showing the Bent Hair Lock,
the sixth lock up from the bottom.

Obverse: *Date:* 1 centered. 4 centered. *Tip of pole points to:* Space between denticles. *LIBERTY:* LI closer than other letters; I opposite space between two denticles. *Points of distinction:* Sixth lock (counting from bottom) bent downward and nearly touching the fifth. Clash marks develop as do mounding and eventually, cracks. *Maris designation:* Large Planchet. *Sheldon designation:* Bent Hair Lock.

Reverse: *Berries left and right:* 8-7. Two top left berries and one top-right berry very small. Lowest berry near bow larger than higher berry. *Upright of second T of STATES opposite:* Denticle, slightly right of its center. *Fraction:* Bar very close to second 0. *Points of distinction:* Left ribbon not connected to knot. With swellings ("mounds") at the upper part of the right wreath and on the lower half of the wreath on both sides. *Sheldon designation:* Mounded Reverse.

Notes: Sheldon believed this to be the second most common 1794 variety. The highest-known grade is AU.

1794, "Shattered Obverse" (usually) • BW-14, S-23, B-7. *Breen dies:* 6-D. *Estimated population:* 75 to 120.

1794, "Shattered Obverse"
(usually) (BW-14, S-23, B-7).

Obverse: Date: 1 centered, bottom serifs minimal or absent. 4 centered, bottom serifs minimal. *Tip of pole points to:* Denticle; pole becomes thicker toward its end. *LIBERTY:* IB closest, I opposite denticle, ERT wide. *Points of distinction:* Top of seventh (counting from bottom) thick. Usu-ally seen with die cracks, although some are from perfect dies. *Maris designation:* Standless 4. *Sheldon designation:* Shattered Obverse.

Reverse: Berries left and right: 6-7. All berries large; later, after relapping for use on BW-16, they are small. *Upright of second T of STATES opposite:* Denticle, slightly left of its center. *Fraction:* Bar wide, covers top of 1 to left and extends beyond second 0 to right. *Points of distinction:* Lower-right pair of leaves have tips close together.

Notes: This variety can be found in AU, but is very rare at this level.

1794, Scarred Head, Full Cheeks • BW-16, S-24, B-8. *Breen dies:* 7-D. *Estimated population:* 1,250 to 1,500.

1794, Scarred Head, Full Cheeks (BW-16,
S-24, B-8), with delicate die crack from
the border through the neck.

Obverse: Date: 1 high. 4 high. *Tip of pole points to:* Denticle, and is close to it. *LIBERTY:* LIBE wide; I opposite left side of denticle. *Points of distinction:* Hair ends in seven very thin locks. Cheek especially rounded, hollow area in hair to left of neck, this being the "scar." Cracks develop, one, then two, which join, and become heavy. There is usually some roughness in the die at the lower region of the neck and between the date and the neck. *Maris designation:* Scarred Head. *Sheldon designation:* Scarred Head, Full Cheeks—Sheldon's father called it the "Apple Cheek" variety.

Reverse: Same die as preceding. *Points of distinction:* A bulge develops and weakens the central inscriptions.

Notes: This variety occurs in Mint State.

1794, Buckled Obverse, No Protruding Leaf Under I of AMERICA • BW-17, S-27, B-9. *Breen dies:* 8-E. *Estimated population:* 45 to 60.

1794, Buckled Obverse, No Protruding Leaf
Under I of AMERICA (BW-17, S-27, B-9).

Obverse: Date: 1 centered. 4 slightly high. *Tip of pole points to:* Denticle, and is close to it. LIBERTY: BE and TY wide, I opposite left side of denticle. *Points of distinction:* Third lock long, sixth lock short. Die bulged horizontally at center, later develops into a crack. *Maris designation:* Egeria (elusive lady). *Sheldon designation:* Buckled Obverse.

Reverse: Berries left and right: 5-6. So tiny as to be an unreliable guide for attribution. *Upright of second T of STATES opposite:* Denticle. *Fraction:* Bar slightly curved down to left. 10 wide, 00 slightly closer to each other. *Points of distinction:* No protruding leaf under I of AMERICA, the leaf is centered on top of the branch. Right branch does not connect to knot, but resumes at knot and continues down to the left.

Notes: Highest-known grades are EF and AU.

1794, No Protruding Leaf Under I of AMERICA • BW-18, S-28, B-10.

Breen dies: 9-E. **Estimated population:** 500 to 750.

1794, No Protruding Leaf Under I of AMERICA (BW-18, S-28, B-10).

Obverse: Date: 1 centered. 4 low. *Tip of pole points to:* Denticle, slightly right of its center. *LIBERTY:* IB and ERT wide, I opposite denticle. *Points of distinction:* Top two locks the same curved shape, heavy, and close to each other. Sheldon says: "The cheek is full, exuberant looking." Relapping causes some weakness. Cracks develop. *Maris designation:* Ornate.

Reverse: Same die as preceding. *Points of distinction:* Faint cracks are seen at the left branch. Clash marks as a triple outline from the top of the head on the obverse are seen in late states.

Notes: This variety occurs in Mint State.

1794, Long Tail on Right Ribbon • BW-20, S-29, B-11. *Breen dies:* 9-F.

Estimated population: 750 to 1,000.

1794, Long Tail on Right Ribbon (BW-20, S-29, B-11).

The curiously long right ribbon and the long tail to the R.

Obverse: Same die as preceding. *Points of distinction:* Die state further advanced. *Sheldon designation:* Tailed Reverse.

Reverse: Berries left and right: 10-8. Three topmost berries at left are stemless. Berry under left upright of M of AMERICA has another berry, disconnected, beyond it; Sheldon considered this to be a berry (giving a count of 8 on the right), Breen did not. *Upright of second T of STATES opposite:* Left part of bold, sharp denticle. *Fraction:* 1 heavy, misshapen, and slightly low. *Points of distinction:* Lettering very close to denticles, especially on the left. Leaf immediately above E of ONE is hollow. Sheldon: "The right ribbon end and the R of AMERICA have long tails, and this is one of the most easily recognized reverses of the series." The ribbon end is particularly distinct and nearly reaches the denticles. A crack is often seen from border through R of AMERICA to the wreath. Bulges develop.

Notes: This variety occurs in Mint State, and it is a rarity so fine.

1794, Marred Field, Long Tail on Right Ribbon • BW-22, S-30, B-12.
Breen dies: 10-F. *Estimated population:* 1,250 to 1,500.

1794, Marred Field, Long Tail on Right Ribbon (BW-22, S-30, B-12). Early (but not earliest) state of the obverse die with tiny island to left of locks 4 and 5, and with clash marks between cap and top of hair. For later die combinations, the obverse was reground. Reverse with distinctively long right ribbon, now well worn and with granularity and bulges, especially near the top.

Detail of island between fourth and fifth locks.

Obverse: Early die state. *Date:* 1 very high; barely touches hair. 4 high. *Tip of pole points to:* Space between denticles. *LIBERTY:* all letters close; TY slightly less close than others, I opposite denticle. *Points of distinction:* Lowest lock with thin C-shaped curl below it. Small raised island in field opposite locks 4 and 5, giving the name *Marred Field.* Some examples are without clash marks. Later impressions are with prominent clash marks between cap and top of head. Sheldon: "The hair is luxuriant, and the cheeks are full. Miss Liberty seems to smile." Also used on BW-24, BW-39, BW-40, BW-41, and BW-42. *Maris designation: Amatory Face* in the 1869 (first) edition; changed in the second edition to *Amiable Face*—seemingly a change from love to friendship. *Sheldon designation:* First Marred Field.

Reverse: Same die as preceding. Well worn by this time. Slightly buckled. Faint clash marks are seen at the upper part of the wreath.

Notes: This variety occurs in Mint State, and is very rare as such.

1794, Marred Field, Long Fraction Bar • BW-24, S-31, B-13. *Breen dies:* 10-G. *Estimated population:* Thousands.

1794, Marred Field, Long Fraction Bar (BW-24, S-31, B-13).

Obverse: Same die as preceding, but a slightly later die state, with clash marks below LIB ground away. Additional flaws ("mars") in left field. *Sheldon designation:* Second Marred Field. He thought this to be an entirely different die. The use of the same obverse die is continued with BW-39, BW-40, BW-41, and BW-42.

Reverse: Berries left and right: 6-6. Fourth berry on the left is partly covered by a leaf. *Upright of second T of STATES opposite:* Denticle. *Fraction:* Very wide fraction bar extending to left and right beyond denominator, the longest on any die of this year. *Points of distinction:* Some leaves on inside of wreath are incomplete. *Sheldon designation:* Long Fraction Bar Reverse.

Notes: Can be found in Mint State.

1794, Dot Between L and I, 7 9 Wide, Four Berries Opposite R •
BW-25, S-NC-8, B-14. *Breen dies:* 11-H. *Recorded population:* 3.

1794, Dot Between L and I, 7 9 Wide, Four Berries Opposite R (BW-25, S-NC-8, B-14). Detail of dot between L and I at BW-26.

Obverse: Date: 1 slightly low. 7 and 9 widely spaced, 9 leans left, 94 close. 4 centered. *Tip of pole points to:* Space between denticles, and is close to it. *LIBERTY:* Dot between bases of L and I (only die with this feature), other letters widely spaced, I opposite space between denticles. *Points of distinction:* Locks of hair except lowest are thin. *Maris designation:* Separated Date.

Reverse: Berries left and right: 6-8. 4 berries close to each other, with 2 on each side of stem, below R of AMERICA. *Upright of second T of STATES opposite:* Space between denticles. *Fraction:* Numerator close to bar, 1 in denominator close to bar. *Points of distinction:* A crack is seen at the upper left.

Notes: Discovered by Willard C. Blaisdell in December 1965. The highest-graded example of this variety is Fine.

1794, Dot Between L and I, 7 9 Wide, Short, Thick Fraction Bar •
BW-26, S-25, B-15.[14] *Breen dies:* 11-I. **Estimated population:** 300 to 400.

1794, Dot Between L and I, 7 9 Wide, Short, Thick Fraction Bar (BW-26, S-25, B-15).

Detail of dot between L and I.

Obverse: Same die as preceding. *Points of distinction:* Clash marks develop.

Reverse: Berries left and right: 8-7. On the left there are 6 large berries and 2 tiny high berries. *Upright of second T of STATES opposite:* Space between denticles. *Fraction:* Bar thick and very short, ends at right edge of 1 and to the left of the center of the second 0. *Points of distinction:* Center dot partly embedded in left upright of N of CENT. Faint clash marks from the obverse are seen at the top of the reverse. Some have a tiny crack from D of UNITED to the wreath.

Notes: This variety occurs in Mint State, but is a great rarity as such. Several AU coins exist.

1794, Dot Between L and I, 7 9 Wide, Wide Fraction Bar With Thin Ends • BW-27, S-26, B-16. *Breen dies:* 11-J. ***Estimated population:*** 750 to 1,000.

1794, Dot Between L and I, 7 9 Wide, Wide Fraction Bar With Thin Ends (BW-27, S-26, B-16). Obverse die relapped, creating weakness in the form of open areas at the lower left of the hair. Parts of the lower right of the Liberty Cap are ground away. The dot between L and I is now very small.

Obverse: Same die as preceding. Die relapped, causing dramatic weakness in the hair to the lower left. Multiple clash marks develop later.

Reverse: *Berries left and right:* 5-6. All are large. *Upright of second T of STATES opposite:* Denticle. *Fraction:* Very wide due to thin lines extending to left and right; extends far beyond Denominator. 1 slightly low. *Points of distinction:* Raised die flaw on left part of O in OF is always present. A crack develops from the rim through E of STATES to the wreath, later joined by another crack from the first S to the wreath.

Notes: This variety can be found in Mint State.

1794, Dot Between L and I, 7 9 Wide • BW-29, S-NC-11, B-17. *Breen dies:* 11-K. ***Recorded population:*** 4.

1794, Dot Between L and I, 7 9 Wide (BW-29, S-NC-11, B-17).

Obverse: Same die as preceding. *Points of distinction:* Late state of the die with certain details weakened by relapping.

Reverse: *Berries left and right:* 6-6. Top-left berries sometimes obscured. Inside berry to right of E of ONE is tiny. *Upright of second T of STATES opposite:* Denticle. *Fraction:* Numerator close to bar and over right part of first 0. Left edge of bar at edge of 1.

Notes: The highest-graded example is VG-8.

1794, Up-turned Locks • BW-30, S-32, B-18. *Breen dies:* 12-K. ***Estimated population:*** 400 to 500.

  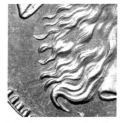

1794, Up-turned Locks (BW-30, S-32, B-18). With cud break on rim above LI. The reverse is heavily damaged from multiple instances of clashing against the obverse die without an intervening planchet.

Detail showing the upturned ends to the locks.

Obverse: *Date:* 1 very low. 4 very low. *Tip of pole points to:* Left part of denticle, and is close to it. *LIBERTY:* Letters widely spaced,

BE widest but only slightly, I opposite denticle. *Points of distinction:* Fourth and sixth locks (counting up from the bottom) have tips turned upward. Some incomplete areas of hair opposite neck and also in another area opposite cap. Sometimes seen with a short rim crack over LI. *Maris designation:* Venus Marina. *Sheldon designation:* Up-turned Locks.

Reverse: Same die as preceding. *Points of distinction:* Now heavily damaged from multiple clashing. Usually seen with a heavy crack from the border through the first S of STATES through the wreath and slightly into the interior.

Notes: Mint State, and a rarity as such.

1794, Up-turned Locks, "Wheel Spoke" Breaks on Reverse • BW-31, S-33, B-19. *Breen dies:* 12-L. *Estimated population:* 20 to 25.

1794, Up-turned Locks, "Wheel Spoke" Breaks on Reverse (BW-31, S-33, B-19).

Obverse: Same die as preceding. *Points of distinction:* Cud break over LI always present, as on the late state of the preceding use. A crack develops from this break down to the cap.

Reverse: Berries left and right: 6-6. Upright of second T of STATES opposite: Denticle. *Fraction:* Bar is closer to the right ribbon than the left; partially covers 1 and extends to half over the second 0. Numerator is left of center on the bar and is over the first 0.

Points of distinction: "Wheel Spoke" reverse, from buckling (actually, sinking of the center of the die) and cracks at several places around the rim. On worn coins the buckling results in ONE / CENT being worn away quickly. *Sheldon designation:* Six "Wheel Spoke" Breaks.

Notes: The highest-grade examples are VF. In 1958, when *Penny Whimsy* was published, Dr. Sheldon noted this: "Nine examples of this famous rarity are now known to us, but unfortunately, three of them are impounded in the American Numismatic Society, and two of the remaining six are injured or burnished coins." It is testimony to the interest in varieties that since 1958 the population has about doubled. Numismatists like nicknames, and "Wheel Spoke" has helped make this variety very popular.

1794, Single Berry Left of Bow • BW-32, S-34, B-20. *Breen dies:* 12-M. *Estimated population:* 30 to 45.

1794, Single Berry Left of Bow (BW-32, S-34, B-20).

Obverse: Same die as preceding. *Points of distinction:* The crack from the cud break to the cap expanded as the die was used.

Reverse: Berries left and right: 5-6. Most berries small. Only a single berry (instead of two) near left ribbon bow; this and the next die are the only ones with this feature. *Upright of second T of STATES opposite:* Space between denticles, but closer to denticle on the left. *Fraction:* Numerator high. Bar thick and barely covers all of the denominator. 1 high, first 0 low and leans right. *Points of distinction:* Lowest leaf on left points to the left foot of the second A of AMERICA. Berry to left of C of CENT also near a leaf tip.

Notes: The highest grades for this variety are VF (most practically) and EF. Dr. Sheldon (1958): "Ten now known to us, eight of them in collectors' hands. . . . Four examples new to the present writer have appeared since *Early American Cents* was written. Still a great rarity, most fervently desired by collectors who are dangerously sick with the cent disease."

1794, 9 in Denticle, Single Berry Left of Bow • BW-34, S-35, B-21.
Breen dies: 13-M. ***Estimated population:*** 45 to 60.

1794, 9 in Denticle, Single Berry Left of Bow (BW-34, S-35, B-21).

Date showing 9 embedded in a denticle, unique among 1794 dies.

Detail of the ribbon bow with a single berry (instead of the usual two) at the left, similar to the reverse of BW-37.

Obverse: Date: 1 very low, close to or touches denticle. 9 embedded in denticle. 4 very low. *Tip of pole points to:* Space between denticles and is close to it. *LIBERTY:* Irregularly spaced, high, and close to denticles; ER widest, R nearly touches denticles, and I opposite left part of denticle. *Points of distinction:* Lowest lock is thinner than normal, higher locks are medium size and all well defined. Rounded cheek on Miss Liberty. Most (but not all) have a crack beginning at the border between E and R extending down through the portrait, and another from the border through the lower part of the cap to the hair, and sometimes other progressions as well. *Sheldon designation:* Delicate Lower Lock.

Reverse: Same die as preceding.

Notes: The highest grades for this variety are VF (most practically) and EF.

1794, Low Head, Single Berry Left of Bow • BW-36, S-NC-1, B-22.
Breen dies: 14-M. ***Recorded population:*** 4.

1794, Low Head, Single Berry Left of Bow (BW-36, S-NC-1, B-22).

Obverse: Date: 1 low. 4 centered, very close to neck and to denticles. *Tip of pole points to:* Denticle, and is close to it; pole is thick and wide. *LIBERTY:* LI close, others widely spaced, RT widest. I close to and opposite denticle. *Sheldon designation:* Low Head.

Reverse: Same die as preceding. *Points of distinction:* A bulge and then a heavy break develop.

Notes: The highest-graded piece is G-4.

1794, Low Head, Single Berry Left of Bow (but different die) • BW-37, S-36, B-23. *Breen dies:* 14-N. *Estimated population:* 45 to 60.

1794, Low Head, Single Berry Left of Bow (but different die) (BW-37, S-36, B-23).

Detail of the ribbon bow with a single berry (instead of the usual two) at the left, similar to the reverse of BW-34.

Obverse: Same die as preceding. *Points of distinction:* Clash marks are seen on later states as is a faint crack.

Reverse: Berries left and right: 6-7. Fourth berry on right is tiny. Only a single berry is near the left ribbon bow; this and the preceding die are the only ones with this feature. *Upright of second T of STATES opposite:* Space between denticles, but closer to denticle on the right. *Fraction:* Numerator high. Bar very thin, barely covers 1, extends to slightly more than halfway over second 0. Second 0 high. *Points of distinction:* Lowest leaf on right points to C of AMERICA. No leaf tip near berry to left of C of CENT. Cracks develop.

Notes: The highest-known grade for this variety is AU.

1794, Distant 1, Single Berry Left of Bow (die as preceding) • BW-38, S-37, B-24. *Breen dies:* 15-N. *Estimated population:* 13 to 19.

1794, Distant 1, Single Berry Left of Bow (die as preceding) (BW-38, S-37, B-24).

Obverse: Date: 1 low and distant from 7. 79 close. 4 low. *Tip of pole points to:* Denticle. *LIBERTY:* IBE wide, 1 opposite denticle just left of its center. *Points of distinction:* In the later state the die is relapped, causing some lightness of detail at the back of the hair. *Sheldon designation:* Distant 1.

Reverse: Same die as preceding.

Notes: The highest grades this variety is known in are VF and EF, and it is very rare in either grade. This is among the more famous varieties of 1794, and it is readily distinguishable at sight. Unknown to

Maris, Frossard, and other students of the series, the first example was located by Lancaster, Pennsylvania, dealer Charles Steigerwalt in the spring of 1900. Though it was unknown to W.W. Hays in his 1893 work, it was included in a New York sale as a "Hays-44" and returned as misattributed. Steigerwalt recognized it as new, and in the 1910 reprint of the Hays text it was added as No. 59. Some old-timers have referred to this as the "Steigerwalt variety."[15]

Numismatic Notes: Regarding Steigerwalt: The June 1900 issue of *The Numismatist* noted this:

> Charles Steigerwalt [the Lancaster, Pennsylvania dealer] has recently bought the collection of the late Mr. Hays, the most valuable part of which was the series of many varieties of the 1794 cent which he had long made an object of study, and which is well known by the late Ed. Frossard's

illustrated monograph upon them. The collection was also rich in New Jersey and Connecticut series. But Dr. Hall, of Boston, has the finest collection of these latter in existence, probably as fine a collection of the 1794 varieties and very probably the finest collection of the U.S. cents known.

In the August issue Steigerwalt invited inquiries concerning the purchase of the Hays Collection of 1794 cents, which he held at $1,000, but would entertain a slightly lower offer. "Further details will be given to any person who really means business and does not inquire out of idle curiosity only."

1794, Marred Field, Single Berry Left of Bow (die as preceding) •
BW-39, S-38, B-25. *Breen dies:* 10-N. **Estimated population:** 45 to 60.

1794, Marred Field, Single Berry Left of Bow (die as preceding) (BW-39, S-38, B-25).

Obverse: Later die state, reworked and strengthened. Dr. Sheldon considered the reworked obverse die to be a different die. See *Walter Breen's Encyclopedia of Early United States Cents 1793–1814* for details. *Date:* The 1 is centered on BW-39, BW-41,

and BW-42 after more regrinding. 4 centered and close to both neck and denticles. *Tip of pole points to:* Between denticles. *LIBERTY:* All letters close; TY slightly less close than others, I opposite denticle, some letters weak at top due to regrinding. *Points of distinction:* Prominent raised island in field opposite locks 4 to 6. *Maris designation:* Amiable Face. *Sheldon designation:* Third Marred Field.

Reverse: Same die as preceding.

Notes: The highest grade this variety is found in is AU.

1794, Marred Field, Fatal [Reverse] Break Variety • BW-40, S-NC-2,
B-26. *Breen dies:* 10-O. **Recorded population:** 2.

1794, Marred Field, Fatal [Reverse] Break Variety (BW-40, S-NC-2, B-26).

Obverse: Same die as preceding. *Points of distinction:* Cracks develop near the left border, followed by additional cracks. In the late state much of the detail is missing at D and ST at the upper left.

Reverse: Berries left and right: 7-6. Berry under left upright of M of AMERICA. *Upright of second T of STATES opposite:*

Denticle. *Fraction:* Bar extends from right edge of 1 to halfway over second 0. 1 over first 0. *Points of distinction:* Pair of leaves above E of ONE complete. Leaf points to the right of the bottom-right serif of T of CENT. Ribbons widely spread and not near fraction. Right ribbon bow touches stem of leaves. Denticles large and pointed. The die is broken from the border above E of UNITED through the D, and in this general area, raising the relief of the field, probably ending its service. *Sheldon designation:* Fatal Break Variety.

Notes: The two examples are graded Mint State (held by the ANS) and VG-10.

1794, Marred Field, "Sprawled Ribbon Ends" • BW-41, S-39, B-27. *Breen dies:* 10-P. **Estimated population:** 20 to 25.

1794, Marred Field, "Sprawled Ribbon Ends" (BW-41, S-39, B-27).

Obverse: Same die as preceding. Some later impressions with light clash marks between top of cap and hair. Cracks are more prominent than earlier.

Reverse: Berries left and right: 7-6. Berry under center of M of AMERICA. *Upright of second T of STATES opposite:* Denticle. *Fraction:* Bar extends from right edge of 1 to left of center of second 0. 1 over first 0.

Points of distinction: Pair of leaves above E of ONE has bottom leaf with only the tip. Leaf points to the bottom-right serif of T of CENT. Ribbons widely spread and not near fraction. Right ribbon bow nearly touches stem of leaves. Denticles large and pointed, the largest on any 1794 cent reverse. Found with a crack from the rim near the 1 of the denominator, across the ribbon and into I of UNITED. Dr. Sheldon knew of only one coin lacking this crack. In the late state the center sinks, causing a buckling on the coin and weakness at the lettering. *Sheldon designation:* Sprawled Ribbon Ends.

Notes: The highest grades for this variety are EF and AU, and it is rare at either level.

1794, Marred Field • BW-42, S-40, B-28. *Breen dies:* 10-Q. **Estimated population:** 30 to 45.

1794, Marred Field (BW-42, S-40, B-28).

Obverse: Same die as preceding. *Points of distinction:* Cracks are even more prominent now.

Reverse: Berries left and right: 7-7. *Upright of second T of STATES opposite:* Denticle, slightly right of its center. *Fraction:* Bar extends from right edge of 1 to slightly past center of second 0. 1 over first 0. First 0 low, and second 0 high. *Points of distinction:* Ribbon bow is high above knot. Denticles have rounded ends. Light cracks develop.

Notes: The highest-graded examples are AU and Mint State (exceedingly rare).

1794, Truncated Hair Locks, Most Berries Are Tiny • BW-44, S-41, B-30. *Breen dies:* 16-S. **Estimated population:** 300 to 400.

1794, Truncated Hair Locks, Most Berries Are Tiny (BW-44, S-41, B-30). Late state of the reverse die.

Obverse: Date: 1 low. 7 and 9 close, 9 almost touches denticle. 4 very low. *Tip of pole points to:* Space between denticles. *LIBERTY:* Close to denticles, widely spaced, ER closest, 1 opposite left part of denticle. *Points of distinction:* "Between the cap and the head, two short locks terminate abruptly, one above the pole and one below it." Sometimes with a crack from the border between 7 and 9. Clash marks are removed by light relapping. Further clash marks develop, as do cracks. *Maris designation:* Abrupt Hair. *Sheldon designation:* Truncated Hair Locks.

Reverse: *Berries left and right:* 7-7. 4 inner berries on left are large, all others are tiny. *Upright of second T of STATES opposite:* Denticle. *Fraction:* Bar from about halfway over the 1 to halfway over the second 0.

First 0 low. *Points of distinction:* Denticles short and rounded. The reverse is sometimes perfect, but most often with crack from the border through D, along the top of CE, to N, then into N of ONE, continuing. Various stages of this crack are known.

Notes: The highest-obtainable grade is EF. There is one example in Mint State (held by the ANS).

1794, Truncated Hair Locks, Weak "OF" • BW-45, S-42, B-29. *Breen dies:* 16-R. *Estimated population:* 160 to 200.

1794, Truncated Hair Locks, Weak "OF" (BW-45, S-42, B-29).

Detail of weak OF and wide A and M of AMERICA.

Obverse: Same die as preceding. *Points of distinction:* Light clash marks develop.

Reverse: *Berries left and right:* 6-6. *Upright of second T of STATES opposite:* Space between two denticles and slightly closer to the left one. *Fraction:* Bar covers most of 1 and about two-thirds of the second 0. Numerator over first 0. All digits in denominator lean slightly right. *Points of distinction:* A thin spine extends from the tip of the left stem. OF always light. AM of AMERICA wide. Denticles rounded.

Notes: The highest grades for this variety are AU and Mint State (unique).

1794, Lowest Lock Clipped, No Hook, Weak "OF" • BW-46, S-43, B-32. *Breen dies:* 17-R. *Estimated population:* 750 to 1,000.

1794, Lowest Lock Clipped, No Hook, Weak "OF" (BW-46, S-43, B-32).

Detail showing the lowest lock of hair without a hook at the end.

Obverse: *Date:* 1 very high and over space between denticles. 4 touches neck. *Tip of pole points to:* Denticle, just right of its center. *LIBERTY:* Letters fairly evenly spaced; I opposite space between denticles. *Points of distinction:* Lowest lock clipped at its end, eliminating the hook, tip points downward to the left. No loop under left side of neck. Sheldon: "Here for the first time we see a new set of figures with larger and taller 7, pointed 4, taller, more pointed 1, and a slightly taller 9. This is the beginning of Chapman's Style 3, and in this group [through S-51] the busts are a little smaller and narrower, with the hair in rolled locks over the ear, and the lowest curl only about the same thickness as those above it. The hair is treated in more minute detail, as if to try to delineate the separate hairs. The faces have full, plump cheeks." The die is found perfect or with a crack from the border behind the cap, and sometimes another crack from the border through 7 and 1 to the hair. *Maris designation:* Short Bust.

Reverse: Same die as preceding. *Points of distinction:* Usually seen with a crack from the border through U and the wreath, to C of CENT.

Notes: The highest grades for this variety are AU and Mint State (held by the ANS).

1794, Lowest Lock Clipped, No Hook • BW-48, S-NC-10, B-31. *Breen dies:* 17-T. *Recorded population:* 1.

1794, Lowest Lock Clipped, No Hook (BW-48, S-NC-10, B-31).

Obverse: Same die as preceding.

Reverse: Berries left and right: 6-6. *Upright of second T of STATES opposite:* Denticle, slightly to left of its center. *Fraction:* Bar slants slightly down to left; barely covers 1 and extends most of the way above second 0. 10 wide, 00 closer.

Notes: This example is VG-10. Discovered by Christopher B. Young at the ANA convention, July 27, 1994. The only unique 1794 cent variety. Daniel W. Holmes Jr. Collection.

1794, Lowest Lock Clipped, No Hook, Right Ribbon End Weak • BW-49, S-44, B-33. *Breen dies:* 17-U. *Estimated population:* 1,250 to 1,500.

1794, Lowest Lock Clipped, No Hook, Right Ribbon End Weak (BW-49, S-44, B-33).

Obverse: Same die as preceding. *Points of distinction:* Obverse always seen with crack from the rim through 17, extending left, and always with clash marks. Later cracks develop.

Reverse: Berries left and right: 7-6. Berry under left upright of M of AMERICA. Large berry centered left of C of CENT. *Upright of second T of STATES opposite:* Denticle. *Fraction:* Bar slants, covers 1, and extends most of the way above second 0. 1 high and leans right, 1 and 0 wide, 00 closer. Second 0 weak. *Points of distinction:* Right ribbon end weak. Sometimes with a perfect die, but usually with a crack from the border near O, down to the N of ONE, and sometimes continuing.

Notes: The highest grades for this variety are AU and Mint State (unique).

1794, Lowest Lock Clipped, No Hook • BW-51, S-NC-5, B-34. *Breen dies: 17-V. Recorded population: 2.*

1794, Lowest Lock Clipped, No Hook (BW-51, S-NC-5, B-34).

Obverse: Same die as preceding. *Points of distinction:* Die cracks as on preceding use, now with a bulge.

Reverse: Berries left and right: 7-6. Upright of second T of STATES opposite: Denticle. *Fraction:* Bar extends from right edge of 1 to slightly past center of second 0. 1 leans right, first 0 low. *Points of distinction:* Center dot within left upright of N of CENT near its top. A crack develops and expands. The die was laminated at the center, causing streaks and rough spots.

Notes: Discovered by John Pawling in 1951, thus not included in *Early American Cents* (1949). The two examples are graded, respectively, AG-3 and Fair-2.

1794, Braided Hair • BW-52, S-45, B-35. *Breen dies: 18-V.* **Estimated population:** 30 to 45.

1794, Braided Hair (BW-52, S-45, B-35).

Hair with heavy tresses.

Obverse: Date: 1 very high and over denticle. 4 touches neck. *Tip of pole points to:* Denticle, just right of its center. *LIBERTY:* LI and ER close, I opposite space between denticles. *Points of distinction:* Locks 2 to 6 have delicate points, 2 and 3 are similar to an open claw, and there is a large space between 4 and 5 extending well into the main part of the hair. *Maris designation:* The Plicae. Sheldon: "Called by Maris *The Plicae*, referring to the fact that the hair is partially twisted or coiled into heavy, separate braids which point out behind in quite a novel manner." Whether a modern observer would call the hair *braided* is questionable. The tresses are heavy and bold, however. *Sheldon designation:* Braided Hair.

Reverse: Same die as preceding. *Points of distinction:* Always with die damage in the form of ridges diagonally down to the right from TA of STATES. Sometimes with a tiny crack from the border, to IC, to the nearest leaf, and continuing onward.

Notes: The highest grades for this variety are AU and Mint State (unique).

1794, Braided Hair, Ridge at E of CENT • BW-54, S-46, B-36. *Breen dies:* 18-W. *Estimated population:* 300 to 400.

1794, Braided Hair, Ridge at E of CENT (BW-54, S-46, B-36).

Detail showing the die defect at E of CENT and nearby; this permits instant recognition of the variety.

Obverse: Same die as preceding. *Points of distinction:* Die crack upward from border beyond the date. Sometimes with another crack beginning at the border below C and continuing upward. Many different die states are known.

Reverse: Berries left and right: 6-6. 2 berries near bow are stemless. Upper-left berry very small. *Upright of second T of STATES opposite:* Space between denticles. *Fraction:* Bar extends from center of 1 to near center of second 0. 1 leans right, first 0 low. *Points of distinction:* Die defect caused a prominent ridge at E of CENT.

Notes: The highest grades for this variety are AU and Mint State.

1794, Left Edge of Neck Ends in Sharp Tip • BW-58, S-47, B-39. *Breen dies:* 20-Z. *Estimated population:* 120 to 160.

1794, Left Edge of Neck Ends in Sharp Tip (BW-58, S-47, B-39).

Detail of neck ending in sharp tip.

Obverse: Date: 1 high, doubled denticle to left of its base. 94 close. 4 very high, almost touches neck. *Tip of pole points to:* Slightly right of center of rounded denticle. *LIBERTY:* Left base of R slightly low; I opposite

denticle. *Points of distinction:* Left part of neck ends in a sharp tip instead of blending into the hair, with no loop. Cracks develop. *Maris designation:* Young Head. *Sheldon designation:* Braided Upper Locks.

Reverse: Berries left and right: 6-6. Arranged 2 outside and 4 inside on each branch. *Upright of second T of STATES opposite:* Space between denticles. *Fraction:* Bar extends from right edge of 1 to center of second 0. 10 wider than 00; second 0 slightly low. *Points of distinction:* Small piece or notch out of the bottom of the ribbon bow at left. On most (but not all) a tiny crack begins at the border past the first A of AMERICA to a leaf.

Notes: The highest grades for this variety are VF and EF (exceedingly rare).

1794, Left Edge of Neck Ends in Sharp Tip, Starred Reverse • BW-59, S-48, B-38. *Breen dies:* 20-Y. *Estimated population:* 50 to 60.

1794, Left Edge of Neck Ends in Sharp Tip, Starred Reverse (BW-59, S-48, B-38). Around the reverse border are 94 tiny five-pointed stars. The Adams-Husak coin, the finest known.

Detail of certain of the stars.

Obverse: Same die as preceding. *Points of distinction:* Light clash marks are seen, then removed by lapping.

Reverse: Unique Starred Reverse die. Apparently, 94 tiny five-pointed stars were first placed around the border of the die, for a reason unknown today. Later, the die was completed with normal features, including cutting denticles around the border, some of which took away certain star elements, though most remain and are bold when viewed under magnification. The most famous of all 1794 cent dies. Dr. Sheldon: "Collectors mention it with religious awe." The BW-59 and BW-84 reverses are the only ones of the year with smaller letters than the others. *Points of distinction:* The die buckles and eventually fails.

Notes: The highest grades for this variety are VF and EF (unique).

Numismatic Notes: This variety has attracted continuing excitement ever since its discovery, said to have been by the teen-aged Henry Chapman in the year before he went into business with S. Hudson Chapman to form the Chapman brothers partnership (which endured until 1906). The description of the coin and the scenario of its finding as related by S.H. here:

Reverse. A circle of 94 minute, 5 pointed stars inside the deeply serrated border with some of the stars between or under the points of the serrature. It seems as if the engraver had at first attempted to use this circle of stars as a border, and then, not approving of it, engraved the serrated border to and over them. The stars and points are not equally spaced and the serrature points, therefore, cover some of the stars. At first glance they appear as if they were merely marks dividing the spaces for the serrature points, but each is a perfectly formed, minute, 5 pointed star. . . .

This die was discovered by Henry Chapman during 1877. Dr. Maris, the first man to make a study of the series, was standing between him and the author whilst we were examining a lot of 1794 Cents, when H.C., picking up a specimen and examining it, exclaimed, 'Here is a die with minute stars around the reverse.' Dr. Maris confirmed the discovery and said, 'It was previously unknown.'[16]

The discovery coin was sold to large cent specialist Samuel Bispham. On February 11–12, 1880, his collection was sold by the Chapmans.

On April 6, Joseph Chandler Roach wrote to New York dealer Édouard Frossard about the variety, stating that he owned one and Lorin G. Parmelee of Boston owned another (acquired from Maris). Frossard looked through his inventory and promptly found a fourth.

Soon afterward, E.B. Mason Jr., in his *Numismatic Visitor*, printed this, without bothering to mention the Chapmans, who were competitors in Philadelphia:

For the first time, in any journal we present a description of the new and important discovery of the new and beautiful 'Starred' variety of the U.S. cent of 1794. This coin made its debut at a coin sale in New York last February, and was purchased by a lucky dealer for four dollars and twenty-five cents! A duplicate of this rare piece was picked up in this city in March, and is now for sale at this office. The 'starred' variety differs from the common pieces only on the reverse. Eighty-nine [*sic*] small, fine pointed stars circle around the serrated, or milled border, just between the points, giving to the cent a really handsome appearance. The above pieces are from original dies, and give evidence of considerable circulation and abrasions. . . .

R.C. Davis, the well known numismatist, has after considerable investigation discovered that the starred variety of the 1794 U.S. cent derives its origin from the experimental piece of 1792, known as the 'Eagle on a Rock,' which can only be seen in the Mint Cabinet of coins, this city. Around the edge of the latter are eighty-seven [*sic*] small five pointed stars, bearing an exact resemblance to the stars on the 1794 starred cent. This fact leads to the conclusion that some of the planchets bearing only the stars, were used when the Mint authorities were coining the 1794 cents. This explanation enhances the fictitious value of the three known specimens of the 'Starred 94' now owned by Haseltine, Roach and Mason of this city.

Likely the Haseltine coin was actually owned by J. Colvin Randall, a local dealer and investor who often worked in Haseltine's office. S.K. Harzfeld's auction of November 26–27, 1880, included such a cent, consigned by Randall. Édouard Frossard, in his magazine, *Numisma*, publicized the discovery. It was certainly the item of the year in 1880.

In *Numisma*, that same month, Frossard printed a poem submitted by Thomas S. Collier, entitled, "On the Star-Circled Cent of 1794."

In the almost century-and-a-half since 1880, the Starred Reverse has been the subject of many mentions, articles, and comments. Dr. Sheldon thought the variety was "the whim of an idle hour at the Mint." Don Taxay, in *U.S. Mint and Coinage*, viewed it as a pattern. The present author added comments in the 1982 offering of the John W. Adams Collection of 1794 cents, to this effect: the die was certainly made for a special purpose, whether for a pattern or a proposed regular issue, but, after the tiny five-pointed stars were punched around the periphery, the die was set aside. Rather than waste it, the die was made into a cent reverse.

What really happened may never be known. This unique variety keeps its secret well!

Most 1794, Starred Reverse, cents are in lower grades. Any example in any grade has significant value if some of the stars can be discerned. The finest is the S.S. Forrest Jr. coin, obtained from Spink & Son, London, later found in the John W. Adams Collection, and sold in 2008 as part of the Walter Husak Collection. The present author owned this coin for a time in the 1970s.

In lower grades the date and several stars must be discernible.

1794, Starred Reverse		Cert	Avg	%MS
		7	13.7	0%

Fair-2	AG-3	G-4	VG-8	F-12	VF-20
$9,830	$14,500	$21,330	$29,375	$51,750	$115,000

1794, Left Edge of Neck Ends in Sharp Tip • BW-60, S-NC-9, B-40.

Breen dies: 20-AA. ***Recorded population:*** 2.

1794, Left Edge of Neck Ends in Sharp Tip (BW-60, S-NC-9, B-40), early reverse die state.

1794, Left Edge of Neck Ends in Sharp Tip (BW-60, S-NC-9, B-40), late reverse die state.

Obverse: Same die as preceding. *Points of distinction:* A crack develops and becomes heavy, through the center, to the rim at the upper right.

Reverse: *Berries left and right:* 5-6. *Upright of second T of STATES opposite:* Highest outside leaf on left. *Fraction:* Bar short. Second 0 very close to ribbon. Numerator slightly right of center of first 0. *Points of distinction:* Leaves very close at wreath apex. In its late state the die develops a vertical, bisecting crack. Probably, this occurred soon after it was first used, accounting for its rarity today.

Notes: The two examples, graded VG-7 and AG-3, are both in the Daniel W. Holmes Jr. Collection.

1794, Left Edge of Neck Ends in Sharp Tip, Closed Wreath • BW-61, S-49, B-41. *Breen dies:* 20-BB. ***Estimated population:*** 750 to 1,000.

1794, Left Edge of Neck Ends in Sharp Tip, Closed Wreath (BW-61, S-49, B-41).

Detail from another coin showing the late-state obverse die crack.

The fraction is crowded to the right, and the digits are irregularly aligned.

Obverse: Same die as preceding. During this mating, a large, vertical die crack develops from the border through the left side of E to the hair.

Reverse: *Berries left and right:* 9-6. Largest is under the left upright of M of AMERICA. *Upright of second T of STATES opposite:* Denticle. *Fraction:* Numerator leans right and is close to bar. Bar almost covers 1, extends to slightly past center of second 0, and ends at ribbon. In the denominator 1 is distant and leans right. *Points of distinction:* Leaf tips touch at wreath apex. First S of STATES high; TA close. This is the most extensively mated reverse die of the 1794 year. *Sheldon designation:* Closed Wreath.

Notes: Found in AU and Mint State; both grades are very rare.

1794, Left Edge of Neck Ends in Sharp Tip (different die), Closed Wreath • BW-63, S-50, B-43. *Breen dies:* 22-BB. **Estimated population:** 45 to 60.

1794, Left Edge of Neck Ends in Sharp Tip (different die), Closed Wreath (BW-63, S-50, B-43).

Obverse: Date: 1 very high, almost touches hair. Double denticle below 7. 4 very high, barely touches neck. *Tip of pole points to:* Left part of triangular denticle. *LIBERTY:* Closely spaced, I opposite denticle slightly left of its center. *Points of distinction:* Left part of neck ends in a sharp tip instead of blending into the hair; slight trace of loop above top right of 7. Lowest lock severed behind neck, with space before it resumes. In a later state there is relapping, probably to remove clash marks. In the latest state a crack develops from the 4, extending right, to the tip of the bust, and through the pole. *Sheldon designation:* Short Bust, Detached Lower Lock.

Reverse: Same die as preceding.

Notes: The highest grade this variety is found in is AU.

1794, Second and Fourth Locks Long, Left Edge of Neck Ends in Sharp Tip (different die), Closed Wreath • BW-65, S-51, B-42. *Breen dies:* 21-BB. **Estimated population:** 60 to 75.

1794, Second and Fourth Locks Long, Left Edge of Neck Ends in Sharp Tip (different die), Closed Wreath (BW-65, S-51, B-42).

Obverse: Date: 1 very high, almost touches hair. 4 very high, barely touches neck. *Tip of pole points to:* Space between denticles. *LIBERTY:* IB and TY wide, I opposite denticle slightly left of its center. *Points of distinction:* Left part of neck ends in a sharp tip instead of blending into the hair, with no loop. Second and fourth locks long and with brush-like ends. The obverse is usually perfect, but some have a crack beginning between 1 and 7, going across the top of the 7 to the neck, and curving down to the end of the pole. Sometimes with an additional crack extending from the left border. *Sheldon designation:* Long Locks.

Reverse: Same die as preceding.

Notes: The highest grade this variety is found in is EF.

Detail showing the long second and fourth locks with brush-like ends.

The leaves touch at the top of the wreath, unique among 1794 cent dies.

1794, Date spaced 1 79 4, Closed Wreath • BW-67, S-52, B-44. *Breen dies:* 23-BB. **Estimated population:** 25 to 30.

1794, Date Spaced 1 79 4, Closed Wreath (BW-67, S-52, B-44).

Obverse: *Date:* 1 very high, almost touches hair. 4 very high, barely touches neck. Pole points to right part of rounded denticle. 94 close, date spaced as 1 79 4. *Tip of pole points to:* Right part of denticle, and is close to it. *LIBERTY:* L close to cap, LI close, I opposite denticle. *Points of distinction:* Hair strands bold and coarse. Usually with a crack below the top of the cap to the hair, but a few are from a perfect die. Tom Morley called it the "Bully Head," from its strong, tough-appearing visage.[17] *Sheldon designation:* 1 and 7 Distant.

Reverse: Same die as preceding.

Notes: The highest grade this variety is found in is VF, and it is very rare as such.

1794, Severed Sixth Lock, Closed Wreath • BW-69, S-53, B-45. *Breen dies:* 24-BB. **Estimated population:** 20 to 25.

1794, Severed Sixth Lock, Closed Wreath (BW-69, S-53, B-45).

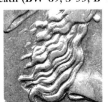

Detail of the severed lock.

Obverse: *Date:* 1 very high, almost touches hair. 4 very high, almost touches neck. *Tip of pole points to:* Center of triangular denticle. *LIBERTY:* L close to cap, RT close, I opposite space between denticles. *Points of distinction:* Hair strands bold and coarse. Tip of sixth lock detached. *Sheldon designation:* Severed Sixth Lock.

Reverse: Same die as preceding.

Notes: The highest grade this variety is found in is EF.

1794, 7 Tilts to Right, Closed Wreath • BW-70, S-54, B-46. *Breen dies:* 25-BB. **Estimated population:** 300 to 400.

1794, 7 Tilts to Right, Closed Wreath (BW-70, S-54, B-46).

Date showing the slanting or tilted 7.

Obverse: *Date:* 1 very high. 7 tilted to the right. 4 very high. *Tip of pole points to:* Space between denticles, slightly closer to denticle on the right. *LIBERTY:* RT close,

I opposite left part of denticle. *Points of distinction:* Hair strands bold and coarse. Sixth lock (counting up from the bottom) detached and forms a small island. Bottom lock ends in a chisel-like point and has a very small hook. Clash marks develop, and in the late state there is a delicate crack

from the left border to the hair. *Maris designation:* Crooked 7. *Sheldon designation:* Slanting 7.

Reverse: Same die as preceding.

Notes: The highest grades this variety is found in are EF and AU.

1794, 7 Tilts to Right, Ribbon Bow With Two Knots, "Crazy A" in STATES • BW-71, S-55, B-47. *Breen dies:* 25-CC. **Estimated population:** 500 to 750.

1794, Tilts to Right, Ribbon Bow With Two Knots, "Crazy A" in STATES (BW-71, S-55, B-47).

Detail showing the "Crazy A" (from another coin).

Obverse: Same die as preceding. *Points of distinction:* The obverse continues with the crack from the preceding use of the die, now sometimes with an additional crack branching off from the first and going down through the hair.

Reverse: *Berries left and right:* 6-5. All large except for the fourth on the left. *Upright of second T of STATES opposite:* Denticle, slightly to right of its center. *Fraction:* Numerator heavy, close to or touching bar, and slightly right of the center of the second 0. Bar extends from left side of 1 to halfway over second 0. First 0 low. *Points of distinction:* "Crazy A" in STATES is high and leans left. Two ribbon knots, one above the other. Leaves are very close at wreath apex. Amateur workmanship. On some coins there is a die crack in the left obverse field. *Sheldon designation:* Big Berries Variety.

Notes: The highest grades this variety is found in are AU and Mint State, very rare at either level.

1794, 7 Tilts to Right, "Office Boy" Reverse • BW-72, S-56, B-48. *Breen dies:* 25-DD. **Estimated population:** 300 to 400.

1794, 7 Tilts to Right, "Office Boy" Reverse (BW-72, S-56, B-48).

Obverse: Same die as preceding. *Points of distinction:* Cracks as preceding, but now more prominent. In a late state the obverse is relapped, removing the clash marks.

Reverse: *Berries left and right:* 8-7. Breen counted 6-7, perhaps overlooking two tiny ones near the branch at top left. *Upright of second T of STATES opposite:* Denticle. *Fraction:* Numerator leans right and touches bar. Bar extends from over 1 to near top center of second 0. *Points of distinction:* Irregular spacing of some letters; TA of STATES connected, T high, etc. Leaf pair with points opposite second A of AMERICA. Lower-right ribbon end partly detached. Two ribbon knots, one high and detached. Dr. Sheldon: "Highly defective reverse. In addition to the nine defective leaves, the bow is incomplete, Amateur workmanship, probably from the same hand as the preceding reverse." Called the "Office Boy" Reverse by John Clapp.

Notes: The highest grades this variety is found in are AU and Mint State, very rare at either level.

1794, 7 Tilts to Right, "Office Boy" Reverse		Cert	Avg	%MS
		(a)		

AG-3	G-4	VG-8	F-12	VF-20	EF-40
$310	$460	$640	$900	$2,580	$7,000

a. Included in certified population for 1794, Head of 1794.

1794, "Pyramidal Head," Button on Cap • BW-74, S-57, B-55. *Breen dies:* 29-JJ. *Estimated population:* Thousands.

1794, "Pyramidal Head," Button on Cap (BW-74, S-57, B-55).

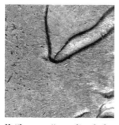

Small "button" or die defect on outside of lower left of the cap.

Obverse: Date: 1 very high. 4 slightly high. *Tip of pole points to:* Denticle, and is close to it. *LIBERTY:* IB wide, I opposite denticle. *Points of distinction:* Hair strands are bold and coarse and are fairly straight in a line slanting down to the left, evocative of the edge of a pyramid. Tiny dot ("button") on outside of lower left of cap—as also seen on BW-84—is really much ado about nothing on examination. Perfect die state or with light parallel cracks from the nose and lower lip to the border, increasing in visibility with die use. *Maris designation:* Pyramidal Head. *Sheldon designation:* Button Variety.

Reverse: Berries left and right: 7-7. *Upright of second T of STATES opposite:* Denticle, slightly to left of its center. *Fraction:* Bar extends from close to upper left of 1 to past center of second 0. 1 in numerator very high. *Points of distinction:* ICA of AMERICA close to denticles. Lowest berry on inside left touches ribbon. Leaves close at wreath apex. An injury to the die is seen over CA. In its late state, die sunk at the center, producing a prominent bulge nearly obliterating the lettering.

Notes: This variety is known in Mint State.

1794, Thick Hair, Wide Date • BW-76, S-58, B-56. *Breen dies:* 30-KK. *Estimated population:* 300 to 400.

1794, Thick Hair, Wide Date (BW-76, S-58, B-56).

Detail showing the thick hair strands.

Obverse: Date: 1 very high. 4 low. *Tip of pole points to:* Denticle, and is close to or touches it. *LIBERTY:* LIBE wide, B slightly low, I opposite space between denticles and slightly closer to denticle on the right. *Points of distinction:* Hair strands bold and coarse. *Maris designation:* Many Haired. *Sheldon designation:* Thick Hair, Wide Date.

Reverse: Berries left and right: 6-7. *Upright of second T of STATES opposite:* Space between denticles. *Fraction:* Numerator leans slightly

right. Bar curved; extends from upper right of 1 to right edge of second 0. First 0 low and near end of denticle. *Points of distinction:* Right stem close to ribbon and points past A. RICA close to denticles. Some have a crack through UNIT, these being in the minority. Clash marks develop, and a crack becomes prominent, eventually generating a rim cud. This last state is very rare.

Notes: The highest grades this variety is found in are EF and AU (exceedingly rare).

1794, Thick Hair, Wide Date, Left Ribbon Bow Double Cut • BW-77, S-59, B-57. *Breen dies:* 30-LL. *Estimated population:* 300 to 400.

1794, Thick Hair, Wide Date, Left Ribbon Bow Double Cut (BW-77, S-59, B-57).

The tilted fraction and the reverse die crack.

Obverse: Same die as preceding. *Points of distinction:* The obverse is found perfect, but also is found with a small crack from between the 9 and the 4 to the neck.

Reverse: Berries left and right: 7-7. *Upright of second T of STATES opposite:* Denticle, slightly to left of its center. *Fraction:* Leans sharply to the right. Numerator to the left of center of bar and over second 0. Bar extends from center of 1 to past center of second 0. 1 high. Second 0 near denticle. *Points of distinction:* Letters on right are close to denticles. Left stem short. Left ribbon bow is double cut at top. Many denticles blended are together except for their tips. The reverse can be found perfect, but often has a crack starting at the border beneath the end of the left ribbon. This continues to expand, eventually becoming heavy.

Notes: This variety is known in Mint State.

1794, Thick Hair, Close Date • BW-79, S-60, B-52. *Breen dies:* 27-HH. *Estimated population:* 200 to 300.

1794, Thick Hair, Close Date (BW-79, S-60, B-52).

Obverse: Date: 1 very high, close to or barely touches hair. 4 close to or barely

touches neck. *Tip of pole points to:* Left part of denticle and nearly touches it. *LIBERTY:* RT close, R close to hair, I opposite right part of denticle. *Points of distinction:* Hair strands bold and coarse. Lock 5, small, and with tip disconnected. There are often clash marks between the hair and LIB, sometimes dramatic. Some coins have a faint crack in the same area. *Maris designation:* Patagonian. *Sheldon designation:* Thick Hair, Close Date.

Reverse: *Berries left and right:* 6-5. *Upright of second T of STATES opposite:* Denticle, slightly to left of its center. *Fraction:* Bar extends from upper left of 1 to past center of second 0. First 0 low. *Points of distinction:* The right leaf of the lowest-inside pair on the right is a simple line and seems to be edgewise. The ribbon bow comes from the knot on the left, and the right ribbon end is high above the knot and does not connect to anything. Denticles heavy and pointed. Light clash marks are seen.

Notes: The highest grades this variety is found in are AU and Mint State (exceedingly rare). Édouard Frossard's 1879 description: "The head large, the ear nearly square. The legend LIBERTY near milling, with the R close to head. In the date, 1 touches the hair, and 4 the bust. The cap and staff touch the milling."

1794, Thick Hair, Close Date, Short Right Stem • BW-80, S-61, B-53.
Breen dies: 27-II. **Estimated population:** 120 to 160.

1794, Thick Hair, Close Date,
Short Right Stem (BW-80, S-61, B-53).

Detail of the reverse showing clash marks
in the form of denticles from the obverse
die. These are most prominent to the left
and right of the end of the left ribbon.

Obverse: Same die as preceding. *Points of distinction:* A faint crack on the preceding use of this die can be more developed but

still is not strong. The incuse marks are still present. An additional mark or crack can sometimes be seen from the rim to the hair left of the 1 in the date.

Reverse: *Berries left and right:* 7-7. *Upright of second T of STATES opposite:* Denticle, slightly to left of its center. *Fraction:* Bar extends from upper right of 1 to center of second 0. First 0 low. *Points of distinction:* Short right stem. Denticles heavy and pointed. Multiple clash marks are seen, most prominently along the bottom border. The obverse die became loose in the press and fell on the reverse die, impressing the denticles into the steel.

Notes: The highest grades this variety is found in are AU and Mint State. Sheldon notes that all of this variety are on planchets that are thicker than usual.

1794, Heavy, Stubby Lower Lock, Short Right Stem • BW-82, S-62, B-54.
Breen dies: 28-II. **Estimated population:** 75 to 120.

1794, Heavy, Stubby Lower Lock, Short Right
Stem (BW-82, S-62, B-54). The obverse has the
usually-seen dramatic break at the left border.

Detail of trephined head.

Obverse: *Date:* 1 very high. 4 high. *Tip of pole points to:* Denticle. *LIBERTY:* IBE wide, I opposite denticle. *Points of distinction:* Hair strands bold and coarse. Lowest lock especially heavy. Locks 4 to 6 weak or incomplete at tips. Usually (but not always) with a large cud break at left border. The obverse is rarely found perfect, but is most often seen with a large "cud" rim break behind the neck, the most dramatic on any 1794 obverse die. *Maris designation:* Trephined Head. *Sheldon designation:* Heavy, Stubby Lower Lock.

Reverse: Same die as preceding.

Notes: This variety is known from EF to Mint State, but is a rarity at any high level. Trephined Head refers to the marked depression in the hair above the highest lock, suggesting that Miss Liberty's skull had been drilled with a saw to remove a circular disc of bone, thus relieving pressure on the brain, from a blood clot, for example.[18]

1794, Fallen 4 in Date (also With Button on Cap) • BW-84, S-63, B-37.
Breen dies: 19-X. *Estimated population:* 500 to 750.

1794, Fallen 4 in Date (also With Button on Cap) (BW-84, S-63, B-37).

Detail showing the "Fallen 4," more properly designated as "High 9."

Obverse: Date: 1 very high. 9 very high, creating illusion of "Fallen 4." The 17 and 4 are about on the same level. *Tip of pole points to:* Space between denticles, and nearly touches denticles. *LIBERTY:* L distant from cap, by the width of the letter L, doubled denticle opposite upper left of I, T over forehead, only die with this characteristic. *Points of distinction:* Tiny dot ("button") on outside of lower left of cap—as also seen on BW-74—but in the present instance the button is often overlooked. Some denticles crude and irregular. Some light clash marks are seen. Probably the most distinctive of the 1794 obverse dies, perhaps cut by a mechanic rather than an engraver. George Clapp called this the Drunken Diecutter's Obverse.

Reverse: Berries left and right: 6-5. Berries near bow are tiny. *Upright of second T of STATES opposite:* Denticle, slightly left of its center. *Fraction:* Bar wide and extends beyond denominator; touches ribbon on right. Numerator very low with 00 running into border. *Points of distinction:* Lettering extremely close to denticles all around. The BW-59 and BW-84 reverses are the only ones of the year with smaller letters than the others. Denticles heavy and crude. Amateurish workmanship overall, matching the only obverse die mated with this reverse. Some light clash marks are seen.[19] Remarkably, this reverse die is a reworking of 1793, Bisecting Obverse Crack, Liberty Cap (BW-27), and other combinations of this die employed in 1793.[20]

Notes: The highest grades this variety is found in are AU and Mint State (unique).

1794, Fallen 4 in Date (also With Button on Cap)		Cert	Avg	%MS
		(a)		
AG-3	G-4	VG-8		F-12
$330	$510	$730		$1,120
VF-20		EF-40		AU-50
$2,420		$6,330		$12,250

a. Included in certified population for 1794, Head of 1794.

1794, Shielded Hair • BW-86, S-NC-6, B-49. *Breen dies:* 26-EE. ***Recorded population:*** 2.

1794, Shielded Hair (BW-86, S-NC-6, B-49).

Obverse: Date: 1 very high, barely touches hair. 4 high. *Tip of pole points to:* Denticle. *LIBERTY:* BER slightly wide, R leans right, I opposite left part of denticle. *Points of distinction:* Denticles deep and heavy at lower left, in effect protecting the hair. Strands of hair are bold and coarse. Tips of third to seventh locks in nearly a straight line. *Maris designation:* Shielded Hair (Maris knew this die from the variety next described).

Reverse: Berries left and right: 5-7 (per Breen). *Upright of second T of STATES opposite:* Denticle, slightly to left of its center. *Fraction:* Numerator tilts right and does not touch bar. Bar from right edge of 1 to nearly center of second 0. Second 0 low. *Points of distinction:* The die is sunken at the center, causing the coin to be raised and the raised part to wear very quickly. There is a crack from the border between D of UNITED and S, extending into the field.

Notes: Both examples are Fine. Discovered by Walter Breen in August 1957, at which time he was the main staff cataloger for the New Netherlands Coin Company.

1794, Shielded Hair, Missing Fraction Bar • BW-87, S-64, B-50. *Breen dies:* 26-FF. ***Estimated population:*** 60 to 75.

1794, Shielded Hair, Missing Fraction Bar (BW-87, S-64, B-50).

Detail of fraction with missing horizontal bar.

Obverse: Same die as preceding.

Reverse: Berries left and right: 7-7. *Upright of second T of STATES opposite:* Denticle, slightly to right of its center. *Fraction:* No fraction bar, one of the most famous reverse dies of the era. *Points of distinction:* Denticles heavy and somewhat pointed. In its late state, the die is bulged at the center and a crack extends from the border through the D of UNITED, continuing inward.

Notes: This variety occurs in Mint State, but is exceedingly rare as such. This variety is widely listed, including in the regular edition of the *Guide Book of United States Coins*, and is one of the most desired rarities of 1794.

1794, Shielded Hair, Missing Fraction Bar		Cert	Avg	%MS
		(a)		

AG-3	G-4	VG-8	F-12
$420	$670	$925	$2,070

VF-20	EF-40		AU-50
$4,580	$9,330		$23,330

a. Included in certified population for 1794, Head of 1794.

1794, Shielded Hair, Short Stems to Wreath • BW-88, S-65, B-51. *Breen dies:* 26-GG. **Estimated population:** Thousands.

1794, Shielded Hair, Short Stems to Wreath (BW-88, S-65, B-51).

Detail of numerator touching fraction bar.

Obverse: Same die as preceding. *Points of distinction:* Clash marks and cracks develop.

Reverse: *Berries left and right:* 7-6. Berries are large except for tiny fifth and small seventh on left; fifth berry easy to miss.

Upright of second T of STATES opposite: Denticle. *Fraction:* Numerator close to bar. Bar extends from center of 1 to past center of second 0. First 0 low. *Points of distinction:* Short stems to wreath. Found perfect or with light cracks.

Notes: The highest grades this variety is found in are AU and MS-60 (exceedingly rare). This is the commonest of all 1794 cents and by far the most often seen of the Shielded Hair varieties. The name is derived "from the deeply-impressed denticles on the left side which give the variety its name, and in effect 'shield' the hair from wear—making the variety fertile ground for overgrading! The *whole coin's* appearance must be assessed in determining grade. In the case of this particular variety, to fail to do so could leave the buyer the 'proud' owner of a F-15 coin in an EF-40 holder!"[21]

1794, Distant 1, Heavy Figures, Split Pole (on most) • BW-90, S-66, B-58. *Breen dies:* 31-MM. **Estimated population:** 30 to 45.

1794, Distant 1, Heavy Figures, Split Pole (on most) (BW-90, S-66, B-58).

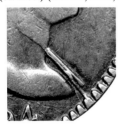

"Split Pole" caused by a die crack.

Obverse: *Date:* 1 low. 4 slightly low. *Tip of pole points to:* Left side of denticle and is distant from it. *LIBERTY:* L close to cap, Y completely over forehead (very unusual), and I opposite left part of denticle. *Points*

of distinction: Hair strands bold and coarse. Found with a perfect die, or with a crack across the neck to the hair, and also from the bottom of the neck across the lowest lock and into the field. Other cracks later develop. *Sheldon designation:* Split Pole Variety, as most (but not all) have a die crack paralleling the pole, making it appear split or doubled. Also, according to Sheldon, Distant 1, Heavy Figures.

Reverse: *Berries left and right:* 6-7. Most berries are very small. *Upright of second T of STATES opposite:* Denticle. *Fraction:* Bar extends from center of 1 to center of second 0. 1 in denominator high. *Points of distinction:* No trace of stems in the unusually narrow space between the ribbon knot and numerator. Clash marks are seen above the wreath and below the ribbon knot.

Notes: VF is the highest grade known for this variety.

1794, MODIFIED HEAD STYLE

BW-94 to BW-99 are in this style. The tip of the lowest lock almost forms a circle, and the tip points upward. The portrait is also in lower relief. Walter Breen attributes this portrait and the finished dies to John Smith Gardner, although there is no documentary support of this. Gardner worked as "acting assistant engraver," later as assistant engraver, until March 31, 1796. Craig Sholley suggests that Robert Scot created all of the portrait hubs, and the modified head dies are those finished by John Smith Gardner with the "circle lock" being his signature. Again, there is no proof of this, but the style change and timing (Scot being involved with silver coinage) are curious.

According to Sheldon, "The heads are a little larger, border, and the whole design is executed in a 'hard, inartistic style, as continued in 1795.' The relief is now almost entirely flat, the hair is braided into five heavy coarse locks, there is little evidence of fine engraving, the features suggest no expression other than a grim stare, or as Maris put it, a Roman stare. He called these the *Roman Plicae.*"

The preceding may be a bit harsh, as these cents—as well as those of 1795 and 1796, continuing the slightly modified design—are highly appreciated. However, the character is changed somewhat, as continued to happen with still later designs, as die making became more routine and less individually artistic.

There are five obverse dies. Check the lower lock first to be sure that a coin is a member of this class. Then check the obverse features, then verify by checking the reverse possibilities, for which there are three dies.

1794, "Marred Hair and Cheek," Lowest Lock Nearly a Circle • BW-94, S-67, B-59. *Breen dies:* 32-MM. **Estimated population:** 300 to 400.

1794, "Marred Hair and Cheek," Lowest Lock Nearly a Circle (BW-94, S-67, B-59).

Obverse: *Date:* 1 closer to curl than to 7. 4 centered. Date widely spaced. *Tip of pole points to:* Denticle, and is not close to it.

LIBERTY: L separated from cap by about the same distance that the bases of I and B are separated. *Points of distinction:* Marks on portrait from contact with the reverse die. End of lower lock nearly a circle, but incomplete. Found perfect or with three faint die cracks. *Maris designation:* Roman Plica. *Sheldon designation:* Marred Hair and Cheek.

Reverse: Same die as preceding.

Notes: This variety is known in Mint State.

1794, Bisecting Obverse Die Crack • BW-95, S-68, B-60. *Breen dies:* 33-MM. *Estimated population:* 45 to 60.

1794, Bisecting Obverse Die Crack (BW-95, S-68, B-60). The bisecting obverse crack is light on this example.

Obverse: *Date:* 1 much closer to 7 than to curl. Tip of 7 low and above denticle. 4 high. *Pole points to:* Left side of denticle. *LIBERTY:* L close to cap. IB wide. *Points of distinction:* Lower lock forms a nearly complete loop ("circle" so called). Appears with a bisecting crack from 8 o'clock to 2 o'clock that varies from very light to heavy.

Reverse: Same die as preceding. *Points of distinction:* Light clash marks are seen.

Notes: The highest grades this variety is known in are EF and AU, and it is rare at either level. Unknown to Maris. First publicized in Édouard Frossard's 23rd Sale, August 3, 1882, lot 548.

1794, Lower Lock a Circle • BW-96, S-69, B-61. *Breen dies:* 34-MM. **Estimated population:** 300 to 400.

1794, Lower Lock a Circle (BW-96, S-69, B-61).

A complete "circle" is formed
at the end of the lower lock.

Obverse: Date: 1 about equidistant from curl and 7. 4 slightly high. 1 was first punched in an inverted position, then corrected (trace of serif as tiny spine at upper-right side of final 1 is sometimes visible). *Pole points to:* Space between denticles. *LIBERTY:* L separated from cap slightly more than the same distance that the bases of I and B are separated. IBER wide. *Points of distinction:* Lower lock forms a complete loop ("circle" so called) by virtue of a tiny spine connecting it to the main lock.

Reverse: Same die as preceding. *Points of distinction:* Dr. Sheldon knew of a single example with a horizontal, bisecting die crack across the reverse, passing through the first T of STATES, the E of CENT, and the second A of AMERICA.

Notes: This variety is known in Mint State.

1794, Lower Lock a Circle • BW-97, S-70, B-62. *Breen dies:* 34-NN. **Estimated population:** 750 to 1,000.

1794, Lower Lock a Circle (BW-97, S-70, B-62).

Obverse: Same die as preceding. Lower lock forms a complete loop ("circle" so called). *Points of distinction:* The die develops crack from denticle down to between TY, eventually to the face.

Reverse: Berries left and right: 6-7. *Upright of second T of STATES opposite:* Denticle, slightly to the left of its center. *Fraction:* Bar extends from center of 1 to center of second 0. 1 in denominator high. Denominator close to denticles. *Points of distinction:* Three leaves (the center one a protruding tip) under D of UNITED. C of AMERICA tilted right. Some injury is seen at the lower right of the wreath. First and last part of border inscription closer to denticles than other lettering.

Notes: This variety is known in Mint State.

1794 • BW-98, S-71, B-63. *Breen dies:* 35-NN. ***Estimated population:*** 750 to 1,000.

1794 (BW-98, S-71, B-63).

Detail showing the curious raised lines on the eyebrow and nose.

Obverse: Date: 1 closer to curl than to 7. 94 close. 4 slightly high. *Pole points to:* Denticle. *LIBERTY:* L close to cap. LI closer than are other letters. *Points of distinction:* Raised parallel die lines at nose and eyebrow (best seen on high-grade coins). The obverse is found perfect and also with a light crack from the border through the tip of the cap and the top of LIBE. Some later coins have other cracks as well. Clash marks are seen in front of the chin and neck, with some traces of AMERICA in the upper field of the obverse on some.

Reverse: Same die as preceding. *Points of distinction:* Clash marks are seen.

Notes: This variety is known Mint State, and is rare as such.

1794 • BW-99, S-NC-3, B-64. *Breen dies:* 36-OO. ***Recorded population:*** 2.

1794 (BW-99, S-NC-3, B-64).

Obverse: Date: 1 high under lowest lock and closer to curl than to 7. 4 high. *Pole points to:* Space between denticles. *LIBERTY:* L about as close to cap as it is to I. IBE very wide. *Points of distinction:* Tips of four upper locks of hair are in a straight line. Top of 1 very close to hair above it.

Reverse: Berries left and right: 6-7. *Upright of second T of STATES opposite:* Denticle, slightly to the left of its center. *Fraction:* Bar extends from upper right of 1 to near center of second 0. In the denominator, 10 widely spaced, 0's lean slightly right. *Points of distinction:* Some letters in AMERICA very close to denticles. Two leaves under D of UNITED. Tip of highest leaf on left points to highest leaf on right, slightly below its tip. Short stem on berry under left upright of M of AMERICA. A light crack is seen from the D of UNITED extending upward to the wreath.

Notes: The two pieces are Fine-12, per conservative grading, (Daniel W. Holmes Jr. Collection) and G-6 (American Numismatic Society). Unknown to Maris. Discovered by Ebenezer Gilbert in the early 1900s.

1794, With Head Style of 1795

BW-101 is the only 1794 issue with this style. The tip of the lowest lock is short and points downward. This design is continued in 1795, earning it the designation *Head of 1795.*

Typical values for 1794, Exact Head of 1795, cents.

1794, Exact Head of 1795	Cert	Avg	%MS
	45	31.9	11%

AG-3	G-4	VG-8	F-12	VF-20	EF-40	AU-50
$300	$450	$660	$850	$2,375	$4,800	$8,500

1794, Exact Head of 1795, Tip of Lowest Lock Points Downward •
BW-101, S-72, B-65. *Breen dies:* 37-OO. **Estimated population:** 500 to 750.

1794, Exact Head of 1795, Tip of Lowest Lock Points Downward (BW-101, S-72, B-65).

Obverse: Date: 179 widely spaced, 94 close. 17 very close to border. *Pole points to:* Denticle. *LIBERTY:* L nearly touches cap. LI and ER close. *Points of distinction:* Tip of lowest lock points downward; no curl. Only 1794 die with this feature. Most show a die crack from the rim to upper left of Y, to lower right of T, to hair. *Maris designation:* '95 Head.

Reverse: Same die as preceding. *Points of distinction:* Found perfect or with a crack from the border diagonally through D of UNITED to the wreath stem.

Notes: The highest grades this variety is known in are AU and Mint State, and it is rare so fine. Walter Breen suggests that these were delivered on December 30, 1794, along with some examples of the preceding variety. This makes the assumption that this, the most modern of 1794 dies, was part of the last pair used, a theory not necessarily consistent with Mint practice of the era.

Numismatic Notes: *Dickeson's 1859 comments about 1794 cents:* Montroville W. Dickeson's *American Numismatical Manual,* 1859, included this about the cents dated 1794:

Of this emission we have discovered but one type; of which 26 varieties have come under our notice, which may be determined mainly by reference to the variations of those of 1793. These cents are somewhat thicker than those that preceded them, the weight of each being increased by about 17 grains;[22] the hair of the goddess, also, does not recede so much from the forehead. The planchets from which they were struck were of good copper, and the milling of the edges being more prominent has protected them from the effect of abrasion, and hence they are frequently found in a fine state of preservation. They are quite plenty, the number issued by the Mint amounted, according to the official statement, to 12,513,300;[23] and the number of dies in a single year excites surprise, the preparation of each die involving much expense.

1795, Liberty Cap

Circulation mintage, Lettered Edge (estimated): 37,000.
Circulation mintage, Plain Edge (estimated): 501,500.

The cents of 1795 are an interesting study in that they comprise several widely differing varieties, but the number of die combinations is small compared to the year before or the year after. All are of the Liberty Cap design with a wreath reverse, similar to the general style of 1794. R.W. Julian and Craig Sholley suggest that the portrait and wreath hubs were likely made by Mint engraver Robert Scot. Some of, or perhaps all of, the working dies were finished by assistant engraver John Smith Gardner, as Scot—as the chief engraver—would have been addressing the silver and gold coinage, which was politically more urgent, himself. The historical records, along with the fact that the dies appear to be hand cut and quite different in design from other Mint products, strongly suggest that the Jefferson Head cents were made outside of the Mint by a man named John Harper.

In this year, the Mint had been busy with silver and gold coin production and with problems arising from the making of dies. The first shipment of cents of this date, amounting to 37,000 coins, was made on December 1, 1795. This is widely given as the entire mintage figure for the lettered edge type, but there is no way to know if it is accurate, as the present-day rarity of lettered-edge coins suggests a higher figure.

Early issues are on thick planchets with lettered edges and a statutory weight of 208 grains, The price of copper was rising in the market, and the direction was given by President Washington on December 27 that henceforth the weight should be reduced to 168 grains. The new coins were made on thinner planchets with plain edges. From December 28 to 31, some 45,000 cents were struck of the new standard. These were delivered on January 1, 1796. From January 16 to March 31, 1796, five more deliveries took place, presumably of 1795-dated coins, amounting to 456,500 cents, giving a total of 501,500 thin-planchet coins of 1795 in all. Afterward there was a long interval before more coins were struck. Dr. Sheldon suggests that this was because new dies were being engraved for the 1796 cents. Julian and Sholley state that Mint records show that the facility was very busy with silver and gold coinage at this time.

The cents of 1795 were sent to banks throughout the country. Prior to this all the United States Mint coins, according to Frank H. Stewart, had been issued only locally in Philadelphia.

One of the thin-planchet varieties was made with a completely reeded edge, as on gold coins of the era, the only large copper cent of this format. The reason it was made is unknown.

The most curious cents of the year are the so-called Jefferson Heads. George H. Clapp and Howard R. Newcomb, in *The United States Cents of the Years 1795, 1796, 1797, and 1800*, discussed the Jefferson Head cents at some length, noting that "the late David Proskey was one of our best-informed students of the large cents of the United States," referencing Proskey's comment from the *Coin Collector's Journal*, March 1880:

> This so-called "Jefferson Head" cent was probably named for the same reason as the Guinea pigs (because they did not come from Guinea, and they are not pigs); the portrait on the piece does not resemble that of Jefferson, nor did he have aught to do with the issue, and last, but not least, *it is not a cent*; but is undoubtedly a counterfeit of the cent of 1795, and was struck somewhere about 1803. The workmanship and style of every portion of the piece show that the dies were never executed at the U.S. Mint; the hair alone would be sufficient to condemn it, no artist employed in the mint since its

establishment would have engraved such a stiff unnatural mass after having for models the beautiful wavy locks which adorn the earlier coins; the figures and letters are totally unlike any used on the cents; the fraction 1/100 is of the size figures found on the issue of 1803; the wreath with its lobster claw leaves and three-looped bow furnishes more evidence of the inexpert tool of an imitator who had before him different types of cents and engraved the least difficult part of each; the short and narrow serrated border on the reverse is unlike any used in 1795, while the absence of the border ornamentation on the obverse, even on the best of them, would indicate that a worn cent was copied. . . .

Dr. Sheldon noted:

> By some the *Jefferson* cents have been regarded as contemporary counterfeits, but others have thought it more likely that these coins were the result of a sort of whimsical experiment on the part of some Mint employee who may have been caricaturing, or merely have been "idly trying his hand." I am inclined to this latter view. At any rate the coins are of entirely different design from any of the regular cents, and they possess quite a personality of their own. Moreover, they certainly circulated as cents, for many of the specimens are in well worn condition, and for a long time the Jefferson has been looked upon with favor by cent collectors—at least as a mystery and a curiosity. . . .

Walter Breen, largely drawing upon information unearthed by R.W. Julian, created a chapter on them for his *Encyclopedia of Early United States Cents 1793–1814:* "Harper's 'Jefferson' Cents."[24] It was revealed that John Harper, a mechanic and saw maker with a factory near Trenton, New Jersey, had visited the Mint during a time when the institution was having problems and Congress had mounted an inquiry into its operations.[25] He sought to obtain a private contract to produce coins.

At his own expense, Harper prepared a coining press and had cent dies cut to produce a quantity of copper coins, examples of which were given to the Congressional committee. Mint Director Elias Boudinot confiscated Harper's dies, but offered him the position of assistant coiner, which the latter declined. By inference, Breen suggests that what were later called Jefferson Head cents were the samples prepared by Harper. Necessarily, they were of different workmanship than the Mint products. As to whether Harper's proposal coins and the Jefferson Heads are one and the same, this can only be assumed, as there is no specific documentation.

While the panorama of 1795 cent varieties is small and the varieties quite diverse, among these are several major rarities, including the Reeded Edge and Jefferson Head issues. Accordingly, most collectors will be content with the less expensive and more available issues.

Typical grades for the Lettered Edge or early issues tend to be low, and the coins are often dark or porous. In contrast, most Plain Edge cents of the typically seen varieties are on smooth planchets of high quality, although relatively few are perfectly centered. The Reeded Edge and Jefferson Head coins exist only in lower grades.

Lettered Edge Varieties

Typical values for 1795, Lettered Edge.
Rare varieties may be worth more.

1795, Lettered Edge		Cert	Avg	%MS
		48	33.4	15%

AG-3	G-4	VG-8	F-12	VF-20	EF-40	AU-50	MS-60BN	MS-63BN
$275	$410	$625	$1,290	$2,290	$6,330	$9,580	$19,170	$39,000

1795, LIBER-TY Hyphenated, 5 Does Not Touch Neck, ONE / CENT High, Lettered Edge • BW-1, S-73, B-1. *Breen dies:* 1-A. *Estimated population:* 60 to 75.

1795, LIBER-TY Hyphenated, 5 Does Not Touch Neck, ONE / CENT High, Lettered Edge (BW-1, S-73, B-1).

Detail showing the die crack appearing as a hyphen in LIBER-TY.

Obverse: *Date:* Serif of 1 close to hair, upper right of 5 close to but distinctly separated from the neck. Base of 5 centered over a denticle. Date distant from border. *Pole points to:* Denticle, slightly left of its center. *LIBERTY:* Always found with the hyphen-like die crack of LIBER-TY, the other parts of which are within the base of the R and extend to the T. BE and RT wide. Upright of T over junction of hair and forehead.

Reverse: ONE / CENT high in wreath. Single leaf to each side of wreath apex. Two leaves opposite D of UNITED. Leaf slightly more than half over E of ONE. Found perfect and later with a crack from the top of U to N to the base of I to below TE to D and beyond. Another delicate crack is sometimes seen from the center of F in OF to the first A of AMERICA to the base of ME to R to the top of I to the rim over C.

Notes: The highest grades this variety is found in are VF and EF, and it is a rarity at either level. First identified by Sylvester S. Crosby and published in J.W. Haseltine's catalog of Crosby's collection, June 1883. Usually seen in low grades.

1795, Top of 5 Overlaying the Neck, ONE / CENT High, Lettered Edge • BW-2, S-74, B-2. *Breen dies:* 2-A. *Estimated population:* 160 to 200.

1795, Top of 5 Overlaying the Neck, ONE / CENT High, Lettered Edge (BW-2, S-74, B-2).

Detail of the date. Note the top of the 5 showing its overlay on the bottom edge of the neck.

Obverse: *Date:* Top of 1 close to hair, but serif distant from curl to the left. Top of 5 high and into the neck, showing flag of 5 overlaying the neck (not buried in it). *Pole points to:* Denticle, slightly right of its center. Tip of pole shallow. *LIBERTY:* Widely spaced. B leans right. Upright of T above junction of hair and forehead. *Points of distinction:* Found perfect and with a crack from the rim below 95, to the top of the 9, and to the neck.

Reverse: Same as preceding. Now, the cracks are more advanced, and on some coins a new crack is seen across TES and beyond. Sometimes cracks are nearly all around the border.

Notes: This variety is known in Mint State. Lot 500 of the Eliasberg Collection Sale, 1996, offered an example of this variety (cataloged by Mark Borckardt) described as:

1795 Lettered Edge. S-74. Low Rarity-4. VF-35. Sharpness of AU-50. Strike: Well centered and sharply detailed. Surfaces: Olive brown obverse with lighter tan reverse. Lightly porous and burnished with the appearance of having been lightly etched. Pedigree: William Cutler Atwater, B. Max Mehl, June 11, 1946, Lot 18 $57.50; Louis E. Eliasberg, Sr.

The original Mehl commentary is illustrative of why it is exceedingly difficult to make modern conclusions about the grade of a coin based on an old-time listing, this from the Atwater catalog:

> Extremely fine, although I doubt if the coin has ever been in circulation. Was purchased as an Uncirculated specimen. Just the barest touch of cabinet friction with unusually sharp impression. Medium olive surface on obverse and very light brown on reverse. Very rare so choice.

1795, 3 Leaves at Apex, ONE / CENT Slightly High, Lettered Edge
• BW-3, S-75, B-3. *Breen dies:* 2-B. **Estimated population:** 300 to 400.

1795, 3 Leaves at Apex, ONE / CENT Slightly High, Lettered Edge (BW-3, S-75, B-3).

Obverse: Same as preceding. *Points of distinction:* Cracks as on the preceding, and with a delicate crack across the tops of RITE to the rim opposite the mouth.

Reverse: ONE / CENT fairly high. At the apex, single leaf left and double to the right, this being definitive for Lettered Edge cents of this date. *Points of distinction:* There is a crack from the rim at the left through the top of ME of AMERICA. Buckling is later seen at this point.

Notes: This variety is known in Mint State. This variety is often granular or on defective planchets. The National Numismatic Collection in the Smithsonian has a Mint State coin overstruck on a Talbot, Allum & Lee token, plain edge except for OF showing from the original T.A.&L. cent.

1795, LIBERTY Not Hyphenated, 5 Touches Neck, 2 Leaves at Apex, ONE / CENT High, Lettered Edge • BW-4, S-76a, B-4a. *Breen dies:* 3-C.
Estimated population: 45 to 60.

1795, LIBERTY Not Hyphenated, 5 Touches Neck, 2 Leaves at Apex, ONE / CENT High, Lettered Edge (BW-4, S-76a, B-4a).

Detail of date. The top of 5 touches the neck.

Obverse: Date: Serif of 1 close to hair, upper right of 5 touches the neck. Base of 5 centered over a denticle, slightly to the left of its center. Date distant from border. *Pole points to:* Denticle, slightly left of its center. *LIBERTY:* L almost touches cap. LI close. Upright of T over hair to left of forehead. *Points of distinction:* Multiple clash marks develop.

Reverse: ONE / CENT high in wreath. Single leaf to each side of wreath apex. Three leaves opposite D of UNITED. Leaf completely over E of ONE ending above right upright of N. *Points of distinction:* Multiple clash marks develop.

Notes: The variety is known in EF to Mint State, and is exceedingly rare at these levels. Some are struck on thin planchets; one of these was graded MS-70 by Dr. Sheldon, but now is graded MS-63.[26]

Plain Edge Varieties

Typical values for 1795, Plain Edge.
Rare varieties may be worth more.

1795, Plain Edge		Cert	Avg	%MS
		209	28.7	11%

AG-3	G-4	VG-8	F-12	VF-20	EF-40	AU-50	MS-60BN	MS-63BN
$190	$320	$480	$960	$1,490	$4,250	$7,000	$10,170	$24,000

1795, RTY Widely Spaced, ONE / CENT High, Plain Edge • BW-5, S-NC-2, B-5. *Breen dies:* 4-C. *Recorded population:* 2.

1795, RTY Widely Spaced, ONE / CENT High, Plain Edge (BW-5, S-NC-2, B-5).

Detail showing part of the word "YORK" and other lettering from the Talbot, Allum & Lee undertype.

Obverse: Date: 1 close to hair, tip of 5 pierces neck. 79 very close, 17 slightly less close, 95 widest in date. *Pole points to:* Space between denticles. *LIBERTY:* Not easily discernible. Breen says RTY widely spaced.

Reverse: Same as preceding.

Notes: Discovered by Walter Breen in a consignment for Lester Merkin's sale of March 1969; AG-3. A second example was found in 1993; Fair-2. Both are struck over Talbot, Allum & Lee cents.

1795, LIBERTY Not Hyphenated, 5 Touches Neck, 2 Leaves at Apex, ONE / CENT High, Plain Edge • BW-8, S-76b, B-4b. *Breen dies:* 3-C. *Estimated population:* Thousands.

Obverse: Same as preceding. *Points of distinction:* Found perfect, as on the Lettered Edges, and also in a later state with a fine crack from the rim at the left of the 1, to the tip of the second hair lock, to the cap, and back to the rim. Sometimes swellings are seen in the left and right field.

Reverse: Same as preceding. *Points of distinction:* Found perfect on early impressions, later with the die crumbling at OF and at the N of ONE and the back of CENT. On some rare examples, a rim break obliterates part of R and all of IC. After most of these had been struck, "the obverse was reground, leaving the pole weaker and severing the second lock from the hair, together with the upper half of the third lock" (Sheldon's comment).

Notes: This variety is known in Mint State. Misstruck, off-center, etc., coins are not rare. Walter Breen calls it the commonest of the Liberty Cap cents.

1795, 5 Touches Neck, ONE / CENT Centered, Dot Within First A of AMERICA, Plain Edge • BW-9, S-77, B-6. *Breen dies:* 3-D. *Estimated population:* 300 to 400.

1795, 5 Touches Neck, ONE / CENT Centered, Dot Within First A of AMERICA, Plain Edge (BW-9, S-77, B-6).

Detail showing the tiny raised dot in the first A of AMERICA.

Obverse: Same as described under BW-4. *Points of distinction:* Found perfect and also

with swelling in the left and right fields, later with a crack extending from the shoulder above the date to the cap and border.

Reverse: Two leaves at wreath apex. ONE / CENT centered within wreath; C low. Five groups of three leaves in the left branch, four groups in the right. Raised dot within upper space of first A of AMERICA. *Points of distinction:* Found perfect and also with many delicate cracks, also with weakening at OF, at NI, and at CENTS, and flattening of most of the leaves in the wreath. This die must have been injured severely by contact with some hard object.

Notes: The highest grades this variety occurs in are AU and Mint State (unique).

1795, ONE / CENT Centered, Dot Within First A of AMERICA, Plain Edge • BW-10, S-NC-3, B-7. *Breen dies:* 3-E. *Recorded population:* 4.

1795, ONE / CENT Centered, Dot Within First A of AMERICA, Plain Edge (BW-10, S-NC-3, B-7).

Obverse: Same as preceding. Now relapped so as to remove many details.

Reverse: Leaf tip under lower-left serif of T of STATES. Rightmost leaf tip of pair to left of O of ON is about halfway up the O. Pair of leaves to left of C of CENT extend nearly to its top; berry above left-most leaf in pair. *Points of distinction:* A bulge develops at the top, probably early in the life of the die, accounting for the rarity of the variety.

Notes: Grades are Poor-1 to AG-3. Discovered by Jack H. Beymer in July 1979 and published in April 1980.

1795, Pole Connected to Denticle, ONE / CENT Centered, Plain Edge • BW-11, S-78, B-8. *Breen dies:* 5-F. ***Estimated population:*** Thousands.

1795, Pole Connected to Denticle, ONE / CENT Centered, Plain Edge (BW-11, S-78, B-8).

Detail showing date and the pole connecting to a denticle.

Obverse: Date: Serif of 1 close to hair, upper right of 5 touches the neck. Base of 5 centered over a denticle left of its center. Date distant from border. Compare to BW-4. *Pole points to:* Denticle, and runs into it, a definitive feature. *LIBERTY:* L distant from cap. All letters close. T well over hair to left of forehead. *Points of distinction:* Found perfect and with a faint crack under the jaw near the neck. On some examples the die is slightly eroded at the top of the 5, connecting that digit to the neck.

Reverse: Leaf tip under upright of T of STATES. Rightmost leaf tip of pair to left of O of ON is about even with the base of the O. Pair of leaves to left of C of CENT extend about halfway up the letter; no berry above leftmost leaf in pair. *Points of distinction:* Multiple clash marks are seen.

Notes: This variety is known in Mint State.

1795, Date Spaced 1 79 5, Reeded Edge • BW-13, S-79, B-9. *Breen dies:* 6-G. ***Recorded population:*** 5.

1795, Date Spaced 1 79 5, Reeded Edge (BW-13, S-79, B-9), a rarity. The finest known example.

Obverse: Date: Spaced as 1 79 5 with 79 close. 1 close to hair and 5 close to neck. *Pole points to:* Left side of denticle. *LIBERTY:* BE wide. Top of T low. Bottom of Y low. *Points of distinction:* Upright of Y over junction between hair and forehead.

Reverse: Three leaves at apex. 14 leaves to the left, 18 to the right. 7 berries on each branch. Triple leaf below OF. This die was also used to coin 1796, Three Leaves Opposite OF, Single Leaf Over O of ONE, Reverse of 1794 (BW-43), and 1796, Three Leaves Opposite OF, Reverse of 1794 (BW-44, BW-45, BW-46, BW-47, and BW-48).

Notes: The finest is the Daniel W. Holmes Jr. coin variously graded as VG-8 and 10, other examples are Good and VG. With a fully reeded edge, unique among early cents, but similar to the edge of gold coins of the era. Struck in a collar, for reasons unknown. The reeding is not entirely regular (based on an examination by Jack Robinson in January 1989). Today this is one of the most "celebrated" varieties among early cents, in terms of collector comment. An example in any grade, if shown at an EAC meeting, is bound to attract interest. One example is a holed brockage, ex Homer K. Downing and Charles Ruby.

Numismatic Notes: The first publication of this variety seems to have been in the W.A. Lilliendahl Collection that was cataloged by William Harvey Strobridge with assistance from Edward Cogan, which was sold in 1,232 lots from May 26 to 28, 1862, in one of the most popular auction venues of the time: Bangs, Merwin & Co., Irving Building, 594–596 Broadway, New York.

The cent was described as, "1795 Thick die, milled edge, in excellent preservation, and excessively rare." This coin is not traced today, as evidenced by all known examples being in very low grades.[27]

THE JEFFERSON HEADS

1795, Jefferson Head, Lettered Edge • BW-15a and b, S-NC-1, B-10a and b. *Breen dies:* 7-H. *Recorded population:* 3.

1795, Jefferson Head, Lettered Edge (BW-15a, S-NC-1, B-10a).

Obverse: "Jefferson Head" portrait of Miss Liberty. No ribbon. Small date. Only the one die for the various Jefferson Head varieties.

Reverse: Highest leaf pair on the left at apex is mostly over the lower leaf pair on right side of apex. Leaf above O of ONE points to the left, past the tops of the letters. *Points of distinction:* In the late state, two cracks at the left.

Notes: Two minor edge variations: BW-15a (1 known) with FOR in large letters and leaf after DOLLAR pointing downward. Discovered in June 1974 by Anthony Terranova and Joseph Rose. Fine-12 with obverse scratch. BW-15b (2 known), occurring in VF-20 and Fair-2.

1795, Jefferson Head, Lettered Edge • BW-16a, S-NC-4, B-11a. *Breen dies:* 7-I. *Recorded population:* 2.

1795, Jefferson Head, Lettered Edge (BW-16a, S-NC-4, B-11a).

Obverse: Same as preceding.

Reverse: Highest leaf pair on left at apex is slightly over a leaf on the right side of the apex. Leaf above O of ONE points to N.

Notes: Lettered edge. Leaf after DOLLAR points upward. Discovered by Curtis Ray Whitson in August 1991. G-5 (Daniel W. Holmes Jr. Collection) and Poor, holed.

1795, Jefferson Head, Plain Edge • BW-16b, S-80, B-11b. *Breen dies:* 7-I. *Estimated population:* 45 to 60.

1795, Jefferson Head, Plain Edge (BW-16b, S-80, B-11b).

Obverse: Same as preceding.

Reverse: Same as preceding.

Notes: VF is the highest grade known. This is the plain-edged version and the only readily collectible example of the Jefferson Head, although it is rare. Beware of electrotypes (see Numismatic Notes). The finest is VF-35 (per Breen). One example is known struck over a Liberty Cap cent with Lettered Edge, earlier in the Homer K. Downing Collection, later in the Daniel W. Holmes Jr. Collection.

Numismatic Notes: W.E. Woodward in his sale of the Levick, Emery, Ilsley, and Abbey Collections, October 18 through 22, 1864, offered lot 671, "1795 Sometimes called the 'Jefferson Head,'" an early use of this term.

Édouard Frossard's description (*Monograph*, 1879):

> Jefferson Head. The head is entirely different from any variety of this or other dates. The profile is in a nearly straight line from the hair to the point of nose; the lips pouting, the chin pointed, the hair straight, with a few thin locks at the end, one of which forms a long double curl under the bust, and points at 1 in date. There is no band around the hair. The legend LIBERTY in large letters, widely spaced, is equally distant from cap, head and edge. The date between 179 wide, the 5 a little nearer 9. *Reverse:* ONE CENT in centre large; the legend and the fractional denominator also large. The wreath bears large elongated leaves, nearly all double and forked, pointing in every direction, with apparently eleven berries on the left, and twelve on right branch. Struck on a thick planchet; only traces of milling are discernable on the obverse, and but little on reverse. Edge plain; diameter 29 mm.

Mention of an example was printed under "Replies to Correspondents," in *Mason's Coin Collectors' Herald*, March 1880, in answer to a query from A.C.L. of Hartford:

> We sold the celebrated 'Jefferson Head' cent 1795 some years ago to the late A.S. Robinson for $90. It has a queer history. Bought by us for one dollar and a half in 1868, sold to [J. Colvin] Randall for $10, sold by Mr. R. at auction to Mr. Haseltine for $145, thence to Mr. Fewsmith for about the same amount; thence transferred to us in 1872, with the above result. Now owned by a large manufacturer in Massachusetts and valued at $300. We have had three specimens, all poor—besides the latter which is the finest known of the 'Jefferson Head' variety.

Mason had electrotypes made of a coin owned by J. Colvin Randall and offered them for sale for 50¢ each. In that era electrotypes were widely bought and sold as "fillers." The British Museum supplied electrotypes of its coins on special order, and in the early 1900s the American Numismatic Society did the same (without reference here to Jefferson Head cents). Some of Mason's electrotypes survived to the modern era and are occasionally confused with originals.

1795, Jefferson Head, Plain Edge		Cert	Avg	%MS
		1	10.0	0%

AG-3	G-4	VG-8	F-12	VF-20
$13,750	$23,750	$33,330	$56,670	$121,250

1796, Liberty Cap
Circulation mintage (assumed): 109,825.

This was a year of change. It seems that early in 1796 the Mint was busy striking cents from 1795-dated dies. Then came the production of 1796, Liberty Cap, cents, with deliveries extending from May 12 to June 8. These were ostensibly comprised of 109,825 coins—a figure which is per a comment in *Mason's Coin and Stamp Collectors' Magazine*, December 1867. Though *Mason's* is not necessarily a reliable source, in this instance the periodical quoted a Mint officer. The change to the Draped Bust motif began afterward, with the first deliveries of the new design on October 12.

The heads on 1796, Liberty Cap, cents are in slightly higher relief than are those of 1795, in some instances resulting in the reverses being more shallowly defined, as more copper had to flow into the deep obverse die in the coining press. This also had the effect of the reverses wearing down more quickly once the coins were placed into circulation. On many lower-grade 1796 cents in existence today, the obverse is a grade or two higher than the reverse. On the obverse of coins from certain dies, if Miss Liberty is oriented with the profile of her face more or less vertical, the date can be off center to the left. On the same coins, if the date is centered at the bottom, the profile is tilted back.

The reverses are subtly different from earlier Liberty Caps in that the denticles are smaller and the leaves are thinner. All have a single leaf at each side of the wreath apex, the so-called Reverse of 1795. Certain 1796 reverses were later used in 1797 and 1798.

Director Boudinot, on December 22, 1795, suggested to the Secretary of State that planchets be imported, and on March 1, 1796, he ordered ten tons of copper, with the planchets to weigh seven pennyweights, from William L. Coltman of London. In the following October he wrote to Coltman that the planchets had arrived on the *Rebecca* under Captain James Hughes, and were badly executed—having been cut from coarse rolled sheet copper almost as rough as cast iron—and were not clean.[28]

As a class, the 1796, Liberty Cap, cents are scarcer than those of the year before. The quality of the planchets varies, due no doubt to the acquisition of copper from diverse sources. Examples are available in all grades from well worn to the very occasional Mint State. Apart from the basic type, there are no particular varieties that have attracted attention beyond specialists. Among the varieties, some are quite scarce, but none are impossibly rare or expensive. Thus, this is the first year for which the completion of a full set of Liberty Cap die combinations is a possibility.

Typical values for 1796, Liberty Cap.
Rare varieties may be worth more.

1796, Liberty Cap	Cert	Avg	%MS
	141	25.7	11%

G-4	VG-8	F-12	VF-20	EF-40	AU-50	MS-60BN
$430	$640	$1,375	$2,725	$6,000	$13,500	$27,830

1796, No Triple Leaves on Outside of Right Branch • BW-1, S-91, B-1.
Breen dies: 1-A. **Estimated population:** 400 to 500.

1796, No Triple Leaves on Outside
of Right Branch (BW-1, S-91, B-1).

Obverse: Date: 1 below hair. Numerals widely and about evenly spaced, but 96 slightly closer. 6 below neck. *Pole points to:*

Space between denticles. *LIBERTY:* L close to cap. Fairly closely spaced. *Points of distinction:* There is a die bulge from the rim to the nose and in the left field, the intensity of which increases with subsequent strikes. Sometimes there is a crack from the back of the lower hair and another through the center of 6 in the date.

Reverse: Outside triple leaves opposite IT and ED. C of CENT distant and leans right. *Points of distinction:* This variety exists from a perfect die and also with a crack through the second S of STATES and from the rim to I of AMERICA. Similarities between this reverse die and that used to coin BW-2 indicate that BW-1 may have been the first 1796, Liberty Cap, struck, rather than the last, as is often thought.[29]

Notes: This variety is known in Mint State.

1796, Closest Date, Pole Very Close to Bust • BW-2, S-81, B-2. *Breen dies:* 2-B. **Estimated population:** 300 to 400.

1796, Closest Date, Pole Very Close to Bust (BW-2, S-81, B-2).

Obverse: *Date:* 1 barely touches hair. 17 very wide, 79 closer, 96 closest. 6 close to neck. *Pole points to:* Space between denticles, and is very close to the bust. *LIBERTY:* L barely touches the cap. BER wide. *Points of*

distinction: Typically seen with a rough area from the left rim to the cap. Sometimes with a light crack from below the nose to the rim, and another from the rim, past the right of Y, and to the nose.

Reverse: Outside triple leaves opposite IT, ED, and CA. *Points of distinction:* This die was used to coin BW-2 and 1798, Style 2 Hair, Small 8, Style 2 Letters, Reverse of 1795 (BW-3). Relapped in a later state.

Notes: The highest grades for this variety are AU and Mint State (unique). Dr. Sheldon observed diameters from 28 mm to 30.5 mm for this variety.

1796, Closest Date, Pole Very Close to Bust, Triple Leaf Opposite AM • BW-3, S-82, B-3. *Breen dies:* 2-C. **Estimated population:** 75 to 120.

1796, Closest Date, Pole Very Close to Bust, Triple Leaf Opposite AM (BW-3, S-82, B-3).

Obverse: Same as preceding. *Points of distinction:* A faint bulge develops in the field. Some die chips are seen.

Reverse: Outside triple leaves opposite IT, ED, AM, and CA. *Points of distinction:* This die was used to coin BW-3, BW-4, BW-5, and 1798, Style 1 Hair, Large 8, Style 1 Letters, Reverse of 1795 (BW-2). A small crack is from the base of E of AMERICA to the adjacent R.

Notes: The highest grades for this variety are EF and AU. This variety is difficult to find with good eye appeal.

1796, Triple Leaf Opposite AM • BW-4, S-83, B-4. *Breen dies:* 3-C. **Estimated population:** 120 to 160.

1796, Triple Leaf Opposite AM (BW-4, S-83, B-4).

Obverse: *Date:* 1 below hair. 17 very wide, 79 closer, 96 closest. 6 close to neck. *Pole points to:* Denticle. *LIBERTY:* L close to but does not touch the cap. IB wide. Base of Y low. *Points of distinction:* Breen reports only two examples of this variety without the break between the end of the pole and the bust. Examples are known with a rim break from the left of B, along the top of

RTY, and to the rim. Die scaling is seen across the lower edge of the cap and in front of the mouth.

Reverse: Same as preceding. This die was used to coin BW-3, BW-4, BW-5, and

1798, Style 1 Hair, Large 8, Style 1 Letters, Reverse of 1795 (BW-2).

Notes: AU is the highest grade known. This variety is difficult to find with good eye appeal.

1796, Date Slopes Down to the Right • BW-5, S-84, B-5. *Breen dies:* 4-C.
Estimated population: 300 to 400.

1796, Date Slopes Down to the Right (BW-5, S-84, B-5).

Detail showing date sloping down to the right and becoming closer to the denticles.

Obverse: Date: 1 close to hair. Date slopes down to the right so that the 6 is slightly closer to the denticles than to the neck.

Definitive. *Pole points to:* Denticle, and is distant from neck. *LIBERTY:* LIBER wide. T partly over junction between hair and forehead (also definitive). *Points of distinction:* Liberty's mouth is slightly open. Denticles are thin and widely spaced. A sinking of the die caused a swelling at 6. This is the most distinctive die among the 1796 obverses.

Reverse: Same as preceding. This die was used to coin BW-3, BW-4, BW-5, and 1798, Style 1 Hair, Large 8, Style 1 Letters, Reverse of 1795 (BW-2). *Points of distinction:* Sometimes with a crack through the top of the letters in OF.

Notes: This variety is known in Mint State.

1796, Date Slopes Down to the Right • BW-6, S-85, B-6. *Breen dies:* 4-D.
Estimated population: 60 to 75.

1796, Date Slopes Down to the Right (BW-6, S-85, B-6).

Detail of the reverse showing irregularity of the denticles.

Obverse: Same as the preceding.

Reverse: Outside triple leaves opposite UN, IT, ED, and CA. Segment of a leaf covers branch below center of M. Three leaves opposite O of ONE; two leaves near T of CENT; leaf tip under left edge of O in OF. Numerator is too far right above the bar; bar is closer to left ribbon than to the right. Denticles opposite CA and lower are irregular in size and spacing. *Points of distinction:* On a later state the die is relapped, removing some of the lower-relief features.

Notes: This variety can be found in VF to AU, the latter unique. This variety is difficult to find with good eye appeal.

1796, Date Slopes Down to the Right • BW-7, S-86, B-7. *Breen dies:* 4-E. *Estimated population:* 45 to 60.

1796, Date Slopes Down to the Right (BW-7, S-86, B-7).

Obverse: Same as the preceding.

Reverse: Outside triple leaves opposite UN, ED, RI, and CA. Three leaves opposite O of ONE; two leaves near T of CENT; leaf tip far past left edge of O in OF and closer to S.

Notes: The highest grades this variety is found in are EF and AU, extremely rare at either level. This variety is difficult to find with good eye appeal.

1796, Date Slopes Down to the Right • BW-8, S-87, B-8. *Breen dies:* 4-F. *Estimated population:* 300 to 400.

1796, Date Slopes Down to the Right (BW-8, S-87, B-8).

Reverse: Outside triple leaves opposite UN, IT, ED, and A. Two leaves opposite O of ONE; three leaves below T of CENT. *Points of distinction:* This die was used to coin BW-8, BW-9, BW-10, and 1798, Style 1 Hair, Large 8, Style 2 Letter, Reverse of 1795 (BW-1). Multiple clash marks are seen.

Obverse: Same as the preceding. *Points of distinction:* Some later impressions have a light crack from the denticles under 7, across the bust and the end of the pole, in an arc to the border above.

Notes: The highest grades this variety is found in are AU and Mint State (unique).

1796, Club Pole • BW-9, S-88, B-9. *Breen dies:* 5-F. *Estimated population:* 120 to 160.

1796, Club Pole (BW-9, S-88, B-9).

Obverse: Date: About evenly spaced, but 96 slightly closer. 1 near hair, 6 near neck. *Pole points to:* Space between denticles. "Club

Pole" variety, with pole thicker at the end, somewhat like a baseball bat. *LIBERTY:* L touches cap. BE wide. *Points of distinction:* Sometimes with a small crack from the denticles through the right side of 7 to the neck.

Reverse: Same as the preceding. This die was used to coin BW-8, BW-9, BW-10, and 1798, Style 1 Hair, Large 8, Style 2 Letter, Reverse of 1795 (BW-1).

Notes: The variety can be found in are VF to AU, the latter exceedingly rare.

1796 • BW-10, S-89, B-10. *Breen dies:* 6-F. ***Estimated population:*** 300 to 400.

1796 (BW-10, S-89, B-10).

Detail of 6 touching neck.

Obverse: Date: 1 close to hair. Widely spaced, but 96 slightly closer. 6 barely touches neck. *Pole points to:* Space between denticles and is distant from them. *LIBERTY:* IBERT wide. *Points of distinction:* Denticles are large and some are irregular. Clash marks develop and a bulge is seen at the bottom border.

Reverse: Same as the preceding. This die was used to coin BW-8, BW-9, BW-10, and 1798, Style 1 Hair, Large 8, Style 2 Letter, Reverse of 1795 (BW-1). *Points of distinction:* Clash marks develop.

Notes: The finest example of this variety is a unique EF-40. Despite the large population, the finest attainable is only VF or so. Eye appeal is a problem on most examples.

1796 • BW-11, S-90, B-11. *Breen dies:* 6-G. ***Estimated population:*** 30 to 45.

1796 (BW-11, S-90, B-11).

Obverse: Same as the preceding. *Points of distinction:* A rare late state has a crack through the top of LIBER.

Reverse: Outside triple leaves opposite UN, ED, and C. Two leaves opposite O of ONE; two leaves below T of CENT. Numerator 1 is too far right above the bar. Denticles are heavy and closely spaced. *Points of distinction:*

This die was used to coin BW-11 and 1797, Reverse of 1795 (BW-1); 1797, Plain Edge, Wide 1 7 97 Date, Reverse of 1795 (BW-2a); 1797, Gripped Edge, Wide 1 7 97 Date, Reverse of 1795 (BW-2b); 1797, Reverse of 1795, Plain Edges (BW-3a); and 1797, Reverse of 1795, Gripped Edge (BW-3b). This variety exists from a perfect die and also with a short crack above N of ONE. The dies are usually oriented in the same direction.

Notes: This variety can be found in Mint State, and it is extremely rare as such. This is the most difficult 1796, Liberty Cap, to locate in any grade, and as most lack good eye appeal, the challenge is even greater in this respect.

Draped Bust (1796–1807)

**1796, 6 Berries Left and Right, Leaf Tip Opposite D,
Reverse of 1797, Large Fraction (BW-65, S-119, B-40).**

Designer: *Robert Scot.* **Weight:** *168 grains (10.89 grams).*
Composition: *Copper.* **Diameter:** *Average 29 mm.* **Edge:** *Plain.*

The Draped Bust cent made its debut in 1796, following a coinage of Liberty Cap cents the same year. The motif, from a drawing by Gilbert Stuart, was first employed on certain silver dollars of 1795.

The new design proved to be very durable and was used through and including 1807. While the 1799 is a classic rarity and the 1804 is elusive, enough exist of most other dates that finding a choice one will be no problem. As a rule, the earlier dates are scarcer than the later ones. Generally, they are struck on high-quality planchets, many of which were imported from Boulton & Watt, of Birmingham, England.

Most cents of this type are well worn, some nearly smooth. Such levels as Fine and Very Fine are readily available and form the basis of many collections. At the EF and AU levels the coins are progressively scarcer. Mint State coins are rare for most varieties, except for some that were part of the famous Nichols Find (described below).

Striking can vary in quality. Some areas of the denticles are apt to be weak, and on the reverse the higher leaves in the wreath are often lightly defined. This is apt to vary from one variety to another. Though the planchet quality is generally good, many dark and porous coins are in the marketplace. Except for rare die varieties, one can be choosy and cherrypick for quality.

THE NICHOLS FIND

Chances are excellent that if you encounter a Mint State 1796 or 1797 copper large cent, it will be linked by pedigree to the famous Nichols Find (also known as the Goodhue-Nichols Find).

According to numismatic tradition, these pieces came from an original bag of cents obtained in late 1797 or early 1798 by Benjamin Goodhue, who was born in Salem, Massachusetts, in 1748 and died there in 1814. Goodhue, a Federalist, was a representative to Congress from 1789 to 1796 and a senator from 1796 to 1800. He is said to have been the grandfather of Mrs. Nichols.

If Goodhue obtained the pieces at the Mint, it would probably have been after November 21, 1797, for during 1797 coins were only delivered by the coiner to the treasurer from November 22 to December 18. Blank planchets had been imported recently from Matthew Boulton of Birmingham, England, such planchets being remarkable for their high quality (in sharp contrast to those made within the Mint, often from copper of uncertain purity and often irregular). As a result, coins in collections today, and attributed to this hoard, are apt to have particularly smooth and glossy surfaces.

It is believed that Goodhue gave the coins to his daughters, who continued to pass them down in the family. Eventually, they were distributed from the Salem area.

One account quotes a rumor that the coins came from Major C.P. Nichols of Springfield, Massachusetts.[30]

In any event, by 1858 or 1859, the numismatic community was aware of the coins, at which time they traded for about $1 each. By 1863 all of the pieces had been dispersed—apparently by David Nichols—by which time they had a market value of about $3 to $4 apiece.

Another story suggests, citing an erroneous date, that they were dispersed to collectors, "perhaps just prior to 1863," and that "David Nichols of Gallows Hill, near Salem, passed them out at face value."[31]

The assigning of the quantity of 1,000 pieces to the hoard is assumed from Mint records that show in 1797 that the Mint regularly issued cents in bags of 1,000 and boxes of 5,000 coins. As at least several hundred examples are known to exist today, the estimate of 1,000 may be reasonable.

This first-person account by John Robinson, of Salem, Massachusetts, sheds further light on the quantity in this statement, although by the time he saw the coins it is probable that some had already been paid out:

> I began in 1857 with a bright copper cent of that year I found in my mother's purse, and a handful of coins from the Far East from an old sea chest of my father's. Additions were gained by looking over the coins in the tills of the Salem shopkeepers who allowed me to poke over their silver and copper coins unrestricted. The old tollhouse on Beverly Bridge furnished an almost Uncirculated cent of 1823, and a beautiful cent of 1800 over 1799 came from a Salem shoe shop. These were obtained at one cent each.
>
> The older collectors helped us, too, and David Nichols, living near Gallows Hill, would occasionally open the bag of mint-bright cents of 1796 and 1797 and give us one of each. The lot came, it was said, from the Hon. Benjamin Goodhue, who received them in part pay for his services in the U.S. Senate. As I remember them at the time there were about 50 or 60 of each date in the bag.[32]

Today, the typical Nichols Find cent is apt to be glossy brown with somewhat prooflike fields, toned a medium brown. Varieties attributable to this source include 1796, 6 Berries Left and Right, Leaf Tip Opposite D, Reverse of 1797, Large Fraction (BW-65); 1797, Berries: 6-6 (BW-13); and 1797, Closest Date, Berries 6-6 (BW-21).

Examples of 1798, Style 1 Hair, Large 8 Embedded in Drapery (BW-15), which was not in the Nichols Find, appear to have been struck on planchets from the same Boulton lot and were probably made very early in 1798.[33]

Design Details

On the obverse the head of Miss Liberty faces to the right, her hair behind, some tied with a ribbon at the back, and other tresses falling to her shoulder. Her bosom at the lower right is draped in cloth. The letters of LIBERTY are above her head, and the date is between the bust and the bottom border. Denticles are around the border. The same design was used on half cents from 1800 to 1808, as described earlier.

The reverse is of the same general style as that used on the Liberty Cap cents, but somewhat more standardized—this increasingly being the case for most coinage designs as the years progressed and technology became more advanced.

The wreath is open at the top and tied with a ribbon bow below. Some early dies have one leaf to each side of the wreath apex, the so-called Reverse of 1795, but most in this series have one leaf at the upper left and two at the upper right.

Around the outside of the wreath is the inscription UNITED STATES OF AMERICA. At the center in two lines is ONE CENT. The fraction 1/100 is below the ribbon bow. Denticles are around the border.

The portrait and wreath hubs were made by Robert Scot, chief engraver at the Mint, from a drawing by Gilbert Stuart. It appears that various Mint employees assisted in the making of the working dies—apparently including at least one mechanic or other person not skilled as a die sinker, as evidenced by the glaring errors on several different 1802 reverses. Craig Sholley, in his studies of contemporary Mint records, found them incomplete for this period. Accordingly, it is not known if an apprentice or laborer was assigned to the chief coiner's department.

1796, Draped Bust

Circulation mintage (assumed): 363,375.

The first delivery of Draped Bust cents took place in October 1796, according to figures supplied to *Mason's Coin and Stamp Collectors' Magazine*, December 1867, by a Mint official. William E. DuBois and some others at the Mint were interested in the history of the institution at that time, but certain of the information Mint people supplied was not reliable. That said, we can only assume that these figures may be correct, but acknowledge that we have no way of verification. The annual *Report of the Director of the Mint* gave calendar-year figures which often, including for 1796, were not relevant to the actual number of coins struck bearing that date.

Prior to 1836, the Mint often reused serviceable dies (including obverses) from prior years. Also, the Mint would occasionally hold over coins struck at the very end of a year and deliver them in early January of the next. The figures in the *Annual Report of the Director of the Mint* are thus merely the number of coins *delivered* during that year and have little relevance to the actual number of coins bearing any given date. As noted earlier, this created many "mintages" for coins that did not bear the calendar-year date, such as 12,170 half cents struck in 1799 from earlier dies.

Mint Director Robert Maskell Patterson, who served from 1835 to 1851, disliked this practice, feeling that the official figures should represent the date on the coins. He essentially put an end to this arrangement, and (with some exceptions) the figures from 1836 on (especially for copper) do represent the coins struck for that date.

The 1867 account noted that 363,375 Draped Bust (presumably) cents were delivered through and including November 24, 1796. Craig Sholley found that the treasurer's account book corroborates the figure, but gives December 31 as the final delivery date. However, this is an accounting date and not necessarily the exact date the coiner delivered the coins to the treasurer. Also, as Dr. Sheldon pointed out, additional 1796-dated coins were struck in 1797, as evidenced by the fact that their reverses were also used—in an earlier die state—on some cents with 1797 obverses.[34]

Draped Bust cents of this date come in two easily discernible reverse styles: with one leaf at each side of the wreath apex—Reverse of 1795—and with one leaf on the left and two on the right—Reverse of 1794, and also the Reverse of 1797. In the following listing the Reverse of 1795 varieties are listed first, for ease of attribution. The Sheldon and Breen texts comingle them. Certain obverse dies mated with Reverse of 1795 dies were also mated with Reverse of 1797 dies and are listed in the Reverse of 1797 section. As a general rule, denticles on 1796, Draped Bust, cents are not prominent, and some show hardly any denticles at all, this being particularly true of obverses. Obverse denticles tend to be long and thin, while those on the reverse are variously long and thin or short and somewhat pointed.

Cents of this type and date are usually seen in circulated grades, from well worn upward. At the EF level most are rare, and AU and Mint State coins range from very rare to extremely rare. Exceptions are provided by Nichols Find varieties, often seen in Mint State. However the demand for them by seekers of "trophy coins," who are usually not interested in other varieties in lesser grades, has always furnished a strong market when they cross the auction block.

Cents of this date and type are generally rare. Unlike the situation for collectors a generation ago, nearly all are expensive, even at the Good and VG levels. As always, cherrypicking for quality is advised.

ONE LEAF EACH SIDE OF WREATH APEX— 1796 WITH REVERSE STYLE OF 1795

The nearly dozen different varieties can be easily distinguished by checking the obverse first and then the three-leaf clusters on the reverse. Remarkably, each of the different reverses has a different cluster arrangement.

Typical values for 1796, Draped Bust, cents with the Reverse of 1795. Rare varieties may be worth more.

1796, Draped Bust, Reverse of 1795			Cert	Avg	%MS
			19	23.6	5%

G-4	VG-8	F-12	VF-20	EF-40	AU-50	MS-60BN	MS-63BN
$490	$850	$1,580	$2,940	$6,375	$12,875	$19,500	$28,830

1796, Numerals 796 Equidistant From Border, Reverse of 1795 •
BW-15, S-97, B-20. *Breen dies:* 13-J. **Estimated population:** 300 to 400.

1796, Numerals 796 Equidistant From Border, Reverse of 1795 (BW-15, S-97, B-20).

Obverse: Bases of 796 each about the same distance from the border, which is definitive for an obverse mated with a Reverse of 1795. *Points of distinction:* From a perfect

die, but also seen with a crack over TY developing into a rim break and a break at the right rim.

Reverse: Outside triple leaves opposite UN, IT, ED, and CA. Only Style of 1795 reverse with this configuration among 1796 cents. Four berries on each branch. In fraction, first 0 leans right and is distant from 1.

Notes: The highest-known grades for this variety are EF and AU, and it is very rare at these levels.

1796, 96 Close, 6 Does Not Lean Sharply Right, Reverse of 1795 •
BW-16, S-98, B-21. *Breen dies:* 14-J. **Estimated population:** 120 to 160.

1796, 96 Close, 6 Does Not Lean Sharply Right, Reverse of 1795 (BW-16, S-98, B-21).

Obverse: 179 wide, 96 close, 6 does not lean sharply right; knob of 6 is just slightly

farther right than the curve below it; bottom of 9 only slightly higher than bottom of 7 (Compare to BW-32). *Points of distinction:* There is a crack from the rim to the upper right of Y.

Reverse: Same as preceding. *Points of distinction:* Seen with a perfect die and also with a crack at the first A of AMERICA.

Notes: This variety can be found in Mint State, and is very rare so fine.

1796, 96 Close, 6 Does Not Lean Sharply Right, Reverse of 1795 •
BW-17, S-99, B-22. *Breen dies:* 14-K. **Estimated population:** 45 to 60.

1796, 96 Close, 6 Does Not Lean Sharply Right, Reverse of 1795 (BW-17, S-99, B-22).

Obverse: Same as preceding. *Points of distinction:* Some die deterioration is seen at the throat. There is a crack from the rim

to the upper right of Y. Sometimes seen with a crack from the rim behind the shoulder, up through the ribbon to B to the rim.

Reverse: Triple leaf cluster opposite D and ER. Only Style of 1795 reverse with this configuration among 1796 cents.

Notes: VF is the highest grade known. This variety is difficult to find with good eye appeal.

1796, T Over Junction of Hair and Forehead, Reverse of 1795 •
BW-20, S-NC-4, B-23. *Breen dies:* 15-K. **Estimated population:** 30 to 45.

1796, T Over Junction of Hair and Forehead, Reverse of 1795 (BW-20, S-NC-4, B-23).

Obverse: T over junction of hair and forehead, the only obverse die with this feature

mated with a Reverse of 1795, and thus definitive. 17 very close; 796 evenly spaced and slightly wider. *Points of distinction:* This die was used to coin BW-20, BW-40, and BW-53.

Reverse: Same as preceding. *Points of distinction:* On a rare late state there is a crack from the rim to the top of TES.

Notes: VG is the highest grade known.

1796, Date Hyphenated 17-96, Reverse of 1795 • BW-24, S-NC-2,
B-31. *Breen dies:* 19-Q. **Reported population:** 11.

1796, Date Hyphenated 17-96, Reverse of 1795 (BW-24, S-NC-2, B-31). For detail of hyphen see BW-26.

Obverse: Date with hyphen-like flaw causing it to read 17-96. Date widely spaced. 6 close to drapery. Rough patch in the field below the ribbon knot. *Points of distinction:*

This die was used to coin BW-24, BW-25, BW-26, BW-27, BW-55, and BW-56.

Reverse: Outside triple leaves opposite UN, D, ME, and CA. Only Style of 1795 reverse with this configuration among 1796 cents. O in OF slightly low and leans right. Lowest leaf in cluster of three close to junction of AM. 1 of denominator far left and touches or nearly touches ribbon. T of CENT leans slightly to the right.

Notes: The highest grade known is EF (unique), followed by Fine, then VG.

1796, Date Hyphenated 17-96, Reverse of 1795 • BW-25, S-96, B-32.

Breen dies: 19-R. ***Estimated population:*** 20 to 25.

**1796, Date Hyphenated 17-96,
Reverse of 1795 (BW-25, S-96, B-32).
For detail of hyphen, see BW-26.**

Obverse: Same as preceding. *Points of distinction:* This die was used to coin BW-24, BW-25, BW-26, BW-27, BW-55, and BW-56.

Reverse: Outside triple leaves opposite IT, D, and AM. Only Style of 1795 reverse with this configuration among 1796 cents. *Points of distinction:* From a perfect die and also with a crack across the die from T of UNITED, to M of AMERICA, and to the rim.

Notes: VG and Fine are the highest grades. Most range from Poor to AG-3. Walter Breen: "20 currently known."

1796, Date Hyphenated 17-96, Reverse of 1795 • BW-26, S-93, B-34.

Breen dies: 19-T. ***Estimated population:*** 300 to 400.

**1796, Date Hyphenated 17-96,
Reverse of 1795 (BW-26, S-93, B-34).**

Detail showing the hyphenated date.

Obverse: Same as preceding. *Points of distinction:* A rough area in the left field below the ribbon knot is always present. Some have a light crack through the date. This die was used to coin BW-24, BW-25, BW-26, BW-27, BW-55, and BW-56.

Reverse: Outside triple leaves opposite IT, ED, M, and ER. Only Style of 1795 reverse with this configuration among 1796 cents. Five berries on the left branch, four on the right. Fraction bar tilts to the right. Second 0 high. *Points of distinction:* Early impressions are from a perfect die, after which cracks develop at AMERICA and expand to include the lower-right ribbon and fraction.

Notes: This variety is known in Mint State.

1796, Date Hyphenated 17-96, Reverse of 1795 • BW-27, S-95, B-35.

Breen dies: 19-U. ***Estimated population:*** 30 to 45.

**1796, Date Hyphenated 17-96,
Reverse of 1795 (BW-27, S-95, B-35).**

Obverse: Same as preceding. *Points of distinction:* With cracks and also with die deterioration at ER. This die was used to coin BW-24, BW-25, BW-26, BW-27, BW-55, and BW-56.

Reverse: Outside triple leaves opposite UN, ED, and RI. Only Style of 1795 reverse with this configuration among 1796 cents. The leftmost leaf in the pair opposite C of CENT is skeletal and overlaps the stem. Fraction well centered and spaced; first 0 slightly low.

Notes: EF and AU are the highest grades known, and examples are exceedingly rare at those levels.

1796, 6 Leans Sharply Left, Reverse of 1795 • BW-30, S-116, B-36.
Breen dies: 20-V. ***Estimated population:*** 60 to 75.

1796, 6 Leans Sharply Left, Reverse of 1795 (BW-30, S-116, B-36).

Detail of leaning 6 in date.

Obverse: 6 leans sharply left so that the knob is about centered over the rest of the digit; knob very close to drapery; definitive for an obverse die mated with a Reverse of 1795. Die used with BW-30 and BW-68.

Reverse: Outside triple leaves opposite UN, ED, and ER. Only reverse with this configuration. NITE wide, ST wide. Numerator close to or touches fraction bar; bar nearly touches the left ribbon.

Notes: VF is the highest grade known. This variety is difficult to find with good eye appeal.

1796, 96 Close, 6 Leans Sharply Right, Reverse of 1795 • BW-32, S-92, B-28. *Breen dies:* 18-N. ***Estimated population:*** 300 to 400.

1796, 96 Close, 6 Leans Sharply Right, Reverse of 1795 (BW-32, S-92, B-28).

Detail of leaning 6 in date.

Obverse: 6 leans so far right that the knob at the top is farther to the right than is the curve below it; bottom of 9 much higher than bottom of 7; definitive for an obverse die mated with a Reverse of 1795 die (compare to BW-16). *Points of distinction:*

This die was used to coin both BW-32 and BW-54. Seen from a perfect die and also with cracks, including at the base of RTY nearly to the rim and another in front of the face. Later, more cracks develop, and the die shatters.

Reverse: Outside triple leaves opposite N, D, and CA. Only Style of 1795 reverse with this configuration among 1796 cents. First T of STATES leans slightly right. Lowest leaf of group of three points to the left foot of the second A of AMERICA; stem points to right foot of the same letter. Fraction well spaced and somewhat delicate; first 0 slightly low. *Points of distinction:* Seen from a perfect die and also with a rim break at the end of the right ribbon.

Notes: This variety is known in Mint State, and it is very rare as such.

ONE LEAF LEFT AND TWO LEAVES RIGHT AT APEX—1796 WITH REVERSE STYLE OF 1794

This arrangement is adapted from that given in *Walter Breen's Encyclopedia of Early United States Cents 1793–1814.* The reverse configuration is the key to identifying the varieties easily. The Style of 1794 coins have leaf clusters modified by hand, there being only three dies used. One reverse has no three-leaf clusters on the reverse and is identifiable by a two-leaf cluster below OF. The other two have a three-leaf cluster below OF (as do Reverse Style of 1797 coins, with the position varying slightly). These other two dies have other differences, as described, differentiating them from the Style of 1797.

In contrast, the Style of 1797 coins which were made with a punch with all of the leaves in place and with only *one* three-leaf cluster in the wreath (the cluster at the outside top of the right-hand wreath).

Typical values for 1796, Draped Bust, cents with the Reverse of 1794. Rare varieties may be worth more. Some varieties are priced individually, as follows.

1796, Draped Bust, Reverse of 1794	Cert	Avg	%MS
	30	14.1	0%

G-4	VG-8	F-12	VF-20	EF-40	AU-50	MS-60BN
$410	$875	$1,680	$2,750	$6,250	$12,625	$19,000

1796, Leaf Pair Opposite OF, Numerator Merged Into Fraction Bar, Reverse of 1794 • BW-40, S-101, B-25. *Breen dies:* 15-M. **Estimated population:** 60 to 75.

1796, Leaf Pair Opposite OF, Numerator Merged Into Fraction Bar, Reverse of 1794 (BW-40, S-101, B-25).

Detail of numerator merging into fraction bar.

Obverse: Correct LIBERTY spelling. Upright of T over junction of hair and forehead. Definitive in combination with this reverse. *Points of distinction:* This die was used to coin BW-20, BW-40, and BW-53. Clash marks develop, then a crack through ERTY.

Reverse: Leaf pair (instead of cluster of three) opposite OF, definitive for a Reverse of 1794 die. Denticles have rounded ends. Numerator merged into the fraction bar; first 0 low. Single leaf below C of CENT.

Notes: There is a Mint State (ANS) example, then grades drop down to EF.

1796, Leaf Pair Opposite OF, Numerator Merged Into Fraction Bar, Reverse of 1794 • BW-41, S-102, B-26. *Breen dies:* 16-M. **Estimated population:** 120 to 160.

1796, Leaf Pair Opposite OF, Numerator Merged Into Fraction Bar, Reverse of 1794 (BW-41, S-102, B-26).

Obverse: Correct LIBERTY spelling. Upright of T over hair. Definitive in combination with this reverse. *Points of distinction:* From a perfect die and also with a crack from the rim through BE to the hair.

Reverse: Same as preceding. *Points of distinction:* From a perfect die and also with a crack at the top of AMERI.

Notes: EF is the highest grade known.

1796, "LIHERTY", Leaf Pair Opposite OF, Numerator Merged Into Fraction Bar, Reverse of 1794 • BW-42, S-103, B-27. *Breen dies:* 17-M. **Estimated population:** 120 to 160.

1796, "LIHERTY", Leaf Pair Opposite OF, Numerator Merged Into Fraction Bar, Reverse of 1794 (BW-42, S-103, B-27).

Obverse: The intended B in LIBERTY appears as an H, the result of the B being punched backwards and then corrected. Definitive in combination with the Reverse of 1794. This die was used for both BW-42 and BW-70.

Reverse: Same as preceding. *Points of distinction:* A crack develops at the top of AMERI.

Notes: Exists in AU and Mint State (unique). This distinctive error is one of the most popular of the era.

1796, "LIHERTY", Leaf Pair Opposite OF, Reverse of 1794		Cert	Avg	%MS
		(a)		

G-4	VG-8	F-12	VF-20	EF-40	AU-50
$750	$2,250	$4,670	$8,000	$19,625	$40,000

a. Included in certified population for 1796, "LIHERTY", Reverse of 1797, Large Fraction.

1796, Three Leaves Opposite OF, Single Leaf Over O of ONE, Reverse of 1794 • BW-43, S-108, B-12. *Breen dies:* 7-H. **Estimated population:** 120 to 160.

1796, Three Leaves Opposite OF, Single Leaf Over O of ONE, Reverse of 1794 (BW-43, S-108, B-12).

Obverse: Date: Widely spaced and close to denticles. 7 very close to denticle. 6 touches

denticle. Knobs of 9 and 6 half cut off from defective punch. *LIBERTY:* LIB widely spaced. *Points of distinction:* Denticles wide and closely spaced. Some are from a perfect die, and others display light cracks.

Reverse: Three leaves opposite OF. Seven berries in left branch with *just one* near the ribbon bow. Leaf points to inside of right foot of second A of AMERICA. Single leaf over O and another over N of ONE. Leaf below C of CENT distant from berry to left of C. *Points of distinction:* This die was used to coin BW-43, BW-44, BW-45, BW-46, BW-47, and BW-48 and 1795, Date Spaced 1 79 5, Reeded Edge (BW-13). Seen with the right ribbon attached, or in a later state, disconnected.

Notes: The highest grades known for this variety are EF and AU; it is very rare at these levels.

1796, Three Leaves Opposite OF, Reverse of 1794 • BW-44, S-107, B-13.[35] *Breen dies:* 8-H. **Estimated population:** 45 to 60.

1796, Three Leaves Opposite OF, Reverse of 1794 (BW-44, S-107, B-13).

Obverse: Date: Positioned low, with 7 lowest. Knobs of 9 and 6 half cut off from defective punch. 6 closer to denticles than to drapery. *LIBERTY:* LI slightly wider

than IB. RT wide. Base of Y low. Tip of lower-right serif of T above junction of hair and forehead. *Points of distinction:* A massive cud break develops at the rim at top of Y and extends to the right. Coins with this break are especially rare.

Reverse: Same as preceding. *Points of distinction:* The die has been relapped to remove clash marks.

Notes: The highest grades known for this variety are Fine and VF (very rare). This variety is difficult to find with good eye appeal.

1796, Three Leaves Opposite OF, Reverse of 1794 • BW-45, S-106, B-14. *Breen dies:* 9-H. **Estimated population:** 75 to 120.

1796, Three Leaves Opposite OF, Reverse of 1794 (BW-45, S-106, B-14).

Obverse: Date: 1 and 96 distant from denticles, 7 close. Knobs of 9 and 6 half cut off due to the same defective punch. 6 leans slightly to the right. *LIBERTY:* IBE wide. ER closest. Tip of lower-right serif of T above junction of hair and forehead. *Points of distinction:* From a perfect die, or with light cracks.

Reverse: Same as preceding. *Points of distinction:* Cracks develop in later states.

Notes: AU is the highest grade known.

1796, Three Leaves Opposite OF, Reverse of 1794 • BW-46, S-109, B-15. *Breen dies:* 10-H. **Estimated population:** 200 to 300.

1796, Three Leaves Opposite OF, Reverse of 1794 (BW-46, S-109, B-15).

Obverse: Date: Fairly evenly spaced. Curved along and not close to denticles,

except for base of 7. Knob of 9 half cut off, from a defective punch. 6, using the same punch but inverted, has the knob patched. *LIBERTY:* Letters fairly evenly spaced. IB slightly closer than are any others. Tip of lower-right serif of T very slightly to the right of the junction of the hair and forehead. *Points of distinction:* A crack develops from the lowest curl through the top of 1796, and later a crack extends from the rim through T to the hair.

Reverse: Same as preceding. *Points of distinction:* Seen with the right ribbon attached, or in a later state, disconnected. On a late state, part of right stem is missing near bow knot.

Notes: VF and EF are the highest known grades.

1796, Three Leaves Opposite OF, Reverse of 1794 • BW-47, S-110, B-16. *Breen dies:* 11-H. *Estimated population:* 500 to 750.

**1796, Three Leaves Opposite OF,
Reverse of 1794 (BW-47, S-110, B-16).**

Obverse: Date: 6 in date is much closer to denticles than is any other digit (compare to the next). 179 wide, 96 close; knobs on 9 and 6 half cut off. 6 leans right with the

knob beyond the curve below. *LIBERTY:* Repunched left uprights of L and I. Base of T above bases of R and Y. *Points of distinction:* On all examples a die crack connects 96 at their centers. Also used for BW-50.

Reverse: Same as preceding. *Points of distinction:* Late die state with part of stem missing. Cracks develop.

Notes: This variety is known in Mint State. According to Walter Breen, the most available cent variety among 1796 issues of both types.

1796, Three Leaves Opposite OF, Reverse of 1794 • BW-48, S-111, B-17. *Breen dies:* 12-H. *Estimated population:* 60 to 75.

**1796, Three Leaves Opposite OF,
Reverse of 1794 (BW-48, S-111, B-17).**

Obverse: Date: 1 farther from hair than on the preceding variety. 6 in date is much closer to denticles than is any other digit (compare to the preceding, which is similar). 179 wide, 96 close; knobs on 9 and 6

half cut off. 6 leans slightly right with the knob about even with the curve below. *LIBERTY:* LI close, other letters wide. Tip of lower-right serif on T over junction of hair and forehead. *Points of distinction:* Usually seen with light cracks.

Reverse: Same as preceding. *Points of distinction:* Seen with the right ribbon attached, or in a later state, disconnected. Cracks develop in later states.

Notes: The highest grades are VF to AU (unique). This variety is difficult to find with good eye appeal.

1796, Three Leaves Opposite OF, Leaf Pair Over O of ONE, Reverse of 1794 • BW-49, S-NC-5, B-18. *Breen dies:* 12-I. *Reported population:* 8.

**1796, Three Leaves Opposite OF,
Leaf Pair Over O of ONE, Reverse
of 1794 (BW-49, S-NC-5, B-18).**

Obverse: Same as preceding.

Reverse: Three leaves opposite OF. Seven berries in left branch with *two* near the ribbon bow. No leaf under second A of AMERICA. Leaf pair over O and another over N of ONE. Leaf below C of CENT very close to berry to left of C.

Notes: The highest grade reported by Walter Breen is Fine-15. This variety was discovered by Howard R. Newcomb and published by George H. Clapp in "New Varieties of 1796 Cents," *The Numismatist,* January 1934.

1796, Three Leaves Opposite OF, Reverse of 1794 • BW-50, S-112, B-19. *Breen dies:* 11-I. *Estimates population:* 75 to 120.

1796, Three Leaves Opposite OF, Reverse of 1794 (BW-50, S-112, B-19).

Obverse: Same as BW-47. *Points of distinction:* Always with light die cracks.

Reverse: Same as preceding. *Points of distinction:* Most have a light crack from the rim to the second T of STATES to a leaf tip. In its latest state the die sinks at the center, and coins are bulged in this area.

Notes: EF to AU (exceedingly rare) are the highest grades for this variety. This variety is difficult to find with good eye appeal.

ONE LEAF LEFT AND TWO LEAVES RIGHT AT APEX—1796 WITH REVERSE STYLE OF 1797

The Style of 1797 coins were made with a punch with all of the leaves. There is just one three-leaf cluster in the wreath, and it is at the upper outside of the right-hand wreath. The berries, stems, lettering, and fraction were added by hand, providing differences that can aid in attribution.

The fractions on the Reverse Style of 1797 coins come in two sizes: small and large. Walter Breen used this as a convenient way to separate four of the die varieties, a method continued here.

Typical values for 1796, Draped Bust, cents with the Reverse of 1797. Rare varieties may be worth more. Some varieties are priced individually, as follows.

1796, Draped Bust, Reverse of 1797		Cert	Avg	%MS
		23	19.8	13%

AG-3	G-4	VG-8	F-12	VF-20	EF-40	AU-50	MS-60BN	MS-63BN	MS-63RB	MS-65BN
$250	$440	$810	$1,520	$2,500	$4,690	$6,500	$11,250	$17,625	$28,250	$60,000

1796 WITH REVERSE STYLE OF 1797—SMALL FRACTION

There are only four combinations under this heading. By checking the obverse and reverse they can be identified easily enough, although as two of them are very rare, those are not likely to be encountered.

1796, T Over Junction of Hair and Forehead, Reverse of 1797, Small Fraction • BW-53, S-100, B-24. *Breen dies:* 15-L. *Estimated population:* 45 to 60.

1796, T Over Junction of Hair
and Forehead, Reverse of 1797,
Small Fraction (BW-53, S-100, B-24).

Obverse: T over junction of hair and forehead. Definitive in combination with this reverse. *Points of distinction:* This die was used to coin BW-20, BW-40, and BW-53.

Reverse: Five berries to the left and five to the right. Outside berry opposite left upright of M of AMERICA, definitive for use with this reverse. CENT is very low. Fraction too far right, with bar close to ribbon. *Points of distinction:* Usually from a perfect die, but the ANS has one with a significant crack at STATES.

Notes: EF is the highest grade known. This variety is difficult to find with good eye appeal.

1796, Reverse of 1797, Small Fraction • BW-54, S-NC-1, B-29. *Breen dies:* 18-O. *Estimated population:* 20 to 25.

1796, Reverse of 1797, Small
Fraction (BW-54, S-NC-1, B-29).

Obverse: 6 leans so far right that the knob at the top is farther to the right than is the curve below it; bottom of 9 much higher than bottom of 7; definitive for an obverse die mated with a Reverse of 1797, Small Fraction, die. *Points of distinction:* This die was used to coin both BW-32 and BW-54. Always with light cracks.

Reverse: Five berries on the left branch, four on the right. No outside berry below first A of AMERICA.

Notes: F and VF are the highest grades known, and examples are rare as such; usually VG or so is the highest grade seen. Once Non-Collectible, changed to *Now-Collectible.*

1796, Date Hyphenated 17-96, Reverse of 1797, Small Fraction • BW-55, S-94, B-30. *Breen dies:* 19-P. *Estimated population:* 30 to 45.

1796, Date Hyphenated 17-96, Reverse of
1797, Small Fraction (BW-55, S-94, B-30).

Detail of low fraction, with low first 0.

Obverse: Date with hyphen-like flaw causing it to read 17-96. Date widely spaced. 6 close to drapery. Rough patch in the field below the ribbon knot. *Points of distinction:* This die was used to coin BW-24, BW-25, BW-26, BW-27, BW-55, and BW-56. Clash marks are seen near the portrait. A light crack develops at and near the rim including ER.

Reverse: Five berries on each branch. Leaf touches left serif of left foot of second A of AMERICA, definitive in combination with this obverse. Fraction low; first 0 low.

Notes: VF and EF are the highest grades, the latter exceedingly rare. This variety is extremely hard to find with good eye appeal.

1796, Date Hyphenated 17-96, Reverse of 1797, Small Fraction •
BW-56, S-NC-3, B-33. *Breen dies:* 19-S. *Estimated population:* 20 to 25.

1796, Date Hyphenated 17-96, Reverse of 1797, Small Fraction (BW-56, S-NC-3, B-33).

Obverse: Same as preceding. *Points of distinction:* A weakness develops at ER. This die was used to coin BW-24, BW-25, BW-26, BW-27, BW-55, and BW-56.

Reverse: Six berries in the left branch, five in the right, diagnostic in combination with this obverse. Tip of top leaf on the right ends between S and O in OF. Left stem thicker than the right stem. CENT low, T tilts to the right. *Points of distinction:* In later die states there is a rim break at TE of UNITED.

Notes: Fine and VF are the highest grades, the latter exceedingly rare.

1796 WITH REVERSE STYLE OF 1797—LARGE FRACTION
The Stemless Wreath variety, BW-60 is immediately distinguishable. This die was also used in 1797. Walter Breen groups the others, With Stems, into two categories: Wide Date and Close Curved Date. These are not immediately distinguishable by sight, except by experts. Accordingly, the other guidelines must be used, in combination in all instances with pictures.

1796, Stemless Wreath, Reverse of 1797, Large Fraction • BW-60,
S-NC-7, B-46. *Breen dies:* 26-BB. *Recorded population:* 3 known.

1796, Stemless Wreath, Reverse of 1797, Large Fraction (BW-60, S-NC-7, B-46).

Obverse: Date: 7 low. 9 high, 6 highest and touching drapery. *LIBERTY:* IBER wide.

Reverse: Stemless Wreath.

Notes: 3 are known, not counting a partial impression of the dies on a previously struck *half cent.* One is in the ANS, another was found by Rod Burress in 1999, and the third was bought on the Internet by Dan

Demeo in 2007. The curious half cent was identified in 1994 by Mark Borckardt.[36] The highest grades are Fine (half cent overstrike), Good, and AG-3. This variety is now known as Sheldon NC-7, though earlier listed in *Early American Cents* as NC-6. This listing was canceled, as it was thought that the only known example, in the American Numismatic Society, was altered from a 1797, Stemless Wreath, cent. In November 1994, Mark Borckardt met with Denis Loring and John Kleeberg at the ANS, and Loring confirmed that the Borckardt coin was indeed what had earlier been called NC-6. That number now being occupied by another variety, the new designation NC-7 was given.[37]

1796, No Ribbon Knot, Reverse of 1797, Large Fraction • BW-62, S-117, B-37. *Breen dies:* 21-W. **Estimated population:** 30 to 45.

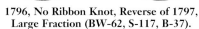

1796, No Ribbon Knot, Reverse of 1797, Large Fraction (BW-62, S-117, B-37).

Obverse: Date: Widely spaced. 9 distant from denticles. 6 closest to denticles and centered over two of them. *LIBERTY:* B leans right. BE and RT wide. *Points of distinction:* Clash marks and cracks develop.

Reverse: No ribbon knot, an engraving error; definitive. Five berries on each side of the wreath. Tip of highest-right leaf between ES of STATES, seen only on this and BW-64 within this style. *Points of distinction:* Some have a crack from the rim to the right side of the D.

Notes: The highest-graded examples are EF and AU, and very rare as such. This variety is difficult to find with good eye appeal.

1796, Top of 6 Overlays Drapery, Reverse of 1797, Large Fraction • BW-63, S-NC-6, B-38. *Breen dies:* 22-W. **Recorded population:** 3.

1796, Top of 6 Overlays Drapery, Reverse of 1797, Large Fraction (BW-63, S-NC-6, B-38).

Obverse: Date: 1 close to or touches hair. 6 overlays drapery. Compare to BW-67. 179 close, 96 wider. *LIBERTY:* Upright of T over forehead. *Points of distinction:* Crack at D of UNITED.

Reverse: Same as preceding.

Notes: Discovered by Denis Loring at the 1970 ANA Convention. Both examples are AG-3.

1796, 6 Berries Left and Right, Berry Opposite D, Reverse of 1797, Large Fraction • BW-64, S-118, B-39. *Breen dies:* 22-X. **Estimated population:** 30 to 45.

1796, 6 Berries Left and Right, Berry Opposite D, Reverse of 1797, Large Fraction (BW-64, S-118, B-39).

Obverse: Same as preceding.

Reverse: Tip of highest-right leaf between ES of STATES, seen only on this and BW-62 within this style. Six berries on each branch; berry opposite D of UNITED, this definitive within the style. Denominator widely spaced, with 10 especially so. *Points of distinction:* Most are struck from a perfect die, but some have a crack from under the end of the left ribbon to below 1 of 100, which develops into a break.

Notes: VF and EF are the highest grades known, the latter exceedingly rare. This variety is almost impossible to find with "nice" surfaces.

1796, 6 Berries Left and Right, Leaf Tip Opposite D, Reverse of 1797, Large Fraction • BW-65, S-119, B-40. *Breen dies:* 22-Y. **Estimated population:** 300 to 400.

1796, 6 Berries Left and Right, Leaf Tip Opposite D, Reverse of 1797, Large Fraction (BW-65, S-119, B-40).

Detail of two connected denticles over TA of STATES.

Obverse: Same as preceding. *Points of distinction:* All have a crack from the denticles, to the lower curl, to the bases of 17, and then back to the rim; also a crack from the denticles below the 6 to the bust and into the field.

Reverse: Six berries left and six right. Leaf tip opposite D of UNITED; definitive within the style. Fraction wide, with 1 in denominator near ribbon. *Points of distinction:* Two denticles over TA of STATES are connected. A crack is sometimes seen over AT, and other minor cracks can be in evidence.

Notes: The Nichols Find contained many Mint State coins of this variety. Surfaces are often prooflike. Walter Breen estimated that "several hundred" of this die combination were found. *However,* in grades such as VG to VF this variety is a significant rarity.

1796, Reverse of 1797, Large Fraction, 1 of 100 Too Far Left • BW-66, S-113, B-41. *Breen dies:* 23-Z. **Estimated population:** 45 to 60.

1796, Reverse of 1797, Large Fraction, 1 of 100 Too Far Left (BW-66, S-113, B-41).

Obverse: Date: Close to denticles, 6 closest and over a pointed denticle. Knob on 9 half cut off, knob on top of 6 patched with a blob.

LIBERTY: LIBE wide. L leans left. *Points of distinction:* Die cracks are in the date area.

Reverse: Six berries left and five right. Denominator too far left, with 1 near ribbon. Left ribbon recut on its right side. *Points of distinction:* This die was used to coin BW-66, BW-67, BW-68, and 1797, Berries: 6-5 (BW-22).

Notes: VF is the highest grade known. This variety is difficult to find with good eye appeal.

1796, Top of 6 Overlays Drapery, Reverse of 1797, Large Fraction, 1 of 100 Too Far Left • BW-67, S-114, B-42. *Breen dies:* 24-Z. **Estimated population:** 60 to 75.

1796, Top of 6 Overlays Drapery, Reverse of 1797, Large Fraction, 1 of 100 Too Far Left (BW-67, S-114, B-42).

Obverse: Date: Fairly evenly spaced. Tip of 1 very close to hair. 96 high, top of 6 overlays drapery. Compare to BW-63. Knobs on 9 and 6 half cut off. *LIBERTY:* Fairly evenly spaced. ER very close to hair. Upright of T over junction of hair and forehead, unusual on dies of this date. *Points of distinction:* This variety is found from a perfect die and also with cracks at TY, later a rim break in that area.

Reverse: Same as preceding. *Points of distinction:* There is always a crack from the rim to the second T of STATES. Later impressions have a crack at adjacent A, which

expands to become a small break at the rim. This die was used to coin BW-66, BW-67, BW-68, and 1797, Berries: 6-5 (BW-22).

Notes: VF and EF are the highest grades known.

1796, 6 Leans Sharply Left, Reverse of 1797, Large Fraction, 1 of 100 Too Far Left • BW-68, S-115, B-43. *Breen dies:* 20-Z. *Estimated population:* 300 to 400.

1796, 6 Leans Sharply Left, Reverse of 1797, Large Fraction, 1 of 100 Too Far Left (BW-68, S-115, B-43).

Obverse: 6 leans sharply left so that the knob is about centered over the rest of the digit; knob very close to drapery; definitive for an obverse die mated with a Reverse of 1795. *Points of distinction:* Perfect-die

impressions exist, after which the die developed many cracks and, eventually, a break at the rim at TY. Die used with BW-30 and BW-68.

Reverse: Same as preceding. *Points of distinction:* Some clash marks are seen in the field. This die was used to coin BW-66, BW-67, BW-68, and 1797, Berries: 6-5 (BW-22). BW-68 was struck *after* 1797, Berries: 6-5 (BW-22).

Notes: VF and EF are the highest grades known. This variety is difficult to find with good eye appeal.

1796, Reverse of 1797, Large Fraction, 1 of 100 Nearly Touches Ribbon • BW-69, S-105, B-44. *Breen dies:* 25-AA. *Estimated population:* 45 to 60.

1796, Reverse of 1797, Large Fraction, 1 of 100 Nearly Touches Ribbon (BW-69, S-105, B-44).

Obverse: *Date:* 17 wide, 79 slightly closer, 96 close. 6 first punched low, then repunched in present position. *LIBERTY:* LI and BER

wide. *Points of distinction:* Clash marks are seen, later multiple. Cracks develop.

Reverse: Six berries left and five right. Second A of AMERICA close to side of ribbon. 1 in denominator too far left and nearly touches the ribbon.

Notes: VF or so is the highest grade for this variety, but mention has been made of a unique Mint State coin.

1796, "LIHERTY", Reverse of 1797, Large Fraction, 1 of 100 Nearly Touches Ribbon • BW-70, S-104, B-45. *Breen dies:* 17-AA. **Estimated population:** 200 to 300.

1796, "LIHERTY", Reverse of 1797, Large Fraction, 1 of 100 Nearly Touches Ribbon (BW-70, S-104, B-45).

Detail showing the "H" in LIHERTY.

Obverse: Intended B in LIBERTY appears as an H, the result of the B being punched backwards and then corrected. Definitive

in combination with the Reverse of 1797. This die was used for BW-42 and BW-70. *Points of distinction:* From a perfect die, or with a crack at the drapery at the right. In a late state a cud break is seen over TY.

Reverse: Same as preceding. *Points of distinction:* From a perfect die or with several cracks.

Notes: EF is the highest grade known.

1796, "LIHERTY", Reverse of 1797, Large Fraction		Cert	Avg	%MS
		13	26.5	8%

G-4	VG-8	F-12	VF-20
$710	$2,080	$4,750	$5,930

EF-40	AU-50	MS-60BN	MS-63BN
$17,500	$30,000	$70,000	$125,000

1797, Draped Bust
Mintage (per Mint Report): 897,510.

Cents of 1797 were made in many different varieties. The earliest ones were probably from a Reverse of 1795 style die with a single leaf at the top of the wreath apex. This die was mated with three obverses. The Gripped Edge variety, discussed below, was part of that series.

Other 1797 cents have the later reverse style with one leaf at the upper left and two at the upper right. These were made with punches incorporating the wreath and its leaves, with berries, stems, lettering, and the fraction added by hand, creating many variations.

In addition to the Gripped Edge, many other varieties have faint lines on the edges, prompting this comment in *Penny Whimsy:*

> Many of the varieties are more or less marked or "milled" on the edges, with faint diagonal lines in patches, but never evenly, and never entirely around the edge. Since the process probably had to do with the preparation of the planchets, and not with the striking of the coins themselves, the presence or absence of traces of milling is a condition of no great concern to the student of die variation.

On April 26, 1797, Director Boudinot ordered 15 tons of planchets from Boulton & Watt, which arrived on the *Adriana* and were quite satisfactory. In contrast, when 9,296 pounds weight of planchets arrived from the Governor & Company of copper mines on the *William Penn* they proved to be a bad lot. These cost £11 a ton more than those from Boulton & Watt. "They were concave and convex and had to be cleaned and milled before being struck. These were the second lot of inferior planchets from the same concern resulting in nearly everything else being ordered from Boulton & Watt."[38]

Some coins from the Boulton & Watt planchets were included in the famous Nichols Find (see details under the introduction for 1796 cents).

Among the varieties of this year the several Stemless Wreath coins from two different reverse dies have always been popular. This type of error is also found among cents of other dates, as well as in some half cent varieties. Otherwise, the field of varieties is standard to the casual observer, but can be differentiated by berry counts, letter positions, and other usual methods. LIBERTY is slightly farther to the right on the typical 1797 coin, with the T over or close to the junction of the hair and forehead. Walter Breen notes that some varieties have the B from a punch with the upper-left serif too short or completely missing. Sometimes this defect was repaired by hand.

Most 1797 cents in the marketplace are in worn grades. AU and higher coins range from scarce to rare, except for certain Nichols Find pieces in Mint State, often with prooflike surfaces.

The following listing begins with Reverse of 1795 coins, then Reverse of 1797 with Stemless Wreath, then the others.

ONE LEAF EACH SIDE OF WREATH APEX—1797 WITH REVERSE STYLE OF 1795

The varieties under this listing are from a single reverse die combined with three different obverses.

1797, Reverse of 1795 • BW-1, S-NC-1, B-1. *Breen dies:* 1-A. **Reported population:** 9.

1797, Reverse of 1795 (BW-1, S-NC-1, B-1).

Obverse: Date: About evenly spaced. 7 close to drapery. *LIBERTY:* The most widely spaced of any 1797 die. T is mostly over the forehead. *Points of distinction:* The ANS example has a crack at BERT.

Reverse: Outside triple leaves opposite UN, ED, and C. Two leaves opposite O of ONE; two leaves below T of CENT. Numerator 1 is too far right above the bar. Denticles are heavy and closely spaced. *Points of distinction:* This die was used to coin 1797 BW-1, BW-2a, BW-2b, BW-3a, BW-3b, and 1796 (BW-11).

Notes: Walter Breen enumerates six coins, the finest VF-25, the others AG-3 to VG-8.

1797, Plain Edge, Wide 1 7 97 Date, Reverse of 1795 • BW-2a, S-120a, B-2a. *Breen dies:* 2-A. **Estimated population:** 200 to 300.

1797, Plain Edge, Wide 1 7 97 Date, Reverse of 1795 (BW-2a, S-120a, B-2a).

Obverse: Date: First three digits of the date are spaced widely as 1 7 97. Definitive with this reverse. 7 close to drapery. *LIBERTY:* IB and TY close. Upright of T over hair. *Points of distinction:* The die deteriorated

from "perfect" to rough. A crack develops at the left and continues through the date.

Reverse: Same as preceding. *Points of distinction:* Some are from a perfect die, and the others have a crack from the denticles past the left of U of UNITED.

Notes: AU and Mint State (unique) are the highest grades known.

1797, Plain Edge, Wide 1 7 97 Date, Reverse of 1795			Cert	Avg	%MS
			8	16.6	0%

G-4	VG-8	F-12	VF-20	EF-40	AU-50
$225	$410	$875	$2,250	$6,625	$22,500

1797, Gripped Edge, Wide 1 7 97 Date, Reverse of 1795 • BW-2b, S-120b, B-2b. *Breen dies:* 2-A. *Estimated population:* 750 to 1,000.

Obverse: Same as preceding.

Reverse: Same as preceding.

Notes: AU and Mint State (unique) are the highest grades known. This variety is "Gripped Edge" in the form of irregularly spaced notches on the edge. The purpose of this is unknown. Enough of these exist that they are plentiful in the marketplace.

Numismatic Notes: Early mentions of what is called the Gripped Edge today:
    Mason's Coin Collectors' Herald, June 1880:

> Another Rare Variety of U.S. Cents. For the first time we make public the discovery of a 1797 cent with an indented periphery, resembling a lettered edge, caused by the clamps holding the planchets to prevent turning in the dies.

Mason's Coin Collector's Magazine and Coin Price Current, December, 1890:

The Indented Edge 1797 Cent. A collector in San Francisco has forwarded a very fine 1797 U.S. cent, with indented edge, and wishes to dispose of it, unless he can learn its true history. We would be pleased to have an article from any of the experts in the U.S. Mint or elsewhere, concerning the origin of the Indented Edge 1797 Cent. That it was a Mint issue, with its peculiar irregular reeded edge, we have no doubt, and it may be true that owing to the planchets moving or jumping during coinage that clamps with teeth were used to hold the planchets in position. Who knows? The Editor.

1797, Gripped Edge, Wide 1 7 97 Date, Reverse of 1795	Cert	Avg	%MS
	12	26.6	0%

G-4	VG-8	F-12	VF-20	EF-40	AU-50
$240	$450	$925	$2,250	$7,500	$20,000

1797, Reverse of 1795, Plain Edge • BW-3a, S-121a, B-3a. *Breen dies:* 3-A. *Estimated population:* 10 to 15.

1797, Reverse of 1795, Plain Edge (BW-3a, S-121a, B-3a).

Obverse: Date: Date compact. 17 closer than are the other numerals. Base of 7 over denticle. *LIBERTY:* Closely spaced. LI slightly wider than IB. Upper left of B defective. Upright of T over junction of hair and forehead. *Points of distinction:* The die states range from perfect through various progressions of die cracks.

Reverse: Same as preceding. *Points of distinction:* With a die crack from the denticles past the left of U of UNITED and some other tiny cracks.

Notes: The highest grades for this variety are VG (exceedingly rare), then Good. *Copper Quotes by Robinson* advises that there are many low-grade fakes of this variety.

1797, Reverse of 1795, Plain Edge	Cert	Avg	%MS
	(a)		

AG-3	G-4
$2,250	$4,830

a. Included in certified population for 1797, Plain Edge, Wide 1 7 97 Date, Reverse of 1795.

1797, Reverse of 1795, Gripped Edge • BW-3b, S-121b, B-3b. *Breen dies:* 3-A. *Estimated population:* 300 to 400.

1797, Reverse of 1795, Gripped Edge (BW-3b, S-121b, B-3b).

Obverse: Same as preceding.

Reverse: Same as preceding.

Notes: With Gripped Edge. This variety exists in Mint State, and is exceedingly rare as such.

1797, Reverse of 1795, Gripped Edge	Cert	Avg	%MS
	(a)		

G-4	VG-8	F-12	VF-20
$275	$520	$1,320	$3,250

EF-40	AU-50	MS-60BN
$11,500	$25,000	$50,000

a. Included in certified population for 1797, Gripped Edge, Wide 1 7 97 Date, Reverse of 1795.

ONE LEAF LEFT AND TWO LEAVES RIGHT AT APEX— ONLY ONE THREE-LEAF CLUSTER IN WREATH— 1797 WITH REVERSE STYLE OF 1797

The Style of 1797 coins were made with a punch with all of the leaves. There is just one three-leaf cluster in the wreath, and it is at the upper outside of the right-hand wreath. The berries, stems, lettering, and fraction were added by hand, providing differences that can aid in attribution. Cents of this style comprise the vast majority of issues of the year.

The Stemless Wreath varieties are listed first, as attribution is simplified, thereby reducing the number of "regular" coins following.

STEMLESS WREATH VARIETIES

1797, Stemless Wreath • BW-6, S-NC-8, B-26. *Breen dies:* 18-R. *Recorded population:* 1.

1797, Stemless Wreath (BW-6, S-NC-8, B-26).

Obverse: Date: Medium width. 79 wide. Base of each digit is over a denticle. *LIBERTY:* Defective B. LI slightly wider than IB. LI closest to denticles. T mostly over hair, partly over forehead. *Points of distinction:* Die break (piece removed from the die) "hangs down" from the denticles far to the left of L, and extends to opposite the second ribbon. This die was used to coin

BW-6, BW-7, BW-34, and BW-35. A die break becomes even more prominent.

Reverse: Stemless Wreath, first die. Tip of leaf under right part of D of UNITED. Outside leaf of pair under center of M of AMERICA. Leaf close to but does not touch C of CENT. *Points of distinction:* This die was used to coin BW-6 and BW-10.

Notes: This coin is VF-25 with the sharpness of a higher grade. It resides in the Daniel W. Holmes Jr. Collection. This variety, unknown when *Early American Cents* and *Penny Whimsy* were compiled, was found by Ed Kucia in 1980 and confirmed as a new variety at the Early American Coppers convention in 1985.[39]

1797, Stemless Wreath • BW-7, S-131, B-27. *Breen dies:* 18-S. **Estimated population:** 500 to 750.

1797, Stemless Wreath (BW-7, S-131, B-27).

Obverse: Same as preceding. *Points of distinction:* Often with a small crack below the right of the R and a tiny crack from the end of the nose. This die was used to coin BW-6, BW-7, BW-34, and BW-35.

Reverse: Stemless Wreath, second die. Tip of leaf under center of D of UNITED. Outside leaf of pair under right upright of M of AMERICA. Leaf connected to C of CENT.

Notes: EF is the highest grade known.

1797, Stemless Wreath (BW-7)		Cert	Avg	%MS
		23	24.8	4%

G-4	VG-8	F-12	VF-20	EF-40
$250	$530	$1,180	$2,500	$8,875

1797, 17 Wide, Stemless Wreath • BW-8, S-132, B-28. *Breen dies:* 19-S. **Estimated population:** 45 to 60.

1797, 17 Wide, Stemless Wreath (BW-8, S-132, B-28).

Obverse: Date: 1 heavy, other numerals lighter. Second 7 lowest at its base, but is centered between a denticle and the drapery. *LIBERTY:* BE very wide, TY slightly wide. B defective. E over low area of hair wave. Upright of T over junction of hair and forehead. *Points of distinction:* A slight bulge develops in the right field.

Reverse: Same as preceding. *Points of distinction:* Some have a rim break opposite IC of AMERICA.

Notes: This coin can be found in Mint State (unique), then VF is the next-highest grade. Usually seen in low grades.

1797, 17 Wide, Stemless Wreath (BW-8)		Cert	Avg	%MS
		(a)		

G-4	VG-8	F-12	VF-20
$440	$940	$2,750	$4,750

a. Included in certified population for 1797, Stemless Wreath (BW-7).

1797, Second 7 Nearly Touches Short Denticle, Stemless Wreath • BW-9, S-133, B-29. *Breen dies:* 20-S. **Estimated population:** 60 to 75.

1797, Second 7 Nearly Touches Short Denticle, Stemless Wreath (BW-9, S-133, B-29).

Detail of low second 7 and fused denticles.

Obverse: Date: Low. First 7 over denticle. Second 7 lower and nearly touches a *shorter* denticle; the next two denticles to the right are fused together. *LIBERTY:* I leans right.

B leans right and is not defective. E over low area of hair wave. Upright of T over junction of hair and forehead. *Points of distinction:* Lower-right part of the drapery is usually weakly struck. This die was used to coin both BW-9 and BW-36. Incuse marks from wreath are in front of throat, with traces elsewhere. V-shaped break from rim to top of RT.

Reverse: Same as preceding. *Points of distinction:* Often with a crack at the top of STATE and a light rim break over IC.

Notes: VF is seen occasionally, there is one EF (ANS).

1797, 2nd 7 Nearly Touches Short Denticle, Stemless Wreath (BW-9)	Cert	Avg	%MS
	(a)		

G-4	VG-8	F-12	VF-20
$440	$940	$2,750	$4,690

a. Included in certified population for 1797, Stemless Wreath (BW-7).

1797, 7 Embedded in Drapery, Stemless Wreath • BW-10, S-143, B-31.

Breen dies: 21-R. *Estimated population:* 45 to 60.

1797, 7 Embedded in Drapery, Stemless Wreath (BW-10, S-143, B-31).

Obverse: Date: Second 7 close to shortened denticle and, at the top, is embedded in the drapery. *LIBERTY:* IB and ER close. B leans right. R has tiny right serif extension, Breen's "Style II, curled tail to R," the only 1797 obverse die with this feature. Upright of T over hair. *Points of distinction:* This die also used to strike BW-37.

Reverse: Stemless Wreath, first die (also see BW-6 above). Tip of leaf under right part of D of UNITED. Outside leaf of pair under center of M of AMERICA. Leaf close to but does not touch C of CENT. *Points of distinction:* This die was used to coin both BW-6 and BW-10. Clash marks are seen and there is a light crack near D of UNITED.

Notes: EF is the highest grade known.

1797, 7 Embedded in Drapery, Stemless Wreath (BW-10)	Cert	Avg	%MS
	(a)		

G-4	VG-8	F-12	VF-20	EF-40
$440	$940	$2,670	$4,560	$10,170

a. Included in certified population for 1797, Stemless Wreath (BW-7).

WREATH WITH STEMS VARIETIES

For this extensive series of reverse dies, the distribution of berries left and right furnishes a quick guide to differentiating varieties prior to checking other features. The Breen chronology, less the varieties earlier described, is followed.

Typical values for 1797 cents With Stems.
Rare varieties may be worth more.

1797, With Stems	Cert	Avg	%MS
	179	34.2	20%

G-4	VG-8	F-12	VF-20	EF-40	AU-50	MS-60BN	MS-63BN
$200	$350	$530	$1,160	$2,260	$3,750	$6,560	$12,560

1797, "Island" in Field Before Throat, Berries: 5-5, Left Bow and Ribbon Disconnected From Knot, Small Fraction • BW-12, S-134, B-4.

Breen dies: 4-B. **Estimated population:** 120 to 160.

1797, "Island" in Field Before Throat, Berries: 5-5, Left Bow and Ribbon Disconnected From Knot, Small Fraction (BW-12, S-134, B-4).

Detail of the reverse, showing amateurish die punching at the center, hardly the work of an experienced die sinker.

Obverse: *Date:* High above denticles. 1 barely touches hair. 7's are lowest and each is over a denticle. 97 close. Second 7 barely touches drapery. *LIBERTY:* LI wider than IB. BER wide. B defective. E touches hair.

T mostly over forehead. *Points of distinction:* Prominent raised "island" in field before throat, from a chip out of the die; definitive. Swelling behind the lower curls and neck. Die scratch connects 97.

Reverse: *Berries left and right:* 5-5. *Fraction:* First 0 is very low. Bar extends from over left edge of 1 to just past center of second 0. Small Fraction, the only such size among 1797 cents. *Points of distinction:* Lowest leaves on right are incomplete. Bottom of left bow and top of ribbon are very weak or not attached to knot. Letters in ONE / CENT are amateurishly punched and poorly aligned. Occurs in early state with perfect die (rare) and later with a crack from E of AMERICA to the wreath. Cracks develop and a bulge renders indistinct the letters NE of ONE.

Notes: EF and AU are the highest grades known, the latter exceedingly rare. Some have raised beads on the edge, an aspect not publicized in earlier generations and not well studied today.

1797, Berries: 6-6 • BW-13, S-135, B-5. *Breen dies:* 5-C. **Estimated population:** 300 to 400.

1797, Berries: 6-6 (BW-13, S-135, B-5).

Obverse: *Date:* Base of both 7's low, and each over a space between denticles. Upper right of second 7 barely touches drapery. *LIBERTY:* LI very close, B defective. Upright of T over junction of hair and forehead. *Points of distinction:* Crack from C of AMERICA to the rim; some have a light crack from I to nearby leaf.

Reverse: *Berries left and right:* 6-6; one of two dies with this arrangement. See BW-21 for the other. *Points of distinction:* Lowest berry on right partly overlaps stem. Leaf slightly separated from C of CENT. In denominator, 10 wider than 00.

Notes: Mint State coins are seen with frequency, from the Nichols Find, this also being true for the other 6-6 berries variety. However, the demand for them is so strong that there is always a lot of attention in the auction room when one is offered. Some show original mint color, more than any other from this source. The passion for "trophy coins" has led to a "push" toward liberal grading of this variety.[40]

1797, Berries: 5-4 (only die) • BW-14, S-NC-6, B-6. *Breen dies:* 5-D. *Recorded population:* 2.

1797, Berries: 5-4 (only die)
(BW-14, S-NC-6, B-6).

Obverse: Same as preceding. *Points of distinction:* A bulge develops across the lower left, near the center.

Reverse: Berries left and right: 5-4; definitive.

Notes: AG-3 and G-4. This variety was discovered by Ray Chatham in 1958.

1797, Berries: 5-4 (only die) • BW-15, S-136, B-7. *Breen dies:* 6-D. **Estimated population:** 300 to 400.

1797, Berries: 5-4 (only die)
(BW-15, S-136, B-7).

Obverse: Date: 1 and first 7 lean right. 17 wide, 79 wider, 97 close. First 7 very close to denticle; second very close to or touches denticle. *LIBERTY:* L closest to denticles. LI and ER close. B not defective. Upright of T over hair.

Reverse: Same as preceding. *Points of distinction:* Perfect die or with a light crack from the rim, through U to the wreath, and then back to the rim. Crack from left of E of AMERICA to the wreath, continuing back to the C and to the rim.

Notes: AU is the highest grade known.

1797, Berries: 6-5 • BW-16, S-137, B-8. *Breen dies:* 6-E. **Estimated population:** 500 to 750.

1797, Berries: 6-5 (BW-16, S-137, B-8).

Detail of second A of AMERICA and ribbon.

Obverse: Same as preceding. *Points of distinction:* A crack develops on the rim at the lower left.

Reverse: Berries left and right: 6-5. *Fraction:* Numerator is directly over first 0. Fraction bar ends at edge of 1. *Points of distinction:* Tip of leftmost leaf in pair opposite space between E and D of UNITED. Right foot of second A of AMERICA touches ribbon. One of two reverse 6-5 dies used to coin 1797 cents. See BW-22 for the other. Some have swelling at UNI and RICA, leading to obliterating IC and part of the adjacent A. Crack from rim below 00 through ribbon and stem.

Notes: AU is the highest grade known.

1797, Closest Date, Berries: 5-5, Incomplete Leaf Opposite T of UNITED, Spine From Bar to Left Ribbon, 1 of 100 Nearly Touches Ribbon • BW-17, S-122, B-9. *Breen dies:* 7-F. **Estimated population:** 30 to 45.

1797, Closest Date, Berries: 5-5, Incomplete Leaf Opposite T of UNITED, Spine From Bar to Left Ribbon, 1 of 100 Nearly Touches Ribbon (BW-17, S-122, B-9).

Obverse: *Date:* Base of both 7's low and each over a denticle. Upper right of second 7 nearly touches drapery. *LIBERTY:* LIB close. B not defective. Upright of T over junction of hair and forehead. *Points*

of distinction: Die states range from perfect to with cracks at AMERICA. Sheldon's "Closest Date."

Reverse: *Berries left and right:* 5-5. *Fraction:* Spine on fraction bar to or near left ribbon. 1 in denominator leans right, is distant from 0, and almost touches the ribbon. *Points of distinction:* Outside leaf opposite T of UNITED is incomplete (compare to BW-28). Leaf left of C of CENT is simply an arc. Cracks develop.

Notes: Fine and VF are the highest grades known, the latter exceedingly rare. This variety is usually found with a dark, porous surface.

1797, Closest Date, Berries: 5-5, Short Fraction Bar • BW-18, S-NC-2, B-10. *Breen dies:* 7-G. **Estimated population:** 20 to 25.

1797, Closest Date, Berries: 5-5, Short Fraction Bar (BW-18, S-NC-2, B-10).

Obverse: Same as preceding.

Reverse: *Berries left and right:* 5-5. Four berries are without stems. *Fraction:* Frac-

tion bar very short and covers neither the 1 or the second 0. *Points of distinction:* A light crack through the top of ED of UNITED is seen, as is a break in the denticles over D ST, later expanding.

Notes: Discovered by Howard R. Newcomb in 1944 (the same year his book on 1816 to 1857 cents was published). VG and Fine are the highest grades known, the latter being very rare.

1797, Closest Date, Berries: 5-5, Short Fraction Bar With Spine to Right, Distant 1 in Fraction • BW-20, S-NC-3, B-11. *Breen dies:* 7-H. **Estimated population:** 25 to 30.

1797, Closest Date, Berries: 5-5, Short Fraction Bar With Spine to Right, Distant 1 in Fraction (BW-20, S-NC-3, B-11).

Obverse: Same as preceding.

Reverse: *Berries left and right:* 5-5. *Fraction:* 1 in the denominator is far to the left. Fraction bar short, but does extend halfway over second 0 (compare to the preceding), this not including a tiny engraver's scratch or spine extending to the right. *Points of distinction:* Eventually, a heavy rim cud is seen over TES.

Notes: Discovered by Henry C. Hines in 1944. Known only in grades of Fine (very rare) and below.

1797, Closest Date, Berries: 6-6 • BW-21, S-123, B-12. *Breen dies:* 7-I. *Estimated population:* 120 to 160.

1797, Closest Date, Berries: 6-6 (BW-21, S-123, B-12).

Detail of fused denticle pair over TA of STATES.

Obverse: Same as preceding.

Reverse: Berries left and right: 6-6; one of two dies with this arrangement. See BW-13 for the other. *Fraction:* In denominator 10 closer than 00. *Points of distinction:* Lowest berry on right adjacent to stem. Fused denticle pair above space between TA. Leaf solidly touches C of CENT. Seen without and later with minor cracks.

Notes: This variety is usually seen in Mint State from the Nichols Find, this also being true for the other 6-6 variety. The present variety is the least often encountered from that source.[41]

1797, Berries: 6-5 • BW-22, S-NC-5, B-13. *Breen dies:* 8-J. *Estimated population:* 20 to 25.

1797, Berries: 6-5 (BW-22, S-NC-5, B-13).

Detail of short fraction bar.

Obverse: Date: 179 evenly spaced, 97 close. Upper right of second 7 barely touches drapery. *LIBERTY:* B defective. TY farther below denticles than are other letters. T very slightly right of junction of hair and forehead. *Points of distinction:* The die develops a crack through ERTY, then a rim break.

Reverse: Berries left and right: 6-5. *Fraction:* Numerator is right of center of first 0. Fraction bar ends between 1 and 0. *Points of distinction:* Tip of leftmost leaf in pair opposite center of D of UNITED. Right foot of second A of AMERICA is separated from ribbon. One of two reverse 6-5 dies used to coin 1797 cents. See BW-16 for the other. This die was also used to coin 1796, Reverse of 1797, Large Fraction, 1 of 100 Too Far Left (BW-66); 1796, Top of 6 Overlays Drapery, Reverse of 1797, Large Fraction, 1 of 100 Too Far Left (BW-67); and 1796, 6 Leans Sharply Left, Reverse of 1797, Large Fraction, 1 of 100 Too Far Left (BW-68).

Notes: Discovered by Pittsburgh dealer A.C. Gies in 1935. VF and EF are the highest grades known, the latter very rare.

1797, Berries: 5-5, E of AMERICA Over M, Right Ribbon Hollow, Denominator Spaced Widely • BW-23, S-124, B-14. *Breen dies:* 9-K. **Estimated population:** 30 to 45.

1797, Berries: 5-5, E of AMERICA Over M, Right Ribbon Hollow, Denominator Spaced Widely (BW-23, S-124, B-14).

Obverse: Date: 17 very slightly wider than 797. *LIBERTY:* LIB close. B without defect. R touches hair. Upright of T over junction of hair and forehead. *Points of distinction:* Obverse swellings are more extensive than on the previous use of this die.

Reverse: Berries left and right: 5-5. *Fraction:* Fraction bar short and closer to right ribbon. Denominator digits very wide, with first 0 low. *Points of distinction:* E of AMERICA over *faint* traces of an erroneous M. Leaf point under slightly left of center of M. Level point of right ribbon is weak. With swelling at OF.

Notes: F to VF are the highest grades known, the latter being especially rare. Nearly always seen in lower grades. BW-23 is easily confused with BW-31, so check both descriptions.

1797, Swelling at 97 and Drapery, Berries: 5-5, E of ONE Directly Over T • BW-24, S-125, B-15. *Breen dies:* 9-L. **Estimated population:** 45 to 60.

1797, Swelling at 97 and Drapery, Berries: 5-5, E of ONE Directly Over T (BW-24, S-125, B-15).

Obverse: Same as preceding. *Points of distinction:* Now with swelling at 97 and drapery, extending into right field. In late states the swelling obliterates the entire date.

Reverse: Berries left and right: 5-5. *Fraction:* Small fraction bar far from denominator 1 and ends over left part of second 0; 1 much closer to left ribbon than 0 is to right. *Points of distinction:* E of ONE directly over T. F in OF and second A are light, as copper went to create the swelling opposite this point in the coining press.

Notes: VF is the highest grade known. Usually found in low grades.

1797, Fused Denticles at 4 O'Clock, Berries: 5-5, E of ONE Directly Over T • BW-25, S-126, B-16. *Breen dies:* 10-L. **Estimated population:** 300 to 400.

1797, Fused Denticles at 4 O'Clock, Berries: 5-5, E of ONE Directly Over T (BW-25, S-126, B-16).

Obverse: Date: Second 7 over a denticle; left top very close to drapery, right top touches drapery. *LIBERTY:* LIB close. B defective. Upright of T over junction of hair and forehead. *Points of distinction:* Defect joins denticles at 4 o'clock on rim; expands to become a large crack and break. This die state, impressive to view, is not particularly rare.

Reverse: Same as preceding. *Points of distinction:* Found from a perfect die and also with light cracks.

Notes: AU is the highest known grade.

1797, Deep Dip In Wave Under E, Berries: 5-5, E of ONE Directly Over T • BW-26, S-127, B-17. *Breen dies:* 11-L. **Estimated population:** 120 to 160.

1797, Deep Dip In Wave Under E, Berries: 5-5, E of ONE Directly Over T (BW-26, S-127, B-17).

Detail showing deep dip between hair waves.

Obverse: Date: Fairly evenly spaced. Second 7 about equidistant from denticles and drapery, and visibly separated from each. *LIBERTY:* LI close. B not defective. Under the upright of E the hair wave is "angular," per the literature—actually a deeper dip or trough between two waves—as compared to all other dies of the year. Upright of T over junction of hair and forehead. *Points of distinction:* Some are from a perfect die, and others have a crack beginning at the denticles opposite the ribbon knot.

Reverse: Same as preceding. *Points of distinction:* Always with two light cracks.

Notes: VF and EF are the highest grades known, the latter extremely rare.

1797, Berries: 5-5, Spine on Fraction Bar to Right • BW-27, S-141, B-18. *Breen dies:* 12-M. **Estimated population:** 120 to 160.

1797, Berries: 5-5, Spine on Fraction Bar to Right (BW-27, S-141, B-18).

Obverse: Date: 17 wide, 97 close. Second 7 distant from drapery. Sometimes the knob on the 9 is weak. *LIBERTY:* BE wide. B defective, but later patched. Upright of T over junction of hair and forehead.

Reverse: Berries left and right: 5-5. *Fraction:* Small fraction bar ends over left side of first 0. Spine extends from fraction bar to right ribbon. *Points of distinction:* F in OF repunched. AM touches. C of CENT attached to leaf. Some die injury around the wreath. Often seen with one or more cracks on the lower part of the coin.

Notes: VF is a reasonable objective, but an EF and an AU are recorded.

1797, 7 Distant From Drapery, Berries: 5-5, Incomplete Leaf Opposite T of UNITED • BW-28, S-NC-4, B-19. *Breen dies:* 13-N. *Reported population:* 3.

1797, 7 Distant From Drapery, Berries: 5-5, Incomplete Leaf Opposite T of UNITED (BW-28, S-NC-4, B-19).

Obverse: Date: Second 7 distant from drapery. *LIBERTY:* BE and RTY wide. BER higher above the hair than usual. B not defective. Upright of T over junction of hair and forehead. *Points of distinction:* A crack is in the right field.

Reverse: Berries left and right: 5-5. *Fraction:* Short fraction bar ends between 1 and 0 and halfway over second 0. *Points of distinction:* Leaf opposite T of UNITED incomplete. Leaf left of C of CENT skeletal (compare to BW-17).

Notes: Discovered by Dr. Sheldon in 1934, early in his interest in the subject. Fine is the highest grade known.

1797, R on Head, Berries: 5-5 • BW-30, S-138, B-20. *Breen dies:* 14-N. *Estimated population:* Thousands.

1797, R on Head, Berries: 5-5 (BW-30, S-138, B-20).

Obverse: Date: 179 about evenly spaced, 97 slightly closer. Bases of 7's each over a denticle. Second 7 very close to drapery. *LIBERTY:* LIB closer to denticles. B without imperfection; sharp curl point under upright. Left of R barely touches head. Upright of T over junction of hair and forehead. *Points of distinction:* Sometimes with a light crack from Y into the field.

Reverse: Same as preceding. *Points of distinction:* Some have light cracks at STATES. Usually swollen at OF.

Notes: This variety exists in Mint State.

1797, Berries: 5-5, Spine From Stem to U, Line to Right of Fraction Bar • BW-31, S-139, B-21. *Breen dies:* 15-O. *Estimated population:* Thousands.

1797, Berries: 5-5, Spine From Stem to U, Line to Right of Fraction Bar (BW-31, S-139, B-21).

Detail of line between the fraction bar and right ribbon.

Obverse: Date: Ends of 7's point to spaces between denticles. Second 7 about equidistant from drapery and denticles, and visibly separated from each. *LIBERTY:* IB close. B without imperfection. R close to hair. Upright of T over junction of hair and forehead. *Points of distinction:* Sometimes from a perfect die, but usually with extensive cracks, these very interesting to view.

Reverse: Berries left and right: 5-5. *Fraction:* Short fraction bar begins to right of 1 and ends over left part of second 0. *Points of distinction:* Spine from left stem to U. Line past bar to right, to ribbon, but not connected to it.

Notes: BW-23 is easily confused with BW-31, so check both descriptions. This variety exists in Mint State. This is far and away the most often seen of the 1797 cent varieties.[42]

1797, Broken T Obverse, Berries: 5-5, Spine From Stem to U, Line to Right of Fraction • BW-32, S-140, B-22. *Breen dies:* 16-O. *Estimated population:* Thousands.

1797, Broken T Obverse, Berries: 5-5, Spine From Stem to U, Line to Right of Fraction (BW-32, S-140, B-22).

Detail showing broken T.

Obverse: Date: 17 wide. Second 7 close to drapery. *LIBERTY:* ER wide. B defective. Top bar of T broken. Upright of T over junction of hair and forehead, but mostly over hair. *Points of distinction:* Typically seen with a light crack from the denticles up to the left. A later state has a crack downward from Y, and still later with swelling at the date.

Reverse: Same as preceding. *Points of distinction:* Bulges and cracks develop.

Notes: Though thousands exist, this variety is scarcer than BW-31. This variety exists in Mint State.

1797, R on Head, Berries: 5-5, M Over E • BW-33, S-128, B-23. *Breen dies:* 17-P. *Estimated population:* 300 to 400.

1797, R on Head, Berries: 5-5, M Over E (BW-33, S-128, B-23).

Detail of M over erroneous E.

Obverse: Date: 1 over denticle; touches hair. Upper-left serif and upper-right corner of second 7 touch drapery; bottom opposite space between denticles. *LIBERTY:* BER wide. B without defect. R touches hair. Upright of T over junction of hair and forehead. *Points of distinction:* Examples can be found from a perfect die as well as with cracks that become extensive.

Reverse: Berries left and right: 5-5. *Points of distinction:* M of AMERICA over erroneous E. Many denticles are fused at the bottom border. Multiple clash marks, mostly light, are seen. Walter Breen says at least 12 sets can be discerned, indicating very careless press operation. Cracks develop.

Notes: AU is the highest grade known.

1797, Berries: 5-5, M Over E • BW-34, S-129, B-24. *Breen dies:* 18-P. **Estimated population:** 45 to 60.

1797, Berries: 5-5, M Over E (BW-34, S-129, B-24).

Obverse: See description under BW-6. *Points of distinction:* This die was used to coin BW-6, BW-7, BW-34, and BW-35. On most examples a crack begins at the denticles above the ribbon, extends into the field and then back to the rim. Walter Breen knew of only two without this feature.

Reverse: Same as preceding.

Notes: VF and EF are the highest grades known. Most examples are in lower grades.

1797, Berries: 5-5 • BW-35, S-130, B-25. *Breen dies:* 18-Q. **Estimated population:** 750 to 1,000.

1797, Berries: 5-5 (BW-35, S-130, B-25).

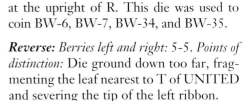

Detail of severed ribbon ends.

Obverse: Same as preceding. *Points of distinction:* The crack behind ribbon is advanced on this use of the die. Often with a tiny crack at the upright of R. This die was used to coin BW-6, BW-7, BW-34, and BW-35.

Reverse: *Berries left and right:* 5-5. *Points of distinction:* Die ground down too far, fragmenting the leaf nearest to T of UNITED and severing the tip of the left ribbon.

Notes: AU and low-range Mint State are the highest grades known.

1797, 7 Embedded in Drapery, Berries: 5-5, Spine From Bar to Right Ribbon • BW-36, S-NC-7, B-30. *Breen dies:* 20-T. **Recorded population:** 1.

1797, 7 Embedded in Drapery, Berries: 5-5, Spine From Bar to Right Ribbon (BW-36, S-NC-7, B-30).

Obverse: See description under BW-9. *Points of distinction:* This die was used to

coin BW-9 and BW-36. Now a large crack extends from the rim, above the end of the drapery, to the bottom of the throat.

Reverse: Thin spine extends from fraction bar to near right ribbon (compare to BW-20). Upper-left serif of D partly missing.

Notes: Unique. VG-7. Daniel Holmes Jr. Collection. Discovered by Julius Reiver in October 1968.[43]

1797, 7 Embedded in Drapery, Berries: 5-5, Spine From Bar to Right

Ribbon • BW-37, S-142, B-32. *Breen dies:* 21-T. **Estimated population:** 30 to 45.

**1797, 7 Embedded in Drapery,
Berries: 5-5, Spine From Bar to
Right Ribbon (BW-37, S-142, B-32).**

Obverse: This die was also used to strike BW-10, see for description.

Reverse: Same as preceding.

Notes: VF is the highest grade known.

1798, 8 Over 7, Draped Bust

Mintage (per Mint Report*): Part of the total for 1798.*

There are two overdated obverse dies and two reverse dies that combine to create a total of three varieties. The most often seen is BW-3. All are collectible, although, except for specialists, most buyers opt for a single example. The typical coin is apt to be in a grade from Good to Fine or VF. Walter Breen knew of no Mint State examples, but William C. Noyes reports an MS-60 coin of BW-3.

Both Sheldon and Breen mix the 1798, 8 Over 7, overdate among regular dates. However, it is thought that most readers consider the overdate to merit a special listing of its own.

1798, 8 Over 7, Closely Spaced Overdate, 8 Touches Drapery • BW-1,

S-150, B-6. *Breen dies:* 4-E. **Estimated population:** 50 to 70.

**1798, 8 Over 7, Closely Spaced Overdate,
8 Touches Drapery (BW-1, S-150, B-6).**

Obverse: Date: Date spaced closely. Upper right of 8 touches drapery; definitive. *LIBERTY:* ER wide. Center of E over highest wave of hair. T mostly over hair and only slightly over forehead. *Points of distinction:* Very thin, long denticles.

Reverse: Left stem points to center of U. Fraction bar ends over upper right of 1 in denominator. Leaf edge is noticeably into

the bottom-right part of T of CENT. *Points of distinction:* This die was used to coin BW-1 and 1798, Style 1 Hair, Large 8, 8 Very Low (BW-11). Some are bulged at S OF A.

Notes: In his census William C. Noyes lists the R.E. Naftzger Jr. coin as EF-45, the finest recorded. VF is a more achievable objective.

1798, 8 Over 7,		Cert	Avg	%MS
Closely Spaced Overdate, 8 Touches Drapery (BW-1)		(a)		

G-4	VG-8	F-12	VF-20
$510	$1,875	$4,500	$8,330

a. Included in certified population for 1798, 8 Over 7, Widely Spaced Overdate, 8 Distant from Drapery (BW-3).

1798, 8 Over 7, Closely Spaced Overdate, 8 Touches Drapery • BW-2, S-151, B-7. *Breen dies:* 4-F. **Estimated population:** 200 to 300.

1798, 8 Over 7, Closely Spaced Overdate, 8 Touches Drapery (BW-2, S-151, B-7).

Detail showing the overdate and long, thin denticles.

Obverse: Same as preceding. *Points of distinction:* In this use a bulge develops in the left field. Eventually, cracks develop, and a rim break is seen at the lower right.

Reverse: Left stem points to lower left of U. Fraction bar ends over space between 1 and 0 in denominator; closer to 1 than to 0. Leaf edge barely overlaps the outer part of the lower-right serif of T of CENT. *Points of distinction:* Some are from a perfect die, others have light cracks.

Notes: EF and AU are the highest grades known, the latter extremely rare.

1798, 8 Over 7, Closely Spaced Overdate, 8 Touches Drapery (BW-2)		Cert	Avg	%MS
		(a)		

G-4	VG-8	F-12	VF-20	EF-40
$360	$800	$3,000	$7,500	$17,500

a. Included in certified population for 1798, 8 Over 7, Widely Spaced Overdate, 8 Distant from Drapery (BW-3).

1798, 8 Over 7, Widely Spaced Overdate, 8 Distant From Drapery • BW-3, S-152, B-13. *Breen dies:* 10-K. **Estimated population:** 500 to 750.

1798, 8 Over 7, Widely Spaced Overdate, 8 Distant From Drapery (BW-3, S-152, B-13).

Obverse: Date: Date spaced widely. Upper right of 8 distant from drapery; definitive. *LIBERTY:* ER close. Lower left of E over highest wave of hair. Upright of T over junction of hair and forehead. *Points of distinction:* Short, thick denticles. There is a light crack from the denticles to the hair, and on some there is another crack to the ends of the knot.

Reverse: Top-right leaf tip below right edge of S. Crossbar of E of AMERICA connected to serif above. Left stem is very thick at the end and points past U to lower left of N. Fraction bar closer to left ribbon.

Denominator widely spaced and with the tops of the digits all on about the same level (unusual, as the first 0 is often lower); 1 leans right. *Points of distinction:* This die was used to coin BW-3 and 1798, Style 1 Hair, Small 8, Leaf Tip Below Right Edge of S (BW-18).

Notes: EF and AU are the highest grades known, the latter extremely rare. Walter Breen notes that the only AU coin known to him, now graded AU-55, had been graded MS-70 in 1966. This is the overdate most often seen, an ideal choice for those who collect one of each major variety listed in the regular edition of the *Guide Book of United States Coins.*

1798, 8 Over 7, Widely Spaced Overdate, 8 Distant from Drapery (BW-3)		Cert	Avg	%MS
		20	25.7	5%

G-4	VG-8	F-12	VF-20	EF-40	AU-50
$240	$470	$1,120	$3,125	$9,250	$18,000

1798, Draped Bust
Mintage (per Mint Report): 841,745.

The Sheldon text (and others) suggests points for differentiating the dies of this year, the most difficult assignment up to this point in time, as the dies become more stereotyped. These obverse distinctions are:

Large 8 and Small 8: The Large 8 is about 20 percent taller than the adjacent 9. The bottom center is more nearly round than the following. The Small 8 is about the same size as the adjacent 9. The bottom center is elliptical.

Large 8 in date.   Small 8 in date.

Style 1 Hair and Style 2 Hair: The Style 2 has an extra curl on the interior between the outer curl and the drapery. Generally, Style 1 Hair dies also have very long denticles.

Style 1 Hair.   Style 2 Hair.

Style 1 and Style 2 Letters in LIBERTY: Style 1 letters display an R with the lower right delicate, thinner at the bottom, with a serif extending to the right. Style 2 letters display an R with the lower right thicker at the bottom, plus a serif extending to the right. Harry E. Salyards offers this: "I think the best way to differentiate these is to think of the Style 1 'R' as a *gentle slope*, almost like an italic lower case *l* rotated 90 degrees counterclockwise; whereas the Style 2 'R' looks like a *boot*, with the 'heel' almost closing the space toward the upright of the letter."[44]

Style 1 Letters.   Style 2 Letters.

Reverse distinctions include the Type of 1795 with just two leaves at the wreath apex and the type of 1797 with one leaf on the left and two on the right. The latter reverses can be found with Style 1 "R" or Style 2 "R" in AMERICA.

In the present listing the distinctive Reverse of 1795 varieties are listed first. These are followed by the 1797 Style 1 Hair and Style 2 Hair issues, under which Large 8 and Small 8 varieties are noted as is the letter "R" style.

ONE LEAF EACH SIDE OF WREATH APEX— 1798 WITH REVERSE STYLE OF 1795

The varieties under this listing are from two reverse dies (both used earlier in 1796) combined with three different obverses. Interestingly, once you check the reverse, simply checking the *style* of the obverse will permit quick attribution as each die is different. Sometimes called Reverse of 1796.

1798, Style 1 Hair, Large 8, Style 2 Letters, Reverse of 1795 • BW-1, S-155, B-9. *Breen dies:* 6-H. **Estimated population:** 300 to 400.

1798, Style 1 Hair, Large 8, Style 2 Letters, Reverse of 1795 (BW-1, S-155, B-9).

Obverse: Date: Very widely spaced. Tip of 7 points between two denticles. 8 high and close to or touches drapery. *LIBERTY:* Widely and fairly evenly spaced. Upright of T over forehead just past hair. *Points of distinction:* Exceptionally long and spike-like denticles. Some are from a perfect die, while others have one or more cracks.

Reverse: Outside triple leaves opposite UN, IT, ED, and A. Two leaves opposite O of ONE; three leaves below T of CENT. *Points of distinction:* A light crack is from N to above E of ONE. This die was also used to coin 1796, Date Slopes Down to Right (BW-8); 1796, Club Pole (BW-9); and 1796 (BW-10).

Notes: A popular variety usually seen in lower grades, but many EF and finer coins exist, into the Mint State category—which is itself quite rare.

1798, Style 1 Hair, Large 8, Style 2 Letters, Reverse of 1795	Cert	Avg	%MS
	(a)		

G-4	VG-8	F-12	VF-20	EF-40	AU-50
$320	$650	$1,400	$2,625	$7,125	$12,375

a. Included in certified population for 1798, Style 1 Hair, Reverse of 1797.

1798, Style 1 Hair, Large 8, Style 1 Letters, Reverse of 1795 • BW-2, S-156, B-10. *Breen dies:* 7-I. **Estimated population:** 30 to 45.

1798, Style 1 Hair, Large 8, Style 1 Letters, Reverse of 1795 (BW-2, S-156, B-10).

Obverse: Date: 1 close to or touches hair. 17 close. 8 high and touches drapery. *LIBERTY:* Closely spaced. E between two hair high points. Upright of T over junction of hair and forehead. *Points of distinction:* Long spike-like denticles. Some are from a perfect die, and others have a crack starting at the denticles at the lower right.

Reverse: Outside triple leaves opposite IT, ED, A, and CA. *Points of distinction:* This die was also used to coin 1796, Closest Date, Pole Very Close to Bust, Triple Leaf Opposite AM (BW-3); 1796, Triple Leaf Opposite AM (BW-4); and 1796, Date Slopes Down to the Right (BW-5). Always with a light crack at the top from OF at the top extended to the left.

Notes: VF is the highest grade known.

1798, Style 1 Hair, Large 8, Style 1 Letters, Reverse of 1795	Cert	Avg	%MS
	(a)		

G-4	VG-8	F-12	VF-20
$2,330	$5,330	$8,500	$16,875

a. Included in certified population for 1798, Style 1 Hair, Reverse of 1797.

1798, Style 2 Hair, Small 8, Style 2 Letters, Reverse of 1795 • BW-3, S-178, B-26. *Breen dies:* 19-S. *Estimated population:* 30 to 45.

1798, Style 2 Hair, Small 8, Style 2 Letters, Reverse of 1795 (BW-3, S-178, B-26).

Obverse: Date: About evenly spaced. 1 distant from hair. 8 distant from portrait. *LIBERTY:* Fairly evenly spaced and high above head. Upright of T over junction of hair and forehead. *Points of distinction:* Denticles small. Crack in the right field becomes more prominent, and another crack develops through the date.

Reverse: Outside triple leaves opposite IT, ED, and CA. *Points of distinction:* This die was also used to coin 1796, Closest Date, Pole Very Close to Bust (BW-2). Multiple cracks develop.

Notes: Fine and VF are the highest grades known.

1798, Style 2 Hair, Small 8, Style 2 Letters, Reverse of 1795		Cert	Avg	%MS
		(a)		
G-4	VG-8		F-12	VF-20
$2,950	$5,750		$9,670	$23,330

a. Included in certified population for 1798, Style 2 Hair, Reverse of 1797.

ONE LEAF LEFT AND TWO LEAVES RIGHT AT APEX— 1798, STYLE 1 HAIR, WITH REVERSE STYLE OF 1797

Typical values for 1798, Style 1 Hair, cents with the Reverse of 1797. Rare varieties may be worth more.

1798, Style 1 Hair, Reverse of 1797	Cert	Avg	%MS
	76	24.6	1%

G-4	VG-8	F-12	VF-20	EF-40	AU-50	MS-60BN	MS-63BN	MS-63RB
$110	$180	$250	$750	$2,470	$5,330	$10,000	$18,750	$29,000

STYLE 1 HAIR, LARGE 8, STYLE 1 LETTERS

There are six varieties within this group. The obverses and reverses are described in a manner in which each obverse and reverse combination is unique.

1798, Style 1 Hair, Large 8, Leaf Tip Between S and O, Buckled Reverse Die • BW-6, S-144, B-1. *Breen dies:* 1-A. *Estimated population:* 30 to 45.

1798, Style 1 Hair, Large 8, Leaf Tip Between S and O, Buckled Reverse Die (BW-6, S-144, B-1).

Detail of close date.

Obverse: Date: Closely spaced, Sheldon's "Large Close Date," Breen's "Closest Date." 17 slightly wider than 798. 1 and 8 each about centered between bust and denticles. Tip of 7 points to denticle. *LIBERTY:* LIB close. E over space between two high waves. R close to hair. Upright of T over junction of hair and forehead. *Points of distinction:* Denticles long, thin, and widely spaced. Closely spaced over the space between R and T.

Reverse: Top-right leaf tip below space between S and O. Long fraction bar with spine *tilting slightly upward* at right end. 10 slightly closer than 00. *Points of distinction:* A bulge extends from A of STATES across the die to near R of AMERICA. On later impressions, cracks are seen here and there.

Notes: Typically VG is highest in the marketplace, but one each VF and EF have been reported.

1798, Style 1 Hair, Large 8, Spine Connects Bar to Right Ribbon •
BW-7, S-145, B-2. *Breen dies:* 1-B. *Estimated population:* 300 to 400.

1798, Style 1 Hair, Large 8, Spine Connects Bar to Right Ribbon (BW-7, S-145, B-2).

Detail of three heavy denticles over second S of STATES.

Obverse: As preceding. *Points of distinction:* From a perfect die or with a crack, in from the neck, extending to the denticles.

Reverse: Top-right leaf tip below S slightly right of its center. Leaf below left side of C of CENT is skeletal. Fraction bar connects with right ribbon via a spine; definitive. Small, raised die chip directly below ribbon knot (weak on some). Three denticles are heavy and close over second S of STATES. All denticles are bold. *Points of distinction:* Die states vary from perfect to with a bulge at the upper right, later with a crack over OF and with minor cracks elsewhere.

Notes: EF is the highest grade known.

1798, Style 1 Hair, Large 8, Spine From Stem to U • BW-8, S-146, B-3.
Breen dies: 2-C. *Estimated population:* 45 to 60.

1798, Style 1 Hair, Large 8, Spine From Stem to U (BW-8, S-146, B-3).

Obverse: Date: Fairly evenly spaced. 1 closer to hair than to denticles. 8 closer to denticles than to drapery. *LIBERTY:* IB and RTY close. Hair under R unfinished. Upright of T over junction between hair and forehead, more over forehead. *Points of distinction:* This is a very curious die, that underwent various relapping and strengthening, also used on BW-9.

Reverse: Top-right leaf tip below space between E and S. Left stem has a spine projecting from its end; on high-grade examples this connects to U. In the denominator the 1 is to the left of the end of the bar.

Notes: VF is typical highest, but single EF (ANS) and Mint State coins have been reported.

1798, Style 1 Hair, Large 8, 1 Lower Than First 0 in Fraction, Second 0 Almost Touches Ribbon • BW-9, S-147, B-4. *Breen dies:* 2-D. *Estimated population:* 60 to 75.

1798, Style 1 Hair, Large 8, 1 Lower Than First 0 in Fraction, Second 0 Almost Touches Ribbon (BW-9, S-147, B-4).

Detail of low 1 in denominator.

Obverse: Same as preceding, but reworked, with loop added below drapery, hair strengthened under R (R now touches hair).

Reverse: A of STATES slightly low and leans right. Top-right leaf tip below right corner of E. C of CENT low, T high. Tiny fraction bar. 1 lower than adjacent 0 (definitive); second 0 far right and nearly touches ribbon. *Points of distinction:* Light cracks develop.

Notes: VF and EF are the highest grades known, and examples are very rare as such.

1798, Style 1 Hair, Large 8, Hollow Area in Lower Curls • BW-10, S-148, B-11. *Breen dies:* 8-J. *Estimated population:* 750 to 1,000.

1798, Style 1 Hair, Large 8, Hollow Area in Lower Curls (BW-10, S-148, B-11).

Detail showing hollow or flat area in lower curls.

Obverse: Date: 1 closer to hair than to denticles. 98 slightly close. 8 almost touches denticles and is distant from drapery. *LIBERTY:* BE slightly wide. B leans slightly right. R close to hair. Upright of T over junction of hair and forehead. *Points of distinction:* Hollow or flat area at inside outer edge of lower curls from excess relapping of the die. Die states vary from perfect to later states with light cracks, then heavy cracks and a cud break over ERT.

Reverse: Berry below left side of E of UNITED has a long stem and does not touch leaves. Top-right leaf tip below S slightly left of its center. ONE / CENT irregularly aligned. *Points of distinction:* There is a light crack at the top of UNITED and extending to the right. Later states have a crack at the top of AMERICA. This die was used to coin BW-10 and BW-14.

Notes: This variety exists in Mint State.

1798, Style 1 Hair, Large 8, 8 Very Low • BW-11, S-149, B-5. *Breen dies:* 3-E. *Estimated population:* 60 to 75.

1798, Style 1 Hair, Large 8, 8 Very Low
(BW-11, S-149, B-5).

Detail of slanted fraction bar.

Obverse: Date: 179 close. 1 and 8 closer to denticles than to bust. *LIBERTY:* LIB close. Prominent curl between B and E. R lower than E and close to head. Upright of T over junction of hair and forehead, closer to forehead. *Points of distinction:* Defects develop in the right obverse field.

Reverse: Berry below left side of E of UNITED has a long stem and does not touch leaves. Top-right leaf tip below S slightly left of its center. Small spine from left of fraction bar (not visible on all examples). Bar slants down to right; covers about half of 1 and left part of second 0. *Points of distinction:* This die was also used to coin 1798, 8 Over 7, Closely Spaced Over-date, 8 Touches Drapery (BW-1). Some are bulged at S OF A.

Notes: This variety has a very low top range, with the finest variously graded as net F-12 and F-15, and the next dozen no better than VG.[45]

STYLE 1 HAIR, LARGE 8, STYLE 2 LETTERS

There are only two varieties in this category, making their attribution easy.

1798, Style 1 Hair, Large 8, 7 Almost Touches Denticle • BW-14, S-153, B-12. *Breen dies:* 9-J. *Estimated population:* 300 to 400.

1798, Style 1 Hair, Large 8, 7 Almost
Touches Denticle (BW-14, S-153, B-12).

Obverse: Date: 179 close, 98 wide. 7 almost touches a denticle. 8 about halfway between denticles and drapery. *LIBERTY:* I leans slightly right. ERT close. T mostly over hair. *Points of distinction:* Fused denticles over space between B and E. Some are from a perfect die, and others have one or more cracks. In its latest state there is a break connecting the rim to the bust.

Reverse: Berry below left side of E of UNITED has a long stem and does not touch leaves. Top-right leaf tip below S slightly left of its center. ONE about evenly spaced. *Points of distinction:* This die was used to coin BW-10 and BW-14. Peripheral cracks expand as the die is used.

Notes: Known only in circulated grades. EF is the highest-known grade.

1798, Style 1 Hair, Large 8 Embedded in Drapery • BW-15, S-154, B-8.

Breen dies: 5-G. **Estimated population:** 75 to 120.

1798, Style 1 Hair, Large 8 Embedded in Drapery (BW-15, S-154, B-8).

Obverse: Date: 1 about equidistant from hair and denticles. 17 wide. 8 high and into the drapery. *LIBERTY:* IBE wide. R close to hair. T mostly over hair. *Points of distinction:* Denticles long and spike-like. Some are from a perfect die, and others have a crack from the drapery to the denticles.

Reverse: Top-right leaf tip below S slightly right of its center. O of ONE distant from N; N close to E. Berry left of bow has its own stem. *Points of distinction:* A swelling can be seen among certain of the peripheral letters.

Notes: EF plus a single Mint State are the highest grades recorded.

STYLE 1 HAIR, SMALL 8, STYLE 2 LETTERS

This format includes 10 different die varieties, two of which Dr. Sheldon rated as Non Collectible, the only such rarities among 1798 issues. Careful examination of both sides will permit identification.

1798, Style 1 Hair, Small 8, Leaf Tip Below Right Edge of S • BW-18, S-NC-1, B-14. *Breen dies:* 11-K. **Recorded population:** 6.

1798, Style 1 Hair, Small 8, Leaf Tip Below Right Edge of S (BW-18, S-NC-1, B-14).

Obverse: Date: 79 close. 8 slightly closer to denticles than to drapery. *LIBERTY:* I leans slightly right. RTY slightly wide. T mostly over hair. *Points of distinction:* A crack develops at the upper right, eventually connecting to the hair.

Reverse: Top-right leaf tip below right edge of S; definitive. Crossbar of E of AMERICA connected to serif above. Left stem is very thick at the end and points past U to lower left of N. Fraction bar closer to left ribbon. Denominator widely spaced and with the tops of the digits all on about the same level (unusual, as the first 0 is often lower); 1 leans right. *Points of distinction:* This die was also used to coin 1798, 8 Over 7, Widely Spaced Overdate, 8 Distant from Drapery (BW-3).

Notes: The "best" coin has EF sharpness, *but* with a deep scratch in the right obverse field, suggesting various "net" grades ranging from F-12 to VF-20.[46]

1798, Style 1 Hair, Small 8, Three Fused Denticles Below 9 • BW-19, S-157, B-15. *Breen dies:* 12-L. **Estimated population:** 750 to 1,000.

1798, Style 1 Hair, Small 8, Three Fused Denticles Below 9 (BW-19, S-157, B-15).

Detail of fused denticles.

Obverse: Date: 98 very slightly wide. Three fused denticles below 9; definitive. 8 about equidistant from denticles and drapery. *LIBERTY:* High above head. Fairly closely spaced. B leans right. E centered over high wave. Upright of T over hair. *Points of distinction:* Sometimes from a perfect die, but more often with die crumbling and, in a later state, a crack through 798.

Reverse: Top-right leaf tip below center edge of S. Raised area within C of AMERICA; Breen suggests that it is the remnant of an erroneous T. Ribbon segments are weak. Numerator 1 is left of center above bar. Bar extends from upper right of 1 to about halfway over second 0. 10 wide, 00 closest. *Points of distinction:* Some are from a perfect die, and others have one or two light cracks among the border letters. Rust developed on the die in later use.

Notes: This variety is known in Mint State.

1798, Style 1 Hair, Small 8, Rim Break Over RTY, Leaf Tip Between S and O, Left Stem Too Short • BW-20, S-NC-2, B-16. *Breen dies:* 13-M. *Recorded population:* 6.

1798, Style 1 Hair, Small 8, Rim Break Over RTY, Leaf Tip Between S and O, Left Stem Too Short (BW-20, S-NC-2, B-16).

Obverse: Date: 79 wide. *LIBERTY:* Very widely spaced. T mostly over forehead. *Points of distinction:* On all a large rim cud

is seen at RTY and to the left and right, indicating this die must have had a problem very early.

Reverse: Top-right leaf tip below space between S and O; definitive. AMERICA widely spaced (normally the spacing is close and AME in particular are tight or touching at their bases). C of CENT separated from leaf. Left stem too short. 6 berries left, 5 right.

Notes: The highest-graded example is VG-8.

1798, Style 1 Hair, Small 8, Left Stem Too Short • BW-21, S-158, B-17. *Breen dies:* 14-M. *Estimated population:* 120 to 160.

1798, Style 1 Hair, Small 8, Left Stem Too Short (BW-21, S-158, B-17).

Obverse: Date: 17 close, 98 wide. 17 closest to denticles. 8 slightly closer to drapery than to denticles. *LIBERTY:* LI close. E and R

each over a wave. Upright of T over hair. Y slightly low. *Points of distinction:* Center curl behind shoulder is a flat area at its center. Loop under drapery incomplete at left. In its late state there are three nearly vertical, nearly parallel die cracks in the left field.

Reverse: Same as preceding. *Points of distinction:* Some are from a perfect die, and others show cracks around the border letters.

Notes: EF to AU are the highest grades known, the latter extremely rare.

1798, Style 1 Hair, Small 8, Three Vertical Cracks in Left Field, 1 of 100 Distant to Left • BW-22, S-159, B-18. *Breen dies:* 14-N. **Estimated population:** 200 to 300.

1798, Style 1 Hair, Small 8, Three Vertical
Cracks in Left Field, 1 of 100 Distant
to Left (BW-22, S-159, B-18).

Detail of distant 1 in denominator.

Obverse: Same as preceding. *Points of distinction:* Always with three nearly vertical, nearly parallel die cracks in the left field (but compare to BW-21, sometimes seen in this state).

Reverse: Top-right leaf tip below S very slightly to the right of its center. Right stem very close to leaf and points to left foot of A. Fraction bar with thin spine at right. 10 widely separated with 1 left of the bar. *Points of distinction:* With cracks among the letters around the border. This die was used to coin both BW-22 and BW-26.

Notes: There is a coin of Mint State in the ANS, otherwise EF and AU are the highest grades available.

1798, Style 1 Hair, Small 8, Lines From Denticles to ER of AMERICA • BW-23, S-160, B-21. *Breen dies:* 17-P. **Estimated population:** 30 to 40.

1798, Style 1 Hair, Small 8, Lines From Denticles
to ER of AMERICA (BW-23, S-160, B-21).

Detail showing crude alignment of letters.
Likely, workmen who had little artistic
skill prepared certain dies in this era.

Obverse: Date: 1 slightly closer to hair than to denticles. 98 wide. 8 about centered between drapery and the top of a denticle. *LIBERTY:* Widely spaced, ERT closest. Lower-left serif of E over high wave of hair. T over junction between hair and forehead. *Points of distinction:* Some are from a perfect die, and others have a light crack from the denticles, extending to the neck, upper drapery, and hair.

Reverse: Top-right leaf tip below S very slightly to the left of its center. Lower-left serifs of E of STATES and F are mostly missing. Lines from denticles to ER of AMERICA. *Points of distinction:* This die was used to coin BW-23, BW-25, and BW-43. This is an earlier *stage* of the die, later reworked, used to coin BW-24.[47] Some are from a perfect die, while others have cracks among the border letters.

Notes: This variety exists in Mint State, and is rare so fine.

1798, Style 1 Hair, Small 8, Large Berries, Serif of C of CENT a Tiny Spine • BW-24, S-161, B-22. *Breen dies:* 17-Q. *Estimated population:* Thousands.

1798, Style 1 Hair, Small 8, Large Berries, Serif of C of CENT a Tiny Spine (BW-24, S-161, B-22).

Obverse: Same as preceding. *Points of distinction:* Cracks develop and expand.

Reverse: Top-right leaf tip below S very slightly to the left of its center. Top serif of C of CENT is a tiny downward spine.

Berries are very large. Numerator centered over bar and high above it. Fraction bar centered between ribbons and extends from right side of 1 to near center of second 0. Compare to BW-27. *Points of distinction:* This die in an earlier *stage* was used to coin BW-23, BW-25, and BW-43. Afterward it was reworked to coin the presently described BW-24.[48] Cracks and bulges develop over the life of the die, and there is a large rim break at the upper left.

Notes: Readily available in EF or slightly finer grades. However, AU and Mint State are both very rare.

1798, Style 1 Hair, Small 8, Incomplete Hair Below ER, Full Knob on 9, Lines From Denticles to ER of AMERICA • BW-25, S-162, B-23. *Breen dies:* 18-P. *Estimated population:* 120 to 160.

1798, Style 1 Hair, Small 8, Incomplete Hair Below ER, Full Knob on 9, Lines From Denticles to ER of AMERICA (BW-25, S-162, B-23).

Obverse: Date: 1 without upper-left serif. Full knob on 9. 8 centered between denticles and drapery. *LIBERTY:* ERT wide. Upright of T over hair. *Points of distinction:* Highest waves of hair below ER are low

and incomplete (compare to the next). Clash marks develop. A crack extends from the rim to the ribbon.

Reverse: See BW-23. *Points of distinction:* This die was used to coin BW-23, BW-25, and BW-43. This is an earlier *stage* of the die, later reworked, used to coin BW-24.[49] Some are from a perfect die, and others have a light crack beginning in the denticles between S of STATES and O. Clash marks are at the top of the die.

Notes: There is one example of Mint State (ANS), otherwise VF is the highest grade.

1798, Style 1 Hair, Small 8, Incomplete Hair Below ER, Knob on 9

Incomplete • BW-26, S-163, B-19. *Breen dies:* 15-N. **Estimated population:** 120 to 160.

1798, Style 1 Hair, Small 8, Incomplete Hair Below ER, Knob on 9 Incomplete (BW-26, S-163, B-19).

Obverse: Date: 1 about equidistant from hair and denticles. Partial knob on 9. 8 twice as close to denticles than to drapery.

LIBERTY: IB closest. Upright of T over hair. *Points of distinction:* Highest waves of hair below ER are low and incomplete (compare to the preceding). The die began to crack apart, with cracks increasing in heaviness with later impressions.

Reverse: See BW-22. *Points of distinction:* This die was used to coin BW-22 and BW-26. The die, already with cracks, is now seen with more, most heavy.

Notes: VF is the highest grade known.

1798, Style 1 Hair, Small 8, Large Berries, Serif of C of CENT Normal • BW-27, S-164, B-20. *Breen dies:* 16-O. **Estimated population:** 120 to 160.

1798, Style 1 Hair, Small 8, Large Berries, Serif of C of CENT Normal (BW-27, S-164, B-20).

Obverse: Date: 1 close to and almost touches hair. 79 close. 8 closer to drapery than to denticles. *LIBERTY:* LIB close. I leans right. E and R over high hair waves. Upright of T over hair. *Points of distinction:* A few were struck from a perfect die, but

most have swelling, sometimes extensive, near the bottom border.

Reverse: Top-right leaf tip below S is left of S's center, but not quite below serif. E of STATES and F have short left serifs. Lowest leaf on the right is incomplete. C of CENT has normal serif. Left branch thick at end. Right ribbon bow weak on its right side. Large berries. Numerator centered over bar and high above it. Bar centered between ribbons and extends from right side of 1 to left side of second 0. 10 very slightly closer than 00. Compare to BW-24.

Notes: AU is the highest grade known.

ONE LEAF LEFT AND TWO LEAVES RIGHT AT APEX— 1798, STYLE 2 HAIR, WITH REVERSE STYLE OF 1797

Typical values for 1798, Style 2 Hair, cents with the Reverse of 1797. Rare varieties may be worth more.

1798, Style 2 Hair, Reverse of 1797	Cert	Avg	%MS
	198	31.0	4%

G-4	VG-8	F-12	VF-20	EF-40	AU-50	MS-60BN	MS-63BN	MS-63RB
$90	$160	$300	$640	$2,050	$3,600	$8,070	$16,500	$26,670

STYLE 2 HAIR, LARGE 8, STYLE 2 LETTERS

This format includes just three varieties, all of which share the same obverse. Accordingly, attribution is by the reverse die. The features at and near CENT are definitive.

1798, Style 2 Hair, Large 8 • BW-29, S-165, B-31. *Breen dies:* 23-U. **Estimated population:** 120 to 160.

1798, Style 2 Hair, Large 8
(BW-29, S-165, B-31).

Obverse: *Date:* Date low. 79 close. *LIBERTY:* High above head. LIB and ER slightly close. TY unusually wide. Upright of T over hair. *Points of distinction:* Highest

hair waves under ER are shallow. Die chip gives Miss Liberty a little wart below her chin.

Reverse: Prominent stem on leaf pair below T of CENT; serif on C is light (but not a spine); berry opposite C touches branch. *Points of distinction:* Some are from a perfect die, and others have a crack from the denticles, to between I and C, and to a berry.

Notes: VF and EF are the highest grades known, the latter being extremely rare.

1798, Style 2 Hair, Large 8 • BW-30, S-166, B-32. *Breen dies:* 23-V. **Estimated population:** Thousands.

1798, Style 2 Hair, Large 8
(BW-30, S-166, B-32).

Obverse: Same as preceding.

Reverse: Little or no stem on leaf pair below T of CENT; serif on C is a spine; berry opposite C touches branch. *Points of distinc-*

tion: All display a crack from the denticles, through E of UNITED, to the leaves and other lower areas, and to the second 0 to the rim. Some others have additional cracks.

Notes: Available in Mint State. One of the most often seen varieties of 1798. Years ago this was a popular variety to alter to "1799," but the reverse crack serves to quickly identify such deceptions. "This is a very difficult coin to find with nice surfaces. There are probably only 30 to 40 that are truly choice."[50]

1798, Style 2 Hair, Large 8 • BW-31, S-167, B-33. *Breen dies:* 23-W. **Estimated population:** Thousands.

1798, Style 2 Hair, Large 8
(BW-31, S-167, B-33).

Detail showing flow marks in the field from an extremely worn die.

Obverse: Same as preceding. *Points of distinction:* The crack present on the previous use has expanded, and on some coins there are additional cracks. The die was worn far past what would have been a normal useful life.

Reverse: Little or no stem on leaf pair below T of CENT; serif on C is normal; berry opposite C is on a stem and does not touch the branch. *Points of distinction:* Multiple cracks occur, and a rim cud develops at the top of the first T of STATES.

Notes: Another readily available variety. AU and a couple of Mint State exist. As AU coins exist in fair numbers, some will probably "graduate" to become Mint State. There is a difference of opinion among experts as to the actual grades of the finest pieces. Walter Breen lists more than a dozen AU and MS examples, while some others suggest the actual population is no more than half that many.[51]

STYLE 2 HAIR, SMALL 8, STYLE 2 LETTERS

This format is the most extensive within the 1798 year and thus provides the greatest challenge for distinction. Attention to details on both sides, including comparing with the photographs, will result in the correct die-variety attribution.

1798, Style 2 Hair, Small 8, Leaf Tip Under Center of D of UNITED
• BW-34, S-168, B-27. *Breen dies:* 20-J. ***Estimated population:*** 300 to 400.

1798, Style 2 Hair, Small 8, Leaf Tip Under Center of D of UNITED (BW-34, S-168, B-27).

Obverse: Date: Fairly evenly spaced, 98 very slightly wider. 1 slightly closer to hair than to denticles. Tip of 7 opposite space between denticles. 8 significantly closer to drapery than to denticles. *LIBERTY:* IB closest. B leans slightly right. E and R over waves of hair. Upright of T over hair. *Points of distinction:* Multiple clash marks are seen in the latest state.

Reverse: Style 2 letters. Top-right leaf tip below center of S. Very long stem to the berry right of T of CENT. Fraction bar closer to left ribbon. 10 closer than 00. *Points of distinction:* Cracks are present on all examples.

Notes: AU is the highest grade except for one Mint State.

1798, Style 2 Hair, Small 8 • BW-35, S-169, B-28. *Breen dies:* 20-T. ***Estimated population:*** 300 to 400.

1798, Style 2 Hair, Small 8 (BW-35, S-169, B-28).

Obverse: Same as preceding. *Points of distinction:* A small rim break develops between 9 and 8. Bulges develop.

Reverse: Style 2 letters. Top-right leaf tip slightly left of center of S. Left stem slightly shorter than right. Fraction bar is heavy and slopes down to the right slightly. 1 in denominator high. *Points of distinction:* Light clash marks are on all.

Notes: AU is the highest grade known.

1798, Style 2 Hair, Small 8 • BW-36, S-170, B-29. *Breen dies:* 21-T. **Estimated population:** 300 to 400.

1798, Style 2 Hair, Small 8 (BW-36, S-170, B-29).

Obverse: Date: Fairly evenly spaced. 1 and 8 distant from bust. *LIBERTY:* Fairly evenly spaced, including ERT (compare to next). E over wave. T mostly over hair. *Points of distinction:* Some are from a perfect die, but most have a crack from the denticles through the ribbon ends, ending at the denticles behind the lowest curl. A crack develops from the rim, through T, and to the hair.

Reverse: Same as preceding.

Notes: The base of the date is into the border on many pieces. Several EF examples and one Mint State example exist.

1798, Style 2 Hair, Small 8 • BW-37, S-171, B-30. *Breen dies:* 22-T. **Estimated population:** 120 to 160.

1798, Style 2 Hair, Small 8 (BW-37, S-171, B-30).

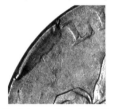

Detail of rim cud to the left of L.

Obverse: Date: Fairly evenly spaced. 1 is slightly closer to hair than to denticles. 8 is closer to drapery than to denticles. *LIBERTY:* E over wave. ER closer than RT. Upright of T over hair. *Points of distinction:* A close copy of the preceding die. A rim cud is to the left of L. On some there is a crack from the rim over T, through Y, and to the denticles on the right edge.

Reverse: Same as preceding.

Notes: EF and AU are the highest grades known, the latter very rare.

1798, Style 2 Hair, Small 8 • BW-38, S-172, B-34. *Breen dies:* 24-X. **Estimated population:** 750 to 1,000.

1798, Style 2 Hair, Small 8 (BW-38, S-172, B-34).

Obverse: Date: Serif of 1 is closer to hair than base is to denticles. Base of 7 over denticle. 98 slightly wide. 8 closer to denticles than drapery, and over a denticle.

LIBERTY: High above head. IB close; both letters lean slightly right. T mostly over hair. *Points of distinction:* Some are from a perfect die, but most have denticle clash marks at the upper rim. On later strikings the die deteriorates further.

Reverse: Style 2 letters. Top-right leaf tip under serif of S. Left stem slightly shorter than right. Fraction bar slopes down to the right slightly. 1 in denominator high. *Points of distinction:* Some are from a perfect die, others have a light crack from the left ribbon to A of AMERICA, and in a later state some appear with a heavy break over ICA.

Notes: AU and lower-range Mint State are the highest grades known, and all examples are rare at these levels.

1798, Style 2 Hair, Small 8 • BW-40, S-173, B-38. *Breen dies:* 27-BB. *Estimated population:* 300 to 400.

1798, Style 2 Hair, Small 8 (BW-40, S-173, B-38).

Detail of cud over RTY.

Obverse: Date: Fairly evenly spaced. Serif of 1 closer to hair than base is to denticles. 7 points to space between denticles. 8 closer to denticles than to drapery. *LIBERTY:* LI close. I leans slightly right. BER wide. E and R over waves. Upright of T

over hair. Base of Y low and with patched lower-left serif. *Points of distinction:* Some are from a perfect die, but most have a cud over RTY, and on the latest impression this expands to the left.

Reverse: Style 2 letters. Top-right leaf tip under serif of S. Lower-left serif of E of STATES incomplete. Left stem slightly shorter than right. Berry left of bow touches the stem. Pair of leaves opposite RI touch the stem. Numerals in denominator evenly spaced. *Points of distinction:* This die was also used to coin 1799, 9 Over 8 (BW-1). Most are from a perfect die, but some have a crack at the top of NITE. In the latest state, quite rare, there is a rim break at CA.

Notes: This variety exists in Mint State, and is elusive as such.

1798, Style 2 Hair, Small 8, Spine on Top of 1 of 1798, Raised Chips Below Ribbon • BW-41, S-174, B-35. *Breen dies:* 25-Y. *Estimated population:* 750 to 1,000.

1798, Style 2 Hair, Small 8, Spine on Top of 1 of 1798, Raised Chips Below Ribbon (BW-41, S-174, B-35).

Obverse: Date: Tiny spine extends upward from top of 1. 17 close. 8 closer to drapery than to denticles. *LIBERTY:* High over head. BERT wide. E and left upright of R over waves. T mostly over hair. Left-bottom

serif of Y patched. *Points of distinction:* Problems develop, including a short crack at the lower left. The die is relapped to remove multiple clash marks.

Reverse: Style 2 letters. Top-right leaf tip under serif of S. A of STATES leans slightly right; lower-left serif of E incomplete. Numerator 1 leans slightly left. 1 in denominator closer to bar than other numerals. *Points of distinction:* There is a light crack near the fraction, and on some later impressions there are clash marks in that area.

Notes: AU is the highest grade known.

1798, Style 2 Hair, Small 8 • BW-42, S-175, B-36. *Breen dies:* 25-Z. **Estimated population:** 200 to 300.

1798, Style 2 Hair, Small 8 (BW-42, S-175, B-36).

Obverse: Same as preceding. *Points of distinction:* The die in this use, relapped, develops a small rim crack at the lower-left rim.

Reverse: Style 2 letters. Top-right leaf tip under serif of S. Lower-left serif of E incomplete. Left stem slightly shorter. *Points of distinction:* On this later state other cracks eventually develop, some so light as to be seen only on high-grade examples. Eventually there is a rim break engulfing the top of the U.

Notes: EF, or slightly finer, is the highest grade available.

1798, Style 2 Hair, Small 8, Lines From Denticles to ER of AMERICA • BW-43, S-176, B-24. *Breen dies:* 19-P. **Estimated population:** 120 to 160.

1798, Style 2 Hair, Small 8, Lines From Denticles to ER of AMERICA (BW-43, S-176, B-24).

Obverse: Date: Low and fairly evenly spaced. *LIBERTY:* LIB slightly closer than other letters. T mostly over hair. Not often found from a perfect die. Most have a crack which starts at the lower right and extends upward.

On later strikings this expands, such as in the next use of the die, for BW-44.

Reverse: See BW-23. Style 2 letters. *Points of distinction:* With two or more cracks. This die was used to coin BW-23, BW-25, and BW-43. This is an earlier *stage* of the die, later reworked, used to coin BW-24.[52]

Notes: EF and AU are the highest grades known, and examples are very rare as such. One EF coin in the ANS is struck over a British Conder token with "N ANGLE" visible on the edge, from part of a longer inscription.[53]

1798, Style 2 Hair, Small 8, Style 1 Reverse Letters, Parts of Ribbon Missing • BW-44, S-177, B-25. *Breen dies:* 19-R. **Estimated population:** 75 to 120.

1798, Style 2 Hair, Small 8, Style 1 Reverse Letters, Parts of Ribbon Missing (BW-44, S-177, B-25).

Obverse: Same as preceding. *Points of distinction:* Now always with vertical die crack in right field, as is already seen in late states of BW-43.

Reverse: Style 1 letters (thinner lower right of R). Top-right leaf tip under center of S. Berry opposite upright of E of UNITED fused into leaf. IC widely spaced. Berry to right of T of CENT has long stem. Parts of both ribbons are missing, most dramatically leaving a raised "island" past A. Numerator to slight right of center above fraction bar.

Notes: VF is the highest grade known.

1798, Style 2 Hair, Small 8 • BW-45, S-179, B-37.[54] *Breen dies:* 26-AA. **Estimated population:** 750 to 1,000.

1798, Style 2 Hair, Small 8 (BW-45, S-179, B-37).

Obverse: Date: Low. 98 slightly wide and about on the same level. *LIBERTY:* Widely spaced. E and R over high waves of hair. Serifs at base of Y are mostly gone. T

mostly over hair. *Points of distinction:* Clash marks develop, and are removed by relapping, after which additional clash marks are sustained.

Reverse: Style 2 letters. Top-right leaf tip under serif of S. E of AMERICA first punched upside down, then corrected. CE slightly wider than usual. *Points of distinction:* Clash marks develop, and are removed by relapping.

Notes: This variety exists in Mint State.

1798, Style 2 Hair, Small 8, Patch of Hair Missing Below Ear • BW-46, S-180, B-41. *Breen dies:* 29-EE. **Estimated population:** 40 to 55.

1798, Style 2 Hair, Small 8, Patch of Hair Missing Below Ear (BW-46, S-180, B-41).

Detail of missing hair.

Obverse: Date: Low. 79 slightly closer. 8 higher than other numerals. *LIBERTY:* IB close. Both letters lean slightly right. Upright of T over hair. *Points of distinction:* Patch of hair missing below ear to the left. Nearly horizontal crack in the left field and a light crack at the top of ER.

Reverse: Style 2 letters. Top-right leaf tip under serif of S. Leaf opposite T of UNITED weak. R of AMERICA has a straight tail from reworking (not Style 1). Left stem shorter and thinner than right. *Points of distinction:* As the die deteriorates, a large rim cud is seen above TATE.

Notes: VF is the highest grade known.

1798, Style 2 Hair, Small 8, Berries 6 Left and 5 Right, Large Heavy Fraction • BW-47, S-181, B-42. *Breen dies:* 29-FF. **Estimated population:** 300 to 400.

1798, Style 2 Hair, Small 8, Berries 6 Left and 5 Right, Large Heavy Fraction (BW-47, S-181, B-42).

Detail of the fraction showing 00 over smaller 00 in the denominator.

Obverse: Same as preceding. *Points of distinction:* The crack at the left expands, and there is an additional crack.

Reverse: Style 2 letters. Top-right leaf tip under serif of S. Large fraction with heavy features. The denominator of the fraction shows 00 over a previous smaller 00.

Notes: AU and Mint State are the highest-known grades, and examples are rare as such.

1798, Style 2 Hair, Small 8, Style 1 Reverse Letters, Line Connects Right Ribbon and A • BW-48, S-182, B-43. *Breen dies:* 30-GG. *Estimated population:* 160 to 200.

1798, Style 2 Hair, Small 8, Style 1 Reverse Letters, Line Connects Right Ribbon and A (BW-48, S-182, B-43).

Detail of line between second A of AMERICA and ribbon.

Obverse: Date: 79 slightly closer. 8 closer to drapery than to denticles. *LIBERTY:* BE and RT slightly wide. T above hair but close to junction. *Points of distinction:* Flat area in hair above first hair strand over 1.

Reverse: Style 1 letters. Top-right leaf tip slightly left of center of S. CENT low. A die scratch forms a ridge from the right ribbon to A; definitive.

Notes: Singles are AU and Mint State, otherwise grades are EF and lower.

1798, Style 2 Hair, Small 8, High Top Serif on 7 • BW-50, S-183, B-44. *Breen dies:* 31-GG. *Estimated population:* 45 to 60.

1798, Style 2 Hair, Small 8, High Top Serif on 7 (BW-50, S-183, B-44).

Obverse: Date: Low and evenly spaced. High top serif on 7. *LIBERTY:* LIB close, IB closest. E and R over high waves. Upright of T over hair but close to junction. *Points of distinction:* Compare to the following, especially LIBERTY.

Reverse: Same as preceding.

Notes: VF and EF are the highest-known grades. Comment from Harry E. Salyards: "This is an excellent variety to illustrate the perils of assigning a high rarity rating to a not-particularly-distinctive variety, which looks very similar to . . . a very common variety—in this case, the S-184 that follows. Sheldon called the S-183 an R-8 in *Early American Cents*, having seen all of *two* examples. By the time of publication of *Penny Whimsy* it was down to an R-7; by the revised EAC rarity ratings in the early 1980s, it was down to an R-6; and now it's considered no better than an R-5."[55]

1798, Style 2 Hair, Small 8, High Top Serif on 7 • BW-51, S-184, B-45.

Breen dies: 32-GG. ***Estimated population:*** 1,250 to 1,500.

1798, Style 2 Hair, Small 8, High Top Serif on 7 (BW-51, S-184, B-45).

Obverse: *Date:* Low and about evenly spaced. High top serif on 7. *LIBERTY:* Widely spaced. Uprights of E and R over high waves. Upright of T over junction of hair and forehead, but slightly more over hair. *Points of distinction:* Compare to the preceding, especially LIBERTY.

Reverse: Same as preceding.

Notes: This variety exists in Mint State, and is rare so fine.

1798, Style 2 Hair, Small 8, Thick Fraction Bar Slopes Down to Right • BW-52, S-185, B-46.

Breen dies: 32-HH. ***Estimated population:*** 500 to 750.

1798, Style 2 Hair, Small 8, Thick Fraction Bar Slopes Down to Right (BW-52, S-185, B-46).

Detail of fraction with thick, sloping bar.

Obverse: Same as preceding. *Points of distinction:* Multiple cracks are seen on all.

Reverse: Style 2 letters. Highest-right leaf below serif of S (slightly more left than usual). Fraction bar overly thick and sloped down to right. Numerator over 0, but left of center of the bar. *Points of distinction:* On early impressions a clash mark with denticles is above ERICA. This fades, but other clashes appear. In a late state there is a rim cud over IC.

Notes: EF is the highest-known grade.

1798, Style 2 Hair, Small 8, Style 1 Reverse Letters, Crack from Fraction to ME • BW-53, S-186, B-39.

Breen dies: 28-CC. ***Estimated population:*** 750 to 1,000.

1798, Style 2 Hair, Small 8, Style 1 Reverse Letters, Crack from Fraction to ME (BW-53, S-186, B-39).

Obverse: *Date:* Low. 79 slightly close. *LIB-ERTY:* LIB and ER close. E and R over high waves. Upright of T over hair. Lower-right serif of Y short. *Points of distinction:* Always with a light crack at TY to the right rim.

Reverse: Berry left of bow is distant from the stem. Pair of leaves opposite RI overlap and hide the stem. *Points of distinction:* Crack from rim beginning below the fraction, continuing through the lower right of the fraction and the leaf tips, and curving up to the right through ME is always present on the 1798 coins. This die was also used to coin 1799, 9 Over 8 (BW-2). The 1799, 9 Over 8, overdate was struck first. The rim cud over IC has expanded, and other cracks appear.

Notes: A single example in Mint State is reported, otherwise grades are EF and lower.

1798, Style 2 Hair, Small 8 • BW-54, S-187, B-40. *Breen dies:* 28-DD. **Estimated population:** Thousands.

1798, Style 2 Hair, Small 8 (BW-54, S-187, B-40).

Obverse: Same as preceding. *Points of distinction:* The crack has expanded, and other cracks eventually develop.

Reverse: Style 2 letters. Top-right leaf tip under serif of S. Left branch short. Top-left berry droops. Fraction bar short. *Points of distinction:* Some coins are from a perfect die, and others have one or more cracks.

Notes: This variety exists in Mint State. Breen believes this is the commonest variety of 1798.

1799, 9 Over 8, Draped Bust

Mintage (per Mint Report): Unknown.

The production of 1799-dated cents is unknown but was smaller than any other year in the series; most of the cents in the 1799 Mint Report were from dies dated 1798. The 1799, 9 Over 8, overdate cent, nearly always seen in lower grades, is usually lumped with the 1799 perfect date in terms of publicity and respect among non-specialists. The 1799 date, while not the most famous of the large cents (that honor probably goes to the 1793 issues), is far and away the rarest. Generally, a collector of cents by date will opt to acquire just a "1799," whether it is an overdate, as here, or the more available perfect date.

The overdate exists in two varieties, sharing a common obverse die. Both reverse dies are very well made and resemble each other very closely, except for very minor details as described. Both were also used to coin 1798-dated cents.

The 1799, 9 Over 8, is highly prized by specialists, and a great deal of attention accompanies the auction offering of an example in, say, Very Fine.

The *Mint Report* for calendar year 1799 gives a delivery figure of 904,585. However, virtually all of these cents were dated 1798. No one knows why the Mint bothered preparing just two 1799-dated dies, with one being an overdate of 1798, but it seems likely that the Mint simply did not wish to go a full year without issuing any coins with the 1799 date. This odd turn of events thus lead to the single scarcest date in the large cent series. This theme was repeated in 1803, when the Mint again over-estimated the number of dies needed (albeit for a different reason) leading to the next scarcest date, the 1804.[56]

1799, 9 Over 8 • BW-1, S-NC-1, B-1. *Breen dies:* 1-A. **Recorded population:** 8.

1799, 9 Over 8 (BW-1, S-NC-1, B-1). For detail of overdate see BW-2.

Obverse: Date: About evenly spaced, but 99 is slightly wider. The 9 Over 8 overdate figure is very clear, with the under 8 bold, and is distant from the drapery. *LIBERTY:* IB close. E and R over high waves of hair. Upright of T over hair.

Reverse: Berry left of bow touches the stem. Pair of leaves opposite RI touch the prominently raised stem. *Points of distinction:* This die was also used to coin 1798, Style 2 Hair, Small 8 (BW-40).

Notes: Breen records the best as the Fine-12 Geiss coin (this grade being per Breen), listed in *Penny Whimsy* as VF-20. Others are VG-7 and lower. This variety was discovered by Dr. Sheldon in B. Max Mehl's Frederic W. Geiss Collection sale, February 18, 1947, lot 48.

1799, 9 Over 8 • BW-2, S-188, B-2. *Breen dies:* 1-B. **Estimated population:** 175 to 225.

1799, 9 Over 8 (BW-2, S-188, B-2).

Detail of the overdate.

Obverse: Same as preceding. *Points of distinction:* The die fails with a curving break at the right side of LIBERTY. A rare late die state shows triple cracks at LIBERTY. At this time the average life for a coining die was about 40,000 impressions.

Reverse: Berry left of bow is distant from the stem. Pair of leaves opposite RI overlap and hide the stem. *Points of distinction:* This die was also used to coin 1798, Style 2 Hair, Small 8, Style 1 Reverse Letters, Crack From Fraction to ME (BW-53). The 1798 was struck first. A very rare late die state shows a crack from the rim to the second 0, up through three leaf tips to ME, and to the rim.

Notes: A single AU example is followed by several grades of VF. Examples are mostly in low grades and are often porous or corroded. This variety is rare in grades of VG and upward, with pleasing, smooth surfaces.

1799, 9 Over 8 (BW-2)	Cert	Avg	%MS
	7	8.4	0%

AG-3	G-4	VG-8	F-12	VF-20
$3,630	$5,670	$13,500	$20,330	$32,000

1799, Draped Bust
Mintage (per Mint Report*): Unknown.*

The production of 1799-dated cents is unknown but was smaller than any other year in the series; most of the cents in the 1799 Mint Report were from dies dated 1798. The 1799 cent, sharing honors with the 1799, 9 Over 8, overdate, has been the most famous date in the series, ever since numismatics became a popular hobby in the 1850s. Nearly all are well worn, in grades such as About Good to VG, usually porous, corroded, or with other detractions—what Jack Robinson, William C. Noyes, and others might call "scudzy." Properly graded VG, Fine, and VF coins, if on smooth planchets and with excellent eye appeal, are very highly prized.

Over the years there has been much speculation as to why most examples show extensive wear, including the theory that the copper was especially soft. However, tests on the cents using the Mohs scale of hardness (devised to test minerals) have shown that the copper does not measurably differ from other cents of the era. Probably, the mintage quantity was very small, and it was only by chance that no Mint State examples were saved.

In the 19th century, a time when it was not generally realized in numismatic circles that calendar-year mintage figures were not necessarily relevant to the number of coins struck with that *date*, several theories arose as to why the 1799 cent was so rare, when the mintage was liberal. See Numismatic Notes for BW-1.

There is only one die variety of the perfect date 1799 cent.

Typical values for 1799 cents.

1799			Cert	Avg	%MS
			42	11.8	2%

AG-3	G-4	VG-8	F-12	VF-20
$3,170	$4,750	$9,100	$15,330	$27,000

1799 • BW-1, S-189, B-3. *Breen dies:* 2-C. **Estimated population:** 800 to 1,000.

1799 (BW-1, S-189, B-3). This is the Henry C. Hines Collection example, AU, considered to be the finest known.

Obverse: *Date:* Perfect (not overdated) second 9. 99 close. Second 9 distant from drapery. *LIBERTY:* High above head. LIB and ER slightly close. E and R over high waves of hair. Upright of T over hair.

Reverse: Tip of highest outside leaf under serif of S. Berries very large. Figures in the denominator are heavy and closely spaced, 00 being slightly closer. Bar extends from upper left of 1 to left side of second 0. *Points of distinction:* On the latest state, two small rim breaks occur at the upper right.

Notes: The finest by a good measure is the AU-50 coin commonly referred to as the "Hines cent." The coin turned up in England in the 1920s and was sold by A.H. Baldwin & Sons, Ltd. Later owners included Frank H. Shumate, Elmer Sears, and Wayte Raymond, the last selling it to Henry Hines for a reported $2,500.[57] From Hines it went to Robert Henderson, founder of the Sheraton Hotel chain. In 1947 it crossed the block in Numismatic Gallery's ANA Convention sale and sold below market value at $1,500.

In September 1958, it was the star attraction, or should have been, at Abe Kosoff's sale of the Dr. James O. Sloss Collection. There was not as much "buzz" as was hoped for (Q. David Bowers, who was present, noted), and it went quietly to R.E. Naftzger Jr., in whose collection it remained until 1992. The cent went through several hands, into the Daniel Holmes Collection, auctioned by Ira and Larry Goldberg in 2009. For that offering the catalogers, Bob Grellman and Chris Victor-McCawley, called it AU-55, but NGC raised the bar by many numbers and certified it as MS-62. Another high-grade (for a 1799) cent was also owned by Hines, and was sold in 1952 by New Netherlands Coin Co. as part of the Homer K. Downing Collection. This sale provided the first deeply researched and extensively annotated catalog by that company, starting a tradition that quickly became famous.

Most coins of this variety are low grade and with problems, as noted above. It is a possibility that some of the nicer examples of this and other scarce varieties owe their survival to J.N.T. Levick and others who were allowed to enter the Mint circa 1857 to search through the old coppers that had been redeemed for the new small cents.[58] As Dr. Sheldon and others point out, overgrading is rampant for coins of this date. For the typically available well-worn coin it is difficult to find an example with a nice balance, having both LIBERTY and the date well defined.[59]

Numismatic Notes: Édouard Frossard, *Monograph of United States Cents and Half Cents Issued Between the Years 1793 and 1857,* 1879:

In nearly every 1799 cent we have examined, the legend or date was weak. From the fact that the two last numbers of the date appear weak and even indistinct, collectors should not hastily reject the piece as spurious; the impression itself may have been light, and the indistinct date may be caused by a softness in the metal, the lack of a properly milled border, or the closeness of the curls of the 9 to the rim, causing the date to be easily abraded or worn by friction while in circulation. Nevertheless, the boasted rarity of this piece has undoubtedly acted as an incentive to dishonest practices on the part of numismatic tinkers and others, who wished (and still wish) to produce specimens that can pass as genuine among credulous or inexperienced collectors. We therefore caution those collectors in whose eyes an altered or forged coin is an abomination, and who want none but genuine specimens in their cabinets, to closely examine by means of a lens, or to submit to those more experienced than they, before purchasing, any specimen on which rests the slightest shadow of doubt.

One thing is certain, either the 1799 cents change ownership with amazing rapidity, or the number available to collectors has vastly increased. At any rate, the difficulty experienced by Mr. Mickley, when first in search of a specimen of this date to complete his set of cents, no longer exists, and fair to good specimens can easily be obtained when wanted. We have had as many as seven 1799 cents, from which to make a selection, when desiring to purchase a fine specimen for a private collection. In condition there was but little difference between them, they ranking at what may be called "very good for date," but in price they ranged all the way from $20 to $100—the last by no means the best.

On the rarity of the 1799 cent: From the *American Journal of Numismatics,* October 1882:

A Very Scarce Penny: A good story is told by numismatists regarding the big pennies of the year 1799, and was originated by the late Dr. M.W. Dickeson, who had a sly method of creating a market for his goods. The tale was to the effect that some years ago in Salem, Mass., someone conceived the idea that it would be a good thing to send all the pennies they could get to Africa; so a ship was loaded up after the coin had been secured, and in due course of time it arrived in that very warm country. Here the work of trading began, and the bright and shining coppers were traded off with the female natives for oils and other merchantable articles. The African bored holes in the coins and used them for necklaces, ear-rings, nose-rings and other ornaments. The result of this was that the pennies were very scarce. The story is generally believed by coin collectors, and as a result a good penny of the year 1799 commands all the way from $15 to $25, according to the degree of perfection.

Mr. E. Mason, Jr., the numismatist, has another version to give regarding the scarcity of this coin. He said that the records of the Mint for the years 1798–99 show that over 700,000 pennies were coined, but that on account of the method of keeping the accounts, it was impossible to tell just how many there were each year.

"The cause of the scarcity," Mr. Mason said, "lies in the fact that the coins were imperfectly struck off. The date on the bottom seemed to be very soft, and it readily wore off. I have had some three or four thousand of these pennies, and I believe I have seen as many more with the date completely obliterated. There are pennies of other years that are more difficult to obtain than those of 1799, and if there were so many of them in Africa, it would pay to send an agent there to hunt them up, and we would have had a man there long ago. Some time ago it was said that the pennies of 1812 were commanding large figures, and that only a few were in existence. They can be had readily for three or four cents apiece."—*Philadelphia Record*.

Mehl's Numismatic Monthly, February 1908, ran:

Rare Copper Cents.
Coin Collector's Theory to
Account for Their Scarcity.

That some of the rarest and most valuable of the United States cents, particularly those dated 1799 and 1804, owe their scarcity to the fact that Fulton built the steamboat *Clermont* is the theory held by some coin collectors. They believe that thousands of the old time large copper cents went toward making the copper boiler for the pioneer steamboat.

This theory would explain the mystery that has long puzzled coin collectors as to the reason for the almost total disappearance of the cents of the dates mentioned. The first cents struck at the United States Mint at Philadelphia were of large size. The copper blanks, or planchets, were imported from England, being sent over in kegs. Copper at this period was a scarce article in this country, with the exception of the small quantity produced at the only copper mines then known in the United States, those at Granby, Conn., nearly all the metal used here came from England.

Builders of steam engines in those days were of the opinion that boilers

constructed of iron were unsafe and impracticable and as a consequence boilers were made of copper, all the boilers that came from England being, it is said, constructed of that metal. Fulton was likewise of the belief that copper was the only fit metal to be used in boilers. It is likewise possible that, finding a scarcity of metal with which to construct the boiler of the *Clermont*, he finally resorted to the most convenient source of supply, which happened to be the large United States copper cents.

Of course, the cost of such a boiler would represent a large sum, but it is on the records that the steam frigate *Fulton*, another ship, launched in 1815, the year of the inventor's death, had a boiler entirely constructed of copper which alone cost the large sum of $23,000. That the supply of cents of this period was large enough to meet such a demand is also likely enough. From 1793 to and including 1795, 1,066,033 cents were coined and in 1796, 974,000 were struck.[60]

Joseph Mickley and the 1799 cent: One of numismatics's favorite twice-told tales involved Joseph J. Mickley, early numismatist in Philadelphia. He was a repairer of violins, pianos, and other instruments. His home was open to fellow collectors, who enjoyed many evenings of camaraderie there. Today he is remembered as one of the most famous people in the hobby.

Edward Groh, another early collector—and, at the age of 20, one of five founders of the American Numismatic Society, in March 1858—outlived most of his peers. On October 20, 1901, an interview with him was printed in the *New York Times*. Groh told the reporter about the coin collecting scene of 30 or 40 years earlier. The veteran numismatist lamented that in early times it was possible to track down rare issues and find bargains among coins in circulation, but now it had become a "very matter-of-fact science and study." Further:

The story of Mickley's chase after the 1799 cent illustrates the difference of methods then and now. Mr. Mickley wasn't a collector when he started to hunt for that cent, but he had been born in the year 1799, and wanted the coin for a pocket piece. Nowadays he would have found out the whereabouts of every cent of that mintage simply by consulting any dealer in town. As it was, he had to go about it in the old way. Now it happens that the 1799 cent is the rarest known, and it was years before Mr. Mickley had his ambition to possess one fulfilled. By that time he had become so interested in examining coins and consulting with collectors all over the country that he had become quite an enthusiast on the subject himself. When he died a few years ago he left one of the finest private coin collections in the country.

Actually, Mickley, who began collecting coins by 1817, sold most of his collection to W. Elliot Woodward in 1867.[61] Mickley died on February 15, 1878.

The Abbey 1799 cent: The name of pioneer numismatist Lorenzo Abbey is remembered today through the so-called "Abbey cent," a particularly nice example of the rare 1799 year. On September 8, 1863, his collection was auctioned by Henry Leeds & Co., New York City. In 1996 this was cataloged by Mark Borckardt as part of the Eliasberg Collection sale.

Abbey is said by some to have bought the 1799 cent circa 1844, but accounts vary. Historian E.J. Attinelli recalled the collector and his holdings, but described his entry into coins as a transaction involving Augustus B. Sage, which would have taken place circa 1858:[62]

This was a coin sale, succeeding one of furniture, etc. The owner of the coins was the gentleman whose name is perpetuated in the celebrated 'Abbey Cent' of 1799, which, notwithstanding so many years have elapsed, since it was brought to the notice of the numismatic public, still maintains its position as one of the finest known. Mr. Abbey is a native of [New York state], having been born in Herkimer County, on the 14th of January, 1823. He has long been a resident of [New York City], carrying on an extensive business in needles, fishing-hooks, and tackle.

His introduction to numismatology occurred through the following incident: Mr. John Martense, a friend of his and a numismatist, having a duplicate Unc. cent of 1826, presented it to Mr. Abbey, stating that it was worth about $5; being somewhat incredulous, he took it to Mr. [Augustus B.] Sage, who at once offered Mr. Abbey $7 for the cent. Somewhat astonished by finding fine coins to have such a value, he at once applied himself in diligent search for others, and with some considerable success. The very next day he procured from a grocer's till the rare 'large head Nova Eborac.' The 1799 cent above alluded to, he bought for $25 from Mr. Rogers in Fulton St., who had bought it from a countryman for $2. Among other pieces he thus brought to the knowledge of numismatists, were the 'Washington half dollars' in copper, the 1802 half dime, subsequently sold in Mr. Lilliendahl's sale for $380, and other fine or rare pieces.[63]

Samuel Abbott Green: Samuel Abbott Green began collecting coins when he found a rare 1799 cent in circulation, sometime around 1846.[64] His interest grew, and in time he became prominent in the Boston Numismatic Society. He eventually served on the 1870 and 1872 Assay Commissions and as a co-editor of the *American Journal of Numismatics.*

Where is this coin today?: In the June 1917 issue of *The Numismatist,* Dr. Robert Cornell Jr. of Philadelphia, paid for a half-page notice that stated:

I think I am correct in assuming that there has never yet been discovered a 1799 cent Uncirculated, but the foremost dealers and many prominent collectors have assured me that my specimen, almost Uncirculated, is the finest known. I cannot compete with the unlimited bids which have recently been the rule in sales where coins that I would consider fit associates for the 1799 have been sold. If I can get a suitable offer for my small collection of choice cents, many having original red, some brilliant, I will sell it.

1800, 1800 Over 1798, Draped Bust
Mintage (per Mint Report): A small part of the 1800 figure.

It seems that, in 1800, unfinished dies were held in the engraver's department, including a 1798 die and several in which all digits except the last had been entered, as 179. Each of these was overdated to read 1800. The supply arose from the Mint having overestimated the coinage for 1798, believing that planchet shipments from Boulton & Watt would arrive on a routine basis. Delays were experienced, and problems resulted.

Today there are a remarkable 11 different die combinations of overdates for this year. The 1800, 1800 Over 1798, varieties are listed here, all from the single obverse die (with Style 1 Hair), followed by the 1800, 180 Over 179, varieties in a separate section. Among the 1800, 1800 Over 1798, two are rare, the first with only three known and the second with slightly more than a dozen. The remaining two are obtainable easily enough.

1800, 1800 Over 1798, 1 Right of Center of Small Fraction Bar • BW-1, S-NC-5, B-3. *Breen dies: 2-B. Recorded population: 3.*

1800, 1800 Over 1798, 1 Right of Center of Small Fraction Bar (BW-1, S-NC-5, B-3).

Obverse: Date: Very compact. 7 bold under the 8. Loop of 9 visible within first 0; part of the top of the 9 visible above it. Traces of the center of the 8 within the second 0, and a small trace above it. 1 and second 0 about equidistant from bust and denticles. *LIBERTY:* ER slightly wide. E over wave, R almost touching wave. Upright of T over hair.

Reverse: Numerator, 1, far to the right of the center of the very small bar. Bar extends from upper right of 1 to above left side of second 0; definitive. Bar much closer to the left ribbon than to the right ribbon. *Points of distinction:* A heavy rim cud is seen at the upper right, extending well into AME.

Notes: Discovered by D. Stanley Q. West in 1965 and published in 1968, thus not included in *Penny Whimsy* or other early references.[65] The three examples are VG-10 (discovery coin), AG-3, and AG-3.

1800, 1800 Over 1798 • BW-2, S-NC-6, B-4. *Breen dies: 2-C.* **Recorded population:** 13.

1800, 1800 Over 1798 (BW-2, S-NC-6, B-4).

Obverse: Same as preceding.

Reverse: Numerator, 1, centered above fraction bar. Bar extends from above center of 1 to above center of second 0. Bar equidistant between the two ribbons.

Notes: Walter Breen records the highest as "VF-25, sharpness of EF-40, but repaired at D ST." At one earlier time it was auctioned as AU.

1800, 1800 Over 1798 • BW-3, S-190, B-5. *Breen dies: 2-D.* **Estimated population:** 300 to 400.

1800, 1800 Over 1798 (BW-3, S-190, B-5).

Obverse: Same as preceding. *Points of distinction:* Some are from a perfect die, and others have one or two cracks.

Reverse: First S of STATES low. Numerator, 1, is very slightly left of center above fraction bar. Bar extends from upper right of 1 to slightly past center of second 0.

Notes: This variety exists in Mint State, and is rare as such. Priced after BW-4.

1800, 1800 Over 1798, 1 in Numerator Too High • BW-4, S-191, B-2. *Breen dies: 2-A.* **Estimated population:** 300 to 400.

1800, 1800 Over 1798, 1 in Numerator Too High (BW-4, S-191, B-2).

Detail of overdate.

Obverse: Same as preceding.

Reverse: Numerator, 1, is very slightly left of center above the short fraction bar. Bar extends from upper right of 1 to slightly past center of second 0. In denominator the 1 is very high. Bar is closer to right ribbon than to left. *Points of distinction:* With a clash mark over STAT and a prominent mounding at the fraction, as well as various cracks. This die was also used to coin 1800, 180 Over 179, Serif of 7 at Upper Left of 8 (BW-6). Comment by Harry E. Salyards: "Sheldon, of course, considered the NC-1 [1800, 180 Over 179, Serif of 7 at Upper Left of 8 (BW-6), in this text] a different reverse die. Much of the difficulty comes from having to compare two almost-completely hubbed reverse dies, as seen on two traditional die varieties—one of which, the NC-1, shows no distinguishing cracks, and is known by only three examples; the other of which is available by the hundreds, and is full of cracks and clashes!"[66]

Notes: EF and AU are the highest grades known.

1800, 1800 Over 1798 (BW-3 and BW-4)	Cert	Avg	%MS
	21	27.7	5%

G-4	VG-8	F-12	VF-20	EF-40	AU-50
$225	$650	$1,750	$3,000	$7,250	$17,000

1800, 180 Over 179, Draped Bust

Mintage (per Mint Report*): Part of the total for 1800.*

Among the unused dies on hand in 1800 were five that were partially completed as 179. The 7 and 9 were overpunched with an 8 and 0, and in the empty space a final 0 was added.

All have Style 2 Hair (interior curl left of drapery). Check the fraction on each reverse die, as this feature has more idiosyncrasies than any other part of the die.

Typical values for 1800, 180 Over 179, cents.
Rare varieties may be worth more.

1800, 180 Over 179	Cert	Avg	%MS
	58	24.0	7%

G-4	VG-8	F-12	VF-20	EF-40	AU-50	MS-60BN
$120	$220	$410	$775	$2,600	$4,830	$9,375

1800, 180 Over 179, Serif of 7 at Upper Left of 8 • BW-6, S-NC-1, B-1.

Breen dies: 1-A. ***Recorded population:*** 3.

1800, 180 Over 179, Serif of 7 at Upper Left of 8 (BW-6, S-NC-1, B-1).

Detail of overdate.

Obverse: *Date:* 180 closer than 00. 1 closer to hair than to denticles. Upper-left serif of 7 at upper left of 8, but a different die from the somewhat similar BW-9; top of 8 higher than other numerals. Traces of 9 within first 0. Second 0 about equidistant between denticles and drapery. *LIBERTY:* IB slightly close. Left of E and left of R each over high wave. Upright of T over hair.

Reverse: Numerator, 1, is very slightly to the left of center above short fraction bar. Bar extends from upper right of 1 to slightly past center of second 0. In denominator the 1 is very high. Bar is closer to right ribbon than to left. *Points of distinction:* This die was also used to coin 1800, 1800 Over 1798, 1 in Numerator Too High (BW-4). See note under 1800, 1800 Over 1798, 1 in Numerator Too High (BW-4).

Notes: The three examples are F-12, VG-8, and G-6.

1800, 180 Over 179, "Horned 8", Fraction Bar Tilts Down to Right •
BW-7, S-192, B-6. *Breen dies:* 3-E. ***Estimated population:*** 300 to 400.

1800, 180 Over 179, "Horned 8", Fraction Bar Tilts Down to Right (BW-7, S-192, B-6).

Detail of overdate.

Obverse: *Date:* 18 close. 1 closer to hair than to denticles. Top serif and upper right of 7 visible above 8, creating a "Horned 8." Upper loop of 9 and ball of 9 bold within first 0. Second 0 closer to denticles than to drapery. *LIBERTY:* IB close.

ER wide. Left of E and left of R each over high wave. T mostly over hair, slight part over forehead. Base of Y slightly low.

Reverse: Lower-left serif of E of STATES missing. Fraction bar tilts down to right and is distant from 10, but close to second 0. Closer to the left ribbon than to the right. Numerator, 1, is very slightly left of the center above short fraction bar. Bar extends from upper right of 1 to slightly past center of second 0. In denominator the 1 is very high. Bar is closer to right ribbon than to left. *Points of distinction:* Always with an arc-like crack from the rim through the fraction, up to the right to the rim at I. Later, other cracks appear.

Notes: A single example in Mint State is followed by an AU, then at least two EF.

1800, 180 Over 179, "Horned 8", Square Left End, Pointed Right End to Fraction Bar • BW-8, S-193, B-7. *Breen dies:* 3-F. ***Estimated population:*** 120 to 160.

1800, 180 Over 179, "Horned 8", Square Left End, Pointed Right End to Fraction Bar (BW-8, S-193, B-7).

Detail of overdate.

Obverse: Same as preceding.

Reverse: Stemless leaf pair below T of CENT. Fraction bar square at left end, pointed at right. Numerator centered over it. Bar extends from upper right of 1 to center of second 0. *Points of distinction:* Most often with a crack at the fraction bar and to the left. Another at E of AMER-ICA. Sometimes with cud break at the rim below the fraction.

Notes: A single Mint State is followed by an EF, then multiple graded at the VF level. Dr. Sheldon knew of no more than a dozen when *Early American Cents* was published in 1949. Since then many have been found—testimony to the appeal and effective use of Sheldon's text.

1800, 180 Over 179, Serif of 7 at Upper Left of 8, Horizontal Top of 7 in Upper Loop • BW-9, S-194, B-8. *Breen dies:* 4-G. **Estimated population:** 400 to 500.

1800, 180 Over 179, Serif of 7 at Upper Left of 8, Horizontal Top of 7 in Upper Loop (BW-9, S-194, B-8).

Detail of overdate.

Obverse: *Date:* 1 closer to hair than to denticles. 18 slightly wide. Serif of 7 protrudes from upper left of 7, but a different die than BW-6, described earlier; horizontal element of 7 prominent within upper loop. 9 and ball prominent within first 0, and outline of top of 9 protrudes above it. *LIBERTY:* Base of L slightly low. RTY wide. E and R over high waves of hair. T above hair. *Points of distinction:* Often with rim deterioration above RTY.

Reverse: First S of STATES slightly low. In fraction, numerator 1 is closer to bar than any denominator figures and is slightly to the left of center. 1 in denominator is closer to bar than either 0. *Points of distinction:* With crack from the second 0 to A at the right. Additional cracks appear, eventually resulting in a prominent rim cud below the fraction.

Notes: This variety exists in Mint State.

1800, 180 Over 179 • BW-10, S-195, B-9. *Breen dies:* 4-H. **Estimated population:** 40 to 60.

1800, 180 Over 179 (BW-10, S-195, B-9).

Obverse: Same as preceding. *Points of distinction:* With a rim cud at right of T and all of Y.

Reverse: CE extremely close, ENT separated. Thin fraction bar. Numerator, 1, centered over bar. Both 1's about the same distance from the bar. *Points of distinction:* With a crack from the denticles to the second 0 into ICA. Some mounding in the same area.

Notes: A single AU (ANS) is followed by several of grade VF.

1800, 180 Over 179, Top of 7 Above 8 • BW-11, S-196, B-10. *Breen dies:* 5-I. **Estimated population:** Thousands.

1800, 180 Over 179, Top of 7 Above 8 (BW-11, S-196, B-10).

Detail of overdate.

Obverse: *Date:* 180 close, 00 very slightly wider. Top of 7 protrudes above 8; definitive. Upper loop of 9 and ball prominent in first 0. *LIBERTY:* IB close. E and R over high waves of hair. TY slightly low. Upright of T over hair.

Reverse: First S of STATES quite low. Numerator, 1, slightly to left of center of bar, and is slightly closer to the left ribbon.

Bar from upper right of 1 to slightly left of the center of second 0. *Points of distinction:* A light crack is at ES of STATES.

Notes: AU is the highest grade known.

1800, 180 Over 179, "Horned 8", "Hook" Below Second S • BW-12, S-NC-2, B-11. *Breen dies:* 6-J. *Estimated population:* 12 to 20.

1800, 180 Over 179, "Horned 8", "Hook" Below Second S (BW-12, S-NC-2, B-11).

Obverse: Date: 180 close. Serif and upper right of 7 visible above 8; "Horned 8," but a different die from that described earlier. *LIBERTY:* LI close. Upright of T over hair. *Points of distinction:* A crack extends from the rim opposite the bust, up to the right, and a short distance into the field. This develops into a cud in the latest stages.

Reverse: "Hook" below second S of STATES, the trace of an earlier-punched letter. In fraction, numerator 1 centered. Both 1's about the same distance from the bar. Bar extends from upper right of 1 to above center of the second 0, and is closer to right ribbon. *Points of distinction:* This die was also used to coin 1800, "Q" Variety (Triangle Past First 0), Right Serif of T Over Forehead, "Hook Below Second S" (BW-20).

Notes: VG and Fine are the highest grades known, the latter very rare.

1800, Draped Bust
Mintage (per Mint Report): 2,822,175.

The cents of 1800 (perfect date) are all with Style 2 Hair. The die varieties are often quite similar, making close attention to the descriptions—and especially the photographs—very important. Checking the spacing of LIBERTY, the date numerals, and the layout of the fraction on the reverse can be especially useful. On BW-20 the right serif of the T is over the forehead; on all other dies in this group the T is completely over the hair, though sometimes barely.

Save for two rarities, the varieties are collectible, although several are elusive in high grades. Most cents of this year are found well worn, leading some to suggest that the copper used was especially soft, but there is no proof of this.

Typical values for 1800 cents.
Rare varieties may be worth more.

1800	Cert	Avg	%MS
	134	25.7	10%

AG-3	G-4	VG-8	F-12	VF-20	EF-40	AU-50	MS-60BN	MS-63BN	MS-65BN
$45	$90	$165	$340	$550	$2,270	$3,750	$6,250	$13,625	$17,500

1800, "Q" Variety (Triangle Past First 0), Right Serif of T Over Forehead, "Hook Below Second S" • BW-20, S-197, B-12. *Breen dies:* 7-J.
Estimated population: Thousands.

1800, "Q" Variety (Triangle Past First 0), Right
Serif of T Over Forehead, "Hook Below
Second S" (BW-20, S-197, B-12).

Detail of fanciful "Q."

Obverse: Date: 18 close. Die defect within first 0 and a triangular defect far past its lower right (in fact, next to the second 0), giving rise to the somewhat far-fetched nickname of "Q" variety or "18Q0." A useful guide for quick identification as all have this feature. *LIBERTY:* IB close. Lower-left serif of Y defective. Right serif of T over forehead, but the rest of the letter is over the hair (only such die in this group). *Points of distinction:* All have a V-shaped break from the border to between I and B.

Reverse: "Hook" below second S of STATES, the trace of an earlier-punched letter. In fraction, numerator, 1, centered. Both 1's about the same distance from the bar. Bar extends from upper right of 1 to above center of the second 0, and is closer to right ribbon. *Points of distinction:* This die was also used to coin 1800, 180 Over 179, "Horned 8", "Hook" Below Second S (BW-12). Usually with one or two small cracks, later a rim break over AT of STATES.

Notes: This variety exists in Mint State.

1800 • BW-21, S-198, B-19. *Breen dies:* 10-Q. *Estimated population:* 30 to 45.

1800 (BW-21, S-198, B-19).

Obverse: Date: Fairly evenly spaced. Serif of 1 very close to curl, base distant from denticles. Second 0 closer to drapery than to denticles, and centered over a denticle. *LIBERTY:* Letters close, IB perhaps closest. E and R over high waves. Lower-left serif of Y weak. *Points of distinction:* Typically with clash marks above and near TY.

Reverse: Numerator, 1, slightly right of the center of bar. Bar from upper right of 1 to just before center of the second 0, and slants down slightly to the left. Denominator 1 much closer to the bar than is second 0. Both 0's about the same distance below the bar. *Points of distinction:* Crack from ribbon to top of 1. Light crack at ICA to past the end of the right ribbon.

Notes: VG is the highest-known grade. This has the lowest top grade of *any* Sheldon-numbered 1800 variety.[67]

1800 • BW-22, S-199, B-14. *Breen dies:* 9-L. ***Estimated population:*** 120 to 160.

1800 (BW-22, S-199, B-14).

Obverse: Date: Widely and fairly evenly spaced. Serif of 1 prominent and very close to curl, base distant from denticles. Second 0 closer to denticles than to drapery. Both 0's light at their bases. *LIBERTY:* LIB close. E and R over high waves.

Reverse: Berry opposite E of UNITED has no stem and is wedged between leaf point below and leaf stem above. Numerator, 1, very slightly right of the center of bar. Bar begins over upper right of 1 and ends slightly before center of second 0. First 0 low. *Points of distinction:* Some are from a perfect die, but more often this variety appears with cracks, the die finally failing in the upper section.

Notes: There is one example of grade AU (ANS), followed by several VF pieces.

1800 • BW-23, S-200, B-15. *Breen dies:* 9-M. ***Estimated population:*** 300 to 400.

1800 (BW-23, S-200, B-15).

Obverse: Date: Widely and fairly evenly spaced. Serif of 1 small and very close to curl, base distant from denticles. Second 0 closer to denticles than to drapery. *LIBERTY:* LIB close, IB closest. E and R are each slightly right of the center of a hair wave. *Points of distinction:* Typically struck

so that the denticles are short at the upper left and larger at the lower right. Bulges develop, as do cracks.

Reverse: Serif on C of CENT a tiny spine. Numerator, 1, slightly left of the center of bar and leans slightly left; slightly closer to left ribbon than to the right ribbon. Bar begins over right corner of 1 and ends just before center of second 0. Bar is slightly closer to left ribbon. First 0 low. *Points of distinction:* Nearly always with one or more cracks. This die was first used to coin BW-33, then reworked to coin BW-23.[68]

Notes: VF is the highest grade known.

1800 • BW-24, S-NC-3, B-16. *Breen dies:* 9-N. ***Estimated population:*** 25 to 30.

1800 (BW-24, S-NC-3, B-16).

Obverse: Same as preceding.

Reverse: Serif on C of CENT a tiny spine. Spike at top of I of AMERICA. Numerator, 1, close to and centered over bar; closer to left ribbon. Bar begins over right corner of 1 and ends just before center of second 0. First 0 low.

Notes: Single examples of EF and VF are followed by multiple at the VG level.

1800 • BW-25, S-201, B-17. *Breen dies:* 9-O. **Estimated population:** 75 to 120.

1800 (BW-25, S-201, B-17).

Obverse: Same as preceding. *Points of distinction:* A crack is seen at the left of 1 of 1800.

Reverse: No stems to leaves left of O of ONE. Numerator, 1, close to and centered over bar. Bar begins over right corner of 1 and ends over center of second 0. Both 0's low. *Points of distinction:* Multiple cracks develop.

Notes: VF is the highest grade known.

1800, Spike on Right Side of Right Ribbon • BW-26, S-202, B-18. *Breen dies:* 9-P. *Estimated population:* 75 to 120.

1800, Spike on Right Side of
Right Ribbon (BW-26, S-202, B-18).

Detail showing spike on right ribbon.

Obverse: Same as preceding. *Points of distinction:* Now with much heavier cracks through the lower-left obverse. These probably caused the die to fail, accounting for the elusive nature of this variety today.

Reverse: Raised projection or spike on outside of right ribbon about one-third up from its tip. Numerator, 1, very slightly left of center. Bar thickest about one-third of the distance from its right edge, and tapers to become thinner to the left and right. Bar begins over right corner of 1 and ends just before center of second 0. All denominator numerals are low and closer to being on the same level than usually seen. Denticles thin and closely spaced. *Points of distinction:* This die was first used to coin BW-26, then reworked to coin BW-27 and 1801 (BW-4).[69] Multiple cracks develop. Some have swelling that consumes TATE and extends to other areas.

Notes: EF and AU (especially rare) are the highest grades known.

1800, Die Chips in Field Opposite Nose • BW-27, S-203, B-29. *Breen dies:* 19-V. *Estimated population:* 300 to 400.

1800, Die Chips in Field Opposite
Nose (BW-27, S-203, B-29).

Detail showing a string of die
chips in the field beyond the nose.

Obverse: Date: Evenly spaced. Tiny serif of 1 very close to curl; base of 1 distant from denticles. Second 0 closer to drapery than to denticles. *LIBERTY:* ER wide. E mostly over wave, left upright of R over wave. *Points of distinction:* Connected string of die chips in field past nose, closer to denticles. This die was continued in use far beyond retirement age.

Reverse: AM slightly separated, ME touch. Numerator, 1, high and slightly left of the center of bar. Bar begins part-way over the 1 and ends slightly past center of second 0. Denominator 1 particularly heavy. First 0 low. *Points of distinction:* This die was first used to coin BW-26, then reworked to coin BW-27 and 1801 (BW-4).[70]

Notes: This variety exists in Mint State, and is very rare as such.

1800 • BW-28, S-204, B-25. *Breen dies:* 16-T. *Estimated population:* 120 to 160.

1800 (BW-28, S-204, B-25).

Obverse: Date: Serif of 1 almost touches hair above it but is spaced from curl. 18 close, 00 widest. Second 0 is about centered between the denticles and drapery and is over a space between denticles. *LIBERTY:* LIB close, BE slightly wide. Left of E and

R over waves. *Points of distinction:* Always with clash marks and sometimes with a crack in the right field. Late die states have a rim break at the right.

Reverse: C of CENT barely touches leaf. Left wreath stem short. Numerator, 1, fairly close to bar and centered over it, also centered over the 0 below. Bar begins part-way over 1 and ends over center of the second 0. First 0 low. 1 and second 0 are about equidistant from the bar. Bar closer to right ribbon. Otherwise, quite similar to BW-28.

Notes: AU is the highest grade known.

1800, Flat Spot in Hair Above 1 • BW-29, S-205, B-26. *Breen dies:* 17-T. *Estimated population:* 120 to 160.

1800, Flat Spot in Hair Above 1 (BW-29, S-205, B-26).

Detail of bald spot in hair.

Obverse: Date: 18 wide, 80 close, 00 closest. 1 and 8 closer to bust than to denticles. *LIBERTY:* Uprights of E and R over high waves. ER and TY wide. Upright of T over hair but barely. Y slightly low. *Points of distinction:* Above the hair strand above the 1 is a flat or "bald" spot with no hair; definitive. Most have a horizontal crack at the left, from the hair toward the rim.

Reverse: Same as preceding.

Notes: This variety exists in Mint State.

1800 • BW-30, S-206, B-27. *Breen dies:* 17-U. **Estimated population:** 300 to 400.

1800 (BW-30, S-206, B-27).

Obverse: Same as preceding, but flat spot has been repaired by adding hair. *Points of distinction:* The horizontal crack in the left field is slightly larger as it extends toward the left rim.

Reverse: C of CENT barely touches leaf. Left wreath stem short. Numerator, 1, fairly close to bar and centered over it, also centered over the 0 below. Bar begins part-way over 1 and ends slightly before center of the second 0. First 0 low. 1 much closer to bar than is second 0. Bar closer to left ribbon. Otherwise, it is quite similar to BW-28 and BW-29. *Points of distinction:* On most, a triangular rim cud below the first 0 is seen, with various cracks.

Notes: EF is the highest grade known.

1800, Low L, Rim Break at Fraction • BW-31, S-207, B-28. *Breen dies:* 18-U. *Estimated population:* 300 to 400.

1800, Low L, Rim Break at Fraction (BW-31, S-207, B-28).

Obverse: Date: 1 much closer to hair than to denticles. 00 wide. Second 0 about equidistant from denticles and drapery and is centered over a space between denticles.

LIBERTY: L low (unusual). LIB close, LI closest. Uprights of E and R over waves. Upright of T over hair but barely. *Points of distinction:* Some have a small crack from the hair to T.

Reverse: Same as preceding. *Points of distinction:* The state is advanced, still with the prominent rim cud at the bottom, but with additional development.

Notes: VF and EF are the highest grades known, the latter quite rare.

1800, Die Failure Above TY • BW-32, S-208, B-21. *Breen dies:* 12-S. *Estimated population:* 300 to 400.

1800, Die Failure Above TY (BW-32, S-208, B-21).

Obverse: Date: Serif of 1 almost touches curl. 00 slightly close. Second 0 much closer to denticles than to drapery. *LIBERTY:* LIB

slightly close. Uprights of E and R over waves. RTY wide. Upright of T over hair, but barely. *Points of distinction:* Most, but not all, have die failure at the rim over TY.

Reverse: Numerator, 1, slightly left of center of bar and about the same distance from it as is the 1 in the denominator. 1 in denominator closer to bar than second 0 (which leans left). Bar slightly closer to right ribbon than to the left.

Notes: VF is the highest grade known.

1800 • BW-33, S-NC-4, B-22. *Breen dies:* 13-S. **Reported population:** 9.

1800 (BW-33, S-NC-4, B-22).

Obverse: Date: 1 close to hair and distant from denticles. 00 slightly close. *LIBERTY:*

LIB close. E and R over waves of hair. Y slightly low. *Points of distinction:* This die was first used to coin BW-33, then reworked to coin BW-23.[71] Cracks develop, resulting in die damage, including a very large cud break at the left rim.

Reverse: Same as preceding.

Notes: There is a single example of AU, VG is the next-highest grade.

1800 • BW-34, S-209, B-23. *Breen dies:* 14-S. **Estimated population:** 300 to 400.

1800 (BW-34, S-209, B-23).

Obverse: Date: 1 much closer to hair than to denticles. 18 wide. Second 0 about equidistant from denticles and drapery, and centered over a denticle. *LIBERTY:* Very closely spaced, especially LIB and ERT. E and upright of R over waves. Y slightly

low. *Points of distinction:* Prominent clash marks are seen near the portrait. The die fails, causing indistinct areas.

Reverse: Same as preceding. *Points of distinction:* Found perfect and later with very light rim break under 00 to right ribbon end; also, light crack from rim to top of AM, through center of ER, near the bottom of ICA, and from right foot of A to ribbon end. This develops into rim cud below the fraction, extending to the right.

Notes: There is a single example of Mint State, then several occur in AU.

1800 • BW-35, S-210, B-24. *Breen dies:* 15-S. **Estimated population:** 30 to 45.

1800 (BW-35, S-210, B-24).

Obverse: Date: Closely spaced, 18 closest. 1 close to hair. Denticles often off the planchet. *LIBERTY:* IB close. Uprights of

E and R over waves. Y slightly low. *Points of distinction:* Early impressions have a crack at ER, continuing past the hair to near the right rim. The die fails further with continued use.

Reverse: Same as preceding. *Points of distinction:* The die deteriorates, cracks are seen, and a rim break is over M of AMERICA and another over the space between I and C.

Notes: EF and AU are the highest grades known, and the variety is very rare as such.

1800 • BW-36, S-211, B-13. *Breen dies:* 8-K. **Estimated population:** 400 to 500.

1800 (BW-36, S-211, B-13).

Obverse: Date: Evenly spaced. 1 and second 0 closer to bust than to denticles. *LIBERTY:* Closely spaced. E and R over hair waves. Base of Y slightly low. *Points of distinction:* Swelling and die failure continue. In its late state, the die has a crack at the bottom of 18.

Reverse: Numerator, 1, slightly to left of the center of heavy bar and spaced from it the same distance as the 1 in the denominator; numerator, 1, is slightly closer to the left ribbon than to the right. Bar extends from upper right of 1 to center of second 0. 1 and second 0 about the same distance from bar. Bar is slightly closer to the right ribbon. *Points of distinction:* Some have a light crack from E to S of STATES.

Notes: This variety exists in Mint State, and is very rare at this level.

1800, Tiny Spike at Center Inside of C of CENT • BW-37, S-212, B-20.
Breen dies: 11-R. **Estimated population:** 300 to 400.

1800, Tiny Spike at Center Inside of C of CENT (BW-37, S-212, B-20).

Detail of spike on C in CENT.

Obverse: Date: 1 much closer to hair than to denticles. 18 wide. Second 0 closer to denticles than to drapery. *LIBERTY:* IBE

wide. E and upright of R over hair curls. TY low. Lower-left serif of Y defective. *Points of distinction:* A crack is seen on many, from the denticles to the hair, and another is from the denticles to the forehead, continuing into the portrait.

Reverse: Tiny spike at center inside of C of CENT. Right stem slightly heavier than the left stem and diagonally tapered to a point at lower right. Numerator, 1, centered over bar, and it and bar about equidistant between the ribbons. Bar begins left of the center of denominator 1, above the vertical left edge of 1, and ends over center of second 0. First 0 slightly low. Second 0 leans left.

Notes: AU is the highest grade known.

1801, Draped Bust
Mintage (per Mint Report): 1,362,837.

The cents of 1801 can be divided into two groups, as Dr. William H. Sheldon and Walter Breen divided them in the past. The first group has the first 1 in the date with a serif, while the second 1 in the date lacks this feature. As the 1 with serif is the style of 1800, and as the second 1 in all instances is blunt, it can be assumed that the Serif 1's were made as incomplete dies with the date as 180, probably in 1800, when the Serif 1 was still in use. In 1801 the dies were completed using the Blunt 1 punch whose use was initiated that year. The second group comprises dies with both 1's blunt, which were created entirely in 1801.

Spice is added to the 1801 cent roster by egregious blunders among the reverse dies. *Three* dies have 1/000 instead of the correct 1/100; another is similar, but with the erroneous first 0 in the denominator overpunched with a 1 (one of the first-mentioned dies corrected); and the third blunder is the most famous of all errors in the large cent series: in addition to the fraction appearing as 1/000, the left stem of the wreath is missing and UNITED appears as IINITED. A mechanic or other workman—not an engraver!—probably made these curious dies. Luckily, all three error types exist in sufficient numbers that they are readily collectible. What a numismatic playground!

As with 1800-dated cents, apart from the error varieties, the details of the fraction are perhaps the best guide to attributing the reverses in your first run-through.

Typical values for 1801 cents.
Rare varieties may be worth more.
Some varieties are priced individually, as follows.

1801	Cert	Avg	%MS
	120	25.1	7%

AG-3	G-4	VG-8	F-12	VF-20	EF-40	AU-50	MS-60BN	MS-63BN
$40	$70	$175	$375	$600	$1,930	$4,050	$8,500	$17,375

1801 With First 1 in Date With Pointed Top Serif
1801 • BW-1, S-213, B-1. *Breen dies:* 1-A. ***Estimated population:*** 600 to 800.

1801 (BW-1, S-213, B-1).

Obverse: Date: First 1 with serif near curl, base distant from denticles. 80 low; 01 slightly wide. Second 1 closer to denticles than to drapery. *LIBERTY:* LI and RT close. Uprights of E and R over hair waves. T mostly over hair, but with tip of lower-right serif barely over forehead. Y slightly low. *Points of distinction:* Four wavy cracks are always seen in the field, an indication of improperly tempered die steel that caused the die surface to sink and coins to have mounding.[72]

Reverse: Left stem shorter than the right. Numerator, 1, is centered on fraction bar and close to it. Both the numerator and the bar are about centered between the ribbons. Bar begins over upper right of 1 and ends near center of second 0. 100 is distant from bar; numerals evenly spaced; first 0 slightly low. *Points of distinction:* A crack extends from the numerator upward, through E of AMERICA to the denticles. More cracks develop, and in a late state there is a rim cud in the denticles left of the fraction (not clear on all examples).

Notes: This variety exists in AU and Mint State, and is very rare at either level.

1801 • BW-2, S-214, B-2. *Breen dies:* 2-A. ***Estimated population:*** 300 to 400.

1801 (BW-2, S-214, B-2).

Obverse: First 1 with serif near curl, base distant from denticles and over a space between denticles. 80 close. Second 1 closer to denticles than to drapery and over a space between denticles. *LIBERTY:* LIB close. E and upright of R over hair waves. Upright of T over hair. *Points of distinction:* The rim fails at RTY, and later a cud develops in that area.

Reverse: Same as preceding. *Points of distinction:* Cracks expand, including two diagonal cracks that are more or less parallel at the lower right. The rim break is slightly larger.

Notes: This variety exists in Mint State.

1801 • BW-3, S-215, B-4. *Breen dies:* 3-A. ***Estimated population:*** 75 to 120.

1801 (BW-3, S-215, B-4).

Obverse: First 1 with serif near curl. 180 close. Numeral 0 much closer to denticles than to drapery. *LIBERTY:* LIB close. E and upright of R over hair waves. Upright of T over hair. *Points of distinction:* Cracks develop below the ribbon, close to the hair. In a late state, the die fails above TY, and bulges are seen. Used first on BW-4.

Reverse: Same as preceding. *Points of distinction:* The die fails, causing mounding, clash marks are seen in areas, and cracks develop.

Notes: This variety exists in AU and Mint State (unique).

1801 • BW-4, S-NC-1, B-3. *Breen dies:* 3-B. ***Estimated population:*** 20 to 25.

1801 (BW-4, S-NC-1, B-3).

Obverse: Same as preceding. *Points of distinction:* Coined before BW-3, and with the obverse in an earlier die state.

Reverse: AM slightly separated, ME touch. Numerator, 1, high, and slightly left of the center of bar. Bar begins part-way over the 1 and ends slightly past center of second 0. Denominator 1 particularly heavy. First 0 low. *Points of distinction:* Clash marks are seen at the top border. This die was first used to coin 1800, Spike on Right Side of Right Ribbon (BW-26), then reworked to coin BW-4 and 1800, Die Chips in Field Opposite Nose (BW-27).[73] On this mating there are die incusations and problems at the top and upper-right border and nearby letters.

Notes: High grades are Mint State (unique) followed by VF and multiple Fine examples.

1801 • BW-5, S-NC-5, B-9. *Breen dies:* 6-F. ***Recorded population:*** 4.

1801 (BW-5, S-NC-5, B-9).

Obverse: *Date:* First 1 slightly closer to hair than to denticles, centered over a denticle. 01 slightly wide. Second 1 over a denticle and slightly closer to drapery than to denticle. *LIBERTY:* LIB and RT close. E and upright of R over hair waves. Upright of T, over hair and has a shortened bottom-right serif. *Points of distinction:* This was a very durable obverse in terms of mating with multiple reverses.

Reverse: Berry to the upper left of O of ONE has stem downward, unlike any of the other three reverses mated with this obverse. Numerator 1 close to bar. Bar begins over right side of 1 and ends over center of 0. First 0 slightly low. *Points of distinction:* The known examples have a retained cud at the upper left, encompassing most of STATES, where the die had cracked and sunk, effectively raising the field on the struck coin in this area. Note that "ATES" is visible within this umbrella-shaped area, even on the Fair-2 coin.

Notes: Grades are Fair-2 and Poor-1. While the details of the obverse die can be gained from its later use on other varieties, the reverse information is incomplete.

1801, Fraction Bar Connected to Right Ribbon • BW-6, S-NC-2, B-10.
Breen dies: 6-G. ***Reported population:*** 9.

1801, Fraction Bar Connected to
Right Ribbon (BW-6, S-NC-2, B-10).

Obverse: Same as preceding.

Reverse: Scratch from right side of fraction bar goes to right ribbon. Numerator, 1, slightly closer to the left ribbon than to the right. Bar begins slightly right of center of denominator 1. First 0 slightly low.

Notes: VG is the highest grade known.

1801, Three Errors Reverse • BW-7, S-219, B-11. *Breen dies:* 6-E. ***Estimated population:*** 750 to 1,000.

1801, Three Errors Reverse
(BW-7, S-219, B-11).

Detail showing the three errors: the meaningless fraction 1/000, left wreath stem missing, and IINITED instead of UNITED.

Obverse: Same as preceding. *Points of distinction:* Some have ERTY indistinct due to die deterioration.

Reverse: The famous Three Errors Reverse. The fraction appears as the mathematically meaningless 1/000, the left stem to the wreath is missing, and UNITED appears as IINITED. The latter was caused by first punching the U upside down, then correcting it. This die is also somewhat unusual in that there is a tiny space between C of CENT and the leaf, whereas they are usually connected. *Points of distinction:* This die, first used on BW-7, was also used to coin BW-14. Cracks develop and a cud is seen at the lower left, the final iteration of a prominent crack in this area. Likely, this die was made by a mechanic, not a skilled engraver.

Notes: This variety exists in AU and Mint State. It is fortunate that this popular variety is readily obtainable in the marketplace, although most are well worn.

In lower grades the three errors must all be discernible.

1801, Three Errors Reverse (BW-7)		Cert	Avg	%MS
		20	20.6	10%

AG-3	G-4	VG-8	F-12
$110	$275	$700	$1,750

VF-20	EF-40		AU-50
$4,250	$12,750		$28,750

1801, 1/000 Error, Berry Directly Right of Top of E of ONE • BW-8, S-220, B-12. *Breen dies:* 6-H. *Estimated population:* 300 to 400.

1801, 1/000 Error, Berry Directly Right of Top of E of ONE (BW-8, S-220, B-12).

Detail showing the 1/000 error fraction, one of several different dies with this mistake.

Obverse: Same as preceding. *Points of distinction:* A crack extends from the lower rim upward, forming an arc to the right, then traveling to the second 1, and on to the denticles. The rim deteriorates, causing cuds below the date and to the left and right. Clash marks are near the portrait.

Reverse: Error fraction 1/000. One of three 1801 dies—also see BW-16 and BW-17—with this feature. Left foot of A of STATES slightly high. ONE in normal position; E distant from leaf pair above it; berry horizontally opposite upper right of E. Highest leaf tip on right under right part of S. No thorn from lower-left wreath stem. *Points of distinction:* Cracks develop and expand. A cud is seen above AM.

Notes: EF is the highest grade known.

In lower grades the error fraction must be visible.

1801, 1/000 Error, Berry Directly Right of Top of E of ONE (BW-8)			Cert	Avg	%MS
			(a)		

AG-3	G-4	VG-8	F-12	VF-20	EF-40
$120	$220	$410	$1,050	$2,250	$4,375

a. Included in certified population for 1801, 1/000 Error, Thorn on Stem at Left (BW-17).

1801, Highest Right Leaf Tip Right of S, Fraction Spaced as 1 00 •

BW-9, S-NC-4, B-14. *Breen dies:* 8-J. *Recorded population:* 9.

1801, Highest Right Leaf Tip Right of S, Fraction Spaced as 1 00 (BW-9, S-NC-4, B-14).

Obverse: Date: Serif of first 1 points to top part of curl. 80 close. 1 distant from drapery. *LIBERTY:* LIBE slightly close. Uprights of E and R over hair waves. Upright of T over hair, but close to forehead.

Reverse: Highest-right leaf tip is to the right of the S, the only die of this class (with first 1 having serif) with this feature. Numerator, 1, right of the center of bar. Bar starts over center of denominator 1 and ends over left edge of second 0. 10 very wide—compare to BW-18. *Points of distinction:* This die was used to coin BW-9 and BW-15.

Notes: VG is the highest grade known.

1801 With First 1 in Date With Blunt Top (No Pointed Serif)

1801, Corrected Fraction • BW-11, S-221, B-5. *Breen dies:* 4-C. *Estimated population:* 750 to 1,000.

1801, Corrected Fraction (BW-11, S-221, B-5).

Detail showing the corrected fraction.

Obverse: Date: First 1 about equidistant from curl and denticles. 01 slightly wide. Second 1 closer to drapery than to denticles. *LIBERTY:* LIB close. Uprights of E and R over high hair waves. Upright of T over hair. Lower-left serif of Y long. Compare to BW-12—the same die in a later state.

Reverse: Erroneous 1/000 die with first 0 overpunched with the correct 1. Space between C of CENT and leaf (usually these touch); T high. Perhaps cut by a mechanic. This is a different die from the Corrected Fraction of 1803. *Points of distinction:* A rim cud is at the top right and another is over STA.

Notes: A very popular variety that is readily available in the marketplace. This variety exists in Mint State.

1801, Corrected Fraction	Cert	Avg	%MS
	4	26.5	25%

AG-3	G-4	VG-8	F-12	VF-20
$120	$310	$600	$1,200	$2,330

EF-40	AU-50	MS-60BN	MS-63BN
$5,330	$7,250	$16,670	$30,830

1801 • BW-12, S-216, B-6. *Breen dies:* 4-D. **Estimated population:** Thousands.

1801 (BW-12, S-216, B-6).

Detail showing N leaning in CENT.

Obverse: Same as preceding. *Points of distinction:* Certain features, such as LIBERTY,

can be indistinct due to die damage. Indeed, even high-grade coins are notoriously mushy looking. Compare the obverse of this variety with that of the same die earlier, as it appears on BW-11.

Reverse: N of CENT leans right. 1 is centered over bar. Bar begins left of the center of 1 and continues to above the center of the second 0. Bar leans slightly down to the right and is closer to right ribbon. 100 fairly evenly spaced. First 0 very slightly low. *Points of distinction:* OF is often indistinct. A rim break is seen over STA.

Notes: This variety exists in Mint State.

1801, T Over Forehead • BW-13, S-217, B-7. *Breen dies:* 5-D. **Estimated population:** 15 to 20.

1801, T Over Forehead (BW-13, S-217, B-7).

Obverse: Date: Upright of first 1 closer to denticles than to hair. 80 close. Second 1 closer to denticles than to hair. *LIBERTY:*

Positioned far right. LIB close. B and E over high waves of hair. T completely over forehead; only die in this category with this feature.

Reverse: Same as preceding. *Points of distinction:* Most show evidence of die failure near the bottom border.

Notes: EF and AU are the highest grades known for this variety, and it is very rare as such.

1801, Three Errors Reverse • BW-14, S-218, B-8. *Breen dies:* 5-E. **Estimated population:** 30 to 45.

1801, Three Errors Reverse (BW-14, S-218, B-8).

Obverse: Same as preceding. *Points of distinction:* In the late state a bulge is at ERTY and a slight bulge at the left of the lowest curl. This state is rare.

Reverse: This die was also used to coin BW-7, see entry for details.

Notes: Far the rarer of the two matings with the Three Errors Reverse. Fine and VF are the highest grades known.

In lower grades the three errors must all be visible.

1801, Three Errors Reverse (BW-14)		Cert	Avg	%MS
		(a)		

AG-3	G-4	VG-8	F-12	VF-20
$675	$1,375	$2,375	$9,000	$19,000

a. Included in certified population for 1801, Three Errors Reverse (BW-7).

1801 • BW-15, S-222, B-16. *Breen dies:* 9-J. **Estimated population:** 1,250 to 1,500.

1801 (BW-15, S-222, B-16).

Detail of rim cud at IB in LIBERTY.

Obverse: Date: 1's each equidistant from denticles and bust. 80 close. *LIBERTY:* LIB close. Uprights of E and R over hair waves. Upright of T over hair. *Points of distinction:* A cud is over IB. Clash marks through LIBERTY are on some coins.

Reverse: See BW-9. *Points of distinction:* This die was used to coin BW-9 and BW-15. In its latest use, examples of which are very rare, there is a large rim break over NITE.

Notes: This variety exists in Mint State. One of the more plentiful varieties of the era.

1801, 1/000 Error, Berry Opposite Center of E of ONE • BW-16, S-NC-3, B-15. *Breen dies:* 9-K. **Estimated population:** 25 to 30.

1801, 1/000 Error, Berry Opposite Center of E of ONE (BW-16, S-NC-3, B-15).

Detail showing error fraction.

Obverse: Same as preceding.

Reverse: Error fraction 1/000. One of three dies—also see BW-8 and BW-17—with this feature. Highest leaf tip on right slightly right of S. ONE too high, E close to leaf pair above it; berry opposite center of E. No thorn at end of stem at the left. This die was later altered to create the Corrected Fraction die of 1803: 1803, Lump Under Chin, Corrected Fraction 1/100 Over 1/000 (BW-5).[74]

Notes: VG is the highest grade known.

In lower grades the 1/000 error must be visible.

1801, 1/000 Error, Berry Opposite Center of E of ONE (BW-16)	Cert	Avg	%MS
	(a)		

Fair-2	AG-3	G-4	VG-8
$550	$1,225	$3,250	$8,500

a. Included in certified population for 1801, 1/000 Error, Thorn on Stem at Left (BW-17).

1801, 1/000 Error, Thorn on Stem at Left • BW-17, S-223, B-17. *Breen dies:* 9-L. **Estimated population:** Thousands.

1801, 1/000 Error, Thorn on Stem at Left (BW-17, S-223, B-17).

Detail showing the 1/000 error fraction, one of several different dies with this mistake.

Obverse: Same as preceding. *Points of distinction:* The rim break on the earlier use is expanded here, and on a later state another is seen at the lower right.

Reverse: Error fraction 1/000. One of three dies—also see BW-8 and BW-16—with this feature. Highest leaf tip on right under right part of S. ONE in normal position; E distant from leaf pair above it; berry above and right of upper right of E. Thorn at the end of the stem at the left. *Points of distinction:* A light crack from the denticles to the right side of D of UNITED is seen on most coins. This die was also used to coin 1802, 1/000 Error Fraction (BW-1).

Notes: This variety exists in Mint State. This variety is one of the most often seen of this year.

In lower grades the 1/000 error must be visible.

1801, 1/000 Error, Thorn on Stem at Left (BW-17)		Cert	Avg	%MS
		37	24.6	5%

AG-3	G-4	VG-8	F-12
$115	$230	$410	$780

VF-20	EF-40		AU-50
$1,680	$2,925		$6,940

1801, Fraction Spaced as 1 00 • BW-18, S-224, B-13. *Breen dies:* 7-I. *Estimated population:* Thousands.

1801, Fraction Spaced as
1 00 (BW-18, S-224, B-13).

Obverse: Date: About evenly spaced numerals. First 1 slightly closer to hair than to denticles. Second 1 is slightly closer to denticles than to drapery. *LIBERTY:* LIB close and higher than adjacent E. Uprights of E and R over high waves of hair. Upright of T over hair. Y low and has lower-left serif missing.

Reverse: Highest-right leaf tip under center of S. Numerator, 1, very high, slightly right of the center of bar, and much closer to ribbon knot than to bar. Denominator spaced as 1 00—compare to BW-9; 1 closer to bar than 00. *Points of distinction:* Clash marks are seen. Cracks develop, and in the latest state there is a rim break above F in OF.

Notes: This variety is one of the most often seen of this year. AU is the highest grade known.

1802, Draped Bust
Mintage (per Mint Report): 3,435,100.

There are 20 die combinations of the 1802 cent, 11 of which have engraving errors! In April 1802, the second bill to abolish the Philadelphia Mint was introduced in Congress. Although change was made, uncertainty as to the future may have affected the quality of work.[75]

The normal wreath of the year has 5 berries to the left and 5 to the right. Error dies omit one berry on the right, either opposite E of ONE or T of CENT. A T of LIBERTY, punched over a previous erroneous Y, accounts for another erring die. Missing stems and wrong fractions make up the other error dies. These distinctive errors are an advantage for attribution. Remarkably, the error coins all have generous populations, and some are common. In the following listing the error varieties are listed first, leaving only nine to be deciphered by other means.

Penny Whimsy notes:

> Taken as a whole, the cents of this year are commoner, probably, than those of any other date before 1816. Among the twenty known varieties there are only two unobtainable rarities (NC-1 and NC-2), and these two involve but a single die which is not duplicated on commoner coins. Yet the 1802's have been largely neglected by collectors, perhaps because they contain only three varieties which may be said to possess dramatic peculiarities—the 000 denominator, which is a carry-over from 1801; the stemless wreath; and the stemless wreath with extra "S" and extra fraction bar. According to Mint records, 3,435,100 cents were coined during the calendar year 1802, a record not broken until 1817.

The key word in the above is *dramatic*, as there certainly is no lack of interesting varieties with less obvious peculiarities.

The typical 1802 cent shows extensive wear, although many EF and AU coins can be found, as can scattered Mint State examples. All of the planchets were imported from Boulton & Watt of Birmingham, England and were of good quality.

Check for an error die first, then if a coin does not match, continue in the following section.

Typical values for 1802 cents not from error dies.
Rare varieties may be worth more.
Some varieties are priced individually, as follows.

1802	Cert	Avg	%MS
	385	30.4	3%

G-4	VG-8	F-12	VF-20	EF-40	AU-50	MS-60BN	MS-63BN	MS-63RB	MS-65BN	MS-65RB
$35	$65	$140	$300	$500	$1,200	$2,200	$4,750	$12,000	$23,000	$43,750

1802, Error Die, Varieties

1802, 1/000 Error Fraction • BW-1, S-228, B-4. *Breen dies:* 3-C. **Estimated population:** 750 to 1,000.

1802, 1/000 Error Fraction (BW-1, S-228, B-4).

Detail showing the 1/000 error fraction, one of several different dies with this mistake.

Obverse: *Date:* Fairly evenly spaced. 1 close to hair and distant from denticles; centered over space between denticles. 2 closer to drapery than to denticles. *LIBERTY:* BE slightly wide. E and upright of R over hair waves. Upright of T over hair. Lower-left serif of Y defective. *Points of distinction:* Loop under drapery is above 80 and curved downward. This die was also used to coin BW-17.

Reverse: Error fraction 1/000. Highest leaf tip on right is under right part of S. ONE in normal position; E distant from leaf pair above it; berry above and right of upper right of E. Thorn at the end of the stem at the left. *Points of distinction:* This die was also used to coin 1801, 1/000 Error, Thorn on Stem at Left (BW-17). Several cracks are seen. Eventually, severe sinking of the die obliterates ATES.

Notes: This variety exists in Mint State. As there is only one 1802 reverse die with the 000 feature, the other descriptions can be ignored if a coin meets this criterion.

In lower grades the error fraction must be visible.

1802, 1/000 Error Fraction		Cert	Avg	%MS
		20	39.6	20%

AG-3	G-4	VG-8	F-12	VF-20
$80	$200	$325	$575	$950

EF-40	AU-50	MS-60BN	MS-63BN	MS-65BN
$1,970	$3,330	$8,130	$15,500	$25,000

1802, Stemless Wreath, Single Fraction Bar • BW-2, S-231, B-9. *Breen dies:* 6-E. *Estimated population:* Thousands.

1802, Stemless Wreath, Single Fraction Bar (BW-2, S-231, B-9).

Obverse: *Date:* Fairly evenly spaced; 2 very slightly wider. 1 close to hair, distant from denticle, and centered over denticle. 2 much closer to drapery than to denticles. *LIBERTY:* LIB close. E and R over waves of hair. Y slightly low. Upright of T over hair. *Points of distinction:* Typically with a crack at the bottom of 802 and from the rim through R, the base of T, and under Y, passing through the field in front of the nose and branching opposite the mouth into two finer cracks, which pass to the rim opposite the chin and the neck.

Reverse: No stems to wreath; single fraction bar; definitive for attribution. *Points of distinction:* Clash marks and light cracks are usual for this variety. In the final stage, quite rare, a piece fell out of the die between two long cracks at the top of the wreath.

Notes: This variety exists in Mint State. As there is only one reverse die with stemless wreath and single fraction bar, the other descriptions can be ignored if a coin meets these criteria.

In lower grades both errors must be visible.

1802, Stemless Wreath, Single Fraction Bar		Cert	Avg	%MS
		44	30.9	5%

AG-3	G-4	VG-8	F-12
$60	$110	$200	$425

VF-20	EF-40	AU-50	MS-60BN
$850	$2,250	$3,380	$7,670

1802, E Close Over Dip Between Waves, T Mostly Over Forehead, Three Errors: Stemless Wreath, Double Fraction Bar, Extra Earlier S • BW-3, S-241, B-20. *Breen dies:* 14-M. *Estimated population:* 1,250 to 1,500.

1802, E Close Over Dip Between Waves, T Mostly Over Forehead, Three Errors: Stemless Wreath, Double Fraction Bar, Extra Earlier S (BW-3, S-241, B-20).

Detail showing stemless wreath and double fraction bar. **Detail showing extra second S of STATES.**

Obverse: Date: 1 is slightly closer to hair than to the denticle below it; base of 1 is triangular or pyramidal, rather than left and right serifs being horizontal. 18 wide. 2 slightly closer to drapery than to denticles. *LIBERTY:* IB close. E over dip between two waves of hair; unusual. *Points of distinction:* T mostly over forehead; unusual.

Reverse: No stems to wreath; double fraction bar; definitive. Second S of STATES blundered with bold traces of an extra earlier

S below it. ONE is too high. *Points of distinction:* This die was also used to coin 1803, Three Errors: Stemless Wreath, Double Fraction Bar, Extra Earlier S (BW-1). The 1803 coin was minted first. A light crack from F in OF to the nearby A expands and eventually develops into a rim cud. Another rim crack above TATE eventually develops into a rim cud over AT.

Notes: AU and Mint State are the highest grades, the later being particularly rare. As there is only one reverse die with stemless wreath and double fraction bar, the other descriptions can be ignored. In a way this is a "Three Errors" reverse! This seems to be yet another example of a mechanic (not engraver) sinking a die.

Lower grades must have the Stemless Wreath and Double Fraction Bar visible, but not necessarily the Extra S.

1802, Three Errors: Stemless Wreath, Double Fraction Bar, Extra Earlier S	Cert	Avg	%MS
	(a)		

AG-3	G-4	VG-8	F-12
$60	$115	$205	$440

VF-20	EF-40	AU-50
$900	$2,375	$4,070

a. Included in certified population for 1802, Stemless Wreath, Single Fraction Bar.

OTHER 1802 VARIETIES
1802, Berries: 5 Left, 4 Right, No Berry Opposite E of ONE • BW-4, S-238, B-11. *Breen dies:* 7-G. *Estimated population:* 120 to 160.

1802, Berries: 5 Left, 4 Right, No Berry Opposite E of ONE (BW-4, S-238, B-11).

Obverse: Date: 1 closer to hair than to the denticle over which it is centered. 18 slightly wide. 2 closer to drapery than to denticles. *LIBERTY:* IB closest. Uprights of E and R over hair waves. Lower-right serif of T is barely over forehead. Y slightly low and with lower-left serif defective. *Points of distinction:* Denticles typically weak or missing on lower part of the coin.

This die was used to coin both BW-4 and BW-12. Clashing has further injured the die on this combination.

Reverse: No berry opposite E of ONE. Denticles short and with rounded ends.

Points of distinction: Cracks appear, and a rim break to the left pendant of T, across the tops of ATE, and back to the rim over S is seen in the latest state.

Notes: VF is the highest grade known.

1802, T Over Junction of Hair and Forehead, Berries: 5 Left, 4 Right, No Berry Opposite T of CENT, Bar Tilts Down to the Left • BW-5, S-234, B-14. *Breen dies:* 9-J. *Estimated population:* 200 to 300.

1802, T Over Junction of Hair and Forehead, Berries: 5 Left, 4 Right, No Berry Opposite T of CENT, Bar Tilts Down to the Left (BW-5, S-234, B-14).

Detail showing fraction bar sloping down to the left.

Obverse: Date: 1 very close to hair and distant from denticles. 2 closer to drapery than

to denticles. *LIBERTY:* BE and RTY wide. E centered over dip between two waves of hair. Upright of T over junction of hair and forehead. *Points of distinction:* An early die clash led to a rim break over B. This progresses to cover much of BERT, the so-called "dripping paint" break.

Reverse: No berry opposite T of CENT. Fraction bar tilts slightly down to the left, and is closer to the denominator 1 than to the second 0. Bar is much closer to the right ribbon than to the left. *Points of distinction:* Found with crumbling of the die along the lower edges of bottom pair of leaves on right branch, and along right stem.

Notes: This variety exists in Mint State. As there are three obverses mated to this reverse, and as there is another reverse without a berry to the right of T, the details need to be studied closely when attributing a coin to this variety.

1802, Left of E Over Wave of Hair, Berries: 5 Left, 4 Right, No Berry Opposite T of CENT, Bar Tilts Down to the Left • BW-6, S-235, B-15. *Breen dies:* 10-J. *Estimated population:* 300 to 400.

1802, Left of E Over Wave of Hair, Berries: 5 Left, 4 Right, No Berry Opposite T of CENT, Bar Tilts Down to the Left (BW-6, S-235, B-15).

Obverse: Date: 1 and 2 are each about equidistant between the denticles and the bust. *LIBERTY:* Left uprights of E and R over

waves of hair. Upright of T over hair. *Points of distinction:* A rim break develops at TY and expands. On the latest state, there is a heavy arc-like die crack from the rim into the field at the right, extending into the neck, and continuing behind the head to the left.

Reverse: Same as preceding. *Points of distinction:* Seen with a crack from rim between E and S, through right branch and I, and to rim.

Notes: This variety exists in AU and Mint State.

1802, E Centered Over Wave of Hair, Berries: 5 Left, 4 Right, No Berry Opposite T of CENT, Bar Tilts Down to the Left • BW-7, S-236, B-16. *Breen dies:* 11-J. ***Estimated population:*** Thousands.

1802, E Centered Over Wave of Hair, Berries: 5 Left, 4 Right, No Berry Opposite T of CENT, Bar Tilts Down to the Left (BW-7, S-236, B-16).

Obverse: *Date:* 1 and 2 each closer to the bust than to the denticles. 02 close.

LIBERTY: E and R centered over waves of hair. Lower-right serif of T defective; T over hair. *Points of distinction:* A light crack extends from below 1, upward, and then into the field at the left.

Reverse: Same as preceding. *Points of distinction:* In this pairing, the last use of the die, additional cracks are seen. The upper reverse demonstrates a latticework of cracks, with a rim cud ultimately developing over ST.

Notes: This variety exists in Mint State.

1802, T Over Hair, Berries: 5 Left, 4 Right, No Berry Opposite T of CENT, Bar Tilts Up to the Left • BW-8, S-239, B-17. *Breen dies:* 12-K. ***Estimated population:*** 300 to 400.

1802, T Over Hair, Berries: 5 Left, 4 Right, No Berry Opposite T of CENT, Bar Tilts Up to the Left (BW-8, S-239, B-17).

Detail showing fraction bar sloping up to the left.

Obverse: *Date:* 1 much closer to hair than to denticles. 2 slightly closer to drapery than to denticles. *LIBERTY:* LIB and ER close. Uprights of E and R over waves of hair. Upright of T over hair. *Points of distinction:* Crack off forelock and through

the field in front of the nose becomes progressively heavier, extending to the rim, opposite the mouth. Another crack develops off the underside of the nose, joining the former crack at the rim. The die sinks between these cracks, forming an "elephant trunk" off Liberty's face.

Reverse: No berry opposite T of CENT. Fraction bar tilts sharply up to the left, and is much farther from denominator 1 than from the second 0. Bar is slightly closer to the left ribbon than to the right. *Points of distinction:* Clash marks are seen at RICA, and later elsewhere. A crack develops across the die above its center.

Notes: AU is the highest grade known. As there are three obverses mated to this reverse, and as there is another reverse without a berry to the right of T, the details need to be studied closely when attributing a coin to this variety.

1802, T Over Junction of Hair and Forehead, Berries: 5 Left, 4 Right, No Berry Opposite T of CENT, Bar Tilts Up to the Left •
BW-9, S-240, B-18. *Breen dies:* 13-K. **Estimated population:** 200 to 300.

1802, T Over Junction of Hair and Forehead, Berries: 5 Left, 4 Right, No Berry Opposite T of CENT, Bar Tilts Up to the Left (BW-9, S-240, B-18).

Obverse: *Date:* 1 slightly closer to hair than to denticles. 2 equidistant between drapery and denticles. *LIBERTY:* LIB close. E over dip between waves of hair. Upright of T over junction of hair and forehead. *Points of distinction:* Typically (but not always) with a crack upward from the lower rim, through the drapery, and through the bust to in front of the eye. Clash marks are the norm.

Reverse: Same as preceding. *Points of distinction:* Cracks are more extensive than on the previous use.

Notes: This variety exists in EF and AU, and is rare as such. Multiple VF coins exist.

1802, T in LIBERTY Punched Over Y, Highest Right Leaf Over Right Edge of S • BW-10, S-232, B-12. *Breen dies:* 8-H. **Estimated population:** Thousands.

1802, T in LIBERTY Punched Over Y, Highest Right Leaf Over Right Edge of S (BW-10, S-232, B-12).

Detail of T over Y.

Obverse: *Date:* 1 very high, nearly touching hair, and distant from denticles. 2 slightly closer to drapery than to denticles. *LIBERTY:* IBE close, E leans right. Uprights of E and R over high waves of hair. T cut over an erroneous Y. Parts of the arms of the Y can be seen to each side of the upper part of the upright of the T, especially on the right; definitive. Y mostly over hair, but slightly over forehead. *Points of distinction:* Light clash marks are often seen at the top. Many have a break in the denticles below 18, which eventually extends to involve five denticles, centered under the 1.

Reverse: Highest leaf on right under right edge of S; definitive. Outer leaf tip under first T of STATES. Medium-size berries. Fraction bar nearly touches left ribbon. Nearly always with clash marks between denticles and AMERICA. *Points of distinction:* Several cracks can be seen, the extent of which expanded as the coinage progressed. A rim break forms at the left above ATE.

Notes: This variety exists in Mint State.

1802, T in LIBERTY Over Y, Highest Right Leaf Over Lower-Left Serif of S • BW-11, S-233, B-13. *Breen dies:* 8-I. *Estimated population:* 500 to 750.

1802, T in LIBERTY Over Y,
Highest Right Leaf Over Lower-Left
Serif of S (BW-11, S-233, B-13).

Obverse: Same as preceding. *Points of distinction:* On this use a further three-denticle rim break develops.

Reverse: Highest leaf on right under lower-left serif of S; definitive. Outer leaf tip under right edge of first S of STATES. Large berries. Space between fraction bar and left ribbon. *Points of distinction:* Several cracks are usually seen.

Notes: AU is the highest grade known.

1802, Lower-Right Serif of T Is Slightly Over Forehead, Berry Directly Right of Top Serif of O of ONE • BW-12, S-237, B-10. *Breen dies:* 7-F. *Estimated population:* 750 to 1,000.

1802, Lower-Right Serif of T Is Slightly
Over Forehead, Berry Directly Right of
Top Serif of O of ONE (BW-12, S-237, B-10).

Obverse: See BW-4. *Points of distinction:* Usually seen with a crack through ERTY. This die was also used to coin BW-4.

Reverse: Highest-right leaf tip under lower-left serif of S. Berry directly right of top serif of E of ONE. Fraction bar extends from upper right of 1 to *past center* of second 0. Bar is much closer to the right ribbon than to the left. *Points of distinction:* Multiple light cracks are the rule.

Notes: This variety exists in Mint State.

1802, E Close Over Dip Between Waves, T Mostly Over Forehead, Thorn From Left Stem to U • BW-13, S-242, B-19. *Breen dies:* 14-L. *Estimated population:* 750 to 1,000.

Detail showing thorn from stem to U.

1802, E Close Over Dip Between Waves,
T Mostly Over Forehead, Thorn From
Left Stem to U (BW-13, S-242, B-19).

Obverse: See BW-3. *Points of distinction:* Some, but not all, clash marks seen on the previous use of the die have been removed.

Reverse: Highest-right leaf tip under center of S. Thorn from left stem to U; definitive. Bold center dot over left upright of N. Numerator, 1, centered high above bar. Bar begins at the upper right of 1 and extends to just short of the center of the second 0. 100 very widely spaced. *Points of distinction:* This die was also used to strike

1803, "Unicorn Variety," 3 Embedded in Drapery (BW-6) and 1803, Unfinished Hair Below E (BW-28). A crack is seen at the left over part of UNITED.

Notes: AU is the highest grade known. Walter Breen notes that it is likely that this variety was struck in 1803 and was delivered by the coiner on February 22 of that year.

1802, 1 Touches Hair, Highest-Right Leaf Tip Right of S, Berry Opposite Upper Right of E of ONE • BW-14, S-225, B-1. *Breen dies:* 1-A. *Estimated population:* 400 to 500.

1802, 1 Touches Hair, Highest-Right Leaf Tip Right of S, Berry Opposite Upper Right of E of ONE (BW-14, S-225, B-1).

Obverse: Date: 1 touches hair; definitive. 2 much closer to drapery than to denticles. *LIBERTY:* IB close. E and R over waves of

hair. Upright of T over hair. Y slightly low. *Points of distinction:* Multiple die clashes across the end of the bust, and across and below 802, lead to a typical rim break below 802. Unclashed early state coins are rare.

Reverse: Highest-right leaf tip to right of S; definitive. Berry opposite the upper-right tip of E of ONE; only die with berry in this position. *Points of distinction:* Cracks develop, and eventually a cud eliminates most of E of STATES.

Notes: This variety exists in Mint State.

1802, 1 Touches Hair, Highest-Right Leaf Tip Left of Center of S • BW-15, S-226, B-2. *Breen dies:* 1-B. *Estimated population:* 400 to 500.

1802, 1 Touches Hair, Highest-Right Leaf Tip Left of Center of S (BW-15, S-226, B-2).

Obverse: Same as preceding. *Points of distinction:* In this usage there is always a rim break below 802. Additionally, a crack develops, curving from the right rim to the end of the nose, eventually extending up along it to the forehead and the upper rim above B.

Reverse: Highest-right leaf tip left of the center of S. Medial side of both bow loops incomplete. Right foot of A lower than adjacent left foot of M and right lower foot of M below adjacent left foot of E. Compare to BW-19, where ME join at base. Left, club-like stem shorter than the right stem. Fraction bar heavy and closer to the right ribbon than to the left. Numbers distant from it. Bar begins over the space between 1 and 0 and ends just short of the center of the second 0. 10 closer than 00. *Points of distinction:* A light crack is at the top of the letters at the upper right.

Notes: This variety exists in Mint State.

1802, 1 Does Not Touch Hair, Highest-Right Leaf Tip Left of Center of S • BW-16, S-NC-1, B-3. *Breen dies:* 2-B. **Estimated population:** 35 to 50.

1802, 1 Does Not Touch Hair, Highest-Right Leaf Tip Left of Center of S (BW-16, S-NC-1, B-3).

Obverse: Date: 1 and 2 are closer to bust than to denticles. *LIBERTY:* R over wave of hair. Upright of T over hair. Lower-left serif of Y defective. *Points of distinction:* Loop under drapery is above 802 and is *straight* except at its leftmost part. Most commonly seen with a bisecting crack from the border, through the right of B, into Liberty's hair, curving in front of the ear to cross the neck and drapery, and continuing to the rim to the right of 2—this being light on early impressions, heavier on later ones. Still later, another crack develops.

Reverse: Same as preceding. *Points of distinction:* Clash marks are seen. A light crack is through AMERI.

Notes: VF and EF are the highest grades known, and example are rare as such. This variety was Non-Collectible when *Early American Cents* was published in 1949.

1802 • BW-17, S-227, B-5. *Breen dies:* 3-B. **Estimated population:** 750 to 1,000.

1802 (BW-17, S-227, B-5).

Obverse: See BW-1. *Points of distinction:* This die was also used to coin BW-1.

Reverse: Same as preceding. *Points of distinction:* Multiple clash marks are seen.

The crack described earlier now extends farther to the left to F in OF.

Notes: This combination is often seen with prominent clash marks on the obverse from the wreath, seen behind the hair and under the hair ribbon—as well as, most prominently, in front of the forehead and under the chin—prompting Dr. Sheldon to call it the Cobweb Variety. This variety exists in AU and Mint State, the latter being very rare.

1802 • BW-18, S-229, B-6. *Breen dies:* 4-B. **Estimated population:** 500 to 750.

1802 (BW-18, S-229, B-6).

Obverse: Date: 1 slightly closer to hair than to denticles. 18 wide. 8 low and leans right. 2 about centered between denticles and drapery. LIBERTY: L lower than I. IB much closer than LI. E and R over waves of hair. Upright of T over hair. Lower-left serif of Y longer than right. *Points of distinction:* Usually with cracks near the top border.

Reverse: Same as preceding. *Points of distinction:* Here, in its last use, cracks develop into cud breaks, first over TES and then over AME as well.

Notes: This variety exists in Mint State.

1802, Highest-Right Leaf Tip Under Left Edge of S, Left Stem Short
• BW-19, S-NC-2, B-7. *Breen dies:* 4-D. *Estimated population:* 18 to 22.

1802, Highest-Right Leaf Tip Under Left Edge of S, Left Stem Short (BW-19, S-NC-2, B-7).

Detail showing bottom-right serif of M under bottom-left serif of E.

Obverse: Same as preceding. *Points of distinction:* With a crack through BERTY, as in the latest state of the preceding use.

Reverse: Highest-right leaf tip under left edge of S. ME joined at base. Compare to BW-15, BW-16, BW-17, and BW-18, where right lower foot of M is below the adjacent left foot of E. Left stem short. Fraction bar closer to left ribbon than to right. Bar begins over upper right of 1 and extends to above center of second 0. 10 wider than 00.

Notes: VF and EF are the highest grades known, but examples are very rare so fine. Most are VG or lower. Walter Breen notes that only one was known to Dr. Sheldon when *Early American Cents* was published in 1949. When *Penny Whimsy* came out in 1958 the population was three, which increased to at least 15 when Breen's *Encyclopedia* was released in 2000. As has often happened, Sheldon's NC for Non-Collectible can be called *Now*-Collectible.

1802 • BW-20, S-230, B-8. *Breen dies:* 5-D. *Estimated population:* Thousands.

1802 (BW-20, S-230, B-8).

Obverse: *Date:* 1 and 2 are closer to the bust than to the denticles. 1, 8, and 0 are each centered over a denticle and are level with one another. 80 close. *LIBERTY:* LIB very close. L slightly lower than I. Uprights of E and R over hair waves. Upright of T over hair. Y slightly low. *Points of distinction:* In this use, another crack is seen at the lower right.

Reverse: Same as preceding. *Points of distinction:* Multiple horizontal cracks develop through the upper reverse, with die sinking eventually obliterating TES.

Notes: This variety exists in AU and Mint State, especially rare in the latter category.

Numismatic Notes: The Hidden Find: The Charles Stetson Collection, cataloged by W. Elliot Woodward, was auctioned on January 21 and 22, 1889. Stetson lived in Quincy, Massachusetts, and was born in 1832. Lot 26, an 1802 cent, was described as, "Nearly red, Uncirculated; extremely fine, in almost Proof condition; one of the few known as the Hidden Find, discovered many years ago in R.I.; very rare."[76] As Arthur Conan Doyle did in his Sherlock Holmes detective stories—with mysterious references such as the "giant rat of Sumatra"—Woodward and his contemporaries printed many asides in their catalogs, some of which were probably recognized at the time by the knowing ones, but which left most readers clueless. A certain William E. Hidden was a well-known antiquarian and numismatist around the turn of the 20th century (his collection was sold by Thomas Elder in 1916); could he have been associated with the Hidden Find?

1803, Draped Bust
Mintage (per Mint Report): 3,131,691.

The year 1803 saw an unprecedented production of cents. Struck on high-quality planchets imported from Boulton & Watt, the coins were attractive and problem free. Many were struck from 1802-dated dies.

Today, cents of this year, comprising two dozen different die combinations, are, for the most part, readily collectible.

There are two obverse styles, the Small Date and the Large Date. Reverses come with Small Fraction and Large Fraction. Errors are plentiful, as was the situation in 1802. These errors include a stemless wreath, also with a double fraction bar; two dies with the 1 in the numerator way too high; another with double fraction bar (but with the correct two stems to the wreath); a corrected error fraction; and one with the top of the 3 in the date embedded in the drapery. In many cases, dies were likely made by a workman from the coining department.[77]

These errors are listed first below (Group 1), then the Large Dates as there are just two of them (Group 2), then the remaining Large Fractions in combination with Small Dates (Group 3), and finally the remaining Small Date, Small Fraction varieties. In this way the last category can be studied on its own.

Within the Small Fraction varieties there are many dies that are quite similar. These have been divided into: Coins with unusual features as headlined (Group 4). Coins with 3 (1803) touching or nearly touching the drapery (Group 5). Remaining Small Date, Small Fraction varieties not yet classified (Group 6).

To follow this method, start at the beginning of the 1803 varieties and go downward until your coin is identified. This method does not reflect the order in which the coins were struck and, in some instances the use of the same die on two varieties may not have adjacent Bowers-Whitman numbers (but such dies are cross-referenced).

Typical values for 1803 cents.
Rare varieties may be worth more.
Some varieties are priced individually, as follows.

1803	Cert	Avg	%MS
	253	31.4	7%

AG-3	G-4	VG-8	F-12	VF-20	EF-40	AU-50	MS-60BN	MS-63BN
$65	$140	$300	$600	$1,400	$2,500	$5,000	$15,000	$30,000

GROUP 1: 1803, ERROR DIES

1803, Three Errors: Stemless Wreath, Double Fraction Bar, Extra Earlier S • BW-1, S-243, B-1. *Breen dies:* 1-A. ***Estimated population:*** 750 to 1,000.

1803, Three Errors: Stemless Wreath, Double Fraction Bar, Extra Earlier S (BW-1, S-243, B-1). Earlier S (below second S in STATES). Die also used *later* to coin 1802, E Close Over Dip Between Waves, T Mostly Over Forehead, Three Errors: Stemless Wreath, Double Fraction Bar, Extra Earlier S (BW-3)— see enlarged illustrations there.

Obverse: Date: Small Date with blunt 1. 1 closer to hair than to denticles and is centered over the space between two denticles. 18 slightly close. 3 very close to, but does not touch, drapery. *LIBERTY:* IB very close. Uprights of E and R over hair waves. Upright of T over hair. Y slightly low; lower-left serif repaired. *Points of distinction:* Early in the life of the die a crack develops from the curl on the neck, across the throat, and slightly into the right field. Later, a rim break develops opposite nose and forehead, eventually extending upward through the denticles above, and down to the tops of TY.

Reverse: No stems to wreath; double fraction bar; definitive. Second S of STATES blundered with bold traces of an earlier S below it. ONE is too high. In a way this a "Three Errors" reverse! *Points of distinction:* Usually with clash marks at ERICA, later removed. Crack from rim, to 3, and on to drapery. Die possibly made by a mechanic. This die was used to coin both 1802, E Close Over Dip Between Waves,

T Mostly Over Forehead, Three Errors: Stemless Wreath, Double Fraction Bar, Extra Earlier S (BW-3) and 1803 (BW-1). The 1803 coin was minted *first*.

Notes: There is only one 1803 variety with this reverse. This is one of the most popular varieties of the year. Examples are readily available, and a few are known in Mint State. Quoting *Penny Whimsy:* "In this marriage, the reverse is always found *without* the cracks noted for the 1802 marriage, demonstrating, as Newcomb points out, that this particular 1803 cent must have been struck before some of the 1802 cents were struck. The same thing is encountered four or five times among the early cents, and probably indicates that when a number of dies were still in good condition and not worn out, the transition from one date to the next was sometimes accomplished more or less gradually, with occasional returning to a die of the earlier date, perhaps in order to 'use it up.' They had to be thrifty at the Mint, especially with Congress in session almost next door, and many a congressman looking for something to 'correct.'"[78]

In lower grades all three errors must be visible.

1803, Stemless Wreath, Double Fraction Bar, Extra Earlier S			Cert	Avg	%MS
			12	32.8	17%

AG-3	G-4	VG-8	F-12	VF-20
$75	$160	$300	$570	$970

EF-40	AU-50	MS-60BN	MS-63BN
$2,250	$4,500	$10,000	$17,000

1803, Lump Under Chin (on most), 1 of Numerator Far Too High, Tip of Highest Outside-Right Leaf Under S • BW-2, S-246, B-4. *Breen dies:* 3-D. *Estimated population:* 200 to 300.

1803, Lump Under Chin (on most), 1 of Numerator Far Too High, Tip of Highest Outside-Right Leaf Under S (BW-2, S-246, B-4).

Detail showing carelessly punched fraction with numerator too high, bar tilting slightly down to the left, and 1 punched more deeply and much closer to the bar than the other two digits.

Obverse: Date high, with 1 and 3 close to bust. Fairly evenly spaced. *LIBERTY:* IB closest. E and R over waves of hair. Upright of T over hair. *Points of distinction:* Top of hair unfinished just below highest horizontal strand, from relapping of the die. This die was used to coin BW-2, BW-4, BW-5, and BW-29. Lump under chin on all except early strikes. This combination was the *first* use of the obverse die.

Reverse: Numerator, 1, far too high, close to the ribbon knot, and distant from the fraction bar; bar over 1 of denominator; definitive. Compare to BW-3. Tip of highest outside-right leaf under S of STATES. *Points of distinction:* Found perfect, and with crack from rim to left of first S through tops of STA. Later, the rim becomes heavily broken over STA.

Notes: Most (but not all) have a lump under the chin, Sheldon's "Mumps Obverse." EF and AU are the highest grades known, and examples are very rare in the latter category.

1803, 1 of Numerator Far Too High, Tip of Highest Outside-Right Leaf Between E and S • BW-3, S-NC-1, B-9. *Breen dies:* 4-I. *Estimated population:* 30 to 45.

1803, 1 of Numerator Far Too High, Tip of Highest Outside-Right Leaf Between E and S (BW-3, S-NC-1, B-9).

Detail showing high 1 in numerator.

Obverse: Date: 1 slightly farther from hair than 3 is to drapery; centered over a denticle. 18 close. *LIBERTY:* LIB close. Uprights of E and R over waves of hair. Upright of T over hair. Lower-left serif of Y repaired. *Points of distinction:* This die was used to coin BW-3, BW-30, and BW-31. In this use the die was reground to remove clash marks, after which, seemingly per the usual, more are sustained.

Reverse: Numerator, 1, far too high, close to the ribbon knot and distant from the fraction bar; bar *not* over 1 of denominator; definitive. Compare to BW-2. Tip of highest outside-right leaf between E and S of STATES; definitive. *Points of distinction:* Of those seen by Walter Breen, just one had a crack at NITED.

Notes: VF and EF are the highest grades known, and examples are very rare as such. Most are Fine or lower.

1803, Lump Under Chin, Double Fraction Bar • BW-4, S-248, B-6.
Breen dies: 3-F. ***Estimated population:*** 120 to 160.

1803, Lump Under Chin, Double
Fraction Bar (BW-4, S-248, B-6).

Detail showing double fraction bar,
the first faint above the second.

Obverse: Same as BW-2. Lump under chin. "Mumps Obverse." *Points of distinction:* This die was used to coin BW-2, BW-4, BW-5, and BW-29. In this use the lump remains prominent, and a slight bulging is seen at the lower right.

Reverse: Double fraction bar, the first light and above the other; definitive. *Points of distinction:* A crack is over MERI.

Notes: This variety exists in AU and Mint State, the latter being extremely rare. Most are in lower grades.

In lower grades the Double Fraction Bar must be visible.

1803, Lump Under Chin, Double Fraction Bar		Cert	Avg	%MS
		(a)		

AG-3	G-4	VG-8	F-12
$120	$230	$520	$1,150

VF-20	EF-40	AU-50
$2,350	$6,000	$11,000

a. Included in certified population for 1803.

1803, Lump Under Chin, Corrected Fraction 1/100 Over 1/000 • BW-5, S-249, B-7. *Breen dies:* 3-G. ***Estimated population:*** 750 to 1,000.

1803, Lump Under Chin, Corrected Fraction
1/100 Over 1/000 (BW-5, S-249, B-7).

Detail showing corrected fraction,
an alteration of the die used to coin
1801, 1/000 Error, Berry Opposite
Center of E of ONE (BW-16).

Obverse: Same as preceding. Lump under chin. "Mumps Obverse." *Points of distinction:* This die was used to coin BW-2, BW-4, BW-5, and BW-29. With a crack at the right of the date, which expands and ends in a rim break.

Reverse: This die was first employed as the 1801, 1/000 Error, Berry Opposite Center of E of ONE (BW-16) die, then was corrected later to its present form.[79] *Points of distinction:* A crack at ERIC expands, eventually resulting in a rim cud over RIC.

Notes: This variety exists in Mint State. There is only one 1803 variety with this reverse. An eagerly sought and quite available variety.

In lower grades the fraction must be clear.

1803, Lump Under Chin, Corrected Fraction 1/100 Over 1/000	Cert	Avg	%MS
	14	30.6	7%

AG-3	G-4	VG-8	F-12	VF-20
$85	$170	$370	$630	$1,010

EF-40	AU-50	MS-60BN	MS-63BN
$2,350	$4,830	$10,500	$18,000

1803, "Unicorn Variety," 3 Embedded in Drapery • BW-6, S-245, B-2.

Breen dies: 2-B. **Estimated population:** 300 to 400.

1803, "Unicorn Variety," 3 Embedded in Drapery (BW-6, S-245, B-2).

Detail of clash mark protruding from forehead.

Obverse: Date: 3 embedded into drapery; definitive. Fairly evenly spaced. 1 closer to hair than to denticles. *LIBERTY:* L slightly low. LIB close, IB closest. Uprights of E and R over hair waves. Upright of T over hair. Y slightly low. *Points of distinction:* Clash marks are in the field. One of these protrudes from the forehead, giving rise to the designation, "Unicorn Variety."

Reverse: ONE high; berry to right and slightly higher than center of crossbar. Tiny die scratch connects left stem with U. Numerator over first 0, and about the same distance from the bar. Bar begins slightly right of 1 and ends left of the center of second 0. 100 spaced widely. *Points of distinction:* This die was used to strike BW-6, BW-28, and 1802, E Close Over Dip Between Waves, T Mostly Over Forehead, Thorn From Left Stem to U (BW-13). With extensive cracks and a rim break over N of UNITED. Later the rim breaks at RICA.

Notes: This variety exists in Mint State.

GROUP 2: 1803, LARGE DATES (TWO SIZES OF FRACTIONS)

1803, Large Date (Pointed 1), Large Fraction • BW-8, S-265, B-23.

Breen dies: 14-S. **Estimated population:** 120 to 160.

1803, Large Date (Pointed 1), Large Fraction (BW-8, S-265, B-23).

Detail of the date.

Obverse: Date: Large Date with pointed 1; definitive. 1 and 3 both touch bust. 03 close. *LIBERTY:* LIB close, ER slightly close. Uprights of E and R over hair waves.

Upright of T over hair. *Points of distinction:* Arc-like raised lines are to the right of the drapery, probably from a lathe. Seen with a perfect die and also with cracks. Also see BW-9.

Reverse: Large Fraction; definitive in combination with this obverse. Slightly larger letters than the following—BW-9. OF and AMERICA closer than on BW-9. *Points of distinction:* Occasionally from a perfect die in its early use, but often with a network of cracks.

Notes: EF and AU are the highest grades known. It is thought that the Large Dates were among the last cents struck with the 1803 date. Just one obverse die was made with this style. This variety and the next, listed in the regular edition of the *Guide Book of United States Coins*, are in very strong demand.

1803, Large Date (Pointed 1), Large Fraction		Cert	Avg	%MS
		(a)		

AG-3	G-4	VG-8	F-12	VF-20	EF-40
$125	$260	$550	$1,200	$2,000	$6,500

a. Included in certified population for 1803.

1803, Large Date (Pointed 1), Small Fraction • BW-9, S-264, B-24.
Breen dies: 14-R. *Estimated population:* 60 to 75.

1803, Large Date (Pointed 1), Small Fraction (BW-9, S-264, B-24).

Obverse: Same as preceding. *Points of distinction:* With a crack through the right of 1, upward, then curving back to the rim. Another crack forms later.

Reverse: Small Fraction; definitive in combination with this obverse. Smaller letters than on the preceding—BW-8. OF and AMERICA much farther apart than on BW-8. Extra berry below first T of STATES. *Points of distinction:* This die was used to coin BW-9 and BW-19. The cracks are more extensive on this use, and die failure eventually blanks out STA.

Notes: VF is the highest grade known. This variety is in great demand, due in part to its listing in the regular edition of the *Guide Book of United States Coins*.

GROUP 3: 1803, SMALL DATE, LARGE FRACTIONS
This group combines three obverse dies with three reverses to create five different varieties. The reverses all have Large Letters, with OF and AMERICA spaced closer than on the Small Fraction varieties.

1803, Small Date, Large Fraction, Outside Berry Below T of STATES, Short Fraction Bar • BW-11, S-257, B-16. *Breen dies:* 10-N. *Estimated population:* 750 to 1,000.

1803, Small Date, Large Fraction, Outside Berry Below T of STATES, Short Fraction Bar (BW-11, S-257, B-16).

Detail of the obverse, showing arcs from lathe work.

Detail of the late state of the reverse, showing mounding at STATES from the sinking of the die surface.

Obverse: Date: 1 and 3 closer to bust than to denticles. 1 is very far from the curl and is over a denticle. *LIBERTY:* LIB close; IB closest. ER close. E and R over waves of hair. T is repunched low on the left and is thicker than normal at that point; T is over hair. *Points of distinction:* High-grade impressions show raised arcs on the bust, from a lathe during the die-finishing process.

Reverse: Outside berry below T of STATES; definitive within this group.

Short fraction bar starts over left part of first 0 (definitive within this group), ends left of center of second 0. *Points of distinction:* Multiple cracks develop, and eventually severe die sinking develops, obliterating STATES—as well as much of the date in the corresponding spot on the obverse, due to insufficient metal flow to fill the corresponding part of the obverse die.

Notes: Readily available in the marketplace, including a handful of Mint State.

1803, Small Date, Large Fraction, Leaf Tip Under Left Serif of E of UNITED • BW-12, S-258, B-17. *Breen dies:* 10-O. *Estimated population:* Thousands.

1803, Small Date, Large Fraction, Leaf Tip Under Left Serif of E of UNITED (BW-12, S-258, B-17).

Detail of line through D.

Obverse: Same as preceding. *Points of distinction:* In this use the die is relapped to remove clash marks, after which more appear. A bulge develops to the left of the lowest curl.

Usually with a crack from the rim, through the 1, to curls, back to rim. Lathe lines are still visible on high-grade examples.

Reverse: Leaf tip under left serif of E of UNITED; definitive within this group. T of CENT close to, but does not touch, leaf; definitive within this group. Fraction bar starts above right side of 1 and ends close to center of second 0. Bar is closer to the right ribbon than to the left. A diagonal die line, apparently the slip of an engraving tool, causes a raised line from the rim diagonally through the upper right of the D of UNITED. *Points of distinction:* Clash marks develop.

Notes: Plentiful in Mint State (in the context of early cents) and thus an ideal candidate for a type set.

1803, Small Date, Large Fraction • BW-13, S-259, B-18. *Breen dies:* 11-O. *Estimated population:* 120 to 160.

1803, Small Date, Large Fraction (BW-13, S-259, B-18).

Obverse: Date: 1 and 3 closer to bust than to denticles. 1 over space between denticles. Ball on 3 weak. *LIBERTY:* LI wide. IB and ER slightly close. Uprights of E and R over waves of hair. Lower-left serif of T long; right serif short, and while over the hair, is closer to the forehead than on any die of this group. *Points of distinction:* Extensive clash marks develop.

Reverse: Same as preceding. *Points of distinction:* A very few have a crack from the rim left of the first S, connecting the tops of TAT, and back to the rim over the left edge of E. In the latest state there is a rim break over TAT.

Notes: This variety exists in AU and Mint State, and examples are very rare at these levels. Nearly all are in lower grades. Dr. Sheldon called this the "Ghost 3" variety due to the weak ball at the bottom.

1803, Small Date, Large Fraction, Fraction Bar Closer to Left Ribbon
• BW-14, S-260, B-19. *Breen dies:* 11-P. *Estimated population:* Thousands.

1803, Small Date, Large Fraction, Fraction Bar Closer to Left Ribbon (BW-14, S-260, B-19).

Obverse: Same as preceding. *Points of distinction:* Except for a rare early state of this use, the die has been relapped to remove clash marks, and certain features were strengthened, including the bottom of the 3, which had become weak. Additional clash marks develop. A crack develops from T to the hair.

Reverse: Fraction bar starts above right side of 1 and ends close to center of second 0. Bar is longer than the preceding. Bar is closer to the left ribbon than to the right; definitive within this group. *Points of distinction:* A small rim break is seen over the space above the second S of STATES and the O in OF. This was struck after some examples of BW-15 had been struck. After BW-14 was struck, BW-15 was continued in production. Multiple clash marks.

Notes: This variety exists in Mint State.

1803, Small Date, Large Fraction, Corner of 3 in Drapery • BW-15, S-261, B-20. *Breen dies:* 12-P. *Estimated population:* 500 to 750.

1803, Small Date, Large Fraction, Corner of 3 in Drapery (BW-15, S-261, B-20).

Obverse: Date: Corner of 3 in drapery; definitive in this group. *LIBERTY:* LIBE close; LI closest. E and R over waves of hair. Upright of T over hair. *Points of distinction:* A small die defect or "spur" extends to the right at the bottom of the forehead. Most have an arc-like crack from between 8 and 0, upward through Liberty's shoulder and hair, and then down to the rim at the left. This expands on late states, and mounding is also seen. Altered to create the spurious 1804, "Restrike" from mismatched dies.

Reverse: Same as preceding. *Points of distinction:* Many clash marks are seen.

Notes: This variety exists in AU and Mint State, and examples are very rare in the latter category. This obverse die was discarded as scrap metal by the Mint. Years later it was altered outside of the Mint to read "1804" and was used to make the so-called 1804 "restrikes."

GROUP 4: 1803, SMALL DATE, SMALL FRACTIONS, WITH UNUSUAL FEATURES AS HEADLINED

This group comprises two varieties with characteristics that are unusual among the remaining coins. Each boldface headline is definitive.

1803, T Over Junction of Hair and Forehead • BW-18, S-252, B-11.
Breen dies: 5-J. **Estimated population:** 750 to 1,000.

1803, T Over Junction of Hair and Forehead (BW-18, S-252, B-11).

Obverse: Date: Spaced as 1 8 03. 1 and 3 closer to bust than to denticles. *LIBERTY:* LIB close. E over dip between two hair waves. Upright of T over junction of hair and forehead; definitive. *Points of distinction:* Usually (but not always) with a crack at the base of the date. This enlarges and other problems occur, including a rim cud.

Reverse: Numerator, 1, high and centered over first 0. Bar begins at upper left of 1 and ends slightly before center of second 0. Bar closer to right ribbon than to left. *Points of distinction:* This die was used to coin both BW-18 and BW-30, with BW-18 being struck second. Crack through E of UNITED continues to wreath, then expands to near O in OF, and on to rim. Clash marks are seen.

Notes: This variety exists in Mint State, and examples are extremely rare as such.

1803, Outside Berry Below First T of STATES • BW-19, S-263, B-22.
Breen dies: 13-R. **Estimated population:** 300 to 400.

1803, Outside Berry Below First T of STATES (BW-19, S-263, B-22).

Obverse: Date: 18 slightly close, 80 wider, 03 closest. Top of 3 touches or almost touches drapery. *LIBERTY:* IB closest. E and R over hair waves. Upright of T over hair. *Points of distinction:* This die was used to coin BW-19 and BW-25. Die flaws as in the preceding use of the die. Now with a crack at the base of the date, which expands to form a cud.

Reverse: Extra berry below first T of STATES; definitive within this group. *Points of distinction:* This die was used to coin BW-9 and BW-19. Cracks develop, most notably one at the upper left, beginning past D of UNITED, extending to the wreath, and exiting through the left side of the O in OF.

Notes: This variety exists in AU and Mint State, and it is especially rare in the latter category.

GROUP 5: 1803, SMALL DATE, SMALL FRACTIONS, WITH 3 OF 1803 TOUCHING OR NEARLY TOUCHING DRAPERY
1803, 3 Touches Drapery • BW-21, S-253, B-12. *Breen dies:* 6-K. **Estimated population:** 500 to 750.

1803, 3 Touches Drapery (BW-21, S-253, B-12).   **Detail showing die chip in denominator.**

Obverse: Date: 1 closer to hair than to denticle; centered over a denticle. 803 closer to denticles than is the 1. 03 close. *LIBERTY:* LIB close. E and upright of R over hair waves. Upright of T over hair. Y slightly low. *Points of distinction:* Usually with a crack to the right of date, which later expands. In the latest state there is a rim break at 180. Eventually a break develops in the denticles and extends from below the 0 in the date, to the left, and past the lateral margin of Liberty's lowest curl.

Reverse: Dash (chip) after second 0 in denominator; definitive within the group. Berry centered opposite top edge of E of ONE. Bottom serifs of T's complete. *Points of distinction:* Usually with one or more cracks, although perfect die impressions exist.

Notes: This variety exists in AU and Mint State, the latter being extremely rare.

1803, 3 Touches Drapery • BW-22, S-254, B-13. *Breen dies:* 7-L. *Estimated population:* 1,250 to 1,500.

1803, 3 Touches Drapery (BW-22, S-254, B-13).

Detail showing missing serif on T's.

Obverse: Date: 1 closer to hair than to denticle; centered over a denticle. 03 close. 3 closer to denticles than any other numeral. *LIBERTY:* LIB close. I leans right, with lower-left serif above adjacent serif of L. E and upright of R over hair waves. Upright of T over hair. Y slightly low. *Points of distinction:* Perfect die, or with a crack from the right of 3 to drapery, augmented by other breaks, and culminating in a rim cud at the lower right.

Reverse: Fraction bar covers second 0; definitive within the group. Numerator is twice as close to the bar as it is to the ribbon knot. The bottom-right serifs on all T's are missing.

Notes: Although this is in the same population range as the preceding, the present coin is fairly plentiful in Mint State, no doubt the result of some undocumented hoard. EF and AU coins are likewise easy to find.

1803, 3 Touches Drapery • BW-23, S-255, B-14. *Breen dies:* 8-L. *Estimated population:* Thousands.

1803, 3 Touches Drapery (BW-23, S-255, B-14).

Obverse: Date: 1 very close to hair, and is centered over a denticle. 03 close. 3 much closer to denticles than is any other numeral.

LIBERTY: LIB close; IB closest. E and R over waves of hair. Upright of T over hair; lower-right serif defective. Y slightly low, and with bottom serifs defective. *Points of distinction:* Clash marks are seen, and increase as the die continues in use.

Reverse: Same as preceding. *Points of distinction:* A crack at ST becomes a rim cud over STAT. A light crack is at the right.

Notes: This variety exists in Mint State.

1803, 3 Touches Drapery • BW-24, S-256, B-15. *Breen dies:* 9-M. **Estimated population:** 300 to 400.

1803, 3 Touches Drapery (BW-24, S-256, B-15).

Obverse: *Date:* 1 closer to hair than to denticles; centered over space between two denticles. 03 close. All numerals about the same distance from denticles. *LIB-ERTY:* IB closest. LI and ERT slightly close. E and R over waves of hair. Upright

of T over hair; lower-left serif long. Y slightly low. *Points of distinction:* The die deteriorates, and a crack develops from the rim, upward through the 8, into the bust, curving to the right, and exiting through the end of the drapery. Bulges develop.

Reverse: Fraction bar too far left: begins over the center of 1, ends over the left side of the second 0. Lower-right serif on second T of STATES missing; present on other T's. *Points of distinction:* With multiple cracks.

Notes: This variety exists in AU and Mint State.

1803, 3 Nearly Touches Drapery • BW-25, S-262, B-21. *Breen dies:* 13-Q. **Estimated population:** 200 to 300.

1803, 3 Nearly Touches
Drapery (BW-25, S-262, B-21).

Obverse: *Date:* Spaced as 18 04. 1 closer to hair than to denticles; centered over denticle. All numerals about the same distance from denticles. *LIBERTY:* Letters close; IB closest. E and left upright of R over

waves of hair. Upright of T over hair. Lower-right serif of Y defective. *Points of distinction:* This die was used to coin both BW-19 and BW-25. With linear ridges caused by die cuts or flaws in the right field and on the bosom.

Reverse: Leaf point under upright of D; definitive within the group. Berry nearly opposite center of E of ONE. Both stems short. Bottom serifs of T's complete. *Points of distinction:* Almost all are from a perfect die state. Later, there is a crack at STATES.

Notes: VF is the highest grade known.

GROUP 6: REMAINING 1803, SMALL DATE, SMALL FRACTIONS

1803, Unfinished Hair Below E • BW-28, S-244, B-3. *Breen dies:* 2-C. **Estimated population:** 120 to 160.

1803, Unfinished Hair
Below E (BW-28, S-244, B-3).

Obverse: Same as BW-6. For its present use, it has been relapped, giving an unfinished or plain area below the strand beneath E. *Points of distinction:* Clash marks are seen in front of the neck and throat.

Reverse: Numerator about centered between ribbon knot and the fraction bar below. Bar extends from upper right of 1 to center of second 0. *Points of distinction:* This die was used to strike BW-6, BW-28, and 1802, E Close Over Dip Between Waves, T Mostly Over Forehead, Thorn From Left Stem to U (BW-13).

Notes: EF and AU are the highest grades known.

1803, Lump Under Chin, Point on Left Wreath Stem, Short Fraction Bar • BW-29, S-247, B-5. *Breen dies:* 3-E. *Estimated population:* 300 to 400.

1803, Lump Under Chin, Point on Left Wreath Stem, Short Fraction Bar (BW-29, S-247, B-5).

Obverse: See BW-2. Here in its later state with a lump under the chin, the "Mumps

Obverse." *Points of distinction:* This die was used to coin BW-2, BW-4, BW-5, and BW-29.

Reverse: A point or thorn is at the end of the left stem. Numerator about centered between ribbon knot and the very short bar below. *Points of distinction:* With cracks at UNITED.

Notes: This variety exists in AU and Mint State, the latter being extremely rare.

1803, Loop Under Drapery Very Faint or Missing, Fraction Bar Close to Second 0 • BW-30, S-250, B-10. *Breen dies:* 4-J. *Estimated population:* 300 to 400.

1803, Loop Under Drapery Very Faint or Missing, Fraction Bar Close to Second 0 (BW-30, S-250, B-10).

Obverse: Date: See BW-3. *Points of distinction:* This die was used to coin BW-3, BW-30, and BW-31. Multiple clash marks develop, nearly a dozen totally.

Reverse: See BW-18. *Points of distinction:* This die was used to coin BW-18 and BW-30, with BW-30 being its earliest use.

Notes: This variety exists in Mint State.

1803, Loop Under Drapery Very Faint or Missing, Fraction Bar Distant From Second 0 • BW-31, S-251, B-8. *Breen dies:* 4-H. *Estimated population:* 750 to 1,000.

1803, Loop Under Drapery Very Faint or Missing, Fraction Bar Distant From Second 0 (BW-31, S-251, B-8).

Obverse: Same as preceding. Drapery loop weak. *Points of distinction:* Various cracks are seen. This die was used to coin BW-3, BW-30, and BW-31, here in its final use.

Reverse: E of ONE leans right. NT of CENT low. Fraction bar is very short and is about centered between the numerator and the denominator.

Notes: This variety exists in Mint State.

Detail showing distant second 0.

1804, Draped Bust

Circulation mintage: 200,000 (estimated).

The 1804 is the most famous cent rarity after 1799. The published mintage of 756,838, without question, was mostly composed of earlier dates. A modern population of about 1,200 1804-dated coins has been suggested, as has a survival rate of two percent. This formula would project an original mintage of about 60,000 for 1804-dated cents. The Mint used a more durable die steel beginning in the 1800 to 1802 years. As Adam Eckfeldt became accustomed to the forging requirements, the new steel dramatically increased the die life. This caused some problems with overestimating the number of dies to be prepared. Accordingly, in 1804 the calendar-year coinage was mostly from earlier dated dies on hand.[80] Facts are scarce.

In 1859, in his *American Numismatical Manual*, Dr. Montroville W. Dickeson noted that, in circulation, one 1804-dated cent could be found for every 30 cents of 1805. The author had been acquainted with cents for quite some time and also wrote of finding 1793 issues at face value.

Only one die variety is known, BW-1, which exists in three die states: S-266a, from unbroken dies; S-266b, with a break (which begins as a crack) at ERT at the top of the obverse die; and S-266c, with an obverse break, and with a reverse break connecting the top of MERIC. As most cents have these cuds, the broken dies must have been employed for a significant time. Elsewhere among early coppers, large cud breaks on both sides would usually flag a die pair for removal, making such coins a scarcer die state.

No fully Mint State 1804 cents exist today by the standards generally used up until a few years ago. Recently some of these cents have been graded Mint State, despite the fact that this represents a lowering of standards.[81] As often, opinions are aplenty, and buyers can form their own. 1,200 or so exist in circulated grades. "Gradeflation" is probably here to stay, as grades go up, and up some more, although the coins themselves do not change. No doubt, "Uncirculated" examples will become more available as old-time conservative grading fades from view.

Grades are typically Good to Fine, although quite a few VF pieces exist. EF and AU coins are very elusive. Many retooled and burnished coins are in numismatic circulation.

The so-called "restrike" of this date is actually a spurious concoction, as neither the obverse nor the reverse die was ever used in 1804. Sometime in the 1860s an unknown person took a rusted, broken obverse die of 1803, Small Date, Large Fraction, Corner of 3 in Drapery (BW-15); tooled and lapped it and amateurishly changed the last digit from a 3 to a 4; and combined it with a reverse of 1820 (Newcomb-12), the latter being a different design (with continuous wreath) than that employed in 1804. Apparently, the intent was to create a "filler" for cent collectors, and not to deceive. Multiple examples of this curious cent began to appear on the market in 1868 and attracted notice at the time.[82] In the years since then, the 1804 "restrike" has been popular in its own right, and many numismatists aspire to have an example of this and also the 1823 "restrike" in their collections. Most are in Mint State with brown toning, often with some traces of lighter color. The dies were used for restriking multiple times over the years and are still in existence today.

1804, Original • BW-1a, b, and c; S-266a, b, and c; B-1. *Breen dies:* 1-A. **Estimated population:** 750 to 1,000.

1804, Original (BW-1c, S-266c, B-1).
A high-grade 1804 cent in the latest die state with cud breaks on obverse and reverse rims. This is the rarest cent date of the 19th century.

Obverse: *Date:* Blunt 1, crosslet 4. Numerals about equally spaced and distant from denticles. *LIBERTY:* IB close. Uprights of E and R over hair waves. Upright of T over hair. *Points of distinction:* This variety exists from a perfect die and also with a light crack, then, later, a rim cud break over RTY.

Reverse: Large letters. Large fraction. E of CENT leans right. Long stems to all berries except the two lowest on outside left. *Points of distinction:* Early impressions developed a crack over MERIC that developed into a cud break.

Notes: AU is the highest grade known, although some have been called Mint State (see overview). With perfect obverse this is known as BW-1a. With cud break on obverse and no break on reverse this is BW-1b. With cud breaks on both sides this is BW-1c. On all the 0 of 1804 is opposite O in OF, reflecting slight rotation of the dies. The population and mintage estimates are from Craig Sholley. Many collectors endeavor to obtain each of the three die states.

1804, Original		Cert	Avg	%MS
		86	17.4	1%

AG-3	G-4	VG-8	F-12
$1,375	$2,250	$3,800	$5,500

VF-20	EF-40	AU-50	MS-60BN
$8,830	$17,330	$44,670	$133,330

1804, "Restrike" From Mismatched Dies • BW-3, S-unlisted, B–un-numbered. **Estimated population:** 400 to 700.

1804, "Restrike" From Mismatched Dies (BW-3, S-unlisted, B–un-numbered).

Obverse: 1803, Small Date, Large Fraction, Corner of 3 in Drapery (BW-15) obverse die, rusted and cracked, altered to read "1804."

Reverse: 1820, Large Date (N-12), reverse die, rusted, worn, and relapped, thus removing detail. New denticles added around the border. Originally, this die was paired with a 1820, Matron Head.

Notes: Fantasy "restrike," so called, from two dies, neither of which was used in 1804. This variety is known in Mint State.

Numismatic Notes: Reminiscence by Edward Groh (1901): Edward Groh, born in New York City on June 2, 1837, became interested in numismatics about 1855. In 1858 he was a founder of the American Numismatic Society. On October 20, 1901, the *New York Times* printed an interview with him, which included this:

Generally speaking, all the money that has become worth more than face value has been absorbed by amateurs, or has fallen into the hands of dealers. The only way to gather rare pieces is to buy off dealers or to attend auction sales of private collections. When I was a young fellow, things were different. Take the 1804 cent for instance. One was sold in this city not many months ago for $200. I remember finding a half dozen of those very coins when I was a boy, simply by examining the change that passed through my hands. It paid one to examine change then. I never let a single piece slip by unnoticed.

Commentary concerning the "Restrike" (1907): Lancaster, Pennsylvania dealer Charles Steigerwalt commented in *The Numismatist*, February 1907, about the "restrikes" of the 1804 and 1823 cents. Concerning the 1804:

It was supposed that the 1804 came from the same source as the 1823, but the originator of those disclaimed any knowledge of the 1804. An effort was made in a recent sale catalogue to throw an air of mystery around this 1804. That is simply ridiculous. The obverse has been identified as an 1803, but if that date was too common, a crude 4 was cut over the 3 and a reverse of the period after the fraction was omitted, probably of about 1816 or later, was used in striking these abominations. By whom struck is unknown, but it was at a period long after, when the dies were rusty, and certainly not at the Mint.

1804, "Restrike" From Mismatched Dies		Cert	Avg	%MS
		176	49.6	48%

AU-50	MS-60BN	MS-63BN	MS-63RB
$980	$1,230	$1,620	$2,580

1805, Draped Bust
Mintage (per Mint Report*): 941,116.*

There are three die varieties of this year, two of which are common and the third slightly scarce. Two obverse and two reverse dies were used. The mintage figure for this calendar year undoubtedly includes many coins of earlier dates, particularly 1803.

In his *Encyclopedia*, Walter Breen commented, "Between December 1950 and December 1953 I attributed over 30,000 unpicked large cents." This 'observation series' became the basis for the rarity ratings in *Penny Whimsy*. In his 1879 *Monograph*, Édouard Frossard gave this comment, "The 1805 cents are rare in very fine or uncirculated condition, [and in other states are also] not very common."

Cents of this date tend to have relatively few problems. Most are light or medium brown.

Typical values for 1805 cents.
In Mint State, BW-2 and BW-3 are worth more.

1805	Cert	Avg	%MS
	49	39.4	18%

G-4	VG-8	F-12	VF-20	EF-40	AU-50	MS-60BN
$60	$125	$290	$530	$1,300	$2,500	$5,670

1805, Blunt 1, Outside Leaf Under O in OF • BW-1, S-267, B-1. *Breen dies:* 1-A. **Estimated population:** Thousands.

1805, Blunt 1, Outside Leaf Under O in OF (BW-1, S-267, B-1).

Detail showing blunt 1 in date.

Obverse: Date: Blunt 1; definitive. 5 much closer to drapery than 1 is to hair. 05 close. *LIBERTY:* All letters fairly close, IB closest. Uprights of R and E over waves of hair. Upright of T over hair. Y low and with defective bottom serifs. *Points of distinction:* Later reground to remove clash marks.

Reverse: Tip of highest-left leaf under left serif of S. Outside leaf tip under O in OF. T of CENT touches leaf. Numerator high. Bar much closer to right ribbon than to left. *Points of distinction:* Some have a crack over AM and a crack from the first S of STATES to T and to the wreath.

Notes: Three times more populous than BW-3 (according to Breen). This variety exists in Mint State. Some high-quality fakes by the "Bay Area counterfeiter," made in the 1970s, exist. Authentication or certification (by a leading service) is recommended.[83] As to genuine coins, they are very plentiful in the marketplace, including in EF, AU, and the lower Mint-State ranges. This is the only variety for which Mint State coins are occasionally seen, but at low levels.

1805, Blunt 1, Outside Leaf Under F in OF • BW-2, S-268, B-2. *Breen dies:* 1-B. **Estimated population:** 300 to 400.

1805, Blunt 1, Outside Leaf Under F in OF (BW-2, S-268, B-2).

Obverse: Same as preceding. *Points of distinction:* Additional clash marks develop, and mounding or bulging is seen in the left and right fields.

Reverse: Tip of highest-left leaf past right side of S. Outside leaf tip under F in OF. T of CENT does not touch leaf. Numerator high. Bar about equidistant from left and right ribbons. 00 close. *Points of distinction:* This die was used on BW-2 and BW-3 and 1806 (BW-1).

Notes: This is the scarcest by far of the three varieties of the year. Exists in AU and is rare as such. Most are VF or lower. The highest recorded by Walter Breen is AU-50.

1805, Pointed 1, Outside Leaf Under F in OF • BW-3, S-269, B-3. *Breen dies:* 2-B. ***Estimated population:*** Thousands.

1805, Pointed 1, Outside Leaf Under F in OF (BW-3, S-269, B-3).

Detail showing pointed 1 in date.

Obverse: *Date:* Pointed 1; definitive. 1 touches hair. 80 wide. 5 touches, or nearly touches, drapery. *LIBERTY:* IB very close. E and upright of R over wave of hair. Upright of T over hair; bottom serifs heavy. *Points of distinction:* A crack develops through the base of 180. Clash marks occur and are most obvious on later impressions.

Reverse: Same as preceding.

Notes: This variety exists in AU and Mint State, the latter quite rare.

1806, Draped Bust

Mintage (per **Mint Report***): 941,116.*

The 1806 cent has always been viewed as a slightly scarce date. However, examples are easy to find, including in EF, AU, and low Mint State grades. Most are attractive and are one or another shade of brown. The reported mintage figure seems overly generous and must include cents of some earlier date(s). Only one die variety is known.

In his *American Numismatical Manual*, 1859, Dr. Montroville W. Dickeson described two varieties that are not known today: "We have seen one variety of this cent which was struck from the altered die of 1805, which must have been broken or discarded, as it is the only specimen we have met with. We have also seen another variety on which 1/000 occurs."

	Cert	Avg	%MS
1806	78	32.0	10%

G-4	VG-8	F-12	VF-20	EF-40	AU-50	MS-60BN
$150	$325	$520	$1,030	$2,500	$4,500	$9,500

1806 • BW-1, S-270, B-1. *Breen dies:* 1-A. ***Estimated population:*** Thousands.

1806 (BW-1, S-270, B-1).

Obverse: *Date:* Pointed 1 is very slightly closer to hair than to the denticle over which it is positioned. 80 slightly wide. 6 barely touches drapery; left side of top of inner curve irregular. *LIBERTY:* L slightly low. IB very close. E and R over hair waves. Upright of T over hair. *Points of distinction:* Perfect die impressions exist, followed by those with a crack at the lowest curl and partially to the denticles, with a raised area to the left of the lowest curl, and also extending to the right of the date.

Reverse: Tip of highest-left leaf just past right of S. Numerator slightly closer to ribbon knot than to fraction bar. 00 close. *Points of distinction:* This die was also used on 1805, Blunt 1, Outside Leaf Under F in OF (BW-2) and 1805, Pointed 1, Outside Leaf Under F in OF (BW-3).

Notes: Exists in Mint State. Walter Breen quotes Benjamin H. Collins's description of an 1806 cent with Pointed 6, unknown today, stating that its possible existence is logical as the 1807, 7 Over 6, overdates possibly (but not certainly) have the 6's pointed.

1807, 7 Over 6, Draped Bust

*Circulation mintage (per **Mint Report***): Part of the total for 1807.*

The 1807, 7 Over 6, overdate exists in two varieties, both of which are avidly sought. The first listed is by far the rarer and is in exceptional demand, as it is listed in the regular edition of the *Guide Book of United States Coins.*

Examples of either variety are usually attractive and problem-free.

1807, 7 Over 6, Small 7 Over 6, Blunt 1 • BW-1, S-272, B-2. *Breen dies:* 2-A. *Estimated population:* 60 to 75.

1807, 7 Over 6, Small 7 Over 6, Blunt 1 (BW-1, S-272, B-2).

Detail of overdate.

Obverse: Date: Blunt 1 (definitive) high above denticles and very close to hair. 7 punched over a (possible) Pointed 6, which is still mostly visible, and boldly. Upper right and left of 7 touch drapery. *LIBERTY:* Widely spaced. IB slightly close. Uprights of E and R over hair waves. Upright of T over hair, but with lower-right serif close to forehead. Y slightly low. *Points of distinction:* In the latest state, rare, a crack develops from the rim, through R, and to the eyebrow.

Reverse: Tip of highest-left leaf slightly left of S. Numerator centered over fraction bar and slightly closer to bar than to ribbon knot. 00 close. *Points of distinction:* This die was used to coin BW-1, BW-2, and 1807, "Comet" Variety (For Most), Small Fraction, Bar Not Connected to Ribbon (BW-1).

Notes: EF and AU are the highest grades known, and examples are very rare as such.

1807, 7 Over 6, Small 7 Over 6, Blunt 1	Cert	Avg	%MS
	4	16.5	0%

AG-3	G-4	VG-8	F-12	VF-20
$1,750	$3,250	$8,000	$17,000	$24,330

1807, 7 Over 6, Large 7 Over 6, Pointed 1 • BW-2, S-273, B-3. *Breen dies:* 3-A. **Estimated population:** Thousands.

1807, 7 Over 6, Large 7 Over 6,
Pointed 1 (BW-2, S-273, B-3).

Detail of overdate.

Obverse: Date: Pointed 1 (definitive) centered over denticle and closer to hair. 18 closer to denticles than are other numerals. 80 close. Large, very heavy 7, with thick base, over Pointed 6. 7 very close to drapery. *LIBERTY:* LIB slightly close. E and R over hair waves. Upright of T over hair.

Points of distinction: A tiny horizontal crack begins at the rim at about 7 o'clock. Bulges become prominent.

Reverse: Same as preceding. *Points of distinction:* Perfect die impressions exist. Later states transition to having a crack from the rim, through C of AMERICA, and to the opposite leaf, indicating this was the last combination using this die.

Notes: Exists in Mint State. This is a very popular and easily collectible variety.

1807, 7 Over 6, Large 7 Over 6, Pointed 1		Cert	Avg	%MS
		71	26.7	10%

G-4	VG-8	F-12	VF-20
$110	$210	$375	$630

EF-40	AU-50	MS-60BN
$1,430	$2,630	$6,900

1807, Draped Bust
Mintage (per Mint Report*): 829,221.*

The perfect date, or non-overdated, 1807 is known in four die varieties, two of which are common. Most famous is the "Comet Variety," number BW-1. Most cents of this date are attractive and range from light to dark brown.

1807, "Comet" Variety (for most), Small Fraction, Bar Not Connected to Ribbon • BW-1, S-271, B-1. *Breen dies:* 1-A. **Estimated population:** Thousands.

1807, "Comet" Variety (for most),
Small Fraction, Bar Not Connected
to Ribbon (BW-1, S-271, B-1).

Obverse: Date: High above denticles. 1 nearer hair than denticles. 18 slightly wide. Upper right of 7 close to drapery. *LIBERTY:* ERT slightly wide. Uprights of E and R over waves of hair. Upright of T over

hair, but right serif is close to the forehead; right serif is short. *Points of distinction:* When seen with the die flaw behind the head, this is known as the "Comet Variety." Later, the "comet" becomes heavier, and clash marks are seen. In the final state, there is a bulge at 7, rendering the digit indistinct.

Reverse: See 1807, 7 Over 6, Small 7 Over 6, Blunt 1 (BW-1). Bar not connected to ribbon and A. C of CENT touches leaf. *Points of distinction:* This die was also used to coin 1807, 7 Over 6, Small 7 Over 6, Blunt 1 (BW-1), and 1807, 7 Over 6, Large 7 Over 6, Pointed 1 (BW-2).

Notes: Exists in Mint State. The "Comet Variety" is among the best known of the Draped Bust cents. The appellation lends itself well to coin sale descriptions, such as "Great Comet Appears." Indeed, the early die state without the "comet" (the die sank slightly in this position) attracts little interest, making the "Comet" a member of that curious category in which a damaged, worn, or broken die can be more valuable that a perfect one.[84] In the 1895 catalog of the Winsor Collection, the Chapman brothers described a coin as "1807 Comet variety." Earlier, in the June 1890 offering of the Parmelee Collection, David U. Pro-

skey and Harlan P. Smith simply noted that the variety has a "bar-like defect in die from hair to border." S.H. Chapman noted this is "commonly called the Comet variety" in his April 1923 catalog of the Beckwith Collection.[85]

"Comet" must be visible.

1807, "Comet" Variety		Cert	Avg	%MS
		26	32.4	19%

G-4	VG-8	F-12	VF-20
$130	$290	$600	$1,070

EF-40	AU-50	MS-60BN	MS-63BN
$3,280	$4,250	$12,000	$28,670

1807, Small Fraction, Connected By Line to Ribbon and A • BW-2, S-274, B-4. *Breen dies:* 4-B. *Estimated population:* 500 to 750.

1807, Small Fraction, Connected By Line to Ribbon and A (BW-2, S-274, B-4).

Obverse: Date: Lower than the preceding. 1 much closer to the hair than to the denticles. 80 slightly wide. 7 about centered between drapery and denticles. *LIBERTY:* IB close; lower right of I slightly lower than nearby left serif of B. E and R over

waves of hair. Upright of T over hair, but right serif is close to forehead. Y slightly low and with lower-right serif pointed.

Reverse: A die scratch connects the right side of the bar with the ribbon and the A; definitive. C of CENT is close to, but does not touch, the leaf. *Points of distinction:* Die failure has caused mounding and weakness. Several cracks are seen.

Notes: EF and AU are the highest grades known, and examples are quite rare as such. Worth more than BW-4, especially in high grades.

1807, Base of B Level With E, Large Fraction • BW-3, S-275, B-5. *Breen dies:* 4-C. *Estimated population:* 400 to 500.

1807, Base of B Level With E, Large Fraction (BW-3, S-275, B-5).

Obverse: Same as preceding. *Points of distinction:* In a late state, a crack is through the top of LIBERTY.

Reverse: Left stem short and stubby. Tip of highest-left leaf under S and slightly left of its center. Fraction large. Bar begins over center of 1 and continues to left of the center of second 0. 00 close. Second 0 leans left.

Notes: EF and AU are the highest grades known. Worth more than BW-4, especially in high grades.

1807, Base of B Above E, Large Fraction • BW-4, S-276, B-6. *Breen dies:* 5-C. ***Estimated population:*** Thousands.

1807, Base of B Above E,
Large Fraction (BW-4, S-276, B-6).

Obverse: Date: Low, similar to the preceding. Fairly evenly spaced. 7 about centered between drapery and denticles. *LIBERTY:* L slightly low. B higher than E. ERT wide. E and R over waves of hair. Upright of T over hair. Y slightly low. *Points of distinction:* With a swelling at the rim below the lowest curl. In a later state there are rim breaks in the denticles above LIBE.

Reverse: Same as preceding.

Notes: Exists in Mint State. The dies are often rotated. Walter Breen: "Arguably the commonest of all Draped Bust cents."

1807, Base of B Above E, Large Fraction		Cert	Avg	%MS
		23	20.6	0%

G-4	VG-8	F-12	VF-20
$110	$220	$410	$620

EF-40	AU-50		MS-60BN
$1,400	$3,000		$5,230

CLASSIC HEAD (1808–1814)

1810, 10 Over 09 (BW-1, S-281, B-1).

Designer: *John Reich.* **Weight:** *168 grains (10.89 grams).*
Composition: *Copper.* **Diameter:** *Average 29 mm.* **Edge:** *Plain.*

The Classic Head design by John Reich, assistant engraver at the Mint, was introduced in 1808 and was continued through 1814. Today, all dates are available, with no major rarities, although those of 1809 are considered to be scarcer than the others. Generally, the earlier dates are seen on light-brown planchets and are somewhat casually struck, with many design details weak or absent. Cents of 1814 are often dark and porous.

Finding a sharply struck Classic Head cent, with smooth, attractive fields, and of a brown (rather than gray or black) color, will be a great challenge, involving the inspection of many coins. Lightness of striking is the rule for the vast majority of cents of this type. On the obverse the points to look for include sharpness of the denticles, star centers, hair details, and leaf details. On the reverse, the high parts of the leaves and the denticles are checkpoints. The center lettering is usually quite sharp.

When found, an ideal piece will probably not cost much more than an average example of its date and grade, for most buyers are not oriented toward seeking quality. Grading numbers alone suffice for all but dedicated specialists.

Most examples are well worn, in grades from Good to VF or so. EF coins are scarce by comparison, and AU pieces are scarcer yet. Mint State coins are quite rare and tend to be at lower levels such as MS-60 or MS-61. Any coin conservatively graded as MS-63 or higher is very rare.

All planchets for these cents were imported from Boulton & Watt of Birmingham, England, a firm well known for the excellent quality of its products. The last shipment recorded from that source arrived on April 15, 1812, on the eve of the War of 1812, after which business was not recommenced with this British supplier until after the conflict. Afterward, supplies on hand were used until they were exhausted. As noted in chapter 1, in 1814 the price of copper metal had risen to the point that many cents were melted by speculators. This wholesale destruction no doubt made earlier cent issues rarer than the mintage figures indicate.

Craig Sholley suggests that either the Mint or Boulton & Watt may have begun adding a lubricant to the planchet, or that the British supplier may have begun utilizing a different source, or different ore base, that contained impurities. Whatever the reason, extant coins from later Classic Head years tend to be dark, porous, or both—quite unlike the Draped Bust issues.

The Classic Head series seems to have instituted a Mint policy whereby obverse and reverse dies were replaced at the same time. Earlier, the procedure had been for the pressman to examine the dies as they were being used, then if one die or another became unfit, to remove it and replace it with another. Accordingly, in earlier times, the same obverse die could be mated with two or more reverses, and vice versa. From 1808 through 1814, each obverse is matched with a single distinctive reverse not used elsewhere within that year.

No cents were struck with the date 1815, due to the unavailability of planchets; Mint records show that the supply was exhausted as of October 27, 1814. Mintage resumed late in 1815, using dies dated 1816, of the Matron Head design.

Design Details

The Classic Head, by assistant engraver John Reich, features Miss Liberty facing to the left, with a band in her hair inscribed LIBERTY. Years ago, this was sometimes called the Turban Head, although no turban is present. In 1879, Édouard Frossard, in *Monograph of United States Cents and Half Cents Issued Between the Years 1793 and 1857*, used this nomenclature.

Seven stars are at the border to the left, and six stars are to the right. The date is between the head and the bottom border.

The obverse die was created with a hub punch with the portrait of Miss Liberty. Details of the LIBERTY word were punched by hand into the headband. Seven stars to the left and six to the right were added by individual punches; thus, they vary slightly in their spacing. The dates were added by single punches, one at a time.

The term *Classic Head* seems to have originated with E.D. Mason Jr. in *Mason's Coin and Stamp Collector's Magazine*, February 1868. The design is distinctive, and was also used on half cents (beginning in 1809). Years later, in 1834, it was revived by chief engraver William Kneass and used, with slight modifications, on $2.50 and $5 gold coins.

The reverse, also probably by Reich, is a departure from the previous style. A continuous wreath tied with a ribbon bow at the bottom encloses the inscription ONE / CENT. Around the border is UNITED STATES OF AMERICA. The reverse is from a punch including the wreath and berries, ONE / CENT, and the line under the last word. Accordingly, there are no variations in count or position among any of these features. The letters around the periphery were added by hand, and provide the opportunity to identify die varieties. The position of certain leaf tips in relation to the letters, particularly the second S in STATES, is a handy guide.

1808, Classic Head

Mintage (per **Mint Report***): 1,009,000.*

There are three varieties of the 1808, each struck from a separate die pair. The typical BW-1 and BW-2 have light striking in areas, usually the stars, while BW-3 is sharper on average.

Most 1808 cents show extensive wear, but attractive AU and (usually lower) Mint State grades come on the market now and again, particularly when fine collections cross the auction block.

Typical values for 1808 cents.
Rare varieties may be worth more.

1808		Cert	Avg	%MS
		97	35.0	18%

G-4	VG-8	F-12	VF-20	EF-40	AU-50	MS-60BN	MS-63BN
$110	$275	$500	$920	$2,620	$5,500	$8,000	$15,670

1808 • BW-1, S-277, B-1. *Breen dies:* 1-A. ***Estimated population:*** 750 to 1,000.

1808 (BW-1, S-277, B-1).

Obverse: Frame line in front of L of LIBERTY bulges outward to the left. Rim and denticles at the bottom of the border are weak.

Reverse: Leaf tip under second S of STATES slightly right of its center. Leaf tip under the beginning of the serif to the right of the center of upright of F in OF. *Points of distinction:* Sometimes the die is perfect, but more often there are cracks.

Notes: The bottom of the obverse is usually weak, as is the corresponding area of the reverse (the top left, at STATES). Sometimes Star 1 is very weak, giving rise to the nickname of "12 Stars" variety. This variety exists in Mint State and is rare as such.

1808 • BW-2, S-278, B-2. *Breen dies:* 2-B. ***Estimated population:*** 300 to 500.

1808 (BW-2, S-278, B-2).

Obverse: Frame line straight. All stars on the right are about evenly spaced. *Points of distinction:* On the late state there are rim breaks, including near stars 8, 10, and 11.

Reverse: Leaf tip is under right edge of second S of STATES on sharp impressions; otherwise very slightly left of the right edge. Leaf tip under center of upright of F in OF.

Notes: This variety exists in Mint State and rare as such. It is by far the scarcest variety of the year.

1808 • BW-3, S-279, B-3. *Breen dies:* 3-C. **Estimated population:** Several thousand.

1808 (BW-3, S-279, B-3).

Obverse: Frame line straight. Stars 9 and 10 are more closely spaced than are any other stars on the right. *Points of distinction:* This variety occurs with a perfect die and also injured, with the stars on the right blended into the rim and other distortions. Dr. Sheldon: "This die must have come into violent contact with something hard." A light crack develops from the rim, to star 3, and to the chin. On the latest state there is a rim break at 10 o'clock.

Reverse: Leaf tip under second S of STATES very slightly to the right of its center. Leaf tip under center of upright of F in OF.

Notes: This variety exists in Mint State and is rare as such.

1809, Classic Head
Mintage (per Mint Report): 222,867.

For many years the 1809 has been considered the key date of the Classic Head type. In actuality, cents of this date are fairly plentiful, and in worn grades they are not difficult to find. There is only one die pair.

The obverse is usually flatly struck in some areas, with indistinct star centers and a thin or incomplete border, although there are exceptions. The reverse is usually sharper. The color can vary from light brown to quite dark. Most examples show wear, often extensive. At the EF and AU levels the 1809 *is* somewhat scarce. Well over a dozen examples have been graded Mint State over the years, though usually in lower ranges. Presumably, the Mansion House find (see Numismatic Notes) had higher-level Mint State coins that were secreted about the time of their coinage.

In his 1879 *Monograph*, Édouard Frossard noted: "This date is very scarce, and seldom found in fine condition. The impression of the obverse is light, the milling slight and low; hence specimens which have been in circulation are generally much worn about the edge."

1809				Cert	Avg	%MS
				61	31.2	8%

G-4	VG-8	F-12	VF-20	EF-40	AU-50	MS-60BN
$275	$450	$775	$1,630	$4,500	$8,570	$13,830

1809 • BW-1, S-280, B-1. *Breen dies:* 1-A. **Estimated population:** 750 to 1,000.

1809 (BW-1, S-280, B-1). An example with a remarkably sharp strike.

Obverse: Only die of the year. Star 13 close to date. *Points of distinction:* Some are from a perfect die state, but most are usually cracked from star 11 to near the point of the upper ribbon. Extensive clash marks are seen on later states.

Reverse: Berry under upright of T of UNITED. Leaf tip under center of second S of STATES. *Points of distinction:* Some are from a perfect die, but usually this variety is seen with one or more cracks. The reverse is nearly always sharper than the obverse. Later, small cracks develop, and in its late state the die loses a small piece below E of STATES.

Notes: This variety exists in Mint State.

Numismatic Notes: *A cornerstone find:* Thomas Birch & Sons' June 21, 1871, sale of the M.W. Nickerson consignment offered as Lot 183 an 1809 large cent, "One of nine taken from the cornerstone of the Mansion House, Philadelphia; extremely rare."[86]

Years earlier the Mansion House, located at 122 South Third Street, was considered to be one of the leading stopping places in the city, with its well-known contemporaries including the U.S. Hotel (opposite the Bank of the United States), City Hotel, National Hotel, Washington Hotel, and Congress Hall.[87]

1810, 10 Over 09, Classic Head
Mintage (per Mint Report*): Part of the total for 1810.*

There is just one die pair for the 1810, 10 Over 09, overdate, making classification easy. An 1809 die, different from the one actually used for coinage in 1809, was overpunched with 1 and 0 digits. Some lightness of striking at the star centers is usual, but there are many exceptions.

The typically found coin shows extensive wear. At the AU level this variety is rare, and in Mint State few are found.

1810, 10 Over 09	Cert	Avg	%MS
	43	30.5	12%

G-4	VG-8	F-12	VF-20	EF-40	AU-50	MS-60BN	MS-63BN
$110	$225	$500	$900	$2,230	$3,750	$9,000	$18,330

1810, 10 Over 09 • BW-1, S-281, B-1. *Breen dies: 1-A.* **Estimated population: Thousands.**

1810, 10 Over 09 (BW-1, S-281, B-1).

Detail of overdate.

Obverse: Overdate. Just one die.

Reverse: Tip of leaf under second S of STATES.

Notes: In their late state the dies became worn and grainy, resulting in flow lines in the fields, particularly on the obverse, and distending of the outermost star points. This variety exists in Mint State.

1810, Classic Head

Mintage (per Mint Report): 1,458,500.

On each of the four obverse dies the highest tuft of hair, on the outside about B of LIB-ERTY, was finished by hand, resulting in some slight differences. Cents of this date are much better struck than those of the year preceding, but some lightness of the stars is normal. The color tends to be a pleasing light brown.

Typical values for 1810 cents.
Rare varieties may be worth more.

1810	Cert	Avg	%MS
	118	33.9	14%

G-4	VG-8	F-12	VF-20	EF-40	AU-50	MS-60BN	MS-63BN
$100	$200	$450	$850	$1,700	$3,570	$8,170	$17,000

1810 • BW-1, S-282, B-3. *Breen dies: 3-C. Estimated population: 750 to 1,000.*

1810 (BW-1, S-282, B-3).

Obverse: Star 1 closer to denticle than to bust. Stars 5 and 6 closer than are stars 6 and 7. *Points of distinction:* Cracks develop through certain of the stars.

Reverse: Tip of leaf at right edge of second S of STATES. Tip of leaf opposite right edge of N of UNITED.

Notes: This variety exists in Mint State.

1810 • BW-2, S-283, B-4. *Breen dies: 4-D. Estimated population: 750 to 1,000.*

1810 (BW-2, S-283, B-4).

Obverse: Star 1 close to denticle and distant from bust. Left top of T of LIBERTY at same level as top of adjacent R.

Reverse: Tip of leaf slightly past second S of STATES.

Notes: This variety exists in Mint State.

1810 • BW-3, S-284, B-5. *Breen dies: 5-E. Estimated population: 400 to 500.*

1810 (BW-3, S-284, B-5).

Obverse: Star 1 close to denticle and distant from bust; innermost point repunched. Left top of T of LIBERTY lower than top of adjacent R.

Reverse: Tip of leaf far past second S of STATES. Bottom of EN of CENT close; top of NT more widely spaced. Tops of UNI touch or nearly touch.

Notes: This variety exists in Mint State.

1810 • BW-4, S-285, B-2. *Breen dies:* 2-B. **Estimated population:** 750 to 1,000.

1810 (BW-4, S-285, B-2).

Obverse: Star 1 slightly closer to denticle than to bust, and well separated from each. Stars 3 and 4 are more widely spaced than are any others on the left. *Points of distinction:* A crack develops through the base of 10 and connects the stars at the right.

Reverse: Tip of leaf at right edge of second S of STATES. Tip of leaf opposite left serif of I of UNITED. Bottom of EN of CENT and top of NT about equally spaced.

Notes: This variety exists in Mint State.

Numismatic Notes: A fantasy "restrike" of the 1810 cent was made sometime around the 1850s. The obverse die is the same as used on BW-4, but rusted and cracked. The reverse die is the same as used on the fantasy "restrike" 1804—1804, "Restrike" From Mismatched Dies (BW-3)—originally used on the 1820, Large Date (N-12). Only two examples are known, both struck in tin.

1811, 1 Over 0, Classic Head
Mintage (per Mint Report): Part of the total for 1811.

This variety, from a single pair of dies, usually comes on a dark planchet, somewhat rough, perhaps due to a lubricant on the Boulton & Watt planchets or the use of a different source of metal by that firm.

The striking is usually fairly good, save for some slight lightness at the star centers, particularly toward the bottom. Nearly all examples show extensive wear. In his *Encyclopedia*, Walter Breen knew of no example better than AU-55, this being the only Classic Head cent variety for which Mint State coins are not recorded—at least per conservative grading practice.

However, in his *American Numismatical Manual*, 1859, Dr. Montroville W. Dickeson states this: "We are indebted for ours to an unopened keg returned to the Mint from Charleston, South Carolina." We can only read this and weep. Probably, this was years prior to 1859 and the pivotal 1855 Kline sale (see chapter 4), and Mint officials considered the cents to be of no special value.

1811, 1 Over 0	Cert	Avg	%MS
	23	28.9	13%

G-4	VG-8	F-12	VF-20	EF-40	AU-50
$200	$425	$950	$2,170	$5,920	$14,170

1811, 1 Over 0 • BW-1, S-286, B-2. *Breen dies:* 2-B. **Estimated population:** 300 to 400.

1811, 1 Over 0 (BW-1, S-286, B-2).

Detail of overdate.

Obverse: Overdate with 0 boldly visible under final 1.

Reverse: Point of leaf under second S of STATES. Raised dash under upright of E of ONE.

Notes: A previously unused 1810 die was overdated. AU is the highest grade known.

1811, Classic Head

Mintage (per Mint Report): 218,025.

Similar to the overdate, the "normal" or "perfect" 1811 date is often found dark and porous. Other examples are a light brown.

Striking varies, but some light striking at certain star centers and high areas of the leaves is the rule, not the exception. The typical coin shows extensive wear, but VF and EF examples are not hard to find. Mint State coins are very elusive and are usually in lower ranges of that classification.

1811	Cert	Avg	%MS
	69	31.8	16%

G-4	VG-8	F-12	VF-20	EF-40	AU-50	MS-60BN	MS-63BN
$175	$325	$650	$1,330	$3,070	$7,330	$13,330	$20,000

1811 • BW-1, S-287, B-1. *Breen dies:* 1-A. ***Estimated population:*** 750 to 1,000.

1811 (BW-1, S-287, B-1).

Obverse: Normal or perfect date (not over-date). *Points of distinction:* Rim breaks develop opposite stars 2 to 4. In the final state, rare, there is a rim break near the star 9.

Reverse: Point of leaf slightly past second S of STATES.

Notes: This variety exists in Mint State.

1812, Classic Head

Mintage (per Mint Report): 1,075,500.

The difference between a Large Date and a Small Date 1812 cent is not obvious at a quick glance. A comparison of the two will show a taller 1 in the Large Date. In the Small Date the 1 is shorter than the 2; in the Large Date they are about the same height. There are four die combinations this year—in each case, a unique use of an obverse matching a unique use of a reverse. The sharpness of strike varies, but usually some of the obverse stars are flat at their centers.

Most cents of this date are well worn, although perhaps 25 or so Mint State examples exist per conservative grading, significantly more if graded liberally. Higher-grade coins are often of the BW-3 variety. Surfaces are often dark and somewhat granular. As is true of all Classic Head cents, cherrypicking within a given grade can yield dividends.

Typical values for 1812 cents.
Rare varieties may be worth more.

1812	Cert	Avg	%MS
	59	33.7	8%

VF-20	EF-40	AU-50	MS-60BN	MS-63BN
$1,000	$2,000	$4,000	$10,000	$20,000

1812, Large Date • BW-1, S-288, B-3. *Breen dies:* 3-C. **Estimated population:** 750 to 1,000.

1812, Large Date (BW-1, S-288, B-3).

Obverse: Large Date.

Reverse: Berry under lower-left serif of first T of STATES. Tip of leaf past second S of STATES.

Notes: This variety exists in Mint State.

1812, Large Date • BW-2, S-289, B-4. *Breen dies:* 4-D. **Estimated population:** Thousands.

1812, Large Date (BW-2, S-289, B-4).

Obverse: Large Date.

Reverse: Berry directly under upright of first T of UNITED, the only reverse with this feature.

Notes: This variety exists in Mint State.

1812, Small Date • BW-3, S-290, B-2. *Breen dies:* 2-B. **Estimated population:** Thousands.

1812, Small Date (BW-3, S-290, B-2).

Obverse: Small Date. Star 1 closer to denticles than to bust; points to slightly left of the center of a denticle. *Points of distinction:* Breen notes that "there is a small hoard of Mint State specimens," but no other information is given.

Reverse: Berry under lower-left serif of first T of STATES; tip of leaf under second S. Berry under space between A and M of AMERICA.

Notes: This variety occurs in Mint State.

1812, Small Date • BW-4, S-291, B-1. *Breen dies:* 1-A. **Estimated population:** 750 to 1,000.

1812, Small Date (BW-4, S-291, B-1).

Obverse: Small Date. Star 1 is about equidistant from the bust and the denticles and points to the space between denticles.

Points of distinction: A crack develops and expands, in the latest state through the entire base of the date and connecting through all of the stars.

Reverse: Berry under lower-left serif of first T of STATES; tip of leaf under second S. Berry under right foot of first A of AMERICA.

Notes: This variety exists in AU and Mint State, the latter being very rare.

1813, Classic Head

Mintage (per Mint Report): 418,000.

Cents of 1813 follow the general rule for classic head cents, particularly the later ones: the surfaces are often granular and the color dark. These variations may suggest different sources for the copper.

Typical values for 1813 cents.
Rare varieties may be worth more.

1813	Cert	Avg	%MS
	150	38.8	12%

VF-20	EF-40	AU-50	MS-60BN	MS-63BN
$925	$1,875	$3,400	$8,500	$16,250

1813 • BW-1, S-292, B-2. *Breen dies:* 2-B. **Estimated population:** 1,000 to 1,250.

1813 (BW-1, S-292, B-2).

Obverse: Stars 6 and 7 and stars 12 and 13 close.

Reverse: Berry under space between S and T of STATES. *Points of distinction:* Cracks developed as the die was used.

Notes: This variety exists in Mint State.

1813 • BW-2, S-293, B-1. *Breen dies:* 1-A. **Estimated population:** 750 to 1,000.

1813 (BW-2, S-293, B-1).

Obverse: Stars 6 and 7 widely apart; stars 12 and 13 close. Star 13 closer to date than on BW-1.

Reverse: Berry under upright of first T of STATES. *Points of distinction:* This die, by that time very rusted, was combined in the 1860s with a damaged 1823 obverse and was used to make 1823 "restrike" cents (see 1823 Cents).

Notes: This variety exists in Mint State. It is called 1813/12, an overdate, by Walter Breen, such feature being noticeable only on very high-grade pieces of the earliest die state. This nomenclature is hardly ever used, and it is generally considered to be a regular date.

1814, Classic Head

Mintage (per Mint Report): 357,830.

R.W. Julian suggests that the cents of this date, delivered from the coiner to the Mint treasurer on October 27, were deposited at face value in the Bank of Pennsylvania in December. By that time, the treasurer of the United States had advised against paying out cents, possibly as the market price for copper was at a high level. At that time, and in other times when copper was scarce or expensive, industrial concerns would buy kegs of copper cents and melt them to secure a supply of the metal.[88] Further coinage was suspended, as the supply of planchets had been exhausted.

Cents of 1814 are easily enough collected today. Of all Classic Head cents, the two die varieties of 1814 are best known for being dark and porous. Although occasional examples are seen at the Mint State level, none have been observed with original mint color.

1814, Crosslet 4 • BW-1, S-294, B-1. *Breen dies:* 1-A. **Estimated population: Thousands.**

1814, Crosslet 4 (BW-1, S-294, B-1).

Obverse: Crosslet 4. Base of 4 higher than the base of adjacent 1.

Reverse: Tip of leaf slightly past second S of STATES.

Notes: This variety is found in Mint State.

1814, Crosslet 4		Cert	Avg	%MS
		69	29.8	13%

G-4	VG-8	F-12	VF-20
$80	$200	$400	$875

EF-40	AU-50	MS-60BN	MS-63BN
$1,800	$3,200	$6,500	$12,750

1814, Plain 4 • BW-2, S-295, B-2. *Breen dies:* 2-B. **Estimated population: Thousands.**

1814, Plain 4 (BW-2, S-295, B-2).

Obverse: Plain 4. Base of 4 on about the same level as the base of adjacent 1. *Points of distinction:* Die deterioration at the throat continues to the chin and the mouth, creating the "Bearded Variety." A crack develops from the rim to the 11th star, continuing to the curl, later becoming heavy and joining the rim.

Reverse: Tip of leaf under second S of STATES. *Points of distinction:* A rim break is above D of UNITED and on the latest state also above TA of STATES.

Notes: This variety exists in Mint State.

Numismatic Notes: *Gold in 1814 cents:* The May 1858 issue of *Historical Magazine*

included these replies to a question about 1814 cents:

> United States Cent, 1814: Cents coined in 1814 may be occasionally met with, though I think them quite rare. I have several in my possession. On looking over large quantities at various times, I have never met with a single genuine one of 1815. The records of the Mint state that the amount of copper coinage for 1814 was $3,578.30, but none was coined the succeeding year, according to the records, though I have no doubt some few were struck off.
>
> *Madison*
> *Baltimore, March 6, 1858.*

Another Reply.—Cents of the coinage of 1814 are occasionally met with in circulation. I have a number of them in my possession. A reference to the tables of the Mint, containing a statement of its operations in different years, shows that in 1814 $3,578.30 worth of copper was coined, and that no cents were minted in 1815 or 1828.

I have heard it stated that the scarcity of copper, incident to the war of 1812, was the reason that so few cents were coined in 1813 and 1814, and that none were coined in 1815.

How the absurd story that the cents of 1814 contained gold originated, I am unable to explain. Chemical tests have, in several instances, been applied to the cents of that year, but the presence of gold has never yet been detected.

B.H.H. Troy, N.Y., March 5, 1858.

B.H.H. was B.H. Hall, a numismatist and researcher in the 1850s. Little is known today about Hall. However, he was an active correspondent with Charles I. Bushnell about both Vermont copper coinage (dated 1785–1788) and Fugio cents (dated 1787). In 1858 he provided information to John Hickcox for use in his book.

In the *American Numismatical Manual*, 1859, Dr. Montroville W. Dickeson partially explained the gold rumor: "Additional value has been attached to the issue of this year in consequence of the rumor that it contained gold lost at the Mint at that time. Many cling to them with much tenacity on that account—the slightest basis for credulity being ardently responded to."

The Fulton rumor: The July 1872 issue of the *Journal of Numismatics* noted that in 1814 Robert Fulton built a steamship for the United States called the SS *Fulton*. "One rule he uniformly observed was to have in use copper and not iron boilers; the latter, he thought, were too liable to explosion, and the explosion of iron he believed, would be very disastrous. Wherefore, the boiler of the *Fulton*, which vessel was built in the time of the last British war with the United States, when copper was very scarce and dear, was composed in part of the copper coined cents."

There seems to be no reason to give credence to this comment.

1814, Plain 4		Cert	Avg	%MS
		79	27.6	11%

G-4	VG-8	F-12	VF-20	
$80	$200	$400	$875	

EF-40	AU-50	MS-60BN	MS-63BN	
$1,800	$3,200	$6,500	$12,500	

MATRON HEAD (1816–1839)

**1829, Large Letters (N-1). Mint State
with a generous amount of original color,
rare and remarkable for any variety of this date.**

Designer: *Robert Scot. Later modifications made by Christian Gobrecht.*
Weight: *168 grains (10.89 grams).* **Composition:** *Copper.*
Diameter: *27.5 mm.* **Edge:** *Plain.*

The Matron Head cent, first coined in 1816, has variously been described as numismatically beautiful or artistically ugly—displaying beauty strictly in the eyes of the beholder. Without doubt, the earlier-discussed 1793 Chain, with Miss Liberty appearing to be in a "fright," is exceedingly delightful to numismatists today, never mind that Miss Liberty may not have won a beauty contest. So it may be with the Matron Head cent—the design is what it is, we are used to it, and in its own way it is quite appealing to many specialists. Indeed, it is one of the most numismatically popular motifs in early-1800s coinage, with coins issued from 1816 until 1839, familiarly called the "middle dates."

The basic obverse and reverse designs remained the same until 1835, when modifications were made by Christian Gobrecht, who had been signed as a staff engraver in September of that year. Slightly different styles were continued through 1839, including such curiously named varieties as the *Silly Head* and *Booby Head.* The culmination was the Braided Hair type of late 1839, inaugurating the next major type in the series.

Alexander Vattemare, a Frenchman who visited the United States at least twice in the period from the late 1830s to the 1850s in promotion of a literary and cultural exchange program, visited the Mint and collectors, conducted interviews, and wrote a book, *Collection de Monnaies et Médailles de l'Amérique du Nord de 1652 à 1858*, which was published in Paris in 1861.[89] He claimed that the model for Scot's Liberty head of 1816 was the wife of Director Patterson, but no verification of this has been found.[90]

As noted, from late 1835 through 1839, a number of distinctly different portraits were created in the copper cent series, no doubt by Christian Gobrecht. Perhaps he used the cent series as an experimental ground for ideas that might later be adopted to higher denominations. In the spring of 1836, steam presses were used for the first time at the Philadelphia Mint to strike cents, and perhaps the advent of this power provided a reason for modifying designs. This change may have affected size, relief, or other aspects of the coins, the details of which are now forgotten, and are known to us only by the study of the coins themselves.

There are many die varieties across the series that range from common to unique, according to Howard R. Newcomb's *United States Copper Cents 1816–1857.* The interest in these varieties is extensive, due in no small part to specialist works written about them by John D. Wright and William C. Noyes, plus discussions in *Penny-Wise.* Individual treatment of those varieties, which often differ only by minor details, is beyond the scope of the present text. Many dates and varieties apart from the Newcomb varieties beckon, and such obvious and popular differences as Small Letters and Large Letters and different portrait styles are enumerated below.

Circulated examples of Matron Head cents and the later revisions of the design exist in approximate relationship to their mintages. Generally, fewer of the early dates are found, and the average grade is lower. Coins from 1816 through the 1820s are common in grades such as Good and VG, although many Fine and VF pieces exist. For the 1830s, Fine to Very Fine is typical, plus many EF and AU coins.

Those of 1816 to 1820 (particularly 1818 and 1820) are readily available in Mint State from the famous Randall Hoard. Otherwise, Mint State coins are generally scarce in the type, although those of the 1830s are more available than those of the 1820s. Those of the 1830s are seen with the most frequency, especially for the years 1836 to 1839.

In general, copper cents of this era are fairly well struck *except* for the stars. And, of course, this is a big exception. Relatively few of the earlier years have full centers on all of the stars, and in many instances they are quite flat. While 1816, 1817, and 1821 do 1823 tend to be darkly hued, sometimes even close to black, most other dates are a pleasing brown. Of course, even in the problem years there are many examples where the color is brown. Surface quality is usually good, with the result that coins in grades as low as Very Good and Fine can be a delight to the eye and pleasing to own. This statement would be difficult for a specialist in silver or gold coins to understand, but show a copper specialist a smooth VG 1823 or 1839, 9 Over 6, cent and you'll likely receive a compliment.

Regarding striking, such as on the stars, denticles, and higher areas of the hair on the obverse and wreath leaves on the reverse, this differs from one die variety to another. Specialized texts such as the William C. Noyes and John D. Wright books mentioned below are a guide to such. This is important, as there is no sense chasing a perfect strike if one does not exist for a given variety.

A set of the different *major* varieties we list can be acquired for very reasonable cost in grades from VF to AU, excepting a handful of scarce issues—and even these, such as 1823, 1824, 4 Over 2, and 1839, 9 Over 6, in particular, are not impossible—and can always be represented by lower-grade coins. In Mint State there is a lot of value in the marketplace at the MS-60 to MS-63 level, cherrypicked for quality. Mint State cents with significant mint red attract a lot of attention and usually cost much more. There is unlimited opportunity for cherrypicking, for some MS-60 coins are finer than those graded MS-63. The opposite is true, of course, and such are the pieces to avoid. As in other series, certain dates have "personalities" all their own. As an example, an 1823, 3 Over 2, cent is apt to be quite dark, even black. In contrast, nearly all 1836 cents are light brown.

While some usable obverse dies were probably held over and used later, from 1816 onward the calendar-year mintages are a much more reliable indicator of year-date production than Mint figures were for cents dated earlier. What seems to be the major exception to this rule is 1823, for which no mintage figure is known. Probably, the cents from this year were included in the 1824 accounting.

For all Matron Head dies, the dates were punched into dies one digit at a time. The use of a four-digit logotype or *gang punch* was not initiated until 1840, this being in the second year of the Braided Hair series.

Proof cents were made in small quantities and are very rare for all dates. This is a highly technical area, and careful study is recommended. In the opinion of Q. David Bowers, many "Proofs," including certified examples, are not true Proofs at all.

The middle-date cents are fascinating to explore, indeed one of the most interesting areas in early-1800s numismatics. A great *advantage* for you is that striking and die quality is not mentioned at all on certified holders and is not often noted in descriptions of coins for sale. Accordingly, cherrypicking for quality offers many opportunities, as *most* of these cents either have some weakness of striking (most notably at the star centers), or are struck from tired dies with grainy surfaces, or both.

The following listings from 1816 to the end of the series do not include Whitman numbers as we do not treat all of the many die varieties. Instead, we highlight the "at sight" varieties that are the most popular as does, for example, the regular edition of the *Guide Book of United States Coins.* If you are interested in all the die varieties, these books are your passport: *United States Copper Cents 1816–1857,* by Howard R. Newcomb, 1944, remains the standard reference, with Newcomb numbers (N-1, N-2, etc.), which received numerous additions from later scholars. *United States Large Cents 1816–1839,* by William C. Noyes, 1991, and *The Cent Book, 1816–1839,* by John D. Wright, 1992, both offer large illustrations of varieties in combination with useful information.

THE RANDALL HOARD

Among United States large cents of the early years of the Matron Head design (sometimes referred to as the Coronet design), nearly all are very elusive in Mint State, except for 1816 through 1820. Today, many of these exist, with 1818 and 1820 being by far the most numerous. Such coins are commonly attributed to the Randall Hoard. Cents dated 1816 are in the minority in this regard and are not even mentioned in some historical accounts of the hoard and may be from another source.[91] The number of coins involved is not known, but it seems likely that about 5,000 to 10,000 were found in a small keg.

It seems that these came to light in the 1860s. John Swan Randall, of Norwich, New York, wrote the details to Edward D. Cogan on January 7, 1870, by which time such coins had attracted attention in the numismatic marketplace. E.B. Mason Jr. had called them *restrikes*, because of their brightness:

> I should not sell coin that I knew or believed to be re-strikes without letting it be known. The bright, Uncirculated cents I have sold of 1817, 1818, 1819, 1820, and 1825, I am very sure *are not re-strikes*. I bought them of Wm. H. Chapman & Co., dry goods merchants of this village, and the head of the firm, W.H.C., informed me that he got them of a wholesale merchant in New York, who informed him that he got them from a merchant in Georgia; that he took them as a payment on a debt, and that the Georgia merchant wrote him that they were found since the war in Georgia buried in the earth.
>
> Mr. Chapman said to me that he was in New York about the time the cents were received there, and that the merchant who had (ditto) thought they were too large to use, and did not know what to do with them; and that he (Chapman) thinking that his customers here would be pleased with bright cents, offered ninety cents a hundred for them, which was immediately taken. Chapman & Co. commenced paying them out here, and their bright appearance and old dates made many think they were counterfeits, and they were called 'Chapman's counterfeits,' and the firm stopped paying them out.
>
> I then went to the store and asked W.H. Chapman if he had disposed of many of his bright cents. He replied, 'No. I made a bad bargain,' and laughed about their being regarded as his counterfeits. I then offered to take them at the price he paid— ninety cents a hundred—and he was very willing to let me have them. They were loose together in a small keg, and the great mass of them were of 1818; and a great many, though apparently Uncirculated, were more or less corroded or discolored. I enclose herewith one of the 1817 and 1818, discolored on one side and bright on the other, From this statement, you will see that there can be very little doubt about their being the genuine issues of the United States Mint of their respective dates.
>
> *Very respectfully, John Swan Randall*

The typical example seen today with a Randall Hoard pedigree is a mixture of bright original red with flecks and stains of deep brown or black. Few if any are pristine (uncleaned, undipped) full mint red. As late as the 1950s it was not unusual to see groups of Randall Hoard coins in dealers' stocks. By the 1990s the supply had become widely dispersed, and when seen such coins were apt to be as isolated examples. It is a matter of debate today whether the hoard contained significant coins dated 1825, as this year is hardly ever seen with a brightness and flecks similar to that of the earlier hoard coins.

DESIGN DETAILS

On the obverse the head of Miss Liberty faces to the left, her face having a serious or even severe aspect. On most dies her hair is tied with *plain* hair cords in a bun behind her head, and additional tresses fall behind her neck. Above her forehead a tiara or diadem is lettered LIBERTY. Beginning in 1835, modifications were made, including the adoption of *beaded* hair cords in 1837. On all, the date digits were punched individually, as were the stars, creating variations that are easily observed today.

The reverse motif is similar to that used from 1808 to 1814. A continuous wreath tied with a ribbon bow at the bottom encloses the inscription ONE / CENT, with a line under the latter word (except for certain varieties of 1839). Around the border is UNITED STATES OF AMERICA. There are variations in the size of the lettering.

The 1816 design is attributed to Robert Scot. Modifications from 1835 to 1839 are attributed to Christian Gobrecht.

1816, Matron Head
Mintage (per Mint Report*): 2,820,982.*

There are nine known die combinations among 1816, Newcomb-1 to Newcomb-9. Seven different obverse dies were used. Assuming that the mintage figure for this year includes only Matron Head cents and none from the earlier type, this yields an average mintage per die of 402,000 coins.

All but one are hard to find in Mint State and when seen are usually in lower ranges, this comment being generally true of other Matron Head cents of this decade, except for Randall Hoard coins. N-1 and N-3 are rare. The solitary exception for the 1816 date is provided by N-2, of which William C. Noyes comments, "Major part of Randall Hoard with thousands of spotty Mint State examples. However, few, if any, true MS-65s can be found."

Cents of 1816 are easily available as a date in nearly any grade desired, although examples at the EF and AU levels are scarcer than lower grades and are also scarcer than Mint State. Many are dark in color, this being true of 1817-dated cents, as well, and for the later dates in the Classic Head series. Mint State coins are rare except for N-2, as noted above.

Typical values for 1816 cents. Rare varieties may
be worth more. Mint State values are for N-2 only.

1816		Cert	Avg	%MS
		309	54.1	57%

G-4	VG-8	F-12	VF-20	EF-40	AU-50	MS-60BN	MS-63BN	MS-63RB	MS-65BN	MS-65RB
$25	$50	$75	$150	$220	$350	$650	$850	$1,600	$2,400	$3,600

1816 • Newcomb-1 to Newcomb-9. *Estimated population:* Many thousands.

A high-grade example of 1816 (N-2), probably from the Randall Hoard. The color is original, and spotting is considerably less than usually seen. Some lightness of strike and erosion of the denticles is normal for N-2. Overall, it is a remarkable coin.

Notes: This is the first of the Randall Hoard dates. Randall Hoard coins tend to average around MS-63 and MS-64, with spotting. Some have been stripped down and recolored a glossy brown (a color never present when the hoard was found). Certified coins for this or any other Matron Head date represent the tiniest fraction of the population in collectors' hands. The highest certified are four MS-66BN, four MS-65RB, and two MS-65RD. Probably, several thousand Mint State coins exist, but 1816 is far scarcer date than are 1818 and 1820.

Numismatic Notes: The new design and working dies were probably ready by August 1815 because Patterson thought that the planchets might arrive from England as early as September.[92] However, it was not until about November 20 that the *Coromandel*, carrying the invoice from Boulton, actually docked at Philadelphia. The kegs of blanks were in the hold (as ballast) and thus were unloaded last, or nearly so. All were in the Mint by December 11. As Boulton promised in his letter of May 1815, costs of the copper planchets were down significantly from 1812. The average planchets in 1815 cost 8.057 mills while the corresponding cost in 1812 had been 9.057 mills. The profit to the government was thereby much higher, offsetting other Mint expenses. The cost was lower for other reasons than merely the price of raw copper. The end of the war in early 1815 had reduced insurance rates as well as the special dockage fees charged by the British government as part of a series of wartime taxes.

Patterson ordered that coinage begin as soon as possible, and it is known that several thousand pieces had been struck by December 31, when the annual report of the director noted that cent coinage had resumed. Almost certainly Scot had dated the dies with the year 1816, probably because it was expected that nothing would be released to the public until after January 1. For reasons that are not quite clear at present, the coinage of cents was very slow in late December and early January. It is known, from a letter of Patterson to Boulton, dated December 27, that Mint officials were not completely pleased with the quality of the 1815 planchet delivery. According to Patterson, the blanks were "not quite round" and not sufficiently "milled up" on the edges. This may have required slight modifications to the dies or coin press. There is a second possibility for delay of coinage. On December 30, 1815, John White was paid $53.50 by Mint Treasurer James Rush for cutting a screw. The accounts do not say that this was for a coining press or, if so, which one, but almost certainly it was for a damaged coining press, likely the cent press. The repair could also have been for the half dollar press; coinage was also delayed here, inexplicably, until after January 1.

Copper coinage resumed within a few days of the January 11, 1816, fire and was strong for the next several weeks. On February 3, several kegs, which contained 183,500 coins, were sent to the Bank of Pennsylvania. The rest were all forwarded to the same bank by February 26, for a total coinage of 465,500 from the 1815 Boulton planchet shipment. Only one press was used at this time, as there was no urgency to the coinage. With the delivery, on February 26, of 89,000 cents to the Bank of Pennsylvania, the Mint was once more out of planchets. However, in the latter part of 1815, Patterson had managed to persuade the Treasury that sufficient funds were on hand for the additional needed 20 tons of copper, and that amount had been ordered. This shipment was not received until late May 1816.

1817, Matron Head
Mintage (per Mint Report): 3,948,400.

There are 17 different die combinations of 1817 cents, N-1 to N-17. N-16 is the unique 15-Star variety described separately below, leaving 16 varieties with the normal 13 stars.

Mint State examples of this year are easy to find, with N-3, N-6, N-8, N-13, and N-14 (in particular) being those most often seen in this grade, nearly all attributable to the Randall Hoard. N-10 is likewise available in Mint State, but is much scarcer. Circulated examples are mostly Good to Fine and are often dark in color, this also being true for 1816 and the later dates in the Classic Head series. EF and AU coins are on the scarcer side, and for some varieties AU and Mint State pieces are rare.

A die state of N-9 develops a lump at the top of the head opposite star 9. This has been called the "Mouse Variety" or "Mouse Top Variety" and is popular for that reason (see Numismatic Notes below). These are easily enough obtained, except at the Mint State level.[93]

Detail of the "mouse" on N-9, sometimes called a "crown" or "royal crown" in numismatic folklore.

Typical values for 1817 cents.
Rare varieties may be worth more.

1817	Cert	Avg	%MS
	434	53.4	56%

G-4	VG-8	F-12	VF-20	EF-40	AU-50	MS-60BN	MS-63BN	MS-63RB	MS-65BN	MS-65RB
$25	$40	$70	$150	$195	$290	$525	$800	$1,200	$1,775	$2,700

1817 • N-1 to N-15, N-17. *Estimated population:* Many thousands.

A high-grade Mint State example of N-9, the "Mouse Variety." This die break has been the subject of fanciful tales over the years.

Notes: This is a very common date among early Matron Head cents. Except for Randall Hoard coins, Mint State coins range from scarce to rare. The typical grade encountered is Good to Fine. Choice EF and AU coins are much scarcer. Many circulated coins tend to be on the dark side.

Numismatic Notes: Mouse Variety: The Portsmouth (New Hampshire) *Daily Chronicle*, Tuesday, February 15, 1887, included what was likely a reference to what we call the "Mouse Variety" today:

> No Great of a Lion: 'Two big copper cents, issued in 1817,' says the Philadelphia *Call*, 'are among the rarest in the coin collection of the Philadelphia Mint. These have the Liberty head well defined, but on the top of the head, over the liberty cap, is a small

protuberance, which, under the microscope, appears as a crown. This was cut in the die by an English engraver, who thus set the British crown over the American liberty head.'

It is more commonly known that the back hair of the maiden who represents Liberty on our standard silver dollars is done up in semblance of a lion's head when viewed upside down. As it is also the work of an English artist, the lion may be taken for a British lion. The engraver, however, was considerate enough to put the animal under Liberty's cap, which acts in a measure as a cage or an extinguisher, although the fierce creature shows a disposition and an ability to get out and roar at almost any time, the maiden's attention being attracted in another direction. . . .

Similarly, but a few years later, in *The Numismatist*, December 1891, in a column of queries:

> R.A., Dublin. encloses the following from his scrapbook, and desires to know whether it is true or not. Will some of our correspondents give us light on the subject? 'Two big copper

cents issued in 1817 are among the rarest in the coin collection of the Philadelphia Mint. These have the Liberty Head well defined, but on top of the head over the cap is a small protuberance which, under a microscope, appears as a crown. This was cut in the die by an English engraver, who thus covertly set the British Crown over the American Liberty Head.'

1817, 15 Obverse Stars • N-16. *Estimated population:* 1,250 to 1,500.

1817, 15 Obverse Stars (N-16). The famous 15-Star variety. Nearly all known examples are in circulated grades.

Notes: Newcomb-16 has 15 stars on the obverse instead of the usual 13, the only instance of such an error in the series. The reason for this is unknown. For many years this has been a "must have" coin for even casual collectors of cents. As if the uniqueness of the stars were not enough, the 1 in the date is blunt instead of having a pointed top serif, the only such cent of the era with a blunt 1. As there is only one die combination for the 15-Stars, the obverse is unique and definitive. The reverse, however, which has no unusual features, was also mated to create the normal star-count N-1. All seen of N-16 have been struck from what seem to be non-parallel die faces in the coining press, resulting in deep boldness of the denticles at the lower left of the reverse and lightness in some other areas of both sides.

This variety is quite scarce in the context of 1817-dated cents overall, but enough exist that an example can be found without difficulty. Nearly all show extensive wear. Attractive EF and AU coins are rare, and Mint State coins are even more so. Some years ago Q. David Bowers was offered two "MS-65" coins by a leading cent expert. Upon examination, they were found to be MS-60 at best. "You need to be liberal for the 15-Star," he was told, "for there are none finer than this." An estimated 15 to 25 true Mint State coins are known, most around the MS-60 level.

A related scenario is implied in the McCawley-Grellman description of a coin (illustrated above) offered in 2009 in Larry and Ira Goldberg's sale of the Ted Naftzger Collection of Middle Dates, lot 47. Graded MS-65BN by PCGS, the catalogers added their own opinion, "Del Bland says MS-60+. Our grade is MS-63." This is one of many examples, in the Naftzger catalog as well as in offerings by others, in which grade opinions can vary widely.

1817, 15 Obverse Stars		Cert	Avg	%MS
		45	50.2	24%
G-4	VG-8	F-12		VF-20
$35	$50	$150		$350
FF-40	AU-50	MS-60BN		MS-63BN
$675	$1,075	$3,150		$4,500

1818, Matron Head

Mintage (per Mint Report*): 3,167,000.*

Cents of the year 1818 comprise 10 different die varieties, N-1 to N-10, none of which is an instant-eye or *Guide Book of United States Coins* variety.

Randall Hoard cents come to the fore in 1818 and in 1820, these being the two most encountered years from that hoard. For 1818 the hoard varieties are N-1, N-7, and N-10, with N-10 being one of the two most plentiful die combinations in this hoard. William C. Noyes suggests that thousands exist of this coin alone. This particular variety is nearly always found with a die crack connecting all of the stars and the date. Very curiously, 1820, Large Date (N-13), the other very common hoard coin, has a similar encircling crack.

Apart from hoard coins, Mint State examples are generally scarce, and for some varieties are rare. The typical 1818 is apt to be Good to Fine and of a brown color.

Detail of 1818 (N-3), showing star 1 low and opposite the tip of the neck.

Detail of 1818 (N-10), showing star 1 significantly to the left of the tip of the neck. Most die varieties among early Matron Head cent dates can be easily identified, after some practice.

Typical values for 1818 cents.
Rare varieties may be worth more.

1818						Cert	Avg	%MS		
						728	58.4	76%		

G-4	VG-8	F-12	VF-20	EF-40	AU-50	MS-60BN	MS-63BN	MS-63RB	MS-65BN	MS-65RB
$25	$40	$70	$150	$190	$290	$475	$675	$960	$1,800	$2,800

1818 • N-1 to N-10. **Estimated population:** Many thousands.

An exceptionally high quality 1818 (N-10) Mint State cent from the Randall Hoard, with characteristic encircling die cracks caused by improper annealing of the steel die (not from extensive use of the die).

Notes: The rarest die variety is N-4, nearly all of which are in circulated grades. The hand-punched date numerals and stars of this and other cents of the era make them fairly easy to differentiate using the Newcomb, Wright, or Noyes texts. Certain Randall Hoard coins are plentiful, with N-10 being especially so, and thus ideal for anyone selecting an example of the date. Most have abundant original mint red, usually with some spotting.

1819, 9 Over 8, Matron Head

Circulation mintage (estimate): Several hundred thousand.

A single 1819, 9 Over 8, die is known. The production probably ran to several hundred thousand coins, creating a variety that is easily collectible today. The overdate feature is easily discerned. Most are in circulated grades, although enough Mint State coins exist that finding one will not be a problem. Gems are rare, however.

1819, 9 Over 8				Cert	Avg	%MS
				111	51.0	41%

G-4	VG-8	F-12	VF-20	EF-40	AU-50	MS-60BN	MS-63BN
$30	$50	$150	$250	$360	$560	$1,125	$1,900

1819, 9 Over 8 • N-1. *Estimated population:* Several thousand.

1819, 9 Over 8 (N-1).

Detail of the overdate.

Notes: Stars 2 and 4 are repunched. Common in all circulated grades. Scarce in Mint State, but enough are around that finding one will be no problem. A typical conservative (EAC) grade is MS-60, translating to two or three points higher in the popular marketplace.

1819, Matron Head

Mintage (per Mint Report*): 2,671,000.*

Known to the extent of nine varieties, N-2 to N-10, this date can be compared to others of its era, except that for 1819 there are far fewer Randall Hoard coins, these being N-8 and N-9. Less often seen in Mint State are N-2 and N-6. All nine varieties are readily collectible, with several being scarce, N-7 the scarcest, and a rarity in Mint State. Most examples are in worn grades, VG to Fine being common, probably as retrieved from circulation by enthusiasts in the 1850s. At the EF and AU level the 1819 is quite a bit scarcer.

Typical values for 1819 cents.
Rare varieties may be worth more.

1819		Cert	Avg	%MS
		341	53.5	58%

G-4	VG-8	F-12	VF-20	EF-40	AU-50	MS-60BN	MS-63BN	MS-63RB	MS-65BN
$25	$45	$110	$175	$325	$475	$875	$1,250	$1,750	$2,000

1819 • N-2 to N-10. *Estimated population:* Many thousands.

1819 (N-8). Some stars are flat at the center, this being true of the vast majority of Matron Head cents of all years.

Notes: An estimated 500 to 800 examples each are known of N-8 and N-9, from the Randall Hoard. These usually have generous mint color with some spotting.

1820, 20 Over 19, Matron Head

Mintage (per **Mint Report***): Part of the total of 1820.*

The Mint must have been overoptimistic in 1819, for it seems that early in 1820 at least three unused obverse dies were on hand. Two of these, N-2 and N-3, were overdated by punching 20 separately over the last two digits, from a 2 punch and a small 0 punch. The other, N-1, may be 1820, 182 Over 181, as there is no trace of a final 9. This die has a large 0. William C. Noyes calls these the Large Overdate (N-1) and Small Overdate (N-2 and N-3) varieties respectively.

The position of the under-digit 1 beneath the 2 provides identification of each variety. The N-1 variety has the 1 centered under the 2, N-2 has the 1 under the left part of the 2, and N-3 has the 1 under the right part of the 2. All three dates are illustrated here.

As a standard variety the 1820, 20 Over 19, overdate is readily collectible, most being N-1, of which multiple thousands are estimated to exist. N-2 and N-3 are scarcer, although there are enough in the marketplace that specialists can find them. Curiously, N-3 is the variety most often seen at the gem level. Otherwise, typical grades are VG and Fine. EF and AU coins are slightly scarce.

| Detail of 1820, 20 Over 19, Large Overdate (N-1). 1 centered under the 2. The 0 is very large, in curious contrast to the adjacent small 2. No clear trace of a 9 can be seen under the final figure. | Detail of 1820, 20 Over 19, Small Overdate (N-2). 1 under left part of 2. All digits are about the same size. The 1 is distant from the 8. Traces of the knob of the 9 can be seen protruding from the lower left of the 0, and traces of the loop of the 9 can be seen within it. | Detail of 1820, 20 Over 19, Small Overdate (N-3). 1 under right part of 2. All digits are about the same size. The 1 is distant from the 8. Traces of the inner loop of the 9 are prominent within the 0. |

Typical values for 1820, 20 Over 19, cents.
Rare varieties may be worth more.

1820, 20 Over 19	Cert	Avg	%MS
	55	43.4	33%

G-4	VG-8	F-12	VF-20	EF-40	AU-50	MS-60BN	MS-63BN	MS-63RB	MS-65BN	MS-65RB
$30	$60	$150	$300	$420	$775	$1,500	$2,300	$3,375	$5,250	$10,500

1820, 20 Over 19 • N-1 to N-3. *Estimated population:* Many thousands.

1820, 20 Over 19, Small Overdate (N-3).

Notes: These three overdate varieties are interesting, available, and easy to identify, suggesting the possibility for a small specialized collection. Each of the overdates has a "personality" of its own. Most examples are of the 1820, 20 Over 19, Large Overdate (N-1) variety. Mint State coins seem to be scarcest for N-1, although this is the most available variety in circulated grades.

1820, Matron Head
Mintage (per Mint Report*): 4,407,550.*

There are 15 die combinations of the 1820 cent, grouped into Large Date (with large 0) and Small Date (small 0). In addition there are two styles of the digit 2. These are described in the Notes below.

This is a very common date, as the mintage suggests. There are, however, three very scarce varieties (N-4, N-6, and N-14) and several others that are slightly scarce. Randall Hoard coins are very common for N-13, seen with a distinctive series of cracks connecting the stars and the date—a cousin to 1818 (N-10) in this regard. The N-13 is one of the better struck of the hoard varieties and is a good candidate for a type set. Less often seen from the same source, but plentiful, are N-10 and N-12 to N-15. Mint State examples of other varieties range from very scarce to rare. Circulated coins are aplenty, typically in VG or Fine. EF and AU coins are scarce in comparison. Most have a medium-brown color.

Detail of 1820, Small Date (N-8), showing detail of the date with inner curl on 2. This strike shows blank planchet area beyond the denticles, revealing that the denticles on this die were added in the form of pellets.	Detail of 1820, Large Date (N-13), showing detail of the date with knob on 2. Although this is called a "knob," it is simply a thicker area.

1820, Small Date • N-4 to N-8, N-14. *Estimated population:* Together with Large Date, many thousands.

Notes: Small 0 of 1820. There are two types of 2 digits, one with a delicate inner curl and one with a heavy end of irregular shape sometimes called a "knob," as follows: N-4: 2 with inner curl; N-5: inner curl; N-6: inner curl; N-7: inner curl; N-8: inner curl; N-14: 2 with knob.

Together with 1820, Large Date, common in all grades including Mint State, although certain varieties are rare, as noted above.

Numismatic Notes: See next entry.

Typical values for 1820, Small Date. Rare varieties may be worth more.

1820, Small Date		Cert	Avg	%MS
		35	52.4	54%

EF-40	AU-50	MS-60BN	MS-63BN
$300	$500	$950	$1,350

MS-63RB	MS-65BN		MS-65RB
$2,250	$2,900		$4,200

1820, Large Date • N-9 to N-13 and N-15. *Estimated population:* Together with Small Date, many thousands.

1820, Large Date (N-13). This is the most plentiful of the Randall Hoard coins. It is instantly identifiable by the signature die cracks linking the stars and the date. Although not sharp in all details, the N-13 is one of the better-struck varieties of the year. The uniformity of mint color on the obverse, without flecks or stains, is remarkable.

Notes: Large 0 of 1820. There are two types of 2 digits, one with a delicate inner curl and one with a heavy end of irregular shape sometimes called a "knob," as follows: N-9: 2 with inner curl; N-10: knob; N-11: knob; N-12: knob; N-13: knob; N-15: inner curl.

Together with Small Date, common in all grades including Mint State, although certain varieties are rare, as noted above.

Numismatic Notes: Excess supply of copper cents: From *Niles' Register,* November 18, 1820: "Mint of the United States. Philadelphia Nov. 1820. The public are informed that the coinage of copper will be discontinued, for some time, at the Mint of the United States. A large supply of cents, however, is now ready for distribution; and, on application, will be furnished, to any reasonable amount, in exchange for an equal amount in specie, or paper (notes or drafts) receivable in any of the banks in Philadelphia; or on evidence of credit being entered in favor of the Treasury of the United States, in the Bank of the United States, or any of its branches. Shipments will be made agreeable to order; insurance effected and paid, and an adequate allowance made for freight to any port in the United States, to which vessels are cleared out from Philadelphia. Application to be made to the treasurer of the Mint. James Rush. Nov. 10."

High-grade examples elusive: In 1859, in his *American Numismatical Manual,* Dr. Montroville W. Dickeson wrote: "The slight milling of the edges of these coins render good specimens difficult to be obtained." Milling is a correct (but, today, largely forgotten) term describing the raised rims. They are low on many 1820 cents, making the coins more susceptible to wear, and making high-grade examples rarer than would otherwise be the case.

Typical values for 1820, Large Date. Rare varieties may be worth more.

1820, Large Date	Cert	Avg	%MS
	99	58.2	74%

EF-40	AU-50	MS-60BN	MS-63BN
$210	$325	$450	$600

MS-63RB	MS-65BN		MS-65RB
$825	$1,250		$2,000

1821, Matron Head
Mintage (per **Mint Report***): 389,000.*

The 1821 cent has the lowest mintage of any Matron Head up to this point in time. The actual coinage of 1821-dated coins is not known, but it probably approximated the *Mint Report* figure. There are two die varieties, each fairly common, but the N-1 is slightly less plentiful than the N-2. This fits in well with the mintage figure, as the average life for a die was about 400,000 impressions at the time, but with wide variations. We have no way of knowing if the calendar-year mintage was all dated 1821, but if it was, considering that there were two obverse dies, the production per die was far less than typical. R.W. Julian suggests that it was not until about 1836 that calendar-year figures accurately represented coins dated with the same year.[94] Even then, there were occasional exceptions. Reverses tended to outlive obverses; both reverse dies were reused in 1822.

As a *date* the 1821 is a key issue, not in a class with the 1823, but one of the scarcest years in the Matron Head series. Typical grades are VG to Fine or so. EF and AU coins are scarce. Many coins of this year and the next two are on the dark side. Mint State coins are rarities, and were it not for the Boston find (see Numismatic Notes for N-1 and N-2), they would be extreme rarities. In any market season a nice high-grade 1821 cent at auction attracts a lot of attention.

Typical values for 1821 cents.

1821	Cert	Avg	%MS
	119	33.2	9%

G-4	VG-8	F-12	VF-20	EF-40	AU-50	MS-60BN	MS-63BN	MS-63RB
$100	$200	$450	$900	$1,650	$3,150	$8,875	$15,500	$28,500

1821 • N-1 and N-2. *Estimated population:* 3,000 to 4,500.

From a small group found in Boston a generation ago, this N-2 is one of only a handful of 1821 circulation-strike cents with original mint color. In the field inside the denticles the original compass scribe line is seen, used during the die preparation process to help position the elements.

Notes: On N-1 star 13 points to a denticle; on N-2 it points to the space between denticles. There is no significant price difference between the varieties in circulated grades. Estimated 5 to 7 Mint State known of N-1, 15 to 20 of N-2 (in *The Cent Book,*

John D. Wright suggests as many as 27). At the AU level fewer than 80 are estimated to exist.

Numismatic Notes: A significant find: In 1821 a particular building was constructed in Boston, and to memorialize the event at least seven new copper cents were placed in its cornerstone. In 1981 the structure was razed, and the long-forgotten pieces came to light. These coins were attributed as two examples of N-1 and five of N-2. Both N-1 coins were called Mint State-63 by the cataloger, while four of the five examples of N-2 were graded MS-63 and the fifth MS-60. These were sold at auction by New England Rare Coin Galleries in 1981, six of the pieces went to Garry Fitzgerald and one to R.E. Naftzger Jr.[95]

1822, Matron Head
Mintage (per Mint Report*): 2,072,339.*

As a date, the 1822 is slightly scarce. Across the 14 known die combinations, none is really common, and several are rare, with the laurels going to N-14, of which just six are known—the best in Fine grade. Mint State coins come on the market with regularity, but for certain varieties are unknown. The average coin in numismatic hands is probably VG or fine. Quite a few exist at the EF level, somewhat fewer for AU. Generally, these are fairly well struck, on smooth planchets, and possessing excellent eye appeal. The hue is often dark.

Typical values for 1822 cents.
Rare varieties may be worth more.

1822	Cert	Avg	%MS
	201	45.5	27%

G-4	VG-8	F-12	VF-20	EF-40	AU-50	MS-60BN	MS-63BN	MS-63RB	MS-65BN	MS-65RB
$30	$50	$100	$200	$425	$700	$1,200	$1,800	$3,000	$4,900	$12,000

1822 • N-1 to N-14. *Estimated population:* Many thousands.

A gem 1822 (N-2) with a significant amount of original mint red. Very few cents of any variety of this year have any mint color. Most are quite dark. The stars are very sharp, except for a few with slight weakness at the centers.

Notes: On average, cents of this date are fairly well struck. Possibly 100 to 200 Uncirculated coins are known, mainly in lower levels and hardly ever with a trace of mint red. In the AU range there are probably fewer than 1,000. Estimates vary widely among specialists.

1823, 3 Over 2, Matron Head

Mintage (per Mint Report*): Included in the* 1824 *report.*

The mintage of the 1823, 3 Over 2 is unknown, but it was likely very small. No cents were struck in calendar year 1823, leading to the conclusion that dies (this and the "perfect date") of this year were used later, probably in 1824. The overdate is scarce as a basic "date," actually an overdate, but the only variety, N-1, would not otherwise attract much notice on its own. In Mint State the variety is a great rarity, and at the AU level they are seldom seen. Some are slightly prooflike. Most are VG to Fine or so. Usually well-struck, and sometimes even needle-sharp, pieces are the rule. Nearly all are dark, and the surface is often unsatisfactory. Cherrypicking is needed to acquire one with good eye appeal within any given grade.

1823, 3 Over 2	Cert	Avg	%MS
	78	23.5	0%

G-4	VG-8	F-12	VF-20	EF-40	AU-50	MS-60BN
$200	$400	$1,000	$2,000	$3,100	$5,750	$13,750

1823, 3 Over 2 • N-1. *Estimated population:* 1,000 to 1,250.

1823, 3 Over 2 (N-1).

Notes: Difficult to find with good eye appeal. Mint State coins by typical market grading probably number 5 to 7, or, per EAC strict grading, about half of that. Probably 10 to 15 can be called AU.

1823, Matron Head

Mintage (per Mint Report*): None.*
Mintage (estimate): 20,000 to 40,000.

There is no specific mintage record for the 1823 "perfect date" (non-overdate), as no cents were coined in this calendar year. There is just one variety, N-2. The production was no doubt small, probably only in the tens of thousands. The reverse die was reused in 1824. In the *American Numismatical Manual*, 1859, Dr. Montroville W. Dickeson gave this mintage:

> The number coined—obtained through letters from Washington—was 12,250.* This coinage is not acknowledged in the Mint report, it being, from that authority, one of the years of non-coinage. The copper of this emission is pure and soft, hence the cents are much worn, and can be rarely found in a condition worthy of preservation. They command a premium. (*See *State Papers, first* Session, 18th Congress, vol. ii. Doc. 152.)

While this figure is probably far too low, it reflects that in the cradle days of numismatics the 1823 was considered to be rare. Today the 1823 remains the rarest by far of all dates from 1816 to 1857.

The fact that numismatists were allowed to sort through cents that were shipped to the Mint for redemption after the large coppers were discontinued is very significant. Likely, 1823 cents were picked out, while most—if not all—other dates from 1816 onward were ignored unless they were in high grades. Accordingly, if this is true, the survival rate of 1823 cents is much higher than other years of the era, pointing to a very low mintage. If, say, 1,000 cents of this date exist today, and the survival rate was just two percent or three percent of the mintage—a figure that Walter Breen and some others have used for certain early coins—this would indicate a mintage of 33,000 to 50,000 or so. If the survival rate was higher due to numismatists picking these coins out from shipments, and was five percent or so, that would indicate a mintage of just 20,000. These can only be guesses, but the mintage of 1823-dated cents must have been very small.

On the obverse the stars are lightly or flatly struck, most noticeably at the left, although the denticles are usually well defined. Similar to the 1823, 3 Over 2, most coins are somewhat dark, but the average surface quality is better on N-2. The typical coin is VG or Fine. VF pieces are scarce in the context of dates of the era, and EF and AU examples are rare. The reverse die was later used to coin 1824, 4 Over 2 (N-5).

So-called "restrikes" were made with this date, first appearing in 1867. These are fantasy combinations of the 1823 obverse, now rusted and damaged, with an irrelevant reverse from 1813. All are in Mint State, or close, today. See details below, including in Numismatic Notes.

1823 • N-2. *Estimated population:* 800 to 1,200.

1823 (N-2). Of all dates in the Matron Head series, the 1823 is by far the rarest. The illustrated coin is one of few high-level Mint State coins known.

Notes: Probably 8 to 12 Mint State coins exist, the finest being the Naftzger coin (illustrated here). At the AU level an estimated 25 to 40 exist. Estimates vary widely. As no mintage figure has been published, the 1823 is one of the most unappreciated coins of its era. "Restrikes" were made in copper (see below), but some were struck in silver—these off-metal pieces are beyond the scope of the present listings.

1823, "Restrike" later die state. These were made over a long period of time from the 1860s onward. The dies still exist today.

Numismatic Notes: The 1823 "restrike": In the *American Numismatical Manual,* 1859, Dr. Montroville W. Dickeson did not mention this coin, suggesting that it was unknown at the time. It is likely that, similar to the "restrike" half cent of 1811 and cent of 1804, someone used dies discarded by the Mint as "scrap iron." Many various dies were owned by Joseph J. Mickley (although this pair seems to have taken a different path; see below), and other were held past 1950 by Wayte Raymond.[96] The 1823 restrikes began appearing in quantity in 1867. Before then, $3 each was asked for an 1823-dated cent.[97] Early restrikes are from an uncracked obverse die. Later, a bisecting crack extends from 10 o'clock down to the right to 4 o'clock, and another crack extends from between 7 and 8 o'clock into the portrait. The dies were used at later times, in the meantime deteriorating further. They were still in existence in the 1950s when C. Douglas Smith offered them to Q. David Bowers, and they are probably held by a collector today. As these were struck over a long period of time, there are multiple states of die cracks, rim erosion, and other dete-

rioration. Some in Mint State have traces of mint red or yellowish red.

In February 1907, in *The Numismatist,* Lancaster, Pennsylvania, dealer Charles Steigerwalt told of the "restrikes" of the 1804 and 1823 cents. Concerning the latter: "While at a recent sale, information regarding the 1823 was given by an aged collector, who told how, years ago, he had found the dies in New York, probably sold with old iron from the Mint, brought them to Philadelphia, had a collar made, which was lacking, and the coins struck by a man named Miller in 7th Street, that city. Later the dies came into possession of a then leading dealer there and, when his store was sold out in 1885, the writer finding them among a lot of old dies purchased, they were at once destroyed so effectually that no more will ever come from that source. These coins never saw the Mint and are counterfeits pure and simple."

1823, Original		Cert	Avg	%MS
		43	23.8	5%

G-4	VG-8	F-12	VF-20
$250	$500	$1,500	$3,000

EF-40	AU-50	MS-60BN
$4,375	$8,750	$19,250

1823, "Restrike"		Cert	Avg	%MS
		61	63.3	97%

AU-50	MS-60BN	MS-63BN
$925	$1,250	$1,500

1824, 4 Over 2, Matron Head
Mintage (per Mint Report): Part of the 1824 total.

In terms of basic overdates, the 1824, 4 Over 2, is one of the most desired in the later series. The overdate feature is very bold and can be seen with the naked eye. One obverse die was mated with two reverses to create the only two varieties, N-1 and N-5—the second being especially elusive today. Nearly all of both varieties are in lower grades. A handful of Mint State N-1 coins exist (for N-5, see Numismatic Notes), but an EF or an AU is a very respectable high grade for this variety. The Eliasberg Collection N-1 was AU.

Light striking is seen on the obverse stars on N-1, with N-5 on average being slightly sharper. Typical grades are VG to Fine or Very Fine. Most have a brown color and nice eye appeal.

Typical values for N-1. N-5 in any grade is worth much more.			
1824, 4 Over 2	Cert	Avg	%MS
	40	38.1	13%

G-4	VG-8	F-12	VF-20	EF-40	AU-50	MS-60BN
$60	$100	$300	$750	$1,500	$2,500	$6,000

1824, 4 Over 2 • N-1 and N-5. *Estimated population:* 1,500 to 2,000.

1824, 4 Over 2 (N-1).

Detail of the date on 1824, 4 Over 2 (N-1).

Notes: Two unused 1822 obverse dies were overdated, this and the 1823, 3 Over 2. An estimated 4 to 6 Mint State coins exist and perhaps 15 to 25 AU examples. EF coins are scarce. N-5 is rarer in all grades.

Numismatic Notes: *More about the N-5:* As for high-level examples of the N-5, the Naftzger Collection, generally featuring choice and gem middle-date cents, checked in with a Very Fine example. With wide variables in reported grades, it is difficult to know "who's on first," so to speak. A coin owned by the late Garry Fitzgerald has been reported as MS-65 in William C. Noyes' *United States Large Cents 1816–1839* (1991) and as AU-55 in *The Official Condition Census for U.S. Large Cents 1793–1839* (1995) by Noyes, Del Bland, and Dan Demeo. It is generally agreed that the American Numismatic Society has a Mint State coin, but if any others exist, their status is not universally agreed upon. The reverse die for 1824, 4 Over 2 (N-5) is the same as used for the 1823 (N-2).

1824, Matron Head
Mintage (per Mint Report): 1,262,000.

The 1824 cent is one of the scarcer dates among early Matron Head issues, but is generally not recognized as such. Three obverse dies were used, each varying slightly in their spacing left to right, in combination with three different reverses, as N-1 to N-4. N-1 is quite common, the other three are slightly scarce.

The typical coin is lightly struck on some of the stars, but is generally sharp in most other details. Most are in grades from VG to VF, but enough EF and AU coins exist that finding one will be no problem. Mint State coins are scarce, and choice and gem pieces are especially so. Few have even a tinge of mint color. In all grades the usual 1824 cent is brown and with nice eye appeal.

Typical values for 1824 cents.
Rare varieties may be worth more.

1824						Cert	Avg	%MS		
						123	44.7	20%		

G-4	VG-8	F-12	VF-20	EF-40	AU-50	MS-60BN	MS-63BN	MS-63RB	MS-65BN
$40	$75	$150	$300	$500	$850	$2,400	$4,000	$5,000	$8,000

1824 • N-1 to N-4. *Estimated population:* Many thousands.

Notes: 150 to 250 Mint State coins (estimates vary widely). 500 to 1,000 AU.

1824 (N-2).

1825, Matron Head

Mintage (per Mint Report): 1,461,100.

Cents of 1825 are slightly scarce in higher grades. This year and others of the era, except for the enigmatic 1823, seem to survive approximately in proportion to their mintages. Accordingly, 1824 is slightly scarcer than 1825, and 1825 is slightly scarcer than 1826. Also, as the years pass, the survival rate is higher. For instance, of any given 100,000 cents struck during 1816 and the same number made in 1825, more 1825s survive.

There are 10 varieties among 1825 cents, N-1 to N-10, none of which is really common. They range from slightly scarce to rare. In the aggregate there are enough that as a *date*, 1825 is common. Grades range from well worn to Mint State. Striking is usually typical for the era: sharp except for some of the stars, especially those on the left. Most have a brown color.

Typical values for 1825 cents.
Rare varieties may be worth more.

1825						Cert	Avg	%MS		
						154	44.9	29%		

G-4	VG-8	F-12	VF-20	EF-40	AU-50	MS-60BN	MS-63BN	MS-63RB	MS-65BN
$30	$50	$100	$150	$340	$650	$1,850	$2,750	$4,700	$7,500

1825 • N-1 to N-10. *Estimated total population:* Thousands.

Notes: The die varieties are all collectible and often have significant differences in the spacing of the date numerals and the positions of the stars. Extant are 180 to 280 Mint State coins (estimates vary widely) and 600 to 1,100 AU.

1825 (N-7). This example displays well-struck stars, including at the centers. As a class such coins are rare among Matron Head cents of the era. Many of the denticles on both sides are indistinct, not unusual for the type.

1826, 6 Over 5, Matron Head
Circulation mintage (estimated): 200,000.

The 1826, 6 Over 5, overdate is one of the least easily discerned major varieties listed in the regular edition of the *Guide Book of United States Coins*. It cannot be quickly identified by examining the date, and only high-grade examples show traces of this feature. Designated as N-8, the 1826, 6 Over 5, is priced only as a generic 1826 when the overdate cannot be discerned. As has been pointed out many times, including by Chris Victor-McCawley and J.R. (Bob) Grellman Jr. in the offering of the Naftzger Collection, "there is some discussion whether or not this is a true overdate." At the upper inside of the 6 there is an artifact that might be the flag of a 5, and at the lower-outside-left of the 6 is a slight extra curve that might be from an earlier 5. Under high magnification on a high-grade example the overdate seems to be convincing. On lower-grade coins, the answer seems to be *no*.

An 1826, 6 Over 5, in *any* grade can be identified by die characteristics. The date is spaced as 1 8 26, with the first three digits widely spaced and the last two very close— unique among 1826 obverse dies. The innermost point of star 6 points *below* the top edge of the coronet—also distinctive among 1826 dies. Even for high grades of this date, some which are not identified as such in the marketplace, this is a handy guide for cherrypicking overdates rather than perfect dates!

The usual coin has some lightness on the stars, but they are sharper than on many other varieties of the era. Denticles are weak or incomplete in areas. Most are brown color and have nice eye appeal.

The overdate must be visible under magnification.

1826, 6 Over 5	Cert	Avg	%MS
	17	55.2	53%

EF-40	AU-50	MS-60BN	MS-63BN	MS-63RB	MS-65BN
$1,240	$2,000	$3,900	$7,750	$11,375	$22,000

1826, 6 Over 5 • N-8. *Estimated population:* 1,000 to 1,250.

1826, 6 Over 5 (N-8). The overdate feature on this variety is very subtle.

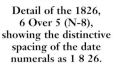

Detail of the 1826, 6 Over 5 (N-8), showing the distinctive spacing of the date numerals as 1 8 26.

Closer view, showing the overdate features.

Notes: Only a tiny percentage show the overdate feature. Readily available in higher grades, which are often found not identified as N-8, but rather as a perfect-date variety.

1826, Matron Head

Mintage (per Mint Report*): 1,517,425.*
Circulation mintage (estimated): 1,300,000.

The 1826 is the date in the 1821 to 1829 range that is most often seen in high grades. There are seven varieties: N-1, N-3 to N-7, and N-9. N-8 is the earlier discussed 1826, 6 Over 5, and N-2, listed by Newcomb in 1944, is no longer recognized. A collection of varieties is easily enough assembled. Although some are scarce, specialists are scarcer yet, making them relatively inexpensive. All are available in Mint State, to varying degrees. N-7 is rated as the most common.

The typical 1826 is likely VG to Fine or so. VF coins are plentiful, as are EF pieces, and AU examples are not hard to find. Mint State coins are usually brown, sometimes with a trace of mint color. Most have some lightness on the stars and some incomplete denticles, although occasional exceptions are found.

Typical values for 1826 cents.
Rare varieties may be worth more.

1826	Cert	Avg	%MS
	241	50.2	37%

G-4	VG-8	F-12	VF-20	EF-40	AU-50	MS-60BN	MS-63BN	MS-63RB	MS-65BN
$25	$40	$75	$150	$250	$450	$900	$1,500	$2,650	$3,100

1826 • N-1, N-3 to N-7, and N-9. *Estimated population:* Thousands.

1826 (N-3). The obverse of this example retains most of the original compass scribe line, used for positioning the stars.

Notes: For reasons unknown today, the 1826 is seen more often in Mint State than the 1824 and 1825. EF and AU coins are readily available as well. In the context of Matron Head cents from 1821 to 1829, this is the most frequently encountered. 300 to 500 Mint State coins (estimates vary widely) exist, along with 800 to 1,400 AU.

Numismatic Notes: *A hoard in Boston:* In the 1940s a man doing some work in the Boston harbor area made a remarkable discovery. The man was working in what was left of an old building that had been the office of a customs agent or toll-taker of some kind in the early 1800s. Cemented into the floor of the structure was a little metal vault or strongbox. The top was pried off, revealing an old-time version of a piggy bank. All in a heap were dozens of large cents dated 1826, and no others. Grades ranged from worn nearly smooth up to lustrous Uncirculated, or close to it. Apparently, some long-forgotten person took a fancy to this particular date and each time an 1826 cent was found in the course of commerce it was dropped through a slot in the floor into this tiny chamber. This must have gone on for many years, judging from the wide variation in grades.

As large cents did not circulate much after 1857 and not at all after the summer of 1862, presumably this cache was formed in the 1840s or 1850s, after which it was untouched for the best part of a century. Perhaps the original depositor passed away and never told anyone about the cents, or perhaps he realized that their value was insufficient to warrant tearing up the floor. The hoard was acquired by Oscar G. Schilke, well-known Connecticut numismatist and one-time president of the New York Coin Club. For several years afterward, he had a good trading stock of cents of this date![98]

1827, Matron Head
Mintage (per Mint Report): 2,357,732.

There are 12 die combinations of the 1827 cent, an average of about 200,000 per die pair. However, some are scarce to rare (N-12 being especially so), and others are common, so usage must have varied. It is Q. David Bowers's experience that this date is common in worn grades, but in Mint State is slightly scarcer than the lower-mintage 1826. Hard facts are elusive, and those who have studied market appearances closely have varied opinions.

As the stars were punched by hand, as were the date digits, there are many variations. Likely, the typical method for the engraver was to put the first star near the tip of the coronet, then add stars to the left and right around the border. As spacing varied, this resulted in many observable differences of star 1 in relation to the neck tip and the date. Similarly, the date digits can be widely or compactly spaced.

The usual 1827 is in a grade from VG to Fine or VF, although EF coins are plentiful. At the Mint-State level this date is scarce, and for some of the die varieties, extremely rare or even unknown. The strike, with respect to the stars and denticles, usually has some weakness, but it is better on average than for the several preceding dates. Planchet quality and eye appeal are usually good.

Typical values for 1827 cents.
Rare varieties may be worth more.

1827	Cert	Avg	%MS
	207	47.0	31%

EF-40	AU-50	MS-60BN	MS-63BN	MS-63RB	MS-65BN
$225	$425	$775	$1,400	$2,500	$3,250

1827 • N-1 to N-12. *Estimated population:* Many thousands.

Notes: This variety is available in Mint State.

1827 (N-5).

1828, Matron Head
Mintage (per Mint Report*): 2,260,624.*

Cents of 1828 are popularly collected by two major varieties, Small Date and Large Date, each from a different font of punches. 8 in the Small Date is what is called the *Script 8* in some other series, and has a heavy diagonal down stroke at the center, from the upper left to the lower right. The 8 in the Large Date is sometimes called a *Block 8* and has top and bottom sections separated by a thin horizontal element. As there is not much difference with the 1's and 2's, it would be better to call these varieties Large 8's and Small 8's, from a technical viewpoint.

Detail of the 1828, Large Date (N-12). The most notable differences are in the 8's.

Detail of the 1828, Small Date (N-10).

As the large digits are necessarily more closely spaced, these varieties are often called Small Wide Date and Large Narrow Date, as they have been in the regular edition of the *Guide Book of United States Coins.* Of the 12 varieties, 11 are the Large Date and N-10 is the only Small Date.

Of the Large Date varieties, all are collectible, but several are scarce. N-4 is found only in lower grades, and N-12, save for the Naftzger gem (illustrated), is impossible to find in Mint State. The 1828s usually have some areas of light striking on the stars, but the typical coin is much sharper than are those of the early 1820s. The denticles are usually complete, or nearly so, and on some dies they are very bold. The usual 1828 is VG to Fine or a bit better. EF and AU coins are plentiful. Most are of a brown color and have good eye appeal. Mint State coins are easily found, but they hardly ever appear with significant mint red.

The 1828, Small Date (N-10) is quite common, but as this is the only die variety with that feature, and there are multiples with the Large Date, the Small Date is several times scarcer than the other. The price difference is modest as there are still plenty to go around. Most have some flatness of the stars. The denticles are usually complete, but not bold.

1828, Large Date • N-1 to N-9, N-11, and N-12. *Estimated population:* Many thousands.

1828, Large Date (N-12), one
of 11 Large Date varieties.

Typical values for 1828, Large Date. Rare varieties may be worth more.

1828, Large Date		Cert	Avg	%MS
		73	51.2	32%

G-4	VG-8	F-12	VF-20	EF-40	AU-50
$25	$50	$75	$150	$230	$400

MS-60BN	MS-63BN	MS-63RB	MS-65BN	MS-65RB
$1,250	$1,750	$2,800	$4,250	$10,000

Notes: An estimated 400 to 700 Mint State coins exist, few of which show any mint color. There are many choice and gem examples. EF and AU coins are common.

1828, Small Date • N-10. *Estimated population:* Several thousand.

1828, Small Date (N-10), the only such variety.

1828, Small Date		Cert	Avg	%MS
		19	49.3	42%

G-4	VG-8	F-12	VF-20	EF-40
$30	$70	$100	$200	$310

AU-50	MS-60BN	MS-63BN	MS-63RB	MS-65BN
$650	$1,950	$3,500	$5,500	$20,000

Notes: An estimated 30 to 50 Mint State coins exist, including in the choice and gem categories. EF and AU coins are plentiful.

1829, Matron Head
Mintage (per Mint Report*): 1,414,500.*

Cents of 1829 are usually classified in two categories: Large Letters (on the reverse) and Medium Letters, the latter sometimes called Small Letters. The Medium Letters coins (N-3, N-5, and N-9) all share the same reverse. Large Letters coins (N-1, N-2, N-4, and N-6 to N-8) combine several obverses and reverses. There are two sizes of 1's, although these are not often noticed. All have Large 1's, except N-7 to N-9, which have Small 1's.

The Large Letters coins are readily available in all grades, including choice and gem Mint State. Striking varies, and usually there is some flatness at certain star centers and, often, on the hair. This particular date is well known in this regard. Denticles, depending on the variety, range from small to prominent, but are usually full.

Medium Letters coins are scarce across the board for the three varieties, with N-9 being rare, with only one reported in Mint State. While the striking is not quite as flat as a pancake, in numismatic equivalents it comes close. Light areas are prominent on both sides, due to spacing the dies too far apart in the coining press. Most are VG to Fine or so. At the EF level they are rare, and AU coins are rarer yet. Mint State coins are very rare. The eye appeal of both styles of 1829 cents is usually very good.

Cents of 1829 are the last of the years that can be called slightly scarce. After this time, all are more plentiful. The average grade of surviving pieces rises as well.

1829, Large Letters • N-1, N-2, N-4, and N-6 to N-8. *Estimated population:* Many thousands.

1829, Large Letters (N-1). Mint State with a generous amount of original color, rare and remarkable for any variety of this date.

Notes: Per general market grading, Mint State coins are estimated to be around 125 to 250, few with mint red, and most in lower levels. EF and AU coins are easy to find.

Typical values for 1829, Large Letters. Rare varieties may be worth more.

1829, Large Letters		Cert	Avg	%MS
		39	48.0	38%

G-4	VG-8	F-12	VF-20	EF-40
$25	$40	$90	$175	$250

AU-50	MS-60BN	MS-63BN	MS-63RB
$440	$825	$1,500	$3,000

1829, Medium Letters • N-3, N-5, and N-9. *Estimated population:* 750 to 1,000.

1829, Medium Letters (N-5). Areas of light striking are seen on both sides. This is the Naftzger coin graded MS-64 by PCGS.

Notes: Mint State coins are very rare. Per conservative EAC grading, only a handful exist. Per grading used elsewhere, perhaps 10 to 20 survive. Grading in coppers is, of course, the eternal question and will never be resolved to everyone's satisfaction. AU examples are rare.

Typical values for 1829, Medium Letters. Rare varieties may be worth more.

1829, Medium Letters		Cert	Avg	%MS
		15	43.0	20%

G-4	VG-8	F-12	VF-20
$50	$150	$350	$500

EF-40	AU-50	MS-60BN	MS-63BN
$1,150	$2,500	$7,000	$10,500

1830, Matron Head
Mintage (per Mint Report): 1,711,500.

Similar to the cents of the preceding year, the 1830 cents are found with Large Letters and Medium Letters on the reverse. The first are common as a class and are readily available in all grades. This is comprised of N-1 to N-5 and N-7 to N-11. The Medium Letters cents, N-6, are rare in any grade and very rare in AU.

Among 1830 Large Letters cents the 10 varieties range from common to very rare, the latter being the case for N-9. Striking varies, but usually there is some lightness, particularly on the stars, and the denticles can be light. Mint State coins are often seen, usually a lustrous brown and with good eye appeal, among the common varieties. For some others, no Mint State coins have been recorded. The average grades of coins in the marketplace is Fine or better, although VG coins can be found as well. EF and AU coins are plentiful. Nearly all have good eye appeal.

The finest known, the Naftzger Collection coin, has been graded 60+ and 63 in specialized references—this being EAC grading—and MS-67 by PCGS. This is one of the very rarest of the major cent varieties listed in the regular edition of the *Guide Book of United States Coins.*

1830, Large Letters • N-1 to N-5 and N-7 to N-11. *Estimated population:* Many thousands.

1830, Large Letters (N-1). The compass scribe line inside the denticles is often called the "inner ring."

Typical values for 1830, Large Letters. Rare varieties may be worth more.

1830, Large Letters			Cert	Avg	%MS
			87	48.0	37%

G-4	VG-8	F-12	VF-20	EF-40	AU-50
$30	$50	$90	$125	$210	$325

MS-60BN	MS-63BN	MS-63RB	MS-65BN	MS-65RB
$550	$1,000	$1,900	$2,700	$3,600

Notes: Per general market grading, Mint State coins are estimated to be around 125 to 250, few with mint red, and most in lower levels. EF and AU coins are easy to find.

1830, Medium Letters • N-6. *Estimated population:* 250 to 400.

1830, Medium Letters (N-6), the finest known example, and a major rarity as such. The sharpness is outstanding on both sides, save for a trivial lightness on the hair.

Notes: Only one Mint State coin has been recorded. EF and AU coins are collectible, but are very rare, with a population of perhaps 20 to 30 combined.

1830, Medium Letters			Cert	Avg	%MS
			7	36.0	14%

G-4	VG-8	F-12	VF-20	EF-40	AU-50
$100	$350	$750	$1,500	$2,000	$4,100

1831, Matron Head
Mintage (per Mint Report): 3,359,260.

The cents of 1831 and 1832 are in many ways comparable. Both have very large mintages, both have Large Letters and Medium Letters styles, and both are common in all grades.

For the 1831 the Large Letters varieties are N-1, N-6 to N-10, and N-14, and the Medium Letters are N-2 to N-5 and N-11. N-13 isn't used and does not exist. The Large Letters coins are much more numerous, but enough exist of both the Large Letters and Medium Letters to fill the demand. Some varieties are scarce. Striking is usually good, with stars full or nearly so, but there are some flat exceptions. Denticles are usually bold, again with some exceptions. The average grade is perhaps Fine or a bit better. Planchet quality is excellent, and across the various grades most have good eye appeal.

1831, Large Letters • N-1, N-6 to N-10, and N-14. *Estimated population: Many thousands.*

1831, Large Letters (N-6).

Notes: This variety exists in Mint State.

Typical values for 1831, Large Letters. Rare varieties may be worth more.

1831, Large Letters	Cert	Avg	%MS
	84	53.3	54%

EF-40	AU-50	MS-60BN	MS-63BN
$150	$250	$400	$700

MS-63RB	MS-65BN	MS-65RB
$1,150	$1,800	$3,500

1831, Medium Letters • N-2 to N-5 and N-11. *Estimated population:* Many thousands.

1831, Medium Letters (N-3).

Notes: Perhaps about one-third to half as many examples exist for this variety as for the Large Letters. This variety exists in Mint State.

Typical values for 1831, Medium Letters. Rare varieties may be worth more.

1831, Medium Letters	Cert	Avg	%MS
	42	51.7	43%

EF-40	AU-50	MS-60BN	MS-63BN
$200	$350	$750	$1,600

MS-63RB	MS-65BN	MS-65RB
$2,750	$2,300	$3,700

1832, Matron Head
Mintage (per Mint Report): 2,362,000.

There are only three die varieties for this date, and two of them are slightly scarce. This calls into question the published mintage figure, which would imply that well over a million would have been struck of the common N-3. The only explanation is that in calendar year 1832 the Mint used earlier-dated dies. R.W. Julian has suggested that figures are incorrect for certain *half cents* of the era, and it seems they are for cents as well. A more reasonable estimated output is about 200,000 or so coins for N-3 and fewer for N-1 and N-2, perhaps yielding 300,000 or so cents actually *dated* 1832.

These are found in the Large Letters style, this being the common N-3, and two of the Medium Letters style, N-1 and N-2. Most have lightness at the star centers. Other details, including the denticles, are often bold, but there are exceptions. Both styles are common in all grades, but the Medium Letters coins are less so. Nearly all have nice eye appeal.

1832, Large Letters • N-3. *Estimated population:* Many thousands.

1832, Large Letters (N-3).

Notes: This variety exists in Mint State.

1832, Large Letters		Cert	Avg	%MS
		29	56.4	59%

EF-40	AU-50	MS-60BN	MS-63BN
$150	$250	$375	$650

MS-63RB	MS-65BN	MS-65RB
$1,000	$2,300	$3,300

1832, Medium Letters • N-1 and N-2. *Estimated population:* Many thousands.

1832, Medium Letters (N-1).

Notes: Perhaps only half as many examples as for the Large Letters variety. This variety exists in Mint State.

Typical values for 1832, Medium Letters.

1832, Medium Letters		Cert	Avg	%MS
		27	59.6	63%

EF-40	AU-50	MS-60BN	MS-63BN
$200	$550	$900	$1,200

MS-63RB	MS-65BN	MS-65RB
$2,250	$2,900	$4,500

1833, Matron Head
Mintage (per Mint Report*): 2,739,000.*

There are six die combinations this year, N-1 to N-6, again casting suspicion that in calendar year 1833, as in 1832, earlier-dated dies were used for part of the production. On the other hand, certain of the dies show *extreme wear* as evidenced by grainy fields and indistinct denticles. Perhaps the die steel was very strong and resisted cracking. The answer may await further study. All have Large Letters on the reverse, seemingly illogical, as smaller letters would have reduced metal flow, permitting the stars to be sharper. Indeed, slightly later in this series, Small Letters would become standard. Very early die states of N-4 show traces of a 2 under the 3—an overdate.

While N-4 is slightly scarce, the other of the five varieties are in generous supply, and there are far more than enough to fill the needs of specialists. All are readily available in Mint State, to varying degrees of availability. These include many at the choice and gem levels. Striking varies. Those from tired dies (such as the Naftzger coin above, which is certified as PCGS MS-66) are apt to be weak and grainy. Those from fresh dies are typically very lustrous. These would seem to furnish ample opportunity for cherrypicking, as most buyers in the marketplace don't seem to care. Most coins have brown surfaces and nice eye appeal. Significant mint color is rare.

1833 • N-1 to N-6. *Estimated population:* Many thousands.

1833 (N-3), an impression from
an extensively worn obverse die.

Typical values for 1833 cents. Rare varieties may be
worth more.

1833			Cert	Avg	%MS
			252	52.6	46%

EF-40	AU-50	MS-60BN	MS-63BN
$150	$250	$375	$750

MS-63RB	MS-65BN	MS-65RB
$1,500	$2,600	$3,700

Notes: Well over 1,000 Mint State coins
are estimated, and far more than that exist
at the EF and AU levels.

1834, Matron Head
Mintage (per Mint Report*): 1,855,100.*

Cents of 1834 are known to exist in seven die combinations. Variables include large or
small 8 in the date, large or small stars, and—on the reverse—large or medium letters.
These variables can be organized into four classes, each of which are listed in the regular edition of the *Guide Book of United States Coins* and are avidly collected:

**1834, Large 8, Large Stars, Large Let-
ters:** N-6 (quite scarce) and N-7 (Proofs
only). Circulation strikes of this variety are
usually seen in lower grades. They are in
strong demand.

**1834, Large 8, Large Stars, Large Letters (N-6).
Second scarcest of the 1834 die combinations,
and the only variety with these features.**

1834, Large 8, Large Stars, Medium

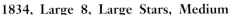

**1834, Large 8, Large Stars, Medium Letters (N-5).
Far and away the rarest combination of the year,
and the only combination with these features.**

Letters: N-5 (the rarity of the year). This
variety is in extreme demand due to its
listing in popular references beyond the
large cent specialty. The illustrated coin is
from the Naftzger Collection and was
graded MS-60 by William C. Noyes, a
grade which was confirmed independently
by Chris Victor-McCawley and J.R. (Bob)
Grellman Jr. PCGS certified the coin as
MS-65.[99]

1834, Large 8, Small Stars, Medium Letters: N-3 (common) and N-4 (slightly scarce).

1834, Large 8, Small Stars, Medium Letters (N-3). One of two die combinations with these features. Common. This particular example has a so-called "Double Profile," or doubled outline to the face, from die "chatter," the result of a loosely fitted obverse die in the coining press.

1834, Small 8, Large Stars, Medium Letters: N-1 (very common) and N-2 (very common).

1834, Small 8, Large Stars, Medium Letters (N-1). One of two die combinations with these features. The commonest of the styles.

Striking varies, but most have lightness among the stars. Denticles are usually complete, but can be weak. Some are struck from tired dies. Most are in lower grades, VG to Fine and VF being typical. The commoner die combinations are likewise the ones easiest to find in Mint State. This year is a delight for cherrypickers, for coins graded high can have low eye appeal and vice versa.

Proofs: N-7 was made only in Proof format. This is the only Proof in the Matron Head series made from dies which were not also used to coin circulation strikes.

1834, Large 8, Large Stars, Large Letters • N-6. *Estimated population: 300 to 500.*

1834, Large 8, Large Stars, Large Letters (N-6).

Notes: Very rare in Mint State, with possibly 10 to 20 extant per general market grading, fewer than 5 by EAC grading. Many exist at the EF and AU levels although most are well worn.

Numismatic Notes: See 1834, Small 8, Large Stars, Medium Letters.

1834, Large 8, Large Stars, Large Letters		Cert	Avg	%MS
		13	45.2	8%

VG-8	F-12	VF-20	EF-40
$150	$300	$400	$575

AU-50	MS-60BN		MS-63BN
$1,300	$2,625		$4,000

1834, Large 8, Large Stars, Medium Letters • N-5. *Estimated population:* 100 to 150.

1834, Large 8, Large Stars, Medium Letters (N-5).

Notes: Extremely rare in Mint State, with possibly 7 to 12 extant per general market grading, fewer than 4 by EAC grading.

Numismatic Notes: See 1834, Small 8, Large Stars, Medium Letters.

1834, Large 8, Large Stars, Medium Letters	Cert	Avg	%MS
	5	50.2	20%

VG-8	F-12	VF-20
$750	$1,500	$2,500

EF-40	AU-50	MS-60BN
$3,700	$6,500	$10,250

1834, Large 8, Small Stars, Medium Letters • N-3 and N-4. *Estimated population:* Many thousands.

1834, Large 8, Small Stars, Medium Letters (N-3).

Notes: Easily available from low grades to Mint State.

Numismatic Notes: See 1834, Small 8, Large Stars, Medium Letters.

Typical values for 1834, Large 8, Small Stars, Medium Letters.

1834, Large 8, Small Stars, Medium Letters	Cert	Avg	%MS
	32	50.0	34%

EF-40	AU-50	MS-60BN	MS-63BN
$140	$240	$350	$625

MS-63RB	MS-65BN	MS-65RB
$925	$1,400	$3,000

1834, Small 8, Large Stars, Medium Letters • N-1 and N-2. *Estimated population:* Many thousands.

1834, Small 8, Large Stars, Medium Letters (N-1).

Notes: Easily available from low grades to Mint State.

Numismatic Notes: Late in 1834 the government of Venezuela ordered 100,000 cents, and these were shipped. In 1835 the Venezuelan government ordered a million more cents. It is not known how many, *if any*, were shipped of the 1835 coins.[100] If any were, likely they consisted of, say, up to a half dozen different die varieties, perhaps accounting for the rarity of certain of these today.

Typical values for 1834, Large 8, Small Stars, Medium Letters.

1834, Small 8, Large Stars, Medium Letters	Cert	Avg	%MS
	74	54.5	50%

EF-40	AU-50	MS-60BN	MS-63BN
$140	$240	$350	$625

MS-63RB	MS-65BN	MS-65RB
$925	$1,400	$3,000

1835, Matron Head and Matron Head Modified
Mintage (per Mint Report*): 3,878,400.*

The mintage of this year is very generous, touching a new high. There are 18 different die combinations, N-1 to N-19, with N-7 found to be the same as N-17 and thus now just a single variety.

The cents of 1835 are found in three styles. It seems likely that the first two were made under the engravership of William Kneass. Christian Gobrecht, hired in September, would be a logical choice as the author of the new Head of 1836 motif (a slight revision of the earlier style) as well as various other portrait changes through the end of the middle date series. All cents of this year have Medium Letters on the reverse.

The die varieties that are common are also easy to find in Mint State, after which there are challenges. For N-18, a grade of Very Fine would be a notable example. The Naftzger coin was graded EF-40 by McCawley and Grellman, and PCGS designated it as AU-58.

Many coins of this year, including surviving Mint State examples, are struck from tired dies showing graininess and deterioration. Eye appeal is often lacking. It would seem that an MS-60 coin, sharply struck and from fresh dies, would be a better buy (and at a fraction of the price) than an MS-65, weakly struck and from tired dies. For this date there is ample opportunity for cherrypicking for quality.

The styles and the relevant Newcomb numbers:

1835, Large 8, Large Stars: N-1 (common) and N-9 (slightly scarce).

1835, Small 8, Small Stars: N-2 (very scarce), N-3 (very scarce), N-4 (rare), N-5 (slightly scarce), N-6 (very common), N-10 (rare), N-11 (rare), N-12 (rare), N-13 (very scarce), N-18 (very rare), and N-19 (very rare).

1835, Head of 1836: N-7 (incorporating N-17, a later die state; very common), N-8 (very common), N-14 (scarce), N-15 (scarce), and N-16 (scarce). The new head is more petite-appearing, has the cheek more rounded, and as a quick point of identification, the bust is slightly longer and thus extends slightly farther to the left. The stars are small.

1835, Large 8, Large Stars • N-1 and N-9. *Estimated population:* Many thousands.

1835, Large 8, Large Stars (N-1).

Typical values for 1835, Large 8, Large Stars.

1835, Large 8, Large Stars			Cert	Avg	%MS
			13	53 7	46%

VG-8	F-12	VF-20	EF-40	AU-50
$100	$150	$250	$360	$700

MS-60BN	MS-63BN	MS-63RB	MS-65BN	MS-65RB
$1,125	$1,700	$2,375	$2,550	$4,600

Notes: Fewer examples exist than for the next two styles. Many Mint State coins exist, and they are easy to acquire. Striking and die quality can be low.

1835, Small 8, Small Stars • N-2 to N-6, N-10 to N-13, N-18, and N-19.
Estimated population: Many thousands.

1835, Small 8, Small Stars (N-6).

Notes: Mint State coins of the common varieties are easy to find, but often these are from tired dies or have striking problems.

Typical values for 1835, Small 8, Small Stars. Rare varieties may be worth more.

1835, Small 8, Small Stars		Cert	Avg	%MS
		47	46.9	30%

VF-20	EF-40	AU-50	MS-60BN
$150	$190	$375	$475

MS-63BN	MS-63RB	MS-65BN	MS-65RB
$675	$1,400	$1,750	$3,750

1835, Head of 1836 • N-7 (N-17), N-8, and N-14 to N-16. *Estimated population:* Many thousands.

1835, Head of 1836 (N-8), with modified portrait.

Notes: Mint State coins of the common varieties are easy to find, but often these are from tired dies or have striking problems.

Typical values for 1835, Head of 1836. Rare varieties may be worth more.

1835, Head of 1836		Cert	Avg	%MS
		94	53.5	40%

VF-20	EF-40	AU-50	MS-60BN
$100	$150	$250	$350

MS-63BN	MS-63RB	MS-65BN	MS-65RB
$550	$900	$1,300	$2,000

1836, Matron Head Modified
Mintage (per Mint Report): 2,111,000.

In March 1836, following the ceremonial striking of medalets, a steam press was first employed for the coinage of the cent denomination. Seven die combinations are known for this date, N-1 to N-7. The most often seen is N-3, usually with a rim cud at the sixth star, making it instantly identifiable. This may well be the most common Matron Head cent of the decade.[101] Certain die varieties range from scarce to rare.

Continuing the trend of the time, the Mint used dies over an extended life span, creating many coins with grainy fields and mushy denticles. Weakly struck stars are the rule. Even the more available varieties are hard to find with a combination of decent (never mind needle-sharp) strike, frosty surfaces (from fresh dies), and good eye appeal. In this context this "common" date is actually rare if well-struck coins are desired, again yielding many opportunities for cherrypicking.

Typical values for 1836 cents.
Rare varieties may be worth more.

1836			Cert	Avg	%MS
			213	53.1	48%

EF-40	AU-50	MS-60BN	MS-63BN	MS-63RB	MS-65BN	MS-65RB
$125	$250	$350	$550	$900	$1,300	$2,000

1836 • N-1 to N-7. ***Estimated population:*** Many tens of thousands.

Notes: Common in all grades, including Mint State, but certain die varieties are rare.

1836 (N-3) with distinctive rim cud at star 6. This is one of the more plentiful varieties of the era.

1837, Matron Head Modified
Mintage (per Mint Report*): 5,558,300.*

The mintage this year hit a new record. There are 16 known die varieties, reflecting extended average use of die pair. More telling is the number of *different* dies. In this year 12 obverses turned out an average of 436,000 coins each! This "economy" is vividly evident in the quality of the coins struck, which, once again, are often from tired dies, sometimes relapped. Striking was done casually, and many coins have weak stars or denticles or both. These shortcomings are typically more evident on the obverse than the reverse. Once again, this year is a cherrypicker's delight.

In this year a new portrait was introduced, attributed to Christian Gobrecht. Instead of having Plain Hair Cords as before, and dating back to 1816, Miss Liberty now has Beaded Hair Cords, which were continued for the rest of the type. The Plain Hair Cord coins come with Medium Letters and Small Letters on the reverse. These styles yield the following combinations:

1837, Plain Hair Cords, Medium Letters: N-1 to N-4, N-6, N-7 (combined with N-8, same pair, N-8 the *earlier* die states), and N-13 to N-17.

1837, Plain Hair Cords, Small Letters: N-5. Scarce, and the key to this trio of styles. This coin is always a classic, due to its listing in the regular edition of the *Guide Book of United States Coins.*

1837, Beaded Hair Cords: N-9 to N-12.

1837, Plain Hair Cords, Medium Letters • N-1 to N-4, N-6, N-7 (N-8), and N-13 to N-17. *Estimated population:* Many thousands.

1837, Plain Hair Cords, Medium Letters (N-1). The obverse die was well used by this point, with a grainy rather than lustrous surface. Lightly struck stars. Remarkable original mint color.

Notes: Common in Mint State, scarcer with significant original mint color.

Typical values for 1837, Plain Hair Cords, Medium Letters. Rare varieties may be worth more.

1837, Plain Hair Cords, Medium Letters		Cert	Avg	%MS
		149	59.0	66%

EF-40	AU-50	MS-60BN	MS-63BN
$125	$250	$350	$550

MS-63RB	MS-65BN	MS-65RB
$775	$1,200	$2,300

1837, Plain Hair Cords, Small Letters • N-5. *Estimated population:* 750 to 1,000.

1837, Plain Hair Cords, Small Letters (N-5). This is the key issue among the three styles of the year. Only one die variety combined these features.

Notes: Estimated 100 to 200 Mint State coins known (or 25 to 50 by EAC grading). Many EF and AU coins exist.

1837, Plain Hair Cords, Small Letters		Cert	Avg	%MS
		24	55.0	50%

EF-40	AU-50	MS-60BN	MS-63BN
$125	$250	$375	$600

MS-63RB	MS-65BN	MS-65RB
$825	$1,500	$2,600

1837, Beaded Hair Cords • N-9 to N-12. *Estimated population:* Many thousands.

1837, Beaded Hair Cords (N-11).

Notes: Common in Mint State, scarcer with significant original mint color.

Typical values for 1837, Beaded Hair Cords.

1837, Beaded Hair Cords		Cert	Avg	%MS
		75	58.8	61%

EF-40	AU-50	MS-60BN	MS-63BN
$110	$200	$325	$500

MS-63RB	MS-65BN	MS-65RB
$775	$1,200	$1,900

1838, Matron Head Modified
Mintage (per Mint Report*): 6,370,000.*

This mintage and part of the 1837 mintage combine to break all coinage records to this point. The Panic of 1837, which had its roots in late 1836 and early 1837, became a reality on May 10, 1837, when banks stopped paying out silver and gold coins. There arose a strong demand for copper coins, and the Mint rushed to fill it, being joined by private manufacturers who issued millions of "Hard Times tokens."

Cent coinage for 1838 was comprised of 15 different varieties, N-1 to N-16, with N-11 and N-13 being different die states of the same combination. As 11 obverse dies were involved, this indicates an average coinage of 579,000 coins per die! Quality is all over the map—from very sharp and from fresh dies, to pieces from tired dies, with mushy denticles and flat stars. This is yet another cherrypicker's playground.

Typical values for 1838 cents.
Rare varieties may be worth more.

1838	Cert	Avg	%MS
	815	56.2	60%

EF-40	AU-50	MS-60BN	MS-63BN	MS-63RB	MS-65BN	MS-65RB
$120	$225	$335	$575	$925	$1,325	$2,150

1838 • N-1 to N-11 (N-13), N-12, and N-14 to N-16. ***Estimated population:*** Many tens of thousands.

Notes: The commonest Matron Head cent. Common in all grades. Mint State coins tend to be brown or with partial mint color, rarely full "red."

1838 (N-4).

1839, 9 Over 6, Matron Head Modified
Circulation mintage (estimated): 20,000 to 40,000.

The 1839, 9 Over 6, is one of the most interesting overdates in the series. In 1839 a die of 1836 with Plain Hair Cords was overdated with a 9, creating an 1839 cent with Plain Hair Cords—a style that had been discontinued two years earlier. Inexplicably, Howard Newcomb thought the overdate to be a die break, apparently not noticing the Plain Hair Cords feature. 1839 was a time of transition (see next listing), and the Matron Head was discontinued late in the year. It is easy to envision that a survey was taken of the Matron Head dies on hand, so as to use them up, and this one from several years earlier was found. In later states a horizontal crack developed across the obverse, expanded, and led to the retirement of the die. The mintage must have been very small. The reverse die was used on 1839, Silly Head (N-4 and N-9).

Today this overdate is nearly always seen in lower grades, with VG to Fine or the occasional VF being usual. Any higher grade is a rarity. The illustrated coin has been variously graded by EACers as MS-60 (William C. Noyes) and 63 (McCawley and Grellman), and by PCGS as MS-65.

1839, 9 Over 6	Cert	Avg	%MS
	48	14.0	0%

VG-8	F-12	VF-20	EF-40
$1,500	$3,000	$5,000	$9,000

1839, 9 Over 6 • N-1. *Estimated population:* 200 to 350.

1839, 9 Over 6 (N-1), the overdate with anachronistic Plain Hair Cords. 1824, 4 Over 2 (N-1).

Detail of the overdate.

Notes: Only one Mint State coin is known, perhaps 3 to 5 AU, and 15 to 20 EF. Most of the others are Fine or Very Fine.

1839, Matron Head Modified
Mintage (per Mint Report): 3,128,661.

Of all dates in the Matron Head series, cents of 1839 are the most diverse and, because of that, likely the most interesting. It seems that in 1839 Christian Gobrecht was contemplating many changes. Already, in 1838, the Braided Hair design was adopted on the $10 eagle, in 1839 it would be employed on the $5 half eagle, and then, in 1840, on the $2.50 quarter eagle—these being all of the gold denominations at the time. The silver series had been revised recently, beginning with the Gobrecht dollar in 1836 and the use of the Liberty Seated motif in the other denominations, including the half dime (1837), dime (1837), quarter dollar (1838), and half dollar (1839).

In 1839 the engraver experimented with some new portraits, including those we know as the Silly Head and the Booby Head. Problems of striking had been endemic to the Matron Head series since day one, with the obverse stars in particular causing problems. By 1839, the Small Letters style of reverse had helped solve that, as less metal flow was needed in the press in the area of the reverse die opposite the stars on the obverse.

Toward the end of the 1839 year, the Braided Hair design—an adaptation of that used on the gold coins—was made standard for the cent. The 1839, 9 Over 6, is discussed in the preceding section, and the 1839, Braided Hair, is in the following section. That leaves these three main styles of Matron Head cents, all of which are with Beaded Hair Cords:

1839, Head of 1838: This is the style of the preceding year (and also late 1837) without a "browlock" or protruding wave of hair above the forehead, and with the back of the shoulder covered by hair. There is a line under CENT on the reverse. Varieties N-2 (slightly scarce) and N-3 (very common) comprise this style. *Quick identification:* No browlock.

1839, Silly Head: This variety appears with prominent browlock (curl of hair projecting to the left at the top of the forehead). Hair surrounds the back of the shoulder and base of T of LIBERTY, with the serifs of T touching the hair. There is a line under CENT on the reverse. Varieties N-4 (very common) and N-9 (slightly scarce) comprise this style. ***Quick identification:*** With browlock, line under CENT.

1839, Booby Head: This variety appears with prominent browlock. Hair surrounds the back of the shoulder, and T of LIBERTY is embedded in the hair, with no serifs visible. There is no line under CENT on the reverse. Varieties N-5 (quite scarce), N-6 (scarce), N-7 (slightly scarce), N-10 (quite scarce), N-11 (very common), N-12 (very scarce), N-13 (slightly scarce), N-14 (quite scarce), and N-15 (rare) comprise this style. ***Quick identification:*** With browlock, no line under CENT.

Striking quality varies, and some are from tired dies. Mint State coins are readily available for the common die varieties. Circulated coins average Fine or Very Fine, with EF and AU coins being abundant. Most are a brown color and have nice eye appeal.

1839, Head of 1838 • N-2 and N-3. *Estimated population:* Thousands.

1839, Head of 1838 (N-2).

Notes: This variety exists in Mint State.

Typical values for 1839, Head of 1838.

1839, Head of 1838		Cert	Avg	%MS
		93	56.0	46%

VG-8	F-12	VF-20	EF-40	AU-50
$40	$65	$100	$130	$240

MS-60BN	MS-63BN	MS-63RB	MS-65BN	MS-65RB
$340	$550	$1,000	$1,450	$2,000

1839, Silly Head • N-4 and N-9. *Estimated population:* Many thousands.

1839, Silly Head (N-9). Prominent browlock on forehead. Right side of neck truncation blends into hair. Line under CENT. This is an extraordinary coin with nearly full original mint red. The stars are quite sharp, but the denticles are mushy.

Notes: This variety exists in Mint State.

Typical values for 1839, Silly Head.

1839, Silly Head		Cert	Avg	%MS
		126	51.6	48%

VG-8	F-12	VF-20	EF-40	AU-50
$50	$100	$150	$225	$400

MS-60BN	MS-63BN	MS-63RB	MS-65BN	MS-65RB
$850	$1,200	$2,200	$2,850	$3,900

1839, Booby Head • N-5 to N-7 and N-10 to N-15. *Estimated population:* Many thousands.

1839, Booby Head (N-11). Prominent browlock on forehead. Right side of neck truncation ends in a square with point or corner visible. No line under CENT. Full original mint red. Sharp stars. Obverse denticles weak.

Notes: This variety exists in Mint State.

Typical values for 1839, Booby Head.

1839, Booby Head			Cert	Avg	%MS
			209	53.4	52%

VG-8	F-12	VF-20	EF-40	AU-50
$50	$100	$150	$200	$350

MS-60BN	MS-63BN	MS-63RB	MS-65BN	MS-65RB
$740	$1,300	$2,325	$2,925	$4,100

BRAIDED HAIR (1839–1857)

1856, Upright 5 in Date (N-8).

Designer: *Christian Gobrecht.* **Weight:** *168 grains (10.89 grams).*
Composition: *Copper.* **Diameter:** *27.5 mm.* **Edge:** *Plain.*

The Braided Hair type, introduced in 1839, continued uninterrupted until 1857. The coins of the earlier years in this date range are referred to as the Petite Head type, while later issues are referred to as the Mature Head—although they both have braided hair. Production was generous, with the result that a set of dates is easily enough collected today, although there are many rare die varieties. The earlier dates, as well as 1857, are not seen as often as the others.

Of special interest are two well-known die blunders in which the four-digit logotype, introduced in 1840, was entered in the die at least partially upside down and then corrected. Thus, we have 1844 over 81, and 1851 over 81. In both instances, the full inverted date is not visible, but just traces of it are. Beyond these are hundreds of die varieties with minute differences, the later ones differentiated mainly by small differences in the date logotype positions. *United States Copper Cents 1816–1857,* by Howard R. Newcomb, 1944, is the standard reference for the Braided Hair cent, but it requires a great deal of patience to use. There are no photographs, and "stock" line drawings plus adjectives are used instead. Essential, and more convenient, is the *Attribution Guide for United States Large Cents 1840–1857,* by J.R. (Bob) Grellman Jr. Before the listing for each year, there is a guide to basic characteristics. Such extra study is worthwhile, because, if the discipline of large copper cents appeals to you, there is the added allure that exceedingly rare varieties are often available for the price of "regular" examples of any given date. Even if they are classified properly, these rare varieties are often reasonably priced—as collector demand is not great—creating a heaven for cherrypicking.

The striking quality of cents of the 1839 to 1857 era varies from issue to issue. Generally, the earlier dates are better struck, but even these are apt to have some weakness. Points to check are star centers (in particular), denticles, and then the hair and leaf details. Generally, the denticles on coins of the 1850s range from weak in areas to "mushy" or indistinct. Some cents of the 1850s have rough patches in the fields from lamination or from grease or debris adhering to the dies. Planchet quality is usually good. Many dies were used beyond their normal life, and these became rough and granular, giving streaky and grainy effects ("flow lines" if radial) to the fields of such pieces.

Among Mint State coins, most from 1839 through and including 1849 are generally seen with brown surfaces or brown with tinges of red. Only rarely are any seen with full *original mint red*, although the deficiency of retained brightness has been made up in spades by large numbers of pieces being dipped. It is buyer beware, and even among certified coins there are many recolored, processed, etc, pieces. These are not necessarily undesirable to own, providing you know what they are and do not pay "original mint color" price for them. Again, great care should be taken either by you, an experienced friend, or a dealer/advisor. Certain die varieties from 1850 to 1856 are frequently seen in Mint State with nearly full original color, usually with some flecks, and are mostly from small hoards. Cents of 1857 are nearly always brown or with some tinges of mint color, scarcely ever with full *original* color. Again, cherrypicking opportunities abound.

Circulated coins exist in approximate proportion to their mintages; although, note that the saving percentage is higher for the later dates. Likely, two percent to three percent of the original mintages survive today. Grades of Fine and Very Fine are about par for the 1840s; Very Fine and Extremely Fine, for the 1850s. For 1857, EF and AU are typical.

Proofs were made in small quantities of certain of the earlier years. In 1856 and 1857, production of Proofs increased, with the result that these dates, while scarce today, do come on the market with some frequency. Certain Proofs of the 1844 to 1849 era—namely 1844 (N-8), 1845 (N-14), 1846, Small Date (N-22 and N-24), 1847 (N-42), 1848 (N-19), and 1849 (N-18)—share a common reverse die. Some, or all, may be restrikes made in the late 1850s and later.[102]

The curtain came down on the large copper cent after the coinage of January 1857, and the abolition of the denomination under the Act of February 21 of that year. However, in 1868, during a period when the Mint was making all sorts of rare patterns, restrikes, and delicacies for collectors, some imaginative person, identity unknown, produced perhaps a dozen or so 1868 large copper cents—identical in design and appearance to those of the 1850s, but bearing the 1868 date.

DESIGN DETAILS

Christian Gobrecht created this new portrait. This being part of a redesign of the copper and gold series—commencing with the 1838 $10 gold and completed with the half cent and $2.50 gold in 1840—the design is not a modification of anything done earlier. The head of Miss Liberty is compact, facing left with a tiara or diadem inscribed LIBERTY and her hair, circled with beads, in a knot at the back of her head. Thirteen stars surround most of the periphery, and the date is below.

Cents of 1839 and 1840 have the head tilted forward in relation to the date, the 1841 and 1842 cents are also tilted, but less so, and this is also true of the 1843 cents of the earlier type. The earlier heads are more delicate, leading Kenneth Bressett, editor of the *Guide Book of United States Coins*, to designate these as *Petite Heads*, a nomenclature we follow here. In 1843 the transition was made to an upright portrait, the *Mature Head*.

Most cents after 1843 are less delicate in appearance than are those of earlier dates, and the dies are more stereotyped.

Numerals were punched individually into the 1839 die and the 1840, Large Date, dies, after which four-digit logotypes came into use.

The reverse design of cents from 1839 to early 1843 is similar to that used on later Matron Heads, with a continuous wreath with a ribbon below, ONE / CENT within, and around the border in small letters, UNITED STATES OF AMERICA. In 1843 a transition was made to a heavier wreath and larger letters, a style continued through to the end of the series.

1839, Braided Hair

Circulation mintage (estimated): 200,000 to 300,000.

Just one die pair, N-8, was used to coin the 1839, Braided Hair. The number struck is not known, but was likely 200,000 to 300,000, considering that 13 obverse dies were used this year (12 of the earlier type) to strike 3,128,661 coins, averaging about 240,000 coins per obverse die. In the context of cents of that date, N-8 is common. If star 1, star 13, and the date are aligned horizontally, the portrait leans forward. This orientation was adjusted in later years.

Striking varies from weak to sharp, but it is usually quite good. Examples are available in all grades from VG to Mint State. In this last category, choice and gem coins with excellent eye appeal are available. As the first year of the type, this variety has always drawn a lot of attention, and offerings of high-grade examples always meet with an enthusiastic reception.

Proofs: None.

1839, Braided Hair				Cert	Avg	%MS
				66	54.7	55%

VG-8	F-12	VF-20	EF-40	AU-50	MS-60BN	MS-63BN	MS-63RB	MS-65BN	MS-65RB
$50	$75	$150	$205	$430	$700	$1,075	$1,425	$3,625	$7,250

1839, Braided Hair • N-8. *Estimated population:* 4,000 to 6,000.

1839, Braided Hair (N-8).

Notes: An estimated 40 to 50 are known in Mint State. In *The Cent Book,* 1991, John D. Wright estimated equal to or more than 30, stating "it is amazing how many really choice examples are around," and called the variety "mega-common" across all grades.

1840, Braided Hair

Mintage (per Mint Report*): 2,462,700.*

Cents of 1840 are found in Large Date and Small Date varieties. This was a year of transition, and the Large Dates were punched in by hand, one digit at a time. The Small Date coins, made later, represent the first use of a four-digit logotype, in which all digits were punched into a die at once. Accordingly, the Large Date obverses vary in the alignment of the digits, whereas the dates on the Small Date obverses are all identical.

Certain of the portraits have a "hole in the ear," a round depression immediately above the earlobe.[103] This is seen on some other dies of this era. These are not delineated here, but are treated in detail in the Grellman text.

In one variety of 1840, Small Date Over Large 18 (N-2), 1840 is punched over the large digits 18, which were punched into the die by hand in 1839 and never finished. Rather than make the die a Large Date 1840 by punching in two more individual numbers, the four-digit Small Date logotype punch was used, creating one of the most unusual varieties in the series.

Detail of the 1839, Braided Hair, with individual digits punched into the die. A partially completed die with only 18 was used to create the 1840, Small Date Over Large 18 (N-2).

Detail 1840, Small Date Over Large 18 (N-2), with undertype hand-punched 18 figures at left, under the 18 of the logotype.

The varieties listed here are these:

1840, Small Date Over Large 18: N-2 only. In 1839 this die was prepared as 18, with the last two spaces left blank, to be filled in when the die was used. The 8 is of the *script* type. All figures were punched by hand. As the third digit was not added, this allowed the die to be used for 1839, if needed, or the new decade, 1840. In 1840 the four-digit logotype was used for the first time. In this instance the logotype is applied with a straight orientation, rather than the curved style used with singly-applied digits in 1839. The logotype also uses a *block* 8 instead of script. The die was punched with the 1840 date, leaving abundant traces of the earlier 18. In addition to producing a large quantity of circulation strikes, this die pair was also given a mirror finish and used to strike Proofs.

1840, Large Date: N-5 to N-10. The digits were punched individually into each die and thus vary in alignment. The figures are large and are arranged in a gentle curve. These were the first 1840 dies made.

1840, Small Date: N-1, N-3, N-4, and N-12. These varieties are punched with the four-digit logotype, comprised of small figures about evenly spaced; the top of the block-type 8 is smaller than the bottom; there is a plain (not crosslet) 4. These were the last dies made.

For each of the above styles, typical grades range from VG upward, with VF being about the median. Mint State coins are scarce, and choice and gem pieces are rare. Only a few have significant original mint color.

Proofs: Mirror Proofs were struck of N-2, in addition to circulation strikes.

1840, Large Date • N-5 to N-10. *Estimated population:* More than 30,000.

1840, Large Date (N-6).

Notes: This variety occurs in Mint State.

Typical values for 1840, Large Date.

1840, Large Date		Cert	Avg	%MS
		91	56.7	55%

EF-40	AU-50	MS-60BN	MS-63BN
$85	$200	$300	$500

MS-63RB	MS-65BN	MS-65RB
$1,150	$1,200	$2,500

1840, Small Date Over Large 18 • N-2. *Estimated population:* More than 5,000.

1840, Small Date Over Large 18 (N-2).

Notes: This variety occurs in Mint State.

1840, Small Date Over Large 18		Cert	Avg	%MS
		8	43.6	38%

EF-40	AU-50	MS-60BN	MS-63BN
$300	$450	$950	$1,800

MS-63RB	MS-65BN	MS-65RB
$2,250	$2,675	$5,000

1840, Small Date Over Large 18, Proof		Cert	Avg	%MS
		8	56.3	

PF-60	PF-63BN	PF-63RB	PF-65BN
$4,500	$7,000	$10,500	$20,000

1840, Small Date • N-1, N-3, N-4, and N-12. *Estimated population:* More than 22,000.

1840, Small Date (N-3).

Notes: This variety is available in Mint State.

Typical values for 1840, Small Date.

1840, Small Date		Cert	Avg	%MS
		83	50.0	39%

EF-40	AU-50	MS-60BN	MS-63BN
$85	$200	$300	$500

MS-63RB	MS-65BN	MS-65RB
$1,150	$1,200	$2,500

1841, Braided Hair

Mintage (per **Mint Report***): 1,597,367.*

Cents of the year 1841 are all of the same standard appearance—the dies possess no significant blunders or date-size variations, yielding simplicity in the resulting coins, so to speak—not that this is desirable! The varieties run from N-1 to N-7, with N-1 known only in Proof format. Circulation strikes are plentiful and can be obtained in nearly any grade desired. Typical examples range from VG to VF. Mint State coins are easy enough to find and usually are lustrous brown or brown with some traces of original color. As always, coins from worn-out dies, with weak stars, or with weak denticles are abundant in the marketplace. Choice coins are easy enough to find within the date (but vary with certain die varieties) and cost no more than coins of average quality.

Proofs: All are of the N-1 variety, a combination used only for Proofs. While hardly common overall, this date is the most available Proof cent of this era, until the coins of the mid-1850s. The reason for this surplus is unknown, although it was an inaugural year (for William Henry Harrison, who caught cold at the swearing-in event and died within the month), and there may have been some ceremony attached to this happenstance.

Typical values for 1841 cents.

1841		Cert	Avg	%MS
		141	54.8	51%

VG-8	F-12	VF-20	EF-40	AU-50	MS-60BN	MS-63BN	MS-63RB	MS-65BN	MS-65RB
$40	$50	$100	$160	$275	$525	$1,100	$1,350	$1,825	$3,000

1841, Proof • N-1. *Estimated population:* 45 to 60.

1841, Proof		Cert	Avg	%MS
		20	64.3	

PF-60	PF-63BN	PF-63RB	PF-65BN
$4,000	$6,000	$9,500	$16,000

1841 • N-2 to N-7. *Estimated population:* More than 35,000.

Notes: This variety occurs in Mint State.

1841 (N-5). Extensive die cracks are seen through the date and stars.

1842, Braided Hair

Mintage (per Mint Report): 2,383,390.

Cents of this date can be found in two styles, Small Date (N-1 and N-2) and Large Date (N-3 to N-9, but N-3 and N-8 being different states of the same dies). Although both the Small Date and Large Date are common overall, there are more of the Small Dates.

Typical examples of either date size range from VG to VF or so, but higher grades are plentiful as well. Mint State coins have brown surfaces or are brown with some mint color. Occasionally a "RD" Large Date comes on the market. For any high-grade examples, cherrypicking for fresh dies and a sharp strike will pay dividends. Check the star centers. Coins from tired dies will be grainy, rather than lustrous, and may have flow lines.

Proofs: N-1 (Small Date) Proofs were made. These combinations were also used to make circulation strikes.

1842, Small Date • N-1 and N-2. *Estimated population:* More than 12,000.

1842, Small Date (N-2).

Notes: This variety exists in Mint State.

Typical values for 1842, Small Date.

1842, Small Date	Cert	Avg	%MS
	47	53.6	49%

EF-40	AU-50	MS-60BN
$90	$220	$375

MS-63BN	MS-63RB	MS-65BN
$650	$1,300	$2,200

1842, Small Date, Proof	Cert	Avg	%MS
	6	64.4	

PF-60	PF-63BN	PF-63RB	PF-65BN
$4,500	$7,000	$11,000	$20,000

1842, Large Date • N-3 (N-8) to N-7 and N-9. *Estimated population:* More than 35,000.

1842, Large Date (N-3).

Notes: This variety is available in Mint State.

Typical values for 1842, Large Date. Rare varieties may be worth more.

1842, Large Date	Cert	Avg	%MS
	121	53.6	50%

EF-40	AU-50	MS-60BN	MS-63BN
$85	$150	$300	$500

MS-63RB	MS-65BN	MS-65RB
$850	$1,800	$3,000

1843, Braided Hair

Mintage (per Mint Report*): 2,425,342.*

This was a year of transition, yielding three main styles that have been avidly collected for a long time. The change was made from the Petite Head, leaning forward, to the Mature Head. In the second, Miss Liberty is positioned upright and is less delicate in her features. Large Letters were used on the reverse for this year, replacing the Small Letters in use since 1839. Changes of this nature were also made on other denominations. Why the Small Letters were discontinued is not known. In fact this change is surprising, as the smaller font facilitated sharpness of strike by decreasing the necessary amount of metal flow. Furthermore, many numismatists of today find the Small Letters more attractive.

Sharpness varies, but in general the Petite Head type is better than the Mature Head varieties. As usual, check the star centers and denticles first, and then check for graininess in the field from tired dies. There are many sharp, attractive coins in the marketplace, but overall they are in the minority.

The three styles for this year:

1843, Obverse and Reverse of 1842: N-2, N-3, N-8 through N-12, and N-14—N-10 being a die state of N-15. Petite Head obverse, Small Letters reverse. This is the most often seen style of the year.

1843, Obverse of 1842 and Reverse of 1844: N-4. Petite Head obverse, Large Letters reverse. This is the key issue of the year, with just one die combination. Although it is common—several thousand exist—it is seen much less often than the two other styles.

1843, Obverse and Reverse of 1844: N-5, N-6, N-16, and N-17. Mature Head obverse and Large Letters reverse, the style used from this point through 1857.

Proofs: Proofs were struck of N-12 (used for circulation strikes as well) and N-14 (used only for Proofs).

1843, Obverse and Reverse of 1842 • N-2, N-3, N-8 to N-10 (N-15), N-11, N-12, and N-14. *Estimated population:* More than 25,000.

1843, Obverse and Reverse of 1842 (N-8). Petite Head. Small Letters.

Notes: This variety is known in Mint State.

Typical values for 1843, Obverse and Reverse of 1842. Rare varieties may be worth more.

1843, Obverse and Reverse of 1842			Cert	Avg	%MS
			153	56.4	63%

EF-40	AU-50	MS-60BN	MS-63BN
$85	$160	$300	$450

MS-63RB	MS-65BN		MS-65RB
$875	$1,750		$2,750

1843, Obverse of 1842, Reverse of 1844 • N-4. *Estimated population:* More than 3,500.

1843, Obverse of 1842 and Reverse of 1844 (N-4). Petite Head. Large Letters.

Notes: This variety exists in Mint State.

1843, Obverse of 1842, Reverse of 1844	Cert	Avg	%MS
	53	53.2	47%

EF-40	AU-50	MS-60BN	MS-63BN
$210	$320	$825	$1,500

MS-63RB	MS-65BN	MS-65RB
$1,850	$2,300	$4,000

1843, Obverse and Reverse of 1844 • N-5, N-6, N-16, and N-17. *Estimated population:* More than 12,000.

1843, Obverse and Reverse of 1844 (N-6). Mature Head. Large Letters. This is the style used for the rest of the series.

Notes: This variety exists in Mint State.

Typical values for 1843, Obverse and Reverse of 1844. Rare varieties may be worth more.

1843, Obverse and Reverse of 1844	Cert	Avg	%MS
	43	48.2	42%

EF-40	AU-50	MS-60BN	MS-63BN
$150	$275	$550	$900

MS-63RB	MS-65BN	MS-65RB
$1,500	$2,100	$3,500

1843, Proof	Cert	Avg	%MS
	9	64.4	

PF-60	PF-63BN	PF-63RB	PF-65BN
$5,075	$8,125	$14,500	$20,500

1844, Braided Hair

Mintage (per Mint Report): 2,398,752.

Cents of this year are numbered from N-1 to N-8, with N-6 and N-7 being different states of the same combination. Most numismatists, except for dedicated collectors of Newcomb varieties, seek a regular 1844 and an example of N-2, the last being a blunder. The 1844 logotype was first punched in an inverted position, heavier on one side, with the number 184 impressed into the die. It was then corrected by overpunching 1844 in the correct orientation. This variety is commonly called 1844 over 81, the *81* being the upside-down 18. This error variety is somewhat scarce in relation to 1844 cents overall.

The typical 1844, including the error die, is about as expected: there is some lightness of the stars, often from overused dies. Mint State coins can be blotchy if with partial mint color, suggesting that the best choice is a consistent brown.

Proofs: N-8 was used to strike Proofs only.

Typical values for 1844 cents.
Rare varieties may be worth more.
Some varieties are priced individually, as follows.

1844		Cert	Avg	%MS
		183	54.2	49%

VG-8	F-12	VF-20	EF-40	AU-50	MS-60BN	MS-63BN	MS-63RB	MS-65BN	MS-65RB
$40	$50	$100	$140	$255	$450	$750	$1,225	$1,750	$2,800

1844 • N-1 and N-3 to N-7. *Estimated population:* More than 45,000.

Notes: This variety exists in Mint State.

1844, Proof • N-8. *Estimated population:* 12 to 20.

1844, Proof	Cert	Avg	%MS
	7	64.4	

PF-60	PF-63BN	PF-63RB	PF-65BN
$6,000	$13,000	$20,000	$30,000

1844, 1844 Over 81 • N-2. *Estimated population:* More than 6,000.

1844, 1844 Over 81 (N-2).

Detail of overdate.

Notes: In 1883, Frank Andrews, in *An Arrangement of United States Copper Cents*, gave this: "A curved line from near right top of first 4, defects, or outlines also seen at top of 8 and final 4." This variety occurs in Mint State.

1844, 1844 Over 81		Cert	Avg	%MS
		31	47.5	32%

VG-8	F-12	VF-20	EF-40	AU-50
$65	$100	$200	$325	$650

MS-60BN	MS-63BN	MS-63RB	MS-65BN
$1,350	$2,750	$4,000	$5,500

1845, Braided Hair
Mintage (per Mint Report*): 3,894,804.*

Similar to those of 1841, the cents of 1845 are all similar at first glance, with no die blunders or specific varieties that attract interest other than by specialists. There are 11 die combinations listed by J.R. (Bob) Grellman Jr., being N-1 to N-15, with some former stand-alone Newcomb numbers now realized as die states of other numbers within that series.

The quality is about the same as other cents of this era: often with flat star centers and lightness elsewhere or from dies that were used beyond retirement age. Mint State coins are usually brown or brown with a tinge of mint color (often not well blended). Most "brilliant" coins which appear for this year through 1849 are only brilliant by virtue of dipping. There are many cherrypicking opportunities.

Proofs: N-14 was only coined in Proof format. This is the only unquestioned Proof variety.[104]

Typical values for 1845 cents.
Rare varieties may be worth more.

1845		Cert	Avg	%MS
		303	56.0	61%

EF-40	AU-50	MS-60BN	MS-63BN	MS-63RB	MS-65BN	MS-65RB
$75	$135	$225	$375	$800	$1,200	$2,500

1845 • N-1 to N-13, N-15. *Estimated population:* More than 90,000.

Notes: This variety exists in Mint State.

1845 (N-11).

1845, Proof • N-14. *Estimated population:* 12 to 15.

1845, Proof		Cert	Avg	%MS
		5	63.8	

PF-60	PF-63BN	PF-63RB	PF-65BN
$4,250	$8,000	$15,000	$23,000

1846, Braided Hair
Mintage (per Mint Report*): 4,120,800.*

The 1846 cents can be divided into Small Date, Medium Date, and Tall Date varieties. A summary of the sizes:

1846, Small Date: N-1 to N-10, N-15, and N-18 to N-22. These comprise 14 different obverse dies, as two inadvertent double listings occur.

Detail of 1846, Small Date (N-3). Deep impression of the four-digit logotype. The thick or lumpy 1 has a thick lower-left serif and a thin lower-right serif; the lower-right outside curve of 8 is cut off; 4 is misshapen with the left point cut off, the serif at right irregular, and the lower-left serif too small; 6 with area of left side of the digit flat. The 1 in the date is only lumpy on deep impressions of the logotype. On deep impressions the upper part of the 6 is closer to the top curve of the lower part of the digit.

Detail of 1846, Small Date, Proof (N-22), with digits more lightly impressed into the die, plus some reduction of the size of the numerals due to polishing to create a Proof surface. Accordingly, the digits appear slightly smaller and more widely spaced.

Detail of 1846, Small Date (N-4). Logotype as preceding, but here with all four digits double punched.

1846, Medium Date: N-11, the only variety.

Detail of 1846, Medium Date (N-11). Base of 1 high, base of 6 low, 4 somewhat misshapen.

1846, Tall Date: N-12, N-13 (same dies as N-23 and N-26 in different states), N-14, and N-16. Four different obverse dies.

Detail of 1846, Tall Date (N-12).

Of the preceding, the Small Date is most often seen in the marketplace, with the Tall Date being quite a bit scarcer, and the Medium Date being scarcest of all. However, on an absolute basis at least several thousand Medium-Date cents exist, so they are readily collectible, though at a premium in comparison to the others.

The same careless striking and use of dies until they wore out yields another year for which cherrypicking can pay great dividends. Obtaining one of each of the three date styles can be done as quickly as a wink, including in Mint State, if you do not care about sharpness of strike and freshness of dies. If you do, set aside several *months*—or perhaps longer!—to complete the trio. Mint State coins are typically brown or brown with some traces of red. Very few have full original mint color.

Proofs: N-22 (Small Date) and N-24 (Tall Date) are known only in Proof format, with no related circulation strikes.[105] A few examples of N-1 (Small Date) are also considered to be Proof, but this variety is usually seen as a circulation strike.[106]

1846, Small Date • N-1 to N-10, N-15, and N-18 to N-22. *Estimated population:* More than 70,000.

1846, Small Date, Proof (N-22).

Notes: This variety is known in Mint State.

Typical values for 1846, Small Date. Rare varieties may be worth more.

1846, Small Date			Cert	Avg	%MS
			254	55.3	62%

EF-40	AU-50	MS-60BN	MS-63BN
$75	$135	$225	$350

MS-63RB	MS-65BN		MS-65RB
$750	$1,200		$2,000

1846, Medium Date • N-11. *Estimated population:* More than 4,000.

Notes: This is the key to the date-size series this year. Known in Mint State.

1846, Medium Date			Cert	Avg	%MS
			31	57.6	71%

EF-40	AU-50	MS-60BN	MS-63BN
$90	$175	$275	$450

MS-63RB	MS-65BN	MS-65RB
$950	$1,425	$2,850

1846, Tall Date • N-12 to N-14 and N-16. *Estimated population:* More than 15,000.

Notes: This variety is known in Mint State.

Typical values for 1846, Tall Date. Rare varieties may be worth more.

1846, Tall Date		Cert	Avg	%MS
		50	49.7	46%

VG-8	F-12	VF-20	EF-40	AU-50
$50	$60	$100	$200	$360

MS-60BN	MS-63BN	MS-63RB	MS-65BN	MS-65RB
$750	$1,225	$1,700	$2,150	$4,250

1846, Proof • *Estimated population:* 15 to 20.

1846, Proof		Cert	Avg	%MS
		2	66.0	

PF-60	PF-63BN	PF-63RB	PF-65BN
$4,250	$8,250	$15,500	$24,000

1847, Braided Hair
Mintage (per Mint Report): 6,183,669.

Cents of 1847 follow suit with those of 1846 in that, under careful study, the appearance of the date digits can be very curious. In several instances a smaller 7 is seen protruding from under the large or final 7, and sometimes traces of other digits are seen as well.

All 1847 cents are of the same "Large Date" size. Varieties are numbered N-1 to N-43, but—allowing for several delistings and several combinations of die states—the ultimate number of die pairs, as listed in the Grellman text, is 31. In addition to the curious "Large Over Small 7" varieties, there are other repunchings not listed here.

Dies with Large 7 over Small 7, sometimes showing other digits as well, include:

N-1: N-1 shows the entire date repunched, with evidence of earlier figures at the bottom.

Detail of 1847 (N-1).

N-2 (and 31, the same in a later state) and N-18: Top of small 7 protrudes above top of final 7. These are two different dies, each with the small 7 in a slightly different position. The N-18 also has

Detail of 1847, Large 7 With Small 7 Above (N-2).

clear repunching at the top of the 8 and is the rarer of the two varieties.

N-3 (and N-33, same dies): Upper-left part of small 7 in front of upper left of final 7. Delicate traces of other numerals are seen as well.

Detail of 1847, Large 7 With Small 7 to Left (N-3).

For nearly all of the 1847 varieties, cherrypicking will pay rich dividends, as many coins have weak stars and other areas, or they are from dies that were kept in the press too long.

Proofs: N-42 was struck only in Proof format and is the only unquestioned Proof of this year. Other supposed "Proofs," including varieties listed in the Breen text and some by Newcomb, are merely prooflike circulation strikes.[107]

Typical values for 1847 cents.
Rare varieties may be worth more.
Some varieties are priced individually, as follows.

1847	Cert	Avg	%MS
	673	57.5	65%

EF-40	AU-50	MS-60BN	MS-63BN	MS-63RB	MS-65BN	MS-65RB
$75	$135	$225	$350	$600	$950	$1,900

1847 • N-1 to N-43, except the following. *Estimated total population:* More than 120,000.

Notes: This variety is known in Mint State.

1847, Large 7 With Small 7 Above • N-2 (N-31) and N-18. *Estimated population:* More than 9,000 as a group.

1847, Large 7 With Small 7 Above (N-2).

Notes: This variety exists in Mint State.

Typical values for 1847, Large 7 With Small 7 Above. N-18 is worth more.

1847, Large 7 with Small 7 Above	Cert	Avg	%MS
	30	53.8	50%

VG-8	F-12	VF-20
$75	$100	$200

EF-40	AU-50	MS-60BN
$400	$750	$1,000

1847, Large 7 With Small 7 to Left • N-3 (N-33). *Estimated population:* More than 3,000.

1847, Large 7 With Small 7 to Left (N-3).

Notes: This variety is known in Mint State.

Typical values for 1847, Large 7 With Small 7 to Left.

1847, Large 7 with Small 7 to Left	Cert	Avg	%MS
	(a)		

VG-8	F-12	VF-20	EF-40
$50	$75	$100	$200

AU-50	MS-60BN	MS-63BN	MS-63RB
$400	$600	$750	$1,000

a. Included in certified population for 1847, Large 7 with Small 7 Above.

1847, Proof • N-42. *Estimated population:* 12 to 15.

1847, Proof	Cert	Avg	%MS
	1	64.0	

PF-60	PF-63BN	PF-63RB	PF-65BN
$4,250	$8,000	$15,000	$23,000

1848, Braided Hair
Mintage (per Mint Report): 6,415,799.

There are 32 different die combinations this year, intermittently numbered from N-1 to N-46. Beyond these 32, there are different die states of the same pair, which were given different numbers, and two varieties which have been delisted. The date numerals seem to be from a single four-digit logotype, but spacing can vary depending upon the depth of the punch into the die and the polishing or lapping done to the completed die.

The same suggestions apply as for earlier years: cherrypicking can pay great dividends as there is a wide variation in sharpness and quality among coins in the marketplace.

For the really dedicated specialist there is a monograph on this particular date, *Major Die States of 1848 Large Cents,* by Daniel Argyro (1995). Using the standard line drawing from the Newcomb 1944 book he added lines and indications to point out die cracks, die lines, and date alignments.

The 1848, Small Date, is a contemporary *counterfeit* made in large quantities. Examples are highly prized today.

Proofs: N-19 is found only in Proof format, the only unquestioned Proof die combination of this year.

Typical values for 1848 cents.
Rare varieties may be worth more.

1848	Cert	Avg	%MS
	714	56.3	59%

EF-40	AU-50	MS-60BN	MS-63BN	MS-63RB	MS-65BN	MS-65RB
$75	$130	$225	$350	$600	$925	$1,850

1848 • N-1 to N-18 and N-20 to N-46. *Estimated population:* More than 140,000.

Notes: This variety is known in Mint State.

1848, Proof • N-19. *Estimated population:* 20 to 30.

1848, Proof	Cert	Avg	%MS
	10	64.7	

PF-60	PF-63BN	PF-63RB	PF-65BN
$5,000	$9,500	$15,000	$23,000

1848, Proof (N-19).

1848, Braided Hair, Small Date (Counterfeit)

The 1848, Small Date, cent, a contemporary counterfeit, has attracted the interest of numismatists for a long time, especially after its listing by Wayte Raymond in the *Standard Catalogue of United States Coins*. Examples are struck from dies that imitated the federal design. Production must have been from somewhat crude facilities, for double and slightly off-center striking is typical.

Various Mint correspondence addresses counterfeit copper cents, though mostly in connection with giving this designation to what we know today as Hard Times tokens. In 1849 an investigator, F.C. Treadwell, was put on the trail of the flood of counterfeit 1848 cents. He enlisted the help of James Paar, of 77 Mott Street, who turned in this report to Treadwell:

New York, November 12, 1849

Dear Sir:

Yours came duly to hand and I have taken some pains and believe I have succeeded in finding the location of our New York Mints. I am certain that large quantities of cents are made here and put into circulation. We have now hundreds of thousands of dollars [worth of cents] and the stock daily increasing. The cent makers are in companies . . . who get them into circulation amongst their brethren, the pawnbrokers. Some of these pawnbrokers use from $200 to $500 worth of cents weekly and pay them out at 96 to the dollar to people who are necessitated to come within their grasp. . . .

About a month since a man hired a room in the Congress Mills, 172 Forsythe street, from John Coull, for the purposes, as he stated, to manufacture cents for the Mint. Instead of commencing to manufacture, he brought in about 30 kegs of planchets which he said that the Mint had refused to stamp on account of their being tarnished. He brightened them up by a chemical process which took him nearly a month to do and when finished put them up into kegs again and sent them out to one of our Mints. This was last week. I have no doubt but that they are in the act of being stamped at this time. Mr. Coull had the curiosity to follow them to the supposed Mint and was admitted through the front premises with the exception of one room, which was kept private. There are those other places in the same neighborhood where the business is transacted but perhaps the same commission. There are others out of this state, but not far from New York. I have the houses and locations of these manufacturers and can furnish them to any officer who may call on me if the United States Mint thinks my statements sufficient to warrant proceedings against the parties.

On Friday evening last a girl called at a grocery in the Bowery for [illegible] and paid 18 cents in new bright cents of 1849. She was asked where she got so many new pennies. She said 'I got them out of the keg.' 'Well, where did the keg come from?' 'Oh, why we make them.' 'Who makes them?' She tells the name of the parties and leaves her own name and address.

One of the parties named has been selling cents for a long time at from 2-1/2 to 15 per cent off the price (face value). I have more information but consider this enough to trouble you as the US Mint [illegible]. I have sent a few specimens. The five bright ones are what the girl paid at the grocery, which you may exhibit if you think proper.

I am, dear sir, yours,
James Paar.

At the Mint the coins were examined by chief engraver James B. Longacre and chief coiner Franklin Peale and found to be counterfeit.[108]

1848, Small Date (Counterfeit) • *Estimated population:* 12 to 15.

1848, Small Date (Counterfeit).

Notes: VF or so is the highest known grade.

1848, Small Date (Counterfeit)	Cert	Avg	%MS
	0	n/a	

VG-8	F-12	VF-20
$6,000	$7,000	$10,000

1849, Braided Hair

Mintage (per Mint Report*): 4,178,500.*

For 1849 there are 20 different die combinations recorded. These are listed from N-1 to N-30, including some that are die states of others and three that have been delisted. The 1849 date seems to have been applied with a four-digit logotype. An early state of N-8 has a line outside of the lower right of the 9 and has been called an "overdate" by some. However, this is not convincing when viewed under high magnification, and there are no specific traces of an undertype 8 in the open bottom center or the left of the 9.

Most have light striking in areas, usually most notably on the obverse stars or denticles. Quality and cherrypicking opportunities are similar to the preceding date. This is the last year in which Mint State coins are very rare with much original color. From 1850 to 1856 they are easily found.

Proofs: N-18 occurs only in Proof format. Other alleged "Proofs" are prooflike circulation strikes according to Grellman.[109] Per contra, Denis Loring considers some strikings of N-30 to be Proofs.[110]

Typical values for 1849 cents.
Rare varieties may be worth more.

1849	Cert	Avg	%MS
	417	55.8	55%

EF-40	AU-50	MS-60BN	MS-63BN	MS-63RB	MS-65BN	MS-65RB
$120	$200	$325	$525	$1,000	$1,350	$2,475

1849 • N-1 to N-17 and N-19 to N-30. *Estimated population:* More than 100,000.

1849 (N-22, late die state of N-6).

Notes: This variety is known in Mint State.

1849, Proof • N-18. *Estimated population:* 20 to 25.

1849, Proof	Cert	Avg	%MS
	3	64.3	

PF-60	PF-63BN	PF-63RB	PF-65BN
$4,250	$8,500	$16,000	$25,000

1850, Braided Hair
Mintage (per Mint Report): *4,426,844.*

Cents of 1850 comprise 20 different die combinations, given as most of the numbers in the range from N-1 to N-28. A single four-digit logotype seems to have been used. Differentiating styles of this year, the date was heavier if the logotype was punched deeply into the die, and in such instances the ball of the 5 is close to the vertical line above it. On lightly punched dies there is a significant space between the 5 and the vertical line.

As cents of this date, indeed of the decade, were in circulation for just a short time, nearly all grade Fine or higher, most VF or higher. EF and AU coins are common, as are Mint State examples. Among the last category, there are many examples from old-time hoards with extensive original color and brilliance, but coins with brown surfaces or brown with partial mint color are much more common. N-7 is the hoard variety most often seen. Striking and die quality varies, again furnishing ample opportunity for cherrypicking.

Proofs: About 10 Proofs are known of N-11, struck before the same combination was used to make circulation issues.

Typical values for 1850 cents.
Rare varieties are worth more.

1850	Cert	Avg	%MS
	934	60.4	79%

EF-40	AU-50	MS-60BN	MS-63BN	MS-63RB	MS-65BN	MS-65RB
$80	$160	$240	$290	$400	$700	$1,225

1850 • N-1 to N-28. *Estimated population:* More than 100,000.

Notes: This variety is known in Mint State.

1850 (N-15).

1851, Braided Hair
Mintage (per Mint Report): 9,889,707.

Coinage this year hit a record high, producing a mintage figure not closely approached by any other year. As a result, cents of 1851 comprise a record 42 different die combinations. These have been assigned most numbers in the range from N-1 to N-45. N-11, N-28, and N-32 have been delisted. N-42 is uncertain and is under study. A single four-digit logotype seems to have been used.

N-3 is the most important of these varieties—a blundered die, called "1851 Over 81." This blunder was caused by a logotype being first punched in an inverted position, then corrected with a regularly oriented logotype—an error related to the 1844/81 coin. The sharpness of the 1851/81—never strong to begin with—fades with die use, and later impressions hardly show the blunder. Accordingly, the only N-3 cents with a premium value are those with the error distinct. These are common on an absolute basis, but they form only a tiny fraction of the extant 1851 cents. Mint State coins with significant original color are very rare.

Detail of 1851,
1851 Over 81 (N-3).

Usual grades for an 1851 cent range from Fine or higher, and most are VF or higher. EF and AU coins are common, as are Mint State examples. Among the last category are many examples from old-time hoards with extensive original color and brilliance, although these bright examples are a small minority of the Mint-State population overall. Most are brown or brown with partial mint color. Striking and die quality varies, again furnishing ample opportunity for cherrypicking.

Proofs: None.

Typical values for 1851 cents.
Rare varieties may be worth more.
Some varieties are priced individually, as follows.

1851	Cert	Avg	%MS
	1,345	58.8	70%

EF-40	AU-50	MS-60BN	MS-63BN	MS-63RB	MS-65BN	MS-65RB
$60	$125	$180	$230	$350	$650	$1,200

1851 • N-1, N-2, and N-4 to N-45. *Estimated population:* More than 225,000.

Notes: This variety occurs in Mint State.

1851, 1851 Over 81 • N-3. *Estimated population:* Thousands exist.

1851, 1851 Over 81 (N-3).

Notes: This variety is known in Mint State.

1851, 1851 Over 81	Cert	Avg	%MS
	89	57.9	69%

F-12	VF-20	EF-40	AU-50
$100	$200	$275	$375

MS-60BN	MS-63BN	MS-63RB	MS-65BN
$750	$1,250	$1,650	$2,700

1852, Braided Hair
Mintage (per Mint Report*): 5,063,094.*

Cents of 1852 are found in 19 different die combinations, an impressive panorama. These have been assigned continuous numbers from N-1 to N-23, with N-2, N-9, N-13, and N-19 delisted. A single four-digit logotype seems to have been used.

Similar to other cents of the era, those dated 1852 were in circulation for just a short time, nearly all grade Fine or higher, most VF or higher. EF and AU coins are common, as are Mint State examples. Among the last category are many examples from old-time hoards with extensive original color and brilliance. Most of these are the N-8 variety. Among the entire population of Mint State coins, most are brown or red and brown. Once again, striking and die quality varies, furnishing ample opportunity for cherrypicking.

Proofs: A few Proofs were struck of N-24. Three examples are known today.[111]

Typical values for 1852 cents.
Rare varieties may be worth more.

1852	Cert	Avg	%MS
	1,271	60.3	75%

EF-40	AU-50	MS-60BN	MS-63BN	MS-63RB	MS-65BN	MS-65RB
$60	$125	$180	$230	$350	$635	$1,150

1852 • N-1 to N-33. *Estimated population:* More than 120,000.

Notes: This variety is known in Mint State.

1852 (N-16).

1853, Braided Hair
Mintage (per Mint Report*): 6,641,131.*

Cents of 1853 are found in 33 different die combinations, an impressive panorama. These have been assigned continuous numbers from N-1 to N-33, with no sharing of a number and no deletions. A single four-digit logotype seems to have been used.

Most are in grades of VF upward, with EF and AU examples being common. Mint State coins are plentiful as well, but, similar to other dates of the decade, are only a tiny fraction of the entire population. Many have significant red, most are brown or red and brown. The brilliant cents most often seen are those of the N-25 variety. Light strikes are common, as are impressions from tired dies. Specialists consider the striking of cents of this date to be among the poorest of the era. Again, cherrypicking will pay dividends, as certified holders make no mention of these problems.

Proofs: None.

Typical values for 1853 cents.
Rare varieties may be worth more.

1853	Cert	Avg	%MS
	2,016	60.2	75%

EF-40	AU-50	MS-60BN	MS-63BN	MS-63RB	MS-65BN	MS-65RB
$60	$125	$180	$230	$350	$635	$1,150

1853 • N-1 to N-33. *Estimated population:* More than 140,000.

1853 (N-10).

Notes: This variety occurs in Mint State.

Numismatic Notes: Hoard notes: In August 1891 this notice appeared in *The Numismatist:* "In the vaults of the Central National Bank of Lynn, Massachusetts, are a lot of 1853 cents that have remained there since they came from the Mint in that year, and are perfect and Uncirculated. Charles G. Bailey of 134 Chestnut Street, Lynn, an official of the bank, has them for disposal at reasonable prices."

In addition to the preceding, Walter Breen said quantities of Mint State examples of 1853 N-25 were from caches discovered in the 1930s, possibly from bank reserves. "There may have been a full keg or more of 1853 cents, which would mean at least a ballpark figure of about 14,000 coins." [112] The present author has found no verification of this or any other huge hoard of Mint State large cents being discovered in the early 1930s, but they may have been. It is said that dealer Elmer Sears found 1,000 or so Mint State coins. In any event, it is highly unlikely that any quantity even remotely reaching 14,000 Mint State coins exists. Breen "facts" are sometimes questionable.

1854, Braided Hair

Mintage (per Mint Report): 4,236,156.

For 1854 there are 29 die combinations, numbered from N-1 to N-30, with N-15 delisted. There are logotype and punch variations.

Quality varies, as expected, for less care was spent on coining cents than for any other denomination. As with other cents of the era, this circumstance pays nice dividends for cherrypickers. The typical grade is VF upward, with EF and AU being common. Most Mint State coins are red or red and brown, but brilliant examples are often met with.

Proofs: Beginning with this year, Proofs were made in more significant quantities, perhaps a couple dozen all told. These are of the N-12 variety, a combination also used to make circulation strikes. "There is very little difference between the final Proofs struck and the first circulation strikes from these dies."[113]

Typical values for 1854 cents.
Rare varieties may be worth more.

1854	Cert	Avg	%MS
	1,072	58.9	67%

EF-40	AU-50	MS-60BN	MS-63BN	MS-63RB	MS-65BN	MS-65RB
$60	$125	$180	$230	$350	$650	$1,200

1854 • N-1 to N-30. *Estimated population:* More than 100,000.

Notes: This variety exists in Mint State.

1854 (N-25).

1854, Proofs • N-12. *Estimated population:* 20 to 25.

1854, Proof	Cert	Avg	%MS
	5	64.6	

PF-60	PF-63BN	PF-63RB	PF-65BN
$4,750	$8,500	$10,000	$14,000

1855, Braided Hair
Mintage (per Mint Report*): 1,574,829.*

The mintage dropped sharply this year, probably due to the rising cost of copper. Patterns of lighter weight and smaller diameter were made, continuing a program launched in 1850. Cents (and half cents) were a profit center at the Mint, and profits were being diminished.

Cents of 1855 were made in two main styles:

Upright 55 in Date: N-1 to N-8, and N-12. N-13 has been assigned, but is a different die state of N-5. The net is 10 different die combinations.

Detail of 1855, Upright 55 (N-4).

Slanting (Italic) 55 in Date: N-9 to N-11, or three die combinations. Later states of N-9 are of the famous *Knob on Ear* variety. The die deteriorated at the center and pieces fell out, causing a prominent lump on the coins. These command a premium and are listed separately here and in various popular guides. N-11 was made only in Proof format.

Detail of 1855, Slanting 55 (N-9).

Detail of 1855, Slanting 55, Knob on Ear (N-9 in a later state).

Both of these styles are very common (N-9 and N-10 are each common in their own right), but there are more of the Upright 55. Typical grades are VF upward. High-level examples are plentiful. The 1855 N-4 with Upright 55 is easy to find with nearly full mint red, and N-5 is seen in this condition with some frequency as well. Otherwise, most Mint State coins are brown or brown with traces of red. As there is no hoard variety among the Slanting 55 coins, these are much harder to find with full original color.

Proofs: Proofs are of the N-10 and N-11 (Slanting 5's) varieties. N-11 was made only in Proof format.

1855, Upright 55 • N-1 to N-8 and N-12. *Estimated population:* More than 30,000.

1855, Upright 55 (N-4).

Notes: This variety exists in Mint State.

Typical values for 1855, Upright 55. Rare varieties may be worth more.

1855, Upright 55		Cert	Avg	%MS
		335	58.8	65%

EF-40	AU-50	MS-60BN	MS-63BN
$60	$125	$180	$230

MS-63RB	MS-65BN	MS-65RB
$350	$635	$1,150

1855, Slanting 55 • N-9 to N-11. *Estimated population:* More than 7,000.

1855, Slanting 55 (N-10).

Notes: This variety exists in Mint State.

Typical values for 1855, Slanting 55. Rare varieties may be worth more.

1855, Slanting 55		Cert	Avg	%MS
		88	59.0	61%

EF-40	AU-50	MS-60BN	MS-63BN
$65	$130	$200	$275

MS-63RB	MS-65BN	MS-65RB
$650	$1,250	$2,000

1855, Slanting 55, Proof • N-10 and N-11. *Estimated population:* 50 to 65.

Notes: Examples are about equally divided between N-10 and N-11.

1855, Slanting 55, Proof		Cert	Avg	%MS
		10	64.5	

PF-60	PF-63BN	PF-63RB	PF-65BN
$4,500	$6,000	$8,750	$12,000

1855, Slanting 55, Knob on Ear • N-9. *Estimated population:* Several thousand.

Notes: This variety is known in Mint State.

The knob must be prominent to merit these prices. Otherwise, regular 1855, Slanting 55, values apply.

1855, Slanting 55, Knob on Ear		Cert	Avg	%MS
		128	56.7	50%

VF-20	EF-40	AU-50	MS-60BN
$150	$180	$310	$455

MS-63BN	MS-63RB	MS-65BN
$760	$1,375	$2,325

1856, Braided Hair

Mintage (per Mint Report*): 2,690,463.*

The mintage was modest this year, again in view of the high prevailing copper prices. Cents of 1856 are usually collected by the two major styles, Upright 5 and Slanting or Italic 5:

1856, Upright 5: N-6 to N-12, or seven die combinations. N-20 is of this style, but is a state of N-8.

Detail of 1856, Upright 5 (N-8).

1856, Slanting *or* Italic 5: N-1 to N-5, N-13, N-14, N-16 to N-19, N-21, and N-22, or 15 die combinations. Examples of N-14 are said to exist in large quantities from bank hoards of the 1930s, per Breen's 1988 *Encyclopedia*, but such coins are not common today.

Detail of 1856, Slanting 5 (N-21).

Both styles are very common in all grades from VF or so to Mint State. Most Mint State coins are brown or brown with some original color. Full original color coins are scarcer than for the immediately preceding years. The striking is usually quite good *except* for the star centers. Coins with sharp stars are in the minority. Cherrypicking will pay dividends, but not as richly as for earlier years.

Proofs: N-5 (Slanting 5) was struck in Proof format only. Likely, more than 100 were made.

1856, Upright 5 • N-6 to N-12. *Estimated population:* More than 20,000.

1856, Upright 5 (N-8).

Notes: This variety occurs in Mint State.

Typical values for 1856, Upright 5. Rare varieties may be worth more.

1856, Upright 5		Cert	Avg	%MS
		220	59.2	64%

EF-40	AU-50	MS-60BN	MS-63BN
$65	$130	$200	$270

MS-63RB	MS-65BN		MS-65RB
$365	$675		$1,200

1856, Slanting 5 • N-1 to N-5, N-13, N-14, N-16 to N-19, N-21, and N-22.
Estimated population: More than 45,000.

1856, Slanting 5 (N-21).

Notes: This variety occurs in Mint State.

Typical values for 1856, Slanting 5. Rare varieties may be worth more.

1856, Slanting 5		Cert	Avg	%MS
		333	57.7	62%

EF-40	AU-50	MS-60BN	MS-63BN
$65	$130	$200	$270

MS-63RB	MS-65BN		MS-65RB
$365	$675		$1,200

1856, Slanting 5, Proof • N-5. *Estimated population:* 65 to 80.

1856, Slanting 5, Proof	Cert	Avg	%MS
	21	64.8	

PF-60	PF-63BN	PF-63RB	PF-65BN
$4,000	$5,000	$7,000	$12,500

1857, Braided Hair
Mintage (per Mint Report): 333,456.

The last year of issue, 1857, is an interesting study in itself. Struck only in January of that year, and to the extent of 333,456 pieces, the 1857 cent comes in Large Date and Small Date varieties, and is scarcer than even the low mintage figure would indicate. Many, probably most, were held back at the mint and melted. It is unlikely that even half the mintage was released. Craig Sholley suggests that the Mint released 140,000 cents.[114] However, the Mint supplied anyone who asked for cents of this date, as part of the above 140,000. Assuming that perhaps 10,000 to 20,000 exist today—strictly a guess—many of these probably were acquired by curio dealers and others at the time to be sold to collectors.

Interestingly, the 1857 cent is hardly ever seen with much original mint brilliance. The typical Mint State coin is apt to be lustrous brown or brown with some minor evidences of lighter color. A coin with *original* surfaces and full color would be a rarity. Most such pieces have been dipped.

There is just one die combination of the Large Date, N-1, but it is common enough that examples can be easily found. It is much more often seen than the Small Date.

The Small Date is found in four combinations, these being N-3 and N-5, used only for Proofs, and N-2 and N-4, used for circulation strikes. As a class, the Small Dates are common, but N-2 is less often seen than N-4. As these coins circulated for only a short time, typical grades are EF upward. The date is common, and there are enough to supply numismatic needs, but they are not often seen in comparison to earlier dates of the decade. Flat stars are the rule. Otherwise, the eye appeal of an 1857 cent is usually quite good.

Proofs: Proofs were made of N-3 and N-5, both of the Small Date variety. These die pairs were only used to make Proofs. Likely the mintage close to 200 to 300. This is the most readily available Proof large cent as a *date*, but as a *variety* the 1856, Slanting 5 (N-5), is most often seen.

1857, Large Date • N-1. *Estimated population:* 7,000 to 14,000.

1857, Large Date (N-1). An exceptional example with full, original color. Most of this variety and date are brown, or brown with slight tinges of mint color.

Notes: This variety is known in Mint State.

1857, Large Date	Cert	Avg	%MS
	572	58.2	63%

EF-40	AU-50	MS-60BN	MS-63BN
$250	$375	$500	$825

MS-63RB	MS-65BN		MS-65RB
$1,000	$1,350		$2,225

1857, Small Date • N-2 and N-4. *Estimated population:* 3,000 to 6,000.

1857, Small Date (N-4). An exceptional example with full original color.

Notes: This variety is known in Mint State. Typical values for 1857, Small Date.

1857, Small Date		Cert	Avg	%MS
		205	56.1	48%

EF-40	AU-50	MS-60BN	MS-63BN
$250	$380	$515	$850

MS-63RB	MS-65BN	MS-65RB
$1,050	$1,625	$2,450

1857, Small Date, Proof • N-3 and N-5. *Estimated population:* 100 to 125.

Notes: N-3 is slightly more available than is N-5.

1857, Small Date, Proof	Cert	Avg	%MS
	8	65.1	100%

PF-60	PF-63BN	PF-63RB	PF-65BN
$4,750	$5,500	$8,000	$13,000

1868, Braided Hair
Proof mintage (estimate): 12 to 15.

In 1868—by which time the Mint had been creating rare patterns, restrikes, and other issues, secretly filtering them into the numismatic market—a large copper cent was created of the exact Braided Hair type, last regularly issued in 1857. At the time, the same obverse was paired with a new reverse of the three-cent denomination (not relevant to the listing here).

The 1868 large cent is similar on both sides to the 1843 to 1857 Mature Head type. The number struck was not recorded, nor was any information entered into Mint records. Today, it is estimated that 12 to 15 were struck in copper, plus some in copper-nickel (not relevant to the copper version discussed here). *United States Patterns* lists this as Judd-611, although it is not really a pattern.

Today the 1868 large copper cent is a member of that small but highly publicized (except for this cent) and extremely expensive class of "numismatic delicacies" struck after their regular series had ended, with examples having been distributed privately. Others include the 1913, Liberty Head, nickel; the 1804 silver dollar; the 1884 trade dollar; and the 1885 trade dollar.

Most examples of the 1868 large cent are attractive and with brown surfaces.

1868, Proof	Cert	Avg	%MS
	0	n/a	

PF-60	PF-63BN	PF-63RB	PF-65BN	PF-65RB
$11,250	$14,750	$15,980	$18,440	$20,000

1868, Proof • *Estimated population:* 15 to 18.

1868 large cent in copper, the 1843 to 1857 design, a special rarity created for the numismatic market after the Braided Hair design had been discontinued.

Notes: Proof-65 and 66 are the highest grades known. Nearly all are "nice" Proofs, though one lightly circulated example exists.[115]

NOTES

INTRODUCTION

1. Reminiscences of "Coin Crank," not otherwise identified, in *The Numismatist*, April 1894. Possibly a clue: Samuel Abbott Green, mentioned in chapter 4, began his interest circa 1846 (Green died in 1919).

2. Ownership interests in the past have included Empire Coin Company; Bowers and Ruddy Galleries; Bowers and Merena Galleries; now owned by others; and the present Stack's Bowers.

CHAPTER 1

1. Certain sections of this and the next chapter are adapted from the author's other texts including *The History of United States Coinage*, the 1982 catalog of the John W. Adams Collection, *American Numismatics Before the Civil War*, and *The Rare Silver Dollars Dated 1804*, among others.

2. Frank H. Stewart, *History of the First United States Mint*, 1924, pp. 7–8.

3. R.W. Julian, personal communication to the author, February 25, 2009.

4. R.W. Julian, "The Digges Letters," *Seaby's Coin and Medal Bulletin*, October–November 1962; other sources. Digges had seen a "Birmingham production, one of the American cents, the intended coin of America and the 100th part of a dollar," these were further explained as being 1791 cents of the type earlier sent by Obadiah Westwood, another coiner, to members of Congress in hopes of obtaining an order. These conform to Robert Morris's suggestion of December 31, 1791, that coins bear the president's portrait, but not to the Mint Act of April 2, 1792, which specifies otherwise.

5. George Washington, "Third Annual Message," October 25, 1791.

6. *Debates and Proceedings in the Congress of the United States*, 1st Sess., 2nd Congress, pp. 484 ff; *Journal of the House of Representatives of the United States*, 1789–1793, Washington, 1826, 1st Sess., 2nd Congress, pp. 547 ff. Citation provided by Richard K. MacMaster from Michael Sletcher, Internet commentary, April 30, 2009.

7. R.W. Julian, personal communication to the author, February 25, 2009.

8. This attribution to Eckfeldt was probably one of many historical embellishments. Old-timer Eckfeldt was well liked when he worked at the Mint, and afterward he often visited the Mint Cabinet and talked with collectors. Spokesmen for the Mint, most of whom knew little about the early days of the institution, turned Eckfeldt into the hero of the early Mint, giving rise to many legends that were perpetuated in later years (personal communication to the author from Craig Sholley, February 15, 2009).

    The attribution of engraving work to Robert Birch is due to an error made in James Ross Snowden's 1860 work, *A Description of Ancient and Modern Coins in the Cabinet of the Mint of the United States*, copied by *Historical Magazine*. His researcher found mention of a "Bob Birch" in the 1793 accounts, but these payments were for medicine and other work unrelated to dies. The late Carl W.A. Carlson believed that William Russell Birch, an English line engraver who moved to America about this time, was responsible for the Birch cents (R.W. Julian, personal communication to the author, February 25, 2009).

    Today, Jayne Street is known as Ranstead and lies just south of Market Street, close to the location of the first Mint (Leonard Augsburger, personal communication to the author, March 12, 2009).

9. *American Journal of Numismatics*, October 1875; 1792 date of an unattributed newspaper clipping from the scrapbook of J.J. Mickley.

10. In various correspondences his surname was spelled "Drost." There is no reason to believe

that the dies were made by Droz in Europe and shipped to America, although this possibility has been raised over the years.

11. R.W. Julian, "The Mint in 1792," *Numismatic Scrapbook Magazine*, April 1962.

12. Thomas Jefferson's Memorandum Book for 1792; Joel J. Orosz, personal communication to the author, July 27, 2004.

13. Frank H. Stewart, *History of the First United States Mint*, pp. 147, 157, here edited. Note that Thomas Flude, discussed later, appears as "Flute" in this and some other accounts. Flude is probably the correct spelling; Voigt's handwriting in his journal is not always clear. Washington's presence at the foundation laying seems to be from oral tradition in the Kates family, who purchased the old Mint property in 1836 (per a letter from J. Lewis Kates to Frank H. Stewart, April 19, 1915, quoted in Stewart's *History*).

14. James Ross Snowden, *A Description of Ancient and Modern Coins in the Cabinet of the Mint of the United States*, 1860, p. 99, mentions that *three* presses had been imported and were being set up. "These three presses were put into operation in the beginning of October, and were used for striking the half dimes," the account continues. The information was incorrect. No presses were imported; there is no confirmation that three were on hand; and in any event the half dismes had been struck in July before the Mint was built.

15. Frank H. Stewart, *History of the First United States Mint*, p. 202.

16. *Ibid.*, p. 70.

17. *Ibid.*, p. 175. On June 1, 1786, primarily through the efforts of Ogden, the Council and General Assembly of New Jersey granted a coining privilege to a group of entrepreneurs composed of Walter Mould, Thomas Goadsby, and Albion Cox. Goadsby was a businessman and investor, and Cox, later employed as assayer by the Philadelphia Mint, was a skilled silversmith and assayer. Ogden was involved in coinage and the use of this press later at his home in Elizabethtown. Ogden, who had served with distinction in the Revolution, was a stage-line owner who had a contract for delivering mail between New York City and Philadelphia. It was specified that 3,000,000 copper coins be produced, each weighing 150 grains of pure copper. Inscriptions were to be provided by the justices of the State Supreme Court. These were to be valued in commerce at the rate of 15 to a New Jersey shilling. The coiners were to pay to the state on a quarterly basis a royalty of 10 percent of the face value of the coins struck. The contract was to be in effect for two years.

18. Letter from Mint treasurer Benjamin Rush to Dr. Hutchinson, the port physician, August 1793, as cited by Warren A. Lapp, "The Yellow Fever Epidemics in Philadelphia and Their Effect on the First U.S. Mint," *The Numismatist*, April 1971.

19. Bill Eckberg, personal communication to the author, March 3, 2009; other sources.

20. R.W. Julian, personal communication to the author, February 25, 2009.

21. Frank H. Stewart, *History of the First United States Mint*, p. 105.

22. Extensive details can be found in "The Yellow Fever Epidemics in Philadelphia and Their Effect on the First U.S. Mint," by Warren A. Lapp, in *The Numismatist*, April 1971, the source of certain information given here.

23. Frank H. Stewart, *History of the First United States Mint*, p. 87, states that on November 23, Jefferson wrote to Scot enclosing the commission as a Mint engraver, which had been signed by Washington on November 20.

24. Edited and excerpted from a contribution to the September 1943 issue of *The Numismatist* by Damon G. Douglas, who was active in research concerning the copper coinage of the 1780s.

25. Although dies dated 1794 were cut for silver half dimes, they were not used until 1795. Dimes and quarters were first made in 1796. Half eagles ($5) delivered in July 1795 were the first gold coins, soon followed by eagles. Quarter eagles made their appearance in 1796. It was not until decades later that other gold denominations were made: the $1 in 1849, $20 in 1850, and $3 in 1854.

26. "The First Assayer of the United States Mint," *American Journal of Numismatics*, April 1882. Much has been written about Cox, including in the *Colonial Newsletter*, most of which is beyond the scope of the present text. Michael Hodder has done extensive research on his life.

27. Frank H. Stewart, *History of the First United States Mint*, p. 125: on January 7, 1793, Henry Voigt paid $3 for a watchdog, which was a "savage brute named Nero."

28. As cited by R.W. Julian in "The Mint Investigation of 1795," *Numismatic Scrapbook Magazine*, July 1961.

29. Frank H. Stewart, *History of the First United States Mint*, p. 60, states that the resignation was submitted because the director did not like all of the criticism being directed toward the very existence of the Mint. R.W. Julian (letter to the author, March 29, 2000) suggests that DeSaussure did not like the climate in Philadelphia and left for that reason.

30. Citation from Craig Sholley, manuscript for "Adam Eckfeldt, Mint Engraver?" refuting multiple published statements, including those by Walter Breen and Don Taxay, that Eckfeldt engraved dies for coinage in 1792. RG104, *Records of the U.S. Mint at Philadelphia*, Entry 3– Letters Sent.

31. Frank H. Stewart, *History of the First United States Mint*, p. 104.

32. Stewart in his *History of the First United States Mint* devotes many pages to the Rush-Boudinot feud.

33. R.W. Julian, personal communication to the author, February 25, 2009.

34. From Mint records per R.W. Julian, personal communication to the author, March 9, 2009. These seem to have been shipped from the Mint in the quantity of 3,530 on April 16 and 8,640 on May 13, 1799, per an adaptation of the information by Ron Manley, "Original Mintages of 1797 and 1800 Half Cents," *Penny-Wise*, July 15, 2000.

35. Sources include Don Taxay, *U.S. Mint and Coinage*, and Frank H. Stewart, *History of the First United States Mint*.

36. Frank H. Stewart, *History of the First United States Mint*, p. 52.

37. Unrelated to this action, at the time in England it was often the practice to kidnap drunks in pubs and take them to a waiting ship that needed crew members. The term *shanghai* is derived from the same action in China.

38. Harry E. Salyards pointed out (personal communication to the author, March 11, 2009) that Seybert had been reading his Annual Reports very carefully, for the figures comprise these: 1,458,500 cents in 1810, plus 218,025 cents in 1811, plus 1,075,500 cents in 1812, plus 418,000 cents in 1813, equals 3,170,025 coins, or $31,700.25 in value, plus 215,000 half cents in 1810 and 63,140 half cents in 1811 equals 278,140 coins, or $1,390.70 in value. $31,700.25 + $1,390.70 = $33,090 (and 95 cents!).

39. Citation furnished by Craig Sholley.

40. R.W. Julian, "The Philadelphia Mint and Coinage of 1814–1816," *American Numismatic Association Centennial Anthology*, 1991.

41. Sources are many, including secretary of the Treasury William H. Crawford's report to the House of Representatives, February 24, 1820.

42. Such things are interesting to contemplate numismatically. Copper cents were indeed struck in 1815, but no 1815-*dated* cents were made. Half dollars were indeed struck in 1816, but no 1816-*dated* half dollars were made. Many other examples could be cited, including the earlier-mentioned "1799" half cents.

43. By year's end the mintage total for 1816 cents was 2,820,982, equal to slightly more than $28,000—this being far less than the "nearly 47,000 dollars" projected.

44. Frank H. Stewart, *History of the First United States Mint*, p. 133.

45. From the firm of Belles & Harrold.

46. Frank H. Stewart, *History of the First United States Mint*, p. 186.

47. Craig Sholley, personal communication to the author, March 8, 2009.

48. From Mint records. R.W. Julian, personal communication to the author, March 9, 2009.

49. Many accounts were carried in *Niles' Weekly Register*, such as this on May 2, 1818: "Specie. We have the pleasure to notice the arrival of several handsome lots of specie—hoping that some of the banks, which do not pay their debts, will purchase it and do justice to their creditors. Several sums have been received in gold within the past week, as well as 450,000 crowns and 55,000 dollars, in silver, from France; 400,000 dollars from England, and 50,000 from Antigua. The three last arrived in New York in one day."

50. The study of economics was in its infancy in America at the time. A later generation of scholars, not perusing contemporary newspapers and bank records, generally overlooked this depression, which was severe in its time. The first widely studied depression is that which commenced in 1837.

51. *Niles' Weekly Register*, April 15, 1820; Treasury Report dated January 1, 1820, for year 1819; similarly, *Annual Report* for 1819, dated April 10, 1820.

52. *Niles' Weekly Register*, January 6, 1819.

53. Statement issued by the Mint, "Small Change," printed in *Niles' Weekly Register*, June 17, 1820.

54. Citation by Bill Eckberg, March 3, 2009, from George G. Evans's Mint history.

55. Per the research of John Kleeberg, "Washington Counterstamps," presented at the Coinages of the Americas Conference, American Numismatic Society, December 4, 1999. Earlier the dies had been widely attributed to Charles Cushing Wright, including, at one time, by the author.

56. This figure, equal to 2,580 per hour, seems to be too high. In 1800 Director Boudinot said a hand press could turn out about 14,000 coins in a 10-hour day. Of course, there would have been some down time during the day.

57. In *The Granite Monthly*, November 1881, Hon. George Stark contributed an account from the 1828 journal of one of his forebears.

58. Document No. 51, 20th Congress, 2nd Session, House of Representatives. To accompany a bill HR 356 dated January 25, 1829, Mint of the United States.

CHAPTER 2

1. In the 1830s Strickland also designed the Charlotte (North Carolina) Mint building.

2. *Niles' Weekly Register* on August 8, 1829, told more: "We have seen a specimen of the half dime lately issued by the mint, and must pronounce it one of the most beautiful coins our country has produced." Years later, in May 1903, The Numismatist reported that the cornerstone of the second Mint had been found and opened. The stone block, weighing about 300 pounds, concealed what was described as an old-fashioned candy jar, inside of which were found three coins and two newspapers. Descriptions of two of the three coins were left to the imagination, but one was a dime of 1829. The newspapers were Philadelphia periodicals printed on July 3 and 4, 1829.

3. R.W. Julian, personal communication to the author, February 25, 2009.

4. Frank H. Stewart, *History of the First United States Mint*, p. 123.

5. Citation furnished by Craig Sholley. Letter in the National Archives.

6. R.W. Julian, personal communication to the author, February 25, 2009.

7. Probably the engine built in 1829 and 1830 by Rush & Muhlenberg, 30 horsepower (see George Escol Sellers, *Early Engineering Reminiscences*, pp. 72, 75). Adam Eckfeldt disliked the horizontal type of steam engine, which was thought by many technicians to be superior. The Charlotte, Dahlonega, and New Orleans mints used horizontal engines.

8. In a recent year, 1832, the Washington's Birthday centennial parade in Philadelphia was so long that it took two hours to pass a given spot.

9. Certain information, including citation, from the report of Franklin Peale to the Franklin Institute as reported in the *Journal of the Franklin Institute*, September 1846, pp. 307–310.

10. Citation provided by Craig Sholley.

11. R.W. Julian, personal communication to the author, February 28, 2009. D. Hamilton Hurd, *History of Bristol County, Massachusetts*, Philadelphia, J.W. Lewis & Co., 1883. Paul and Bob Carter, "The Taunton Copper Manufacturing Company," *The Numismatist*, February 1972. R.W. Julian, "The Great Copper War," *The Numismatist*, February 1977, tells of a Wisconsin entrepreneur who sought to gain the business,

offering American copper instead of the Peruvian metal mostly used by Crocker. This caused a great disturbance at the time, until the Wisconsin metal was found to be inferior in quality. It was not until 1849 that the company opened a facility in Taunton, near Norton Center.

12. Adapted from extensive accounts in *Niles' Weekly Register*, February 18 and 25, 1837. Flour became plentiful later in the year, as evidenced by this notice in *Niles' Weekly Register*, November 25, 1837, p. 193: "Flour is arriving at New York by the canals at the rate of ten thousand barrels per day." The price of a loaf of bread provided a handy index to consumer prices for many years, including into the early 20th century, in times before reliable economic indices were compiled.

13. Per one report in 1837; the number was constantly changing. There was no uniform gathering of statistics at the time and almost nothing in the way of oversight of banks by the states that chartered them; that would come quickly, however, and by 1840 most had bank commissioners who performed reviews and, sometimes, audits.

14. Bucking the trend, Nathaniel Stevens expanded his textile production operation in North Andover, Massachusetts. His workers were on the job for 76 hours each week and earned an average of $4.50 per week, plus $2 for room and board during that time.

15. Citation from R.W. Julian, personal communication to the author. Also see the listing for the 1848, Small Date, cent in chapter 11.

16. Although modern analysis has revealed traces of silver, unintended by Feuchtwanger.

17. 25th Congress, Document No. 7, House of Representatives, first Session, titled "Substitute for Copper. Memorial Lewis Feuchtwanger, September 13, 1837."

18. *Niles' Weekly Register*, September 16, 1837, p. 41.

19. Copy furnished by Kenneth E. Bressett.

20. Frank H. Stewart, *History of the First United States Mint*, p. 81.

21. J.H. Lanman, "The Commerce of Philadelphia," *Hunt's Merchants' Magazine and Commercial Review*, May 1846, p. 433.

22. Don Taxay, *U.S. Mint and Coinage*, 1966, pp. 181, 182, 190.

23. R.W. Julian, personal communication to the author, February 25, 2009.

24. As quoted in Banker's Magazine, June 1854.

25. Details were later published in *Report of the Secretary of the Treasury, on the State of the Finances, for the Year Ending June 30, 1854*. Washington, D.C. Report to the House of Representatives, Thirty-third Congress, 2nd Session. Ex. Doc. No. 3.

26. Michael F. Moran, *1849: The Philadelphia Mint Strikes Gold*, Atlanta, Whitman Publishing, 2015.

CHAPTER 3

1. Sources include Don Taxay, *U.S. Mint and Coinage*, and Craig Sholley, "Adam Eckfeldt, Mint Engraver?" *Penny-Wise*, September 15, 2000. Sholley quotes the 1795 Boudinot Report found in the *American State Papers–Finance:* "It was also a considerable time before an engraver could be engaged, during which time the chief coiner was obliged to make the dies for himself." There is no record anywhere of his ever having been an engraver.

2. R.W. Julian, personal communication to the author, February 25, 2009.

3. Certain Voigt information is from Karl Moulton, *Henry Voigt, the Man Who Made the Money*, manuscript copy supplied to the author in July 2004.

4. *American Journal of Numismatics*, January 1872, quoting Alden's *Collection of American Epitaphs*, vol. 1, p. 223, New York, 1814.

5. Frank H. Stewart, *History of the First United States Mint*, pp. 37, 87, 104.

6. Don Taxay, *U.S. Mint and Coinage*, p. 75.

7. Robert Scot is sometimes confused with Robert Scott, a contemporary portraitist in Edinburgh.

8. R.W. Julian, personal communication to the author, February 25, 2009.

9. As quoted by William Dunlap, *History of the Rise and Progress of the Arts of Design in the United States*, vol. 2, 1834, pp. 469–470. Dunlap dismissed the talents of Scot as being mediocre, his coin designs "vile."

10. Foster Wild Rice, "Antecedents of the American Bank Note Company of 1858," *The Essay-Proof Journal*, Summer 1961. Rice, a leading authority on the history of bank notes, commented that Scot should not be considered a bank-note engraver without proof.

11. Little factual has been found concerning his eyesight, however (R.W. Julian, personal communication to the author, February 25, 2009).

12. Frank H. Stewart, *History of the First United States Mint*, p. 93. Unrelated to this work, Gardner invented the stenographic telegraph—a method of recording spoken words by means of a graphics system.

13. In his books on half cents and large cents, Walter Breen ascribes the creation of specific portraits of Miss Liberty to Gardner, including the small head for the 1795 half cent and the later style of 1795 cent. There is no evidence to support this connection.

14. Frank H. Stewart, *History of the First United States Mint*, p. 179. On June 30, 1795, Gardner was paid $174.88 for 78 days of engraving dies at the Mint. On September 30, 1795, he was paid $174.72 for 78 days of engraving at the Mint. On March 31, 1796, he was paid $234 for 78 days of work at $3 per day.

15. *American Journal of Numismatics*, October 1875; 1806 date of an unattributed newspaper clipping from the scrapbook of J.J. Mickley.

16. As quoted by Mint officer Patterson DuBois in the *American Journal of Numismatics*, vols. 18–19, July 1883.

17. *Ibid.*

18. R.W. Julian, "The Philadelphia Mint and Coinage of 1814–1816," *American Numismatic Association Centennial Anthology*, 1991. Further from that source: "In lieu of Reich doing the work, Chief Engraver Robert Scot executed the new head of Liberty, which has earned the well-deserved reputation of being one of the worst designs ever to appear on an American coin."

19. Information from Stewart Witham, to the author, 1991. Witham doubted the conventional wisdom that Reich died in Albany in 1833. Also see Witham in the selected bibliography. Also see William Dunlap, *History of the Rise and Progress of the Arts of Design in the United States*, vol. 2, pp. 469–470.

20. However, some of his salary was given to Christian Gobrecht, which precipitated a lawsuit by Kneass's wife.

21. For "Christian Gobrecht *fecit* [made it]."

22. Frank H. Stewart, *History of the First United States Mint*, p. 188.

23. *Ibid.*, p. 188, citing a payment to Gobrecht dated December 30, 1826.

24. Craig Sholley, personal communication to the author, February 15, 2009. Outgoing director of the Mint Moore wrote to Robert Maskell Patterson in June 1835 regarding the hiring of Gobrecht, using the "second engraver" term. Secretary of the Treasury Levi Woodbury used "assistant engraver" (Leonard Augsburger, personal communication to the author, March 12, 2009).

25. This refutes "conventional wisdom," largely from the writings of Walter Breen, that Longacre was incompetent as a die sinker and created such dies.

26. *American Journal of Numismatics*, January 1869, there quoted in some detail, the account being from the Philadelphia Press, January 5, 1869.

27. Frank H. Stewart, *History of the First United States Mint*, p. 106.

28. Certain information is from Craig Sholley, including personal communications to the author in February and March 2009 and manuscript copies of his articles on die preparation.

29. Craig Sholley, personal communication to the author, February 15, 2009.

30. Craig Sholley, personal communication to the author, March 11, 2009.

31. Certain very early silver coins (per the Act of 1792) were made to a fineness of .8924+ silver, later changed to 90 percent. Later, there were exceptions to the 90 percent silver rule, as in the silver three-cent piece of 1851, which was 75 percent silver.

32. Craig Sholley, personal communication to the author, March 8, 2009. Sources include a letter from director of the Mint Elias Boudinot to Matthew Boulton, April 22, 1799, noting that "the press is fed by means of a hopper, instead of being put under by hopper." Conventional wisdom (per Don Taxay and Walter Breen) that automatic feeding was devised in 1793 by Adam Eckfeldt can be dismissed, as Eckfeldt was not at the Mint at that time and there are no records of any payments to him.

33. Adapted from *The American Machinist*, 1893, by Raymond H. Williamson, and reprinted by him in *The Numismatist*, January 1951 (here excerpted). The accuracy of certain of Sellers's recollections has been questioned. Certainly, at age four in 1812 he could not have been a very qualified observer. However, "as I grew older and was better able to understand," indicates that his recollections also included visits at an older age. Frank H. Stewart, *History of the First United States Mint*, p. 124, notes, "Despite the fact the first United States Mint was opened to visitors, I have never been able to find any mention of a visit to it by any person, American or foreign, with the exception of Sellers, who was born and raised near it and played around it as a boy. He described it in his reminiscences with great accuracy and intelligence." In modern times Karl Moulton inspected the register of visitors in the National Archives, expecting to find many entries from the 1820s onward listing Joseph J. Mickley and other collectors, but hardly any were given. Apparently, only a few visitors ever signed it.

34. Don Taxay, *U.S. Mint and Coinage*, p. 96., citing "A View of Philadelphia in 1829." Pennsylvania Magazine, July 1954.

35. Clarified by Craig Sholley, personal communication to the author, March 8, 2009.

36. Some have said that other styles were made during the era of half cents and large cents, including bronzed Proofs with a deep brown surface as seen on many medals of the era. Documentation of the making of such half cents or cents at the Philadelphia Mint is nonexistent.

37. Even on this, not everyone agrees.

38. Notwithstanding this lack of evidence, many present-day collectors accept the Breen comment (per a note from Denis Loring to the author, March 24, 2009).

39. As discussed by the author at length with John J. Ford Jr., Breen's employer at New Netherlands Coin Co. in the 1950s. Ford *always* did the grading, without exception. Unrelated to New Netherlands, Breen wrote many "letters of authentication," for a fee, for "Proofs" in various series, that have been debunked today.

40. In 1854 Alfred Hunter prepared a catalog of "extraordinary curiosities" on display by the National Institute at the Patent Office building, which included numismatic items (cf. Emmanuel J. Attinelli, *Numisgraphics*, 1876, p. 82).

41. R.W. Julian, personal communication to the author, February 25, 2009.

42. *American Journal of Numismatics*, January 1879. The tens of thousands of patterns, restrikes, and other coins privately made and sold from spring 1859 to the summer of 1885 never resulted in any official investigation!

43. The Craig and Dannreuther comments are from a round-robin discussion of the subject with the author in February 2009.

44. Denis Loring takes a different view and believes that there are indeed Proofs dating back to 1817, the date of inception suggested by Breen. Loring points out that many others agree (personal communication to the author, March 24 and April 26, 2009).

45. Recollection published in the *American Journal of Numismatics*, February 1867, penned January 1, 1867.

46. *American Journal of Numismatics*, March 1867.

47. *Mason's Coin and Stamp Collectors' Magazine*, July 1871. While there, Mason offered Clay $6,500 *in gold* to buy the coins, but his bid was declined. The collection went elsewhere, and competing dealer William Harvey Strobridge cataloged the Clay collection for auction on December 5–7, 1871.

48. As viewed in the 1960s. The owner desired to sell these as Proofs or have them auctioned as Proofs. Finally, he sold them at a discounted price, and the buyer proceeded to offer them as Proofs.

49. Denis Loring, personal communication to the author, March 24, 2009.

Chapter 4

1. Billed as the Lord St. Oswald Collection, the sale was held by Christie's. Among those in attendance were three American dealers: Lester Merkin, Norman Stack, and James F. Ruddy (partner with the author in the Empire Coin Company). The present author was in London at the time but did not attend the sale.

2. Emmanuel J. Attinelli, *Numisgraphics*, p. 75. Later, the Library became the repository for many important papers connected with the Mint, including documents and sketches relating to Chief Engraver William Kneass and artist Thomas Sully.

3. Joel J. Orosz, *The Eagle That Is Forgotten: Pierre Eugène Du Simitière, Founding Father of American Numismatics*, Bowers & Merena Galleries, 1988.

4. Born in 1777 in Kilbernie, Ayrshire, Scotland, John Allan emigrated to the United States and secured a position in New York City as a bookkeeper. Several varieties of tokens issued in the late 1850s and early 1860s, from dies by George H. Lovett, bear his portrait on the obverse, in combination with various reverse dies.

5. From *Norton's Literary Letter*, No. 3, 1859. A further description can be found in David F. Fanning's Spring 2004, Price List II.

6. A paragraph in John M. Kleeberg's 1992 essay, "New Yorke in America Token," p. 50, note 7 (published by the American Numismatic Society as part of the proceedings of the Coinage of the Americas Conference), gives biographical information about Bache.

7. A guinea is equal to 21 shillings, or slightly more than $5 in equivalent U.S. money at the time; thus the cabinet cost more than $150, an impressive sum in that era.

8. Vladimir Clain-Stefanelli, "History of the National Numismatic Collections," U.S. Government Printing Office, 1968 and 1970,, is the source for most of the information given here regarding numismatics in Washington, D.C.

9. Reminiscence by R. Coulton Davis, letter to *Mason's Coin and Stamp Collectors' Magazine*, May 1867.

10. Charles Davis, *American Numismatic Literature*, Quarterman Publications, 1992, p. 81, notes that multiple editions were published.

11. *American Journal of Numismatics*, January 1868.

12. *Ibid.*, October 1872; Stearns's article appeared in *Numismatic Chronicle*, vol. 3, July 1840 to January 1841, pp. 123–125. The 1840 letter was addressed to a Mr. Bowditch in England. *American Journal of Numismatics*, July 1874; account by Jeremiah Colburn.

13. From *The Diary of Isaac Mickle 1837–1845*, in two volumes, edited by Philip English Mackey, University of Pennsylvania Press, 1977. Mickle lived from 1822 to 1855.

14. *American Journal of Numismatics*, March 1868. Cogan had no firsthand knowledge of the activities of the Mint in the 1820s and 1830s, for he did not become involved in numismatics until the late 1850s.

15. Walter Breen, *The Numismatist*, March 1951.

16. "Master-coins" may have referred, at least in part, to what would later be called Proof coins.

17. The first successful medal-ruling machine seems to have been devised by Christian Gobrecht in 1817, although Asa Spencer and some others claimed priority.

18. From his obituary, October 1894, the *American Journal of Numismatics*.

19. *American Journal of Numismatics*, July 1899, places his starting date as 1817.

20. Eric P. Newman, in *The Fantastic 1804 Dollar*, Whitman Publishing, 1962, commented to the effect that in 1843 Stickney traded one concoction for another, as the silver dollars dated 1804 were made up from new dies at the Mint in 1834.

21. The story of Stickney's exchange with the Mint was related by Henry Chapman in connection with the sale of the Stickney 1804 dollar in Chapman's June 1907 auction.

22. Letter to Philadelphia dealer Edward D. Cogan on July 2, 1867.

23. From *brummagem*, one of several terms to describe stray coppers that were not issued under any government authority, originating from Birmingham, the English location of many manufacturers of unauthorized coppers (Eric P. Newman, personal communication to the author, March 8, 2009, and his earlier writing).

24. *The Numismatist*, January 1918.

25. *American Journal of Numismatics*, January 1891.

26. Emmanuel J. Attinelli, *Numisgraphics*, p. 8. The sale of Professor Daniel E. Groux's coins and medals in Boston, 1848, may have realized as much or more, but no records of prices have been located.

27. *The Numismatist*, June 1949, commentary by Raymond H. Williamson: "At this sale, an Uncirculated 'Chain' cent of 1793 was knocked down to Brown for his first bid of 10 cents." Brown added to his collection during the decade, including at the Flandin sale in 1855, but he later sold his cabinet and shelf of coin books to Henry Mason Brooks, a Salem, Massachusetts, collector, who in turn sold most of the coins to Joseph Finotti, a Catholic priest. Also see the *American*

Journal of Numismatics, May 1869, and *The Numismatist*, October 1929.

28. Montroville W. Dickeson, *American Numismatical Manual*, 1859, pp. 76–78. Another passenger with a numismatic connection was Mahlon Day, who, circa 1819, had published what is believed to be the first counterfeit detector in America, and who went on to issue *Day's New York Bank Note List and Counterfeit Detecter* [sic]. Day, age 64, had enjoyed a very successful life. His wife and daughter also went down with the ship.

29. *American Journal of Numismatics*, April 1874, notes his activity as taking place circa 1822 to 1827 and possibly other times as well.

30. George Parish Jr., *American Journal of Numismatics*, August 1866. Emmanuel J. Attinelli, *Numisgraphics*, 1876, stated the offering brought $733.62.

31. A.C. Kline was a trade style often adopted by John William Kline, and it may have featured the initials of his wife.

32. Cf. George F. Kolbe, sale of the John W. Adams Library, June 3, 2006, lot 235, a Flandin catalog.

33. Joel J. Orosz, *The Curious Case of the Coin Collectors Kline*, 1997.

34. Letter published in *The Numismatist*, October 1929.

35. *American Journal of Numismatics*, October 1868.

36. Recollection in the *Proceedings* of the 28th annual meeting of the American Numismatic and Archaeological Society held in 1885.

37. Mickley's letter from Europe, November 8, 1872, published in the *American Journal of Numismatics*, January 1873.

38. Lea Alborn, a Swedish engraver he had visited during his European trip, prepared the dies for a 51-millimeter memorial medal struck in his memory.

39. From an unsigned mention of Parmelee in *The Numismatist*, April 1892.

40. Filler in the *American Journal of Numismatics*, July 1875.

41. This comment is at odds with his earlier statement that he had been "engaged in the coin *trade* since the latter part of 1856"; apparently, he meant coin *hobby*.

42. This "almost exclusively" comment contradicts his advertising medal (Washington obverse; dies by Robert Lovett Jr.) issued the *following year*, 1859, which lists coins among several other specialties: EDWARD D. COGAN / DEALER IN BOOKS / COINS, MEDALS / AND / ENGRAVINGS. / 1859 / PHILADELPHIA.

Also see the *American Journal of Numismatics*, March 1866.

43. Also see Jim Neiswinter, "The First Published Study of Large Cents (1859)," *Penny-Wise*, July 15, 2000.

44. Record book in the library of the American Numismatic Society.

45. For related (but not numismatic) information see Benson J. Lossing, *Pictorial Field Book of the Revolution*, vol. 1, 1850, pp. 472–472, and vol. 2, 1850, p. 583. *The Token and Medal Society Journal*, June 1978, included "Riley's Fifth Ward Museum Hotel," by Werner G. Mayer, which has an old print showing the four-story establishment.

46. Quoted by R.H. Williamson in "Large Cents That Survived," *The Numismatist*, July 1949.

47. Reminiscences in the *American Journal of Numismatics*, October 1868.

48. In April 1873, the *American Journal of Numismatics* commented that Prime's 1861 book was a "travesty upon coin science." It was not well received in its time, was referred to as a book suitable for children, and was hardly ever cited. Prime was one of the first Americans to visit Egypt and write about it in detail. In 1864 he was president of the New York Numismatic Society, and on November 22, 1866, joined the American Numismatic and Archaeological Society. He spent his summers in Franconia, New Hampshire, in the White Mountains and had a two-story cabin on Lonesome Lake (the *Granite Monthly*, September 1896, illustrates it).

49. Woodward, the owner, stated that this coin was the most valuable American coin or medal, and, apparently, bidders agreed. At the time, Washington tokens and medals were among the most active series with collectors and dealers.

50. *American Journal of Numismatics*, January 1905.

51. Emmanuel J. Attinelli, *Numisgraphics*, 1876, p. 61.

52. Knox, deputy comptroller of currency at the Treasury department, was an enthusiastic numismatist. He was the author of the Coinage Act of 1873 and an authority on finance and banking in America.

53. Under the description of a set of Numisma in the catalog for the Armand Champa Library I, lot 237.

54. *The Celebrated John W. Adams Collection*, 1982, the comment having been furnished by Adams.

55. D.C. Wismer, "My Collecting Experience," *The Numismatist*, May 1939.

56. Doughty was well known as a writer of fiction stories for boys and other works outside of numismatics. He was well liked and popular in his time. Doughty has been criticized by modern numismatic writers for reasons not known. The

errors in the work, of which there were many, should be attributed instead to Proskey. In 1914, Doughty did some scenario writing for the film serial *The Twenty Million Dollar Mystery*.

CHAPTER 5

1. John J. Ford Jr., personal communication to the author, circa 1955.

2. Information from Charles E. Davis's description of a copy in the Armand Champa Library sale.

3. Notes on the convention published in *The Numismatist*, September 1911. Typical of many accounts, half cents were in the shadow of cent publicity. French had a reputation for slow pay and was reported by Thomas L. Elder as such to Henry Chapman, who circa 1904 to 1919 kept his private "Black List; List of Men Reported Bad." B. Max Mehl, who later handled the French collection, had credit difficulties with him as well. (Per Charles Davis, catalog of the Armand Champa Collection, lot 1143)

4. From the catalog *The Celebrated John W. Adams Collection*, 1982. Also Carl W.A. Carlson, "Garrett, Raymond, and the Ellsworth Collection," The American Numismatic Association Centennial Anthology, 1991.

5. From an early typed sheet by Breen later described by Charles Davis as part of lot 119 in the Armand Champa Library, Sale I catalog, lot 119, with one paragraph titled, "Larceny, Inc."

6. J.E. Lindsay Carter and Barbara Honeyman Heath (who had worked with Sheldon), *Somatotyping: Development and Applications*, Cambridge, 1990, p. 6.

7. Harvey Stack, personal communication to the author, January 2009.

8. For the remaining 36 years of his life, Pearl continued to collect coins actively but never returned to copper. Certain of his holdings were later sold at auction by the author and his firm following Pearl's visit to our office. For personal reasons, Pearl sought anonymity and thus attended only a few numismatic events.

9. Contribution to the John W. Adams Collection of 1794 Cents catalog, 1982.

10. Gordon Wrubel, personal communication to the author, July 10, 1997.

11. Conversation with the author, 1950s.

12. Many sources, including "The Kleeberg Report: An Opposing View," by John M. Kleeberg, a former curator of the American Numismatic Society, as published on the Internet, July 14, 2005.

13. "Sidelights of the Convention," *The Numismatist*, November 1948.

14. Among other problems, he could not reconcile himself with his childhood. In the 1940s and 1950s he told many people that he thought that in reality he was the kidnapped son of Charles and Anne Morrow Lindbergh, and that the finding of the baby's body had been contrived.

15. In December 2008, the club celebrated its 100th anniversary in the same restaurant, a New York City icon decorated with about 20,000 pipes smoked by patrons over the years, old playbills, and other memorabilia.

16. John J. Ford Jr. provided the author with much information on Raymond, Breen, and others in interviews beginning in the mid-1950s.

17. The 17th edition of the *Standard Catalogue of United States Coins and Currency* was the last published by Raymond. Just a single edition was printed beyond that, the 18th, prepared by John J. Ford Jr. Ford. Olga Raymond requested that the present author take over as editor, but commercial interests intervened, along with the perceived difficulty of measuring up to Ford's standards of perfection.

18. Recollection of Charles Wormser to the author, circa 1955.

19. *The Numismatist*, October 1921.

20. Born on February 12, 1912, Bullowa developed an interest in numismatics by the time he was a teenager, and in April 1930 a letter from him about commemoratives was published in *The Numismatist*. After his stint with New Netherlands and service in the Army, in the spring of 1946 he acquired the business of dealer Ira Reed at 37 South 18th Street. Soon, *Bullowa's Coin List* was issued, and it continued for years afterward. John W. Adams made his first serious numismatic purchases in Bullowa's shop. In May 1952 Bullowa married Catherine Elias, a dealer in coins and antique jewelry. After his death on September 12, 1953, the business was continued by Catherine.

21. Letter to the author from Ford's sister, Mary Jane Confort, July 29, 2000.

22. I made it a point to attend most of the New Netherlands sales in New York City in the mid-1950s. At one particular event held in the penthouse of the New Weston Hotel, Ford almost lost his life. A bidder, Pennsylvania attorney and token specialist Don Miller, had spent too much time at the nearby bar. After having had a few drinks too many, he passed a $500 bill around, and it disappeared. A particular Hard Times token, Low No. 1, was to be auctioned, and both Ford and Miller expressed an interest in buying it. I don't remember all the details, but whatever happened, the two became involved in a vicious

argument and shouting match. Miller grabbed Ford and pushed him against a low wall at the side of the rooftop terrace, with the street visible many floors below. A great struggle took place, and it seemed that Ford was about to be thrown to eternity, when a bystander and I, both nearby at the time, rushed to the scene and pulled Miller away, saving Ford. Otherwise there would have been no *Penny Whimsy*, which Ford was in the process of sponsoring for publication.

23. This controversy was played out to great length in the numismatic media and still echoes. Details are beyond the scope of the present text.

24. Advertisement in *The Numismatist*, August 1969.

25. Rather than adding space for modern conversions to Bowers-Whitman and Sheldon numbers, the reader is referred to the listings for 1793.

26. The so-called Melish collection, actually the consignment of Ted Naftzger, was separately cataloged and sold at the Central States Convention in Indianapolis. The author was in attendance.

27. When the book—a write-in bid for a customer who promised to pay a winning price for the lot, so long as the bids from the floor did not exceed his or her stated maximum—bought the coin, there was a big letdown in the audience, as bidding on the floor had been quiet, and everyone had expected fireworks.

Chapter 6

1. *Popular Science*, May 1952.

2. This term is still sometimes used and generally means "among the top finest known" without regard to a specific population.

Chapter 7

1. Certain information is from "History of the Early American Coppers Club, 1966–2002," by Pete Smith, EAC Web site.

2. Personal communication to the author, September 7, 2009.

Chapter 8

1. Ron Manley, "Original Mintages of 1797 and 1800 Half Cents," *Penny-Wise*, July 15, 2000.

2. Listed as a grocer on Gouverneur Street, corner of Front Street, in contemporary directories. R.W. Julian could find no record of any shipment being made to Cilley in the treasurer's ledger, but that is not conclusive, as acknowledgements were not given to all orders (personal communication to the author, March 2, 2009).

3. Although the book bore Snowden's name as author, likely most of the text was prepared by William Ewing Dubois and George Bull (curator of the Mint Cabinet).

4. After Cohen's passing, his daughter Debby handled his numismatic estate and consigned his collection of half cents to Superior Galleries, where it was sold on February 2, 1992.

Chapter 9

1. Bill Eckberg, communication to the author, March 2, 2009.

2. Greg A. Silvis, "An Interview with R. 'Tett' Tettenhorst" *Penny-Wise*, January 2006.

3. Estimate of Jim McGuigan, April 20, 2009.

4. Ronald P. Manley, *Half Cent Die State Book 1793–1857*, 1998, p. 36.

5. *Ibid.*, p. 30.

6. Bill Eckberg, communication to the author, March 2, 2009.

7. R. Tettenhorst, letter to the author, March 16, 2009.

8. *Ibid.*

9. *Ibid.*

10. Frank H. Stewart, *History of the First United States Mint*, 1924, p. 115.

11. *Hobbies* magazine, February 1932. The Detroit collector was Howard R. Newcomb.

12. This crossed the block for $506,000 in 1996, setting the record for *any* copper coin sold up to that point in time.

13. R. Tettenhorst, letter to the author, March 16, 2009.

14. Estimate of Jim McGuigan, April 20, 2009.

15. *American Journal of Numismatics*, June 1866.

16. *Numisgraphics*, 1876, p. 42.

17. R. Tettenhorst, letter to the author, March 16, 2009.

18. Ronald P. Manley, *Half Cent Die State Book 1793–1857*, p. 81.

19. Description (which varies in the literature) suggested by R. Tettenhorst, letter to the author, March 16, 2009.

20. Adapted from the author's, *American Coin Treasures and Hoards*, Bowers & Merena Galleries, 1997.

21. Communication to the author, March 8, 2009.

22. Estimate of Jim McGuigan, April 20, 2009.

23. *Walter Breen's Encyclopedia of United States Half Cents 1793–1857*, American Institute of Numismatic Research, 1983, p. 223.

24. From research by Craig Sholley.

25. R. Tettenhorst, letter to the author, March 16, 2009.

26. Only two were known to Walter Breen. Ronald P. Manley, correspondence with the author, February 23, 2009: "EAC member Ed Fuhrman has discovered 4 or more specimens of this 'variety' unattributed on eBay."

27. *Walter Breen's Encyclopedia of United States Half Cents 1793–1857*, p. 252.

28. *Walter Breen's Complete Encyclopedia of U.S. and Colonial Coins*, Doubleday, 1988, pp. 165–166, gives the name *Henry Chapman* and the 200 estimate. Alternatively, *Walter Breen's Encyclopedia of United States Half Cents 1793–1857*, p. 276, places the number as "many hundreds" and gives the name *Chapman Brothers*.

29. The pedigree of this piece is notable: The reverse was used in 1916 to illustrate the Gilbert text on half cents. Later it was part of the sale of the F.R. Alvord Collection; S.H. Chapman, June 9, 1924, lot 131, where it realized $6, a strong price at the time.

30. Ronald P. Manley, *Half Cent Die State Book 1793–1857*, p. 196, citing Bill Weber's discovery reported in *Penny-Wise* No. 4, 1987.

31. Craig Sholley, research in the National Archives, also noted in *Walter Breen's Encyclopedia of United States Half Cents 1793–1857*.

32. Correspondence between Ronald P. Manley and the author, February 23, 2009.

33. John Dannreuther, correspondence with the author, February 24, 2009.

34. Cf. Bill Eckberg, "The 1809 C5 Over What" *Penny-Wise*, November 2006; also communication to the author, February 25, 2009.

35. R.W. Julian from Mint records (communication to the author, March 8, 2009).

36. *American Numismatical Manual of the Currency or Money of the Aborigines, and Colonial, State, and United States Coins: With Historical and Descriptive Notices of Ech Coin or Series*, p. 213.

37. Estimate per Jim McGuigan, April 20, 2009.

38. Boyd's obituary, by Elston G. Bradfield, appeared in *The Numismatist*, October 1958, p. 1180. He died on September 7, 1958, at the age of 71.

39. Conversation between John J. Ford Jr. and the author, June 27, 1996.

40. Walter H. Breen, "Survey of American Coin Hoards," *The Numismatist*, January 1952, modified by his comments in the same journal, October 1952, p. 1010 (pointing out inaccuracies in the Chapman account, this new information having been gained by Breen from old-time numismatist John F. Jones, who had known and visited Collins); *Walter Breen's Complete Encyclopedia of U.S. and Colonial Coins*, p. 169.

41. R.W. Julian from Mint documents in the National Archives.

42. R. Tettenhorst, letter, March 16, 2009, describing a coin in his collection.

43. R.W. Julian from Mint documents in the National Archives.

44. *Walter Breen's Encyclopedia of United States Half Cents 1793–1857*, p. 338.

45. *Walter Breen's Complete Encyclopedia of U.S. and Colonial Coins*, p. 171; also personal recollection of the author concerning the availability of the coins in the 1950s.

46. *Walter Breen's Encyclopedia of United States Half Cents 1793–1857*, p. 338.

47. *Walter Breen's Complete Encyclopedia of U.S. and Colonial Coins*, p. 171; also personal recollection of the author concerning the availability of the coins in the 1950s.

48. *Walter Breen's Encyclopedia of United States Half Cents 1793–1857*, p. 338.

49. Recollection of the author, who was given her "want list."

50. Robert Schonwalter, *Penny-Wise*, whole number 111, November 15, 1885.

51. Eavenson had been collecting since at least 1894 (listed as new member 221 in *The Numismatist*, October 1894; at that time he worked for the Denver & Rio Grande Railroad and lived in Denver; moving to Eckart, Colorado in 1903). Eavenson's sale had a long run of Proof sets and also included a rare 1838-O half dollar.

52. *Walter Breen's Complete Encyclopedia of U.S. and Colonial Coins* spread the word about Gies. On p. 323 he related, concerning Barber dimes, that he "obtained rolls of all of them;" on p. 358 he credited Gies with having rolls of all Barber quarter dollars; on p. 410 he said the same thing about Barber halves. William Pukall and Wayte Raymond were also credited with having most or all Barber coins in roll form, also a highly unlikely scenario.

53. Ford, conversation with the author, June 27, 1996; Ford worked for Stack's, New York City, circa 1941–1942 and saw the Gies coins at that time.

54. Bill Eckberg, communication to the author, March 3, 2009.

55. Putnam-Woodward connection courtesy of Karl Moulton, letter, September 10, 1996, with enclosures.

56. Coins were first struck in Carson City in 1870; first reviewed by the Assay Commission in 1871.

In 1863 (the year for which coins were being reviewed by the Assay Commission in 1864) there were two active mints, Philadelphia and San Francisco.

57. Certain information is from Francis Pessolano-Filos, *The Assay Medals, the Assay Commissions, 1841, 1977*, pp. 155, 159, 162, and 168.

58. Those stored at the Mint were melted by spring 1857, per an account of Director James Ross Snowden in *A Description of Ancient and Modern Coins in the Cabinet of the Mint of the United States.* Philadelphia: J.B. Lippincott, 1860 (this excellent book was mostly researched and written by George Bull, who was then curator of the Mint Cabinet, and William Ewing DuBois).

59. Citation suggested by Bob Vail. Copy of Woodward's sale catalog furnished by Karl Moulton.

60. Charles French, conversation with the author.

61. For several years in the 1950s and early 1960s the author and partner James F. Ruddy bought every 1856 they could find, after determining that although they were priced about the same as other dates of this period, they were much scarcer in the marketplace.

62. Craig Sholley, letter to the author, January 18, 2001. Also, early in 1857 large copper cents were paid out to the extent of 100,000 coins, again until February 28.

63. A small number of 1857 half cents have a depression in the right obverse field below the hair bun. This struck-through error was first described by Mark Borckardt in the May 1976 issue of *Penny-Wise*.

CHAPTER 10

1. A reference to the new small-size Flying Eagle cent launched in May 1857.

2. 1858 essay provided by Anthony Bongiovanni Jr. As a student, Ingersoll must have made diligent inquiry in an era in which no general numismatic texts were available, probably consulting various *Annual Reports of the Director of the Mint* to learn about distribution patterns of cents. Ingersoll later became treasurer of the Academy of Music, Haverhill, Massachusetts, a popular entertainment venue from the early 1880s onward. Thanks also to Dennis Tucker and David Sundman for information.

3. Breen died in 1993, and Borckardt organized his notes and helped with the publication in 2000. As this was a "Breen book," the considerable research of others, including that of Borckardt and modern contributors to *Penny-Wise*, was not added.

CHAPTER 11

1. Silver coins in the form of 1792 half dismes were struck in July at the home of John Harper, before the Mint cornerstone was laid, and soon reached circulation. The first gold coins would not be delivered until summer 1795.

2. "The Mint Investigation of 1795," *Numismatic Scrapbook Magazine*, July 1961.

3. In the present cross-references below, "Crosby" is spelled out in full, to avoid confusion with other "C" authors such as S. Hudson Chapman and Roger S. Cohen Jr., although both described copper coins other than 1793 cents.

4. The estimated mintages of 1793 Chain cents are by Mark Borckardt, contribution to the Eliasberg Collection catalog, 1996; based on a distribution of an estimated 1,000 examples surviving across all five varieties.

5. Stetson, born in 1832, lived in Quincy, MA, and enjoyed hoarding cents of his birth date.

6. "The Mint Investigation of 1795," *Numismatic Scrapbook Magazine*, July 1961.

7. "The Strawberry Leaf Cent. A Reappraisal," essay in *America's Large Cent,* Coinage of the Americas Conference, American Numismatic Society, 1998.

8. Jim Neiswinter, communication to the author, March 30, 2009.

9. As written by Charles Davis, Armand Champa Library III, lot 2566.

10. Jim Neiswinter, in "Reverses Revisited: S-63 Is the Reworked S-13," *Penny-Wise*, July 2006, presented photographic overlays demonstrating that the reverse of S-13 of 1793 was reworked to create S-63 of 1794.

11. Jim Neiswinter, communication to the author, March 30, 2009.

12. Denis Loring, communication to the author, March 6, 2009, contributed to these comments.

13. From the catalog, *The Celebrated John W. Adams Collection*, 1982, Also, Carl W.A. Carlson, "Garrett, Raymond and the Ellsworth Collection," 1991.

14. Incorrectly plated in the Breen *Encyclopedia.*

15. Steigerwalt, "1794 cents," *The Numismatist,* July 1906, as cited in *Walter Breen's Encyclopedia of Early United States Cents 1793–1814*, Bowers and Merena Galleries, 2000, p. 149.

16. S. Hudson Chapman, *The United States Cents of the Year 1794*, 1926, p. 20. S.H. was born in 1857, Henry in 1859. In 1877 they were both in the employ of Philadelphia dealer J.W. Haseltine.

17. Harry E. Salyards, communication to the author, February 7, 2009.

18. *Ibid.*

19. Pete Smith, in "Observations on the Starred Reverse Cent," *Penny-Wise,* January 15, 1989, debunked an earlier-published theory by Walter Breen that the reverse die for S-48 was used earlier for S-63, by using photographic overlays.

20. Jim Neiswinter, in "Reverses Revisited: S-63 Is the Reworked S-13," *Penny-Wise,* July 2006, presented photographic overlays demonstrating that the reverse of S-13 of 1793 was reworked to create S-63 of 1794.

21. Harry E. Salyards, M.D., communication to the author, February 7, 2009.

22. Not a correct statement; the standard remained the same as 1793.

23. An error. The number of one-cent pieces minted with the 1794 date is not known with certainty, but it is far short of 12+ million. The *Guide Book of U.S. Coins* suggests 918,521, while *Walter Breen's Complete Encyclopedia of U.S. and Colonial Coins* states that 807,500 were made.

24. R.W. Julian, "The Harper Cents," *Numismatic Scrapbook Magazine,* September 1964.

25. Harper had a previous relationship with the Mint. In 1792, incoming equipment for the Mint, then planned, later under construction, had been set up in Harper's coach house in Philadelphia on Sixth Street above Chestnut, opposite Jayne Street. A press made by Mint mechanic Adam Eckfeldt was used to strike certain coins there (per *The Historical Magazine,* September 1861). Other accounts suggest Harper's *cellar.*

26. *Walter Breen's Encyclopedia of Early United States Cents 1793–1814,* p. 63.

27. *Ibid.,* p. 257.

28. Frank H. Stewart, *History of the First United States Mint,* 1924, p. 71.

29. Denis Loring, communication to the author, March 6, 2009.

30. Walter H. Breen, "A Survey of American Coin Hoards," *The Numismatist,* January 1952.

31. William H. Sheldon, *Penny Whimsy,* p. 189.

32. *The Numismatist,* August 1917.

33. From the author's 1997 book, *American Coin Treasures and Hoards,* which includes a long list of Nichols Find citations.

34. *Penny Whimsy,* p. 179.

35. Incorrectly plated in the Breen *Encyclopedia.*

36. Mark Borckardt, letter to the editor of *Numismatic News,* November 27, 2007. Among specialists not everyone agrees that the misstruck *half cent* should qualify as a *cent* of this variety and be included in the population.

37. *Walter Breen's Encyclopedia of Early United States Cents 1793–1814,* p. 365.

38. Frank H. Stewart, *History of the First United States Mint,* p. 72.

39. Details are in *Penny-Wise,* May 15, 1985, and in *Walter Breen's Encyclopedia of Early United States Cents 1793–1814,* p. 424.

40. Harry E. Salyards, communication to the author, March 17, 2009.

41. *Ibid.*

42. *Ibid.*

43. *Penny-Wise,* November 15, 1968.

44. Harry E. Salyards, communication to the author, March 17, 2009.

45. Harry E. Salyards, communication to the author, March 18, 2009.

46. *Ibid.*

47. Bill Maryott, "Die Varieties, Die Stages, Die States, and the Theory Behind Coining," *Penny-Wise,* March 2009, calls these die *stages,* as the die was reworked after heating and annealing.

48. *Ibid.*

49. *Ibid.*

50. Harry E. Salyards, communication to the author, March 18, 2009.

51. *Ibid.*

52. Bill Maryott, "Die Varieties, Die Stages, Die States, and the Theory Behind Coining," *Penny-Wise,* March 2009, calls these die *stages,* as the die was reworked after heating and annealing.

53. For example, the 1791 Liverpool Halfpenny has the edge lettered PAYABLE IN ANGLESEY LONDON OR LIVERPOOL X.

54. Incorrectly plated in the Breen *Encyclopedia.*

55. Harry E. Salyards, communication to the author, March 18, 2009.

56. Text of this comment from Craig Sholley, February 15, 2009.

57. Obituary of Henry C. Hines, *The Numismatist,* February 1949. The cent was described as "Uncirculated."

58. Suggestion by Craig Sholley, communication to the author, February 15, 2009.

59. Harry E. Salyards, communication to the author, March 18, 2009.

60. Craig Sholley states (communication to the author, March 8, 2009) that during the War of 1812 the price of copper soared to 80¢ per pound, or about twice the face value of copper coins!

61. Mickley, recollection in the *American Journal of Numismatics*, June 1868.

62. *Ibid.*, p. 24.

63. The Abbey 1799 cent was sold as part of the Louis E. Eliasberg, Sr., Collection, May 1996, lot 510; various pedigree information was related in the catalog, including a chronology from John J. Ford Jr., February 17, 1953 (in which was stated that the coin was purchased by Abbey from a dealer named Rogers on Fulton Street for $25, circa 1844–1846, and was retained by Abbey until he sold it in a private transaction in 1856). After the Eliasberg sale, some corrections to the pedigree were made. In 1875, Abbey, in South Orange, New Jersey, published a small sheet offering large cents for sale, unrelated to the famous 1799.

64. American Journal of Numismatics, January 1891. The January 1, 1882, issue of Frank Leslie's Illustrated Newspaper includes his biography, on the occasion of Abbott having been recently elected mayor of Boston.

65. *Penny-Wise*, September 15, 1968.

66. Harry E. Salyards, communication to the author, March 18, 2009.

67. *Ibid.*

68. Bill Maryott, "Die Varieties, Die Stages, Die States, and the Theory Behind Coining," *Penny-Wise*, March 2009, calls these die *stages*, as the die was reworked after heating and annealing.

69. *Ibid.*

70. *Ibid.*

71. *Ibid.*

72. The "perfect die" mentioned in the Breen *Encyclopedia* as having been discovered by Tom Warfield in 1951 seems to be fictitious, a case of Breen mis-remembering. In any event, no such perfect die has ever been seen by specialists such as Jack H. Robinson and Harry E. Salyards (per note to the author, March 20, 2009).

73. Bill Maryott, "Die Varieties, Die Stages, Die States, and the Theory Behind Coining," *Penny-Wise*, March 2009, calls these die *stages*, as the die was reworked after heating and annealing.

74. *Ibid.*

75. *Penny Whimsy*, p. 13.

76. This grade description would be impossible to translate into today's terms.

77. R.W. Julian, communication to the author, March 8, 2009.

78. Congress moved from Philadelphia to Washington in 1800 and thus was not "almost next door" in 1802 or 1803.

79. Bill Maryott, "Die Varieties, Die Stages, Die States, and the Theory Behind Coining," *Penny-Wise*, March 2009, calls these die *stages*, as the die was reworked after heating and annealing.

80. Craig Sholley, communication to the author, February 15, 2009.

81. Denis Loring, communication to the author, March 6, 2009. Also see Bill Noyes, *et al.*, *The Official Condition Census for U.S. Large Cents 1793–1839*, which uses "EAC standards," in which the top two are listed as AU-50, followed by EF listings.

82. *Mason's Coin and Stamp Collectors' Magazine*, March 1869.

83. In the early 1970s the author assisted the Secret Service in the identification of fake 1877, 1909-S, and certain other coins. The counterfeiter was found, and claimed that he used genuine coins as a base and then added metal to them. The Secret Service dropped the case as it could not determine that, legally, these were counterfeits. They were not willing to share any further information. Jack Beymer identified other suspected fakes, including the 1809 cent.

84. Other examples include the 1922 "plain" cent struck from a worn, filled 1922-D die; the 1937-D, 3-Legged Buffalo, nickel; and the 1800, AMERICAI, silver dollar.

85. Per notes by Mark Borckardt in the Eliasberg Collection catalog, 1996.

86. Citation furnished by Bob Vail.

87. G.M. Davison, *The Traveller's Guide Throughout the Middle and Northern States, and the Provinces of Canada*, Saratoga Springs, New York, 1834, p. 69.

88. *Annals of Congress*, 14th Congress [convened in 1815], First Session, p. 694.

89. Vattemare's work, never printed in English (although a Spanish edition was published in 1904), was based upon the cabinet of the Bibliothéque Nationale in Paris, not upon cabinets he had observed during his travels in the United States, although American coins were discussed.

90. R.W. Julian, "The Philadelphia Mint and Coinage of 1814–1816," *American Numismatic Association Centennial Anthology*, 1991.

91. However, in most modern references and citations the 1816 is included; e.g., John D. Wright, The Cent Book, 1992, p. 4, concerning 1816 Newcomb-2: "Possibly a few thousand Mint State examples survive from the Randall Hoard circa 1867."

92. R.W. Julian, "The Philadelphia Mint and Coinage of 1814–1816," American Numismatic Association Centennial Anthology, 1991.

93. Another variety, N-8, has slight traces of a "mouse" in the later obverse die state.

94. Comments to the author during the preparation of this manuscript.

95. John D. Wright, The Cent Book, 1992, pp. 81–82. James L. Halperin, letter to the author, July 1, 1996. New England Rare Coin Auctions, October 1981 Long Beach Sale, lots 58–64. The "brightest," graded as MS-64 RD (the plate coin in this text), the Naftzger coin, was sold as lot 116 by Larry and Ira Goldberg in the Naftzger sale of February 2009.

96. And offered for sale by New Netherlands Coin Company, privately, after Raymond's death (personal recollection of the author).

97. Mason's Coin and Stamp Collectors' Magazine, March 1869.

98. Recollection of Oscar G. Schilke to Q. David Bowers, circa 1959.

99. To list all such instances of wide discrepancies would involve a lot of space. Occasional mentions, as here, are simply to remind readers that opinions can differ dramatically, and to use great care when paying strong premiums for coins that have exceptionally high grades attached.

100. R.W. Julian, "U.S. Half Cent Thrives Despite Second Rate Treatment," Numismatic Scrapbook Magazine, October 1972.

101. In the 1950s, when it was possible to buy wholesale lots of cents by the thousands and sort them, this was the variety most often encountered from its era. Typically, these lots had scarce dates (but not varieties) and EF or finer coins had been picked out beforehand.

102. Denis Loring, communication to the author, April 26, 2009.

103. For descriptions of these see John R. Grellman Jr., The Die Varieties of United States Large Cents 1840–1857, 2001. Variations in digit alignment for the Large Date coins are also described.

104. John R. Grellman Jr., in The Die Varieties of United States Large Cents 1840–1857, debunks Breen "Proofs" (Proof coin Encyclopedia) for N-2 and 5, and questions N-8.

105. John R. Grellman Jr., Ibid., debunks certain other Breen-listed "Proofs."

106. Denis Loring, communication to the author, March 25, 2009.

107. John R. Grellman Jr., The Die Varieties of United States Large Cents 1840–1857.

108. From R.W. Julian, "New York Coiners Plague Hobby with Bogus 1848, 1849 Cents," Numismatic Scrapbook Magazine, June 24, 1972, who gives many more details.

109. John R. Grellman Jr., The Die Varieties of United States Large Cents 1840–1857.

110. Communication to the author, April 26, 2009. PCGS has certified an N-30 as Proof-64.

111. Denis Loring, communications with the author, March 25 and April 26, 2009. Other "Proofs" of this year have turned out to be circulation strikes.

112. Walter Breen's Complete Encyclopedia of U.S. and Colonial Coins, p. 211; also personal recollection of the author concerning the availability of the coins in the 1950s. These comments are not otherwise confirmed.

113. Denis W. Loring, communication to the author, April 26, 2009.

114. Craig Sholley, communication to the author, January 18, 2001.

115. Denis Loring, communication to the author, March 25, 2009.

SELECTED BIBLIOGRAPHY

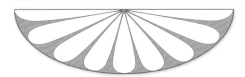

Selected bibliography of works relating to half cents and early cents as well as Mint history. Other sources are cited in the text and the end notes. The author gained additional knowledge by consulting a large body of auction catalogs and price lists over many years.

Adams, John W. *United States Numismatic Literature. Volume I. Nineteenth Century Auction Catalogs.* Mission Viejo, CA: George Frederick Kolbe Publications, 1982.

——*United States Numismatic Literature. Volume II. Twentieth Century Auction Catalogues.* Crestline, CA: George Frederick Kolbe Publications, 1990.

Adelson, Howard. *The American Numismatic Society 1858–1958.* New York City, NY: American Numismatic Society, 1958.

American Journal of Numismatics. New York City, NY, and Boston, MA: Various issues 1866 to 1912.

Argyro, Daniel. *Major Die States of 1848 Large Cents.* Buffalo, NY: Published by the author, 1995.

Asylum, The. Published by the Numismatic Bibliomania Society, various issues 1980s onward.

Attinelli, Emmanuel J. *Numisgraphics, or A List of Catalogues, Which Have Been Sold by Auction in the United States. . . .* New York City, NY: Published by the author, 1876.

Bathe, Greville and Dorothy. *Jacob Perkins: His Inventions, His Times & His Contemporaries.* The Historical Society of Pennsylvania, Philadelphia, 1943.

Boka, Jon Alan. *Provenance Gallery of the Year 1794, United States Large Cents.* San Ramon, CA: Falcon Books, 2005.

Borckardt, Mark, and William Metropolis. "Restriking the Issues: The Large Cent Restrikes of 1804, 1810, and 1823." *America's Large Cent.* American Numismatic Society, Coinage of the Americas Conference, November 9, 1996. Published 1998.

Bowers, Q. David. *The History of United States Coinage as Illustrated by the Garrett Collection.* Published for The Johns Hopkins University, Baltimore.

First printing, Los Angeles, California: Bowers and Ruddy Galleries, Inc., 1979.

——*The American Numismatic Association Centennial History.* Wolfeboro, NH: Bowers and Merena Galleries, Inc. on behalf of the American Numismatic Association, 1991. Two volumes.

——*American Coin Hoards and Treasures.* Wolfeboro, NH: Bowers and Merena Galleries, Inc., 1997.

——*The History of American Numismatics Before the Civil War, 1760–1860.* Wolfeboro, NH: Bowers and Merena Galleries, 1998.

Boyd, F.C.C. "Engravers of the U.S. Mint in Philadelphia." *The Numismatist.* July 1940.

Brady, J. D. "Rediscovery of Joseph Wright's Medal of Washington." *ANS Museum Notes 22.* New York City, NY: American Numismatic Society, 1977.

Breen, Walter H. *Walter Breen's Encyclopedia of United States Half Cents.* Southgate, CA: American Institute of Numismatic Research, 1983.

——"Robert Scot's Earliest Device Punches." *America's Copper Coinage 1783–1857.* New York City, NY: American Numismatic Society, 1985. Proceedings of the Coinage of the Americas Conference, November 30 to December 2, 1984.

——*Walter Breen's Complete Encyclopedia of United States and Colonial Coins.* New York City, NY: Doubleday & Co., 1988.

——*Walter Breen's Complete Encyclopedia of United States and Colonial Proof Coins 1722–1989.* Wolfeboro, NH: Bowers and Merena Galleries, 1989.

——"Philadelphia's Original Flying Disks: Early American Coppers—Blanks, Sources, Identifying Marks." *American Numismatic Association Centennial Anthology.* Wolfeboro, NH: Bowers and Merena Galleries, 1991.

——*Walter Breen's Encyclopedia of Early United States Cents 1793–1814.* Wolfeboro, NH: Bowers and Merena Galleries, 2000.

Bressett, Kenneth E., ed; earlier edited by Richard S. Yeoman. *A Guide Book of United States Coins.* Atlanta, GA: Whitman Publishing, various editions 1946 to date.

Cable, Ken. "Delist the 1836 First Restrike Half Cent?" *Penny–Wise.* September 15, 1998.

Carlson, Carl W.A. "Birch and the Patterns of '92." *The Numismatist.* March 1982.

Carothers, Neil. *Fractional Money.* New York City, NY: John Wiley & Sons, Inc., 1930.

Carter, Paul and Bob. "The Taunton Copper Manufacturing Company." *The Numismatist.* February 1972.

Chamberlain, Georgia. "Joseph Wright, First Draughtsman and Diesinker to the United States Mint." *The Numismatist.* December 1954.

——"John Reich, Assistant Engraver to the United States Mint." *The Numismatist.* March 1955.

Clapp, George H. *The United States Cents of the Years 1798–1799.* Sewickley, PA: Published by the author, 1931.

——*The United States Cents 1804–1814.* The Coin Collector Series Number Eight. New York City, NY: Wayte Raymond, Inc., 1941.

Clapp, George H. and Howard R. Newcomb. *The United States Cents of the Year 1795, 1796, 1797 and 1800.* New York City, NY: The American Numismatic Society, 1947.

Cohen, Roger S., Jr. *American Half Cents, the Little Half Sisters.* Baltimore, MD: Published by the author, 1971; second edition, 1982 (with information, including about Proofs, not in the first edition).

Coin Collector's Journal, The. New York City, NY: J.W. Scott & Co., various issues in the 1870s and 1880s.

Coin World Almanac. Sidney, OH: Coin World, 1976 and later editions.

Coin World. Sidney, OH: Amos Press, *et al.*, 1960 to date.

Coinage Laws of the United States 1792–1894. Modern foreword to reprint by David L. Ganz. Wolfeboro, NH: Bowers and Merena Galleries, Inc., 1991.

Coleman, Richard T., Jr. "Proof, Business Strike or Restrike?" *Penny-Wise.* July 15, 1996.

——"Proof Half Cent Update." *Penny-Wise.* September 15, 1996.

——"Series VII Restrikes: The Breen Effect." *Penny-Wise.* November 15, 1998.

——"Coronet Proof Half Cents with a Small Berry Reverse and Doubled T in CENT, Part 3." *Penny-Wise.* January 2004.

——"A Listing of Proof Half Cents of Coronet Head Obverse and Small Berry Reverse." *Penny-Wise.* March 2004.

——"A Listing of Original Proof Half Cents with Classic Head Obverse and Large Berry Reverse, Part 1." *Penny-Wise.* May 2004.

——"A Listing of Original Proof Half Cents with the Classic Head Obverse and Large Berry Reverse, Part 2: 1836." *Penny-Wise.* July 2004.

——"A Listing of First Restrike Proof Half Cents with the Classic Head Obverse." *Penny-Wise.* September 2004.

Craig, John. *The Mint: A History of the London Mint from A.D. 287 to 1948.* Cambridge, UK: University Press, 1953.

Crosby, Sylvester S. "The Cents of 1793." *American Journal of Numismatics.* April 1869.

——*The United States Coinage of 1793—Cents and Half Cents.* Boston, MA: Published by the author, 1897.

Dalton, R., and S.H. Hamer. *English Provincial Token Coinage of the 18th Century.* Boston, MA: Quarterman Publications, 1972. Reprint of the original London edition.

Davis, Charles E. *American Numismatic Literature: An Annotated Survey of Auction Sales 1980–1991.* Lincoln, MA: Quarterman Publications, Inc., 1992.

——"W. Elliot Woodward, a Few Notes and New Plates." *The Asylum.* Winter 1992.

Dickeson, Montroville W. *American Numismatical Manual.* Philadelphia, PA: J.B. Lippincott & Co., 1859.

Dubois, William E. *Pledges of History: A Brief Account of the Collection of Coins Belonging to the Mint of the United States, More Particularly of the Antique Specimens.* Philadelphia, PA: C. Sherman, Printer, 1846; New York: George P. Putnam, 1851.

Dunlap, William. *History of the Rise and Progress of the Arts of Design in the United States.* New York City, NY: George P. Scott & Co., Printers, 1834.

Eckberg, William R. "Who Made the Half Cents of 1793?" *Penny-Wise.* May 15, 2000.

——"How Many Half Cents Are There?" *Penny-Wise.* July 15, 2000.

——"Rarities and Hoard Coins: The 1825–1857 Half Cents." *Penny-Wise.* September 15, 2000.

——"Rarities and Hoard Coins Revisited." June 2002, manuscript.

——"The 1809 C-5, 9 over What?" *Penny-Wise.* November 2006.

Eckberg, William R., and Mike Packard. "Changing Rarities of Half Cents in the Last Half Century." *Penny-Wise.* November 2007.

Evans, George G., ed. *Illustrated History of the United States Mint*. Philadelphia, PA: George G. Evans, various editions of the 1880s and 1890s.

Frossard, Édouard. *Numisma*. Various issues 1877–1891.

Grellman, J.R., Jr. *The Die Varieties of United States Large Cents 1840–1857*. Lake Mary, FL: Published by the author, 1991.

Hickcox, John H. *An Historical Account of American Coinage*. Albany, NY: Joel Munsell, 1858.

Historical Magazine, The. Morrisania, NY. Issues in Series 1, 2, and 3, 1850s and 1860s.

Johnston, Elizabeth B. *A Visit to the Cabinet of the United States Mint, at Philadelphia*. Philadelphia, PA: J.B. Lippincott & Co., 1876.

Julian, R.W. "The Mint Investigation of 1795." *Numismatic Scrapbook Magazine*. July 25, 1961.

——"The Mint in 1792." *Numismatic Scrapbook Magazine*. April 25, 1962.

——"The Copper Coinage of 1794." *Numismatic Scrapbook Magazine*. March 25, 1963.

——"The Beginning of Coinage—1793." *Numismatic Scrapbook Magazine*. May 25, 1963.

——"The Harper Cents." *Numismatic Scrapbook Magazine*. September 25, 1964.

——"The Copper Coinage of 1795." *Numismatic Scrapbook Magazine*. December 25, 1964.

——"The 1796 Copper Coinage." *Numismatic Scrapbook Magazine*. December 25, 1965.

——"New York Coiners Plague Hobby with Bogus 1848, 1849 Cents." *Numismatic Scrapbook Magazine*. June 24, 1972.

——"The Early Half cents 1793–99." *Numismatic Scrapbook Magazine*. January 25, 1973.

——"Half cent Blanks Use Welsh Copper." *Numismatic Scrapbook Magazine*. July 25, 1973.

——"The Cent Coinage of 1793." *Numismatic Scrapbook Magazine*. December 25, 1974.

——"Cent Coinage of 1794–95." *Numismatic Scrapbook Magazine*. January 25, 1975.

——"Cent Coinage of 1796." *Numismatic Scrapbook Magazine*. March 25, 1975.

——"Cent Coinage of 1797." *Numismatic Scrapbook Magazine*. April 25, 1975.

——"British Planchets and Yellow Fever." *Numismatic Scrapbook Magazine*. June 25, 1975.

——"From Shortage to Surfeit: The Cent Coinage of 1799." *Numismatic Scrapbook Magazine*. August 25, 1975.

——"The Philadelphia Mint and Coinage of 1814–1816." *American Numismatic Association Centennial Anthology*. Wolfeboro, NH: Bowers and Merena Galleries, 1991.

——"Aspects of the Copper Coinage, 1793–1796." *America's Large Cent*. American Numismatic Society, Coinage of the Americas Conference, November 9, 1996. Published 1998.

——"The Half Cent Coinage of 1832–1835." *Penny-Wise*. March 15, 2001.

Kleeberg, John. "The Strawberry Leaf Cent. A Reappraisal." *America's Large Cent*. Numismatic Society, Coinage of the Americas Conference, November 9, 1996. Published 1998.

Lapp, Warren A. "Uses and Abuses of U.S. Large Cents." *The Numismatist*. August 1971.

Lapp, Warren A., and Herbert A. Silberman, eds. *United States Large Cents 1793–1857*. Lawrence, MA: Quarterman Publications, 1975.

Loring, Denis W. "An Overview of Proof Large Cents." *America's Large Cent*. American Numismatic Society, Coinage of the Americas Conference, November 9, 1996. Published 1998.

Manley, Ronald P. "A Case for Proof-Only 1831 Half Cents." *Penny-Wise*. May 15, 1996.

——*Half Cent Die State Book 1793–1857*. Published by the author, 1998.

——"A Survey of Half Cent Weights by Date and Planchet Type." *Penny-Wise*. March 15, 1998.

——"Thoughts on the Thin Planchet Lettered Edge Half Cents." *Penny-Wise*. July 15, 1998.

——"Original Mintages of 1797 and 1800 Half Cents." *Penny-Wise*. July 15, 2000.

Maryott, Bill. "Die Varieties, Die Stages, Die States, and the Theory Behind Coining." *Penny-Wise*. March 2009.

Mason's Monthly Illustrated Coin Collector's Magazine. Philadelphia, PA, and Boston, MA: Ebenezer Locke Mason, various issues from the 1860s onward. Titles vary.

McGirk, Charles E. "United States Cents and Die Varieties, 1793–1857." *The Numismatist*. Published serially from October 1913 to December 1914.

McGuigan, James R. "Why Collect Proof Half Cents? The Numbers May Surprise You." *The Coin Dealer Newsletter*. Monthly Supplement, October 10, 1997.

Mickley, Joseph J. *Dates of United States Coins, and Their Degrees of Rarity*. Philadelphia, PA: Published by the author, July 1858.

Neiswinter, Jim. "Joseph N.T. Levick." *America's Large Cent*. American Numismatic Society, Coinage of the Americas Conference, November 9, 1996. Published 1998.

——"The First Published Study of Large Cents (1859)." *Penny-Wise*. July 15, 2000.

——"Reverses Revisited: S-63 Is the Reworked S-13." *Penny-Wise*. July 2006.

New York Times. New York City, NY: Various issues circa 1851–1857.

Newcomb, Howard R. "Half Cents—Originals and Restrikes." *The Numismatist.* March 1933.

——*United States Copper Cents 1816–1857.* New York City, NY: Stack's, 1944.

Newman, Eric P., and Kenneth E. Bressett. *The Fantastic 1804 Dollar.* Racine, WI: Whitman Publishing Company, 1962.

New-York Dispatch. New York City, NY: 1857. Clippings of certain columns by Augustus B. Sage and other numismatic comments, as preserved in a scrapbook by the American Numismatic Society.

New York Herald. New York City, NY: Various issues circa 1857–1861.

Noyes, William C. *United States Large Cents 1816–1839.* Bloomington, MN: Litho Technical Services, 1991.

Noyes, William C., Del Bland, and Dan Demeo. *The Official Condition Census for U.S. Large Cents 1793–1839.* Jon Lusk, Digital Dynamics, 2005.

Numismatic Guaranty Corporation of America Census Report. Sarasota, FL: Numismatic Guaranty Corporation of America, various issues.

Numismatic News. Iola, WI: Krause Publications; succeeded by F+W Publications, 1952 to date.

Numismatic Scrapbook Magazine, The. Lee F. Hewitt, editor. Chicago, IL: Hewitt Brothers; later, Sidney, OH: Amos Press, 1935–1976.

——*Numismatist, The.* Various addresses: American Numismatic Association, 1888 onward.

Orosz, Joel J. *The Eagle That Is Forgotten: Pierre Eugène Du Simitière, Founding Father of American Numismatics.* Wolfeboro, NH: Bowers and Merena Galleries, 1988.

——*The Curious Case of the Collectors Kline.* Wolfeboro, NH: Bowers and Merena Galleries, 1997.

——"Robert Gilmor, Jr. and the Cradle Age of American Numismatics." *The Numismatist.* May 1990.

——"Death of a Numismatic Argonaut," (Lewis Roper, M.C.). *Rare Coin Review.* July–August 2001.

Parish, Daniel, Jr. "List of Catalogues of Coin Sales, Held in the United States from 1828 to the Present Time." Serial article in the *American Journal of Numismatics,* 1866.

PCGS Population Report. Newport Beach, CA: Professional Coin Grading Service, various issues.

Prime, W.C. *Coins, Medals, and Seals.* New York City, NY: Harper & Brothers, 1861.

Raymond, Wayte. *Standard Catalogue of United States Coins and Paper Money* (titles vary). New York City, NY: Scott Stamp & Coin Co. (and others), 18 editions 1934 to 1957.

Romines, Del. "The 1847 'Large over Small 7' Cent." *Penny-Wise.* July 15, 1989.

Sheldon, William H. *Early American Cents.* New York City, NY: Harper & Brothers, 1949.

Sheldon, William H., Dorothy I. Paschal, and Walter Breen. *Penny Whimsy.* New York City, NY: Harper & Brothers, 1958.

Sholley, Craig. "Adam Eckfeldt, Mint Engraver?" *Penny-Wise.* September 15, 2000.

——"Early U.S. Minting Methods. Part I: Die Forging and Hardening." Manuscript supplied by the author.

——"Early U.S. Minting Methods. Part III: The Presses and Striking." Manuscript supplied by the author.

——"The Third Die: Part I: Middle and Late Date Cents." Manuscript supplied by the author.

Silvis, Greg A. "An Interview with R. 'Tett' Tettenhorst." *Penny-Wise.* January 2006.

Smith, Pete. "Observations on the Starred Reverse Cent." *Penny-Wise.* January 15, 1989.

——"W. Elliot Woodward: Early Chronicler." *The Numismatist.* February 1997.

——"Early U.S. Coining Dies in the ANS Collection." *America's Large Cent.* American Numismatic Society, Coinage of the Americas Conference, November 9, 1996. Published 1998.

——"History of the Early American Coppers Club 1966–2006." EAC website: www.eacs.org.

Snowden, James Ross. *A Description of Ancient and Modern Coins in the Cabinet of the Mint of the United States.* Philadelphia, PA: J.B. Lippincott, 1860.

Stauffer, David McNeely. *American Engravers Upon Copper and Steel.* New York City, NY: Grolier Club of New York, 1907.

Stewart, Frank H. *History of the First United States Mint, Its People and Its Operations.* Philadelphia, PA: Frank H. Stewart Electric Co., 1924.

Taxay, Don. *Counterfeit, Mis-Struck and Unofficial U.S. Coins.* New York City, NY: ARCO Publishing, 1963.

——*U.S. Mint and Coinage.* New York City, NY: ARCO Publishing, 1966.

——*Scott's Comprehensive Catalogue of United States Coinage.* New York City, NY: Scott Publications, 1970 (cover date 1971).

Tettenhorst, R. "The Dr. Edwards Copy of the 1796 Half Cent." *Penny-Wise.* July 15, 1988.

Treasury Department, United States Mint, *et al. Annual Report of the Director of the Mint.* Philadelphia, PA; later, Washington, D.C.: 1795 onward, 19th century issues.

Williamson, Raymond H. "Collecting U.S. Large Cents." *The Numismatist.* June 1949.

——"U.S. Large Cents That Survived." *The Numismatist.* July 1949.

Witham, Stewart. *Johann Matthaus Reich, Also Known as John Reich.* Canton, OH: Published by the author, November 1993.

Wright, John D. "A Study on Overdated United States Large Cents." *The Numismatist.* June 1969.

——*The Cent Book 1816–1839.* Bloomington, MN: Litho Technical Services, 1992.

——"The Hiatus." *America's Large Cent.* American Numismatic Society, Coinage of the Americas Conference, November 9, 1996. Published 1998.

About the Author

Q. David Bowers became a professional numismatist as a teenager in 1953. He is chairman emeritus of Stack's Bowers Galleries and is numismatic director of Whitman Publishing. He is a recipient of the Pennsylvania State University College of Business Administration's Alumni Achievement Award (1976); has served as president of the American Numismatic Association (1983–1985) and of the Professional Numismatists Guild (1977–1979); is a recipient of the highest honor bestowed by the ANA (the Farran Zerbe Award); was the first ANA member to be named Numismatist of the Year (1995); and has been inducted into the ANA Numismatic Hall of Fame, one of only 12 living members and the only professional numismatist among these. He has also won the highest honors given by the Professional Numismatists Guild. In July 1999, in a poll published in *COINage*, "Numismatists of the Century," Dave was recognized in this list of just 18 names. He is the author of over 50 books; hundreds of auction and other catalogs; and several thousand articles, including columns in *Coin World* (now the longest-running by any author in numismatic history), *The Numismatist*, and other publications. His books have earned more "Book of the Year Award" honors bestowed by the Numismatic Literary Guild than have those of any other author. He was involved in the sale of five of the six most valuable collections ever sold at auction—the Ambassador and Mrs. R. Henry Norweb Collection ($24 million), the Garrett Collection for The Johns Hopkins University ($25 million), the Harry W. Bass, Jr. Collection ($45 million), the Eliasberg Collection ($55+ million), and the John J. Ford, Jr. Collection (nearly $60 million). When the all-time record for any rare coin ever sold at auction was achieved, a gem 1794 dollar in 2013, he cataloged it and his firm sold it. Dave is a trustee of the New Hampshire Historical Society and a fellow of the American Antiquarian Society, American Numismatic Society, and Massachusetts Historical Society. He has been a consultant for the Smithsonian Institution, Treasury Department, and U.S. Mint, and is research editor of *A Guide Book of United States Coins* (the annual best-selling book in numismatics, the standard guide to prices). In Wolfeboro, New Hampshire, he is on the Board of Selectmen and is the town historian. This is a short list of his honors and accomplishments.

About the Foreword Author

Harry E. Salyards: 2015 marks Harry E. Salyards's 56th year as a coin collector. He has been a member of Early American Coppers for 36 years, and editor of its journal *Penny-Wise* for 29. He is also a 36-year member of the Liberty Seated Collectors Club, a member of the Medal Collectors of America, and a charter member of the John Reich Collectors Society, the Conder Token Collectors Club, and the Numismatic Bibilomania Society. He has special interests in the federal coinage of 1793 through 1807, particularly the large cents of 1794, and the Draped Bust, Small Eagle, dollars of 1795–1798; the Comitia Americana series of medals; the tokens of Thomas Spence; and the political medalets of Henry Clay. His research into his own American ancestors, revealing roots in both 17th-century Massachusetts and 18th-century Virginia, has amplified and enriched his parallel studies in American numismatics, as both his own family, and the coinage of the mints of the United States, came to span the continent. He and his wife, Phyllis Shannon Salyards, are graduates of the University of Nebraska College of Medicine, and retired family physicians, with two grown children and two grandchildren.

Credits and Acknowledgements

Pricing contributors included **Pierre Fricke**, **J.R. (Bob) Grellman Jr.**, **Denis W. Loring**, **Chris Victor-McCawley**, and **Dave Wnuck**.

The American Numismatic Society provided illustrations of several 1793 cents. **Leonard Augsburger** provided information regarding Mint history. **Del Bland** reviewed the manuscript and made suggestions. **Jon Alan Boka** reviewed sections of the manuscript, especially regarding cents of 1794, and made suggestions. **Mark Borckardt**, editor of *Walter Breen's Encyclopedia of United States Large Cents*, reviewed the manuscript, made suggestions regarding rarity and die descriptions, and assisted with obtaining photographs. **Wynn Bowers** reviewed the manuscript and made suggestions. **Greg Cohen** reviewed the manuscript and made suggestions. **John W. Dannreuther** provided advice and information on technical aspects of minting, especially regarding Proofs and date logotypes. **Dan Demeo** provided information about a die variety. **Bill Eckberg** reviewed the half-cent section and helped with several revisions, including estimated populations, historical and technical data, and more, plus general observations on Mint history. **Roberta French** was the main associate for compiling and checking data and assisting with research. **Pierre Fricke** reviewed portions of the manuscript and provided suggestions. **Ira Goldberg** and **Larry Goldberg** provided many illustrations, including of coins from the Roy E. Naftzger and Daniel W. Holmes Jr., collections, constituting a significant percentage of the later dates in the present work. **J.R. (Bob) Grellman Jr.** reviewed the manuscript, made suggestions, and assisted with die-variety and population information. **James Halperin**, **Steve Ivy**, and **Paul Minshull** (**Heritage Auctions**) provided many illustrations. They provided images from the Walter Husak Collection, a significant percentage of the early dates in the present work. **Greg Hannigan** provided illustrations for review. **Daniel W. Holmes Jr.**, encouraged the project. **Walter Husak** provided additional illustrations of many high-quality cents from his collection. **R.W. Julian** read the manuscript, made suggestions, and helped in other ways, especially regarding Mint history. **Denis W. Loring** reviewed the manuscript and made suggestions regarding die varieties, Proofs, populations, and other matters. **Jon Lusk** made suggestions regarding images. **Ron Manley** read much of the front matter and did in-depth analysis of the half-cent section, adding many suggestions and clarifications. **Jim Matthews** reviewed the manuscript and gave ideas. **Jim McGuigan** reviewed the half-cent part of the manuscript and made suggestions, including for estimated populations. **Jack McNamara** reviewed the manuscript and made suggestions. **Patty Moore** helped with proofreading. **Jim Neiswinter** reviewed certain sections of the next, most notably the early years of cents (with focus on 1793), provided photographs, and made suggestions. **Eric P. Newman** reviewed certain sections on Mint history and made suggestions; he also assisted with images from the R. Tettenhorst collection. **Joel J. Orosz** reviewed certain sections on Mint history and 19th-century numismatics and made suggestions. **Michael Printz** provided photographs of coins from an important private collection. **Tom Reynolds** reviewed the manuscript and made suggestions. **Harry E. Salyards** wrote the foreword and made suggestions concerning the text and variety listings. **Thomas Serfass** assisted in providing images from the R. Tettenhorst Collection. **Craig Sholley** reviewed the manuscript and contributed numismatic and historical information, including about die varieties and practices at the Philadelphia Mint. The archives of **Stack's Bowers Galleries** yielded many illustrations, mostly by **Douglas Plasencia**. **David M. Sundman** supplied historical information. **R. Tettenhorst** reviewed the material on half cents and made suggestions, provided coins for photography, and assisted in other ways. **Frank Van Valen** reviewed the manuscript and made suggestions. **Chris Victor-McCawley** reviewed the manuscript and made suggestions. **Alan V. Weinberg** provided images, including of 1792 patterns. **Ray Williams** provided information. **Dave Wnuck** provided information relating to pricing.

While the bibliography gives many sources, in providing information regarding varieties, rarity, and die states, the works of Walter Breen, Roger S. Cohen Jr., J.R. (Bob) Grellman Jr., Ronald P. Manley, William C. Noyes, and William H. Sheldon were particularly helpful. *Penny-Wise*, the journal of Early American Coppers, was essential as well. I also appreciate the "greats" I knew in the past, a list which includes just about everyone active in buying, selling, or doing serious studies on half cents and cents from 1953 onward.

Index